MW01256267

A HOT PEPPER CORN

Richard Baxter's Doctrine of Justification
in Its Seventeenth-Century Context of Controversy

Hans Boersma

REGENT COLLEGE PUBLISHING
VANCOUVER, BRITISH COLUMBIA

National Library of Canada Cataloguing in Publication

Boersma, Hans, 1961–

A hot pepper corn: Richard Baxter s doctrine of justification in its seventeenth century context of controversy / Hans Boersma.

Based on the author s doctoral dissertation (Th.D.), State Univ. of Utrecht, 1993.
Includes bibliographical references and index.
ISBN 1-57383-282-0

1. Baxter, Richard, 1615-1691—Contributions in concept of justification. 2.
Justification—History of doctrines—17th century. I. Title.

BX5207.B3B64 2003   234 .7 092   C2003-905978-2

<I>f in acknowledgment of the favour of his Redemption, he will but pay a pepper corn, he shall be restored to his former possession, and much more.

(Richard Baxter)

If we magnifie one grain of our own pepper to that height that we make it a part of that righteousness by which to stand at Gods tribunall this one grain will sink us down to hell, so hot a poyson is Mr. *Brs* pepper-corn.

(John Crandon)

Contents

Abbreviations

AmQ	*American Quarterly*
ARG	*Archiv für Reformationsgeschichte*
BanT	*Banner of Truth*
BC	*Baxter Correspondence*
BDBRSC	*Biographical Dictionary of British Radicals in the Seventeenth Century*
BJRL	*Bulletin of the John Rylands Library*
BLGNP	*Biografisch lexicon voor de geschiedenis van het Nederlandse Protestantisme*
BQ	*Baptist Quarterly*
BSABR	*Bibliotheca Sacra and American Biblical Repository*
BSHPF	*Bulletin de la Société de l'Histoire du Protestantisme Français*
BSTR	*Bibiotheca Sacra and Theological Review*
BT	*Baxter Treatises*
CaL	*Christianity and Literature*
CalTo	*Calvinism Today*
CCRB	N.H. Keeble and Geoffrey F. Nuttall, *Calendar of the Correspondence of Richard Baxter*
ChH	*Church History*
CHJ	*Cambridge Historical Journal*
ChM	*Churchman*
CO	John Calvin, *Ioannis Calvini Opera quae supersunt omnia,* ed. Guilielmus Baum, Eduardus Cunitz, and Eduardus Reuss.
CoQ	*Constructive Quarterly*
CQR	*Church Quarterly Review*
CR	A.G. Matthews, *Calamy Revised*
CTJ	*Calvin Theological Journal*
DNB	*Dictionary of National Biography*
DNR	*Documentatieblad Nadere Reformatie*
DAPEL	Samuel Halkett and John Laing, *Dictionary of Anonymous and Pseudonymous English Literature*
DaR	*Dalhousie Review*
DWL	Doctor Williams's Library, London
EC	*Eighteenth Century*
ERE	*Encyclopaedia of Religion and Ethics*
ET	*Expository Times*
EvQ	*Evangelical Quarterly*
Foun	*Foundations*

GBD	*General Biographical Dictionary*
Hist	*Historian*
HLQ	*Huntington Library Quarterly*
HThR	*Harvard Theological Review*
Inst.	John Calvin, *Calvin: Institutes of the Christian Religion,* ed. John T. McNeill, trans. and indexed Ford Lewis Battles
JEH	*Journal of Ecclesiastical History*
JHI	*Journal of the History of Ideas*
JPHSE	*Journal of the Presbyterian Historical Society of England*
JRH	*Journal of Religious History*
JThS	*Journal of Theological Studies*
JURCHS	*Journal of the United Reformed Church History Society*
KuD	*Kerygma und Dogma*
MCM	*Modern Churchman*
NeAKG	*Nederlands Archief voor Kerkgeschiedenis*
OiC	*One in Christ*
OS	John Calvin, *Joannis Calvini Opera Selecta,* ed. Petrus Barth and Guilelmus Niesel
PHSGBI	*Proceedings of the Huguenot Society of Great Britain and Ireland*
PHSL	*Proceedings of the Huguenot Society of London*
PMQR	*Primitive Methodist Quarterly Review*
PS	*Prose Studies*
RB	*Reliquiæ Baxterianæ*
ScHR	*Scottish Historical Review*
SCJ	*Sixteenth Century Journal*
TBHS	*Transactions of the Baptist Historical Society*
TCHS	*Transactions of the Congregational Historical Society*
Theol.	*Theology*
ThRef	*Theologia Reformata*
ThTo	*Theology Today*
WCF	Westminster Confession of Faith
WThJ	*Westminster Theological Journal*
ZKG	*Zeitschrift für Kirchengeschichte*

Preface

Upon the completion of this dissertation I wish to express my sincere appreciation to the many people who have assisted in one way or another. In the first place, I thank my supervisor, Prof. Dr. C. Graafland of the University of Utrecht. His interest in Amyraldian theology and in the doctrine of justification has really stimulated my research. His straightforward insistence on twofold justification has contributed in no small measure to my appreciation of Baxter's theology and to my renewed understanding of biblical soteriology. I also would like to mention Prof. Dr. N.H. Keeble of the University of Stirling, Prof. Dr. J.I. Packer of Regent College (Vancouver), Prof. Dr. J. Van den Berg of the University of Leiden, and Prof. Dr. R. Van den Broek of the University of Utrecht for their kind willingness to serve as members of the examination committee. I also express my gratitude for the thorough Reformed theological training which I have received at the Theological College of the Canadian Reformed Churches in Hamilton, Ontario.

I am indebted to the hospitality of a number of people while doing research in London and Cambridge. I wish to mention Mr. and Mrs. Alan Abrams, Rev. Dr. and Mrs. Alan C. Clifford, Rev. and Mrs. David Jones, and the staff of Tyndale House, Cambridge who provide a superb environment for postgraduate theological research. I am indebted to these people not only for their hospitality, but for new friendships as well. I also want to mention the academic advise and other assistance I have received from Dr. Timothy K. Beougher, Dr. Alan C. Clifford, Dr. N.H. Keeble, and Dr. J.I. Packer. I further express my appreciation to those who have granted permission to quote from their unpublished theses. A special thank you goes to my brother, Jan, who has gone over most of my Latin translations and has also made up for my lack of computing skills on numerous occasions.

Of the libraries that I have used I want to make special mention of the Cambridge University Library, where the staff of the rare books room has been unfailingly cooperative in meeting my inordinate requests, and the State University of Utrecht, whose interlibrary loan department has helped me track down material on numerous occasions. I have also enjoyed the help of Dr. Williams's Library, London. I am grateful to the Trustees of this library for allowing me to consult Baxter's manuscripts. Of course, the Trustees are not responsible for the selection that I have made. I also waive any copyright in the extracts that I have made, so far as the exercise of this right might debar other scholars from using and publishing the same material and from working for that purpose on the same manuscripts. I have also been assisted in an invariably cooperative manner by the staff of University Microfilms International in Ann Arbor, Michigan and in Godstone, Surrey.

Last of all, I want to thank my dear wife, Linda, who has sacrificed much patience, assistance, and love during the many years that I have been engaged in full-time studies. I would never have finished this project without her.

A few comments on some matters of style are in order. With regard to the transcription of primary sources, I have everywhere retained the original spelling, except that I have replaced the double "vv" by a "w"; I also have not reproduced the long "s." Where square brackets occur these are part of the original. Words between angle brackets indicate my own additions to an original text. Any translations are mine, except where otherwise indicated. I have consulted the first edition of Baxter's *Aphorismes of Justification* (1649). For the sake of convenience, I also include the page numbers of the 1655 edition between brackets (*e.g., Aphorismes* II.110-11 [pp. 283-84]). References to Baxter's *Practical Works* are given first to the recently reprinted four-volume edition (first edition, 1707) and then, between brackets, to Orme's 23-volume edition of 1830 (*e.g., Works* II.437 [7.129-30]). *CCRB* references follow the numbers of letters rather than volume and page numbers.

Chapter I

Present State of Research

It's no great matter what *Men* deem,
Whether they count me good or bad!
In their applause and best esteem,
There's no contentment to be had.
I stand not to the Bar of Man;
It's thy displeasure makes me sad:
My thoughts and actions thou wilt scan:
If thou approve me I am glad.[1]

(Richard Baxter)

INTRODUCTION

For some, a discussion of Baxter's theology might need justification. Already in 1925, A.R. Ladell commented that "<t>he day to discuss Baxter's theology has long since passed ..."[2] Fortunately, however, subsequent scholarship has not vindicated this judgement. Particularly since the mid-1950s there has been a resurgence in Baxter research. This may in no small measure be attributed to J.I. Packer's dissertation on Baxter, which proved to be a milestone.[3] Research has further been stimulated by the eminent biographical accounts of Baxter by Frederick J. Powicke and Geoffrey F. Nuttall.[4]

---

1. In Linda Jo Samuel Banks, "The Poems of Richard Baxter: A Critical Edition with Notes and Commentary," Diss. Emory Univ. 1967, p. 68.
2. A.R. Ladell, *Richard Baxter: Puritan and Mystic*, pref. W.H. Frere, Studies in Church History (London: Society for Promoting Christian Knowledge; New York: Macmillan, 1925), p. 132.
3. James I. Packer, "The Redemption and Restoration of Man in the Thought of Richard Baxter," Diss. Univ. of Oxford 1954.
4. Frederick J. Powicke, *A Life of the Reverend Richard Baxter 1615-1691* (London: Cape, [1925?]); Frederick J. Powicke, *The Reverend Richard Baxter under the Cross (1662-1691)* (London: Cape, 1927); Geoffrey F. Nuttall, *Richard Baxter* (London: Nelson, 1965).
   Biographies of Baxter are mainly based on his autobiographical account, *Reliquiæ Baxterianæ* (1696), edited by Matthew Sylvester. This work has been published several times in an abridged format: Edmund Calamy, ed., *An Abridgment of Mr. Baxter's History of his Life and Times. With an Account of many others of those Worthy Ministers who were Ejected after the Restauration ... And a Continuation of their History, till the year 1691* (London, 1702); J.M. Lloyd Thomas, ed., *The Autobiography of Richard Baxter*, Everyman's Library, 868 (London: Dent; New York: Dutton, 1931); N.H. Keeble, ed., *The Autobiography of Richard Baxter*, abridged J.M. Lloyd Thomas (London: Dent; Totowa, N.J.: Rowman & Littlefield,1974). For a more complete listing, see N.H. Keeble, *Richard Baxter: Puritan Man of Letters*, Oxford English Monographs (London: Clarendon, 1982), pp. 168-69. This book is based on Keeble's earlier dissertation, "Some Literary and Religious Aspects of the Works of Richard Baxter," Diss. Univ. of Oxford 1973.

Shealy has rightly commented: "Sheer bulk is both a blessing and a problem in Baxter research ..."[5] No author of the seventeenth century can measure up to Baxter in regard to the volume of writings. Perhaps as much as forty percent of his writings are included in his *Practical Works*.[6] The remainder of his publications, which are to a large extent controversial writings, are obviously more pertinent to the present discussion. This published material has been catalogued repeatedly, most recently and comprehensively by N.H. Keeble.[7] The publication of the two-volume *Calendar of the Correspondence of Richard Baxter* in 1991 will doubtless be a great stimulus for further research.[8] This calendar not only lists Baxter's

For contemporary attacks on the *RB*, see *Vindiciæ Anti-Baxterianæ: Or, Some Animadversions On a Book, Intituled Reliquiæ Baxterianæ; Or, The Life of Mr. Richard Baxter* (London, 1696). The author of this anonymous work is generally held to be Samuel Young (William Orme, "The Life and Writings of Richard Baxter," in *Works* 1.725, n. h; 731; Edward Arber, *The Term Catalogues*, Vol. III [London: privately printed, 1903-06], p. 74 [cf. *DAPEL* 6.187]). See also Thomas Long, *Review of Mr. Richard Baxter's life* (London, 1697).

For additional secondary literature on the *RB*, see William Orme, "Life and Writings," in *Works* 1.726-33; Samuel Taylor Coleridge, "Richard Baxter: 1615-1691," in *Marginalia*, Vol. I, ed. George Whalley, Vol. XII of *The Collected Works of Samuel Taylor Coleridge*, Bollingen Series, 75 (London: Routledge and Kegan Paul; Princeton, NJ: Princeton Univ. Press, 1980), pp. 230-61; Roberta Florence Brinkley, ed., "Richard Baxter," in *Coleridge on the Seventeenth Century*, introd. Louis I. Bredvold (1955; New York: Greenwood, 1968), pp. 321-64; Donald A. Stauffer, *English Biography before 1700* (Cambridge, MA: Harvard Univ. Press, 1930), esp. pp. 192-94, 248; Geoffrey F. Nuttall, "The MS. of *Reliquiae Baxterianae* (1696)," *JEH*, 6 (1955), 73-79; Margaret Bottrall, "Richard Baxter," in *Every Man a Phoenix: Studies in Seventeenth-Century Autobiography* (London: Murray, 1958), pp. 111-40; James McJunkin Phillips, "Between Conscience and the Law: The Ethics of Richard Baxter (1615-1691)," Diss. Princeton Univ. 1958, pp. 83-89; Geoffrey F. Nuttall, "The Personality of Richard Baxter," in *The Puritan Spirit: Essays and Addresses* (London: Epworth, 1967), pp. 104-17; Joan Webber, "Richard Baxter: The Eye of the Hurricane," in *The Eloquent "I": Style and Self in Seventeenth-Century Prose* (Madison: Univ. of Wisconsin Press, 1968), pp. 115-48, 281-84; Royce MacGillivray, "Richard Baxter: A Puritan in the Provinces," *DaR*, 49 (1969-70), 487-96; Owen C. Watkins, "*Reliquiae Baxterianae*," in *The Puritan Experience: Studies in Spiritual Autobiography* (New York: Schocken, 1972), pp. 121-43; Karl Joachim Weintraub, "Bunyan, Baxter, and Franklin: The Puritan Unification of the Personality," in *The Value of the Individual: Self and Circumstance in Autobiography* (Chicago: Univ. of Chicago Press, 1978), pp. 228-60, 391-93; Robert S. Paul, "Ecclesiology in Richard Baxter's Autobiography," in *From Faith to Faith: Essays in Honor of Donald G. Miller on His Seventieth Birthday*, ed. Dikran Y. Hadidian (Pittsburgh: Pickwick, 1979), pp. 357-402; Dayton William Haskin, "The Light Within: Studies in Baxter, Bunyan, and Milton," Diss. Yale Univ. 1978, pp. 43-73; Dayton Haskin, "Baxter's Quest for Origins: Novelty and Originality in the Autobiography," *EC*, 21 (1980), 145-61; N.H. Keeble, *Richard Baxter*, pp. 132-55; N.H. Keeble, "The Autobiographer as Apologist: *Reliquiae Baxterianae* (1696)," *PS*, 9 (1986), 105-19; David Cornick, "Richard Baxter: 'Autobiography'," *ET*, 101 (1990), 259-63.

5. William Ross Shealy, "The Power of the Present: The Pastoral Perspective of Richard Baxter, Puritan Divine: 1615-1691," Diss. Drew Univ. 1966, p. 26.

6. Baxter's *Practical Works* were first published in four volumes in 1707 and were re-edited by William Orme in a 23-volume set in 1830. The 1707 edition has been reprinted recently (*The Practical Works of Richard Baxter: With a Preface, Giving Some Account of the Author, and of This Edition of His Practical Works: An Essay on His Genius, Works, and Times; and a Portrait*, 4 vols. [London, 1838; rpt., introd. J.I. Packer (Vol. I), Ligonier, PA: Soli Deo Gloria, 1990-91]).

7. N.H. Keeble, *Richard Baxter*, pp. 156-84. This bibliography is very helpful, especially because it also lists secondary literature on Baxter. It does not mention most of the unpublished dissertations dealing with Baxter's theology. Earlier lists of Baxter's writings appeared in William Orme, "Chronological List of the Works of Baxter," in *Works* 1. 793-99; A.G. Matthews, "The Works of Richard Baxter," *TCHS*, 11 (1930-32), 102-12, 125-39, 189-205, 228-36 (also published as *The Works of Richard Baxter: An Annotated List* [London, 1932]); and Nuttall, *Richard Baxter*, pp. 132-36.

8. *CCRB*, 2 vols. (Oxford: Clarendon, 1991).

unpublished correspondence but also summarizes the contents of each item, gives some significant quotations from them, and adds numerous suggestions for consultation of secondary literature.

One of the prime purposes of this chapter is to come to a delineation of the area which must be investigated in the present study. I will attempt to do this by giving an overview and a brief discussion of the most significant studies which have appeared on Baxter's soteriology. The overview will indicate where Baxter's place in seventeenth-century Calvinist thought needs further analysis. This chapter, therefore, provides justification for the topic under discussion. In doing so, I limit myself to modern scholarly studies on Baxter's soteriology. A number of significant studies have also appeared on Baxter's ecclesiology, and in particular on his views regarding the relationship between church and state. This is a particularly fruitful area of research but falls outside the scope of the present study.[9]

A discussion of the secondary literature on Baxter's soteriology will also bring to the fore some key areas where scholars differ in their interpretation or evaluation of Baxter. The interpretation of Baxter's soteriology is by no means uniform. The present chapter will highlight some of these differences of opinion. I will present my own judgement on these issues and hope to substantiate it in the remainder of the book.

The analysis of the present state of scholarship does not only serve to prove the need for the ensuing discussion. A number of studies discussed in this chapter are unpublished theses. Most of these are largely unknown and are hardly ever referred to in secondary literature.[10] Some indication of the research done on Baxter's soteriology will therefore be beneficial to further work in this area.

---

9. For discussions on Baxter's ecclesiology and his attempts to come to church unity, see Orme, "Life and Writings," in *Works* 1.573-613; Fred. James Powicke, "Richard Baxter (1615=1691) as a Catholic Christian," *PMQR*, NS 31 (1909), 232-47; F.J. Powicke, "Richard Baxter and Comprehension in the English Church," *CoQ*, 7 (1919), 349-67; Irvonwy Morgan, *The Nonconformity of Richard Baxter* (London: Epworth, 1946), pp. 90-116; Sydney C. Carter, *Richard Baxter 1615-1691*, Great Churchmen, 12 (London: Church Book Room Press, 1948), pp. 19-23; A. Morgan Derham, "Richard Baxter and the Oecumenical Movement," *EvQ*, 23 (1951), 96-115; Phillips, "Between Conscience and the Law," pp. 255-82; Geoffrey F. Nuttall, "Presbyterians and Independents: Some Movements for Unity 300 Years Ago," *JPHSE*, 10 (1952), 4-15; R.L. McCan, "The Conception of the Church in Richard Baxter and John Bunyan: A Comparison and Contrast," Diss. Univ. of Edinburgh 1955; Earl Kent Brown, "Richard Baxter's Contribution to the Comprehension Controversy: A Study in Projected Church Union," Diss. Boston Univ. Graduate School 1956; Isolde Jeremias, "Richard Baxters Catholic Theology, ihre Voraussetzungen und Ausformungen," Diss. Georg August-Universität 1956, pp. 141-233; George R. Abernathy, "Richard Baxter and the Cromwellian Church," *HLQ*, 24 (1961), 215-31; A. Harold Wood, *Church Unity without Uniformity: A Study of Seventeenth-Century English Church Movements and of Richard Baxter's Proposals for a Comprehensive Church*, pref. E. Gordon Rupp (London: Epworth, 1963); Sidney H. Rooy, *The Theology of Missions in the Puritan Tradition: A Study of Representative Puritans: Richard Sibbes, Richard Baxter, John Eliot, Cotton Mather, and Jonathan Edwards*, Diss. Amsterdam 1965 (Delft: Meinema, 1965), pp. 111-14; Shealy, "The Power of the Present"; Paul, "Ecclesiology in Richard Baxter's Autobiography."
10. David A. Weir, in his excellent bibliography of federal theology and the covenant idea before 1750, does mention some of these largely unknown studies (*The Origins of the Federal Theology in Sixteenth-Century Reformation Thought* [Oxford: Clarendon, 1990], pp. 170, 172, 178-79).

INCIDENTAL STUDIES (1852-1954)

It is difficult, if not impossible, to classify modern research on Baxter. If, however, for practical purposes, some lines of demarcation must be made, the first one ought to be Packer's influential dissertation, written in 1954. Prior to this date, the analyses of Baxter's theology remain incidental. George P. Fisher, for instance, wrote two articles on Baxter's theology in 1852.[11] These articles give a general overview of Baxter's theology. The first article is entirely based on Baxter's two most systematic treatises, his *Catholick Theologie* (1675) and his only Latin work, *Methodus Theologiæ* (1681). Fisher's reason for restricting his analysis to these two works is that after the earlier doctrinal works "his <*i.e.*, Baxter's> views underwent important changes."[12] The first article deals with Baxter's views of sin, moral ability, Scripture, the Trinity, the decrees, redemption, regeneration, justification, Christian virtue, and eschatology. In the second essay Fisher discusses Baxter's view on the relation between faith and reason, his mediating position in soteriology, his mystical tendency, and his pastoral piety. He also characterizes some of Baxter's works.

The first essay is, for the present purpose, most interesting. The article quotes extensively from the two treatises under discussion. Generally, the author is careful in his interpretation of Baxter's views. Regarding the doctrine of the perseverance of the saints, Fisher argues that Baxter's position changed from an avowal of the doctrine of the perseverance of the saints to the idea that weak Christians may fall away.[13] Of the latter view, Fisher states: "It seemed to him <*i.e.*, Baxter> not an unreasonable hypothesis that, when once converted, they may actually fall away."[14]

Fisher correctly observes that Baxter distinguishes between natural and moral ability. His conclusion regarding the freedom of the will, however, is one-sided: "All men have not only the natural power to repent and believe, but they have such grace as confers *moral* ability, and if faithfully used, would lead finally to their conversion and salvation."[15] This misrepresents Baxter's position. It gives the impression that all men have the moral ability to believe.[16] In actual fact, Baxter explicitly repudiates this Arminian position. Further, the statement that "Christ died for all, but not for all equally" presents only the one side of the coin.[17] Baxter also affirms the equality of Christ's death for all. The relation between these two apparently contradictory notions needs to be addressed. In the second article Fisher concludes that Baxter, despite his professed accord with the Synod of Dort and the

---

11. George P. Fisher, "The Theology of Richard Baxter," *BSTR*, 9 (1852), 135-69; George P. Fisher, "The Writings of Richard Baxter," *BSTR*, 9 (1852), 300-29.
12. Fisher, "Theology of Richard Baxter," 138.
13. Fisher, "Theology of Richard Baxter," 165.
14. Fisher, "Theology of Richard Baxter," 145-46, n. 1. Cf. 164-65.
15. Fisher, "Theology of Richard Baxter," 152. Fisher also comments: "If men do what is in their power, their salvation is sure" ("Writings of Richard Baxter," 313).
16. Elsewhere, Fisher suggests that Baxter "may not always be consistent with himself" ("Theology of Richard Baxter," 162, n.5).
17. Fisher, "Theology of Richard Baxter," 160.

Westminster Assembly, "can hardly be styled a Calvinist." Baxter is Baxterian.[18]

Three years later an anonymous article gives a similar overview of Baxter's theology, this time discussing Baxter's *End of Doctrinal Controversies* (1691).[19] The essay summarizes several doctrines of Baxter's last systematic treatise, quoting extensively from this work, and giving an accurate picture of Baxter's theology. All in all, these three essays present a succinct and admirable overview of Baxter's mature view, despite some minor shortcomings in Fisher's presentation of Baxter's position.

Ladell's *Richard Baxter: Puritan and Mystic* (1925) is a biography of Baxter, preceded by a chapter on Puritanism and nonconformity from 1558 to 1662 and followed by a rather inadequate chapter on Baxter as a mystical theologian. Ladell's erroneous description of Baxter as a mystic is due (1) to his broad description of mysticism as "the science of communion with God," which would fit almost anybody's theology; and (2) to his one-sided emphasis on Baxter's *Saints Rest* (1650).[20] Another point of misunderstanding is that Ladell is under the impression that Baxter becomes so moderate at a later age that he insists more and more "upon the possibility of Salvation including every man."[21]

Irvonwy Morgan's study, *The Nonconformity of Richard Baxter* (1946), begins by placing Baxter in his historical context by recounting the rise of Puritanism and the history of England from the reign of Elizabeth (1558-1603) to the Restoration under Charles II (1660). This is followed by a biographical chapter on Baxter's experiences after the Great Ejection (1662). Following this historical section comes a theological part in which Baxter's views on soteriology, the church, ministry, Scripture, the sacraments, church government, and *adiaphora* are laid out.

For the present purpose, chapter six, dealing with Baxter's theological position, must be briefly reviewed. The presentation of Baxter's position is generally accurate, though somewhat superficial. Baxter's theology is rightly interpreted as being Amyraldian. Morgan sees the difference between Baxter and the Calvinists of his day "in the fact that he *<i.e.,* Baxter> did not believe that God willed that anyone should be damned, but he thought that God did will that the elect should be saved, as a kind of extra grace, as it were."[22] Morgan insists that Baxter stands for

18. Fisher, "Writings of Richard Baxter," 307.
19. "Richard Baxter's 'End of Controversy'," *BSABR*, 12 (1855), 348-85.
20. Ladell, *Richard Baxter*, pp. 134-51. F. Ernest Stoeffler correctly observes that Ladell's focusing on the *Saints Rest* (1650) is responsible for the identification of Baxter as a mystic (*The Rise of Evangelical Pietism*, Studies in the History of Religions, 9 [Leiden: Brill, 1965], p. 93).
21. Ladell, *Richard Baxter*, p. 133.
22. Morgan, *Nonconformity of Richard Baxter*, p. 79. Morgan has rightly been criticized for stating that Baxter taught that many would be saved apart from the elect (Packer, "Redemption and Restoration," pp. 259-60; and Timothy K. Beougher, "The Teaching and Practice of the Puritan Pastor Richard Baxter with Regard to Becoming a 'True Christian'," Diss. Trinity Evangelical Divinity School 1990, pp. 73-74). Cf. Thomas W. Jenkyn's erroneous comment that Baxter's "theory is, that all the elect *are sure* to be saved; and that those who are non-elect *may be* saved, if they believe the Gospel" (Introd., *Making Light of Christ and Salvation, Too Oft the Issue of Gospel Invitations: A Call to the Unconverted to Turn and Live: The Last Work of a Believer; His Passing Prayer, Recommending His Departing Spirit to Christ, to Be Received by Him; Of the Shedding Abroad of God's Love on the Heart by the Holy Ghost*, by Richard Baxter, Works of the Puritan Divines, Baxter [London: Nelson, 1846], p. liii).

justification by faith alone: "So he stands as a fencer fighting two opponents – the Papists, with their doctrine of merit, and the Antinomians, with their ridicule of good works."[23] Although Morgan thus gives a congenial interpretation of Baxter, his picture of Baxter holding to justification by faith alone and rejecting merit needs some qualification.

The third and last section of Hugh Martin's *Puritanism and Richard Baxter* (1954) deals with Baxter. Within this section only a minor part is devoted to his theology.[24] It gives a brief and somewhat superficial exposition of Baxter's ideas on justification and the atonement. The book is informative but relies heavily on secondary literature.[25]

Major Advance (1954-66)

Between 1954 and 1966 at least nine dissertations were written dealing in their entirety with a particular aspect of Baxter's soteriology or with a closely related area. Two other studies also paid considerable attention to Baxter's views on such topics. These studies have significantly advanced the state of Baxter research. Due to differences in interpretation, this second phase of research highlights some of the problem areas.

The most significant impetus in this period came from Packer's dissertation, "The Redemption and Restoration of Man in the Thought of Richard Baxter" (1954). The dissertation begins with a section entitled "The Theologian," in which Puritanism and Baxter's epistemology are discussed. Packer identifies Baxter's logic as "Aristotelianism modified and augmented in the light of the Ramist critique."[26] Packer rightly emphasizes Baxter's trust in reason as an instrument to discover the truth.[27]

The second section deals with anthropology. It carefully describes Baxter's understanding of man's vegetative, sensitive, and mental faculties, the latter being endowed with vital active power, intellect, and will.[28] Baxter's views on man as the image of God are also discussed,[29] as well as God's role as *Dominus*, *Rector*, and *Benefactor*.[30] Concluding an interesting chapter on man's fall and his sinfulness, Packer comments that "all Baxter has to say about man, created and fallen, is entirely consonant with the Reformed and Puritan orthodoxy of his day."[31]

The third section, "The Redemption of the World," needs careful analysis. Packer begins by tracing how Baxter came to his theological position on soteriol-

23. Morgan, *Nonconformity of Richard Baxter*, p. 80.
24. Hugh Martin, *Puritanism and Richard Baxter* (London: SCM, 1954), pp. 131-37.
25. Geoffrey F. Nuttall, rev. of *Puritanism and Richard Baxter*, by Hugh Martin, *JEH*, 6 (1955), 240-41.
26. Packer, "Redemption and Restoration," p. 74. Cf. pp. 32-34, 57-61, 74-76, 82-84.
27. Packer, "Redemption and Restoration," pp. 91-100.
28. Packer, "Redemption and Restoration," pp. 110-23.
29. Packer, "Redemption and Restoration," pp. 123-25.
30. Packer, "Redemption and Restoration," pp. 125-37.
31. Packer, "Redemption and Restoration," p. 167.

ogy. Packer describes covenant theology as holding together the double pivot of Calvinist soteriology: the secret and revealed will of God. Here he locates Baxter's deviation from the Calvinist position: Baxter, along with the school of Saumur, held "that the doctrine of the covenant of grace was exclusively concerned with God's revealed will, and that His secret decree had no place in th<e> definition of it."[32]

In a subsequent chapter Packer gives an accurate analysis of Baxter's views on the atonement, noticing the influence of the Dutch Arminian, Hugo Grotius (1583-1645). Packer maintains that Baxter accepted irresistible grace, since conversion is God's act as divine Proprietor, not his act as Ruler.[33] Packer considers Baxter's assault on limited atonement "largely an attack on a man of straw," since his opponents never denied the free offer of grace.[34] The author takes particular exception to Baxter's theory of the nature of the atonement, preferring the position of John Owen (1616-83) over that of Baxter.[35]

The following chapter describes Baxter's views on justification. Packer observes that what offended people particularly in Baxter's theology was his doctrine of a two-fold righteousness (legal righteousness of Christ and personal evangelical righteousness) and his insistence that faith and works justify in the same kind of causality.[36] Packer describes the charge that Baxter's doctrine of justification was "papist" as "ludicrous."[37] Then Packer comes to what he considers the "root difference between Baxter and orthodox Calvinism":

> To orthodox Calvinism, the law of God is the permanent, unchanging expression of God's eternal and unchangeable holiness and justice. It requires perfect obedience from mankind, on pain of physical and spiritual death, and confers salvation and eternal life only upon those who perfectly obey it. God could not change this law, or set it aside, in His dealings with men, without denying Himself... Baxter's 'political method' led him to a very different idea of God's law. To him, God's justice is merely a rectoral attribute, a characteristic quality of His government, and His laws are no more than means to ends. Like all laws, they may under certain circumstances be changed, if the desired end is attainable by other means.[38]

After locating the root of Baxter's heterodoxy in his concept of the law, Packer concludes the chapter with an appendix on Baxter's harmonizing of Paul and James on justification. Here Packer incorrectly concludes that Baxter's position does not substantially differ from "the normal Reformed view" of men like John Owen and Thomas Manton (1620-77).[39] In a somewhat brief chapter on the sacraments Packer then analyzes Baxter's defense of infant baptism.[40]

---

32. Packer, "Redemption and Restoration," p. 213.
33. Packer, "Redemption and Restoration," pp. 256-57. Cf. pp. 384-91.
34. Packer, "Restoration and Redemption," p. 269.
35. Packer, "Redemption and Restoration," pp. 269-70.
36. Packer, "Redemption and Restoration," pp. 298-303.
37. Packer, "Restoration and Redemption," pp. 302-03.
38. Packer, "Redemption and Restoration," pp. 303-05.
39. Packer, "Redemption and Restoration," p. 308.
40. Packer, "Redemption and Restoration," pp. 309-30.

The fourth section of the dissertation deals with the work of the Holy Spirit and with Antinomianism. Here Packer defends that Baxter holds to irresistible grace and believes that assurance is reserved for stronger Christians only. Packer particularly faults Antinomian thought for its deficient doctrine of sin.[41]

Packer's conclusion is that the "foundation of his <*i.e.*, Baxter's> thought ... was unquestionably Calvinistic."[42] He criticizes Baxter for introducing Arminian elements by adopting Grotius' "political method" of theology: "Baxter ... found the rationale of God's laws and punishments, not in His nature, but in His rectoral relation to man."[43] For Baxter, the necessity of punishing does not lie in God's nature. Baxter, says Packer, goes beyond Amyraldianism, in two ways: (1) by adopting "a thoroughly Arminian construction of the atonement" where Amyraldianism had only insisted on the universal extent of redemption; and (2) by denying the propriety of inquiring about the relation between God's general and his special love. While Baxter thus resolves some of the inherent difficulties in the Amyraldian view, it also brings him closer to the Arminian position.[44] His denial of mystical union as a theological category causes the doctrine of justification to be the "least catholic, because the most reactionary, part of Baxter's theology."[45]

Packer's dissertation needs this rather lengthy summary because of its significant impact on subsequent research. This influence has been largely positive, because Packer's analysis is generally both accurate and thorough. It gives the best analysis of Baxter's theology to date. In particular the attention given to what Packer styles Baxter's "political method," largely derived from Grotius, and the interpretation of Baxter's theology as precise and consistent, rather than a loose amalgamation of ideas, has not failed to contribute positively to further Baxter research.

Packer is mistaken in his analysis, however, when he identifies Baxter's "political method" as "*the* key which unlocks his system."[46] It is my contention that the "political method" unlocks only half of his theology: God's will *de debito*, as *Rector*. The other half is God's will *de rerum eventu*, which is his will as *Dominus Absolutus*. Packer recognizes that Baxter uses this distinction. It seems to me that this should have prevented him from making Baxter's "political method" *the* key to understand his theology.

Further criticism is possible with regard to Packer's identification of Baxter's core mistake: making God's justice into a mere rectoral attribute. The idea that "<t>he demand for retribution was grounded in the nature of government rather than in the nature of God" is, in the whole of Baxter's theology, a false dilemma.[47] It is true that Baxter is of the opinion that Christ's sacrifice satisfies not the law,

---

41. Packer, "Redemption and Restoration," p. 431.
42. Packer, "Redemption and Restoration," p. 457.
43. Packer, "Redemption and Restoration," p. 458.
44. Packer, "Redemption and Restoration," pp. 459-62.
45. Packer, "Redemption and Restoration," p. 470.
46. Packer, "Redemption and Restoration," p. ii (emphasis added).
47. Packer, "Redemption and Restoration," p. 305. Cf. p. 458: "Baxter ... found the rationale of God's laws and punishments, not in His nature, *but* in His rectoral relation to man" (emphasis added).

but only the Lawgiver. But, unlike the Socinian view which he abhors, he does ground the demand for satisfaction in the very nature of God. God is not only *Dominus Absolutus*, but also *Rector*. When the *Rector* is satisfied, God is satisfied in his very nature.[48]

Despite his criticisms of Baxter, Packer constantly remains objective in his analysis. Packer's personal views, therefore, by no means detract from the value of his dissertation as a milestone in Baxter research. One qualifying comment must be made, however, with regard to an essay written by Packer at a later date, in 1969. Here Packer describes Baxter – as theologian – as "something of a disaster." Baxter's political method is described as rationalistic, externalizing sin, obscuring substitutionary atonement, losing sight of the dimension of self-despairing trust, and even as a loss of God.[49] Packer concludes that "Baxter, by the initial rationalism of his 'political method', which forced Scripture into an *a priori* mould, sowed the seeds of *moralism* with regard to sin, *Arianism* with regard to Christ, *legalism* with regard to faith and salvation, and *liberalism* with regard to God."[50] This is an unfortunate denunciation of Baxter's theology, and one that stands in contrast to the balanced approach of Packer's dissertation.

The 1956 dissertation of Isolde Jeremias obviously builds on the groundwork laid by Packer.[51] The dissertation is entitled "Richard Baxters Catholic Theology, ihre Voraussetzungen und Ausformungen." It intends to move beyond Packer by focusing more on Baxter's practical theology and by summarizing Baxter's "Leben und Lehre umfassende katholische Theologie."[52] The set-up is original: Jeremias distinguishes between theory and practice, *Lehr und Leben*. After an introductory section in which Jeremias situates Baxter against the background of Puritanism, she first discusses his theory. Here Jeremias places Baxter's theological system in a Puritan mold. Anthropology, redemption, pneumatology, predestination, and justification are discussed. In the section on practice, the author deals with the two aspects of the Christian life – the individual sphere and the communal life of the church. This section deals with faith, the relation between faith and works, assurance, sin, and perseverance, after which a discussion of the church, the church offices, and the sacraments follows. This leads to the next section, in which the author paints Baxter's ideal: the unity of the catholic church. *Lehr und*

---

48. That Packer misinterprets Baxter on this central point of evaluation is remarkable since Packer is well aware that Baxter criticized Grotius who denied that satisfaction was made to God as God. Packer then proves that for Baxter God must be satisfied as *Dominus Absolutus, Rector*, and as *Benefactor* ("Redemption and Restoration," p. 253).
49. J.I. Packer, "The Doctrine of Justification in Development and Decline among the Puritans," in *By Schisms Rent Asunder*, Proc. of the Puritan and Reformed Studies Conference, 1969 (n.p.: n.p., [1970]), p. 27. This essay has been republished in J.I. Packer, *A Quest for Godliness: The Puritan Vision of the Christian Life* (Wheaton: Crossway, 1990), pp. 149-61. Packer bases his charge that Baxter's "political method" loses God on his incorrect understanding of Baxter, as if Baxter did not ground God's rectorial justice in the nature of God.
50. Packer, "Doctrine of Justification," p. 28.
51. The use of Packer is unfortunately rarely acknowledged. Jeremias adopts the phrase "political method" as interpretative key to Baxter without acknowledging its source (Jeremias, "Richard Baxters Catholic Theology," pp. 68, 92, 203, 276, 298-99, 307, 312, 334-35, 345).
52. Jeremias, "Richard Baxters Catholic Theology," p. 5.

Leben are but steps on the ladder to the highest goal, the unity of the church, which in turn points to God the Creator. Only at this point does Baxter's system become clear.[53] In this last section Jeremias discusses Baxter's ecumenical attitude, his position over against other groups and sects, and gives a final description of his theological *Mittelweg*.

Thus the author combines Baxter's doctrinal, theoretical thought with his practical, pastoral approach: theory and practice are closely related: "Weder 'Lehre' noch 'Leben' sind bei Baxter Ziele in sich selbst, die unabhängig gegeneinander ausgespielt werden können."[54] Baxter's historical significance lies in his merging the theoretical and practical aspects of Puritan theology into a higher, comprehensive unity.[55] Neither *Lehre* nor *Leben* are goals in themselves. Together they form "die Vorstufe der himmlischen Erkenntnis der Liebe." This love is manifested in a national unity of all Christians under the government of God.[56] This entire system, states Jeremias, is built on Baxter's "politischen Methode."[57]

Jeremias' structuring of Baxter's thought is creative, and her emphasis on Baxter's concern for the unity of the church is in agreement with his thinking. Unfortunately, however, Jeremias does not indicate whether she has taken the distinction between theory and practice, with a third, transcending principle being located in the unity of the church, from Baxter's own writings. She merely avers that this was his thinking.[58] But nowhere does Baxter structure his theology in this manner. Indeed, the division is somewhat arbitrary: the entire chapter on faith, listed by Jeremias under the section on practice, might just as well be part of the section on theory. Why should justification be classified under theory, but not the relation between faith and works?

This somewhat arbitrary structure does not mean that the actual description of Baxter's views is inadequate. The dissertation gives a sympathetic and generally correct overview of Baxter's theology. In a few instances, Jeremias is vague or incorrect. She does not make clear, for instance, what exactly the role of faith is in justification. At times she appears to be of the opinion that Baxter accepts the conditionality of faith.[59] Elsewhere, she states that he was often attacked "weil er den Glauben nicht zur Bedingung, sondern zum Mittel für die deklarative Rechtfertigung machte."[60] At the root of this imprecision lies a failure to analyze what Baxter writes regarding the instrumentality of faith. Further, it is not clear whether Baxter is a coherent, logical thinker,[61] or whether he is not.[62]

Also in the mid-1950s, two dissertations have been written on Baxter's ethics:

---

53. Jeremias, "Richard Baxters Catholic Theology," pp. 2-3.
54. Jeremias, "Richard Baxters Catholic Theology," p. 24.
55. Jeremias, "Richard Baxters Catholic Theology," p. 42.
56. Jeremias, "Richard Baxters Catholic Theology," pp. 333-34.
57. Jeremias, "Richard Baxters Catholic Theology," p. 335.
58. Jeremias, "Richard Baxters Catholic Theology," pp. 2-3.
59. *E.g.*, Jeremias, "Richard Baxters Catholic Theology," pp. 99-103.
60. Jeremias, "Richard Baxters Catholic Theology," p. 307.
61. Jeremias, "Richard Baxters Catholic Theology," p. 297. This is in accordance with Packer's judgement.
62. Jeremias, "Richard Baxters Catholic Theology," pp. 41, 52.

"Faith and Works in the Ethical Theory of Richard Baxter," by W. Lawrence Highfill (1954), and "Between Conscience and the Law: The Ethics of Richard Baxter (1615-1691)," by James McJunkin Phillips (1958). These two dissertations have been produced independently of each other.[63] The result is that two very similar topics are dealt with in rather different manners. Highfill begins with two introductory chapters in which he relates the seventeenth-century theological background to Baxter and gives a biographical account. This is followed by an admirable chapter on the relation between faith and works as conditions of justification. Here the author concludes that although Baxter remains "within a Calvinistic framework," he emphasizes man's natural freedom to appropriate the means.[64] This combination of a sympathetic and a critical approach is maintained in the remainder of the dissertation. Highfill describes love to God and self-denial as key virtues for Baxter, from which numerous other virtues arise. Baxter's casuistry, as exhibited in his *Christian Directory* (1673), is based on an interplay between authority and conscience. The Bible is the only inclusive authority for Baxter, since it contains both natural and revealed law.[65] But each person must interpret Scripture through the agency of the Holy Spirit and the use of reason.[66] The conscience is a rational process concerned with human behavior, not a separate faculty.[67] God's law has priority over man's conscience.[68] Highfill illustrates this with examples taken from the *Christian Directory*. He maintains that Baxter manages to avoid the taint of unorthodoxy,[69] but that he "clears the way for undue emphasis on works."[70] Highfill concludes that "the flood of works swells to threatening proportions, and he <*i.e.*, Baxter> is not entirely successful in controlling it."[71]

The title of Phillips' dissertation, "Between Conscience and the Law," explains his methodology in analyzing Baxter's ethics. He places Baxter between the one extreme of an over-emphasis on conscience – which results in Antinomianism – and the other extreme of sole attention to the law – which results in legalism. Phillips, therefore, comes to an analysis which, in a sense, is similar to that of Highfill. There are also differences, however. Highfill maintains that works play a prominent role in Baxter's theology. Phillips seems to assign a smaller place to the law in Baxter's thought. Highfill argues that Baxter veers toward

---

63. Phillips writes that considering the "renaissance of Baxter scholarship, it is surprising that there have been no major studies of his writings on ethics ..." ("Between Conscience and the Law," p. vii). Phillips appears unaware of Highfill's study four years earlier.
64. W. Lawrence Highfill, "Faith and Works in the Ethical Theory of Richard Baxter," Diss. Duke Univ. 1954, p. 107.
65. Highfill, "Faith and Works," p. 226.
66. Highfill, "Faith and Works," pp. 234-39.
67. Highfill, "Faith and Works," p. 239.
68. Highfill, "Faith and Works," pp. 241-42.
69. Baxter manages to avoids unorthodoxy, according to Highfill, because of the following elements: (1) the ultimate cause of justification lies in God's gracious act in Christ's sacrifice, not in any act of man; (2) obedient acts are not consistently separated from justifying faith; (3) Baxter's approach to works is not qualified by any sacramental system; and (4) works as conditions are God's gifts ("Faith and Works," pp. 90-91).
70. Highfill, "Faith and Works," p. 284.
71. Highfill, "Faith and Works," p. 301. Cf. pp. 286, 289.

legalism. Phillips thinks that for Baxter conscience and law are engaged in a moral dialogue. This dialogue prevents Baxter from turning into a mere legalist: "In the last analysis ... one can only be responsible for an accounting of his own calling before God, who searches out the conscience of each believer."[72]

Phillips' structure also differs from that of Highfill. Phillips begins with a broad discussion of the philosophical, scientific, economic and technological, ecclesiological, and theological contexts of Baxter's ethics. Then follows a very informative chapter on the relation between law and conscience in Thomas Aquinas (c. 1227-74), John Calvin (1509-64), the Puritans, and sixteenth- and seventeenth-century Anglicans.[73] This leads to the central issue: the relation between law and conscience in Baxter. Finally, the author discusses the four sections of Baxter's *Christian Directory*.[74]

The result is a balanced discussion of Baxter's ethics. Perhaps Phillips gives too much emphasis on the role of conscience in the moral dialogue. Baxter's aversion from Antinomianism would make him feel utterly uncomfortable with an undue emphasis on unverifiable sources of authority. On soteriological issues, the author sometimes makes unwarranted statements. He argues, for instance, that in Baxter's thought election becomes particularized for certain individuals only on the basis of their performing the conditions of faith and repentance.[75] Phillips' denial that Baxter holds to irresistible grace may also be somewhat one-sided.[76] These are minor blemishes, however, on an otherwise helpful analysis of Baxter's ethics.

A brief overview must be given of William W. Bass' dissertation (1958) on Platonic Influences in John Owen, Richard Baxter, and John Howe (1630-1705).[77] In this dissertation Bass shortens his earlier M.A. thesis on John Owen and complements it with chapters on Baxter and Howe.[78] The dissertation presents a discussion of the revival of Platonism in the Renaissance and a characterization of the Cambridge Platonists. Then the author presents a historical and a theological picture of Puritanism, in which he emphasizes the influence of Ramist logic. The

---

72. Phillips, "Between Conscience and the Law," p. 299. Cf. pp. 187-88, 290. Still, elsewhere Phillips does seem to be of the opinion that Baxter verges in a legalist direction: "If Christ is the norm of a Christian's interpretation of the Scriptures, the legalism which Baxter and his fellow-Puritans reintroduced into Christianity from the Old Testament must be carefully sifted" (p. 335).

73. I am using the term Anglican because Phillips refers to it. Collinson and Tyacke have rightly drawn attention to the fact that the term "Anglican" is an anachronism when referring to the seventeenth century, since the label dates from the nineteenth century (Patrick Collinson, *The Elizabethan Puritan Movement* [Oxford: Clarendon, 1967], pp. 13, 34; Nicholas Tyacke, *Anti-Calvinists: The Rise of English Arminianism c. 1590-1640*, Oxford Historical Monographs [1987; rpt. Oxford: Clarendon, 1991], p. xviii).

74. Baxter's *Christian Directory* is divided into Christian ethics (private duties), Christian ecclesiastics (church duties), Christian economics (family duties), and Christian politics (political and economic duties).

75. Phillips, "Between Conscience and the Law," p. 55.

76. Phillips, "Between Conscience and the Law," p. 250.

77. William W. Bass, "Platonic Influences on Seventeenth-Century English Puritan Theology As Expressed in the Thinking of John Owen, Richard Baxter and John Howe," Diss. Univ. of Southern California 1958.

78. Cf. William Ward Bass, "The Theology of John Owen," M.A. Thesis Univ. of Southern California 1955.

second part of the dissertation gives descriptions of the thinking of Owen, Baxter, and Howe. All three were scholastic, "and to that extent were Platonic."[79]

In the chapter on Baxter, Bass pays particular attention to his doctrine of justification, giving a brief analysis of Baxter's *Aphorismes of Justification* (1649). He rightly concludes that in a rather un-Platonic way, Baxter emphasizes individual responsibility rather than participation of all men in either the first or the second Adam.[80] Baxter does, to a large degree, accept the Ramist emphasis on method. This is especially manifest in his later writings.[81] His strong emphasis on Christianity being a rational religion, combined with his mystic terminology, illustrates a Platonic tendency.[82]

Due to the large area of research, the author unfortunately does not always base his arguments on a sufficiently broad acquaintance with the primary literature.[83] Nevertheless, the dissertation consistently focuses on the influence of Platonic thought patterns. This unifies the various sections into an interrelated whole.

Kevan's study, *The Grace of Law: A Study in Puritan Theology* (1964) bases its evaluation of Baxter's theology mainly on Packer's dissertation.[84] The Puritan understanding of the law is generally depicted as standing mid-way between Antinomianism and Baxter's position. The result is a thorough systematic theological exposition of issues surrounding the relation between law and grace. The study gives an abundance of information, and quotes numerous primary sources. This approach does entail some simplification, however. With some exceptions, the Puritans are usually put together as a monolithic theological entity, with the Antinomians and Baxter constituting the aberrations.[85] This means that little justice can be done to variations in thought patterns and emphases of individual theologians. Baxter also does not oppose the term "merit," as Kevan reluctantly admits he did.[86]

Baxter is discussed as one of seven theologians in "The Doctrine of Regeneration in English Puritan Theology, 1604-1689," a 1965 dissertation written by James L. Shields. In a spirit congenial to experiential Calvinist thought, he discusses the doctrine of regeneration in William Perkins (1558-1602), Richard Sibbes (1577-1635), Richard Baxter, John Owen, Thomas Goodwin (1600-80), Stephen Charnock (1628-80), and John Howe. These theologians are not discussed separately; instead, Shields takes a topical approach. Baxter is characterized as a mediator who "stood for a moderate Calvinism which was to be approached from an experiential perspective."[87]

---

79. Bass, "Platonic Influences," p. 288.
80. Bass, "Platonic Influences," p. 198.
81. Bass, "Platonic Influences," p. 210.
82. Bass, "Platonic Influences," pp. 203-07.
83. Bass states, to some extent correctly, that Baxter rejects irresistible grace. It is not clear, however, what he bases this statement on ("Platonic Influences," p. 184).
84. Ernest F. Kevan, *The Grace of Law: A Study in Puritan Theology* (London, 1964; rpt. Grand Rapids: Baker, 1976), pp. 29-30, 67-68, 146.
85. There are exceptions to this generalizing tendency (*e.g.*, Kevan, *Grace of Law*, pp. 59-60, 77).
86. Kevan, *Grace of Law*, p. 206.
87. James L. Shields, "The Doctrine of Regeneration in English Puritan Theology, 1604-1689," Diss. Southwestern Baptist Theological Seminary 1965, p. 33. Since I only have access to the most pertinent sections of this dissertation I will refrain from a further evaluation of this study.

Sidney H. Rooy has a finely balanced discussion of the theology of Baxter in a separate chapter of his dissertation of 1965, *The Theology of Missions in the Puritan Tradition*.[88] After giving a biographical introduction, Rooy discusses conversion, the role of the church, and the redemption of the world. Not much needs to be said about this dissertation, apart from the fact that it is a study which gives an accurate portrayal of some central themes of Baxter's theology. It is one of the few studies which present an adequate description of his views on the grace given to heathens, and of the possibility that they be saved – a possibility which Baxter thought was only slight. Rooy also makes some illuminating comments on the relation between common and special grace in Baxter's thought: "Universal grace precedes special grace. The former proceeds by degree into the latter, though there is an indiscernable point at which a moral, qualitative difference enters."[89]

The charge of legalism is voiced by N.H. Mair, in his dissertation, entitled "Christian Sanctification and Individual Pastoral Care in Richard Baxter."[90] After an introductory chapter Mair focuses on Baxter's views on sanctification. This is followed by discussions of the form and content of his pastoral care. These chapters consist mainly of extended quotations of some of Baxter's works on pastoral care, along with some comments by way of summary and evaluation. The most significant chapter is the last one, which ties together the various elements from the previous sections. An important recognition in the dissertation is the inseparability of Baxter's doctrinal positions and his practical theology.[91] From a dogma-historical viewpoint, however, the study is of minor significance because of the lack of analysis of Baxter's theological thought patterns. Mair's evaluation of Baxter, which is influenced by the theology of Paul Tillich, is largely negative.[92]

Ecclesiology and practical theology intersect in Shealy's original study, "The Power of the Present: The Pastoral Perspective of Richard Baxter, Puritan Divine: 1615-1691." This dissertation of 1966 does not concern Baxter's soteriology in an immediate sense. Because some aspects of Baxter's concept of the covenant are discussed, however, a few comments are in place. In a first section, on the universal church, Shealy appropriately discusses its relation to God's governance, the spiritual war which continues until death, covenant and baptism, and Scripture. The second section deals with institutionality. Here ministerial authority is discussed in its relationship to magisterial and parental authority. He also pays some attention to the place of ministerial ordination. In the last section, on particularity, Shealy deals with the relationship between the pastor and the local church community. Discipline and communion, and the pastor's teaching and preaching tasks are discussed in this section.

---

88. Rooy, *Theology of Missions*, pp. 66-155.
89. Rooy, *Theology of Missions*, p. 87.
90. N.H. Mair, "Christian Sanctification and Individual Pastoral Care in Richard Baxter: An Analysis of the Relation between Richard Baxter's Understanding of Christian Sanctification and the Form and Content of His Individual Pastoral Direction," Diss. Union Theological Seminary 1966, pp. 232, 269, 280-81. Although Mair charges Baxter with legalism, he thinks that good works "are never regarded by Baxter as meritorious of salvation ..." (p. 132).
91. Mair, "Christian Sanctification and Individual Pastoral Care," pp. 263, 292.
92. Mair, "Christian Sanctification and Individual Pastoral Care," pp. 281-88.

The title of Shealy's dissertation, "The Power of the Present," refers to the authority of the pastor. This authority is one which must be exercised at the present time.[93] This is not meant in an objective, temporal sense, however: "There are no 'objective' events; there are only 'creative' events."[94] The sense of time is not chronological, but covenantal and relational. The absolute decree and the conditional relation are both parts of life.[95] The present is not conditional, but is lived in the presence of God.[96] Faith is a gift of the Holy Spirit.[97] Still, the law constantly confronts man. This means that the decree is carried out conditionally.[98] Shealy correctly emphasizes the covenantal scheme underlying Baxter's theology. But he gives a rather peculiar interpretation of the "eschatological dynamic" in Baxter's thinking.[99] That there is an eschatological drive in Baxter's thought is clear. But this must be regarded in a strictly temporal sense. For Baxter, the covenant relationship with God takes place in time. While Shealy often does grasp Baxter's thought patterns, at other times he is removed from them and makes few references to Baxter to substantiate his arguments.

C.F. Allison is the last author in this second phase of Baxter research. His book, *The Rise of Moralism: The Proclamation of the Gospel from Hooker to Baxter* (1966), offers a critique of the development of the doctrine of justification from the time of Richard Hooker (1554-1600) to that of Richard Baxter. According to Allison, the earlier English Protestants all held that Christ's righteousness was the formal cause of justification. Allison therefore styles them "imputation divines." With Jeremy Taylor (1613-67) a change set in. A generation of "holy living divines" arose. A greater emphasis on works resulted in the requirement of obedience before the grace of justification was granted. What is more, "<f>aith itself became a work which by virtue of its righteousness as a (good) work merited justification."[100]

Allison devotes a special chapter to Baxter's theology and the controversies it provoked.[101] In this chapter he maintains that Baxter sees faith, rather than Christ's righteousness, as the formal cause of justification.[102] It is true that Baxter does not regard Christ's righteousness as the formal cause of justification. But he does not substitute faith in its place, as Allison suggests. Allison is the only one among modern scholars who has reiterated the old charge, common among Baxter's contemporaries, that "it is difficult to distinguish Baxter's position from that of the Council of Trent."[103] This is an unfair criticism, based on a misunderstanding of

93. For this explanation of the title, see Shealy, "Power of the Present," pp. 271, 285, 299.
94. Shealy, "Power of the Present," p. 118.
95. Shealy, "Power of the Present," p. 122.
96. Shealy, "Power of the Present," p. 120.
97. Shealy, "Power of the Present," p. 123.
98. Shealy, "Power of the Present," p. 124.
99. For this phrase, see Shealy, "Power of the Present," p. 33.
100. C.F. Allison, *The Rise of Moralism: The Proclamation of the Gospel from Hooker to Baxter* (London: SPCK, 1966), p. 204.
101. Allison, *Rise of Moralism*, pp. 154-77.
102. Allison, *Rise of Moralism*, pp. 157, 161, 176.
103. Allison, *Rise of Moralism*, p. 163.

what Baxter actually taught. Allison has rightly been criticized for his erroneous position.[104] The misinterpretation is particularly damaging since Allison is of the opinion that the issue of the formal cause of justification constitutes the main dividing point between the earlier "imputation divines" and the later "holy living divines."

RECENT "REVIVAL" (1978-PRESENT)

Between 1954 and 1966 a large number of studies have appeared on Baxter's soteriology, often approaching similar or identical problems from different perspectives. After the publication of Allison's book there has been a period in which very little study has been done in this area. In fact, it was not until 1982 that a new study on Baxter's theory of the atonement was presented.[105] No studies prior to this date dealt with the topic at hand in any extensive way. Also Richards' study of 1982 remained an incidental publication. It is only very recent that there has been somewhat of a "revival" in Baxter research through the work of Gavin McGrath, Timothy Beougher, and Alan Clifford.[106]

First, however, some other studies need attention. Haskin gives some insight in Baxter's allegedly mystical tendency, in his dissertation, "The Light Within: Studies in Baxter, Bunyan, and Milton" (1978).[107] It is Haskin's contention "that Baxter was deeply divided in his thinking about the inner light."[108] Although for much of his life Baxter had great faith in the power of education as a channel of God's grace, this changed in a later period.[109] Haskin's position is quite different from that of Ladell, who avers that Baxter's mystical tendency appears in one of his first publications, *Saints Everlasting Rest* (1650). Haskin is correct in asserting that Baxter, at a later age, comes to place less trust in reason's ability to come to definite answers on theological issues. This goes accompanied by a less favorable evaluation of the subtleties of medieval scholastic theology. This does not mean, however, that Baxter later also comes to a more sympathetic attitude toward the spiritualist "sectaries" whom he opposed in the 1650s.

---

104. Gavin John McGrath, "Puritans and the Human Will: Voluntarism within Mid-Seventeenth Century English Puritanism As Seen in the Works of Richard Baxter and John Owen," Diss. Univ. of Durham, 1989, p. 259; and Beougher, "Conversion, pp. 102-03.
105. David J. Richards, "Richard Baxter's Theory of the Atonement," M.A. Thesis Wheaton College 1982.
106. McGrath, "Puritans and the Human Will"; Beougher, "Conversion"; Alan C. Clifford, *Atonement and Justification: English Evangelical Theology 1640-1790: An Evaluation* (Oxford: Clarendon, 1990). This does not take into consideration the research of N.H. Keeble, which only briefly deals with Baxter's soteriology in his *Richard Baxter: Puritan Man of Letters* (1982). He discusses Baxter's opposition to Antinomianism and his ideas on assurance (pp. 69-73, 132-39).
107. The material on Baxter has been published in revised form in Haskin, "Baxter's Quest for Origins," 145-61.
108. Haskin, "The Light Within," p. 44.
109. Haskin, "The Light Within," pp. 45-46; Haskin, "Baxter's Quest for Origins," 156-57. Haskin does admit that Baxter "was certain that personal illumination was not a function of some mystical experience" ("Baxter's Quest for Origins," 157-58).

James Lincoln Breed, in his dissertation of 1980 on Cotton Mather (1663-1728), deals briefly with Baxter's views on sanctification, since the second largest number of allusions and quotations in Cotton Mather's works are said to come from Baxter.[110] Breed insists that Baxter carefully distinguishes common and special grace.[111] With respect to conversion itself, Breed maintains that in Baxter's thought human reason, when stimulated by the Word of God, inevitably brings the other faculties of the soul into realignment with God's commandments. Sin is only an error of the intellect. It is only unreasonableness. Conversion is a process of concurrence between the Holy Spirit and man's reason.[112] Although Breed captures some of Baxter's emphases – most notably the large role assigned to reason – it is incorrect to state that for Baxter conversion is something primarily of the intellect. This is not Baxter's position, but that of the Huguenot theologian of Saumur, Moyse Amyraut (1596-1664). Baxter maintains that both faculties are involved in sin and conversion, but that the will is preeminent.

A more significant study on Baxter is David J. Richards' "Richard Baxter's Theory of the Atonement" (1982). The central part of this M.A. thesis is a description of Baxter's theory of the atonement. This theory is portrayed as an "eclectic Calvinistic generalism."[113] The author's main criticism of Baxter is his pressing of the Scriptural data into a legal framework: "By expressing his view of the atonement in legal categories, Baxter has been able to produce a more logical and consistent system of thought, but in the process he has necessarily had to let certain Scriptural aspects of the atonement recede into the background or to adapt their meaning to fit his legal categories."[114]

Richards' thesis is accurate in its description of Baxter's view on the atonement. He does not point out that Baxter's "legal" set-up lies anchored in his federal scheme of thought. Also, the various parts of Baxter's theory of the atonement receive only brief analysis. Some aspects are not discussed, such as the prospect of salvation for those for whom the new law has been enacted but who have not heard the Gospel. All in all, the discussion is rather brief, but accurate.

Although Von Rohr's well-known study, *The Covenant of Grace in Puritan Thought* (1986) does not focus on Baxter in particular, some comments are in place because his remarks on Baxter are illustrative of a problem which also appears in Packer's earlier dissertation. Von Rohr repeatedly quotes Baxter in a section dealing with the conditionality of the covenant, but not at all in the part which speaks of the absoluteness of the covenant.[115] This means that only half of Baxter's federal scheme is represented, even if it is the most significant part.

Three authors have recently focused on Baxter's theology: Gavin McGrath, Timothy Beougher, and Alan Clifford. McGrath's dissertation is entitled "Puri-

110. James Lincoln Breed, "Sanctification in the Theology of Cotton Mather," Diss. Aquinas Institute of Theology 1980, p. 267.
111. Breed, "Sanctification," p. 269.
112. Breed, "Conversion," pp. 273-74.
113. Richards, "Richard Baxter's Theory of the Atonement," p. 4. Cf. pp. 2, 10, 15, 104.
114. Richards, "Richard Baxter's Theory of the Atonement," pp. 52-53.
115. John Von Rohr, *The Covenant of Grace in Puritan Thought*, Studies in Religion, 45 (Atlanta: Scholars, 1986), pp. 53-55, 57, 62, 66, 71, 74-75, 78.

tans and the Human Will: Voluntarism within Mid-Seventeenth Century English Puritanism As Seen in the Works of Richard Baxter and John Owen" (1989). As the subtitle indicates, the theme of voluntarism is traced in the thought of Baxter and Owen.[116] McGrath does not ignore the differences between the two but maintains that voluntarism is a unifying factor. He suggests that "Baxter and Owen represent not so much two opposing poles in mid-seventeenth century puritanism as different shades of opinion: agreeing on some points and yet strongly disagreeing on others."[117] Because McGrath detects voluntarism in the thinking of Baxter as well as Owen he is able to present a study which approaches both antagonists in a sympathetic manner.

The dissertation begins with an introductory chapter, which is followed by a discussion of the doctrine of the human will throughout the history of the church. When McGrath comes to the difference between Baxter and Owen on the divine initiative, he focuses on their difference of opinion regarding the conditionality of the covenant. He rightly maintains that for Baxter a condition simply meant that "the actions of one party were merely suspended until the other party performed the necessary condition."[118] In speaking of the human response McGrath presents a careful exposition of Baxter's rejection of the instrumentality of faith: "Interestingly he <i.e., Baxter> turned his opponents' objections right around and argued that an instrument actually suggested that man justified himself."[119] With regard to irresistible grace McGrath states that both Baxter and Owen accept this notion, though Owen bases it on the immutability of God's decree, while Baxter bases it only on the grace of the Spirit in conversion.[120] Again, McGrath sees this difference reflected in the disparate views on the covenant and faith.[121]

In a chapter on the life of grace and the relation between grace and duty, the author is able to posit a remarkable degree of congeniality between Baxter and Owen.[122] McGrath makes no attempt to brush aside the differences between the two on the issue of perseverance. For Baxter, perseverance was a condition. The danger of apostasy "was very real and so concern was absolutely essential but the probability was that the elect, because they were predestined to faith and glory, would persevere."[123]

McGrath has written a thorough thesis. One of the most commendable aspects of it is that it remains objective, despite the obvious temptation to be drawn into the heated debates between Baxter and Owen. What is more, McGrath convincingly demonstrates that both authors have a voluntarist strain in their thinking. At

---

116. McGrath does not use the term "voluntarism" to define any particular school of thought but defines the phrase as "the prominence, but not dominance, of the will's response to God's sovereign initiatives in the divine/human encounter" (p. 3; emphasis throughout in original).
117. McGrath, "Puritans and the Human Will," p. 64.
118. McGrath, "Puritans and the Human Will," p. 186.
119. McGrath, "Puritans and the Human Will," p. 235. Cf. pp. 227-28.
120. McGrath, "Puritans and the Human Will," p. 289.
121. McGrath, "Puritans and the Human Will," p. 291.
122. McGrath, "Puritans and the Human Will," pp. 293-343. Parts of this chapter have been reworked into a popular brochure (Gavin J. McGrath, *Grace and Duty in Puritan Spirituality*, Grove Spirituality Series, 37 [Bramcote: Grove, 1991]).
123. McGrath, "Puritans and the Human Will," p. 364.

the same time, this implies a certain weakness: the serious nature of the differences between Baxter and Owen is not always brought into sharp enough focus. For instance, the difference between the two on the sufficiency of Christ's death must not be underestimated, as McGrath seems to do.[124] I also cannot agree when the author states that for Baxter a condition has no merit,[125] or that with regard to the assurance of faith Baxter only accepts the reflex act "with hesitancy and considerable qualification."[126] The main line of argument, however, is presented in a persuasive manner.

The dissertation of Timothy K. Beougher, entitled "Conversion: The Teaching and Practice of the Puritan Pastor Richard Baxter with Regard to Becoming a 'True Christian'" (1990), gives an overview of several aspects of Baxter's theology. Beougher does not limit himself to Baxter's doctrine of conversion, but also outlines the central aspects of his anthropology, his doctrine of justification, his ecclesiology, and his doctrine of the sacraments. Beougher's interpretation of Baxter is influenced by Packer's work. Also Beougher is of the opinion that Baxter's "political method" is the key to Baxter's doctrine of justification.[127] Thus, Beougher comes to the statement: "Using his political framework, he <i.e., Baxter> interprets the divine attributes as governmental attributes, manifesting themselves in God's legislation and execution of His laws."[128]

Beougher considers Baxter's doctrine of justification as being Calvinist in an orthodox sense. Says Beougher: "I am convinced that, while there were unique features in Baxter's formulation, when seen in light of his entire theology, that <sic> the differences were *largely* verbal."[129] One of the main arguments Beougher adduces for this position is that "Baxter refuses to give any merit whatsoever to man in any of these necessary actions on man's part."[130] The result of this picture of Baxter is a rather positive evaluation of his theology.

That Baxter research continues to arouse controversy is proven by Alan C. Clifford's study, *Atonement and Justification: English Evangelical Theology 1640-1790: An Evaluation* (1990). This study compares John Owen, Richard Baxter, John Tillotson (1630-94), and John Wesley (1703-91), on the points of atonement and justification. The book is "chiefly intended as a reply to John Owen."[131] This creative study witnesses a great deal of existential involvement on the part of the author. Some of his arguments have provoked rather sharp expressions of dissent.[132]

---

124. McGrath, "Puritans and the Human Will," p. 205.
125. McGrath, "Puritans and the Human Will," p. 367.
126. McGrath, "Puritans and the Human Will," p. 379.
127. Beougher, "Conversion," p. iii.
128. Beougher, "Conversion," p. 51.
129. Beougher, "Conversion," pp. 83-84.
130. Beougher, "Conversion," p. 99. Cf. pp. 92, 104.
131. Clifford, *Atonement and Justification*, p. viii.
132. Particularly sharp criticism has come from Paul Helm, rev. in *BanT*, No. 235 (1990), 29-31; and from Stephen C. Perks, "Atonement and Justification: A Review Article," *CalTo*, 1, No. 4 (1991), 26-32. Most reviews, however, have given more balanced evaluation of Clifford's study: Gerald Bray, rev. in *ChM*, 105 (1991), 93-94; D.W. Bebbington, rev. in *JURCHS*, 4 (1991), 567-68; Alister McGrath, rev. in *JThS*, 42 (1991), 397-98; Alan P.F. Sell, rev. in *PHSGBI*, 25 (1991), 293-94, rpt. in *CTJ*, 27 (1992), 116-17; W.R. Ward, rev. in *JEH*, 42 (1991), 326-27; A. Skevington Wood, rev. in *EvQ*, 63 (1991), 287-88.

Although I disagree with Clifford's position that Calvin taught universal atonement, the author does give a lucid exposition of the thought patterns of the various theologians.[133] It is Clifford's contention that Owen's doctrine of the atonement, restricting it to the elect, is couched in an Aristotelian type of "means-end terminology."[134] For Baxter, there are also other ends in the atonement.[135] Clifford charges Owen with three anomalies in his thinking: his acceptance of common grace,[136] his retaining of the free offer of grace,[137] and the fact that true believers continue to be plagued with unbelief.[138] Clifford is of the opinion that all of this is in conflict with Owen's thesis of limited atonement.

In an interesting chapter on the nature of the atonement Clifford spells out the differences between Baxter and Owen. Here again, insists Clifford, it is Owen's use of Aristotelian categories which marks the failure of his commercialist view of the atonement.[139] Clifford does state that Baxter is too dependent on Grotius' governmental view of the atonement.[140] Still, Clifford's analysis clearly favors Baxter's position over that of Owen.

CONCLUSION

The above analysis of secondary literature on Baxter's soteriology indicates that much work has already been done. Practically all aspects of his soteriology have been dealt with in one way or another. Remarkably, however, much disagreement has remained. This disagreement not only concerns the evaluation of Baxter, but often begins at the level of understanding his position as such. These differences in interpretation probably arise from a combination of factors: (1) where Baxter's soteriology, or his theology in general, constitutes but one of a number of issues investigated, some inaccuracies may arise. (2) The scholar's own theological preferences may cause him to present a biased picture of Baxter's theology, whether that be done consciously or unconsciously. (3) Baxter's discussions are often extremely intricate. In a real sense, Baxter is a scholastic theologian. His constant use of distinctions is nearly proverbial among his critics as well as his students. To understand Baxter's theological positions one must go through the arduous process of analyzing the numerous distinctions he makes. Neglecting to sort out the various nuances in these distinctions may easily lead to a misunderstanding of certain aspects of Baxter's theology. (4) Baxter's theological system is a tightly knit unit. Packer has rightly drawn attention to its consistency. Approaching the "Baxterian" system from a somewhat different theological framework may easily

---

133. I have documented my disagreement with the position that Calvin held a straightforward universalist position in "Calvin and the Extent of the Atonement," *EvQ*, 64 (1992), 333-55.
134. Clifford, *Atonement and Justification*, p. 96.
135. Clifford, *Atonement and Justification*, pp. 101-02.
136. Clifford, *Atonement and Justification*, pp. 102-05.
137. Clifford, *Atonement and Justification*, pp. 113-16.
138. Clifford, *Atonement and Justification*, p. 112.
139. Clifford, *Atonement and Justification*, p. 129.
140. Clifford, *Atonement and Justification*, pp. 130-31, 134-35.

result in misunderstanding. Once Baxter's theological method is grasped, the various pieces fit together. Prior to one's unlocking of Baxter's theological system, however, it is often difficult to locate its constitutive elements. This lack of understanding may result in an inaccurate portrayal of his theology.

The disagreements are not restricted to some incidental points. Indeed, it is a much debated question how Baxter's theology must be identified. Of course, Baxter styled himself a "Catholick Christian," an adherent to "meer Christianity."[141] But this does not take away the need to come to a more theologically determined circumscription of his position. Some regard Baxter as a Calvinist.[142] Others, however, interpret his theology as Amyraldian[143] or Arminian.[144] Then again, his theology has been described as Roman Catholic[145] or even Socinian.[146]

---

141. Cf. N.H. Keeble, "C.S. Lewis, Richard Baxter, and 'Mere Christianity'," *CaL*, 30, No. 3 (1981), 27-44.
142. Packer, "Redemption and Restoration," p. 457; Bass, "Platonic Influences," p. 179; Mair, "Christian Sanctification," p. 94; Richards, "Richard Baxter's Theory of the Atonement," pp. 2, 4, 104; Beougher, "Conversion," pp. 83-84.
143. Robert Baillie, *The Letters and Journals of Robert Baillie, A.M. Principal of the University of Glasgow. M.DC.XXXVII.-M.DC.LXII*, ed. David Lang, III (Edinburgh: Ogle, 1842), 324, 369, 390-91. Baillie also considers Baxter "stuffed with grosse Arminianisme" (p. 304). Lewis Du Moulin also charged Baxter with being Amyraldian (*Parænesis* [London, 1656], sigs. g1ᵛ, g4ᵛ). Cf. Keeble, "C.S. Lewis, Richard Baxter, and 'Mere Christianity'," 30.
144. In modern research, most statements that Baxter is Arminian are carefully qualified. C. Graafland typifies Baxter as a Reformed evangelical with Arminian tendencies (*Van Calvijn tot Barth: Oorsprong en ontwikkeling van de leer der verkiezing en het Gereformeerd Protestantisme* [The Hague: Boekencentrum, 1987], p. 201). John F.H. New speaks of "evidence of theological Arminianism" (*Anglican and Puritan: The Basis of Their Opposition, 1558-1640* [London: Black, 1964], p. 127, n. 39). F. Ernest Stoeffler speaks of a "tinge of Arminianism" which could "easily be over-stated" (*Rise of Evangelical Pietism* p. 91).
145. In fact, Baxter was called "Bellarminus Junior," an appellation adopted with some degree of relish in the anonymous *Vindiciæ Anti-Baxterianæ*, pp. 247-48. Thomas Edwards compared the "Baxterian" doctrine to the "Papist" and the "Quaker" positions in three parallel columns, with the "Baxterian" position placed in the middle (*Paraselene dismantled* [London, 1699], pp. 223-82). Edwards' book contains the following epitaph (p. 223), which is also given in Banks, "The Poems of Richard Baxter," p. 816:

    An EPITAPH
                                  * Romish Faith
    Baxter *farewel!* * Hen-Fydd's *Epitome,*
    Rome's *Vatican and Conclave fell in thee;*
    St. Omers *mourn! for thy Disciples will*
    By this find lesser Grist come to thy Mill.
    To say no more, write on his Tomb, Here lies
    The Mirror of Self-Inconsistencies:
    Or rather thus, Papal Conformity,
    Hid *under* Reformation *here doth lie.*

    The charge that Baxter's position is similar to that of Trent has been reiterated by Allison, *The Rise of Moralism*, p. 163.
146. Stephen Lobb associated Baxter with Socinianism in *Growth of Error* (London, 1697), pp. 18-20, 191-98. Baxter was defended against this charge by the anonymous *Plea For the Late Accurate and Excellent Mr. Baxter* (1699). John Owen also came close to accusing Baxter of Socinianism (cf. below, p. 43).

For lack of any proper description, many have finally resorted to the term "Baxterianism" to describe Baxter's theology.[147]

The choice of one's description or appellation is of course intimately interwoven with one's interpretation of Baxter's views. His views on the atonement are closely connected to his doctrine of justification. Some of the questions that must be discussed, therefore, are the following: what does Baxter regard as the extent and the nature of the atonement? What does it mean when he argues that Christ died for all? Did Christ die for all but perhaps not equally for all (Fisher)? What does Baxter's theory of a two-fold righteousness mean exactly? Did Christ merit freedom from the penalty (Kevan)? What is the role of faith? Is it the formal cause of justification (Allison)? What are Baxter's views on the distinction between common and special grace? Does he indeed carefully distinguish the two (Breed)? Is God's grace irresistible (Packer, McGrath) or not (Phillips, Bass)? Is salvation possible for all (Fisher, Ladell)? Perhaps one of the most important questions is: how does Baxter regard the relation between faith and works? Does he at all times shy away from the idea that man merits justification (Morgan, Kevan, McGrath, Beougher)? Does he or does he not want to speak of human conditions within the covenant (Jeremias)? Is Baxter perhaps legalistic in his outlook (Mair) and does he have an undue emphasis on works (Highfill)? Is perseverance an assured promise for all believers or does Baxter's emphasis on the conditionality of the covenant prevent him from insisting on the perseverance of the saints? How does Baxter relate justification and assurance? Does he demand careful introspection or does he only accept the reflex act with hesitancy (McGrath)? These are but some of the questions that arise from the above presentation of the present state of Baxter research. Other questions need to be addressed as they occur in the debates on justification between Baxter and some of his opponents.

Considering the differences in interpretation, it is by no means superfluous to re-investigate some aspects of Baxter's soteriology. The doctrine of justification presents itself as a logical choice: for more than forty years, from the beginning of his writing career – the publication of *Aphorismes of Justification* (1649) – to the very end of his life – the publication of *End of Doctrinal Controversies* (1691) – Baxter was embroiled in debates about justification.

There are two additional reasons why the doctrine of justification in Baxter needs investigation. First, because of the central stature of this doctrine in the range of soteriological concerns, related issues will naturally surface in a discussion of justification. This means that the differences in interpretation with regard to the whole of Baxter's soteriology will be dealt with, albeit from the perspective of the doctrine of justification. Furthermore, although various soteriological questions have been discussed before in a systematic theological manner, Baxter's numerous intensive debates surrounding justification have never before been sub-

---

147. The phrase "Baxterian Faith" was first used in 1654 by John Crandon in his *Aphorisms Exorized* (London, 1654), sig. A3[r]. It soon became a common appellation. William Robertson, in his *Iggeret hammashkil*, spoke of a "*Baxterian* definition" of pardon and of "*Baxterian* principles" ([London, 1655], pp. 29, 48, 51, 56, 58, 63, 65-66, 69-70, 122-23, 141). Thomas Edwards referred to "Baxterianism" throughout his *Paraselene dismantled*.

jected to intensive scrutiny. Both N.H. Keeble and Gavin McGrath have given a stimulus in appendices to their respective dissertations, by presenting bibliographical overviews of the controversies regarding justification between Baxter and his opponents.[148] These controversies are eminently suited to come to a good understanding of Baxter's thinking on justification. If anywhere, it is in his controversial writings that he is forced to come to terms with issues and to develop his arguments and present them at length.

Baxter's controversies concerning justification, therefore, form the subject under investigation in this study. It is my intent to come to an understanding of Baxter's doctrine of justification by means of an analysis of the various controversies. Such an analysis also leads to the identification of an interpretative key to Baxter's theory of justification. It is my contention that Baxter's doctrine of justification must be interpreted against the background of his federal scheme: the relation between the conditional and the absolute covenant, God's legislative will and his will *de rerum eventu* (regarding the actual outcome of events). This bifurcation is central to much of Baxter's thinking and therefore provides the opening into his doctrine of justification. In my analysis of Baxter's understanding of the twofold will of God I will, by and large, refrain from discussing the medieval background to this distinction. As will become clear in this study, the immediate background to Baxter's distinction does not lie in Nominalist theology, but in seventeenth-century high Calvinist theology. Furthermore, due to the rise of scholastic methodologies in seventeenth-century Protestantism, the distinction between the two aspects of God's will became common place. The obvious indirect dependence on medieval scholasticism is, therefore, assumed throughout, rather than explicitly discussed with every reference to the twofold will of God.

A few comments with regard to the structure of the remainder of this study may be in order. The next chapter begins with an overview of Baxter's religious and theological development. This also serves to give some biographical information which will facilitate an understanding of Baxter's position on justification. The same chapter also gives a detailed historical account of his controversies on justification. The isolation of the historical part into a separate chapter allows for a more systematic theological approach in the remainder of this study. The controversial setting of Baxter's theory of justification comes to the fore in chapter three, which deals with the relation between justification and faith in several of his opponents. Baxter rejects their position that faith follows justification *in foro Dei*. His rejection of the high Calvinist doctrine of justification from eternity raises the question how he views the role of faith. Chapter four deals with this question. In this connection, Baxter's doctrine of common grace is discussed, as well as his position that faith in Christ as Savior *and* Lord is part of the condition of justification, and his denial of the instrumentality of faith.

Baxter bases his understanding of the role of faith on his theory of the atonement. Thus, chapter five begins with a discussion of the various influences on his

---

148. N.H. Keeble, "Some Literary and Religious Aspects," pp. 342-44; McGrath, "Puritans and the Human Will," pp. 392-95.

view of the atonement. This is followed by an investigation of the extent and the nature of the atonement. This entails a look at Baxter's solution to the question whether there is a double imputation – of Christ's passive and active righteousness – or a single imputation – of Christ's passive righteousness only. The relation between Christ and the believers in his work as Mediator is carefully scrutinized.

This brings the discussion to the main reason why the polemics between Baxter and his opponents were often heated: Baxter's antagonists feared that he introduced justification by works. As will become clear, Baxter indeed taught a two-fold righteousness: Christ's legal righteousness and one's personal evangelical righteousness. Although Baxter considered this latter aspect as only a small contribution – a "pepper corn" – by way of condition only, his opponents found his "pepper corn" too hot to swallow. It was ultimately this little "pepper corn" which raised the temperature in the debate.

Chapter II

Historical Introduction

Ten Thousand Stars and Candles give one Light,
Concordant Sounds make one sweet Melody.
Two Ears, One hearing Cause, Two Eyes, One Sight;
But Light and Darkness have no Unity.[1]

(Richard Baxter)

THEOLOGICAL DEVELOPMENT UNTIL 1649

Baxter's "Middle Way" Amyraldian?

Baxter's theology is difficult to define. Baxter himself located his position in between Calvinism and Arminianism.[2] He certainly had a high regard for the school of Saumur and for its spiritual father, John Cameron (c. 1580-1625).[3] Many of the works of Salmurian divines had a place in Baxter's library.[4] Among his extensive correspondence in Doctor Williams's Library, London, is a letter from Paul Testard (1599-1650), who, along with Moyse Amyraut, was criticized at the Synods of Alençon (1637) and Charenton (1644) for his universalist position.[5]

---

1. In Banks, "Poems of Richard Baxter," p. 223.
2. Baxter explicitly attempted to reconcile both parties in his *Catholick Theologie* (1675).
3. For Cameron, see *DNB* 8.295-96; Gaston Bonet Maury, "John Cameron: A Scottish Protestant Theologian in France," *ScHR*, 7 (1910), 325-45. For Cameron's theological views, see François Laplanche, *Orthodoxie et Prédication: L'œvre d'Amyraut et la querelle de la grâce universelle*, Études d'histoire et de philosophie religieuses, 59 (Paris: Presses universitaires de France, 1965), pp. 50-57; Brian G. Armstrong, *Calvinism and the Amyraut Heresy: Protestant Scholasticism and Humanism in Seventeenth-Century France* (Madison: Univ. of Wisconsin Press, 1969), pp. 42-70; Stephen Strehle, *Calvinism, Federalism, and Scholasticism: A Study of the Reformed Doctrine of Covenant*, Basler und Berner Studien zur historischen und systematischen Theologie, 58 (Bern: Lang, 1988), pp. 198-205; *CCRB* 116, n.3.
4. See Geoffrey F. Nuttall, "A Transcript of Richard Baxter's Library Catalogue: A Bibliographical Note," *JEH*, 2 (1951), 207-21; and Geoffrey F. Nuttall, "A Transcript of Richard Baxter's Library Catalogue (Concluded)," *JEH*, 3 (1952), 74-100, items 49-50, 231-35, 239-41, 250-51, 265, 279, 336, 448, 460, 464, 527.
5. DWL MS *BC* v, ff. 21ʳ-24ᵛ (*CCRB* 1022). For Amyraut and the Amyraldian controversy, see Jürgen Moltmann, "Prädestination und Heilsgeschichte bei Moyse Amyraut: Ein Beitrag zur Geschichte der reformierten Theologie zwischen Orthodoxie und Aufklärung," *ZKG*, 65 (1954), 270-303; David Sabean, "The Theological Rationalism of Moïse Amyraut," *ARG*, 55 (1964), 204-16; Laplanche, *Orthodoxie et Prédication*; Armstrong, *Calvinism and the Amyraut Heresy*; Roger Nicole, *Moyse Amyraut: A Bibliography with Special Reference to the Controversy on Universal Grace* (New York: Garland, 1981); F.P. Van Stam, *The Controversy over the Theology of Saumur, 1635-1650: Disrupting Debates among the Huguenots in Complicated Circumstances*, Diss. Am-

Amyraut wrote a letter to Baxter, in which he expressed his high regard for the latter.[6]

To identify Baxter as an Amyraldian divine, however, fails to take into account at least four factors. First, Baxter himself disclaimed that the essentials of his teaching were taken from Cameron or Amyraut.[7] Writing to Peter Ince (1615?-1683) in 1653, Baxter comments with regard to John Davenant (1576-1641) and Amyraut:

> I p<ro>fess y<a>[t] I never (to my remembrance) received one opinion from either of y<e>[m], so I am as unapt to yield up my understanding to any man & to goe uppon trust, as most men y<a>[t] ever yet I was acquainted w<i>[th]; & do suspect rather y<a>[t] my fault lies y<a>[t] way; & y<a>[t] I am guilty of overvaluing Davenant & Amyraldus (& more Camero & Baronius) for their agreeing w<i>[th] my iugdm<en>[t], y<a>[n] of captivating mine to theirs.[8]

Second, Baxter's first publication, *Aphorismes of Justification* (1649), does not support the hypothesis that the teachings of Saumur were Baxter's most influential source. The treatise refers only twice both to Cameron and to Amyraut. The frequent references to Hugo Grotius, John Goodwin (1594?-1665), William Bradshaw (1571-1618), John Ball (1585-1640), and George Downham (d. 1634) stand in marked contrast to the paucity of references to the Salmurian divines.[9] Also John Owen, Johannes Maccovius (1588-1644), *The Marrow of Modern Divinity* (1645), and John Saltmarsh (c. 1612-47) occur frequently, albeit that Baxter only uses them as examples of aberrant types of theology.[10] Finally, Baxter often appeals to William Pemble (c. 1592-1623) and William Twisse (1578?-1646), to

---

sterdam 1988, Studies of the Institute Pierre Bayle, Nijmegen (SIB), 19 (Amsterdam: APA-Holland University Press, 1988); Strehle, *Calvinism, Federalism, and Scholasticism*, pp. 206-14; Stephen Strehle, "The Extent of the Atonement and the Synod of Dort," *WThJ*, 51 (1989), 1-23; Stephen Strehle, "Universal Grace and Amyraldianism," *WThJ*, 51 (1989), 345-57.

6. For the Latin text of the letter, see *RB* II.442. Elisabeth Labrousse gives both the Latin text and a French translation, as well as an evaluation of the historical setting of the letter in "Une lettre de Moïse Amyraut à Richard Baxter," *BSHPF*, 119 (1973), 566-75. Cf. *CCRB* 708.

7. Baxter, *Certain Disputations* (London, 1657), sig. b3[v]. Cf. below, p. 198.

8. DWL MS *BC* i, f. 11[v] (*CCRB* 148). Baxter refers to Robert Baronius as "Camero *secundus, vel* Cameroni *secundus*" (*Reduction* [London, 1654], p. 71). For Davenant, see *DNB* 14.101; Morris Fuller, *The Life Letters and Writings of John Davenant D.D. 1572-1641 Lord Bishop of Salisbury* (London: Methuen, 1897); H.R. McAdoo, *The Structure of Caroline Moral Theology* (London: Longmans, Green and Co, 1949), pp. 101-07; Allison, *Rise of Moralism*, pp. 5-14, 127-32; William Robert Godfrey, "Tensions within International Calvinism: The Debate on the Atonement at the Synod of Dort, 1618-1619," Diss. Stanford Univ. 1974, pp. 179-88.

9. Baxter, *Aphorismes* (London, 1649) I.39, 41, 55, 80, 94-95, 146, 331; II.122, 125, 138-39, 143-45, 151 (2nd ed. [Cambridge, 1655], pp. 26, 28, 37, 52, 61-62, 95, 212, 291-92, 301-02, 305-06, 310) (for Grotius); I.18, 52, 54, 183, 187, 306; II.126 (pp. 12, 35-36, 118, 120, 196, 294) (for Goodwin); I.52, 55, 59, 183, 187, 199, 306, 314-15; II.12 (pp. 35, 37, 40, 118, 121, 127, 196, 201, 230) (for Bradshaw); I.54, 197, 222, 317, 332; II.181-85 (pp. 36, 126, 141, 203, 213, 330-32) (for Ball); I.190-91, 234, 254, 282, 289 (pp. 122-23, 149, 162, 180, 185) (for Downham).

10. Baxter, *Aphorismes* II.9, 124-25, 137-45, 151, 181 (pp. 229, 292-93, 301-06, 310, 330) (for Owen); II.9, 124-25, 136, 146, 151 (pp. 229, 292-93, 300, 307, 310) (for Maccovius); I.330; II.8, 76, 99 (pp. 211, 228, 262, 276) (for *The Marrow of Modern Divinity*); I.90, 113, 276, 316; II.35 (pp. 58, 74, 176, 202, 245 [incorrect pagination; sig. O4[r]]) (for Saltmarsh).

whom he has a particularly ambivalent attitude.[11] A third factor which should cause some restraint in identifying Amyraldian influences on Baxter is the fact that he recommends large lists of theologians who all mediate between Arminianism and Calvinism. In these lists, scattered throughout his writings, Baxter mentions not just the theologians of Saumur and the above mentioned theologians, but also others, among whom the most significant are George Lawson (d. 1678), John Preston (1587-1628), Thomas Gataker (1574-1654), Anthony Wotton (1561?-1626), John Gibbon (1629-63), James Ussher (1581-1656), John Strang (1584-1654), Johannes Berg (1587-1658), Conrad Berg (1592-1642), Petrus Van Mastricht (1630-1706), Martin Bucer (1491-1551), and Lewis Le Blanc (c. 1614-75). Baxter singles out the moderate British delegates – George Carleton (1559-1628), Joseph Hall (1574-1656), John Davenant, Samuel Ward (1571-1641), Walter Balcanquhall (1586?-1645), and Thomas Goad (1576-1638) – as well as the Bremen delegates – Matthias Martini (1572-1630), Heinrich Isselburg (1577-1628), and Lewis Crocius (1586-1655) – to the Synod of Dort (1618-19) as representatives of the general theological stand which he supports.[12] As will become clear in the remainder of this study, Baxter appeals to several of these divines on more than one occasion. In the fourth place, it should be noted that there are a number of significant issues on which Baxter registers his dissent from the teachings of the Salmurian professors Moyse Amyraut and Joshua Placaeus (1606-55).[13]

Early Theological Development

If it was not primarily Cameron or Amyraut who influenced Baxter, the question arises what the historical origin of Baxter's "middle way" is. There is no simple answer to this question. Perhaps the best way to describe his theology is to say that it is eclectic.[14] Baxter insists that he is concerned about the truth.[15] Truth is to be

---

11. Baxter, *Aphorismes*, sig. a6ʳ; I.98, 173, 190-91, 222, 254, 282, 294, 297, 300, 303; sig. Q1ᵛ; II.163 (sig. A6ʳ, pp. 64, 112, 122-23, 141, 162, 180, 188, 190, 192, 194; sig. M1ʳ; p. 318) (for Pemble); I.2, 173, 290; II.163, 168, 172-73 (pp. 2, 112, 185, 318, 321, 324) (for Twisse).
12. Baxter, *Saints Rest* (1650), in *Works* III.3 (22.7); *Plain Scripture Proof*, 4th ed. (London, 1656), pp. 193, 275; *Christian Directory* (1673), in *Works* I.733 (5.591); *Confutation* (London, 1654), p. 202; *Of Justification* (London, 1658), p. 167; *Catholick Theologie* (London, 1675) II.286; *Two Disputations* (London, 1675), pp. 47-48; *Answer* (London, 1675), pp. 47, 84; *Breviate* (London, 1690), sig. A2ᵛ; *Defence of Christ* (London, 1690), sig. A6ᵛ, pp. 46-47, 55.
13. Baxter disagreed, for instance, with Amyraut's intellectualist view of faith (*Certain Disputations*, p. 397), with his view of the conditionality of God's decree (*Plain Scripture Proof*, p. 275), and with Placaeus' theory of original sin (*Two Disputations*, pp. 148, 213-24, 229; *Catholick Theologie* II.111).
14. Several scholars have drawn attention to Baxter's eclecticism: Jenkyn, introd., in Baxter, *Making Light of Christ and Salvation*, pp. xlv, l; Geoffrey F. Nuttall, *Richard Baxter and Philip Doddridge: A Study in Tradition* (London: Oxford Univ. Press, 1951), p. 2; Bass, "Platonic Influences," p. 294; Shealy, "Power of the Present," pp. 29-35; Richards, "Richard Baxter's Theory of the Atonement," pp. 2, 4, 10, 15, 104; Beougher, "Conversion," p. 47.
  That eclecticism was by no means uncommon for seventeenth-century Protestant thought has recently been demonstrated in the case of Arminius by Richard A. Muller (*God, Creation, and Providence in the Thought of Jacob Arminius: Sources and Directions of Scholastic Protestantism in the Era of Early Orthodoxy* [Grand Rapids: Baker, 1991]). Although Muller interprets Arminius' theology as "modified Thomism" (p. 271), he repeatedly draws attention to other influences as well. He regards Arminius as an eclectic theologian (pp. 48, 78, 132, 272).
15. DWL MS *BC* i, f. 11ʳ (*CCRB* 148); *Catholick Theologie* II.282; *RB* I.114.

valued, wherever it may be found. This is at least part of the reason why a su-pralapsarian as William Twisse as well as an Arminian as Hugo Grotius, could have a profound impact on Baxter's thinking.[16]

It is possible, however, to say more than just that Baxter created his own amalgam from various theological sources. His upbringing and theological training sheds some light on this matter. As Nuttall says, Baxter's primary schooling in his hometown of Rowton, Shropshire, was "worse than scanty."[17] His father, however, made him read the Scriptures, so that he came "to love the Bible, and to search by degrees into the rest."[18] On Sundays, while the people of the village were dancing under the maypole, Baxter's father was reading the Scriptures. He was, therefore, scorned as a Puritan. Because his father's religious behavior was the cause of mockery, Baxter became convinced "that Godly People were the best, and those that despised them and lived in Sin and Pleasure, were a malignant unhappy sort of People."[19] Baxter's education changed for the better when he was taught by a certain John Owen in the school of Donnington, Wroxeter.[20] At about this time, Baxter read *Bunny's Resolution*, a book written by the Jesuit author Robert Parsons, and edited by Edmund Bunny. Baxter states that God used the book "to awaken my Soul" and to show him "the necessity of resolving on a Holy Life."[21] The book also moderated his attitude toward Roman Catholicism.[22] A book of Richard Sibbes, *The bruised reede and smoaking flax* (1630), and some of William Perkins' works helped to further Baxter's conversion at this time.[23]

Upon the advise of his teacher, Baxter decided not to go to university when he was sixteen. He instead left for Ludlow, where Richard Wickstead, chaplain to the Council of the Welsh Marches, would tutor him. Baxter felt he was "deceived," since Wickstead was a poor scholar and cared little about the education of his student.[24] Baxter could, however, make full use of Wickstead's library. Back home, Baxter taught at the school in Donnington for a few months and then studied some logic under the minister of Wroxeter, Francis Garbett.[25]

---

16. This eclectic tendency in Baxter's thinking means that it is not possible to give a brief overview of the main source(s) of his theology. Instead, it is necessary to trace the impact of individual theologians on Baxter in discussing the particular issues surrounding the doctrine of justification.
17. Nuttall, *Richard Baxter*, p. 2. Baxter describes his teachers as ignorant, immoral and given to excessive drinking (*RB* I.1-2).
18. *RB* I.2.
19. *RB* I.3.
20. *RB* I.1. Cf. Nuttall, *Richard Baxter*, p. 3.
21. *RB* I.3. Baxter comments, however, that "whether sincere Conversion began *now*, or *before*, or *after*, I was never able to this day to know ..." (*RB* I.3).
22. Baxter, *Safe Religion* (London, 1657), sigs. a1ʳ⁻ᵛ: "I was born and bred here among the Professors of the Reformed Catholik Christian Religion. When I was young, I judged of your <i.e., the Romanists'> Profession as I was taught, and the prejudice which I received against it, did grow up with me, as yours doth against us. Yet receiving much good to my soul by *Parsons* Book of Resolution corrected (when I was but sixteen years of Age) it run much in my mind, that sure there were some among you that had the Fear of God." Baxter also recalls his benefit from this book in *Against the Revolt* (London, 1691), pp. 539-40.
23. *RB* I.4.
24. *RB* I.4.
25. *RB* I.5.

Baxter states that his studies of logic led him to a "closer Course of Study."[26] Although he continued to read numerous practical works, he now also engaged in the study of medieval scholasticism, to which he took a particular liking. Baxter comments that next to practical divinity, "no Books so suited with my Disposition as *Aquinus, Scotus, Durandus, Ockam,* and their Disciples ..."[27] Baxter "read all the School men <he> could get ..."[28] At a later age, he came to regret his excessive zeal for scholasticism. Its value was not as great as he first thought.[29]

Yet, Baxter retained a high regard for medieval scholasticism and freely made use of scholastic distinctions and methodology both in his polemical writings and in his systematic treatises. In his controversial writings, he often presents his arguments in syllogistic form. Perhaps more significant are his appeals to scholastic metaphysics and theology to buttress his arguments. The names of Bonaventura (1221-74), Thomas Aquinas, John Duns Scotus (c. 1266-1308), Durandus of Sancto Porciano (c. 1270-1332), Francis Suárez (1548-1617), Diego Álvarez (d. 1631), Diego Hutardo de Mendoza (1503-75), and others are found throughout Baxter's writings.

There has also been some discussion of the influence of Ramist logic on Baxter.[30] Peter Ramus (1515-72) had revolutionized Protestant theological methodology by suggesting that Aristotelian logic be replaced by a method in which self-evident axioms are arranged according to their natural order, going down from universals to singulars by means of bifurcations.[31] There is no denying that to

26. *RB* I.5.
27. *RB* I.6.
28. *RB* I.6.
29. Says Baxter: "In my youth I was quickly past my Fundamentals, and was running up into a multitude of Controversies, and greatly delighted with metaphisical and scholastick Writings (though I must needs say, my Preaching was still on the necessary Points): But the elder I grew the smaller stress I layd upon these Controversies and Curiosities (though still my intellect abhorreth Confusion), as finding far greater Uncertainties in them, than I at first discerned, and finding less *Usefulness* comparatively, even where there is the greatest Certainty" (*RB* I.126). Yet, comments Baxter, "I would not dissuade my Reader from the perusal of *Aquinas, Scotus, Ockam, Arminiensis, Durandus,* or any such Writer; for much Good may be gotten from them: But I would persuade him to study and live upon the essential Doctrines of Christianity and Godliness, incomparably above them all" (*RB* I.127).
30. Jenkyn, introd., in Baxter, *Making Light,* pp. l-li; Packer, "Redemption and Restoration," pp. 32-34, 57-63, 82-84; Mair, "Christian Sanctification," p. 252; Shealy, "Power of the Present," p. 376, n. 1; Keith L. Sprunger, "Ames, Ramus, and the Method of Puritan Theology," *HThR,* 59 (1966), 134, 148; Beougher, "Conversion," pp. 40-42. Most of these references to Ramist influence on Baxter are unfortunately incidental. The subject is worthy of more in depth study.
31. For Ramism, see Kenneth McRae, "Ramist Tendencies in the Thought of Jean Bodin," *JHI,* 16 (1955), 306-23; Perry Miller, "The Marrow of Puritan Divinity," in *Errand into the Wilderness* (New York: Harper & Row, 1956), pp. 48-98; Bass, "Platonic Influences," pp. 64-82; Walter J. Ong, *Ramus: Method, and the Decay of Dialogue: From the Art of Discourse to the Art of Reason* (Cambridge, MA: Harvard Univ. Press, 1958); Peter Toon, *The Emergence of Hyper-Calvinism in English Nonconformity 1689-1765,* pref. J.I. Packer (London: Olive Tree, 1967), pp. 24-25; Sprunger, "Ames, Ramus, and the Method of Puritan Theology," 133-51; John Dykstra Eusden, Introd., in William Ames, *The Marrow of Theology,* trans. and ed. John D. Eusden, foreword Douglas Horton (1968; rpt. Durham, NC: Labyrinth, 1983), pp. 37-47; Robert Letham, "The *Foedus Operum*: Some Factors Accounting for Its Development," *SCJ,* 14 (1983), 457-67; Ames (1968); W. Wilson Benton, "Federal Theology: Review for Revision," in *Through Christ's Word: A Festschrift for Dr. Philip E. Hughes,* ed. W. Robert Godfrey and Jesse L. Boyd III (Phillipsburg: Presbyterian and Reformed, 1985), pp. 195-200; Donald K. McKim, *Ramism in William Perkins' Theology,* American University Studies, Series VII: Theology and Religion, 15 (New York: Lang, 1987).

Baxter "*Method* is a great help to understanding and memory."[32] Baxter owned two copies of Ramus' *Dialectica*,[33] occasionally refers to Ramus,[34] and – most significantly – consciously replaced the method of dichotomies with his own trichotomies.[35] Baxter was convinced that there were *vestigia trinitatis* throughout creation. A true method of theology must be ordered accordingly. Consequently, his main systematic treatise, *Methodus Theologiæ* (1681), abounds with schemes presented in the way of bifid and, especially, trifid distinctions. Thus, Ramus had at least an indirect influence on Baxter's method.

When he was about eighteen, Baxter spent a month in London with Sir Henry Herbert in Whitehall, London. Disheartened by the low spiritual level at court, Baxter returned home around Christmas, 1634.[36] In the next few years, he met with a group of pious nonconformists in Shrewsbury. One of the leaders of this group was Walter Cradock (1606?-59), whose Antinomianism Baxter later deplored.[37] In 1638, he was ordained as deacon and served for nine months as a teacher in Dudley, Worcestershire. He moved to Bridgnorth, Shropshire in 1640, where he became the assistant pastor of the town until he went to Kidderminster, Worcestershire in April, 1641.

To understand Baxter's resolution of a number of theological issues in the next decade it is important to realize that his faith underwent a serious crisis during this early period in Kidderminster. Baxter questioned "the certain Truth of the Sacred Scriptures; and also the Life to come, and Immortality of the Soul."[38] In "the storm of this Temptation" Baxter even questioned if he were really a Christian, since he could not believe that faith might consist with the kind of doubts which he had.[39] Although Baxter overcame this crisis, he continued to struggle with his doubts. He had no question that he needed "daily Prayer, That God would increase my Faith."[40]

---

32. Baxter, *Catholick Theologie* I.i.2. Cf. *RB* I.6: "*Distinction* and *Method* seemed to me of that necessity, that without them I could not be said to know; and the Disputes which *forsook* them, or *abused* them, seem but as incoherent Dreams." Cf. *Answer*, pp. 30-31; *Treatise of Justifying Righteousness* (London, 1676), sig. A4ʳ; *End of Doctrinal Controversies* (London, 1691), pp. 146-47.
33. Nuttall, "Transcript," 207-21; and Nuttall, "Transcript (Concluded)," 74-100, items 327, 512.
34. Baxter, *Saints Rest*, in *Works* III.235-36 (23.135); *Reasons of the Christian Religion* (1667), in *Works* II.94 (21.187).
35. Baxter, *Methodus Theologiæ* (London, 1681), sigs. A5ʳ⁻ᵛ; *RB* III.69. Cf. Packer, "Redemption and Restoration," pp. 82-84.
36. *RB* I.11.
37. Nuttall, *Richard Baxter*, p. 12. For Cradock, see Benjamin Brook, *The Lives of the Puritans: Containing a Biographical Account of Those Divines Who Distinguished Themselves in the Cause of Religious Liberty, from the Reformation under Queen Elizabeth, to the Act of Uniformity, in 1662* (London: Black, 1813), III, 382-86; *DNB* 12.438; Geoffrey F. Nuttall, "Walter Cradock (1606?-1659): The Man and His Message," in *The Puritan Spirit: Essays and Addresses* (London: Epworth, 1967), pp. 118-29; Geoffrey F. Nuttall, *The Welsh Saints 1640-1660: Walter Cradock, Vavasor Powell, Morgan Llwyd* (Cardiff: Univ. of Wales Press, 1957), pp. 18-36; *BDBRSC* 1.186-87.
38. *RB* I.21. Sidney H. Rooy wrongly states that Baxter never doubted the truth of Scripture and Christianity but only the genuineness of his faith in Christ (*Theology of Missions*, p. 69).
39. *RB* I.22.
40. *RB* I.24.

These personal experiences contributed to Baxter's conviction that the degree of certainty varies with the evidence one has. Says Baxter:

> My certainty that I am a Man, is before my certainty that there is a God; for *Quod facit notum est magis notum:* My certainty that there is a God, is greater than my certainty that he requireth love and holiness of his Creature: My certainty of *this* is greater than my certainty of the Life of Reward and Punishment hereafter: My certainty of that, is greater than my certainty of the endless duration of it, and of the immortality of individuate Souls: My certainty of the Deity is greater than my certainty of the Christian Faith: My certainty of the Christian Faith in its Essentials, is greater than my certainty of the Perfection and Infallibility of all the Holy Scriptures: My certainty of that is greater than my certainty of the meaning of many particular Texts, and so of the truth of many particular Doctrines, or of the Canonicalness of some certain Books. So that as you see by what Gradations my Understanding doth proceed, so also that my Certainty differeth as the Evidences differ.[41]

As faith builds on reason, so one can be more certain of things established by reason than of matters established by faith.[42] Faith is an act of elevated reason.[43] It has rightly been commented that in Baxter "there is the recognition that he has not yet arrived and perhaps never will arrive at the final answers to all his questions."[44]

Army Experiences

Baxter's epistemological uncertainty in his early years in Kidderminster did not result in scepticism. Some of the difficulties that he was unable to resolve at an earlier stage came to a head when he entered the army. When the Civil War broke out, Baxter took refuge in the parliamentary garrison of Coventry. During this quiet period, in which he could pursue his studies, he resolved his doubts about infant baptism. Influenced by his reading of two high Calvinists, Pemble and Twisse, Baxter also engaged in a dispute against Samuel Cradock (d. 1654) and Tristram Dimond "to prove *Remission of Sin* (not only Conditional but Actual) to be an *Immediate effect* of Christ's Death, and pleaded for it, *Heb.* 1.3. and *Rom.* 8.32. (and against Universal Redemption) which I since perceive I misunderstood and abused."[45] The arguments of Cradock and Dimond forced Baxter to reevaluate the doctrine of the covenants and justification. He later admitted that up to this point he "had never read one *Socinian*, nor much of any *Arminians* ..."[46]

The real impetus toward the resolution of many theological questions came in the summer of 1645, when Baxter accepted General Whalley's offer to become a chaplain in his parliamentary army. Baxter only stayed with the New Model Army

---

41. *RB* I.128.
42. Cf. Margaret L. Wiley, "Richard Baxter and the Problem of Certainty," in *The Subtle Knot: Creative Scepticism in Seventeenth-Century England* (London: Allen and Unwin, 1952), pp. 172-74.
43. Baxter, *Reasons of the Christian Religion*, in *Works* II.98 (21.200).
44. Wiley, "Richard Baxter and the Problem of Certainty," p. 171.
45. Baxter, *Penitent Confession* (London, 1691), p. 24. For Dimond, see *CR* 164-65. Cf. *CCRB* 10.
46. Baxter, *Catholick Theologie*, I, sig. a2ᵛ.

until February, 1647. But these few years were decisive. Baxter was surprised by
the anti-royalist mood in the army: "I heard the plotting Heads very hot upon that
which intimated their Intention to subvert both Church and State. Independency
and Anabaptistry were most prevalent: Antinomianism and Arminianism were
equally distributed ..."[47] Baxter was astonished that a few "hot-headed Sectaries"
had managed to become "the Soul of the Army."[48] He felt compelled to enter into
debate with the sectarian soldiers:

> I found that many honest Men of weak judgments and little acquaintance with
> such Matters, had been seduced into a disputing vein, and made it too much of their
> Religion to talk for this Opinion and for that; sometimes for State Democracy, and
> sometime for Church Democracy; sometimes against Forms of Prayer, and some-
> times against Infant Baptism, (which yet some of them did maintain); sometimes
> against Set-times of Prayer, and against the tying of our selves to any Duty before
> the Spirit move us; and sometimes about Free-grace and Free-will, and all the Points
> of Antinomianism and Arminianism. So that I was almost always, when I had oppor-
> tunity, disputing with one or other of them ...[49]

In February, 1647 Baxter's health collapsed. He stayed for three months at Rous
Lench, Worcestershire, at the house of Sir Thomas and Lady Rous, convalescing
from his break-down before returning to Kidderminster. The restful period at
Rous Lench was the occasion not only of the writing of the *Saints Everlasting Rest*
(1650) but also of the resolution of issues surrounding the extent of the atonement
and justification. While working on his *Saints Everlasting Rest* Baxter came to
Matthew 25, which appeared to teach justification by works. His grappling with
this chapter, as well as "two or three things" which he remembered from reading
William Twisse, inclined him to moderation regarding the issues on which Arminians and Calvinists disagreed.[50] Despite the fact that his experiences in the army
had prepared Baxter for this change in views, it still happened suddenly: "An
over-powring Light (I thought) did suddenly give me a clear apprehension of those
things, which I had oft reached after before in vain. Whereupon I suddenly wrote
down the bare Propositions (so many of them as concerns Righteousness and
Justification,) and so let them lye by me long after."[51] Lamont rightly comments
that this meant a "genuine turning-point" in Baxter's career.[52] He had now laid the

47. *RB* I.50. Elsewhere, Baxter speaks of the sectarians in the army as "part Arminians, but most
    Antinomians or worse" (*Penitent Confession*, p. 22; cf. *Of Imputation* [London, 1675], p. 22).
48. *RB* I.50.
49. *RB* I.53. Cf. I.54, 56; Nuttall, *Richard Baxter*, pp. 36-37.
50. Baxter, *Aphorismes*, sigs. a7ʳ⁻ᵛ (A6ʳ⁻ᵛ); *Unsavoury Volume* (London, 1654), p. 5; *Confession* (Lon-
    don, 1655), p. 2; *Catholick Theologie*, I, sig. a2ᵛ; *RB* I.107. Cf. *Of Justification*, p. 171. For
    Twisse's influence on Baxter, see below, pp. 66-67, 80-89, 195-97.
51. Baxter, *Unsavoury Volume*, p. 5. In his *Aphorismes*, Baxter writes: I "discovered more in one
    weeke, then I had done before in seventeen yeares reading, hearing and wrangling" (II.110-11 [pp.
    283-84]). Cf. Packer, "Redemption and Restoration," pp. 232-33.
52. William M. Lamont, *Richard Baxter and the Millennium: Protestant Imperialism and the English
    Revolution*, Croom Helm Social History Series (London: Croom Helm; Totowa, NJ: Rowman and
    Littlefield, 1979), p. 67.

groundwork for his doctrine of justification. These basic outlines remained unaltered for the rest of his life.

PRIVATE ANIMADVERSIONS

Anthony Burgess and Richard Vines

What had begun by way of a background study to the *Saints Everlasting Rest* expanded into a treatise all by itself, a treatise which would take up much of Baxter's time in the next few years: *Aphorismes of Justification, With their Explication annexed. Wherein also is opened the nature of the Covenants, Satisfaction, Righteousnesse, Faith, Works, &c.* (1649). The immediate reaction was one of violent opposition. In a letter of September 11, 1649 to his neighboring antipaedo-baptist pastor, John Tombes (1603?-76), Baxter wrote:

> I have voluntarily been more prodigal of my reputation in putting out that Pamphlet of Justification, which I well know was like to blast my reputation with most Divines, as containing that which they judge a more dangerous errour then Anti-pædo-baptism, and the issue hath answered my expectation: I am now so hissed at by them, that I feel temptation enough to schism in my discontents[53]

Admittedly, when Baxter published this letter in 1653, in the third edition of *Plain Scripture Proof*, he commented in a marginal note "that I have found as brotherly loving dealing about them as I could desire, and more then I did expect; and that from the most Divines that I have to do with."[54] Nevertheless, it is evident that the *Aphorismes* created an outcry among many Calvinists in England.[55]

Even the reactions of Richard Vines (c. 1600-56) and Anthony Burgess (fl. 1652), to whom Baxter dedicated his *Aphorismes*, were not entirely positive.[56] It had been a politically astute move to dedicate the book to these divines. Both were respected members of the Westminster Assembly (1643-49). Vines, who was Master

---

53. Baxter, *Plain Scripture Proof*, p. 409.
54. Baxter, *Plain Scripture Proof*, p. 409 (emphasis inverted).
55. Baxter gives an account of the private animadversions received on his *Aphorismes* in *RB* I.107-08. In this account, he gives the following order in which he received the animadversions: Anthony Burgess, John Warren, John Wallis, Christopher Cartwright, George Lawson. Baxter's account, written in 1664, is not completely accurate. He omits the comments he received from Richard Vines and John Tombes. The historical order – as indicated by the date of the receipt of the first letter from each opponent – must be (1) John Warren (August 27, 1649); (2) Anthony Burgess (December 3, 1649); (3) Richard Vines (July 1, 1650); (4) John Tombes (probably May, 1651); (5) George Lawson (perhaps July, 1651); (6) Christopher Cartwright (perhaps May, 1652); (7) John Wallis (June 28, 1652). The dates of (5) and (6) are uncertain and may have to be reversed and perhaps even be placed prior to (4) (cf. below, p. 38; p. 40, n. 123).
56. For Richard Vines, see *GBD* 30.394-96; Brook, *Lives*, III, 230-35; James Reid, *Memoirs of the Lives and Writings of Those Eminent Divines, Who Convened in the Famous Assembly at Westminster, in the Seventeenth Century*, Vol. II (1811, 1815; rpt. Edinburgh: Banner of Truth, 1982), 191-99.*DNB* 58.369-71; *CCRB* 14. For Anthony Burgess, see Reid, *Memoirs*, I, 146-54; *DNB* 7.308; *CR* 86-87; *CCRB* 14.

of Pembroke Hall, Cambridge, had been on the committee which had drafted the Westminster Confession of Faith (1647). Burgess had already demonstrated his opposition to the Antinomians in two treatises, one on the role of the moral law (*Vindiciæ legis: Or, A Vindication of the Morall Law and the Covenants, From the Errours of Papists, Arminians, Socinians, and more especially, Antinomians*, 1646) and one on the doctrine of justification (*The True Doctrine of Ivstification Asserted, and Vindicated, from The Errors of Papists, Arminians, Socinians, and more especially Antinomians*, 1648). But Baxter did not receive the support he was probably hoping for. He writes: "Mr. *Vines* wrote to me applaudingly of it. Mr. *Burgess* thought his Name engaged him to write against it."[57]

Burgess' reaction was, in fact, quite negative. Baxter had heard that Burgess "disliked some things in my Aphorisms" and asked him to specify his objections.[58] In the first letter of a correspondence which extended from December 3, 1649 until June 28, 1650 Burgess commented that there were indeed some doctrinal points which made him "vehemently dissent" from Baxter's *Aphorismes*, such as "many positions about Christs Righteousness, about faiths Justification in your sense, and the Efficacy of new Obedience in this work as well as faith."[59] Since Burgess declined to be specific, Baxter entreated him as yet to send him one or two of his strongest arguments: "I know it is not an hours work with you to do that much; and I would bestow twenty for you."[60] In his reply, Burgess again refused to present Baxter with animadversions on his *Aphorismes*, except that he indicated that the apostle Paul excludes "all works under any notion" from justification.[61] He proposed to meet Baxter in Birmingham to discuss the matter further.[62] But Baxter felt he had to reject the offer because his health was so weak that "a few words do so spend me ..."[63] Baxter's letter had a sense of urgency. He did not mind if – as rumor had it – Burgess would publish a refutation of the *Aphorismes*. But he pleaded with Burgess that "I might but see your Arguments, that before I dye, I might know whether I have erred, and not dye without repenting or recanting: and if I err not; that I might shew you my grounds more fully ..."[64] Baxter then presented a list of 26 questions on which he requested Burgess' comments. Most of these questions dealt with the conditionality of the covenant and with the role of faith and works in justification.

Burgess still refused to give in to Baxter's pleas, having "not time, nor paper" to answer his questions.[65] He wryly remarked that an oral discussion should not

57. *RB* I.107. Cf. Geoffrey F. Nuttall, "Richard Baxter's Correspondence: A Preliminary Survey," *JEH* 1 (1950), 91; *CCRB* 14, n. 2.
58. Baxter, *Of Justification*, p. 159 (emphasis throughout in original). Baxter published his correspondence with Burgess in *Of Justification*, pp. 159-254.
59. Burgess, in Baxter, *Of Justification*, p. 160 (*CCRB* 26).
60. Baxter, *Of Justification*, p. 162 (*CCRB* 35).
61. Burgess, in Baxter, *Of Justification*, p. 164 (*CCRB* 38).
62. Burgess, in Baxter, *Of Justification*, p. 163 (*CCRB* 38).
63. Baxter, *Of Justification*, p. 165 (*CCRB* 39).
64. Baxter, *Of Justification*, p. 165 (*CCRB* 39). Also in his previous letter, Baxter had written: "I may dye in error unrecanted, and you (being now importuned for your help) be guilty of it" (*Of Justification*, p. 162 [*CCRB* 35]).
65. Burgess, in Baxter, *Of Justification*, p. 180 (*CCRB* 40).

take too much energy from Baxter, "because I had been informed of a late solemn conference you had about *Pædobaptism*, which could not but much spend you."[66] Here Burgess referred to the debate between Baxter and John Tombes on January 1, 1650, which had lasted approximately six hours.[67] In a final letter, Baxter consented to meet with Burgess, "if God will shew me so much Mercy, as to enable this restless uncessantly-pained *Sceleton* to such a work ..."[68] He then gave some lengthy arguments defending his views on the conditionality of the covenant and on the relation between faith and works.[69] A conference was finally held in Birmingham in September, 1650, with Baxter and Burgess present, as well as Samuel Wills, rector of Birmingham, and Richard Sargeant, Baxter's assistant.[70] The discussion still left Baxter unconvinced of Burgess' position.

Burgess considered it his duty to warn against Baxter's doctrines of grace. He did so – without mentioning Baxter by name – in a treatise entitled *The True Doctrine of Justification Asserted & Vindicated From the Errours of many, and more especially Papists and Socinians* (1654). It was intended as the second part to his publication of 1648 under a similar title. In his latest publication, he continued to accuse Baxter of making works a cause of justification.[71] The latter was angered by the fact that Burgess "was not pleased to take any notice" of his denials of the causality of works in justification.[72] Therefore, he briefly replied to Burgess in the preface of his *Confession* (1655).[73] Burgess responded in kind in his preface to some sermons on John 17 (1656).[74] This led to Baxter's lengthy disputation against Burgess in *Of Justification* (1658).[75] Baxter now also felt justified in publishing the correspondence which had passed between the two divines. Moreover, by doing so he wanted to prove that he had indeed attempted to prevent a public contest with Burgess.[76] Nevertheless, at this point, Baxter did take the blame for starting the contest "by dishonouring his Name by a temeracious prefixing it to my undigested papers; (though nothing but High estimation, and Affection was my motive.)"[77] In this whole flurry of discussion, both disputants abstained from mentioning each other by name.

Richard Vines, of whom Baxter says that he "wrote to me applaudingly," did not give Baxter his unqualified support either. As the recent *Calendar of the Correspondence of Richard Baxter* makes clear, Vines did have some reservations with regard to the *Aphorismes*. He rejected the idea that works are "secondary

---

66. Burgess, in Baxter, *Of Justification*, p. 176.
67. Baxter, *Plain Scripture Proof*, p. 205.
68. Baxter, *Of Justification*, p. 181 (*CCRB* 43).
69. Baxter, *Of Justification*, pp. 181-250.
70. The account of the conference is dated September 12, 1650. For the account, see DWL MS *BC* i, ff. 263^r-264^v (*CCRB* 48).
71. Burgess, *True Doctrine*, II (London, 1654), 220.
72. Baxter, *Confession*, sig. e1^v.
73. Baxter, *Confession*, sigs. e1^v-e3^r.
74. Burgess, *Expository Sermons* (London, 1656), sigs. A4^r-A5^r. Cf. Baxter, *Of Justification*, pp. 96-101.
75. Baxter, *Of Justification*, pp. 67-156.
76. Baxter, *Of Justification*, sig. A4^v.
77. Baxter, *Of Justification*, sigs. A4^{r-v}.

conditions unto iustification or conditions of a secondary iustification" and disagreed with Baxter's "abdication of faith's instrumentality."[78]

Other Reactions

Apart from the two Westminster divines to whom he had dedicated his treatise, Baxter received private comments on his *Aphorismes* from at least five others. One of them, John Warren (1621-96), had lived in Baxter's house as a school boy when Baxter preached in Bridgnorth. Warren was now vicar of Hatfield Broad Oak, Essex.[79] He sent his animadversions on August 27, 1649. After excusing himself that he had no opportunity to reply immediately (September 11),[80] Baxter came with a lengthy reply on November 7.[81] Thereupon, Warren came with further comments,[82] which again provoked a lengthy reaction from Baxter.[83]

By now, Baxter had become convinced that there were serious shortcomings in his *Aphorismes*. In a postscript to *Plain Scripture Proof*, dated November 12, 1650, Baxter commented:

> Some accuse that Book of obscure brevity, some of inconvenient phrases, some of particular Errours; and most, of erecting a new frame of Divinity. My present purpose is (if God assist) to clear in the next what seems obscure, to confirm what seems to be but nakedly asserted, to manifest the consent of the learned to most that seemeth novel and singular, to adde mnch <*sic*> where I find it defective, to reduce the whole to a better Method, and contract and annex what I had prepared of Universal redemption (because I will not provoke the angry world with any more contentious Volulmns <*sic*>, if I can chuse) and to retract what my friends shall discover to be erroneous.[84]

As it turned out, Baxter's "better Method" had to wait till 1681, when he published his *Methodus Theologiæ*. His *Universal Redemption* was not published until 1694, three years after his death.[85] More important for the present purpose, however, is that in the above statement Baxter appeared to admit that certain things in his *Aphorismes* needed to be clarified and perhaps even retracted. A few years later, he revoked the book in the hope of publishing a revised edition.[86] In the preface to his *Confession*, Baxter wrote: "I find that there are some incautelous passages in my *Aphorisms*, not fitted to their reading that come to suck poyson, and to seek for

---

78. DWL MS *BC* ii, f. 19ʳ (*CCRB* 64 [cf. 44]).
79. For Warren, see *RB* I.107; III.97; *CR* 511; *CCRB* 16.
80. DWL MS *BC* vi, f. 96ʳ (*CCRB* 22).
81. DWL MS *BT* xiv.324, ff. 10ᵛ-111ʳ (*CCRB* 25).
82. DWL MS *BT* vi.198, ff. 94ʳ-115ʳ.
83. DWL MS *BT* vi.199, ff. 116ʳ-199ʳ (*CCRB* 74).
84. Baxter, *Plain Scripture Proof*, p. 345.
85. For the origin of *Methodus Theologiæ*, see *RB* III.69-70, 190; Orme, "Life and Writings," in *Works* 1.468-71; *CCRB* 72, n. 2; 443, n. 1. For the origin of *Universal Redemption*, see appendix A.
86. Despite the many pleas to republish the *Aphorismes*, this never materialized, due to lack of time (*CCRB* 188, n.1, 294, 443). A second edition of the *Aphorismes* was published in Cambridge without Baxter's consent in 1655 (Baxter, *Answer*, p. 10; *Catholick Theologie*, I, sig. a3ʳ; *RB* I.111; *CCRB* 236, n. 8).

a Word to be matter of Accusation, and food for their censuring Opinionative zeal."[87] A little further, he commented: "If any Brother understand not any word in my *Aphorisms* which is here interpreted, or mistake my sense about the Matetr <*sic*> of that Book, which is here more fully opened, I must expect that they interpret That by This."[88] Baxter later argued that these two statements had been a retraction or suspension of his book.[89] Although his comments did not sound like a retraction, Baxter did say that he was "truly ashamed" of the book because of "its indigested passages and imperfections."[90]

James I. Packer rightly notes, however, that the alterations which Baxter had intended to make to his *Aphorismes* were mainly marginal.[91] To the end of his life, he continued to insist that it was "sound Doctrine and useful: But it being my first, is defective in Method and in some words which should have been more clearly and cautelously exprest ..."[92] Baxter's "retraction" concerned only the book as such, not the doctrine which it contained.[93]

John Tombes, whose antipaedobaptist position Baxter consistently opposed, was probably the first to comply with the latter's request for animadversions on his *Aphorismes*.[94] In his letter to Baxter, likely written in May, 1651, the pastor of the neighboring town of Bewdley showed himself congenial to Baxter's position on justification, but did take exception to some points.[95] He questioned the concept of a continued justification as well as the notions that faith means obedience to the Gospel precepts and that faith justifies by receiving Christ as King as well as Savior. He also questioned Baxter's view of the atonement.[96] Before Baxter had

---

87. Baxter, *Confession*, sig. d4[r].
88. Baxter, *Confession*, sigs. e3[v]-e4[r]. Cf. Baxter's admission to Richard Vines on June 16, 1651 that he had been too rash in publishing his *Aphorismes* (DWL MS *BC* ii, f. 20[r]; cf. *CCRB* 68).
89. Baxter, *Answer*, pp. 10-11. Cf. also *Two Disputations*, pp. 4, 44.
90. Baxter, *Unsavoury Volume*, p. 13. Thomas Tully, when reproached by Baxter for judging him by his retracted *Aphorismes*, said he was unable to find any recantation in Baxter's writings (*Letter* [Oxford, 1675]), pp. 6-8.
91. Packer, "Redemption and Restoration," pp. 485-87, which gives a list of ten points in which Baxter would have liked to see changes made.
92. Baxter, *Penitent Confession*, p. 25. Cf. *Plain Scripture Proof*, p. 191; DWL MS *BT* ii.21(1), f. 2[r]; *Confession*, p. 2; *Of Justification*, p. 358; *Answer*, pp. 10, 12; *Of Imputation*, p. 22; *Catholick Theologie*, I, sig. a2[v]; *RB* I.125.
93. Cf. Baxter's comment against Tully: "And that I wrote my *Confession*, and *Disputes of Justification*, as an Exposition of it <*i.e.*, the *Aphorismes*>; and that I *Retracted*, or *Suspended*, or *Revoked*, not the *Doctrine*, but the *Book*, till I had Corrected it, and did disown it as too unmeet an Expression of my Mind, which I had more fully exprest in other *Books*" (*Answer*, pp. 11-12).
94. For Tombes, see Robert Nelson, *The Life of Dr. George Bull, Late Lord Bishop of St. David's. With the History of Those Controversies In which he was Engaged: And an Abstract of those Fundamental Doctrines which he Maintained and Defended in the Latin Tongue*, 2nd ed. (London, 1714), pp. 245-53; Anthony à Wood, *Athenæ Oxonienses: Exact History of All the Writers and Bishops Who Have Had Their Education in the University of Oxford. To Which Are Added The Fasti or Annals of the Said University*, 3rd ed., ed. Philip Bliss, III (London: Rivington, 1813-20), 1062-66; *GBD* 29.440-43; *DNB* 57.2-4; *CR* 487-88; *BDBRSC* 3.245-46; *CCRB* 17; Arthur S. Langley, "John Tombes As a Correspondent," *TBHS*, 7 (1920), 13-18; W.T. Whitley, "Dissent in Worcestershire during the Seventeenth Century," *TBHS*, 7 (1920), 2-4.
95. The date of Tombes' first letter may be derived from the date of Baxter's reply, which is June 9, 1651 (*CCRB* 62).
96. Tombes, in Baxter, *Of Justification*, pp. 325-30. Cf. *Plain Scripture Proof*, pp. 274-76.

an opportunity to mail out his reply, Tombes sent him some additional comments in a letter of June 17.[97] He objected in particular to Baxter's view of the role of the covenant in justification. He also expressed his fear that Baxter would be unable to avoid the opinion of a possible "Intercision of Justification."[98] Baxter, thankful for these "free, candid, rational Animadversions,"[99] wrote extensive replies, first to Tombes' initial letter,[100] and then to his second.[101] Without securing Tombes' permission, Baxter later included their correspondence in *Of Justification*.[102]

The next person to give Baxter his private comments on the *Aphorismes* was George Lawson, rector of More, Shropshire.[103] Lawson sent his animadversions perhaps around July, 1651.[104] On August 5, Baxter returned a reply.[105] Lawson then came with a lengthy rejoinder.[106] Four years later, he reopened the discussion by sending Baxter some papers in reaction to his *Confession*.[107] Baxter did not reply to them, both because he thought that Lawson's papers were intended only for private information and because he did not have all of Lawson's comments.[108] When the latter published his *Theo-Politica* (1659), he again opposed some of Baxter's views. He rejected the notion that Christ as King and Prophet is the

---

97. Tombes, in Baxter, *Of Justification*, pp. 331-32 (*CCRB* 69).
98. Tombes, in Baxter, *Of Justification*, p. 331.
99. Baxter, *Of Justification*, p. 332.
100. Baxter, *Of Justification*, pp. 332-83 (*CCRB* 66). Tombes' first letter is not dated. Baxter's first reply is dated June 9, 1651 (*Of Justification*, p. 383).
101. Baxter, *Of Justification*, pp. 384-96 (*CCRB* 70). This second reply is dated June 20, 1651 (*Of Justification*, p. 384).
102. In the preface to his treatise opposing George Bull's doctrine of justification, Tombes comments: "In the year 1651 I sent some animadversions on Richard Baxter's Aphorisms about justification to him, which he himself published – without consulting me – together with his response in the year 1658." ("Anno 1651 animadversiones quasdam in Aphorismos *Richardi Baxteri* de justificatione ad ipsum misi, quas ipse me inconsulto edidit unà cum responso suo Anno 1658" [*Animadversiones in Librum Georgii Bulli* (Oxford, 1676), sigs. *2ᵛ-*3ʳ].)
103. For Lawson, see *RB* I.107-08; III.69; *DNB* 32.289; *BDBRSC* 2.177-78; *CCRB* 72. For secondary literature on Lawson's political ideas, see A.H. Maclean, "George Lawson and John Locke," *CHJ*, 9 (1947), 69-77; John Bowle, *Hobbes and His Critics: A Study in Seventeenth Century Constitutionalism* (London: Cape, 1951), pp. 86-113; Julian H. Franklin, *John Locke and the Theory of Sovereignty: Mixed Monarchy and the Right of Resistance in the Political Thought of the English Revolution*, Cambridge Studies in the History and Theory of Politics (Cambridge: Cambridge Univ. Press, 1978), pp. 53-130; Conal Condren, "The Image of *Utopia* in the Political Writings of George Lawson (1657): A Note on the Manipulation of Authority," *Moreana*, 18 (1981), 101-05; Conal Condren, "*Sacra* before *Civilis*: Understanding the Ecclesiastical Politics of George Lawson," *JRH*, 11 (1981), 524-35; Conal Condren, *George Lawson's Politica and the English Revolution* (Cambridge: Cambridge Univ. Press, 1989).
104. Lawson's original animadversions are no longer extant. In *CCRB* 72 they are identified as DWL MS *BT* ii.39(2), ff. 190ʳ-193ᵛ; ii.39(3), ff. 195ʳ-206ᵛ; ii.39(4), ff. 208ʳ-210ᵛ; ii.39(7), ff. 226ʳ-229ᵛ; xv.340, ff. 68ʳ-72ᵛ (These last two MSS belong together.); iv.82, f. 183ʳ. This appears incorrect. Most of these manuscripts contain comments on the natural and moral power of the will, which was not the main point of discussion between Baxter and Lawson. The handwriting is also not that of Lawson. The approximate date of Lawson's first animadversions may be identified by the date of Baxter's response, August 5, 1651.
105. DWL MS *BT* vi.197, ff. 52ʳ-93ᵛ (*CCRB* 72).
106. DWL MS *BT* i.9, ff. 99ʳ-150ᵛ (*CCRB* 73). Baxter gave a final review of the debate in *BT* vii.274, ff. 327ʳ-335ᵛ.
107. DWL MS *BC* ii, ff. 177ʳ-185ᵛ (*CCRB* 243, 247).
108. DWL MS *BC* ii, f. 169ʳ (*CCRB* 286).

special object of faith;[109] denied Baxter's distinction between *sententia legis* and *sententia judicis*;[110] maintained that justification is a sentential act of God by his Spirit in man's soul;[111] and denied that continued and consummate justification is by works.[112] But in all of this, Lawson did not mention Baxter by name.

Doubtless, Lawson's comments were more influential on Baxter's thinking than any other reaction which he had received so far:

> The next Animadverter was Mr. *George Lawson*, the ablest Man of them all, or of almost any I know in *England*; especially by the Advantage of his Age and very hard Studies, and methodical Head, but above all, by his great skill in Politicks, wherein he is most exact, and which contributeth not a little to the understanding of Divinity. Though he was himself near the *Arminians* (differing from them in the Point of *Perseverance* as to the *Confirmed*, and some little matters more) and so went farther than I did from the *Antinomians*, yet being conversant with Men of another Mind, to redeem himself from their Offence, he set himself against some Passages of mine, which others marvelled that he of all Men should oppose; especially about the *Object of Faith*, and *Justification*.[113]

It may safely be concluded that Lawson – who by Baxter's testimony leaned more in an Arminian direction than Baxter himself – thought that the *Aphorismes* strayed too far from a Calvinist line of thinking.[114] Baxter's admiration for Lawson is especially noteworthy because Baxter refers to Lawson's "instigating me to the Study of *Politicks*."[115] With regard to the significance of political science for theology, Baxter placed Lawson on a par with Hugo Grotius, whose book on the atonement, *Defensio fidei* (1617), had a great impact on Baxter.[116] Considering Lawson's contribution to Baxter's thinking, it is clear that political categories gave considerable shape to his thought.[117]

Christopher Cartwright (1602-58) of York – of whom Baxter says that "he was a man of good reading as to our later Divines, and was very well verst in the Common Road, (very like *Mr. Burgess*); a very good Hebrician, and a very honest worthy Person" – was one of Baxter's more sympathetic critics.[118] Cartwright carefully distinguished his position from that of the Antinomians: "I do not speak of freedom from all sin as the Antinomians do, as if God did see no sin in his

---

109. Lawson, *Theo-Politica* (London, 1659), pp. 299-301.
110. Lawson, *Theo-Politica*, p. 303.
111. Lawson, *Theo-Politica*, pp. 304-05.
112. Lawson, *Theo-Politica*, pp. 313-15.
113. *RB* I.107. Cf. I.108: "I learnt more from Mr. *Lawson* than from any Divine that gave me Animadversions, or that ever I conversed with ..." Cf. III.69.
114. Maclean goes too far, however, in suggesting that "the two men differed radically both in their religious, and in their political, opinions" ("George Lawson and John Locke," 72).
115. *RB* I.108.
116. Cf. Beougher, "Conversion," pp. 42-45. For the impact of Grotius' governmental view of the atonement on Baxter, see below, pp. 200-02.
117. Packer is correct in noting that Baxter's "political method" is important in Baxter's theological system ("Redemption and Restoration," pp. ii-iii, 132-33, 233-34, 302-03, 305, 330, 458, 462, 465).
118. *RB* I.107. For Cartwright, see also Baxter, *Treatise of Justifying Righteousness*, sigs. A3ʳ⁻ᵛ; *RB* III.172; *DNB* 9.220-21; *CCRB* 949, n. 1.

Children, and they had no sin to be humbled for: but I say, That God doth not impute sin unto them, so as to condemn them for it."[119] Moreover, Cartwright agreed with Baxter that faith is a condition for justification. He even agreed that obedience is a condition for salvation. Cartwright took exception, however, to Baxter's use of the distinction between legal and evangelical righteousness.[120] He disagreed with Baxter's ideas that works have a "*co-interest* with *Faith* in Justification" and that obedience is a condition of justification.[121] Further disagreement surfaced about the instrumentality of faith, the nature of the last judgement, the question whether the afflictions of believers are punishments or not, as well as a number of related issues.[122]

When Baxter received Cartwright's animadversions he wrote a reply and ordered the material in such a way that he first wrote down the particular comment of his *Aphorismes* which was at stake, then Cartwright's animadversion on it, followed by his own reply. This compilation he entitled *An Account of my Consideration of the Friendly, Modest, Learned Animadversions of Mr. Chr. Cartwright of York, on my Aphorisms* (1652).[123] Cartwright came with a renewed reaction to Baxter, which he entitled *Exceptions Against a Writing of Mr. R. Baxters, In Answer to some Animadversions Upon his Aphorisms.* When Cartwright indicated his desire to publish these *Exceptions* and, therefore, requested Baxter to return his manuscript, Baxter was unable to do so, "because they were lost, (and I had no mind to be very inquisitive after them, in order to a Publick view) But some years after his <*i.e.*, Cartwright's> death, they were found again."[124] When, in 1675, Baxter wanted to oppose Thomas Tully's (1620-76) doctrine of imputation he decided to publish his discussion with Cartwright. It was preceded by a treatise on imputation – written three or four years earlier (*Of the Imputation of Christ's Righteousness to Believers*) – and a reply to Tully, and it was followed by a final rebuttal of Cartwright's *Exceptions* (*The Substance of Mr. Cartwright's Exceptions Considered*).[125]

Baxter next received animadversions from John Wallis (1616-1703), a former student of Anthony Burgess, who had recently been appointed as Savilian professor of geometry in Oxford.[126] Wallis was widely studied: a famous mathematician, adept in cryptography as well as in classical languages and theology. To Baxter, however, he was "a stranger w<ho>ᵐ I never saw."[127] Wallis' animadversions are dated June 28, 1652.[128] Baxter replied in a letter of August 3. This letter is no

---

119. Cartwright, *Exceptions* (London, 1675), p. 163.
120. *RB* I.107.
121. Baxter, *Substance* (London, 1675), p. 4.
122. Baxter lists the main points of difference in *Substance*, p. 4.
123. The title page is dated May 26, 1652. Baxter finished the compilation on June 18, 1652 (Baxter, *Account of my Consideration* [London, 1675], p. 294).
124. Baxter, *Treatise of Justifying Righteousness*, sig. A2ᵛ (emphasis throughout in original).
125. Baxter, *Treatise of Justifying Righteousness*, sigs. A3ʳ⁻ᵛ; *RB* III.172; *CCRB* 889.
126. For Wallis, see *RB* I.107; *GBD* 31.28-47; Reid, *Memoirs*, II, 205-14; *DNB* 59.141-45; J.F. Scott, "The Reverend John Wallis, F.R.S. (1616-1703)," in *The Royal Society: Its Origins and Founders*, ed. Harold Hartley (London: Royal Society, 1960), pp. 57-67; *CCRB* 87, 96.
127. DWL MS *BT* ii.21(1), f. 2ʳ. Cf. *Aphorismes* II.111 (p. 284).
128. For Wallis' letter to Baxter, see DWL MS *BT* ii.21(2), ff. 22ʳ-43ᵛ (*CCRB* 87).

longer extant, but Wallis' reply is. Wallis commented that Baxter put "a higher value upon my papers & conceptions than (I fear) they deserve ..."[129] He stated that the few apparent differences of opinion "will be easyly cleared, I hope, if you please but to observe ye difference between Sanctification & Justification ..."[130] Baxter's unfinished reply to Wallis' animadversions was entitled "The Learned, Moderate, Animadversions of Mr John Wallis, Considered."[131] It addressed a number of issues, but most notably the theory of double imputation (of Christ's active as well as passive obedience) and the question whether Christ's sufferings were the *idem* or the *tantundem*, the same as or just as much as the penalty required by the law. The latter question was one of the key issues on which Baxter had expressed his disagreement with John Owen, in his *Aphorismes*. It is impossible to ascertain the precise date of Baxter's reply. It must have been written after the publication of Owen's *Vindiciæ Evangelicæ* (1655) because of Baxter's comment to Wallis that he had left Owen's book unanswered.[132] Baxter never finished his reply to Wallis: "I began to write a Reply, but broke it off in the middle because he little differed from me."[133]

PUBLIC CONTROVERSY: 1649-58

John Owen

Augustus H. Strong makes the comment in his *Systematic Theology* that "Owen was the most rigid, as Baxter was the most liberal, of the Puritans."[134] It is understandable, therefore, that a discussion of the interaction between the theologies of Baxter and Owen conjures up strong emotions, even if Strong's observation is an overstatement.[135] If such personal involvement means that the twentieth-century scholar himself enters the debate as a third party the danger is real that academic integrity gives way to biased judgement, and that a historically inaccurate picture emerges.[136]

---

129. DWL MS *BC* vi, f. 104^r (*CCRB* 96).
130. DWL MS *BC* vi, f. 104^r.
131. DWL MS *BT* ii.21(1), ff. 1^r-21^r.
132. DWL MS *BT* ii.21(1), f. 13^r.
133. *RB* I.107. Another motive for not finishing and publishing the reply to Wallis may have been the fact that a main topic of discussion was the *idem/tantundem* issue. Baxter had resolved not to debate this issue with Owen anymore (cf. below, p. 43, n. 141; p. 337).
134. Augustus H. Strong, *Systematic Theology: A Compendium Designed for the Use of Theological Students* (Old Tappan, NJ: Revell, 1907), p. 47.
135. For Owen, see Andrew Thomson, "Life of Dr Owen," in *Works* 1.xix-cxxi; *DNB* 42.424-28; *CR* 376-77; Peter Toon, ed., *The Correspondence of John Owen (1616-1683): With an Account of His Life and Work*, foreword Geoffrey F. Nuttall (Cambridge: Clarke, 1970); Peter Toon, *God's Statesman: The Life and Work of John Owen: Pastor, Educator, Theologian* (Exeter: Paternoster, 1971); Sinclair B. Ferguson, *John Owen on the Christian Life* (Edinburgh: Banner of Truth, 1987), pp. 1-19; *CCRB* 197, n. 1.
136. One of the few studies which gives an irenic evaluation is the recent dissertation by McGrath, "Puritans and the Human Will."

Another danger is, of course, that one attempts to downplay the differences, even though they are real as well as serious.[137] It is particularly imperative to avoid this latter temptation since the present study is an attempt to get Baxter's distinctive views more sharply in focus. Of course, even if the debate cannot be reduced to an interest in insignificant theological niceties or perhaps to a mutual personal dislike, this does not mean that the personalities of Baxter and Owen did not enter the debate. To begin with, the tendency to prolixity on the part of both authors likely contributed to the protracted nature of the discussions. As the pope told the devil in an anonymous dialogue about Owen and Baxter:

> SHall WE allow these Scribling Fellows to write for ever? They feed the Press as *baxter* feeds his Wolf, and it like their Desires, is as large as Hell; and, like the Horse-Leach, it sucks, and is never satisfied: They have a kind of Ambitious Itch to scrible: Here comes a Heap of *Octavo*'s, there a Heap of *Quarto*'s; and presently another of *Folio*'s ...[138]

It was not only the verbosity of both authors which dragged out the debate. Also less virtuous elements formed a contributing factor. When Baxter opened the fray by expressing his disagreement with Owen rather sharply in an appendix to his *Aphorismes* he did so in a way that inevitably had to provoke the latter's anger. Baxter stated plainly that Owen, in his *Death of Death* (1647), had failed to rebut Hugo Grotius on three counts: (1) Owen had overlooked Grotius' most important arguments; (2) had slightly answered only two; and (3) had finished by saying the same as Grotius did, thereby yielding the whole cause.[139] The invective style of Baxter's reaction to Owen added to the intensity of the debate.

Owen may also have felt insulted because he had already started on a distinguished career, having preached twice before parliament, once in 1646 and once in 1649 on the day after the execution of King Charles I. Baxter displayed a lack of

---

137. William Orme goes as far as to say that an analysis of Owen's *Of the Death of Christ* (1650) "would now be very uninteresting, as he <i.e., Owen> admits himself that the contention lay more about 'expressions than opinions'" (*Memoirs of the Life, Writings, and Religious Connexions, of John Owen, D.D. Vice-Chancellor of Oxford, and Dean of Christ Church, during the Commonwealth* [London: Hamilton, 1820], pp. 120-21). Orme's judgement was not new. Baxter already commented to John Wallis: "I meet with many Learned Divines, y<a>ᵗ think it a matter of meere wordes & no moment whether it were Solutio ejusdem, or Satisfactio; whether Xᵗ paid yᵉ Idem or Tantundem" (DWL MS *BT* ii.21[1], f. 13ʳ).
138. *A Dialogue between the Pope and the Devil, about Owen and Baxter* (London, 1681), p. 1 (no pagination). The anonymous author does not actually refer to the debate between Baxter and Owen but rather laments the popularity of their practical writings.
139. Baxter, *Aphorisms* II.139 (p. 302). Baxter elaborates on these three points in II.139-46 (pp. 302-07). For Owen's *Death of Death* (1647), see Jack N. Macleod, "John Owen and the Death of Death," in *Out of Bondage*, Proc. of the Westminster Conference, 1983 (Nottingham: Westminster Conference, [1984]), pp. 70-87; J.I. Packer, "'Saved by His Precious Blood': An Introduction to John Owen's *The Death of Death in the Death of Christ*," in *Quest for Godliness*, pp. 125-48; Dewey D. Wallace, "The Life and Thought of John Owen to 1660: A Study of the Significance of Calvinist Theology in English Puritanism," Diss. Princeton Univ. 1965, pp. 166-72; Robert Keith McGregor Wright, "John Owen's Great High Priest: The Highpriesthood of Christ in the Theology of John Owen, (1616-1683)," Diss. Iliff School of Theology and Univ. of Denver 1989, pp. 99-115.

sensitivity toward the difference in status between Owen and himself. Aware of this, Baxter commented in 1655:

> One evidence of it <*i.e.*, the charge that Baxter was "hypocritically proud"> which I have heard from the apprehension of others, *viz*, becaus I gave him <*i.e.*, Owen> not his due Titles of honor, is no whit cogent with mee that know the case: and I think my justification is unanswerable: *viz*, that when my papers were written hee was not Doctor, though hee was when they came out of the press.[140]

Baxter had to admit that he "was foolishly drawne in to be ye begiñer" of the controversy[141] and that he had "medled too forwardly with Dr. *Owen*, and one or two more that had written some Passages too near to Antinomianism."[142] Owen's response, *Of the Death of Christ* (1650), was straightforward but not abusive.[143]

When Baxter reopened the debate five years later in his *Confession*, he spoke of Owen as a "sober and learned man."[144] Nevertheless, his discussion of Owen's views was preceded by two chapters in which he rebutted Antinomianism and, in particular, the view that justification by faith is justification *in foro conscientiae* rather than *in foro Dei*.[145] In the chapter dealing with Owen, Baxter made little effort to come to an accurate portrayal of Owen's position and instead gave numerous arguments refuting the notion of justification before faith. He then commented toward the end of the chapter: "AND thus I have shewed you somewhat of the face of these Doctrines of the Antinomians."[146] The implication was never made explicit, but was nevertheless clear: Owen was "enrolled into the troop of Antinomians."[147] Owen, upset by this treatment, complained in his *Vindiciæ Evangelicæ* (1655) that at a conference in London about justification, held shortly before the publication of the *Confession*, Baxter had not even mentioned his intent to publish this confutation.[148] Owen took revenge by quoting various Socinian statements.[149] They were clearly selected with a view to illustrate Baxter's affinity to them.

The debate was therefore held in an acrimonious spirit, which was largely due to Baxter's insensitive attitude. It was one of the few controversies in which not Baxter himself, but his opponent had the last public word. Baxter referred back to

---

140. Baxter, *Certain Disputations*, pp. 484-85.
141. DWL MS *BT* ii.21(1), f. 13^r. Also in his *Admonition* (1654) to William Eyre, Baxter said: "I did impose it as a penalty on my self, not to answer that Book of Mr. *Owens*, till I saw a clear call proving it my duty, because I had been foolishly drawn to be the beginner of the Controversie" (*Admonition* [London, 1654], p. 36).
142. *RB* I.107.
143. Owen could not resist the temptation, however, to make full mileage out of one of Baxter's wrongly construed sentences, the actual meaning of which is the opposite to what he originally intended. The sentence elicited Owen's comment that Baxter "wholly gives up the cause that he pretends to plead, and joins with me ... against Grotius and himself" (*Of the Death of Christ* [1650], in *Works* 10.439).
144. Baxter, *Confession*, p. 219. Cf. pp. 190, 228, 254.
145. Baxter, *Confession*, pp. 150-214.
146. Baxter, *Confession*, p. 289.
147. The expression is from Owen, *Vindiciæ Evangelicæ* (1655), in *Works* 12.601.
148. Owen, *Vindiciæ Evangelicæ*, in *Works* 12.592. For Owen's *Vindiciæ Evangelicæ*, see Wright, "John Owen's Great High Priest," pp. 144-59.
149. Owen, *Vindiciæ Evangelicæ*, in *Works* 12.597-601.

the debate in *Certain Disputations* (1657), only to deny that he had ever classified Owen as an Antinomian, and to complain of being associated with Socinianism.[150]

This denial and complaint concerned not a theological but a personal matter. The only theological comments of Baxter on Owen's position after the latter's *Vindiciæ Evangelicæ* were never made public during Baxter's life-time. In *Universal Redemption*, published in 1694 by Joseph Read, Baxter's one-time assistant, Baxter again dealt with the extent as well as the nature of the atonement. Most likely, this material was partly written between 1647 and 1649 and partly between 1655 and 1657.[151] Baxter's *Universal Redemption* may be regarded as his last reply to Owen, though it remained unpublished during their lifetime. Baxter's determination not to respond to Owen any further may well have been one of the reasons why Baxter never published this manuscript.

This brief overview of the controversy indicates that the personalities of Baxter and Owen did play a role in the course of the debate. Nevertheless, the debate rarely degenerated into discussions on insignificant or secondary aspects of the issues involved. The central core of the questions at hand was constantly in view. These concerned in the first place the extent of the atonement: was redemption universal or was it limited to the elect? A second, and intimately related issue, was the nature of the atonement: was it the *idem*, or was it only the *tantundem* of the penalty threatened in the law? A last issue was formed by the question what exactly constituted the process of justification.[152] Did it begin with the *pactum salutis* and end in one's conscience, or did it follow the condition of faith?[153]

Thomas Blake

One of Baxter's more moderate opponents was Thomas Blake (1597?-1657), pastor of Tamworth, Staffordshire, a town approximately fifty kilometers northeast of Kidderminster.[154] This Presbyterian minister refrained from mentioning Baxter by

---

150. Baxter, *Certain Disputations*, pp. 485-88.
151. Cf. appendix A. Also the unpublished correspondence with John Wallis dealt with an important aspect of Baxter's disagreement with Owen, namely the *idem/tantundem* issue.
152. In medieval interpretations of the doctrine of justification, *processus iustificationis* is a technical term indicating the process in which someone is made righteous (*iustum facere*). I am not using the term here in this precise, restricted sense. The term lends itself, however, for the description of both Owen's and Baxter's understanding of justification because both authors deny that justification is an instantaneous, once for all event. The word "process" therefore serves to indicate the extension of justification, even if it is understood as an entirely forensic concept.
153. Owen identified the last two points as the issues on which Baxter had disagreed with him (*Of the Death of Christ*, in *Works* 10.436). Only, Owen narrows the last issue to the immediate fruits of Christ's death, whereas the actual point in discussion was much broader, as will be demonstrated below.
154. For Blake, see *GBD*.5.396; Brook, *Lives*, III, 269-71; *DNB* 5.179-80; *CCRB* 251.
   For Blake's position on the covenant and the sacraments, see E. Brooks Holifield, *The Covenant Sealed: The Development of Puritan Sacramental Theology in Old and New England, 1570-1720* (New Haven: Yale Univ. Press, 1974), pp. 98-106, 124; James Burton McSwain, "The Controversy over Infant Baptism in England, 1640-1700," Diss. Memphis State Univ. 1986, pp. 304-11. For accounts of the controversy between Baxter and Blake, see *RB* I.110-14; Orme, "Life and Times," in *Works* 1.452, 582-85; Geoffrey F. Nuttall, "Richard Baxter's *Apology* (1654): Its Occasion and Composition," *JEH*, 4 (1953), 69-76.

name when, in his *Vindiciæ foederis* (1653), he opposed some of the ideas in the *Aphorismes*.[155] Neither the theological affinity between the two, nor the reserved manner in which Blake voiced his dissent, prevented the discussion from turning rather heated and, at certain points, personal and insulting. Part of the reason was doubtless Baxter's tendency to major in minors, which could not but exasperate Blake. Baxter was aware of his inclination not just to make innumerable distinctions, but also to be rather acrimonious in debate.[156] His attempt to overcome this weakness did not prevent Blake from feeling insulted.[157]

The debate began with Blake's *Vindiciæ foederis*, in which he took exception to some of Baxter's statements in his *Aphorismes*. Blake published this work "towards the end of *November*," 1652.[158] In this treatise on the covenants Blake took issue with Baxter in three points of doctrine: (1) the "interest that faith, which is short of justifying, gives to Baptisme";[159] (2) whether one is justified by believing in Jesus Christ as King and Teacher as well as by believing in his blood; and (3) whether faith can be said to be an instrument in justification.[160]

Baxter replied in the first part of his *Apology* (1654), which also contained answers to reactions from George Kendall (1610-63), Lewis Du Moulin (1606-80?), William Eyre (c. 1613-70), and John Crandon (d. 1654). This section of the *Apology*, which Baxter wrote in 1653, is entitled *Rich. Baxters Account Given to his Reverend Brother Mr T. Blake of the Reasons of his Dissent from The Doctrine of his Exceptions in his late Treatise of the Covenants*.[161] Here Baxter touched on all three points of debate. It caused a rejoinder from Blake in a treatise on the sacraments. This book, entitled *The Covenant Sealed* (1655), contained three "di-

---

155. As Christopher Cartwright comments in his preface to Thomas Blake, *Covenant Sealed*: "*As soon as I perused his Treatise of the Covenant <i.e., Vindiciæ foederis>, being not unacquainted with Mr. Baxters Aphorismes, I could not but observe how he doth scarce ever name Mr. Baxter (though he name him often) but where he doth approve and commend him ...*" ([London, 1655], sig. ¶2ᵛ). In the "Preface Apologetical" to his *Account* Baxter even comments with regard to Blake's *Vindiciæ foederis* that in it he "found nothing but tenderness and brotherly Love, as to my person; and no such inclination to extreams in his Doctrine, as I found in some others; but much Moderation and Sobriety, as indeed the Gravity, Piety and Integrity of the man, would promise to any that know him" ([London, 1654], sig. A3ʳ).

156. Baxter himself comments: "Because I so well know my own frailty, and proneness to be over-eager and keen and unmannerly in my stile, and the frailty of most Brethren in being Impatient hereof; yea of many in judging themselves wronged when they are not, and making some plain speeches which were but necessary or innocent, to seem proud, contemptuous, and sleighting as to mens persons, racking them to a sense that was never intended, I therefore thought it safest to avoid all occasions of such mistakes, which may be injurious to themselves, as well as to me" (*Account*, sig. A3ᵛ).

157. In his reply to Baxter's *Account*, Blake comments: "But truly Sir, to speak of things, as they are, *I* am apprehensive of not a little gall, in the ink that thou spent upon me, and take my self to be much more bedabled through your writings, than the cause required" (*Covenant Sealed*, p. 550).

158. Blake, *Covenant Sealed*, p. 548. The date on the title page of *Vindiciæ foederis* is 1653.

159. Blake, *Covenant Sealed*, p. 550 (emphasis throughout original).

160. Baxter identifies these three as the main issues between himself and Blake (*Of Justification*, sigs. A3ʳ-ᵛ).

161. Baxter's dedicatory epistle to General Whalley preceding the entire *Apology* dates from March 8, 1654. The preface to the *Account* is dated August 1, 1653 (sig. a3ᵛ).

gressions" touching again on some of the main topics of disagreement.[162] In a lengthy "Postscript" Blake dealt in particular with the question whether faith in Christ as Lord (or King and Teacher) justifies.[163]

The issue of eligibility to the sacraments on the basis of something less than justifying faith, the first point of variance, was readdressed by Baxter in the 542 pages of his *Certain Disputations* (1657).[164] He did not deal directly with the issue of the instrumentality of faith. He had prepared a disputation on this subject, directed against Blake, which was supposed to be included in *Of Justification*. But Baxter "resolved to condemn <it> to perpetual silence" because of Blake's death in June, 1657.[165] It is somewhat unfortunate that Baxter's reply to Blake is no longer extant, since it might shed further light on Baxter's position. Baxter did react to Blake in *Of Justification*, but then on the point whether faith, in its interest in justification, includes faith in Jesus Christ as Teacher and King. This was the second point of disagreement. This disputation, dated November 1656, was already too far in the publication process to be halted as yet. The subject discussed here had also been the first and main issue in Blake's "Postscript" (1655). Closely related to it was the fourth and last disputation in *Of Justification*, in which Baxter argued that the one faith consists of more than one act of faith. Baxter added it because "it is the very heart of our Controversie, which most of our Disputes about the instrumentall Causality of Faith as to Justification, and the other Concomitant, are resolved into."[166] It was the only disputation that was not specifically directed against any opponent in particular.[167]

---

162. Digression I is entitled "Faith which is short of Justifying, entitles to Baptisme" (pp. 113-87); digression II "The seales of the Sacrament are conditionall, and seal conditionally" (pp. 333-49); digression III "Of the Instrumentality of Faith in Justification" (pp. 437-91). Baxter complained of the method used by Blake in *Covenant Sealed*: "As to the present Controversie, it seemed good to Mr *Blake* to begin it with mee; and to my Defens hee hath opposed an angry Reply; not to my whole Book (as I did to that part of his which concerned mee) but to here and there a scrap, disordered and maimed and parcelled as hee thought good" (*Certain Disputations*, sigs. c3ʳ-ᵛ; emphasis inverted). In reality, however, Blake touched on the main points of difference, and did so in a well organized fashion, by means of the three digressions and the "Postscript."

163. At this point in time, Blake had already acquainted himself with Baxter's *Confession* which had been published earlier the same year. Cf. Blake, *Covenant Sealed*, pp. 644, 648.

164. The book consists of five disputations, the third of which – entitled "Whether the Infants of Notoriously ungodly Baptized Parents have Right to bee Baptized" – had been written already two years earlier, before Blake's *Covenant Sealed* (1655) had yet been published. Strictly speaking, therefore, it is not a reaction to Blake. Baxter had earlier declined to publish the third disputation for fear that he might "harden the wicked in their sin ..." (*Certain Disputations*, p. 335). The disputation gives a number of examples of manifestly wicked life styles which Baxter does not deem sufficient to deny people the right to the sacraments (pp. 326-33; cf. sigs. c3ᵛ-c4ʳ). Baxter probably began writing his reply soon after Blake published *Covenant Sealed* (1655): the last disputation is signed October 1, 1655 (p. 523), and the prefatory letter to the associated ministers of Worcestershire dates from January 17, 1657 (sig. A3ᵛ).

165. Baxter, *Of Justification*, sig. A3ᵛ (emphasis throughout in original).

166. Baxter, *Of Justification*, sig. a1ᵛ (emphasis throughout in original).

167. The disputation does not bear any traces of being a reaction specifically directed against Blake. I nevertheless include it at this point in the discussion because of its close affinity to the debate with Blake.

George Kendall and Thomas Barlow

With the controversy between Baxter and George Kendall, rector of Blisland, Cornwall, the debate surrounding the *Aphorismes* entered some new areas: the question of the eternity of God's immanent acts and the difference between common and special grace.[168] Baxter describes his opponent as "a little quick Spirited Man, of great Ostentation and a Considerable Orator and Scholar."[169] In 1653, Kendall published his Θεοκρατία: *Or, A Vindication of the Doctrine Commonly Received in the Reformed Churches Concerning Gods Intentions Of special Grace and Favour to his Elect In the Death of Christ*. This lengthy treatise, prefaced by John Owen, was written in opposition to John Goodwin, the Arminian pastor of an independent church in London, whose *Redemption Redeemed* (1651) advocated universal atonement.[170] Kendall's treatise also contained a digression in which he took exception to a part of Baxter's *Aphorismes*.[171] Kendall maintained in opposition to Baxter that there are no new immanent acts in God, that justification is not just a transient, temporal act, and that faith is an instrument in justification.

Kendall's book came to Baxter's view just before he finished writing his *Account* against Blake.[172] Baxter did not know Kendall, but was impressed with the scholarly nature of the latter's treatise.[173] Not only was it carefully construed in theological respect, it also had serious potential for damaging Baxter's reputation by including him in the same school of thought as a well-known Arminian.[174] Indeed, despite his admission to Vines that Goodwin was a "flatt Arminian," Baxter highly esteemed Goodwin's doctrine of justification, as set forth in the latter's *Impvtatio fidei. Or A Treatise of Justification* (1642).[175] It was, therefore, imperative for Baxter that he lay Kendall's charges to rest, especially where they concerned the simplicity and immutability of God. This he set out to do in *The Reduction of a Digressor*, which he concluded on August 1, 1653.[176] He subsequently published it as the second part of his *Apology* (1654).

---

168. For Kendall, see *RB* I.110; II.206; Wood, *Athenæ Oxonienses*, III, 638-40; *DNB* 30.405-06; *CR* 304-05; *CCRB* 148, n. 6.
169. *RB* I.110.
170. For Goodwin, see *DNB* 22.145-48; *CR* 227. For Goodwin's theological position, see Wallace, "Life and Thought of John Owen," pp. 242-47; Allison, *Rise of Moralism*, pp. 164-65; Von Rohr, *Covenant of Grace*, pp. 94-96, 117-21, 125-26, 137-39; Dewey D. Wallace, *Puritans and Predestination: Grace in English Protestant Theology, 1525-1695*, Studies in Religion (Chapel Hill: Univ. of North Carolina Press, 1982), pp. 130-31, 146-47.
171. Kendall, *Vindication* (London, 1653) I.iv.134-45.
172. Baxter, *Account*, sig. A3ᵛ. Cf. Nuttall, "Richard Baxter's *Apology* (1654)," 70.
173. Baxter, *Account*, sig. A4ʳ.
174. Cf. Baxter's comment that Kendall "thought to get an Advantage for his Reputation, by a Triumph over *John Goodwin* and me; for those that set him on work would needs have him conjoin us both together, to intimate that I was an Arminian ..." (*RB* I.110).
175. DWL MS *BC* ii, f. 20ʳ (*CCRB* 68); Baxter, *Plain Scripture Proof*, p. 193; *Of Imputation*, p. 21. Cf. Lamont, *Richard Baxter and the Millennium*, p. 144. Baxter does think, however, that Goodwin goes too far by alleging that Christ's willingness to die would have been sufficient, were it not that the Jews put him to death (*Account*, p. 114; *Universal Redemption* [London, 1694], p. 144).
176. Baxter, *Reduction*, p. 144. On the same date, Baxter wrote the preface to his *Account* against Blake (*Account*, sig. a4ᵛ).

Kendall did not return to the issues discussed in Baxter's *Reduction*. As Baxter was still busy replying, however, Kendall already broached some related topics: the difference between common and special grace, and the perseverance of the saints. The occasion for this attack lay in some comments which Baxter had made in the second edition of his *Saints Everlasting Rest* (1651) and in *The Right Method For a settled Peace Of Conscience, and Spiritual Comfort* (1653).[177] In the latter treatise, Baxter had stated that he was not certain "that all are elect to salvation, and shall never fall away totally and finally, who sincerely Believe and are Justified."[178] Because of the furor it created, Baxter added an "Apologie" to the second edition, which was published in the same year.[179] The "Apologie," however, did little more than clarify the statement. Kendall, therefore, remarked in his *Sancti sanciti* (1654) – a work which was again prefaced by John Owen – that it was offensive to him

> that Mr. *Baxter* hath cast out somewhat against the maine Doctrine of the Perseverance of the Saints, in his late Directions for keeping peace of Conscience; and that notwithstanding his Apologie he sullies it with several new Arguments as he is pleased to conceive.[180]

Kendall, of the opinion that Baxter had not apologized at all for his comments against perseverance, continued with a rebuttal of Baxter's position in the preface to this book on perseverance.[181]

The situation was particularly troubling for Baxter since Kendall was by no means the only one who objected to the passage on perseverance.[182] Baxter himself reports that "many suspicious Brethren gave out, that I had wrote against the certain Perseverance of the Saints."[183] In order to "avoid offence, and to leave out controversie as much as may be in such practicall Writings," Baxter deleted the controversial section from the third edition of his *Right Method* (1657).[184] In lieu of it, he published *Richard Baxter's Account of His present Thoughts concerning the Controversies about the Perseverance of the Saints* (1657). This booklet first described twelve different views on perseverance and then set out to present Baxter's own position by means of eighteen propositions. Baxter used this opportunity to further explicate his views.

Kendall also took exception to a section in the *Saints Everlasting Rest* where Baxter had written: "Therefore the sincerity of saving grace, as saving, lieth materially, not in the bare nature of it, but in the degree; not in the degree, considered absolutely in itself, but comparatively, as it is prevalent against its contrary."[185] In

---

177. For the controversy surrounding *Right Method*, see Keeble, *Richard Baxter*, p. 16.
178. Baxter, *Right Method* (London, 1653), p. 166.
179. Baxter, *Right Method*, 2nd ed. (London, 1653), sigs. Cc1^r-Cc10^r. Cf. *CCRB* 137.
180. Kendall, *Sancti sanciti* (London, 1654), sig. ****2^r.
181. Kendall, *Sancti sanciti*, sigs. ****2^r-****6^v.
182. *Right Method* was published in May, 1653. By means of various letters Baxter received reports of numerous people being upset with the way in which he handled the doctrine of the perseverance of the saints (*CCRB* 121, 126, 133, 140).
183. Baxter, *Present Thoughts* (London, 1657), p. 1.
184. Baxter, *Present Thoughts*, p. 1.
185. Baxter, *Saints Rest*, in *Works* III.198 (23.27).

a lengthy digression, Kendall attempted to disprove the notion that there is only a difference in degree between common and saving grace.[186] Baxter felt that Kendall had misrepresented his position. In an addition to the fifth edition of the *Saints Rest* (1654), subsequently published also in his *Confession*, Baxter insisted that there was little real difference between his own position and that of Kendall.[187] Asked Baxter: "So oft he <*i.e.*, Kendall> yeeldeth that all sincere Love to God, doth prefer him before all other. Where then is our difference?"[188] Baxter also began writing a more extensive reply. When, in 1655, he happened to be in London, Kendall asked Richard Vines to persuade Baxter that they might meet together with James Ussher and let him determine the controversy.[189] Baxter, who had a high regard for Ussher, "quickly yielded" to this suggestion.[190] Ussher convinced both disputants to put the matter to rest.[191]

Still, Ussher's arbitration did not completely end the controversy over common and special grace. When Baxter wrote his *Certain Disputations* (1657) he reiterated his conviction that Kendall had been mistaken.[192] Still afraid that his clarifications might not be sufficient, Baxter added an extra epistle to the reader in the seventh edition of the *Saints Rest* (1658), which he also included in *Of Saving Faith* (1658).[193] For those who were still afraid that he only made a gradual difference between common and special grace, Baxter once more tried to clarify his opinion. Those who could not appreciate the necessary distinctions in defining the difference between common and special grace Baxter advised to "tear that leaf out of the Book which speaks of this subject, that it may not trouble them."[194]

Kendall also returned to the fray once more. In 1657 he published his *Fur pro Tribunali*, once again prefaced by John Owen, in which he reopened the discussion on the question whether new immanent acts may be ascribed to God.[195] Baxter, though upset that Kendall "broke that promise" to stop the dispute, now decided to leave the issue alone.[196]

---

186. Kendall, *Sancti sanciti* IV.97-142.
187. Baxter, *Confession*, sigs. Aaaa1ʳ-Aaaa4ᵛ (*Saints Rest*, in *Works* III.349-52 [23.466-733]).
188. Baxter, *Confession*, sig. Aaaa4ʳ (*Saints Rest*, in *Works* III.351 [23.472]).
189. For Ussher, see *DNB* 58.64-72; Allison, *Rise of Moralism*, pp. 21-24; R. Buick Knox, *James Ussher Archbishop of Armagh* (Cardiff: Univ. of Wales Press, 1967; Hugh Trevor-Roper, *Catholics, Anglicans and Puritans: Seventeenth Century Essays* (London: Secker & Warburg, 1987), pp. 120-65, 289-92.
190. *RB* I.110.
191. Baxter, *More Proofs* (London, 1675), p. 405; *RB* II.206.
192. Baxter, *Certain Disputations*, pp. 273-74, 442, 476.
193. Baxter, *Saints Rest*, 7th ed. (London, 1658), pp. 830-36 (*Works* III.352-55 [23.474-80]); *Of Saving Faith* (London, 1658), pp. 90-96. Cf. *CCRB* 423. Baxter had additions to the *Saints Rest* printed in *Confession* and *Of Saving Faith* to accommodate those who had bought earlier editions of the *Saints Rest*. These would now not be forced to purchase the new editions (*Of Saving Faith*, p. 90).
194. Baxter, *Saints Rest*, 7th ed., p. 830 (*Works* III.352 [23.474]; *Of Saving Faith*, p. 90).
195. George Kendall, "Dissertatiuncula de novis actibvs immanentibus sintne Deo ascribendi?" in *De Doctrina Neopelagianâ Oratio habita in Comitiis Oxonii Julii 9.1654*, pp. 141-219, in *Fur pro Tribunali* (Oxford, 1657).
196. Baxter, *More Proofs*, p. 405. Cf. *Of Justification*, p. 320. Of course, Baxter himself was not completely innocent of breaking his promise, since he continued to clarify his position against Kendall after 1655. Besides, the material in Kendall's *Fur pro Tribunali* on new immanent acts in God was specifically directed against John Goodwin, not against Baxter.

Baxter's comments in his *Saints Everlasting Rest* on the difference between common and saving grace also caused Thomas Barlow (1607-91) to react in an anonymous addition to *Sincerity and Hypocricy* (1658), a book written by William Sheppard (d. 1675?).[197] Like Kendall, Barlow objected to the notion that there is only a difference of degree between common and special grace. Baxter had learnt – probably through the services of his bookseller, Thomas Underhill – that the anonymous author was the recently appointed provost of Queen's College and librarian of Bodleian Library, Oxford.[198] Baxter, convinced that Barlow had entirely misrepresented his position, responded with *Of Saving Grace* (1658). In it, Baxter reiterated his view on the relation between common and saving grace and argued that he did not really differ with Barlow on the heart of the issue.

Lewis Du Moulin

On "about the very day" that Baxter finished his *Reduction of a Digressor* against Kendall – August 1, 1653 – he was surprised by yet another writing which he could not ignore.[199] This Latin treatise, entitled *De fidei partibus in justificatione Dissertatio*, was written by Colvinus Ludiomaeus. In it, the author published a fragment of a letter which Cyrus Du Moulin, a French pastor, had written to his brother, Lewis, the Camden Reader of ancient history in Oxford.[200] The main part of *De fidei partibus* was a confutation of Cyrus Du Moulin's position from a high Calvinist point of view. Ludiomaeus argued that justification precedes faith in the *ordo salutis*.

Baxter immediately set out to refute the tractate. When he had finished his reply, he received two letters around November, 1653, the one in Latin, the other in English.[201] They both revealed to him that the name of the author of the treatise, Colvinus Ludiomaeus, was an anagram for Ludovicus Molinaeus, or Lewis Du Moulin.[202] It now became clear to Baxter that Lewis Du Moulin had publicly

197. Thomas Barlow, in William Sheppard, *Sincerity and Hypocricy* (Oxford, 1658), pp. 321-416. For Barlow, see Wood, *Athenæ Oxonienses*, IV, 333-41; *GBD* 3.482-87; *DNB* 3.224-29; Allison, *Rise of Moralism*, pp. 141-44; *CCRB* 440. For Sheppard, see *DNB* 52.63-64; Nancy L. Matthews, *William Sheppard, Cromwell's Law Reformer*, Cambridge Studies in English Legal History (Cambridge: Cambridge Univ. Press, 1984); *CCRB* 440. For the dispute between Baxter and Barlow, see *RB* I.117; Orme, "Life and Times," in *Works* 1.462-63; *CCRB* 440.
198. In his reply, *Of Saving Faith* (1658), Baxter refers to Barlow's *Exercitationes aliquot Metaphysicæ de Deo* (1637), and he also comments that "Tradition" has "published" the name of the author of the response to Baxter (*Of Saving Faith*, pp. 5, 87). Baxter also refers to Barlow as the author in *RB* I.117. Keeble and Nuttall suggest that Thomas Underhill was Baxter's informant because he mentions Barlow in a letter written on the very day that he received Sheppard's book from Underhill (*CCRB* 440).
199. Baxter, *Confutation*, sig. lll^r.
200. Peter (1601-84), Lewis, and Cyrus Du Moulin were three sons of the well-known French divine, Pierre Du Moulin (1568-1658). For Cyrus Du Moulin, see *La France protestante*, Eugène and Émile Haag, 2nd ed., ed. M. Henri Bordier, V (Paris: Sandoz et Fischbacher, 1886), 829-30. For Lewis Du Moulin, see *La France protestante*, V, 827-29; *DNB* 39.200; *CR* 172.
201. The approximate date of these letters is clear from the fact that Baxter finished his reply to *De fidei partibus* just before he received William Eyre's *Vindiciæ Justificationis Gratuitæ*, which was in November, 1653 (cf. below, p. 53, n. 224; *CCRB* 149-50).
202. Baxter, *Confutation*, sig.ll2^v (*CCRB* 140-50).

attacked his own brother, although "I have yet no such certainty, as flatly to conclude that he is the undoubted Author ..."[203] But Baxter rightly felt that there was little need to doubt the identification of the author.[204]

Baxter himself was not under attack in Lewis Du Moulin's *De fidei partibus*. That he nevertheless wrote the third part of his *Apology* in opposition to this treatise needed some justification. In his apologetical preface, Baxter came up with twelve reasons why he felt he should oppose Du Moulin.[205] If the author had the right to confute his brother's private letters, Baxter felt that he certainly had the right to confute the author's public writings "which endanger the safety of the Church and Truth."[206] The last reason why Baxter felt compelled to oppose Du Moulin was undoubtedly the main one as well:

> Lastly, I saw more said for the Justification of unbelievers, and against Justification by Faith, in this Book which I confute, then I had before seen in such order, and in so narrow a room; and therefore I thought that the confutation of it might not be unuseful, but might serve instead of the confutation of many, especially it being written in such modest language, which would occasion no wordy altercations or contentions.[207]

Baxter's main motive for opposing Du Moulin lay in the danger which he perceived in the teaching that justification precedes faith.[208]

Lewis Du Moulin's esteem of Baxter soon changed, however. Starting in 1665, he carried on an extensive correspondence with Baxter.[209] Much of this correspondence concerns Du Moulin's Erastian view on the relation between church and state, which clashed with Baxter's insistence that the church has its own disciplinary power.[210] These discussions took place in a good atmosphere. Du Moulin discussed the possibility of translating some of Baxter's works into French.[211] Baxter even came to the conclusion that Du Moulin became "one of those Friends who are injurious to the Honour of their own Understandings by overvaluing me."[212]

---

203. Baxter, *Confutation*, sig. ll2ᵛ.
204. In his autobiography Baxter confidently identifies Ludiomaeus Colvinus as Ludovicus Molinaeus. Also, in a letter of June 9, 1658 Peter Du Moulin, Lewis' brother, thanked Baxter for showing Lewis his error (DWL MS *BC* ii, f. 293ʳ; *CCRB* 459).
205. Baxter, *Confutation*, sigs. lll ʳ-ll2ʳ.
206. Baxter, *Confutation*, sig. ll2ʳ.
207. Baxter, *Confutation*, sig. ll2ʳ.
208. Three years later, Du Moulin also made some passing comments on Baxter's theory of universal redemption in the preface to his *Parænesis ad ædificatores Imperii in Imperio* (1656), accusing him of Amyraldianism (sig. g1ᵛ; cf. sig. g4ᵛ). Baxter denied the charge (*Certain Disputations*, sig. b3ᵛ).
209. *CCRB* 719, 722, 778, 781, 783, 785, 796, 828, 833, 835, 869, 871.
210. For Du Moulin's church political views, see *RB* III.85; F.J. Powicke, "Dr. Lewis Du Moulin's Vindication of the Congregational Way," *TCHS*, 9 (1926), 219-236; Douglas Nobbs, "New Light on Louis du Moulin," *PHSL*, 15 (1936), 489-509; Douglas Nobbs, *Theocracy and Toleration: A Study of the Disputes in Dutch Calvinism from 1600 to 1650* (Cambridge: Cambridge Univ. Press, 1938), pp. 224-45; Geoffrey F. Nuttall, "Dr. Du Moulin and *Papa Ultrajectinus*," *NeAKG*, NS 61 (1981), 205-13.
211. *CCRB* 719, 781, 785.
212. *RB* I.110.

William Eyre

Baxter was barely finished with his confutation of Du Moulin's *De fidei partibus* when another treatise came off the press, which contained a similar teaching: *Vindiciæ Justificationis Gratuitæ. Justification without Conditions; or The Free Justification of a Sinner, Explained, Confirmed, and Vindicated, from the Exceptions, Objections, and seeming Absurdities, which are cast upon it, by the Assertors of Conditional Justification*, written by William Eyre, curate of St. Thomas, Salisbury.[213] The origin of this controversy goes back to 1650, when Eyre, in the weekly lecture for his congregation, denied that faith was a condition for benefiting of the new covenant blessings. In this connection, he asserted that justification precedes faith.[214] A week later, a neighboring minister publicly warned his congregation against Eyre's position. Eyre's sermon created an outcry in the entire town of Salisbury.[215]

The affair had a continuation in April, 1652, when Thomas Warren (1617?-94), rector of Houghton, Hampshire, preached a Wednesday lecture in Salisbury in which he also rejected the notion of justification before faith.[216] After the sermon, Eyre stood up and opposed Warren's views.[217] The next day, Warren attended Eyre's lecture and defended himself when the sermon was finished.[218] The following Wednesday, Benjamin Woodbridge (1622-84), Twisse's successor in Newbury, Berkshire, preached in Salisbury.[219] In his sermon, he opposed Eyre's doctrine of justification.[220] He published this sermon under the title *Justification by Faith: Or, A Confutation Of that Antinomian Error, That Justification is before Faith* (1652).

Baxter warmly commended Woodbridge's sermon.[221] But Eyre was upset, both at what he considered a serious misrepresentation of his judgement and at Baxter's support of Woodbridge.[222] He defended himself against Woodbridge in a

---

213. Baxter says that he "had no sooner finished" his reply to Lewis Du Moulin "but I received this of Mr *Eyre's*" (*Admonition* [London, 1654], sig. A3^r). For Eyre, see Wood, *Athenæ Oxonienses*, III, 885-86; *CR* 187; *CCRB* 116, n. 1. For accounts of the circumstances surrounding Baxter's controversy with Eyre, see *RB* I.111; Wallace, "Life and Thought of John Owen," pp. 250-52; *CCRB* 116, n. 1.
214. William Eyre, *Vindiciæ Justificationis Gratuitæ* (London, 1654), p. 3.
215. Eyre, *Vindiciæ Justificationis Gratuitæ*, pp 3-4.
216. Warren did not, however, use Eyre's name in his sermon (Thomas Warren, *Vnbeleevers No subjects of Iustification* [London, 1654], sig. a3^r, n. *). For Warren, see *DNB* 59.426; *CR* 511-12.
217. Eyre, *Vindiciæ Justificationis Gratuitæ*, p. 5.
218. Eyre, *Vindiciæ Justificationis Gratuitæ*, p. 10.
219. For Woodbridge, see *RB* I.111; III.98; *DNB* 62.385-86; *CR* 543; *CCRB* 539.
220. Woodbridge held to a moderately Calvinist view on justification. Baxter describes him as "a Man of great Judgment, Piety, Ability, and moderate Principles, addicted to no Faction, but of a Catholick Spirit" (*RB* III.98).
221. Baxter, *Right Method*, in *Works* II.886 (9.xvi): "There is a very judicious man, Mr. Benjamin Woodbridge, of Newbury, hath written so excellent well against this error, and in so small room, being but one sermon, that I would advise all private christians to get one of them, and peruse it, as one of the best, easiest, cheapest preservatives against the contagion of this part of antinomianism."
222. Eyre, *Vindiciæ Justificationis Gratuitæ*, sigs. A2^v-A4^v, p. 11.

prefatory epistle to *Christ's Scepter Advanc'd* (1652).[223] He then decided to publish a whole treatise on the issue, entitled *Vindiciæ Justificationis Gratuitæ* (1653).[224] Interestingly, the book received a commendatory epistle from John Owen, who thereby did not promote the credibility of his denial that he taught justification from eternity.[225]

Eyre's treatise also opposed Baxter, who "ascribes a meritoriousness to works, which the Arminians, and Socinians have not dared to do."[226] When Baxter saw the conditionality of the covenant of grace denied and justification before faith asserted in bold terms he felt he had to warn against the seductive nature of Eyre's treatise: "Truly I finde as farre as I can discern, that most of the prophane people in every Parish where yet I have liv'd, are Antinomians; They are born and bred such; and it is the very natural Religion of men ..."[227] Baxter thus published *Rich. Baxter's Admonition to Mr William Eyre of Salisbury* (1654), which he subsequently republished as the fourth part to his *Apology.*[228] The debate between Baxter and Eyre was subsequently reviewed by John Eedes (1609?-67?), who took a mediating position between what he considered the extremes of Eyre and Baxter.[229]

John Crandon

The next disputant to assail Baxter's position was John Crandon, a sectary of Fawley, Hampshire.[230] Crandon's attack was probably the most virulent and the most damaging reaction which Baxter had received until now. As the title page indicated, Crandon's *Mr. Baxters Aphorisms Exorized and Anthorized* (1654) intended to be a "vindication of Justification by meer Grace, from all the Popish and Arminian Sophisms, by which that Author <*i.e.*, Baxter> labours to ground it upon Mans Works and Righteousness."

---

223. Eyre, *Christ's Scepter Advanc'd* (London, 1652), sigs. A3ᵛ-A4ᵛ.
224. According to the title page of Eyre's treatise, it was published in 1654. It had already come out in November of the previous year, however, for Thomason received his copy on November 10, 1653 and Baxter finished his reply on November 26, 1653 (*Catalogue of the Pamphlets, Books, Newspapers, and Manuscripts Relating to the Civil War, the Commonwealth, and Restoration, Collected by George Thomason, 1640-1661* [London, 1908; rpt. Ann Arbor, MI: Univ. Microfilms International, 1977], II, 43; *Admonition*, sig. G4ʳ; cf. Nuttall, "Richard Baxter's *Apology* (1654)," 71).
225. In the recommendatory epistle, Owen commented that he was not familiar with the circumstances of the controversy. He was of the opinion, however, that even among those who seemed to have been enlightened by God there was too much acceptance of "an almost pure *Socinian Justification, and Exposition of the Covenant of Grace.*"
226. Eyre, *Vindiciæ Justificationis Gratuitæ*, p. 190.
227. Baxter, *Admonition*, sig. A3ᵛ.
228. Thomas Warren and Benjamin Woodbridge also reacted to Eyre's *Vindiciæ Justificationis Gratuitæ*, Warren by means of *Vnbeleevers No subjects of Iustification* (1654) and Woodbridge in *The Method of Grace in the Justification of Sinners* (1654). Another reaction came from John Grayle, rector of North Tidworth, Wiltshire, who opposed Eyre in *A Modest Vindication of the Doctrine of Conditions in the Covenant of Grace* (1655) (cf. *CCRB* 116, n. 1).
229. For Eedes, see *DNB* 17.141; Allison, *Rise of Moralism*, pp. 167-68.
230. For Crandon, see *RB* I.110-11; Wallace, "Life and Thought of John Owen," pp. 252-53; *BDBRSC* 1.188-89; *CCRB* 171.

By August, 1652, Crandon's lengthy manuscript had gone to the publisher.[231] It did not immediately come off the press, however, because Henry Bartlett, vicar of Fordingbridge, Hampshire, intervened.[232] He convinced Crandon to let him read the manuscript first and corresponded to Baxter about his dealings with Crandon.[233] Eyre probably also read the book and commented in his *Vindiciæ Justificationis Gratuitæ* that there was "now in the Presse (as I am informed) a large and full answer to his Paradoxicall Aphorismes, by a faithful Servant of the Lord Jesus, *a workman that needs not to be ashamed* ..."[234]

Baxter himself also read Crandon's manuscript prior to its publication. Perhaps he had received a transcription from Bartlett.[235] Baxter appears to have been truly shocked by the violence of Crandon's attack: "Such a piece as I confess my eyes never saw before."[236] Baxter describes his reaction as follows:

> Truly when I read this mans Book, it forced me to say, Oh what a depraved nature hath man! what a dark understanding! what a deceitful heart! what a sad case are our poor people in, when their guides are in such darkness and contention! what a patient God have we! and what reason therefore to be patient with one another?[237]

At first, Baxter refused to reply to all the details of Crandon's book: "And if I must Write as long as slanderers will make me work, or ignorant men need it, then I shall have work enough to do, and my labours be at the command of every mans Vices."[238] Instead, Baxter planned to respond in a general way to his severest critics, especially Eyre and Crandon, in his *Confession*. At the same time, he could clarify any misunderstanding that his *Aphorismes* had caused among "the Orthodox sober Godly Divines."[239]

Baxter thus proceeded to give a confession of his faith, indicating exactly at which points he could not subscribe to the Westminster Standards (1647) and the Canons of Dort (1619) unless he were allowed his own interpretation of these confessional statements.[240] He then gave an exact account of his opinion regarding the role of works in justification.[241] When these first two chapters were finished in the beginning of 1654, however, Baxter saw the published version of Crandon's treatise: "WHen I had written this far, I received Mr. *Crandons* whole book (having

---

231. One of Baxter's correspondents, Henry Bartlett, reported on August 28, 1652 that Crandon's book was in the press (DWL MS *BC* iv, ff. 176[r-v]; *CCRB* 94). For the origin of Baxter's *Unsavoury Volume* against Crandon, see Nuttall, "Richard Baxter's *Apology* (1654)," 72-73.
232. DWL MS *BC* iv, ff. 179[r-v] (*CCRB* 100), vi, f. 133[r] (*CCRB* 121). For Bartlett, see *CCRB* 94.
233. *CCRB* 94, 100, 121, 138, 161. Crandon himself explains the delay in publication as follows: "At length, having finished what I thought fit to be communicated privately to some friends, and not with-holding the view thereof from any that craved it; I suffered it to sleep many moneths, in hope still to see a more learned answer to his worke" (*Aphorisms Exorized*, sig. B1[v]).
234. Eyre, *Vindiciæ Justificationis Gratuitæ*, sig. A4[v] (emphasis inverted).
235. Says Baxter: "I had beforehand got all save the beginning and end, out of the Press, and wrote so much of an Answer as I thought it worthy, before the publication of it" (*RB* I.110-11).
236. Baxter, *Confession*, p. 6.
237. Baxter, *Confession*, p. 7.
238. Baxter, *Confession*, p. 7.
239. Baxter, *Confession*, p. 8.
240. Baxter, *Confession*, pp. 9-28.
241. Baxter, *Confession*, pp. 28-85.

before seen the Monster, *sine Capite & Caudâ*) when I opened it, I found such a name written in its fore-head, as I had thought that dunghill deserved not to be blest with, *viz.* Mr. *Joseph Caryl*, with his Epistle perfixt <*sic*>."[242] The commendatory preface of Joseph Caryl (1602-73) changed Baxter's plan not to give a point by point reply to Crandon's book.[243] The approbation given by this preeminent moderate independent was a sharp blow to Baxter, especially considering the fact that the first edition of the *Saints Everlasting Rest* had carried Caryl's *imprimatur*.

Caryl's preface endorsed Crandon's views on justification by faith without works and on the believers' freedom from the curse of the law. Baxter decided he would attempt to satisfy Caryl on both issues.[244] He added a chapter on each of them.[245] Baxter also felt he should give his reasons for dissenting from Caryl's judgement concerning the substance of Crandon's treatise. This forced him to deal with Crandon's attack in more detail. When this chapter was finished, however, Baxter decided it did not fit in his *Confession*, and instead he added it as the fifth and last part to his *Apology*, which was now finally published.[246] He entitled this section *An Unsavoury Volume of Mr Jo. Crandon's Anatomized: Or a Nosegay of the Choicest Flowers in that Garden, Presented to Mr Joseph Caryl by Rich. Baxter* (1654).[247]

Meanwhile, Baxter continued to write his *Confession*. When he was about half finished he heard that Crandon had died a few weeks after the publication of his attack on Baxter.[248] Although Crandon's death made Baxter wish he had "studied yet harder for more gentle termes," he nevertheless went ahead with the publication of *An Unsavoury Volume* and with the work on his *Confession*.[249] He added a small chapter in which he pointed out how he differed from Roman Catholics with regard to merit.[250] He also gave a description of Antinomianism, as well as a refutation of the position that justification by faith is identical to justification *in foro conscientiae*.[251] He then continued with a lengthy chapter directed specifically against John Owen, in which he opposed the view that justification is from eternity or from the death of Christ.[252] Finally, he buttressed his arguments by appeals to numerous Protestant divines who, Baxter thought, gave as much to works as he did himself.[253] Before publishing his *Confession*, Baxter asked James Ussher, Richard Vines, and Thomas Gataker to peruse it.[254]

---

242. Baxter, *Confession*, p. 85.
243. For Caryl, see *GBD* 8.349-50; Reid, *Memoirs*, I, 193-203; *DNB* 9.253-54; *CR* 103-04; *CCRB* 172.
244. Baxter, *Unsavoury Volume*, sig. I2ʳ; *Confession*, pp. 7, n.; 85-87, 130.
245. Baxter, *Confession*, pp. 85-100, 100-31.
246. Baxter, *Unsavoury Volume*, sigs. I2ʳ⁻ᵛ, p. 84; *Confession*, p. 131.
247. The epistle to the reader in *Unsavoury Volume* is dated March 31, 1654.
248. Cf. the marginal note in *Confession*, p. 203: "I had written hither, before I heard of Mr. *Crandons* death" (emphasis inverted). Cf. *Unsavoury Volume*, sig. I2ᵛ; *RB* I.110.
249. Baxter, *Unsavoury Volume*, sig. I2ᵛ.
250. Baxter, *Confession*, pp. 131-50.
251. Baxter, *Confession*, pp. 150-88, 189-215.
252. Baxter, *Confession*, pp. 215-293. Cf. above, p. 43.
253. Baxter, *Confession*, pp. 293-462.
254. Baxter states that none of the three divines advised him to alter even a word of his *Confession* (*Of Imputation*, p. 32; *Defence of Christ*, sig. A4ᵛ). For Gataker, see Reid, *Memoirs*, I, 284-315; *GBD* 15.334-40; Brook, *Lives*, III, 200-22; *DNB* 21.60-62; Allison, *Rise of Moralism*, pp. 172-74.

William Robertson and John Warner

By 1655, therefore, Baxter had presented his views on justification in his *Aphorismes* and had given a thorough defense of its doctrine against moderate and high Calvinist critical appraisals in his *Apology* and his *Confession*. Nevertheless, the end of the controversies was not yet in sight. When Thomas Hotchkis (c. 1611-93), rector of Stanton, Wiltshire, wrote *An Exercitation Concerning the Nature of Forgivenesse of Sin* (1655), he took exception to the common Protestant distinction between justification and sanctification.[255] Before publishing the treatise, Baxter had privately given him some animadversions and had advised Hotchkis to go ahead with the publication.[256] Baxter also wrote a commendatory epistle to the reader, in which he spoke highly of Hotchkis' work, despite some of its shortcomings.

Hotchkis' treatise was undoubtedly offensive to many high Calvinists, especially because the author took exception to William Twisse's definition of justification. This was unacceptable to William Robertson (d. 1686?), a noted Hebrew scholar and lexicographer in London.[257] He wrote a defense of Twisse against Baxter and Hotchkis, entitled אגרת המשכיל *Iggeret hammashkil. Or, An Admonitory Epistle unto Mr Rich. Baxter, and Mr Tho. Hotchkiss* (1655). Robertson defended that justification was an eternal, immanent act of God. He was, therefore, greatly upset with Baxter's *Reduction of a Digressor* (1654) against Kendall. Robertson also scorned his opponents' apparent lack of knowledge of Hebrew. Baxter refused to reply to Robertson's attack: "To reciprocate gain-sayings with that kinde of men, is an unprofitable and unpleasing thing: The sons of contention in their greatest darkness, are more zealous and unwearied in their generation and work, than the Children of light and peace in theirs."[258]

As noted already, in *Of Justification* Baxter renewed his replies to Thomas Blake, Anthony Burgess, and John Tombes. This book also contained a reply to John Warner (c. 1611-68), vicar of Christchurch, Hampshire.[259] In September, 1657 Warner published his *Diatriba fidei justificantis, qua justificantis*, which carried a commendatory epistle of George Kendall. The treatise had originated from a number of sermons which the author had preached before his own congregation.[260] Warner argued against the absolute necessity of evangelical righteousness.[261] He further maintained that not only our initial, but also our continued justification is by faith alone.[262] The proper object of justifying faith *as justifying* is only faith in Christ as Savior, not as Lord *and* Savior.[263]

---

255. For Hotchkis, see *CCRB* 160.
256. DWL MS *BC* vi, f. 170ʳ (*CCRB* 160); iii, f. 181ʳ (*CCRB* 170).
257. For Robertson, see *DNB* 48.423; *CCRB* 220.
258. Baxter, *Certain Disputations*, p. 481.
259. For Warner, see *RB* I.114; *CR* 510; George Brownen, "John Warner, M.A.: A Forgotten Nonconformist Leader in South-West Hampshire 1646-1668," *CHST*, 7 (1916-18), 280-87; *CCRB* 418.
260. Warner, *Diatriba fidei justificantis* (Oxford, 1657), sig. A1ʳ.
261. Warner, *Diatriba fidei justificantis*, pp. 154-80.
262. Warner, *Diatriba fidei justificantis*, pp. 219-47.
263. Warner, *Diatriba fidei justificantis*, pp. 411-22.

Baxter first read Warner's tractate as a manuscript, without the dedicatory epistle and the epistle to the reader.[264] He immediately set out to write a response. When he saw the published treatise, it appeared that the epistle to the reader contained yet further assaults on his position. Thus, he added a letter to his disputation in which he opposed Warner's epistle to the reader. Before long, Baxter received a private letter from Warner, who – in an attempt to avoid a rebuttal by Baxter – informed him of his *Diatriba fidei justificantis* and told him that he was not really responsible for its publication: after George Kendall had seen the manuscript, another friend had kept it and had refused to return it, unless Warner would consent to have it published.[265] Warner's letter to Baxter was in vain. He had already finished his reply and had sent it to the printer. He wrote a letter to Warner informing him of this fact.[266] In subsequent correspondence, both authors expressed their mutual respect and love, despite their differences of opinion.[267]

PUBLIC CONTROVERSY: 1658-91

Edward Fowler

After 1658, the controversies surrounding justification seemed to have come to end.[268] Neither Baxter, nor any of his opponents, appeared to be willing to return to the fray. This changed in the early 1670s, first of all by the publication of the second edition of Baxter's *Life of Faith* (1670), in which he gave a summary statement of his views on the imputation of Christ's righteousness and refuted high Calvinist notions of justification.[269] A second incident concerned Baxter's support of the strongly moralist stand of Edward Fowler (1632-1714).[270] Fowler, a Latitudinarian rector from Northill, Bedfordshire, and later bishop of Gloucester, wrote a treatise entitled *The Design of Christianity* (1671), in which he set out to prove that inward real holiness was the "ultimate end" of Christ's coming into the

264. Baxter, *Of Justification*, p. 314.
265. DWL MS *BC* iv, f. 159ʳ (*CCRB* 424).
266. DWL MS *BC* iv, f. 163ʳ (*CCRB* 427).
267. DWL MS *BC* iv, ff. 161ʳ⁻ᵛ (*CCRB* 458); iv, ff. 164ʳ⁻ᵛ (*CCRB* 466).
268. In 1658, Baxter published his *Grotian Religion Discovered*. In the preface, he accused Hugo Grotius of being a Papist and defended the Synod of Dort (1618-19) against the Arminianism of Thomas Pierce (1622-91). Baxter's preface led to angry reactions from various Arminians, such as Thomas Pierce, Laurence Womock (1612-86), Thomas Malpas, Peter Heylin (1600-62), and John Bramhall (1594-1663). In the course of the debate, Baxter's views on justification were not under discussion. It is nevertheless interesting to mention the controversy at this point because it confirms the picture of Baxter as a mediating theologian. He was mostly under attack from high Calvinists, but his theology was not appreciated by Arminians either. I hope to deal with Baxter's controversies with these Arminians at a future date.
269. Baxter, *Life of Faith*, in *Works* III.667-84 (12.297-351). This treatise consists of a sermon on Heb 11:1, which Baxter preached as a royal chaplain before King Charles II on July 22, 1660, enlarged in 1670 with a great number of additions (*RB* I.120; cf. Orme, "Life and Writings," in *Works* 1.526-29; N.H. Keeble, "Richard Baxter's Preaching Ministry: Its History and Texts," *JEH*, 35 (1984), 544, 557; *CCRB* 652, n. 1).
270. For Fowler, see *GBD* 15.16-18; *DNB* 20.84-86; *CR* 209; *CCRB* 854.

world.[271] Shortly after the book was published, Baxter received an anonymous letter in which his *Aphorismes of Justification* and other works were charged with "having some hand in breeding such opinions."[272] Baxter was challenged to confute Fowler's views on holiness, justification, and imputed righteousness. Baxter had indeed some minor reservations about Fowler's exclusive attention to holiness as the "design" of Christianity. Nevertheless, he agreed with Fowler's main argument and supported him accordingly in *How Far Holinesse Is the Design of Christianity* (1671).[273] Fowler, greatly appreciative of Baxter's support, wrote him a letter in which he expressed his indebtedness and railed at the pretenses of high Calvinists.[274] In his reply, Baxter mildly censured Fowler for being too censorious of others.[275] In a final letter, Fowler agreed that he was too often tempted to use harsh language against his opponents.[276] His plea for the preeminence of holiness met with an angry response from John Bunyan (1628-88) in *A Defence of the Doctrine of Justification* (1672).[277] Bunyan was convinced that Fowler's *Design* elevated reason, ignored the work of the Holy Spirit, and taught sheer natural morality, along with justification by works. He accused Fowler of Romanism, Socinianism, and Quakerism, as well as of blaspheming the Holy Spirit. This led to an anonymous reply, entitled *Dirt wip't off* (1672).[278] It reacted

271. For Fowler's theological position and the controversy following his publication, see *RB* III.85; Orme, "Life and Writings," in *Works* 1.669-71; John Hunt, *Religious Thought in England: From the Reformation to the End of Last Century*, II (London: Strahan, 1871), 130-35, 307-09; Frederick J. Powicke, *Reverend Richard Baxter*, pp. 53-59; Allison, *Rise of Moralism*, pp. 144-46; Richard L. Greaves, *John Bunyan*, pref. Geoffrey F. Nuttall, Courtenay Studies in Reformation Theology, 2 (Appleford: Sutton Courtenay, 1969), pp. 21, 82-86; Wallace, *Puritans and Predestination*, pp. 164-66; J. Wayne Baker, "*Sola Fide, Sola Gratia:* The Battle for Luther in Seventeenth-Century England," *SCJ*, 16 (1985), 130; Christopher Hill, *A Turbulent, Seditious, and Factious People: John Bunyan and His Church 1628-1688* (Oxford: Clarendon, 1988), pp. 130-35; Isabel Rivers, "Grace, Holiness, and the Pursuit of Happiness: Bunyan and Restoration Latitudinarianism," in *John Bunyan: Conventicle and Parnassus: Tercentenary Essays*, ed. N.H. Keeble (Oxford: Clarendon, 1988), pp. 45-69; T.L. Underwood, "Introduction," in John Bunyan, *Works* 4.xx-xxv; Isabel Rivers, *Reason, Grace, and Sentiment: A Study of the Language of Religion and Ethics in England, 1660-1780*, I: *Whichcote to Wesley*, Cambridge Studies in Eighteenth-Century English Literature and Thought, 8 (Cambridge: Cambridge Univ. Press, 1991), pp. 101, 141-44; Martin I.J. Griffin, *Latitudinarianism in the Seventeenth-Century Church of England*, annotated Richard H. Popkin, ed. Lila Freedman, Brill's Studies in Intellectual History, 32 (Leiden: Brill, 1992), *passim*.
272. Baxter, *How Far Holinesse* (London, 1671), p. 3. The letter is not extant, and its author is unknown. Baxter's only comment regarding the authorship of the letter is "I know not you" (p.21).
273. Baxter finished writing this booklet on August 24, 1671 (*How Far Holinesse*, p. 22).
274. DWL MS *BC* iv, ff. 33[r-v] (*CCRB* 854).
275. DWL MS *BC* iv, ff. 35[r]-36[v] (*CCRB* 857).
276. DWL MS *BC* vi, f. 41[r] (*CCRB* 862).
277. For Bunyan, see *e.g.* Greaves, *John Bunyan*; Hill, *Turbulent, Seditious, and Factious People*; N.H. Keeble, ed., *John Bunyan: Conventicle and Parnassus: Tercentenary Essays* (Oxford: Clarendon, 1988); M. Van Os and G.J. Schutte, eds., *Bunyan in England and Abroad: Papers Delivered at the John Bunyan Tercentenary Symposium, Vrije Universiteit Amsterdam, 1988*, VU-Studies on Protestant History, 1 (Amsterdam: VU Univ. Press, 1990).
278. Secondary scholars usually attribute this book to Fowler himself or to his curate. To regard it as Fowler's own would be in agreement with his admission to Baxter that he tends to react sharply to his opponents. On the other hand, the preface states that "Mr. *Fowler* is much more profitably imployed than to have leisure to return answers to his *wretched Scribbles*, but if he had time lying upon his hands, he will not easily be perswaded to do such bald & rude Scriblers so great an honor" (*Dirt wip't off* [London, 1672], sig. A2[v]; emphasis inverted).

to Bunyan's work in a similarly harsh manner. The book concluded with an abstract of Baxter's defense of Fowler.

Thomas Tully

In 1673 the issues surrounding justification once again became the focus of debate because of Baxter's preface to a book by William Allen on the doctrine of the covenant.[279] Allen's treatise, entitled *A Discourse of the Nature, Ends, and Difference of the Two Covenants*, discussed the difference between the old and the new covenant and presented a defense of the necessity of works for justification. In the preface, Baxter made some comments on what he considered the difference between the "law of innocency" and the "law of grace." He also listed twenty doctrinal statements to which he thought all protestants agreed. These propositions centered around the nature of Christ's atoning work and the significance of sanctification.[280]

Thomas Tully, former principal of St. Edmund Hall, Oxford, chaplain to King Charles II, and, since 1675, dean of Ripon, Yorkshire, reacted both to Baxter's preface and to his *Aphorismes of Justification*.[281] In a lengthy Latin treatise, *Justificatio Paulina sine operibvs* (1674), he attacked Baxter's ideas on imputation and the role of works in justification. He also expressed his dissent from Baxter's views on original sin.[282] Tully's attack was potentially dangerous, seeing it dealt with Baxter's views alongside those of Robert Bellarmine (1542-1621) and George Bull (1634-1710). The latter's doctrine of justification, expressed in his *Harmonia Apostolica* (1670) had created a furor among English Protestants.[283] Baxter was particularly upset with the fact that Tully singled out his *Aphorismes* for an attack, even though they had long since been retracted, while he took no account of Baxter's further writings on justification.[284]

Baxter refers to Tully as someone "whose name is honoured for *Learning* and *Moderation*."[285] Despite this appellation, the debate quickly degenerated. Tully consistently charged that Baxter's theories were Roman Catholic and Socinian in character. Baxter, in return, treated Tully as an Antinomian whose views of imputation subverted the Gospel. Doubtless, the cause of the animosity lay with both

---

279. For Allen, see Murray Tolmie, "Thomas Lambe, Soapboiler, and Thomas Lambe, Merchant, General Baptists," *BQ*, 27 (1977), 4-13; Geoffrey F. Nuttall, "Thomas Lambe, William Allen and Richard Baxter," *BQ*, 27 (1977), 139-40; *CCRB* 473.
280. Baxter's preface is dated June 4, 1672.
281. For Tully, see Wood, *Athenæ Oxonienses*, III, 1055-59; *GBD* 71-73; *DNB* 57.310; *CCRB* 973.
282. Thomas Tully, *Justificatio Paulina* (Oxford, 1674), p. 128. Cf. Baxter, *Two Disputations*, p. 2. For Baxter's controversy with Tully, see Robert Nelson, *Life*, pp. 243-45; Orme, "Life and Writings," in *Works* 1.463-64.
283. For George Bull, see Nelson, *Life*; *DNB* 17.234-38; Allison, *Rise of Moralism*, pp. 118-35; Wallace, *Puritans and Predestination*, pp. 162-64; Henry Chadwick, "Justification by Faith: A Perspective," *OiC*, 20 (1984), 217-18; Alister E. McGrath, "The Emergence of the Anglican Tradition on Justification 1600-1700," *ChM*, 98 (1984), 36-38.
284. Baxter, *Two Disputations*, p. 4; *More Proofs*, p. 343; *Treatise of Justifying Righteousness*, sig. A3ʳ; *Of Imputation*, p. 172; *Answer*, p. 74.
285. Baxter, *Two Disputations*, p. 1.

disputants. Neither of the two authors appeared to be very interested in under-standing the other's motives.

Around the same time that Tully published his attack, Baxter preached a ser-mon at Pinners' Hall, London.[286] The Pinners' Hall lectures were held every Thursday since 1673 and were intended to promote unity between Presbyterians and Independents.[287] The text of Baxter's sermon was Ephesians 1:3: "Blessed be the God and Father of our Lord Jesus Christ, who hath blessed us with all spiritual blessings in heavenly places in Christ." Baxter's comments on imputation and his moderate attitude toward Roman Catholicism infuriated many of the Independ-ents.[288] Two days after Baxter's lecture, Christopher Fowler (1610?-78) opposed him in a sermon on Canticles 2:16 ("My beloved is mine, and I am his").[289] Fowler insisted that Christ and the elect are the same individual persons.[290] Any "true *Protestant*" would accept that Christ's righteousness is the only material cause of justification.[291] Two years later, Thomas Cole (1627?-97) also preached a refuta-tion of Baxter's sermon.[292] Cole argued that the work of faith is no part of our righteousness, and that Christ's imputed righteousness is the "sole and only Right-eousness" by which we are justified in God's sight.[293] Baxter clarified four points in a short tract, entitled *An Appeal to the Light* (1674). He briefly set forth his views on the imputation of Christ's righteousness, on the need for a subordinate personal righteousness, on God's willingness to help when he commands duties, and on the significance of the differences between Protestants and Roman Catho-lics. Tully immediately countered with his *Animadversions upon a Sheet of Mr Baxters entituled An Appeal to the Light* (1675). Tully felt that Baxter had misrep-resented the Calvinist view.[294] He also charged Baxter with concealing his affinity to Roman Catholic notions of justification.[295]

In 1675, Tully received "three several publicke messengers" from Baxter.[296] The first was in the form of a premonition to the third part of Baxter's *More Proofs of Infants Church-membership* (1675).[297] In his preface to this section, Baxter

286. Baxter preached his controverted sermon on August 11, 1674 (Samuel Crisp, "To the Christian Reader," in Tobias Crisp, *Compleat Works* [London, 1690], sig. A3ᵛ; cf. Baxter, *Defence of Christ*, sig. A4ᵛ).
287. The original lecturers were Baxter, Thomas Manton, William Bates (1625-99), William Jenkyn (1613-85) (Presbyterians), John Owen, and John Collins (1632?-87) (Independents). Cf. T.G. Crippen, "The Ancient Merchants' Lecture," *TCHS*, 7 (1916-18), 301; Peter Toon, *Emergence of Hyper-Calvinism*, pp. 50-51.
288. Baxter reported that the city of London "ringeth" of the sermon (*Catholick Theologie* II.263, 283). Cf. *RB* III.103, 154.
289. Samuel Crisp, "To the Christian Reader," in Tobias Crisp, *Compleat Works*, sigs. A4ᵛ-a2ᵛ.
290. Samuel Crisp, "To the Christian Reader," in Tobias Crisp, *Compleat Works*, sig. a1ʳ.
291. Samuel Crisp, "To the Christian Reader," in Tobias Crisp, *Compleat Works*, sig. a2ʳ.
292. Cole preached his sermon on Matt 7:24-27 – the parable of the foundations of rock and sand – on August 8, 1676 (Samuel Crisp, "To the Christian Reader," in Tobias Crisp, *Compleat Works*, sig. a2ᵛ).
293. Samuel Crisp, "To the Christian Reader," in Tobias Crisp, *Compleat Works*, sig. a2ᵛ.
294. Tully, *Animadversions* (Oxford, 1675), sigs. G2ʳ⁻ᵛ.
295. Tully, *Letter* (Oxford, 1675), p. 16; *Animadversions*, sig. G4ᵛ. For Baxter's reply to this charge, see *Answer*, pp. 23-24.
296. Tully, *Letter*, p. 1. The three "messengers" are identified in *CCRB* 973.
297. Baxter, *More Proofs*, pp. 343-44.

took exception to Tully's attack on his theory of original sin. The second "messenger" was Baxter's massive *Catholick Theologie* (1675). It was an attempt to reconcile the varying Protestant doctrines of grace. In this treatise, he briefly referred to Tully, listing him together with a number of Antinomian theologians.[298] The third "messenger" was Baxter's *Two Disputations of Original Sin* (1675). This book consisted of two old disputations which he had used "above twenty years ago" for a meeting of the Worcestershire Association.[299] Thus, Baxter did not give a direct reply to Tully in this book but gave a more systematic exposition of his views on original sin.

Tully reacted angrily to the three affronts in *A Letter to Mr Richard Baxter* (1675). He decided that, after this letter, he would no longer reply to anything that Baxter might decide to write on the various controversies.[300] Baxter, however, came with two more attacks on Tully, both of which were included in his *Treatise of Justifying Righteousness* (1676).[301] The first part was entitled *Of the Imputation of Christ's Righteousness to Believers*.[302] The first five chapters of this first section, in which Baxter gave a history of the doctrine of imputation and presented his own position, had been written in 1672.[303] Baxter apologized for the cursory treatment of the issue, which was due to the haste in which the material had been written.[304] The last three chapters of this section were a direct reply to Tully's *Justificatio Paulina sine operibvs*. The second part of the *Treatise of Justifying Righteousness* was entitled *An Answer to Dr. Tullies Angry Letter*. The remaining three parts of the book contained Baxter's earlier discussions with Christopher Cartwright on twofold righteousness and the role of works in justification.

Tobias Crisp

Baxter was convinced that his controversial writings of the 1650s had been successful in refuting and suppressing Antinomianism.[305] Apparently, he did not think that Tully's attacks signalled a revival of Antinomianism. Any possible high Calvinist vestiges received their final blow in Baxter's *Methodus Theologiæ* (1681). In this Latin tome, on which he had been working for years, he also dealt with numerous questions surrounding the doctrines of the atonement and justification. These expositions went entirely unchallenged.

---

298. Baxter, *Catholick Theologie* II.255.
299. Baxter, *Two Disputations*, p. 11. Baxter published his *Two Disputations* also to defend his doctrine of original sin against Henry Danvers (c. 1622-87), a Fifth Monarchist and antipaedobaptist with whom he was engaged in a dispute on infant baptism (*Two Disputations*, pp. 10-12).
300. Tully, *Letter*, pp. 37-38.
301. The individual parts of this treatise are dated 1675.
302. This part was republished separately in 1679 as *Imputative Righteousness*.
303. The preface to this first section is dated July 20, 1672.
304. Baxter, *Of Imputation*, sigs. A5ᵛ, B1ʳ.
305. In 1664, Baxter recorded his "Thanks to God for the Success of my Controversial Writings against the Antinomians." He comments that this "Sect" has been extinct for many years (*RB* I.111). In January, 1691 Baxter wrote that the errors regarding imputation had "seemed these Thirty Four Years suppressed" (*Defence of Christ*, sig. A2ᵛ; emphasis throughout in original). On the title page of *Scripture Gospel defended*, Baxter speaks of the "sudden reviving of Antinomianism, which seemed almost extinct near Thirty four years."

Because Baxter thought that Antinomianism had been overcome, the republication of the sermons of Tobias Crisp (1600-43) in 1690 by his son, Samuel, meant a shock to him.[306] Crisp's Antinomianism had already been controversial during his lifetime. His sermons, entitled *Christ Alone Exalted*, had first been published after his death, between 1643 and 1683.[307] They had been opposed by Stephen Geree (1594-1656?), John Benbrigge, and Samuel Rutherford (1600-61).[308] Also Baxter had denounced Crisp's views in several of his writings.[309]

The republication of the sermons, along with some additional ones, meant a particularly sharp blow for Baxter because Samuel Crisp had prefaced them with a rebuttal of Baxter's position on imputation. What is more, twelve divines – Presbyterians as well as Independents – placed a declaration in front of the publication in which they testified to the authenticity of the sermons.[310] They stated that they wanted

> to certifie, That we have sufficient reason to believe, that the Sermons now added to them (that were Printed formerly) are the said Dr. *Crisp*'s Sermons; and have been faithfully transcribed from his own Notes, left written with his own Hand, as the said worthy Gentleman, his Son (the transcriber) hath assured the Reader, in that Preface of his own, which is set before the whole Works.[311]

Baxter was enraged by the fact that some Presbyterians, who were closely allied to him, had placed their names in a book which advocated Antinomian doctrine. In another Pinners' Hall lecture, he opposed Crisp's views.[312] Referring to the declaration of the twelve divines, he called out: "Jezabel: What, hang up a Sign to shew

---

306. For Tobias Crisp, see Wood, *Athenæ Oxonienses*, III, 50-51; John Gill, "Memoirs of the Life, etc of Tobias Crisp, D.D.," in Tobias Crisp, *Complete Works*, ed. John Gill, 7th ed. (London, 1832), I, v-viii (incorrect pagination; sigs. b1ʳ-b2ᵛ); Brook, *Lives*, II, 471-75; *DNB* 13.99-100; *GBD* 11.19-21; *BDBRSC* 1.191-92; *CCRB* 160.
307. Crisp's *Christ Alone Exalted* had been published in four parts, in 1643, 1644, 1646, and 1683.
308. Stephen Geree, *Doctrine of the Antinomians* (London, 1644); John Benbrigge, *Christ above all exalted* (London, 1645); Samuel Rutherford, *Survey of the Spirituall Antichrist* (London, 1648).
309. Baxter, *Confutation*, p. 239; *Admonition*, sig. A3ʳ; Pref., in Thomas Hotchkis, *Exercitation* (London, 1655), sig. B3ᵛ; *Confession*, p. 279; *Catholick Theologie* II.255.
    For Crisp's theological position, see Hunt, *Religious Thought*, I, 249-51; Kevan, *Grace of Law*, *passim*; K.M. Campbell, "Living the Christian Life: 4. The Antinomian Controversy of the 17th Century," in *Living the Christian Life*, Proc. of the Westminster Conference, 1974 (n.p.: n.p., [1975]), pp. 70-76; R.T. Kendall, *Calvin and English Calvinism to 1649* (Oxford: Oxford Univ. Press, 1979), pp. 186-88; Mark W. Karlberg, "Reformed Interpretation of the Mosaic Covenant," *WThJ*, 43 (1980), pp. 27-29; Mark Walter Karlberg, "The Mosaic Covenant and the Concept of Works in Reformed Hermeneutics: A Historical-Critical Analysis with Particular Attention to Early Covenant Eschatology," Diss. Westminster Theological Seminary 1980, pp. 150-54; Alan P.F. Sell, *The Great Debate: Calvinism, Arminianism and Salvation*, Studies in Christian Thought and History (Worthing, West Sussex: Walter, 1982), pp. 47-49; Von Rohr, *Covenant of Grace*, *passim*.
310. The twelve divines were Vincent Alsop (d. 1703), Richard Bures (1629-97), John Gammon, John Howe, Thomas Powell, John Turner (d. c. 1692) (Presbyterians); Isaac Chauncy (1632-1712), George Cokayne (1619-91), George Griffith (b. 1619), Increase Mather (1639-1723), Nathaniel Mather (1630-97) (Independents); and Hanserd Knollys (1599?-1691) (Baptist). Cf. Toon, *Emergence of Hyper-Calvinism*, p. 66, n. 4.
311. George Griffith, et al., in Tobias Crisp, *Compleat Works* (1690), sig. A2ʳ.
312. The sermon was held on January 28, 1690 (Samuel Crisp, Pref., in Tobias Crisp, *Christ made Sin* [London, 1691], sig. a2ʳ).

where Jezabel dwelt!"[313] There was an attempt – presumably by John Howe – to calm Baxter down in *Some Considerations of a Certificate to Dr. Crisp's Works* (1690).[314] In *A Conciliatory Judgment* (1690), Thomas Beverley (fl. 1670-1701) attempted to reconcile Baxter and Crisp. According to Beverley, the controversy between the two esteemed divines could be reduced to no more than a "seeming Controversie" between justification and sanctification.[315] In his replies to Howe and Beverley, which he never published, Baxter showed himself utterly unconvinced.[316]

In order to ease the tension, seven of the twelve divines came with a clarification of their declaration.[317] They said that they had never intended to give their approbation of Tobias Crisp's sermons. Their only purpose had been to testify that Samuel Crisp had faithfully transcribed them.[318] Moreover, they had not been aware of the lengthy attack on Baxter which Samuel Crisp had prefaced to the sermons.[319] At the same time, however, they played down Crisp's alleged Antinomianism. The sermons had many positive characteristics, "as to be very apt to make good impressions upon mens hearts."[320] Although the controversy did not prevent the establishment of the "Heads of Agreement" between the Presbyterians and the Independents in London in 1691, the result was a bitter controversy between the two parties, which lasted until 1699 and resulted already in 1694 in the demise of the "Happy Union."[321]

---

313. As reported by Samuel Crisp, Pref., in Tobias Crisp, *Christ made Sin*, sig. a1^v (emphasis throughout in original).

314. *Some Considerations of a Certificate to Dr. Crisp's Works* (London, 1690). The pamphlet is anonymous. Baxter refers to it as follows: "I have seen a printed Paper, though without a name: yet, by ye Style notifying ye Author to be one of ye twelve, & one whom & greatly esteeme ..." (DWL MS *BT* v.143, f. 24^r). Roger Thomas identifies John Howe as the author (*The Baxter Treatises: A Catalogue of the Richard Baxter Papers (Other Than the Letters) in Dr. Williams's Library*, Occasional Paper, 8 [London: Dr. Williams's Trust, 1959], p. 23; "The Break-Up of Nonconformity," in *The Beginnings of Nonconformity*, by Geoffrey F. Nuttall, et al, The Hibbert Lectures [London: Clarke, 1964], p. 41, n. 2). Thomas may well be correct, although I have been unable to find confirmation of this.

315. Thomas Beverley, *Conciliatory Judgment* (London, 1690), p. 3.

316. For Baxter's replies, see DWL MS *BT* v.143, ff. 24^r-26^r (against *Some Considerations*); vii.224, ff. 48^v, 39^r-48^r (against Beverley). Also in his *Defence of Christ* he professes he does not understand why some of the twelve divines prefixed their names to the republication of Crisp's sermons (sig. A2^v). Baxter does not accept the excuse that the errors had been expunged from the sermons (pp. 65-71).

317. The clarification was partly identical to *Some Considerations*. The seven divines were John Howe, Vincent Alsop, Nathaniel Mather, Increase Mather, John Turner, Richard Bures, and Thomas Powell.

318. John Howe, et al., in John Flavel, *Succinct and Seasonable Discourse* (London, 1691), sigs. a3^r, a8^v.

319. Howe, et al., in Flavel, *Succinct and Seasonable Discourse*, sigs. a3^r, a4^r.

320. Howe, et al., in Flavel, *Succinct and Seasonable Discourse*, sig. a5^r (emphasis throughout in original).

321. For the controversy following the publication of Crisp's sermons, see Nelson, *Life*, pp. 260-74; J. Hay Colligan, "The Antinomian Controversy," *TCHS*, 6 (1915), 389-96; Thomas, "Break-Up of Nonconformity," pp. 40-42; Roger Thomas, "Parties in Nonconformity," in *The English Presbyterians: From Elizabethan Puritanism to Modern Unitarianism*, by C.G. Bolam, et al. (London: Allen & Unwin, 1968), pp. 107-12; Roger Thomas, "Presbyterians in Transition," in *English Presbyterians*, pp. 113-25; Hywel R. Jones, "The Death of Presbyterianism," in *By Schisms Rent Asunder*, Proc. of the Puritan and Reformed Studies conference, 1969 (n.p.: n.p., [1970]), pp. 31-38; Baker, "*Sola Fide, Sola Gratia*:," 131-32.

Baxter had set out to write a refutation as soon as he had heard that Crisp's sermons would be republished.[322] This rebuttal, entitled *A Defence of Christ, and Free Grace*, formed the second part of his *Scripture Gospel defended* (1690). As the first part of the same treatise, Baxter decided to publish two older manuscripts on the issue of the imputation of Christ's righteousness. The first of these, *A Breviate of the Doctrine of Justification*, had probably been written in 1677, because of continued "suspicions, aspersions and censures behind my back" by some of the Independents in London.[323] Baxter had especially been upset by the attack on his views on justification by John Troughton (1637?-81) in his *Lutherus redivivus* (1677-78).[324] Baxter had known Troughton, a Presbyterian pastor who had been blind from his youth, from the time Baxter had spent at Coventry. At that time, he had encouraged Troughton's parents to further their son's education, "not foreseeing his snares."[325] Baxter had first given the manuscript of his *Breviate of the Doctrine of Justification* to Samuel Annesley (1620-96), a Presbyterian pastor, at whose house Presbyterians and Independents used to discuss various issues.[326] When, after a year, he had still not heard a response, Baxter decided to publish the treatise, and he wrote a preface to it.[327] As it turned out, however, he waited with its publication for another twelve years, till 1690, because he was afraid "it should kindle New Oppositions."[328]

Annexed to his *Breviate of the Doctrine of Justification*, Baxter also published

---

322. Baxter testifies that he finished his refutation before he had even seen the publication: "SInce the Writing of all that followeth, I have seen the New Edition of Dr. *Crisp's* Sermons ..." (*Defence of Christ*, sig. A2ʳ; emphasis inverted).

323. Baxter, *Breviate*, sig. A4ʳ (emphasis throughout in original). Cf. p. 59. Also in *RB* III.183 Baxter comments: "Continued backbitings about my Judgment concerning justification, occasioned me to write the summ of it in two or three sheets; with the solution of above thirty controversies unhappily rais'd about it." This description of the contents only fits Baxter's *Breviate*. Baxter's comment about "backbitings" in *RB* has incorrectly been interpreted as an allusion to Stephen Lobb's animadversions a year later (*CCRB* 1023). This cannot be correct because Baxter's answer to Lobb (*Scripture Gospel defended*, pp. 75-116), unlike the *Breviate*, does not consist of a summary statement along with the solution of more than thirty controversies.

324. For Troughton, see *CR* 494; *DNB* 57.260; *CCRB* 1224. Troughton's book was published in two parts, in 1677 and 1678. Baxter presumably wrote his *Breviate* after the first part of Troughton's *Lutherus Redivivus* had been published in 1677, since Baxter does not refer to two books of Troughton, but only to one (*Breviate*, sigs. A2ᵛ-A3ʳ). Baxter wrote his preface "near a twelve month" after writing the *Breviate* itself (sig. A4ʳ; emphasis throughout in original). This fits with the reference in *RB* (III.183) to the origin of the *Breviate*, where it is mentioned in the midst of events of 1678 (cf. *CCRB* 1024). At this time, Baxter probably wrote his preface. On the title page of *Scripture Gospel defended* (1690) Baxter says that the *Breviate* was written "about thirteen years past." Also when Baxter replied to *Some Considerations* (1690), he commented: "I thirteen yeares cast by my *Breviate* when I had first shewed it Mʳ Lob, & left it with Dʳ Annesley ..." (DWL MS *BT* v.143, f. 24ʳ).

325. Baxter, *Breviate*, sigs. A3ʳ⁻ᵛ (emphasis throughout in original).

326. Annesley was one of the Presbyterians who preferred unity with the Independents over comprehension. Cf. Thomas, "Parties in Nonconformity," pp. 96-97, 103, 105-06.

327. Baxter, *Breviate*, sig. A4ʳ.

328. Baxter, *Defence of Christ*, p. 2. Cf. pp. 6, 55. Baxter refers to John Troughton on the title page and in the preface of his *Breviate*, as well as on p. 21. This occasioned a hostile letter from Troughton's son, also called John, who was upset that Baxter had insulted his father after his death (DWL MS *BC* v, ff. 57ʳ-58ʳ). Cf. Powicke, *Reverend Richard Baxter*, pp. 175-77; *CCRB* 1224.

an old answer to some animadversions which he had received from Stephen Lobb (d. 1699) in 1678.[329] In the response itself, Baxter had not mentioned Lobb by name. He had referred to him as "an honest judicious moderate Friend."[330] But in 1690, when Baxter for the first time saw Lobb's *The Glory of Free-Grace Display'd* (1680), he was so impressed with this rebuttal of Crisp's views that he decided to reveal the name of the author of the animadversions along with a recommendation of Lobb's refutation of Crisp.[331] In his reply to Lobb, Baxter once again defended his view on the imputation of Christ's righteousness. In the year of his death, 1691, Baxter published his last treatise on the various controverted soteriological issues. It was *An End of Doctrinal Controversies* (1691).[332]

---

329. For Lobb's animadversions, see DWL MS *BC* i, ff. 42^r-47^v (cf. *CCRB* 1023). Baxter received Lobb's animadversions a year after writing his *Breviate*. He immediately set out to write a reply against Lobb (*Breviate*, sig. A4^r). For Baxter's response, see *Scripture Gospel defended* (London, 1690), pp. 75-116. For Lobb, see *DNB* 34.23-24; *CCRB* 1023.
330. Baxter, *Breviate*, sig. A4^r (emphasis throughout in original). Cf. *Scripture Gospel defended*, p. 75.
331. Baxter, *Breviate*, p. 73. As noted above, Lobb later associated Baxter with Socinianism (p. 21, n. 146).
332. For the date of composition of *End of Doctrinal Controversies*, see appendix B.

Chapter III

Justification before Faith

Deliverance here is but begun,
When Christ *[from death]* shall sinners raise,
His grace and we then perfected,
We'll perfectly sing *[his high]* praise.[1]

(Richard Baxter)

Theological Background

BACKGROUND TO BAXTER'S OPPOSITION

Influence of William Pemble and William Twisse

Some of the earliest influences giving shape to Baxter's theology came from high Calvinist authors, such as William Pemble and William Twisse.[2] As Baxter testifies: "I quickly plunged my self into the study of Dr. *Twisse*, and *Amesius*, and *Camero*, and *Pemble*, and others on that subject <*i.e.*, Arminianism>: By which my mind was setled in prejudice against *Arminianism*, without a clear understanding of the case ..."[3] The first manuscript which Baxter produced was a treatise in defense of Pemble's views on conversion. It was "the first Controversie that ever I wrote on," comments Baxter, "but riper thoughts made me burn that Script."[4]

The influence of Pemble and Twisse is unmistakable in Baxter's views of the nature of justification and its place in the *ordo salutis*. Writing about justification from eternity, about the view that pardon of sin is nothing but *velle non punire*, and about justification by faith as being merely justification *in foro conscientiae*, Baxter comments: "I was once drawn my self to some of these opinions by the

---

1. In Banks, "Poems of Richard Baxter," p. 698. Baxter's square brackets indicate alternative rhythms for the second and fourth lines (pp. cviii-cix).
2. For Pemble, see Thomas Fuller, *The History of the Worthies of England* (London, 1662), p. 109; Wood, *Athenæ Oxonienses*, II, 330-31; *GBD* 24.281; Brook, *Lives*, II, 304-05; *DNB* 44.283. For Twisse, see Kendall, "Twissii Vita & Victoria," in *De Doctrina Neopelagianâ* (Oxford, 1657), pp. 63-140; *GBD* 30.118-20; Brook, *Lives*, III, 12-17; *DNB* 57.397-99; Reid, *Memoirs*, I, 37-67.
3. Baxter, *Catholick Theologie* I.i, sig. a2ʳ.
4. Baxter, *Catholick Theologie* II.165. Cf. *Saints Rest*, 4th ed. (London, 1653), sig. O1ʳ (between pp. 160 and 161); Packer, "Redemption and Restoration," p. 393; Jeremias, "Richard Baxters Catholic Theology," p. 88.

meer high estimation of Mr. *Pemble* and Dr. *Twisse*."[5] By the late 1640s Baxter's views had changed dramatically. Throughout the *Aphorismes of Justification* (1649), Baxter criticizes the views of Pemble and Twisse on justification. When, in 1684, Baxter looks back on his earlier views, he admits: "I thought worse of that called *Arminianism* than I should have done ..."[6]

Baxter's early change of opinion regarding the doctrine of justification does not mean that his estimation of Pemble and Twisse shifted accordingly. When George Kendall accuses Baxter of speaking "very slightingly" of the late prolocutor of the Westminster Assembly, Baxter replies:

> I profess still most highly to love and reverence the names of these two blessed excellent men, as formerly I never honoured any two men more. For Dr. *Twiss*, I am more beholden to his Writings for that little knowledge I have then almost any one mans, besides: and for Mr. *Pemble*, for ought I can see in his Book of Justification, he revoked this same error <*i.e.*, that all sins are pardoned as soon as Christ died> which in his *Vindic. Grat.* he hath delivered: sure I am, no two mens Writings have been more in my hands, and few mens names are yet so highly honoured in my heart.[7]

Baxter's eulogy on Pemble and Twisse is more than a polite recognition of the qualities of two divines, extorted by the pressure of opponents. Baxter refers to few authors as frequently in his writings as to Pemble and, especially, Twisse. Many of these occasions are indeed denunciations of their doctrine of justification. Several times, however, Baxter refers to Twisse in a more positive fashion. One of the reasons is that Baxter had derived his distinction between God's *voluntas beneplaciti* and his *voluntas praecepti* from Twisse. More than once, Baxter appeals to Twisse in defense of this distinction.[8] What is more, Baxter also enlists Twisse's support for universal redemption[9] and for the conditionality of the covenant.[10]

It is perhaps difficult to square Baxter's praise for the two high Calvinist divines with his denunciation of their views on justification from eternity as "that error and pillar of Antinomianism."[11] The question is, of course, how to explain

---

5. Baxter, *Reduction*, p. 13. Cf. *Of Imputation*, p. 22: "I had before been a great esteemer of two books of one name, *Vindiciæ Gratiæ*, Mr. *Pembles* and Dr. *Twisses*, above most other books. And from them I had taken in the opinion of a double Justification, one *in foro Dei* as an Immanent eternal Act of God, and another *in foro Conscientiæ*, the Knowledg of that ... ."

6. Baxter, *Whether Parish Congregations* (London, 1684) II.28.

7. Baxter, *Reduction*, p. 13. Cf. Kendall, *Vindication* I.iv.134. Baxter puts up a similar defense when William Eyre accuses him that he mentions Twisse "*slightingly*" (Eyre, *Vindiciæ Justificationis Gratuitæ*, sig. A3ʳ; Baxter, *Admonition*, pp. 3-4). Elsewhere, Baxter speaks of Pemble and Twisse as "both excellent Men" (*End of Doctrinal Controversies*, p. 236), as "those two most excellent famous Divines," and he comments that "as I have excessively honoured them, so do I very highly honour them still" (*Reduction*, p. 135). Cf. *RB* I.73.

8. Baxter, *Aphorismes* I.2-3 (pp. 1-2); *Account of my Consideration*, p. 14; *Confession*, sig. e3ᵛ; cf. *Admonition*, pp. 37-38; *Catholick Theologie* I.i.52; Phillips, "Between Conscience and the Law," p. 50, n. 90.

9. Cf. below, pp. 195-97.

10. Baxter, *Aphorismes* II.173-74 (pp. 324-25); *Confession*, pp. 326-30; *Universal Redemption*, pp. 65, 306-07.

11. Baxter, *Aphorismes* I.173 (p. 112). Cf. *Universal Redemption*, p. 170.

Baxter's seemingly ambivalent attitude toward Pemble and Twisse. The views of these two divines are especially significant because of the constant role they play in the debates between Baxter and his high Calvinist opponents on the relation between faith and justification. Several of Baxter's disputants make their appeal to Pemble and Twisse in defense of justification from eternity.[12] Baxter, while maintaining that the Antinomians all "hold the same thing in substance,"[13] realizes that there are differences between the various authors he opposes. He says that it is the common Antinomian doctrine that justification by faith is "the feeling, assurance, or perswasion of Gods love, or of our pardon and former Justification."[14] In this context, he mentions John Saltmarsh, William Pemble, William Twisse, and Lewis Du Moulin. Baxter then continues to describe a somewhat different view: absolution in heaven and justification differ as part and whole, and justification is terminated in conscience.[15] Although Baxter mentions no one by name, his description of this view makes it clear that he has John Owen in mind. Another description of justification by faith is "that God setteth up a Tribunal in the soul" by which he then publicly – not in conscience – justifies the person.[16] Here Baxter is thinking of George Lawson, with whom he corresponded extensively.[17]

Antinomianism

The influence of Pemble and Twisse on high Calvinists in the mid-seventeenth century, as well as the variety of views among Baxter's opponents, necessitates a close scrutiny both of the doctrine of justification in Pemble and Twisse and in those opponents of Baxter who, like Pemble and Twisse, placed justification before faith. What is more, the influence of Pemble and Twisse is not restricted to high Calvinists such as George Kendall, John Owen, Lewis Du Moulin, William Eyre, John Crandon, and William Robertson. Earlier already, people like Tobias Crisp, Paul Hobson (d. 1666), Henry Denne (d. 1660?), Robert Towne (c. 1593-1663), John Eaton (c. 1575-1642), and John Cotton (1584-1652) had followed Pemble in placing justification in the sight of God before faith.[18]

The theology of these people is often branded as "Antinomian." Some explanatory comments with regard to this classification are necessary, since Baxter's doctrine of justification was partly a reaction against Antinomian theories. He had

---

12. Crandon, *Aphorisms Exorized*, I, sigs. A4ᵛ-a1ʳ; I.xx.245-46; I.xxi.252-54, 259; Kendall, *Vindicatio* I.iv.134; Eyre, *Vindiciæ Justificationis Gratuitæ*, sig. A3ʳ, pp. 21-22, 24, 26, 48, 52, 63, 131-33, 147, 185, 187; Lewis Du Moulin, *De fidei partibus* (London, 1653), pp. 35, 53, 68, 116-19; Robertson, *Iggeret hammashkil*, pp. 25-76.
13. Baxter, *Confession*, p. 190.
14. Baxter, *Confession*, p. 190.
15. Baxter, *Confession*, pp. 190-91.
16. Baxter, *Confession*, p. 191.
17. Cf. Baxter, *Account of my Consideration*, p. 165; Packer, "Redemption and Restoration," p. 290.
18. Cf. Baxter, Pref., in Hotchkis, *Exercitation*, sig. B3ᵛ; *Admonition*, sig. A3ʳ; Norman Brooks Graebner, "Protestants and Dissenters: An Examination of the Seventeenth-Century Eatonist and New England Antinomian Controversies in Reformation Perspective," Diss. Duke Univ. 1984, p. 121.

encountered a high Calvinist view of justification when he was a chaplain in the parliamentary army. There John Saltmarsh taught that justifying faith is a "being perswaded more or lesse of Christs love."[19] Baxter is of the opinion that there are two pillars on which the Antinomian structure – such as that of Saltmarsh – rests: the one is the theory of justification from eternity, the other the denial of the conditionality of the covenant of grace.[20] Elsewhere, Baxter gives forty characteristics of what he considers as Antinomianism.[21] The first characteristic is that justification is an immanent act in God from eternity. Other important characteristics are, in his view, that the elect legally fulfilled the law in Christ as a public person;[22] that the covenant of grace is absolute;[23] that union with Christ precedes faith;[24] that the moral law is abrogated to the believers;[25] that God sees no sin in his people and that, therefore, their afflictions are not punishments;[26] that justification by faith is only God's declaration of absolution to our conscience that we were justified earlier already;[27] that all sin is pardoned at once;[28] that Christ has fulfilled the conditions of the new covenant for us;[29] that one may only act *from* life and not *for* life;[30] that prayer for forgiveness does not concern eternal punishment, but only temporal punishments;[31] and that the Spirit converts people without using instruments.[32]

It is obvious that not all – if any – who hold these and similar tenets would accept being branded as Antinomian. Crandon professes himself "clear from all that is rightly Called, and hath been judged by the reformed Churches and their Champions Antinomianism, *i.e.* oppositeness to the Law."[33] A number of views which Baxter describes as Antinomian, Crandon thinks are acceptable Calvinist teachings. Crandon refuses to accept as Antinomian the following views: (1) that believers are no longer under the curse of the law; (2) that afflictions befalling the believers are not revenging punishments for sin; (3) that believers are not under the law as a covenant of works; (4) that justification is an immanent act in God

---

19. John Saltmarsh, *Free-Grace* (London, 1645), p. 94 (emphasis inverted). Baxter uses this definition of Saltmarsh to give an indication of the Antinomian character of his teaching (*Aphorismes* I.276 [p. 176]; *Confession*, p. 190). For Saltmarsh, see Brook, *Lives*, III, 70-74; *DNB* 50.220-22; Leo F. Solt, "John Saltmarsh: New Model Army Chaplain," *JEH*, 2 (1951), 69-80; *BDBRSC* 3.136-37.

20. Baxter speaks of the doctrine of justification from eternity as "that error and pillar of Antinomianism" (*Aphorismes* I.173 [p. 112]). Later, he maintains that "this opinion, that the Covenant of Grace, which Baptism sealeth, is only to the Elect, and is not conditional, is one of the two master-pillars in the Antinomian fabrick" (*Plain Scripture Proof*, p. 224). Cf. *Confutation*, p. 224; *Of Justification*, pp. 382-83.

21. Baxter, *Confession*, pp. 151-87.

22. Baxter, *Confession*, p. 152.

23. Baxter, *Confession*, pp. 157-58.

24. Baxter, *Confession*, p. 158.

25. Baxter, *Confession*, pp. 161-62.

26. Baxter, *Confession*, pp. 163-65.

27. Baxter, *Confession*, pp. 168-69.

28. Baxter, *Confession*, p. 172.

29. Baxter, *Confession*, pp. 172-73.

30. Baxter, *Confession*, pp. 177-78.

31. Baxter, *Confession*, p. 182.

32. Baxter, *Confession*, pp. 183-84.

33. Crandon, *Aphorisms Exorized*, I, sig. A3ᵛ.

completed in Christ's redemption; (5) that the covenant is absolute; and (6) that Christ satisfied for sins against the Gospel as well as the law.[34]

Crandon's refusal to be classified as an Antinomian indicates the problem in defining the term. There was never a group of preachers or churches identifying themselves as "Antinomian." "Antinomianism" was a term of opprobrium applied by opponents to a number of people whose teaching incorporated a variety of shades and emphases. Also the opponents of the Antinomian position did not all take the same stand within the theological spectrum.[35]

The fact that the differences between spiritualism, hyper-Calvinism, high Calvinism, moderate Calvinism, Arminianism, and Socinianism are fluent shows the difficulty in identifying Antinomianism. It has frequently been associated with spiritualist movements.[36] The reason for this connection lies probably in the fact that contemporary descriptions of Antinomianism made use of such denouncements in order to discredit their Antinomian opponents.[37] Recent historiography, however, has distanced itself from the identification of Antinomianism as an heir to all sorts of spiritualist ancestors. The theological connections between high Calvinism and the writings of those generally classified as Antinomians has induced recent historians to view Antinomianism as "a phase of extreme Calvinism."[38] The latter view is largely correct. Many of the opinions commonly identified as Antinomian stem from an emphasis on the immutability of God, on sovereign, free grace, and on double predestination. That extreme positions may lead to spiritualism is undoubtedly correct, but this does not explain the historical origin of Antinomianism. Antinomianism has clear historical roots in the Calvinist tradition. Of course, there are different degrees in the hardening of high Calvinism toward Antinomianism. Spiritualizing tendencies are akin to Antinomianism. This only serves to indicate that the term "Antinomianism" has no more than relative

34. Crandon, *Aphorisms Exorized*, I, sigs. A3^v-a2^v.
35. J. Wayne Baker distinguishes the leading opponents of Antinomians in England during the seventeenth century into two groups: (1) a more moderate group: Henry Burton, Thomas Bakewell, John Sedgwick, Stephen Geree, Anthony Burgess, Richard Baxter, and Daniel Williams; and (2) an Arminian group: John Goodwin, Laurence Womock, Thomas Pierce, and Edward Fowler ("*Sola Fide, Sola Gratia*," 118-19).
36. Spiritualist movements with which Antinomianism has been associated are Gnosticism, Montanism, Manicheism, Marcionism, medieval mysticism, and Anabaptism. Johannes Agricola, Karlstadt, the Zwickau Prophets, Thomas Münzer, and Nicholas Storch are also often mentioned. Antinomianism has further been connected to the Family of Love, to Seekers, Ranters, Levellers, and Quakers. Cf. J. Macbride Sterrett, "Antinomianism," *ERE*, 1908 ed.; George Arthur Johnson, "From Seeker to Finder: A Study in Seventeenth-Century English Spiritualism before the Quakers," *ChH*, 17 (1948), 299-315; A.H. Newman, "Antinomianism and Antinomian Controversies," *NSHE*, 1949 ed.; Gertrude Huehns, *Antinomianism in English History: With Special Reference to the Period 1640-1660* (London: Cresset, 1951), pp. 11-36; Highfill, "Faith and Works," pp. 14-18; Packer, "Redemption and Restoration," pp. 371, 422, n. 1; Leo F. Solt, *Saints in Arms: Puritanism and Democracy in Cromwell's Army* (Stanford, CA: Stanford Univ. Press; London: Oxford Univ. Press, 1959), pp. 21-24; Kevan, *Grace of Law*, pp. 22-23; Sell, *Great Debate*, pp. 42-43.
37. Cf. Pagitt, *Heresiography* (London, 1645), p. 88; Rutherford, *Survey* (London, 1648), I, 1-354.
38. Wallace, *Puritans and Predestination*, p. 114. Cf. pp. 112-20; Allison, *Rise of Moralism*, pp. 168-72; Toon, *Emergence of Hyper-Calvinism*, pp. 49-69; Richard L. Greaves, "The Origins and Early Development of English Covenant Thought," *Hist*, 31 (1968), 32-34; Curt D. Daniel, "Hyper-Calvinism and John Gill," Diss. Univ. of Edinburgh 1983, pp. 618-30; Graebner, "Protestants and Dissenters."

value. On the whole, it remains imperative to have an open eye for Calvinist influences on what is commonly identified as the Antinomian camp.

Curt D. Daniel, in his excellent overview of the theology of the Baptist hyper-Calvinist, John Gill (1697-1771), observes: "Many writers have described or defined Hyper-Calvinism or Antinomianism in terms of the doctrine of eternal justification."[39] This is certainly Baxter's perspective. To Baxter, any tendency to place justification prior to faith in the *ordo salutis* opens the danger of Antinomianism. Whether or not eternal justification is indeed the hallmark of Antinomianism, Daniel has made it clear that theories which place justification before faith – usually in eternity – are characteristic of those who are commonly identified as Antinomians.[40] Baxter's attitude to these views of justification gives insight into the main doctrinal basis for his opposition to Antinomianism. Considering the pervasive influence of William Pemble and William Twisse, it is understandable that Baxter regards them as the main sources of the Antinomian impact among seventeenth-century high Calvinists, and that he repeatedly criticizes the views of these two widely respected divines. Thus, there is ample reason for an extended discussion of their ideas.

WILLIAM PEMBLE: TWOFOLD JUSTIFICATION

Justification by the Death of Christ

When William Pemble died in 1623 during a visit to his former tutor, Richard Capel (1586-1656), he left two manuscript treatises with his respected teacher.[41] Capel saw to it that they were published, *Vindiciæ fidei* in 1625 and *Vindiciæ gratiæ* in 1627. The two publications of the celebrated reader of divinity in Magdalen College, Oxford found a receptive readership among high Calvinists in the seventeenth century.[42] Pemble's *Vindiciæ gratiæ*, in particular, did much to strengthen the claim of those who maintained that, whatever might happen in time in the relationship between God an man, the elect had been justified long before they had come to faith, or even before they were born.

Pemble's *Vindiciæ gratiæ* excels in clarity. When the author comes to explain how it is possible that sanctification precedes justification – certainly a remarkable position in a book consistently opposing Roman Catholic doctrines of grace – Pemble explains that there is a "double Iustification": justification *in foro divino* and justification *in foro conscientiae*.[43] The former, justification in God's sight, "goeth before all our sanctification." It means actual justification and reconcilia-

---

39. Daniel, "Hyper-Calvinism and John Gill," p. 305. Daniel himself is of the opinion that the key to the Antinomian issue is the question whether or not the law must be used as an incentive in preaching (pp. 631, 645).
40. Daniel, "Hyper-Calvinism and John Gill," pp. 305-30.
41. For Capel, see *DNB* 9.17-18.
42. This is evident from the repeated references to Pemble in Baxter's opponents as well as from the fact that Pemble's books were reprinted both in 1629 and in 1659.
43. Pemble, *Vindiciæ gratiæ*, 2nd ed. (London, 1629), pp. 21-22.

tion by the death of Christ.[44] The latter, justification "in our owne sense," is "but the renelation and certaine declaration of Gods former secret act of accepting Christs righteousnesse to our iustification."[45]

This theory of a twofold justification is central to a correct understanding of Pemble's view on the relation between faith and justification.[46] It is necessary, therefore, to analyze Pemble's view of double justification in some more depth. He discusses this theory in a section on conversion. He describes the moving or impulsive cause of conversion as God's "free-loue to his elect in Christ."[47] When we still lay "in the shadow of death," says Pemble, "euen then God looked on vs with tender compassions, hee pitied vs, he loued vs as chosen vessells prepared for glory ..."[48] Repeatedly, Pemble insists that God "actually loueth" his elect from eternity.[49] This actual love of God precedes the death of Christ and must be traced back to eternity. It even precedes election, since election, like effectual vocation and faith, is a fruit of God's actual love to those whom he will elect.[50]

This does not mean that Pemble adheres to a doctrine of justification from eternity. Baxter wrongly charges Pemble with teaching that justification is an immanent act in God from eternity.[51] It is true that Pemble strongly emphasizes that justification has a firm foundation in eternity, in God's actual love for the elect. But nowhere does Pemble refer to this love of God as justification. Still, he makes an extremely tight connection between election and reconciliation: God's actual love for his elect leads to actual reconciliation by Christ's death. Says Pemble: "If God did actually loue the elect before Christs time, when an actuall reconciliation was not yet made, then much more may hee actually loue the elect after the attonement is really made by Christs death, euen before they doe beleeue it."[52] The scope of Pemble's argument obviously has an anti-Arminian tendency. Opposing the idea that Christ's death only makes reconciliation possible, Pemble maintains that reconciliation is actual upon Christ's death.[53]

Since the elect are actually reconciled by Christ's death, it is understandable that Pemble equates actual reconciliation with justification *in foro divino*. He says that God calls the elect, "with whom being actually reconciled in Christ, hauing iustified them from all their sinnes by his merits, he afterwards sends forth his

44. Pemble, *Vindiciæ gratiæ*, p. 21.
45. Pemble, *Vindiciæ gratiæ*, p. 22.
46. As far as I am aware, Pemble does not make the distinction between justification *in foro divino* and *in foro conscientiae* anywhere else in his writings. This may seem somewhat remarkable, but by no means invalidates the thesis that this distinction is central to his doctrine of justification as he puts it forward in his *Vindiciæ gratiæ*. As the discussion below will make clear, Pemble referred to the same distinction by means of different phrases.
47. Pemble, *Vindiciæ gratiæ*, p. 16.
48. Pemble, *Vindiciæ gratiæ*, p. 16.
49. Pemble, *Vindiciæ gratiæ*, pp. 16-18.
50. Pemble, *Vindiciæ gratiæ*, p. 17.
51. Baxter, *Aphorismes* I.173, 191 (pp. 112, 123). Cf. also Wallace, *Puritans and Predestination*, p. 119.
52. Pemble, *Vindiciæ gratiæ*, p. 17.
53. Says Pemble: "For tis vaine to thinke with the Arminians, that Christs merits haue made God only *Placabilem*, not *Placatum*, procured a freedome that God may be reconciled if hee will, and other things concurre, but not an actuall reconciliation" (*Vindiciæ gratiæ*, p. 23).

holy Spirit into their hearts, calling them from darknesse to light ..."[54] Actual reconciliation and justification both come about by Christ's merits. Pemble is now in a position to comment with regard to justification *in foro divino* that "euen whilst the elect are vnconverted, they are then actually iustified & freed from all sin by the Death of Christ: & God so esteemes of them as free, and hauing accepted of that Satisfaction, is actually reconciled to them."[55]

Pemble does not place justification *in foro divino* in eternity. Without any reservation, however, he situates it at the time of Christ's death. To Baxter, this does little to make Pemble's doctrine more palatable: "Now for Mr. *Pemble*, as he expresly maintains Justification *in foro Dei* to be long before we are born, even on Christs dying, so that is all one to our purpose, as if he maintained it to be from eternity."[56] Indeed, Pemble posits a close connection between reconciliation and the will of God:

> These affections of loue and hatred in God are perpetuall; beeing eternall and vn-changeable acts of his will. Whom he loues he loues alwayes, whom he hates he hates for euer. Nor doth hee as man at any time begin to loue that person, whom before he hated: or hate that person whom before he loued. These things agree not with Gods immutability, or omnisciencie.[57]

This statement is significant because it brings to the fore the reason why Pemble places justification at Christ's death. God's love for his elect is an "eternall and vnchangeable" act of his will. The constancy of God's will may not be compromised by making it in any sense dependent on man's faith. God's hatred to a person does not change into love after a person comes to faith. This is impossible because it would mean that God's will is fickle. For Pemble, the *ordo salutis* has its starting point in the absolute will of God. By his will he loves a certain number of people whom he then elects and, by means of Christ's death, actually justifies and reconciles to himself. These same people are effectually called and brought to faith.

Pemble is convinced that God's attributes of immutability and omniscience are at stake. How can God's affections change if he is immutable? How can he begin to love or hate someone if he knew from eternity whether the person would come to faith or not? Pemble's motivation in placing justification before faith goes back, therefore, to his doctrine of God. To hold on to an actual justification by faith would endanger the sovereignty of God.

Pemble maintains that the elect are actually reconciled and justified at Christ's death. Thus, Christ's sacrifice occupies a central place in Pemble's soteriology. There is some tension, however, between the place of the cross and God's eternal love toward the elect. Pemble maintains that "loue and reconciliation are inseparable ..."[58] God's love to the elect must lead to their reconciliation and justification.

---

54. Pemble, *Vindiciæ gratiæ*, p. 20.
55. Pemble, *Vindiciæ gratiæ*, p. 21.
56. Baxter, *Reduction*, p. 6.
57. Pemble, *Vindiciæ gratiæ*, p. 18.
58. Pemble, *Vindiciæ gratiæ*, p. 17.

Pemble's opponents might well question the need for atonement if God already loved his elect before Christ's sacrifice. If, as Pemble insists, love and reconciliation are inseparable, would one not expect reconciliation and justification to be from eternity? Pemble does not yield to this temptation. To do so, would substantially weaken the significance of the sacrifice of Christ. As it is, Pemble is able to retain the centrality of the cross in his doctrine of justification. The elect are justified at the cross of Christ. Nevertheless, it cannot be denied that Pemble's doctrine of justification displays some tension between God's eternal love to his elect and their actual reconciliation by means of Christ's sacrifice.

Justification by Faith

Another question concerns the place of justification by faith in the *ordo salutis*. It is clear that, for Pemble, faith does not precede, but follows justification in God's sight. At this point, Pemble makes two distinctions. First, he distinguishes between God's love in itself and its manifestation to us. The former "is perpetuall and one, from all to all eternitie, without change, increase or lessening towards euery one of the Elect: But the manifestation of this loue to our hearts and consciences begins in time, at our conuersion, and is variable according to the seuerall degrees of grace giuen ..."[59] Pemble's exposition is unambiguous: the only thing which happens in time is that God's love is manifested to our conscience. This love itself goes back to eternity. We are just not aware of it prior to faith. For this awareness, Pemble uses words such as "manifestation" and "revelation." It is an awareness in the heart, soul, or conscience.

Pemble further distinguishes between God's love to our persons and his love to our "qualities & actions." God's love to the elect as persons "is from euerlasting the same."[60] His love to their qualities and actions begins only when these "become holy by the grace of conuersion: before which time and after too, God is angry euen with his Elect, and testifies his hatred of their sins as much as of any others, by manifold chastisements vpon their persons for their offences."[61] God still punishes his elect because of his hatred of their sins.[62] God's love to the elect is secret.[63] They "feele it not" until their conversion, when God "declares himselfe to bee pleased both with their persons and actions."[64] Baxter regards Pemble's distinction as a contradiction. Baxter states that "the Act and the Actor are so neerly related, that if the act displease God, the Actor must needs, in some measure, or so far, displease him."[65] Speaking of God's castigatory punishments, Baxter comments that "it is not actions that are punished, but men for actions. God was displeased with *David* himself, and not with his actions only."[66]

59. Pemble, *Vindiciæ gratiæ*, p. 18.
60. Pemble, *Vindiciæ gratiæ*, p. 19.
61. Pemble, *Vindiciæ gratiæ*, p. 19.
62. Pemble, *Vindiciæ gratiæ*, pp. 19-20.
63. Pemble, *Vindiciæ gratiæ*, p. 20.
64. Pemble, *Vindiciæ gratiæ*, p. 21.
65. Baxter, *Confession*, p. 236.
66. Baxter, *Confession*, p. 236.

Pemble's distinctions between God's love in itself and its manifestation to us, and between God's love to our persons and his love to our qualities and actions run parallel to the distinction between justification *in foro divino* and *in foro conscientiae*. The former is God's secret, unchangeable love to our persons. The latter is the manifestation, revelation, or declaration of this love to our conscience. This manifestation of God's love "followes our Sanctification, vpon and after the Infusion of Sauing Faith, the onely Instrument of this our Iustification."[67] Thus, in a sense, Pemble does maintain justification by faith. Faith does precede justification. But justification is here not justification in God's sight, but only its manifestation or declaration to one's conscience.

When faith is thus placed in between justification *in foro divino* and justification *in foro conscientiae* it becomes clear why Pemble says that sanctification precedes justification. Sanctification precedes the manifestation of God's love to our conscience. Faith is part of this sanctification which precedes justification in conscience. Pemble has no difficulty in admitting that faith is a "good and holy worke"[68] and that it is "part of our inherent righteousnesse" worked by the Spirit of God.[69] Pemble maintains that faith, as part of our sanctification, follows the infusion of the habit of grace. This habit is a "supernaturall qualitie of holinesse," given to all the elect, "all at once."[70] The operations proceeding from this habit, such as faith, hope, and love, follow from this sanctification and, indeed, are part of it.[71] Since the habit of faith does not precede sanctification, but is merely a part of it, Pemble draws the rather dramatic conclusion that "Faith Properly is not the roote of all other graces, nor the first degree of our sanctification and spirituall life."[72]

Pemble foresees a weighty objection: is it not true that we have no life until we have union with Christ? Does this union not come about by means of faith? Is faith then not the root of all other graces? To escape this conclusion, Pemble resorts to a twofold union. The first union is by the Spirit on his part. This union is wrought "meerely by the holy Spirit" when we are still dead in sin. This grace of conversion precedes both the habit and the act of faith. The second union, by our faith on our parts, follows faith. Says Pemble: "In the first vnion we were insensible of it, and grace is giuen to vs *non petentibus*, that asked not after it: in this second vnion wee are most sensible of its comfort and benefit; and here an augmentation of grace is bestowed on vs *petentes*, earnestly suing for it, and by faith expecting the receiuing of it."[73]

---

67. Pemble, *Vindiciæ gratiæ*, p. 22. When Baxter faces the accusation that he makes sanctification to precede justification by way of condition, he replies: "Mr. *Pemble*, and those that follow him, put Sanctification before all true Justification, (though they call Gods immanent eternal Act, a precedent Justification.)" (*Of Justification*, p. 272).

68. Pemble, *Vindiciæ gratiæ*, p. 22.

69. Pemble, *Vindiciæ gratiæ*, p. 257.

70. Pemble, *Vindiciæ gratiæ*, p. 7. Cf. Graebner, "Protestants and Dissenters," pp. 115-16.

71. Pemble, *Vindiciæ gratiæ*, p. 11.

72. Pemble, *Vindiciæ gratiæ*, p. 12 (emphasis throughout original).

73. Pemble, *Vindiciæ gratiæ*, p. 15. Cf. Baxter's reaction to Pemble's distinction: "I answer, we agree with those men that say so in the matter, but we differ only in the word *union*. We agree that the work of the Spirit causing faith is before faith; but we think that it is not the phrase of Scripture to call that a union on Christs part" (*Confutation*, p. 257).

It is understandable that Pemble's view on the *ordo salutis* became the object of criticism. The bishop of Derry, George Downham (d. 1634), expressed his disagreement with Pemble's views in an appendix to *The Covenant of Grace* (1631).[74] Downham mentions eight points in which he differs from Pemble. The first is the latter's idea that in our first conversion a general habit of grace is infused, which sanctifies all parts and powers of man.[75] Downham then discusses Pemble's views that sanctification precedes justification,[76] that justification precedes faith,[77] and that faith is not the root of the other graces.[78] These points of disagreement all concern Pemble's structuring of the order of salvation. Downham's criticism is echoed in Graebner, who – after commending several aspects of Pemble's theology – remarks:

> Unfortunately, Pemble's theology also contained a glaring weakness which offset its more appealing aspects. By divorcing the divine work of justification and sanctification from the human act of faith, Pemble had, in effect, established a new order of salvation, one in which the graces of justification and sanctification precede the first moment of faith.[79]

Baxter appeals to Downham's criticism of Pemble's *ordo salutis*.[80] His agreement with Downham contrasts with his support of Pemble's theories in an earlier, discarded manuscript. Evidence of this earlier position of Baxter can still be found in his *Saints Everlasting Rest* (1650). Here he adopts Pemble's view that sanctification is identical to the first infusion of the spiritual habit and that sanctification precedes justification.[81] In the fourth edition Baxter retracts this position.[82] Also in his *Confutation* (1654) of Lewis Du Moulin Baxter writes that he used to believe that faith is first given in the seed or the habit, and then in the act. He writes that he took this doctrine from Pemble, and that he "held it fast till lately ..."[83] He now regards the matter as "either unrevealed, or at least uncertain to me. But this is past doubt, that the term *sanctification* is usually taken in Scripture, not for the giving of the first Grace of faith, but for some following sort or degree

74. Downham, *Covenant of Grace* (Dublin, 1631), pp. 197-231. Downham does not mention by name the "learned & godly man" whom he opposes (p. 197). The contents of the appendix, however, places it beyond doubt that Baxter is correct in regarding the appendix as a reaction to Pemble's *Vindiciæ gratiæ*.
   For George Downham (or Downame), see *GBD* 12.297-98; *DNB* 15.395-96. For his views on justification, see Allison, *Rise of Moralism*, pp. 14-18; McGrath, "Emergence of the Anglican Tradition," 31.
75. Downham, *Covenant of Grace*, pp. 197-202.
76. Downham, *Covenant of Grace*, pp. 202-04.
77. Downham, *Covenant of Grace*, pp. 204-09.
78. Downham, *Covenant of Grace*, p. 210.
79. Graebner, "Protestants and Dissenters," p. 119.
80. Baxter, *Confutation*, p. 274.
81. Baxter, *Saints Rest* (London, 1650), pp. 157-60. Cf. Jeremias, "Richard Baxters Catholic Theology," p. 88.
82. Baxter, *Saints Rest*, 4th ed., sigs. O1ʳ-O2ʳ (between pp. 160 and 161). Cf. Packer, "Redemption and Restoration," p. 393, n. 2.
83. Baxter, *Confutation*, p. 200. Cf. p. 274; *Of Saving Faith*, p. 20; *Catholick Theologie* II.164.

of change in our hearts and lives ..."[84] Baxter now considers the opinion of the Salmurian divine, John Cameron, more appealing. Cameron holds the view that the Spirit first causes the act of faith and then the habit by means of the act.[85] But Baxter does not dare to give a definite judgement on the matter. Thus, while he keeps some mental reservation on the question whether acts of faith precede or follow the habit of faith, he adamantly refuses to call the first grace of faith sanctification. He refuses to place sanctification before justification by faith. Of course, Baxter, unlike Pemble, sees justification by faith as justification *in foro divino*. This explains Baxter's concern not to place sanctification before justification in the *ordo salutis*. Pemble does not share this concern: since justification by faith is merely the assurance of justification in conscience, it is acceptable that sanctification precedes it.

Faith and Assurance.

It might be expected that Pemble would take the following step by arguing that faith is simply the assurance in one's conscience that one is justified. But he does not draw this consequence. Instead, he distinguishes a twofold object of faith: (1) the whole revealed will of God, "containing all Histories, Doctrines, Commands, Threatnings, Promises of what kind soeuer";[86] and (2) the "particular Promise of Remission of sinnes and Euerlasting Life by the death of Christ, which in one word we call the Gospel."[87] This distinction corresponds to legal assent and evangelical assent. The former is required as a duty of the moral law and is therefore called legal. The latter is called evangelical because "it assents vnto the speciall promise of grace ..."[88]

Pemble's frequent references to faith as assent are not meant to imply that faith is only located in the intellect. Speaking of the universal and uniform assent to God's entire revealed will, he argues that this assent includes that one "doth most heartily and inwardly acknowledge the truth and goodnesse of these things ..."[89] Faith means that – even if temptations arise – one fixes "the affiance of the heart" on the truth and goodness of God's revealed will.[90] Furthermore, Pemble defines evangelical faith as "a grace of sanctification, wrought by the holy Ghost in euery regenerate man, whereby for his owne particular he trusteth <!> perfectly vnto the promise of Remission of sinnes and Saluation by Christs righteousnesse."[91] Faith is not just intellectual assent. Rather, says Pemble, "this assent is of the whole

---

84. Baxter, *Confutation*, p. 274. Baxter repeatedly opposes Pemble's idea that sanctification, including the first act of faith, precedes justification (*Confutation*, p. 282; *Certain Disputations*, p. 200).
85. Baxter, *Confutation*, p. 274.
86. Pemble, *Vindiciæ gratiæ*, p. 244.
87. Pemble, *Vindiciæ gratiæ*, p. 244.
88. Pemble, *Vindiciæ gratiæ*, p. 245.
89. Pemble, *Vindiciæ gratiæ*, p. 246.
90. Pemble, *Vindiciæ gratiæ*, p. 246.
91. Pemble, *Vindiciæ gratiæ*, p. 257 (emphasis throughout in original).

heart, in Trust, Reliance, Dependance, Adherence, Affiance ..."[92] This assent of faith is also properly called *fiducia*. This *fiducia* "is of the essence of iustifying Faith ..."[93]

It may seem as if Pemble does identify faith and assurance. He does, after all, speak of faith as affiance, as *fiducia*, and states that it is of the essence of faith. As it is, however, he refers to a second kind of *fiducia*. The first *fiducia* is faith. It is the instrument by which the soul "casteth and reposeth it selfe onely vpon Gods Promise in Christ for the obtaining of eternall happinesse."[94] From this first *fiducia* follow both peace of conscience and a second kind of *fiducia*,

> which wee call assurance and full perswasion of the pardon of our sins. This is a fruit of that other *Fiducia* or Trusting vnto the promise it selfe, wherein stands the proper act of iustifying faith. And it followes it, not alwayes presently, but after some time, haply a long time, after much paines taken in the exercise of Faith and other graces.[95]

Assurance is not of the essence of faith, Pemble argues. After the believers have cast themselves on the promise of the Gospel it often happens that "they want ioy in the Holy Ghost, there's no testimony of the Spirit in them, they haue no peace, no sense and inward feeling of Gods loue; and therefore they cannot be assured that their sinnes are pardoned, and that they be in Gods fauour."[96] People with such lack of assurance do have faith, but not the consequent of faith: justification *in foro conscientiae*.

Pemble's view of the *ordo salutis* now comes into sharper focus: from God's will flows his love for some people, whom he then elects. He justifies them in his own sight upon the sacrifice of Christ and calls them in time. This effectual vocation or conversion is followed by the assent of faith, by which the believer puts his trust in God's promise. This may, in due time, lead to a second kind of *fiducia*, the assurance of faith, or justification *in foro conscientiae*.

Faith does not receive a central place in Pemble's theology. It cannot be the condition for justification in God's sight.[97] In fact, faith is not "absolutely neces-

---

92. Pemble, *Vindiciæ gratiæ*, p. 258. Pemble basically identifies assent and affiance. This forces him also to identify truth and goodness, as the respective objects of assent and affiance. He indeed states that the understanding essentially includes the will, and that the will essentially includes the understanding. The object of the understanding and the will are "one and the same. For Truth and Goodnesse are essentially the same thing. In Naturall things it is most plaine, that their Truth and Goodnesse is all one. Their goodnesse is nothing but the Truth of their Beeing in their perfect conformity to Gods vnderstanding and will ..." (*Vindiciæ gratiæ*, p. 202). The distinction between truth and goodness, insists Pemble, originates "not from their Nature, but from our esteeme and conceit of them" (*Vindiciæ gratiæ*, p. 204). At least twice, Baxter mentions Pemble's identification of truth and goodness and of the understanding and the will. He comments: "I shall go on the supposition that his singular opinion is commonly disallowed ..." (*Of Justification*, p. 405; cf. pp. 201-02).
93. Pemble, *Vindiciæ gratiæ*, p. 258.
94. Pemble, *Vindiciæ gratiæ*, p. 258.
95. Pemble, *Vindiciæ gratiæ*, p. 260.
96. Pemble, *Vindiciæ gratiæ*, p. 261.
97. In *Vindiciæ gratiæ*, Pemble does not give faith the role of a condition. Justification, at least inasmuch as it is justification in God's sight, precedes faith. It is nevertheless striking that in his *Vindiciæ fidei* Pemble often refers to faith as a condition. This raises the question how this

sary" in all the elect. This is clear from the case of elect children who die in their infancy. Many of the elect have the graces of sanctification infused in their infancy. After all, infants are as capable of the habits of faith and repentance as adults.[98] Moreover, our initial sanctification, as well as our justification in God's sight, are both benefits which we receive from Christ before we believe. The conclusion must be that faith does not precede all participation in Christ.[99]

Downham criticizes Pemble's views on the nature of justifying faith. In particular, he disagrees with Pemble's view of faith as affiance.[100] Downham maintains that affiance is only a fruit of faith, which follows mental assent and personal application.[101] Baxter does not accept Downham's view that justifying faith is only assent.[102] He is nevertheless of the opinion that Downham has successfully refuted Pemble: affiance is not part of saving faith, but follows the acceptance of Christ.[103]

---

comports with his views on justification as outlined in his *Vindiciæ gratiæ*. Baxter says that Pemble seems to have changed his mind between the writing of *Vindiciæ gratiæ* and *Vindiciæ fidei* (*Aphorismes*, I.191-92 [p. 123]; *Reduction*, p. 13; *Confutation*, p. 323; *Admonition*, pp. 14, 19, 30-31; *End of Doctrinal Controversies*, p. 236). Although Baxter's wording is rather careful, closer scrutiny seems to vindicate his judgement. The only reservation I have is that I have been unable to attain confirmation of Baxter's assertion that Pemble wrote *Vindiciæ gratiæ* before *Vindiciæ fidei*.

Baxter rightly points out that in *Vindiciæ fidei* Pemble has no hesitation at all in speaking of faith as a condition. He distinguishes two covenants: a covenant of works and a covenant of grace. In the former, perfect obedience was the condition. In the latter, faith is the condition: "The law offers life vnto man vpon condition of perfect obedience, cursing the transgressors thereof in the least point with eternall death: The Gospell offers life vnto man vpon another condition, viz. Of repentance and faith in Christ, promising remission of sinnes to such as repent and beleeue" (*Vindiciæ fidei*, 2nd ed. [Oxford, 1629], p. 153; cf. pp. 22-24, 61). Not only does Pemble have no reticence in speaking of faith as the condition of the covenant of grace, also his definition of justification by faith makes clear that he has in mind more than only justification *in foro conscientiae*. Pemble says that "by *Iustification* nothing else is meant; but the gracious act of Almighty God whereby he absolues a beleiuing sinner accused at the Tribunall of his Iustice, pronouncing him iust and acquitting him of all punishment for *Christs* sake" (*Vindiciæ fidei*, pp. 16-17). When Pemble speaks of the conditionality of the covenant of grace, he speaks of conditions of justification *in foro divino*. It is a justification which must "appease the infinite indignation of an angry Iudge," not just the conscience of the believer (*Vindiciæ fidei*, p. 21).

98. Pemble, *Vindiciæ gratiæ*, pp. 23, 45-50. Cf. Graebner, "Protestants and Dissenters," p. 119. Pemble also makes the infusion of the grace of sanctification of infants the basis for infant baptism (p. 47). We may presume that infants of believers have been converted because of the covenant and the promise of God "that he will be the God of the Faithfull and of their Seed" (p. 47).

99. Pemble, *Vindiciæ gratiæ*, p. 23.

100. Downham, *Covenant of Grace*, pp. 211-15.

101. Downham distinguishes between three acts implied in the phrase "believing in Christ": (1) assent, *i.e.*, the willing and voluntary approbation of the mind that Christ is the Savior of all who believe in him. This is a lively, true, and effectual act of the understanding as well as the will. It is properly the justifying act of faith (*Covenant of Grace*, pp. 211-12, 223-31). (2) application, *i.e.*, the belief or assurance that Christ is not only the Savior of all who believe, but also my Savior. By this act of special faith one is also justified in conscience (p. 212). (3) affiance, *i.e.*, resting on Christ for salvation because he is my personal Savior. This is a fruit of faith. Since the promise is not made to all, we must first have justifying faith by way of condition, before we can confidently trust that the promise shall be performed to us (pp. 212-14).

102. Baxter, *Aphorismes* I.254 (p. 162).

103. Baxter, *Aphorismes* I.254, 282 (pp. 161-62, 180); *Account*, p. 94. It is questionable whether Downham's – and, by consequence, Baxter's – criticism of Pemble is really to the point. Pemble indeed argues that saving faith includes affiance. Faith is both assent and affiance. The under-

It may be concluded that Pemble's twofold justification is central to an under-standing of his *Vindiciæ gratiæ*. The distinction between justification *in foro divino* and *in foro conscientiae* corresponds to other distinctions: that between God's love in itself and its manifestation to us; and that between God's love to our persons and his love to our qualities and actions. Although Pemble does not teach justification from eternity, justification *in foro divino* does precede faith: God is actually reconciled by Christ's sacrifice. What is more, his actual love for the elect is from eternity. The result is that faith is not absolutely necessary. It is one of the graces of sanctification which follows justification in God's sight, but it precedes justification *in foro conscientiae*. Pemble does not, however, draw the conclusion that faith is nothing but the assurance of salvation. His distinction between two kinds of *fiducia* prevents such an identification.

WILLIAM TWISSE: JUSTIFICATION FROM ETERNITY

Voluntas beneplaciti *and* voluntas signi

The picture of William Twisse (1578?-1646) as a high Calvinist will provoke little opposition.[104] It is beyond question that he was a strong opponent of the Arminian doctrine of predestination. Most of his publications were written in opposition to Arminian and Jesuit tenets. Baxter certainly confirms this picture when he vehe-mently denounces Twisse's doctrine of eternal justification. Baxter reports with some eagerness that Twisse was questioned in the Westminster Assembly about his view that justification is from eternity.[105] Nevertheless, Baxter does appeal to

---

standing and the will are both involved in faith. In fact, Pemble identifies the two. But it is questionable whether his description of the first *fiducia*, for which he uses both the terms "assent" and "affiance," is really that much different from Downham's concept of assent. The latter also includes both an act of the understanding and an act of the will. Moreover, as noted earlier, Pemble clearly distinguishes between the first *fiducia*, whereby one casts himself on the promise, and the second *fiducia*, the assurance of justification.

Still, there is a difference between Pemble and Downham. For Pemble, justifying faith itself has a personal reference: the believer entrusts himself to Christ. For Downham, justifying faith has no such personal connotation: it is the assent that Christ is the Savior of all who believe. This difference does not mean, however, that Pemble would identify justifying faith as assurance, whereas Downham would separate the two. Both authors regard assurance as a fruit of justifying faith.

104. The scholarly attention which Twisse has received is disproportionate to his influence on Calvin-ist theology in the seventeenth century. As far as I have been able to ascertain, Michael Daniel Bell is correct in his assertion that "a complete study has never been done on Twisse and his methodology ..." ("Propter potestatem, scientiam, ac beneplacitum Dei: The Doctrine of the Ob-ject of Predestination in the Theology of Johannes Maccovius," Diss. Westminster Theological Seminary 1986, p. 177). Bell devotes a separate chapter to a comparison between Twisse and Maccovius on the *objectum praedestinationis* (pp. 169-212). Stephen Strehle gives a brief discus-sion of Twisse's doctrines of God and the decrees in *Calvinism, Federalism, and Scholasticism*, pp. 104-11.

105. Baxter, *Confutation*, p. 276. Cf. *Unsavoury Volume*, p. 8. The WCF explicitly condemns justifica-tion from eternity: "God did, from all eternity, decree to justify all the elect; and Christ did, in the fulness of time, die for their sins, and rise again for their justification: nevertheless they are not justified, until the Holy Spirit doth in due time actually apply Christ unto them" (XI.IV; *Westmin-ster Confession of Faith* [1958; rpt. Glasgow: Free Presbyterian Publications, 1990], p. 59).

Twisse in defense of a twofold will in God and in his pleas for universal redemption and the conditionality of the covenant of grace.[106]

What is more, Baxter's charge that Twisse adhered to eternal justification did not go unchallenged. In 1655, a book written by John Grayle (1614-54), *A Modest Vindication of the Doctrine of Conditions in the Covenant of Grace*, was posthumously published.[107] In this treatise, the author defends the conditionality of the covenant of grace against William Eyre. Attached to Grayle's work is a lengthy preface written by Constant Jessop (c. 1602-58).[108] It is Jessop's contention that Baxter has misinterpreted Twisse in eight related points of doctrine. To prevent any misunderstanding, Jessop writes in a conciliatory vein: "I do very much reverence Mr. *Baxter* for his piety and parts, as also for his love to peace, and zeal for the glory and truth of God, and heartily close with him in warning all, that they do not receive any principles of *Antinomianisme*, upon the credit of any man, especially not on the credit of Doctor *Twisse* ..."[109] Jessop does not defend Twisse in order to oppose Baxter; rather, his aim is to demonstrate that there is very little difference between Baxter and Twisse on justification. Baxter does not give a peremptory judgement on Jessop's reinterpretation of Twisse, but does not seem to have been convinced by it: "And truly I was much taken with that Preface when I read it, and said, Its pity it should be upon mistake: and if it be, me thinks (in that case) I am ready to love his mistake, for the charity in it, and the desirableness of the thing asserted, more then my own ungrateful interpretation, though it should be true."[110]

Jessop alters Baxter's picture of Twisse considerably. First and foremost, Jessop asserts that Twisse nowhere accepts justification from eternity. When Twisse speaks of justification as an eternal act of God he only means "Gods eternal and unchangeable wil and purpose to pardon ..."[111] Second, Jessop argues that Twisse is "farre from asserting remission of sinne to goe before faith ..."[112] Further, Twisse distinguishes between Christ's meriting justification and our actual justification.[113] Twisse also does not limit faith to our knowledge or feeling of God's love. He distinguishes between faith and assurance.[114] Further, Twisse teaches that Christ's righteousness is ours before faith only in the sense that it is meritorious before

---

106. Cf. below, p. 195.
107. For John Grayle, see *DNB* 23.29-30.
108. Constant Jessop, Pref., in John Grayle, *Modest Vindication* (London, 1655), pp. 1-49. For Jessop, rector of Wimborne Minster, Dorset, see *DNB* 29.372.
109. Jessop, Pref., in Grayle, *Modest Vindication*, p. 32. In a letter to Baxter, Peter Ince writes that Jessop had told him that he had left out a more biting passage from the preface (DWL MS *BC* iv, f. 245ᵛ [*CCRB* 221]).
110. Baxter, *Confession*, sig. e3ʳ. Elsewhere, Baxter says that Jessop "hath peaceably and temperately prooved" that he and Twisse are of the same mind regarding the issue of absolution of unbelievers (*Plain Scripture Proof*, p. 484). Since Baxter continues to attribute to Twisse a doctrine of eternal justification, his comment on Jessop's preface is probably more meant as a conciliatory gesture than a real evaluation of Jessop's reading of Twisse.
111. Jessop, Pref., in Grayle, *Modest Vindication*, p. 4.
112. Jessop, Pref., in Grayle, *Modest Vindication*, p. 5.
113. Jessop, Pref., in Grayle, *Modest Vindication*, pp. 6-9.
114. Jessop, Pref., in Grayle, *Modest Vindication*, pp. 9-12.

faith. It is not in our possession, however, until we believe.[115] There is no adoption before the condition of faith is performed[116] Finally, Twisse's assertion that no internal or immanent act in God arises in him *de novo*, is a view to which Baxter himself subscribes as well.[117]

Evidently, Jessop's reinterpretation of Twisse yields a moderately Calvinist outcome. Closer scrutiny of Twisse's position appears to be necessary. It will become clear that the apparent contradictions in Twisse's position are caused by the way in which he applies the distinction between God's decreed will and his revealed will. This finding is most significant to the present study because of the central role of this distinction in Baxter's theology. The structure of Baxter's theology has undergone the pervasive influence of Twisse's high Calvinist theology, regardless of the fact that Baxter takes exception to some key aspects of his doctrine of justification.

In the very beginning of his *Aphorismes of Justification*, Baxter comments that "especially, Doctor *Twisse* frequently" uses the distinction in the will of God between his will of purpose and his will of precept.[118] Twisse indeed uses the distinction throughout his polemical writings.[119] It functions in opposition to the Arminian notions that God has an equal love for all, that he wants all individual people to be saved, and that Christ died for all. The distinction of God's twofold will is central to Twisse's treatise in defense of the Synod of Dort and the Synod of Arles (1620), where the Canons of Dort were accepted as confessional standards. The Canons had been attacked by Daniel Tilenus (1563-1633), the well-known professor of theology at the University of Sedan who had turned Arminian. Tilenus' treatise was entitled *La doctrine des synodes de Dordrecht et d'Alez, mise à l'épreuve de la pratique* (1623). It was the subject of criticism in Twisse's *The Doctrine of the Synod of Dort And Arles, reduced to the practise* (1631?). In his treatise, Twisse distinguishes between the good pleasure of God's will and his law:

> Now like as the act of Gods decree is of the mere pleasure of God, no temporall thing being fitt to be the cause of the æternall decree of God, in like sort, the giving of faith and repentance proceedes merely of the good pleasure of God, according to that, God *hath mercy on whom he will*, Rom.9.18. and to obteyne mercy at the handes of God is to obteyne faith, Rom.11.30. But as for glory and salvation, we doe not say that God, in conferring it, proceedes according to the mere pleasure of his will, but according to a lawe; which is this, *whosoever believeth shall be saved*; which lawe we willingly professe he made according to the mere pleasure of his will, but having made such a lawe, he proceedes according to it.[120]

---

115. Jessop, Pref., in Grayle, *Modest Vindication*, pp. 12-17.
116. Jessop, Pref., in Grayle, *Modest Vindication*, pp. 17-23.
117. Jessop, Pref., in Grayle, *Modest Vindication*, pp. 23-32.
118. Baxter, *Aphorismes* I.1 (pp. 1-2).
119. Strehle draws attention to Twisse's use of the distinction between God's *potentia ordinata* and his *potentia absoluta* and places Twisse in the Nominalist tradition (*Calvinism, Federalism, and Scholasticism*, pp. 109-11).
120. Twisse, *Doctrine of the Synod of Dort*, 2nd ed. (n.p., [1650]), p. 40.

Although he does not use the actual terms here, when he speaks of the good pleasure of God's will and of the law which he has made, Twisse has in mind the scholastic distinction between *voluntas beneplaciti* and *voluntas signi*.[121] He uses the distinction in an effort to maintain both the absolute, secret decree of God and the conditional, revealed law by which he rules mankind. God gives faith and repentance according to his *voluntas beneplaciti*. He gives glory and salvation, however, according to his *voluntas signi*. It is God's secret, decretive will which determines who will receive faith and repentance.[122] It is important to notice that only this *voluntas beneplaciti* may properly be called his will.[123] God's *voluntas signi* is "improperly so called" because it only signifies our duty.[124] This "will" of God merely reveals the condition of glory and salvation. The one is God's secret will, the other his revealed will, his commandment. Twisse therefore writes against Thomas Jackson (1579-1640), the Arminian president of Corpus Christi, Oxford: "<W>hat is it that makes one man more capable of bountifull love and favour then another I know not: what makes him more capable of love in the execution of reward, I know; but what makes him more capable of love in the communication of grace, and in shewing mercy towards him, I know not."[125] Twisse does not know what makes a person capable of God's mercy. He does not know why God bestows faith and repentance on the one while by-passing the other. This belongs to God's *voluntas arcana*. Twisse, does know, however, that God rewards those who have faith and repentance. This is his *voluntas signi*, his revealed or prescriptive will.

Justification and the Role of Faith

Unlike Pemble in his *Vindiciæ gratiæ*, Twisse wants to create room to maintain the conditionality of pardon and salvation. Jessop is correct in drawing attention to

---

121. For this distinction, see Heiko Augustinus Oberman, *The Harvest of Medieval Theology: Gabriel Biel and Late Medieval Nominalism* (Cambridge: Harvard Univ. Press, 1963), pp. 103-10; Francis Oakley, *Omnipotence, Covenant, & Order: An Excursion in the History of Ideas from Abelard to Leibniz* (Ithaca: Cornell Univ. Press, 1984), pp. 114-16. For the use of the distinction in Reformed scholasticism, see Heinrich Heppe, *Die Dogmatik der evangelisch-reformierten Kirche: Dargestellt und aus den Quellen belegt*, ed. Ernst Bizer (Neukirchen: Neukirchener Verlag, 1958), pp. 73-78 (*Reformed Dogmatics: Set Out and Illustrated from the Sources*, ed. Ernst Bizer, foreword Karl Barth, trans. G.T. Thomson [1950; rpt. Grand Rapids: Baker, 1950], pp.85-92]); Richard A. Muller, *Dictionary of Latin and Greek Theological Terms: Drawn Principally from Protestant Scholastic Theology* (Grand Rapids: Baker, 1985), pp. 331-33.
122. Twisse identifies God's *voluntas beneplaciti* with his decree of election and reprobation (*Discovery* [n.p., 1631], pp. 536-37, 559).
123. Twisse, *Discovery*, pp. 536-37, 545, 547. Unlike Twisse, Baxter insists that God's prescriptive will is truly his will: "For God doth not seeme to Will that this or that shall be our duty, and so speake after the manner of men (according to the sense of their *Voluntas signi*) but hee willeth it unfeignedly" (*Aphorismes* I.4 [p. 3]).
124. Twisse, *Discovery*, p. 536. To Twisse, it is not problematic at all, if God's *voluntas beneplaciti* and his *voluntas signi* turn out to be contradictory. God commanded to sacrifice Isaac, but had decreed that Isaac would live. Similarly, God commanded Pharaoh to let Israel go, but he had resolved to harden Pharaoh's heart (*Discovery*, pp. 536, 542, 546-57, 555). Baxter uses these same examples, despite the fact that he is of the opinion that God's prescriptive will is properly so called (*Aphorismes* I.6-7 [pp. 4-5]).
125. Twisse, *Discovery*, pp. 493-94. On the relation between Twisse and Jackson, see Sarah Hutton, "Thomas Jackson, Oxford Platonist, and William Twisse, Aristotelian," *JHI*, 39 (1978), 635-52.

the conditionality of faith as an important factor in Twisse's soteriology. Since the condition of faith precedes pardon and salvation one would expect Twisse to explain the phrase "justification by faith" as meaning that we are justified in God's sight on the condition of faith. This is not the case, however. Rather, Twisse maintains in his *Vindiciæ gratiæ* (1632) that "even before faith and repentance the righteousness of Christ is applied to us, seeing that we pursue efficacious grace by which we believe in Christ and practise penance."[126] Twisse explicitly states that justification and absolution, "as they signify an act of the divine immanent will, are from eternity."[127] Even Arminius admits, says Twisse, that an internal, immanent act in God is from eternity. The real reason why justification cannot be in time is that it does not take the eternity of God seriously: "And it is as impossible for an act of willing to arise anew in God as it is for God himself to begin anew, since in God an act of willing is really the same as God himself ..."[128] Justification is, ultimately, nothing but God's eternal will not to punish the sinner. Justification is *nolle punire*.[129]

Twisse connects the notion of eternal justification to the mediatorial role of Christ when he says that "before faith, this righteousness of Christ was ours, inasmuch as it was performed for us by the intention of God the Father and Christ the Mediator ..."[130] Twisse wants to emphasize the efficacy of Christ's death against Armininianism. The distinction between impetration and application must be understood rightly, says Twisse. The Arminian notion of Christ's death procuring *potentialis redemptio* which becomes *actualis* in the application, is absurd.[131] There is actual redemption and remission through the death of Christ.[132]

---

126. "etiam ante fidem & resipiscentiam applicatur nobis justitia Christi, utpote propter quam gratiam consequimur efficacem, ad credendum in Christum, & agendum pœnitentiam" (Twisse, *Vindiciæ gratiæ* [Amsterdam, 1632], *lib.* I, *pars* 2, *sect.* 25, p. 197).
127. "<J>ustificatio & absolutio, prout significant actum Divinæ voluntatis immanentem, sunt ab æterno" (Twisse, *Vindiciæ gratiæ*, *lib.* I, *pars* 2, *sect.* 25, p. 197).
128. "Et tam impossibile est actum volendi Deo suboriri posse de novo, quam ipsum Deum oriri de novo, quandoquidĕ actus volendi in Deo idem realiter est ipsi Deo ..." (Twisse, *Vindiciæ gratiæ*, *lib.* III, *errat.* 8, *sect.* 7, p. 183).
129. Twisse, *Vindiciæ gratiæ*, *lib.* I, *pars* 2, *sect.* 25, p. 194: "Therefore, remission of sins, if you look at its nature, is simply either the negation of punishment or the negation of the will to punish. To remit sins, therefore, may simply be not willing to punish. But this not willing to punish, as an immanent act in God, was from eternity ... ." ("Remissio enim peccatorum, si quidditatem inspicias, nihil aliud est quam aut punitionis negatio, aut volitionis puniendi negatio. Sit ergo, peccata remittere nihil aliud quam nolle punire. At hoc nolle punire, ut actus immanens in Deo, fuit ab æterno ... .") Cf. Baxter's disagreement with this definition of justification (*Reduction*, p. 98; *Confutation*, p. 182).
130. "ante fidem, hæc Christi justitia nostra fuit, quatenus ex intentione Dei Patris & Christi Mediatoris pro nobis præstitax ..." (Twisse, *Vindiciæ gratiæ*, *lib.* I, *pars* 2, *sect.* 25, p. 197).
131. Twisse, *Vindiciæ gratiæ*, *lib.* 2, *crim.* 4, *sect.* 4, p. 78. Cf. *lib.* 3, *err.* 5, p. 132: "For the theologians teach that our reconciliation with God, or redemption, was truly and properly procured by the death of Christ; also actual reconciliation and redemption, not just their possibility ... ." ("Etenim reconciliationem nostri cum Deo sive redemtionem, morte Christi verè & proprie procuratam esse docent Theologi; Etiam actualem reconciliationem & redemptionem, non autem earundem possibilitatem duntaxat ... .")
132. Twisse, *Vindiciæ gratiæ*, *lib.* II, *crim.* 4, *sect.* 4, p. 78: "Indeed, our interpretation proceeds as follows: Christ acquired efficacious and actual redemption for us by his death, that is, actual remission of sins and reconciliation with God." ("Nostra vero interpretatio sic procedit. Christus morte sua acquisivit nobis redemtionĕ efficacem & actualem, id est actualĕ peccatorŭ remissionĕ, & reconciliationem cŭ Deo.")

Christ's sacrifice and the actual redemption procured by it are central in Twisse's theology. There is a point, however, at which this central role of Christ's death must make room for justification from eternity. In a lengthy digression, Twisse sets out to prove that God, by his *potentia absoluta*, could have pardoned sin without Christ's sacrifice.[133] Twisse uses the distinction between God's absolute and ordained power to weaken the necessity of satisfaction for sin. This indicates a tension between justification from eternity and actual reconciliation by Christ's death. Twisse wants to maintain both, side by side.

If justification is prior to faith – whether that be *ab aeterno* or by Christ's death – what, if any, is the role of faith in justification? After arguing that actual remission of sins and reconciliation with God comes about not in the application, but already in the impetration of redemption, Twisse foresees an objection: is actual remission not the same as justification, and is it, therefore, not by faith? To this objection, he responds that "when the Apostle teaches that we are justified by faith, he only teaches, according to custom, that we are justified by the blood of Christ or because of Christ crucified."[134] In other words, justification by faith simply means justification by faith in Christ. It is justification by Christ.

Twisse is also willing to consider an alternate explanation. In Romans, he insists, justification by faith is forensic absolution. This must be interpreted as follows:

> And in this sense, justification takes place through faith, as someone's absolution is pronounced before the spectacle of a lawsuit and in front of a tribunal of the Judge. For God has set up his tribunal in our hearts, our own conscience prosecutes, terrifies, torments us as the accused according to the law of God. Finally, when at some time the mercy of God thus arises, the Spirit of God, through the voice of the Gospel, raises up, comforts, recreates, and pronounces that our sins have been discharged to us because of Christ. And the Holy Spirit does this by kindling faith in our hearts by which we come to rest in the mercy of God the Father and in the secure satisfaction of Christ the Son.[135]

---

133. Twisse, *Vindiciæ gratiæ, lib.* I, *pars* 2, *sect.* 25, *digr.* 8, pp. 198-207. The proposition Twisse sets out to prove is: "And so to us it appears that it could be claimed that God remits sins, by his absolute power, even if no satisfaction for sins had intervened through the death of Christ the Savior." ("Nobis itaq; videtur asserendū posse Deum, pro potentia sua absoluta, peccata remittere, quamvis nulla intercessisset, per mortĕ Christi Salvatoris, pro peccatis satsifactio" [p. 199].) Baxter is vehement in his disagreement with Twisse on this point (*Aphorismes* II.163 [p. 318]; *Confutation*, p. 322; *More Reasons* [1672], in *Works* II.223 [21.562]; *Methodus Theologiæ* III.i.26; *Universal Redemption*, pp. 477-78). Strehle rightly comments that in Twisse "God is depicted as capable of exonerating the guilty by His "absolute power," and thus excising the present means of salvation, i.e. satisfaction for sin and faith in Christ, as not strictly necessary" (*Calvinism, Federalism, and Scholasticism*, pp. 109-10).

134. "cum docet Apostolus nos fide justificari, nihil aliud ex instituto docet, quàm nos justificari per sanguinem Christi, sive propter Christum crucifixum" (Twisse, *Vindiciæ gratiæ, lib.* II, *crim.* 4, *sect.* 4, p. 79).

135. "Atq; juxta hunc sensum justificatio fit per fidem, quemadmodum coram facie rei, & pro tribunali Iudicis pronuntiatur ejusdem absolutio. Erexit enim Deus tribunal suum in cordibus nostris, conscientia propria juxta legem Dei nos reos peragit, consternit, excruciat: tandem aliquando sic ferente Dei misericordia, Spiritus Dei per vocem Euangelij, erigit, solatur, recreat, & peccata nostra nobis propter Christum dimissa esse pronuntiat; Atque hoc facit Spiritus sanctus accendendo fidem in cordibus nostris qua in Dei patris misericordia, & Christi filij satisfactione securi acquiescamus" (Twisse, *Vindiciæ gratiæ, lib.* II, *crim.* 4, *sect.* 4, p. 79).

Justification by faith means that God sets up his tribunal of justice in our hearts. The forensic justification by faith of which Paul speaks, is simply the pronouncement in our conscience that we are justified.[136] This is not justification itself, however. Twisse speaks of "a kind of judicial and forensic absolution," of absolution which is "as it were" by the mouth of the Judge. Elsewhere, he speaks of "a kind of judicial justification."[137] This pronouncement in conscience is merely *innotescere*.[138] In the application, actual redemption is only made known. This last aspect is but *patefactio* or *manifestatio* of a reconciliation which has already taken place.[139]

This is not to say that this *manifestatio* or absolution in conscience is identical to faith.[140] Twisse, as Pemble before him, does distinguish between faith and the

---

136. Cf. Twisse, *Vindiciæ gratiæ, lib.* I, *pars* 2, *sect.* 25, p. 197: "But the external notification of this one will – by means of a kind of judicial and forensic absolution, which is through Word and Spirit in front of the tribunal of every man's conscience – is that imputation of the righteousness of Christ and also remission of sins and justification, and the absolution which follows faith; for hence it happens that as it were from the mouth of the Judge the absolution is pronounced to us, and thereby the inward purpose of absolving, which was from eternity, is manifested." ("Vnius autem voluntatis notificatio externa, per modum absolutionis, cujusdam judicialis & forensis, quæ fit per verbum & Spiritum, pro tribunali conscientiæ uniuscujusque, hæc est illa justitiæ Christi imputatio, itemque peccatorum remissio, & justificatio, atque absolutio quæ fidem consequitur; Hinc enim fit ut quasi ore Iudicis pronuntietur nobis absolutio, eoque internum absolvendi propositum, quod ab æterno fuit, manifestatur.")
137. Twisse, *Vindiciæ gratiæ, lib.* III, *errat.* 5, p. 132.
138. Twisse repeatedly speaks of *innotescere* to indicate what takes place in one's conscience: "But it is one thing that reconciliation has been procured, another that the same becomes known to us." ("Verùm aliud est, reconciliationem partam esse, aliud eandem nobis innotescere" [*Vindiciæ gratiæ, lib.* III, *errat.* 5, p. 132].) "But those are applied to us through the preaching of the Gospel, not that they take place anew, but that they become known to us ... ." ("Applicãtur autem ista nobis per prædicationẽ Euãngelii, non ut de novo fiãt, sed ut nobis innotescãt ..." [*lib.* II, *crim.* 4, *sect.* 4, p. 78].) "Whence the righteousness of Christ is said to be imputed to us through faith, because it is only discerned through faith, to be imputed to us by God. And only then we are said to be justified, by this kind of justification and absolution from our sins, which produces peace in our consciences." ("Unde dicitur justitia Christi imputari nobis per fidem, quia non nisi per fidem dignoscitur, à Deo nobis imputari: & tum demum justificari dicimur, ejus generis justificatione, atque absolutione a peccatis nostris, quæ pacem ingenerat conscientiis nostris" [*lib.* I, *pars* 2, *sect.* 25, p. 197].) "For if redemption, taken properly, is said to occur before faith, we say that through faith and by faith remission of sins becomes known to our consciences. This remission had indeed been acquired earlier, but not yet become known to us, and therefore could not pacify and calm down our consciences." ("Nam si redemtio proprie dicta fieri dicatur ante fidem, dicimus per fidem & ex fide nobis & conscientiis nostris innotescere remissionem peccatorum, quæ quidem antea acquisita fuit, sed nobis nondum innotuit, & propterea conscientias nostras pacare & tranquillas reddere non potuit" [*lib.* II, *crim.* 4, *sect.* 19, p. 112].)
139. Twisse, *Vindiciæ gratiæ, lib.* II, *crim.* 4, *sect.* 4, p. 79: "Accordingly, we shall be able to distinguish of reconciliation taken in a twofold manner. For God both reconciled us to himself in Christ as to the reality of the matter, and gave in his servants the word of reconciliation as to the evidence and manifestation of the same precious reality. Thus, when we were enemies we are said to have been reconciled to God as to the reality of the matter. But this only happens through the preaching of the Gospel as to the patefaction and the saving communication of the same reality." ("Iuxta ista distinguere poterimus de reconciliatione dupliciter dicta. Nam & *Deus reconciliavit nos sibi in Christo* quoad rei veritatem, & in ministris suis *posuit verbum reconciliationis* quoad ejusdem pretiosæ veritatis evidentiam & manifestationem. Sic *cum inimici essemus* dicimur *reconciliati fuisse Deo* quoad rei veritatem; quod tamen non nisi per Euangelij prædicationem fit, quoad ejusdem veritatis patefactionem, & salutarem communicationem.") Cf. *lib.* I, *pars* 2, *sect.* 25, p. 197.
140. Constant Jessop rightly insists that Twisse does not identify faith and assurance (Pref., in Grayle, *Modest Vindication*, pp. 9-12).

assurance of faith. There is a difference between believing in Christ and believing that Christ has forgiven my sins. The latter follows the former.[141] Twisse is not impressed by his critics' objection that he asks people to believe a falsehood.[142] This charge would only hit home if he would tell people that they must believe that their sins are forgiven. But, says Twisse, "there is no small difference betweene believing in Christ, which we acknowledge to be commanded; and believing that Christ dyed for us, which we finde no where commanded ..."[143]

The failure of Constant Jessop's interpretation of Twisse lies in his misunderstanding of the role of Christ's sacrifice in Twisse's theology. From Twisse's concept of conditionality, Jessop argues that justification must follow faith. The inference may be logical but is not drawn by Twisse. Jessop is forced to admit that Baxter refuses to call Christ's paying of the price actual pardon or reconciliation.[144] But to Twisse the actuality of reconciliation by Christ's blood is central in his argument against the Arminian view of justification. Jessop argues as follows:

> The Doctor <*i.e.*, Twisse>, though he say the remission which Christ hath purchased is actual, *i.e* such a remission which they for whom hee dyed shall actually and infallibly be made partakers of, yet still doth affirme, that none but those which do believe shall partake of it, or obtaine remission of sinnes.[145]

Jessop interprets Twisse's "actual redemption" to mean that it *shall* be actual. Jessop thus takes the angle out of Twisse's objection to the Arminian distinction between the impetration and application of redemption. Twisse and Baxter disagree fundamentally on the question what Christ's death accomplishes. To Baxter, there is no actual redemption or reconciliation wrought by Christ's death. To Twisse's theory of the atonement, the actuality of redemption is a key factor.

From Twisse's liberal use of the concept of the conditionality of pardon and salvation Jessop wrongly infers that justification follows faith. Another wrong conclusion is that when Twisse speaks of justification as an internal and immanent act of God he only means God's purpose to justify.[146] It is difficult to misread

---

141. Twisse, *Vindiciæ gratiæ, lib.* II, *crim.* 4, *sect.* 20, p. 115: "And so we shall proceed along another way and shall say that it is one thing to believe that Christ is our Redeemer, and another to believe truly in Christ ... . Moreover, it should be noticed that an order is given among these things, to believe in Christ and to believe that Christ has redeemed me from sin. The latter is (whatever those itinerant vendors growl in opposition) to believe that my sins have been remitted to me because of the death of Christ. And the former – to believe in Christ – is first; but the latter – to believe that my sins have been forgiven to me because of Christ – is later. For the latter is simply to believe that I have been justified because of Christ." ("Alia itaque via incedamus, & dicamus, aliud esse credere Christum esse redemtorem nostrum, aliud vero credere in Christum ... . Porro advertendum dari ordinem inter ista, *Credere in Christum, & credere Christum me redemisse à peccato*, hoc est (quicquid contra obganniant circulatores isti) credere peccata mea propter mortem Christi, mihi remissa esse. Atque illud, credere scilicet in Christum, prius est; hoc autem credere scilicet peccata mea mihi condonata esse propter Christum, posterius est. Hoc enim nihil aliud est, quam credere me justificatü esse propter Christum.")
142. Cf. Baxter's accusation of Twisse in *Universal Redemption*, pp. 116, 170.
143. Twisse, *Doctrine of the Synod of Dort*, p. 170.
144. Jessop, Pref., in Grayle, *Modest Vindication*, pp. 8-9, 15.
145. Jessop, Pref., in Grayle, *Modest Vindication*, p. 15.
146. Most of the passages from *Vindiciæ gratiæ* to which Jessop appeals, speak of justification by faith. These passages clearly speak of the manifestation of reconciliation in conscience. Cf. Jessop, Pref., in Grayle, *Modest Vindication*, pp. 4-5, 24-29.

Twisse when he posits justification before faith and when he speaks of justification by faith as being nothing but *innotescere*. Jessop is unable to understand Twisse properly because he does not grasp how, on the one hand, Twisse can so clearly speak of conditional pardon and salvation, while, on the other hand, maintaining that justification precedes faith. Being forced to choose which is the "real" Twisse, Jessop opts for the former, who appears more sympathetic to him.

Twisse himself, however, maintains both conditional pardon and justification *ante fidem*. It is easy to see that there is a tension or, perhaps, a contradiction between the two. Twisse is satisfied to accept both positions because he accepts a twofold will in God. By his *voluntas beneplaciti* God gives faith and repentance without any condition. By his *voluntas signi* he sets the condition for pardon, life and salvation. A moderate Calvinist might want to object to Twisse's view that the *voluntas beneplaciti* only speaks of God's decree and, therefore, gives no license to come up with justification before faith. Twisse, however, does not accept this restriction and posits not just an eternal decree but also eternal justification, even if thereby he were to create the impression of two opposing wills in God.

Baxter's Position *versus* High Calvinism

BAXTER'S STARTING POINTS

Justification before Faith and the Twofold Will

Baxter saw it as his task to oppose no less than five high Calvinists on the issue whether justification precedes faith in the *ordo salutis*: John Owen, George Kendall, Lewis Du Moulin, William Eyre, and John Crandon. Baxter refused to reply to the opposition from yet another proponent of justification from eternity, William Robertson.[147] There is certainly no lack of material on which to base an analysis of Baxter's position. It is not sufficient, however, to list his objections to those who place justification before faith in the *ordo salutis*. It is necessary to understand the position from which he works, and which he takes as his starting point in criticizing others.

There are two elements in Baxter's thought which form the basis for his opposition to Antinomianism. He gives an indication of the first element when, at the very end of a long section in which he opposes justification before faith, he writes:

> And that all may take heed of this unhappy model of Theologie that these men have framed, I would earnestly commend to their Consideration this following advice.
> 1. Still keep in your minds a clear Distinction between Gods Rectoral or Legislative Will determining *de Debito, officii, premij, & pœnæ*: and his Will *de rerum existentia & Eventu* as such, determining *de facto* what shall be, and what not; Or between Gods

---

147. Cf. above, p. 56.

Decrees and his Laws. And take heed of confounding these in any point of Theologie; much more in the whole frame. For ought I see, Gods Eternal Decree is the beginning, middle and end of the Antinomians Theologie; It is almost their All.

2. Distinguish carefully between that Decree, Law or Covenant, call it which you will, whereby the Father did, as it were, appoint unto his Son both his work and Reward; and that Law, or Covenant by which both Father and Son do Govern the Church, and make over to us the parts of our salvation. Confounding these hath lost the Antinomians in their Theologie: so that so much of Gods Covenants as they do take notice of, is little more then the Promise of the Father to the Son, and the Absolute discovery of his Decree. They reduce almost all the Covenants to this, and denominate all from this.[148]

Baxter insists that one must distinguish between God's decrees and his laws, as well as between the so-called covenant of redemption between the Father and the Son and the covenant of grace. God's decree is absolute, but the covenant of grace is conditional. Although Baxter does not use the actual terminology here, it is clear that his distinctions run parallel to the distinction between God's *voluntas beneplaciti* and his *voluntas signi*, which Baxter has taken from Twisse. Baxter's adoption of Twisse's bifurcation lies at the basis of his opposition to an *ordo salutis* which places justification before faith. It is Baxter's conviction that those who hold to such an order of salvation fail to distinguish between God's will *de debito* and his will *de rerum eventu*. His opponents only reckon with the latter. Baxter is of the opinion that here lies the foundation of their mistakes in justification. The confounding of these two aspects of God's will "hath lost the Antinomians in their Theologie," in Baxter's judgement.[149]

By applying the distinction of a two-fold will in God Baxter uses one of the structural elements of Twisse's theology. He uses it, however, to argue against Twisse's position that justification is from eternity.[150] Baxter adopts Twisse's distinction between God's *voluntas beneplaciti* and his *voluntas signi*. Rather than placing justification with God's *voluntas beneplaciti*, as Twisse tended to do, Baxter assigns its place to the conditional, revealed will of God.

Threefold Justification Explained

Baxter rarely refers to the bifurcation of God's will in his debates on the relative order between faith and justification. Instead, he takes his starting point for granted: justification must be classified under God's conditional, revealed will. Apart from the distinction between God's decree and his law, there is another distinction which, for Baxter, is important in his opposition to a high Calvinist doctrine of justification. Baxter distinguishes between three kinds of justification: constitu-

---

148. Baxter, *Confession*, p. 290.
149. Baxter, *Confession*, p. 290.
150. Cf. Baxter's comment that remission is not just "*nolle punire*, if you speak it of Gods immanent Will of Purpose, and not of his Will *de Debito* expressed in his Covenant, or his Legislative Will, which Dr. *Twisse* took special notice of as in *præcepto*, and its pitty he had not observed it as well in the Promise and Threatning, which constitute the *Debitum premii & pænæ*, as the Precept doth the *Debitum officii*" (*Reduction*, p. 182).

tive, sentential, and executive. It is a distinction which comes up at various points in the debate. The distinction does not dominate Baxter's arguments against what he considers the Antinomian position of justification. Nevertheless, the distinction is clearly the measuring stick by which he judges the theories of others.

Baxter makes his distinction between constitutive, sentential, and executive justification in numerous places.[151] The first, constitutive justification, is the conformity of the believer to the stipulations of the law of grace. It is also called *iustificatio iuris*. It is a righteousness which always precedes the other two, since "God never judged a man righteous, that was not righteous."[152] This does not mean that constitutive justification is a real, rather than a relative change. Baxter does not confuse justification and sanctification.[153] A person is justified *constitutive* if he is just in relation to the law of grace. Thus, the obligation to punishment is dissolved. Baxter maintains that this conformity to the law of grace is the usual sense in which Scripture speaks of justification.[154] God justifies us this way as King and Benefactor,[155] as Legislator,[156] as Rector.[157] This constitutive justification only means conformity to the law. It is not yet the actual sentence of the Judge. Therefore, Baxter also speaks of constitutive justification as being only a virtual, rather than the actual sentence.[158]

Sentential justification occurs when God or Christ really justifies the believer as Judge and King.[159] This sentential justification is also called *iustificatio per sententiam Iudicis*.[160] It is, as far as the sentence of the Judge goes, "actual,"

---

151. For Baxter's distinctions regarding the nature of justification, see Baxter, *Aphorismes* I.167-93 (pp. 107-24); *Account of my Consideration*, pp. 161-68; *Account*, pp. 3-5; *Reduction*, pp. 96-99; *Confutation*, sig. Mm4^v, pp. 181-86; Pref., in Hotchkis, *Exercitation*, sigs. B9^v-B12^r; *Of Justification*, pp. 10, 24-25, 71-72; *Catholick Theologie* I.ii.69-88, 119-20; *Methodus Theologiæ* III.xxvii.302-04, 318-51; *End of Doctrinal Controversies*, pp. 242-55; Packer, "Redemption and Restoration," pp. 288-92.
152. Baxter, *End of Doctrinal Controversies*, p. 243. Baxter uses this expression more often (cf. *Aphorismes* I.95 [p. 62]; *Reduction*, p. 94; *Of Justification*, p. 340; *Catholick Theologie* I.ii.70, 86, II.239; *Breviate*, p. 7; *Scripture Gospel defended*, p. 98; *Defence of Christ*, pp. 17, 60).
153. Baxter, *Account*, pp. 3-4.
154. Baxter, *Aphorismes* I.184 (p. 119); *Confutation*, p. 181.
155. Baxter, *Of Justification*, p. 24.
156. Baxter, Pref., in Hotchkis, *Exercitation*, sig. B10^r.
157. Baxter, *Reduction*, p. 99.
158. Baxter, *Methodus Theologiæ* III.xxvii.348.
159. Baxter, *Account*, p. 3; *Of Justification*, p. 25; *Catholick Theologie* I.ii.85. Baxter distinguishes between private and public judicial or sentential justification. Moreover, when speaking of public judicial justification, he distinguishes between justification *in foro humano* and *in foro divino*. It is clear, however, that both the private judicial justification – by one's conscience, by angels, or by private people – and the public judicial justification *in foro humano* – by the judgement of domestic, civil, or ecclesiastical authorities – are of less significance. Private justification may either be true or false, and also public justification *in foro humano* need not be according the judgement of God. What really counts is the public sentential justification *in foro divino*. Here, the virtual judgement is through the covenant, promise, or law of grace, which makes and denominates the believer just. The actual justification of the Judge finally gives the sentence by Christ's words to men, by the efficacious and irresistible enlightening of the minds, and by the deeds or the execution itself (*Methodus Theologiæ* III.xxvii.303-04; *End of Doctrinal Controversies*, pp. 245-46).
160. Christ has received all judgement from God (Baxter, *Of Justification*, p. 25). Baxter refers to Acts 17:31 and John 5:22. Christ is the supreme Judge *derivative*, as Mediator according to his human nature. God is the supreme Judge *simpliciter* (*Methodus Theologiæ* III.xxvii.304).

"most full, compleat and eminent" justification.[161] By the sentence of the Judge, the right to impunity is not just declared, but decisively determined "as no more to be controverted."[162] When does this sentential justification take place? Baxter maintains that a certain justification of the conscience is commonly given to those who are justified, although it is often obscure, hesitant, and inconstant.[163] The most full judicial justification follows after death and the resurrection. When Baxter speaks of sentential justification, he has especially the last judgement in view.[164]

The third kind of justification, executive justification, is simply the execution of the sentence. It is the "actuall Liberation from penalty,"[165] *non punire*.[166] It is "the *actual Impunity, removing* of deserved Punishment, and *actual giving posses-sion* of Life and Salvation, which constitutive Justification gave us *Right* to."[167] Sanctification is the beginning of this executive justification, while glorification will be its completion.[168] This executive justification is not restricted to believers. Since also unbelievers have some degree of sanctification, it will be clear that executive justification may take place "by meer providence: and so wicked men are pardoned without a promise, in such measure as God abateth and forbeareth punishing them."[169] It varies in degree according to the degree in which the penal-ty is actually remitted.[170] There is no perfect justification, therefore, as long as sanctification is imperfect.[171] The word "remission" is principally used when it refers to this actual remission of the penalty. When, in constitutive justification, the obligation to the penalty is remitted there is only a *ius ad impunitatem*. The word remission is then used in a less emphatic or direct sense.[172]

Baxter does not distinguish between remission of sin and the imputation of Christ's righteousness as two distinct parts of justification. He inclines to the view that justification does not extend beyond remission of sin, since justification only

---

161. Baxter, *Account*, p. 3. Cf. *Reduction*, p. 97 ("the most perfect of all").
162. Baxter, *Confutation*, p. 182.
163. Baxter, *Methodus Theologiæ* III.xxvii.348: "And mostly the light, or at least sparks, of God's countenance provide the justified with some sense of justification, although to most people it is very obscure, doubtful, and inconstant." ("Et plerumque Justificatis, aliquando vultûs Divini aut Lumen aut scintillæ saltem, Justificationis conscientiam quandam præbent, quamvis pluribus nimis obscuram, dubitantem & inconstantem.") Cf. *Catholick Theologie* I.ii.86.
164. Baxter, *Methodus Theologiæ* III.xxvii.348. Baxter even states that "we know of no such act of God <*i.e.*, justification *per sententiam iudicis*> (properly) but at the particular Iudgement after death, and the last General Judgement" (*Reduction*, p. 183).
165. Baxter, *Of Justification*, p. 24.
166. Baxter, *Reduction*, p. 97; Pref., in Hotchkis, *Exercitation*, sig. B11ʳ.
167. Baxter, *Catholick Theologie* I.ii.86.
168. Since Baxter includes sanctification in executive justification, he identifies, at this particular point, justification and sanctification. As will become clear, however, when Baxter speaks of justification, he usually means constitutive justification, which he distinguishes from sanctifica-tion.
169. Baxter, *Reduction*, p. 97.
170. Baxter, *Reduction*, p. 97.
171. Says Baxter: "For God *perfectly to forgive sin*, while *any sin remaineth* in the soul (especially *habitual*) is a contradiction: For sin it self, though not as *sin*, nor as effected, yet as *permitted* and not healed, is the greatest punishment as was said. And there is no perfect pardon of the punish-ment, while such punishment is continued" (*Catholick Theologie* I.ii.87).
172. Baxter, *Reduction*, p. 183; Pref., in Hotchkis, *Exercitation*, sig. B11ʳ.

restores us to the same condition that we would have been in if Adam had perse-
vered in the state of integrity. Justification does not add any benefits in addition to
the ones that Adam would have had.[173] Pardon is "that *Righteousness* which consisteth in our *right to Impunity*."[174] Since the benefit of Christ's righteousness is
not something which is added to pardon, but is identical with it, Baxter applies the
threefold distinction of justification also to pardon:

> What I have said of Justification, is mostly true of Pardon of Sin: Pardon is threefold,
> 1. Constitutive, which is God's giving us a *Right to Impunity:* This is God's act by
> the pardoning Covenant or Law of Grace. 2. By *Sentence*, judging us so pardoned. 3.
> *Executive*, taking off, or not inflicting Punishment deserved.[175]

Justification and pardon are basically the same. Remission or pardon, however,
denotes more properly the legal or constitutive element of justification, even though
the word "pardon" may also be applied to the sentence of the Judge. The word
justification – which "signifieth very fitly both acts, legal and judicial" – is more
properly applied to the sentence of the Judge than to the Gospel grant of the
Ruler.[176] The most proper way, therefore, to denote the donative and the sentential
aspects, is to speak, respectively, of *remissio iuris* and *iustificatio iudicis*.[177]

Threefold Justification and Thomas Hotchkis

Baxter applies the distinction between constitutive, sentential, and executive justification as the basis from which to assail his opponents. He not only uses his view
of a threefold justification to ward off high Calvinist notions of justification. His
framework also functions in discussions with moderate Calvinists. Thomas Hotchkis,

---

173. Baxter is careful in his judgement: "I am loath to determine so doubtful a Case; But it seems most
     probable to me, that the felicity that *Adam* should have had, and that which Christ will give us, are
     of the same nature; because the Nature and Capacity of man is the same. But what gradual or
     Accidental difference there is, God knows, for I do not" (*Confutation*, p. 235).
     In his *Methodus Theologiæ*, Baxter is less hesitant, saying that "against the liability to punishment
     from sins truly committed, remission of sins is our total righteousness; but not total in an absolute
     sense." ("contra *Reatum Pœnæ* ob peccata *verè commissa*, *Remissio peccatorum* est *tota nostra
     Justitia*: non autem *Tota absolute*" [III.xxvii.321].) Thus, through plenary remission of sin God
     restores (1) the lost favor of God; (2) the help and operation of the Holy Spirit, and, therefore,
     sanctification; (3) the right to eternal life, or the reward of a heavenly inheritance; and (4)
     glorification itself (III.xxvii.321). Baxter adds the qualification that remission is not our total
     justification "in an absolute sense" because despite the fact that Christ has first merited the
     reward, the condition must still be fulfilled: "And therefore the heavenly kingdom is conferred to
     no one as a gift to whom it is not also conferred as a reward." ("Ideóque Regnum cœleste nemini
     obvenit, ut *Donum*, cui etiam non obvenit ut *Præmium*" [III.xxvii.322].) Although the gift and the
     reward are materially the same, formally God does not give the reward – which is a reward of
     merit or of good works – but the gift itself (III.xxvii.321-22).
174. Baxter, *End of Doctrinal Controversies*, p. 255. To be sure, as already indicated above in n. ,
     pardon is not our righteousness in an absolute sense. After all, Baxter insists that one needs
     personal righteousness as the condition to partake of Christ's universal righteousness. Only the
     latter righteousness may be identified with pardon. The former is the condition to be pardoned.
     For a further exposition of Baxter's understanding of twofold righteousness, see below, pp. 273-
     90.
175. Baxter, *End of Doctrinal Controversies*, p. 254.
176. Baxter, *Confutation*, p. 183; Pref., in Hotchkis, *Exercitation*, sig. B10ᵛ.
177. Baxter, Pref., in Hotchkis, *Exercitation*, sigs. B10ᵛ-B11ʳ.

whose attack on William Twisse in *An Exercitation Concerning the Nature of Forgivenesse of Sin* (1655) caused the William Robertson's indignant *Iggeret hammashkil* (1655), defines forgiveness as follows: "Gods pardoning a sinner is, his taking off the sinners obligation to punishment, and consequently in due time the punishment it self ..."[178] Remission has two elements. The *terminus proximus* is the "taking away, or dissolving the obligation of the sinner to punishment." The *terminus remotus* is the "taking away, or the not inflicting of punishment itself."[179]

This definition has several consequences that are repugnant to a high Calvinist definition of justification. First, a reprobate may in some sense be said to be pardoned, "*viz.* with respect to some kind or degree of temporal punishment, either wholly forborn and taken off, or else suspended and delayed for a time."[180] If pardon simply means the non-inflicting of the punishment, the reprobates must, to some extent, share in it. Second, inasmuch as the saints undergo chastisements or punishments their sins have not been pardoned.[181] Pardon of sin may now be total or partial, perfect or imperfect.[182] Third, and most fundamental perhaps, Hotchkis rejects the difference between remission and sanctification.[183] Remission – in the sense of the actual taking away of the punishment – is a real, not just a relative grace:

> That the difference betwixt Sanctification and Justification is not (as hath been commonly said,) That that doth work a real change in a sinner, but this a change barely and purely Relative: for both of them, *viz.* Gods sanctifying, and Gods justifying or pardoning a sinner ... do work in or upon the sinner a real change ...[184]

Baxter, in his preface to Hotchkis' treatise, commends the author for insisting on the necessity for daily prayer for pardon, for maintaining the necessity of works without ascribing any merit to man, and for arguing that final justification is on the condition of perseverance.[185] In none of the three points which high Calvinists might single out for criticism, Baxter would disagree with Hotchkis.[186] Also, in the actual treatise, Hotchkis vindicates Baxter's *Aphorismes of Justification* (1649)

---

178. Hotchkis, *Exercitation*, p. 38.
179. Hotchkis, *Exercitation*, p. 40.
180. Hotchkis, *Exercitation*, p. 66.
181. Hotchkis, *Exercitation*, pp. 67-98.
182. Hotchkis, *Exercitation*, p. 113.
183. Hotchkis, *Exercitation*, pp. 117-19.
184. Hotchkis, *Exercitation*, p. 204.
185. Baxter, Pref., in Hotchkis, *Exercitation*, sig. B12ᵛ.
186. Baxter also agrees with Hotchkis that executive pardon consists partly of sanctification. Speaking of initial executive pardon or justification, Baxter comments: "In *this sense* to *sanctifie* a man, is to *justifie* him *executively*, and so *sententially*" (*Catholick Theologie* I.ii.86). In his preface to Hotchkis' treatise, Baxter attempts to clarify Hotchkis' view that remission is a real change. Baxter explains that when Hotchkis "denyeth Justification to be a change meerely Relative, his Reason is, because it is the same with Remission, and Remission is a real change, *viz.* not punishing. *Ergo, &c.* But note, 1 That he explains himselfe to speake only of Executive Remission, which is nothing to the other two sorts. 2. I thinke executive Remission is not usually called Justification. And therefore I shall still say, that Justification is but a Relative change" (Pref., in Hotchkis, *Exercitation*, sigs. B12ᵛ-C1ʳ).

against the criticism of George Kendall's Θεοκρατία: Or, A Vindication of the Doctrine Commonly Received in the Reformed Churches (1653). Despite his general agreement with Baxter, Hotchkis thinks that "there should more be added for clearing the point ..."[187] He does not appreciate it that Baxter leaves out the element of the effectual taking away of the punishment itself, and that he restricts remission of sin mainly to the dissolution of the obligation to punishment.[188] To put it in Baxter's terminology: Hotchkis regrets it that Baxter only speaks of constitutive pardon and not at all of executive pardon.

Baxter replies to Hotchkis' criticism in his preface to the latter's book. Here Baxter gives a brief exposition of his theory of threefold justification.[189] He then comes with some mild criticism of Hotchkis: "It seems to me that this Reverend Author doth sometime looke only at the executive Remission in his Consectaries; sometime at the Legall Remission; and sometime hee joyneth them together as one."[190] Whereas Hotchkis is of the opinion that Baxter overlooks executive pardon, Baxter argues that Hotchkis should speak more of constitutive pardon. Hotchkis lays himself open for undue criticism because several of the points he wants to make – that the reprobates share in remission of sin; that pardon may be partial and imperfect; and that justification is a real change – are overemphasized because of the nearly sole attention paid to executive remission. Nevertheless, the difference between the two authors remains no more than a matter of emphasis.

Threefold Justification and Cyrus Du Moulin

Baxter construes a similar argument against Cyrus Du Moulin. Du Moulin expresses his disagreement with his brother, Lewis, in a letter to him. In this letter, published by Lewis Du Moulin in his De fidei partibus in justificatione Dissertatio (1653), Cyrus Du Moulin objects to Twisse's theory of justification from eternity.[191] In opposition to Twisse, he distinguishes between justification in God's

---

187. Hotchkis, Exercitation, p. 194.
188. Hotchkis states that Baxter "speaks of Justification or Remission in Law sense, and not in execution, as being another distinct sort or part of pardon" (Exercitation, p. 195). Baxter's Aphorismes (1649) and his Account of my Consideration (written in 1652) only speak of constitutive and sentential justification. The executive element occurs first in Baxter's Apology of 1654 (cf. above, n. 151).
189. Hotchkis, Exercitation, sigs. B9ᵛ-B12ʳ.
190. Baxter, Pref., in Hotchkis, Exercitation, sig. B11ʳ.
191. Cyrus Du Moulin comments: "But as far as I can gather by your words, you do, with Dr. Twiss, seem to acknowledge no other justification, then that in Decree; to wit, that free love of God, whreby <sic> he embraced us in Christ from eternity, and whereby he decreed to absolve us from sin, for his death and obedience; and you seem to disallow of the common distinction of the Decree, and the execution of the Decree." (In Baxter, Confutation, sig. Mm2ᵛ; "Sed quantum possum ex tuis verbis colligere, nullam aliam cum Domino Twisso videris agnoscere Justificationẽ, quam illam quæ in decreto, nimirum gratuitum illum Dei amorem quo nos ob <sic> æterno in Christo amplexus est, & quo decrevit nos propter ejus mortem & obedientiam à peccatis absolvere, & videris improbare distinctionem tritam, decreti & executionis decreti" [in Lewis Du Moulin, De fidei partibus, pp. 126-27]). For English translations I quote from Baxter's translation of the letter in Confutation, sigs. Mm2ʳ-Mm4ᵛ.

decree, actual pardon of the believer, and justification in the life to come.[192] Although he is willing to speak of justification in God's decree, properly speaking sins are only forgiven in this life and in the life to come.[193] Justification by faith is real, proper pardon, insists Cyrus Du Moulin. He admits that it is God's pronouncement to the conscience, but this judicial pronouncement is nevertheless true forgiveness in God's sight.[194]

Baxter has much appreciation for Cyrus Du Moulin's criticism of his brother. He agrees with the Frenchman that justification takes place properly and actually by faith. He thinks that Cyrus Du Moulin still comes too close to the position of his brother, however, when he states that God pronounces this actual judicial sentence in the believer's conscience. Baxter explains his dissent from Cyrus Du Moulin by referring to the distinction between constitutive and sentential justification. Cyrus Du Moulin defines justification as "an act of God the Judge, whereby he pronounceth Righteous, and Absolveth from sin, one that is ungodly and a sinner in himself, and obnoxious to his wrath, of his meer grace, for the perfect obedience of Christ, received by Faith."[195] Justification by faith is an act of God as Judge, a judicial act. This is where Baxter's problem lies with Cyrus Du Moulin:

> His great oversight, in my Judgement is, that he only takes notice of sentential Justification, which is the act of God, as Judge, (besides the decree, which is no Justification,) and not at all of Legal or Testamentary Justification, which is the act of God as Legislator, and Covenanter, and free Donor. It is true, that sentential Justification is most strictly and fully so called: but its as true that Legal or Covenant Justification, is true Justification also, yea and always goes before the former, and is that which the Scripture most commonly means, when it speaks of Justification by faith. Divines call it, Constitutive Justification.[196]

---

192. Cyrus Du Moulin, in Baxter, *Confutation*, sig. Mm2^r: "And this Justification is fitly considered in three distinct seasons: 1. In Gods Decree: 2. When God doth actually pardon the believer: 3. In the life to come, when the sentence of Justification shall be pronounced in the last Judgement." ("& hanc Justificationem in tribus diversis temporibus appositè considerant. 1. In Dei decreto. 2. Cum actu Deus condonat credenti. 3. In vita futura, cum sententia Justificationis in ultimo judicio pronuntiabitur" [in Lewis Du Moulin, *De fidei partibus*, p. 125].)
193. Cyrus Du Moulin, in Lewis Du Moulin, *De fidei partibus*, p. 218 (in Baxter, *Confutation*, sig. MMs^v).
194. Cyrus Du Moulin describes justification by faith as follows: "I think therefore that we must believe, that God doth indeed and properly Justifie a believer and forgive him his sins, as often as after true Repentance and Faith in Christs merit, he giveth to his conscience assurance that such and such a sin is remitted, saying to him as Christ did to the Paralitick man, *Be of good cheer, Son, thy sins are forgiven thee*; and that the act of justification is reitetated <sic>, as oft as the merciful God by his Spirit pronounceth this judgement to the conscience." (in Baxter, *Confutation*, sig. Mm3^r; "Existimo ergo credendum, Deum revera & proprie justificare fidelem & ipsi condonare peccata, quoties post veram pœnitentiam, & fidem in Christi meritum, ipsius conscientiam de tali & tali peccato remisso certum reddit, ipsi dictans quod Christus dicebat paralytico, confide fili, tibi sunt remissa peccata: & toties actum Justificationis reiterari, quoties Deus per spiritum hoc misericors conscientiæ Judicium pronuntiat ..." [in Lewis Du Moulin, *De fidei partibus*, pp. 130-31].)
195. Cyrus Du Moulin, in Baxter, *Confutation*, sig. Mm2^r ("actum Dei Judicis quo impium & peccatorem in sese, & iræ suæ obnoxium, ex mera sua gratia propter perfectam Christi obedientiam fide acceptam pronuntiat justum, & absolvit à peccatis" [in Lewis Du Moulin, *De fidei partibus*, p. 125].).
196. Baxter, *Confutation*, sig. Mm4^v (emphasis inverted).

Baxter's objection to Cyrus Du Moulin is similar to his disagreement with Hotch-kis. He tells both authors that they either do not take constitutive justification into account sufficiently (Hotchkis) or not at all (Du Moulin). While he says to Hotch-kis that he should not place all emphasis on executive justification, he lets Cyrus Du Moulin know that sentential justification is not all. Thus, Baxter judges both authors by means of his own distinction of a threefold justification.

Threefold Justification and George Kendall

Baxter's criticism on Thomas Hotchkis and Cyrus Du Moulin is mild, because he regards them ultimately as allies in his opposition to the theory of justification from eternity. Baxter has no such kinship with George Kendall and Lewis Du Moulin. His criticism of their views is therefore quite sharp.

Kendall's Θεοκρατία: Or, A Vindication of the Doctrine Commonly Received in the Reformed Churches (1653) is directed especially against John Goodwin's Arminian soteriological scheme as set forth in his Redemption Redeemed (1651). Kendall is hesitant in speaking of justification from eternity. There must be a transient act of God involved in justification.[197] The main question, in Kendall's view, is: what exactly is this transient act of God in justification? He expresses his disagreement with Baxter's view that the new covenant or its promulgation is God's transient justifying act. The covenant cannot justify of itself because "it must be beholding to many intervenient causes."[198] If, as Baxter insists, the condition must be fulfilled, this would mean that it is not God, but the believer himself who justifies:

> Its clear in this case of the New Covenant, as in that of the Old: The Covenant ran, The day thou eatest thereof thou shalt die; This was Gods threat; I pray, who brought death into the world, God or Adam? Just so in the New Covenant, Beleeve and be justified; who justifies the believer, God or himself?[199]

The covenant cannot be God's transient justifying act, Kendall insists, because this would still require a condition to be performed. It would imply that man justifies himself. Kendall argues, therefore, that "faith is the real effect which God works by a transient act on a person whom he justifies."[200] Kendall does not simply substitute faith for the covenant as God's transient, justifying act. Rather, God gives faith by means of a transient act. This leads to man's justification when, by faith, he comes to know his justification.

Kendall's view on the relation between God's decree and justification in time will be explored in more detail below.[201] Of special concern at the moment is how Baxter applies his theory of a triple justification to confute Kendall. When the latter states that the covenant is not God's transient act of justification, Baxter

197. Kendall, Vindication I.iv.139.
198. Kendall, Vindication I.iv.140.
199. Kendall, Vindication I.iv.140.
200. Kendall, Vindication I.iv.141.
201. Cf. below, pp. 108-10.

gives a detailed explanation of constitutive, sentential, and executive remission.[202] Apart from the last two, he distinguishes active and passive pardon. Active pardon may be (1) mental, which is God's secret resolution to justify and is less properly called pardon;[203] (2) the very grant of the act of pardon, which is the act of legislation and precedes constitutive pardon; (3) signal, legal, and constitutive, which gives *ius ad impunitatem* by dissolving the obligation to punishment; or (4) the promulgation of this law of grace. Corresponding to these four elements, passive pardon may denote (1) the effects of mental pardon in men's hearts and minds; (2) the law of grace itself; (3) the *ius ad impunitatem* caused by the second act of pardon; or (4) the state that someone is in who has pardon offered to him. After Baxter has given his exposition on active and passive pardon, he states that "besides all this" there is sentential and executive pardon. This implies that the four elements of active and passive pardon may be identified with constitutive justification. They are the four stages in which constitutive justification may be divided. Strictly speaking, constitutive justification is to be identified with the second element of active and passive pardon – the *ius ad impunitatem*.

Having distinguished between active and passive pardon, Baxter comes to the question what Scripture means with justification by faith:

> I think it is the Dissolving of the obligation to punishment, or the giving us a *Jus ad liberationem vel ad impunitatem*, or Gods remitting his *Jus puniendi:* Where the immediate *terminus* is the Dissolution of the obligation, or our *Debitum liberationis, vel jus ad impunitatem*: and the remote *terminus* ... is Impunity it self, or actual liberation from punishment, or *non-punire*.[204]

Baxter's position is almost identical to that of Hotchkis: the immediate *terminus* of pardon is the dissolution of the obligation to punishment; the remote *terminus* is the actual taking away of the punishment, which is executive pardon.[205]

Baxter argues vehemently that the covenant itself justifies: "Doth not the Testament of the Lord Jesus properly convey the Legacy? Doth not Gods Deed of gift of Christ and his Righteousness to us, properly convey? and doth not God properly Give thereby? Why how can a more proper way of Giving be imaginable?"[206] Baxter is of the opinion that by denying the role of the covenant in pardoning sin Kendall has undermined pardon itself. Kendall "disputes against the very formall nature and definition of a pardon: which is to be *an Act of the Rector freeing the guilty from punishment by dissolving the obligation*."[207]

---

202. Baxter, *Reduction*, pp. 96-97.
203. It is worth noting that there is a sense in which Baxter is willing to speak of justification from eternity. He classifies God's secret resolution to justify under God's act of pardon. Properly speaking, however, Baxter reserves God's act of justification to his dissolution of the punishment.
204. Baxter, *Reduction*, p. 98.
205. Baxter makes the same distinction, using the same terminology, in *Confutation*, p. 182.
206. Baxter, *Reduction*, p. 98.
207. Baxter, *Reduction*, p. 99.

Threefold Justification and Lewis Du Moulin

Finally, Baxter opposes his view of a threefold justification to Lewis Du Moulin's
view. Lewis Du Moulin argues against his brother, Cyrus, that justification precedes faith and that "Faith hath no part (or place) in the Definition of justification,
or of Remission of sins."[208] Justification by faith only means "to reveal Christs
Righteousness, to shew it, to make it known, to bring it to the knowledge of the
understanding and conscience."[209] Again, Baxter explains that pardon may either
be constitutive, sentential, or executive.[210] But, says Baxter, "<t>he formal act of
Remission is *Dissolving* the obligation: or *Relaxing* it, or *Giving* Right to impunity ..."[211] There can only be one logical conclusion, in Baxter's view: "And therefore Dr. *Twisse* and you speak unsoundly when you say that Remission of sin is
but *non punire*: Yea, or but *nolle punire*, if you speak it of Gods immanent Will of
Purpose, and not of his Will *de Debito* expressed in his Covenant, or his Legislative Will ..."[212]

The logic of Baxter's conclusion will likely escape his opponents. Baxter
consistently approaches their positions from his own starting points: the distinction between God's will *de debito* and his will *de rerum eventu*, as well as the
distinction of a threefold justification, with its emphasis on constitutive justification. Anything which falls beyond the parameters of this framework fails to measure up to the correct definition of justification or pardon. Baxter's approach has
both a weak and a strong element. On the one hand, his arguments do not always
escape the danger of a fallacious *petitio principii*. Too often, he takes his own
position for granted and uses it to measure the orthodoxy or heterodoxy of his
opponents. On the other hand, by continually asking attention for what he considers the proper view of the nature of justification, Baxter leaves little doubt where
his emphasis lies. He presents a compelling plea for the centrality of God's absolution of the obligation to punishment in the nature of justification.

JUSTIFICATION FROM ETERNITY AND THE NATURE OF GOD

The Eternity of Immanent Acts of God

When, one afternoon in 1655, William Robertson read Baxter's *Reduction of a
Digressor* (1654) against George Kendall, he had a horrible experience. It seemed
as if Baxter looked at him with such a "countenance, the very glances whereof did

---

208. Lewis Du Moulin, in Baxter, *Confutation*, p. 178 ("fidemq; nullas habere partes in definitione
     Justificationis, seu remissionis peccatorum" [*De fidei partibus*, p. 6].). I am quoting the English
     translations of Lewis Du Moulin from Baxter, *Confutation*.
209. Lewis Du Moulin, in Baxter, *Confutation*, p. 178 ("Justitiam Christi revelare, indicare, notam
     facere, in notitiam perferre intellectus & conscientiæ" [*De fidei partibus*, p. 6; emphasis through-
     out in original].).
210. Baxter, *Confutation*, pp. 181-82.
211. Baxter, *Confutation*, p. 182.
212. Baxter, *Confutation*, p. 182.

so much affright me, when either I looked upon it, or when it stared me in the face, that I do profess I could not behold it, nor so much as think upon it, without trembling adversation."[213] Robertson speaks of "that Monster of your mind" which he encountered that afternoon, and he says:

> I never did abhor with greater detestation & indignation the principles of any man, and the defence of them, then I did that one most blasphemous ... Principle of yours, and your defence of it, about the *Immanent acts of God, in his Knowledg and Will:* as if they (or any thing immanent in God) were, or could be, *de novo*, arising or beginning to be in him in time, and not from all eternity; as if there could be any thing in God, which is not God himself, and eternal as himself is.[214]

Robertson's shock came from Baxter's view that God's knowledge and will may originate in him *de novo*. Robertson's comments raise several questions: what does Baxter mean when he says that God's knowledge and will may be said to originate in him *de novo*? Why does Baxter even discuss the possibility of new immanent acts in God if he himself thinks that justification is a transient act? Does Baxter's view indeed impugn the simplicity and immutability of God?

Baxter himself is the cause of the angry outcries from Kendall and Robertson. In his *Aphorismes of Justification* Baxter poses the question whether remission and justification are immanent or transient acts of God. Baxter maintains the latter position. He then adds the comment: "The mistake of this one point was it that led those two most excellent, famous, Divines, Dr *Twisse* and Mr *Pemble*" to their theory of justification from eternity.[215] Baxter comments that it "is much questioned" whether all God's immanent acts are any more eternal than transient acts.[216] What is more, he regards it "quite beyond our understanding to know" whether all God's immanent acts are eternal.[217] To be sure, Baxter only speaks of those immanent acts that have a temporal or external object.[218] He questions, for instance, the eternity of God's knowledge that the world now exists, or that a particular man is sanctified or just.[219]

By his admission that he doubts whether all God's immanent acts are eternal, Baxter allows himself to be side-tracked. He states that it is his view that justification is a transient act of God by enacting and promulgating the new covenant. When he makes some comments on the eternity of God's immanent acts, however, he gives potential opponents the opportunity to call his orthodoxy into question, not only with regard to the doctrine of justification, but also with respect to the very doctrine of God. The discussion on the eternity of God's immanent acts is, in a sense, chimerical: Baxter defines justification as a transient act, makes some

---

213. Robertson, *Iggeret hammashkil*, p. 6.
214. Robertson, *Iggeret hammashkil*, p. 7.
215. Baxter, *Aphorismes* I.173 (p. 112). As noted earlier, Baxter was erroneous in attributing the doctrine of justification from eternity to William Pemble (cf. above, p. 72).
216. Baxter, *Aphorismes* I.173 (p. 112).
217. Baxter, *Aphorismes* I.174 (p. 113).
218. Cf. Baxter, *Reduction*, p. 68: "Remember that we speak not of those Immanent acts whose object is Eternal: but of those that have a temporary object, as the actual existence of things, &c."
219. Baxter, *Aphorismes* I.173 (p. 112).

comments in passing in which he questions the eternity of some of God's immanent acts, and then allows himself to be dragged into a lengthy argument with
Kendall on the latter point.

The impression of an unreal debate is confirmed when Baxter enters on an
extensive discussion of a number of arguments against Kendall. These arguments
are in defense of the notion that God's immanent acts, as they relate to external
objects, originate *de novo*. Some of these arguments concern the divine understanding. Kendall insists that God's knowledge is unchangeable: "God knowes
that that *is to day* which was *not yesterday*, but God as perfectly *knew it yesterday*
as *to day*, and *knew at once* all *the various successions* in time, or did he otherwise, a *change* cannot possibly be avoided, notwithstanding all Mr. *Baxter* al-
legeth to the contrary."[220] Baxter does not accept this argument. Some, says Baxter, will simply reply that if there is no object of knowledge, there can be no
knowledge. These people will hold that "it is unnaturally and improperly called
Science (and so Omniscience) which hath not an Object."[221] Comments Baxter:

> <T>hey will then assume, that *Peter* and *Paul* did not actually exist from eternity:
> Christ did not actually suffer from eternity: and so the actual existence of *Peter* in
> *nunc temporis*, was not an intelligible object from Eternity: and therefore they think
> they may conclude, that it could not be known from Eternity.[222]

If one were to accept this line of argument, it would mean that God knows things
de novo when they come into being *de novo*.

The case is much the same with regard to the divine will. Kendall argues that a
new immanent act of God's will must mean that it is a new act for the better, for
the worse, or indifferent. None of these are acceptable, argues Kendall:

> if for the better, he was not absolutely *perfect before*, as being capable of *bettering*;
> if for the *worse*, he is not so *perfect since* this *act*; as he was *before*, which is to make
> him *lesse* perfect by his *new act*; if *neither*, then is this act such as might as well have
> been *out* as *in*, and then it is an *imperfection* to act so *impertinently*.[223]

Baxter replies to this that "they" will say that a new act of God's will is better for
the creature, and also – relatively or reputatively – better for God, "as God is said
to be Blessed, Glorified, Honoured, Well pleased, Exalted, Magnified, &c. And
thus it may be Better to God, though he receive no real addition of felicity; and so
not Vain or Indifferent."[224]

Baxter also points out that if it is acceptable to speak of a diversity of immanent acts in God it cannot possibly be wrong to ascribe these acts to God *de novo*:

220. Kendall, *Vindication* I.iv.136. Cf. John Crandon's comments in his reaction to this aspect of
Baxter's *Aphorismes*: "But to God who is eternall, dwels in eternity, is eternity, nor circumscribed
with place or time, there is nothing former, or latter, no succession, of present to past, of future to
present, but all at once, and at one view apparent to his eye, or knowledge ..." (*Aphorisms
Exorized* I.xxi.257).
221. Baxter, *Reduction*, p. 17.
222. Baxter, *Reduction*, p. 18. Cf. pp. 59-60.
223. Kendall, *Vindication* I.iv.134.
224. Baxter, *Reduction*, p. 20.

"And are there not the same Reasons for our ascribing to God, the beginning and ending of Immanent Acts, as the Diversity of them? Is not one as consistent with his Immutability, as the other with his simplicity?"[225]

Throughout his reply to Kendall, Baxter relates the arguments of numerous scholastic theologians, both Thomists and Scotists. He consistently refuses, however, to adopt any of these arguments as his own. Indeed, "I think they are *de ignotis*, dreams, fightings in the dark, yet much like your own."[226] If forced to choose any opinion at all with regard to the eternity of God's immanent acts, Baxter will opt for Kendall's position, "but I take the point in Question to be past our reach ..."[227]

Baxter's admission that he does not have a solution to the issue stems from his keen awareness of the distance between God and man. Baxter begins his treatise against Kendall with an exposition in which he argues that it is "one of the greatest sins" of divines to dispute unrevealed things about the nature of God.[228] Our knowledge of God is very limited. There is an enormous difference between God and man. Knowledge and will in God "are not the things that we by those terms use to expres ..."[229] These faculties are ascribed to God only "by a very, very, very low remote Analogy."[230] In fact, Baxter denies any analogy of attribution between God and man. That which is called "knowledge" in God, is only in him and "not in the creature at all."[231] We must speak of God's various attributes only because there is no other way to express ourselves.[232] But we are so at a loss that "you and I can no more tell what that is in God which we call Knowing, Willing, Acting, then my Horse can tell what Reasoning or Discourse is in me, or thereabouts."[233] Baxter is upset by what he regards as Kendall's presumption in pretending to understand God's immanent acts.[234]

Baxter is obviously unwilling to commit himself firmly in the debate. He is only out to prove that the comments in his *Aphorismes* which cast doubt on the eternity of some of God's immanent acts represent an opinion held by numerous scholastics in the past, and that this opinion does not need to lead to a denial of the simplicity and immutability of God. His fear to be presumptuous in speaking of

---

225. Baxter, *Reduction*, p. 25. Cf. pp. 20, 69.
226. Baxter, *Reduction*, p. 19.
227. Baxter, *Refutation*, p. 41. Cf. p. 17: "I think it most sutable to Gods Unity and Simplicity, that all his immanent acts (so called by us) are Himself and are One. But I dare not say I am certain that God cannot be Simple and Perfect, except this be true: both because He is beyond my knowledge, and because the doctrine of the Trinity assureth us that there is in God a true diversity consisting with Unity, Simplicity and Perfection of Essence." Further down, Baxter repeats: "I must again intreat you, and every ingenious Reader, to fasten no opinion on me, but what I own, at least none which I disclaim. If I must be of one side in this Controversie, I will be of Mr. *Kendals* side, and say, that God hath but one act immanent, and that is Eternal. But my thoughts are, that we know not what we talk of when we speak thus, and therefore I will not be of any side in this" (p. 29).
228. Baxter, *Reduction*, p. 7. Cf. pp. 7-11.
229. Baxter, *Reduction*, p. 20.
230. Baxter, *Reduction*, p. 29.
231. Baxter, *Reduction*, p. 33. Cf. p. 10.
232. Baxter, *Reduction*, p. 33.
233. Baxter, *Reduction*, p. 39. Cf. *Account of my Consideration*, p. 158.
234. Baxter, *Reduction*, pp. 28, 39-40, 49.

the being of God makes him stop short of determining the question of the eternity of God's immanent acts.

God's Will to Justify an Immanent Act de novo

Kendall's attack on Baxter has forced him to defend his position. In no way does Baxter want to deny the simplicity and immutability of God. The debate is not only concerned with the doctrine of God, however. Kendall has a strong tendency to place justification in eternity. He declines to call God's decree by the name of justification. He does, however, say that there is "some what like to justification" in the decree to justify.[235] Indeed, the decree "carries in it a remission of them *tantamount* ..."[236]

There is a point at which Baxter is also willing to grant that justification goes back to eternity. Prior to the dissolution of the obligation there is another element in God's active justification: his secret resolution to justify. Baxter calls it pardon in a "less-proper sense."[237] He carefully distinguishes this resolution from God's decree. Kendall is wrong, says Baxter, in thinking that God's decree *de futuro* is the same as God's resolution to justify.[238] Baxter appears to be distinguishing between God's *decretum iustificationis* and his *propositum iustificationis*.[239] Only the latter must be said to begin in time: "Gods Acts of Approving and Disapproving, esteeming just, and esteeming unjust, are diversified and distinguished; so in the same respects they may and must be said to begin and end according to their objects, without any change in God."[240] The change in the object gives the denomination to God's will now to justify the believer.[241] Even where there is a change in God's resolution to justify, however, this is not really a change in God himself: it is only "applied to God speaking after the manner of men (in which manner we are necessitated to speak of God:) ..."[242] The change in God's immanent acts is denominated from the change in extrinsic objects. Still, although it is a change *denominatione extrinseca*, there is a real basis for this denomination in the things denominated, for "else it were delusory and abusive."[243]

Because Baxter asserts that God's resolution to justify arises *de novo*, Kendall's excursion on the eternity of God's immanent acts now appears to be more than just a side-track: it is an excursion with an intimate connection to Baxter's doctrine of justification. For Baxter, pardon is primarily freedom from the obligation to punishment. This change in man's relation to the law of grace necessitates a corresponding change in God's will to punish. There must be a new immanent act of God, a *propositum iustificationis*, before man can be constituted righteous.

---

235. Kendall, *Vindication* I.iv.137 (emphasis throughout in original).
236. Kendall, *Vindication* I.iv.138 (emphasis inverted).
237. Baxter, *Reduction*, p. 96.
238. Baxter, *Reduction*, p. 96.
239. Baxter, *Confutation*, p. 183; *Confession*, p. 217.
240. Baxter, *Confession*, p. 217.
241. Baxter, *Confutation*, p. 183.
242. Baxter, *Reduction*, p. 96.
243. Baxter, *Reduction*, p. 68. Cf. pp. 25-26.

It is not without reason that Baxter has given the numerous arguments of medieval scholastics in favor of new immanent acts of God's will and understanding. Although he comes with a *non liquet*, he is sympathetic to these arguments because they support his position. They undergird his own view that in justification by faith there is a corresponding new act of God's will to justify. As Baxter testifies:

> <W>e may well say, God willed from Eternity the futurition of the worlds Creation, and Christs Death, &c. But now he doth not will their futurition, but their preterition: and that he Loveth now (as believers in Christ) those whom he before Hated as Workers of Iniquity; and that he is satisfied and well-pleased in his Son, and his Sacrifice, who was not so before... And I am sure that Scripture speaks of God in this language, ascribing to him Immanent acts, as new or as ceasing, and as moved by exteriour causes: Therefore this way of speaking is not unfit or intolerable.[244]

Even if Baxter does not really want to appropriate the arguments of the medieval scholastics, his oft-repeated claim that he does not wish to decide the question of the eternity of God's immanent acts for fear of presumption does ring somewhat hollow in face of the fact that he insists that many of God's immanent acts – of which the resolution to justify is certainly one – do arise *de novo*.[245] Baxter wants to maintain the simplicity of God. This makes him stop short of denying the eternity of some of God's immanent acts. He even says that his sympathies, if anywhere, lie with Kendall. His doctrine of justification, however, leads him into the direction of a denial of the eternity of those immanent acts which concern an external object. The very fact that these immanent acts are said to originate *de novo* and that this has *fundamentum in re* means that there is an irreconcilable tension between Baxter's unwillingness to deny the eternity of any immanent acts and his position that some immanent acts do originate *de novo*.

Justification before Faith: Several Views

JOHN OWEN

Ius ad rem *and* ius in re

It would be misleading to argue that there is one standard Calvinist doctrine of

---

244. Baxter, *Reduction*, pp. 29-30.
245. At the end of his discussion with Kendall on the eternity of God's immanent acts Baxter lists approximately seventy proof texts arguing that "God himself in his Word doth ordinarily speak of his own Acts, which we call Immanent, as Beginning or Ending ..." (*Reduction*, p. 74; cf. pp. 74-77). By way of example, the second text which Baxter mentions is Rom 9:25 ("I will call them my people, which were not my people"). Baxter only adds the comment: "Love is an Immanent act" (p. 74). The conclusion must of course be that God's immanent act of love has a beginning.

justification to which Baxter reacts.[246] Not all of Baxter's opponents held to justification before faith. Furthermore, the ensuing discussion will make clear that
there were also varying shades of opinion among those who did accept this particular position. Despite these differences, however, there are common elements in
the positions that will be outlined below: none of them restricts justification to an
act of God which follows faith. All of the views under discussion place at least
some aspect of justification prior to faith. The result is that justification by faith is
interpreted as the enjoyment of something which was, at least in a sense, already
present prior to faith. For a clearer picture of the type of doctrine which Baxter
opposes in his rejection of the view that justification precedes faith it is necessary
to study the views of Baxter's opponents in more detail.

Baxter's most notable antagonist was John Owen. Much of the controversy
between Baxter and Owen concerns the immediate benefits of the atonement. In
his *Death of Death* (1647) Owen – in line with Pemble and Twisse – objects to the
idea that Christ purchased "not salvation, but a salvability."[247] To maintain the
immediate procurement of the benefits of the covenant, Owen distinguishes between stipulations about the future that are *sub conditione* and those that are *sub
termino*.[248] In the former case, the future event is uncertain; in the latter, it is
certain. Having defined the nature of a condition in such a way as to imply uncertainty, Owen concludes that "it oppugns the whole nature of the Deity, and over-
throws the properties thereof, immediately and directly."[249] Owen does acknowledge that the benefits of Christ's death are not received without some intervention
of time. They are granted *sub termino*. The reason for the delay is that Christ's
death is not a physical cause. If it were a physical cause it would immediately
bring about its effect. Since Christ's death is a moral cause, however, a law or
covenant intervenes between the sacrifice and the enjoyment of the benefits.[250]

The use of the distinction between moral and physical causes enables Owen to
maintain a temporal distance between Christ's procuring the benefits and his
actual granting of them. Owen can now make an analogous temporal distance

246. Iain Murray, for instance, is inaccurate when he states that "with respect to the great doctrines of
      salvation" the theology of the Puritans "was united, cohesive and homogeneous," and that Baxter
      is the "one outstanding exception" ("Richard Baxter-'The Reluctant Puritan'?" in *Advancing in
      Adversity*, Proc. of the Westminster Conference, 1991 [Thornton Heath, Surrey: Westminster
      Conference, (1992)], pp. 7-8).
247. Owen, *Death of Death* (1647), in *Works* 10.207.
248. Owen, *Of the Death of Christ*, in *Works* 10.465.
249. Owen, *Of the Death of Christ*, in *Works* 10.465.
250. Owen, *Of the Death of Christ*, in *Works* 10.459, 472. Owen may seem to contradict himself when
      he speaks of the immediate effects of Christ's death as a moral cause. On the one hand, he states:
      "Moral causes do never immediately actuate their own effects, nor have any immediate influence
      into them" (p. 459). On the other hand, he says: "By the death of Christ we are immediately
      delivered from death with that immediation which is proper to the efficiency of causes which
      produce their effects by the way of moral procurement" (p. 472). What Owen likely means, is that
      Christ's death is not immediate in a temporal sense: its benefits are only enjoyed *sub termino*,
      once the new law or covenant has taken effect and is interposed. Christ's death is immediate in a
      logical sense: the enjoyment of its benefits is not dependent on the uncertain fulfillment of
      another cause, as would be the case if the benefits would be granted *sub conditione*.

between *ius ad rem* and *ius in re*.[251] The former is a right to be enjoyed in due time; the latter means the present possession of that to which one already has a right. A man who has an estate has a *ius in re*. The son, however, will enjoy this estate only upon his father's death, though he has a present *ius ad rem*.[252] Owen maintains that Christ's death has procured an *ipso facto* delivery from the curse.[253] This delivery gives the elect a right to justification or *ius ad rem*.

Justification As Terminating in Conscience

It is only a small step from the assertion that Christ has procured an *ipso facto* delivery from the curse to the statement that justification by faith is only the process of becoming conscious of one's justification. It has been stated in Owen's defense that he categorically denies adhering either to justification from eternity or to a justification which is only *in foro conscientiae*.[254] To some extent, such a defense is justified. Owen explicitly disavows justification from eternity and also argues that justification is not only in conscience.[255] While full justice must be done to Owen on this point, it cannot be denied that there is, at the very least, some tension in his thinking. As Gavin McGrath suggests:

> There was, however, a modicum of contradiction in Owen's thought: on one hand, he insisted that the death of Christ merited *ipso facto* the justification of the elect, his death was a cause independent from the faith of the believer; on the other hand, Owen stressed the necessity of faith and repentance, for in the truest sense a person was not justified before personal faith.[256]

The tension in Owen's thought can be put in even sharper terms. Owen not only suggests that *Christ's death* merited justification *ipso facto*, but he goes as far as to suggest that the *elect* thereby acquired a right to justification.

What is more, while Owen does not hold that justification was *in foro conscientiae* alone, this is definitely an essential part of justification. Owen suggests rhetorically "whether absolution from the guilt of sin and obligation unto death, though not as terminated in the conscience for complete justification, do not

---

251. Owen, *Of the Death of Christ*, in *Works* 10.466, 476. Cf. p. 478; *Vindiciæ Evangelicæ*, in *Works* 12.607, 610.

252. Owen, *Of the Death of Christ*, in *Works* 10.466.

253. Owen, *Death of Death*, in *Works* 10.268; *Of the Death of Christ*, in *Works* 10.474-75. J.I. Packer's description of the Calvinist view on redemption may serve as an description of Owen's insight: "Christ did not win a hypothetical salvation for hypothetical believers, a mere possibility of salvation for any who might possibly believe, but a real salvation for his own chosen people. His precious blood really does 'save us all'; the intended effects of his self-offering do in fact follow, just because the cross was what it was. Its saving power does not depend on faith being added to it; its saving power is such that faith flows from it. The cross secured the full salvation of all for whom Christ died" ("'Saved by His Precious Blood'," pp. 133-34). To regard this viewpoint as the general Calvinist stand seems to me an overstatement since it does not do justice to the variety of opinion within Calvinist thought.

254. Allison, *Rise of Moralism*, p. 174; Wallace, "Life and Thought of John Owen," pp. 283-85; Wallace, *Puritans and Predestination*, p. 146; Daniel, "Hyper-Calvinism and John Gill," p. 319.

255. Owen, *Death of Death*, in *Works* 10.276-77; *Vindiciæ Evangelicæ*, in *Works* 12.592, 596, 601-04.

256. McGrath, "Puritans and the Human Will," p. 264.

precede our actual believing ..."[257] Thus, justification is a process. It begins prior to faith and is terminated or completed in the conscience.[258] Owen thinks that this absolution prior to faith may be the justification of the ungodly (Rom 4:5).[259]

Owen bases the *ius ad rem* not only on Christ's purchase, but ultimately on the covenant of redemption between God and Christ.[260] Baxter is correct in stating, in Owen's own words:

> One learned man <*i.e.*, Owen> saith, that, Absolution in heaven, and Justification differ as part and whole; and that Justification is terminated in conscience; and so makes a longer work of Justification, then they that say it is *simul & semel*; or, then I whom Mr. *Cr*<andon> blames for it ...[261]

For Owen, justification begins with the *pactum salutis* between God and Christ and with Christ's atoning sacrifice. Baxter is therefore correct in suggesting that justification from eternity is not far removed from Owen's thinking. The *ius ad rem* is procured for the elect on the twofold basis of the covenant of redemption and Christ's death. This right to justification is a benefit which follows immediately upon the sacrifice.

Justification and Union with Christ

Owen appears to base the *ius ad rem* on the covenant of redemption and the atonement. Elsewhere, however, he links the *ius ad rem* to union with Christ. As C.F. Allison observes:

> A sinner in justification becomes truly righteous as he becomes a member of Christ whose righteousness is thereupon imputed to him in such union. A justified person is truly righteous, then, because he is *in Christ*. Owen places more explicit emphasis on this union with Christ than even Downame does, and perhaps more than anyone of the period with the exception of John Donne.[262]

---

257. Owen, *Of the Death of Christ*, in *Works* 10.470.
258. Owen states explicitly: "Neither yet do I hence assert complete <!> justification to be before believing. Absolution in heaven, and justification, differ as part and whole" (*Of the Death of Christ*, in *Works* 10. 470).
259. Owen, *Of the Death of Christ*, in *Works* 10.470.
260. Owen, *Of the Death of Christ*, in *Works* 10.477. Bass draws attention to the important place of the *pactum salutis* as the basis of Owen's soteriology ("Theology of John Owen," pp. 38-39; Bass, "Platonic Influences," pp. 106-09). Bass suggests that Owen's idea of a covenant of redemption between the Father and the Son stems from his reading of Platonic literature: "His thinking of the covenant was tempered more by the vertical ladder of ascent and descent than in a horizontal development of the covenants of Jehovah who was progressively revealing himself through the course of an eschatological history" (p. 109). Bass correctly draws attention to the importance of the covenant of redemption for Owen's theology. He provides no proof, however, for his assertion that Platonic influences lie at the basis of this concept in Owen.
261. Baxter, *Confession*, pp. 190-91. Baxter gives here a direct quotation of Owen (cf. above, n. 258). Cf. *Confession*, p. 218.
262. Allison, *Rise of Moralism*, p. 175. Union with Christ is a central theme in Owen's theology. Cf. Owen, *Discourse concerning the Holy Spirit* (1674), in *Works* 3.463-67, 478, 516-18; 4.383-86; *Of the Death of Christ*, in *Works* 10.468-71; *Doctrine of the Saints Perseverance* (1654), in *Works* 11.336-41; *Duty of Pastors and People Distinguished* (1644), in *Works* 13.22-22; R.W. De Koey-

Owen is of the opinion that a person is truly righteous in Christ. Strictly speaking, therefore, it is no longer forensic righteousness. The question must be raised whether such a concept of mystical union is compatible with the idea that payment is not made by the debtor but by Christ.[263] Does Owen's concept of mystical union still allow for such a differentiation between the person of Christ and the person united to him? Owen makes some strong statements regarding man's right to justification: "Where merit intercedes, the effect is reckoned as of debt; that which is my due debt I have right unto... They, then, who are under merit have also a right unto that whereof it is the merit."[264] Owen bases this right on the union with Christ. He states that Christ is "their <i.e., those "under merit"> surety, doing that whereby he merited only on their behalf, yea, in their stead, they dying with him ..."[265]

On the one hand, Owen insists that it is the covenant of redemption and the death of Christ which give the *ius ad rem*. On the other hand, he also argues that union with Christ gives the *ius ad rem*. These two positions are incompatible.[266] It is not difficult to see why Owen comes to this confused position. It originates from a combination of two irreconcilable thought patterns. He wants to do justice both to the immediacy, the absolute character, of Christ's benefits – which demands a *ius ad rem* at the time of Christ's sacrificial death – and to the fact that "<n>o blessing can be given us for Christ's sake, unless, in order of nature, Christ be first reckoned unto us."[267] When, on one occasion, Owen links up the *ius ad rem* with the *pactum salutis* and the atonement, and, on another occasion, with union with Christ, this illustrates that he has ultimately not succeeded in separating the *ius ad rem* from the *ius in re*. Having isolated the *ius ad rem* he is uncertain as to its proper position in the process of justification.

---

er, "Pneumatologia: Een onderzoek naar de leer van de Heilige Geest bij de puritein John Owen (1616-1683)," Doctoraalscriptie Rijksuniversiteit Utrecht 1990, pp. 66-67; R.W. De Koeyer, "'Pneumatologia': Enkele aspecten van de leer van de Heilige Geest bij de puritein John Owen (1616-1683)," *ThRef*, 34 (1991), 244; Ferguson, *John Owen on the Christian Life*, pp. 32-36; B. Loonstra, *Verkiezing – verzoening – verbond: Beschrijving en beoordeling van de leer van het pactum salutis in de gereformeerde theologie*, Diss. Utrecht 1990 (The Hague: Boekencentrum, 1990), p. 106; Wallace, *Puritans and Predestination*, pp. 154-55. For a discussion of Owen's views on union with Christ in the context of communion with Christ, see Jonathan Jong-Chun Won, "Communion with Christ: An Exposition and Comparison of the Doctrine of Union and Communion with Christ in Calvin and the English Puritans," Diss. Westminster Theological Seminary 1989, pp. 258-91.

263. Baxter is fearful that a high Calvinist view of imputation leads to the idea that we merit our own justification (cf. below, pp. 236-37).

264. Owen, *Of the Death of Christ*, in *Works* 10.468.

265. Owen, *Of the Death of Christ*, in *Works* 10.468. Cf. *Duty of Pastors and People Distinguished*, in *Works* 13.23.

266. Owen clearly sees the atonement and union with Christ as temporally separate. Union with Christ takes place when the Holy Spirit is first given in regeneration (*Discourse concerning the Holy Spirit*, in *Works* 3.464, 478, 516-17; *Doctrine of the Saints Perseverance*, in *Works* 11.337). Cf. Baxter's comment: "If we are Absolved, Pardoned, Justified, and have Right to heaven from eternity, or before Faith, then we have all these before we are in Christ, or joyned or united to Christ, or are made his members. But the Consequent is false: therefore so is the Antecedent" (*Confession*, p. 283).

267. Owen, *Of the Death of Christ*, in *Works* 10.469. Christ had obtained a right for Peter, though he only received Christ and faith when "the term was expired" (pp. 469-70).

Owen maintains that it is the "ungodly" who are united to Christ.[268] The ungodly are united to Christ prior to faith. It is true, Owen admits that "Christ is ours before and after believing in a different sense."[269] But what exactly is lacking prior to faith? It is God's act of pardoning mercy which is to be "completed in the conscience." It is the "heart's persuasion" regarding God's promise. It is "the soul's rolling itself upon Christ."[270] These are all descriptions of assurance of faith. It seems that only assurance is lacking before faith. This implies a far-reaching identification of faith and assurance.[271] Once faith, or assurance, has been given justification is complete. Owen maintains that the elect do have union with Christ before faith, even though justification is not yet complete at this time. The following process of justification emerges from Owen's argument:

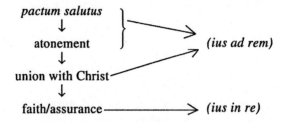

Justification is based on the *pactum salutis* and the purchase of Christ. Because these give the actual right to justification, they must be included in the process of justification. Following Christ's atoning death comes union with Christ, which precedes faith. The right to justification is also connected to this union with Christ. Finally, justification is terminated or completed in the conscience, when one attains assurance of faith.

GEORGE KENDALL

Justification More Than an Immanent Act

John Owen is not alone in disclaiming the theory of justification from eternity. George Kendall, although he is somewhat less unequivocal, also says that God's decree to justify "cannot be called Justification ..."[272] Kendall does say, however,

268. Owen, *Of the Death of Christ,* in *Works* 10.470.
269. Owen, *Of the Death of Christ,* in *Works* 10.470.
270. Owen, *Of the Death of Christ,* in *Works* 10.470.
271. This view is supported by Beeke's careful analysis of Owen's views on assurance. (Joel R. Beeke, "Personal Assurance of Faith: English Puritanism and the Dutch 'Nadere Reformatie:' From Westminster to Alexander Comrie (1640-1760)," Diss. Westminster Theological Seminary 1988, pp. 177-263; and in Joel R. Beeke, *Assurance of Faith: Calvin, English Puritanism, and the Dutch Second Reformation,* American University Studies: Theology and Religion, 89 [New York: Lang, 1991], pp. 213-80. Beeke's 1991 publication is a revised form of his earlier dissertation.) Beeke argues that in an earlier stage Owen held that "assurance is part and parcel of faith" (*Assurance of Faith,* pp. 213-14). The shift away from this close identification of faith and assurance is noted first in Owen's *Doctrine of the Saints' Perseverance* (1654; *Assurance of Faith,* p. 219).
272. Kendall, *Vindication* I.iv.139 (emphasis throughout in original).

that "there is some what like to justification in the eternal decree of God to justifie men."[273] God's decree to remit sins is a remission "tantamount."[274]

The question is, of course, what Kendall means with such statements. He gives some insight in this when he presents a definition of justification:

> *Justification* is by the consent of all men, (I mean Protestants,) a *remission of our sins*, and *accepting of us as righteous*: Now this is either *a meere immanent*, or a *meer transient act*, or *both*. I know no man will say it is a *meer transient* act; there being no *transient act* of God which doth not suppose an *immanent* one, for that *he acts nothing* upon the *creature* but what he *first purposed* in *himself* to *act*; so then an *immanent act* there must be confest, if there be a *transient one* ...[275]

Remission and accepting as righteous cannot be just a transient act. The reason, maintains Kendall, is that there is always an immanent decree lying behind a transient act. The reason why God's transient act in time is not justification all by itself is simply that this act of God presupposes the decree or purpose to justify.

That the immanent act as such does not justify alone is clear, says Kendall, from the fact that an immanent act cannot make a moral or legal change. Such a legal change is necessary in justification, because justification "is on all hands confessed to be *pronouncing* or *declaring of us righteous*."[276] Kendall almost seems to say that the actual pronouncing one righteous is a transient act of God, not an immanent act. When this is coupled with the assertion that God's decree to justify is not justification itself, it would seem that for Kendall justification *in foro Dei* follows faith in the order of salvation.

The Moment of Justification in foro divino

Before jumping to conclusions, however, it is necessary to analyze what Kendall means when he speaks of justification "tantamount." Because of God's decree there is no danger of condemnation for the elect. God no longer presses any charges. Says Kendall:

> <F>or who *shall charge them* <i.e., our sins> *on us, where God decrees to remit them? the conscience* I confess may, so may the *devil* joyning with our *conscience*; but all this while their charge is of no great *danger* to us when God hath *decreed to remit them to us*, and though they may *trouble* us, they cannot *damne* us ...[277]

Following the decree to justify there may be accusations from our conscience, but not from God. Consequently, when Kendall speaks of God's transient act in justification he says that it "signifieth onely a *testimony given by God*, whereby he makes us *know* that we are *justified before God* ..."[278] The only thing which the transient act does, is "prove" God's acceptance, "evidence" his acceptance to us.

---

273. Kendall, *Vindication* I.iv.137-38 (emphasis throughout in original).
274. Kendall, *Vindication* I.iv.138.
275. Kendall, *Vindication* I.iv.138.
276. Kendall, *Vindication* I.iv.139.
277. Kendall, *Vindication* I.iv.138-39.
278. Kendall, *Vindication* I.iv.138.

It is remarkable that Kendall does not distinguish between justification *in foro divino* and *in foro conscientiae* in the sense that the former precedes faith, while the latter follows it. He rejects this easy division because it implies that justification in God's sight is complete prior to faith. Instead, he almost identifies the two when he says that "we are said to be *justified in his sight* when he makes it as it were evident to our *sight*, that we are *justified ...*"[279] It seems, then, that the process of justification begins with God's decree to justify and that it is completed when we become aware of our justification. Only at this point is it possible to say that we are justified in God's sight.

Kendall's thought pattern is similar to that of Owen. In Owen, justification is a process beginning with the covenant between the Father and the Son and terminating in conscience. But there are also some differences between Owen and Kendall. Owen refers to the covenant between the Father and the Son and to Christ's sacrifice as the beginning of the process of justification. Kendall only speaks of God's decree or immanent act. This means the loss of the strong christological element found in Owen. There is also a difference in emphasis: Kendall lacks Owen's clear denial that he teaches justification from eternity. To Kendall, God's decree "hath *much* in it *like* to *justification ...*"[280] Owen simply says that justification is "terminated in conscience." Kendall is far more descriptive with regard to this completion of the process of justification: he speaks of proof, evidence, and testimony whereby God makes known that we are justified in his sight. Still, these differences remain matters of emphasis. There is little material difference between Owen and Kendall in their respective outlines of the nature of justification.

Owen and Kendall allow more room for justification by faith in time than Twisse and Pemble. For the latter two authors justification *in foro divino* was completed either in God's immanent act or by Christ's sacrifice. Anything happening by faith was no longer justification in God's sight. Owen and Kendall do not go quite as far. They consider justification as a process starting in God's decree and terminating in conscience. On the other hand, neither Pemble, nor Twisse went as far as to identify faith and assurance. Owen did take this step. Regardless of these differences, however, it is questionable whether the end result is much different: faith can no longer play a central role in justification in God's sight.

Lewis Du Moulin

Twofold Reconciliation

The key to Lewis Du Moulin's view of justification is his distinction of a twofold reconciliation:

---

279. Kendall, *Vindication* I.iv.138.
280. Kendall, *Vindication* I.iv.138.

The first, by which God is reconciled to us: The second, by which we are reconciled to God. Of the first Reconciliation, *Paul* speaks, when he saith, that we were reconciled when we were enemies, *Rom. 5.10. Col. 1.21. 2 Cor. 5.18,19*. but of the second he speaketh in the next verse, *We beseech you, that ye will be reconciled to God;* which is done when we apprehend the first Reconciliation, and know God Benevolent to us. By and for Christs obedience God is reconciled to us, but by Faith are we reconciled to God.[281]

By distinguishing a *duplex reconciliatio* Du Moulin is able to maintain what he considers to be the full meaning of Romans 4:5: God justifies the ungodly "as ungodly."[282]

Du Moulin speaks of the first reconciliation – by which God is reconciled to us – in three different ways. First, with an appeal to Twisse, he argues that justification is an internal act of God which cannot be renewed.[283] It is done in an instant: "IUstification is an immanent act of God, done in an instant, which puts nothing in the Justified, though in the adult it necessarily createth Faith, as Faith doth Good Works: For Remission of sins is an effect of Christs death, as Faith is of Remission of sin."[284] This act of justification is simply *nolle punire*. The result is that the punishment itself is taken away: *punitionis negatio*.[285] It seems, however, that Du Moulin is hesitant to place justification in the mere will of God without any consideration of Christ's death. When he speaks of justification as an immanent act he adds that remission is an effect of Christ's death.[286] Similarly, with regard to the first reconciliation, Du Moulin comments that "Christs righteousness *was ours*, both in the intention and purpose of God, and in the performance of the Mediator ..."[287] Du Moulin seems reluctant to separate God's will not to punish from Christ's sacrifice. Still, God's *nolle punire* remains his act of justification.

---

281. Lewis Du Moulin, in Baxter, *Confutation*, p. 271 (emphasis inverted; "Prima, qua Deus reconciliatur nobis, Secunda, qua nos reconciliamur Deo. De prima reconciliatione loquitur *Paulus*, cum dicit nos fuisse reconciliatos cum essemus inimici, *Rom. 5.v.10. Coloss.1.v.21. & 2 Cor. 5.v.18,19.* at de secunda agit versu proximo, *rogamus vos ut velitis reconciliari Deo:* quod fit cum primam reconciliationem apprehendimus, & novimus nobis benevolum Deum: per & propter Christi obedientiam Deus reconciliatur nobis, at per fidem reconciliamur Deo" [*De fidei partibus*, pp. 66-67].).

282. Lewis Du Moulin, in Baxter, *Confutation*, p. 266 (emphasis throughout in original; "quà impium" [*De fidei partibus*, p. 64]).

283. Lewis Du Moulin, *De fidei partibus*, pp. 53-54 (in Baxter, *Confutation*, p. 248).

284. Lewis Du Moulin, in Baxter, *Confutation*, p. 249 (emphasis throughout in original; "Justificatio actio Dei est immanens, in instanti facta, quæ nihil in Justificato ponit; quanqnam <sic> in adultis, necessariò creet fidem, ut fides bona opera; nam remissio peccatorum est effectio mortis Christi, ut fides remissionis peccatorum ..." [*De fidei partibus*, pp. 55-56].).

285. Says Du Moulin: "I Said it is an immanent Action: For Remission of sin, if you respect the quiddity, is nothing else then a Negation of punishment: So therefore to remit sin, is nothing else but to Nill to Punish: which act was immanent in God, and followeth not Faith ... ." (In Baxter, *Confutation*, pp. 250-51 [emphasis inverted]; "Dixi esse actionem immanentem: nam remissio peccatorum, si quidd
itatem respicias, nihil aliud est quam punitionis negatio; aut volitionis puniendi negatio. Sic ergo, peccata remittere, nihil aliud est quam nolle punire; qui actus in Deo immanens fuit, nec fidem consequitur ..." [*De fidei partibus*, p. 56].)

286. Lewis Du Moulin, *De fidei partibus*, p. 56 (in Baxter, *Confutation*, p. 249).

287. Lewis Du Moulin, in Baxter, *Confutation*, p. 277; (emphasis inverted; "Justitia Christi, tum intentione & proposito Dei, tum in præstatione Christi Mediatoris nostra fuit ..." [*De fidei partibus*, p. 69].).

Christ's sacrificial death is the second aspect which Du Moulin mentions in connection with God's being reconciled to us. Remission is the effect of the imputation of Christ's righteousness and must, therefore, be seen as distinct from it.[288] This reconciliation with God takes place at Christ's death, so that justification is *simul et semel*.[289] It is caused *uno acto*, by the one sacrifice of Christ on the cross.[290] Against the Arminian scheme of thought, Du Moulin insists that Christ died not just to impetrate remission, but actually to remit the sins of the elect:

> WE must needs admit Remission of sins before faith: nor with a keener sword do we cut the throat of the Arminians, asserting both Reconcilableness and not Reconciliation by Christs death, and potential Remission in Christs death, and not Actual. For Christ dyed not to make Remission of sins possible; nor only to impetrate Remission, but actually to remit the sins of the elect, and confer Remission of sins: Did not our Lord Jesus when he dyed, at least satisfie for all the elect, paying a full price for the sins of all the elect? Did he only obtain in his death, that the elect shall attain remission of sins when they should believe hereafter in Christ?[291]

The second element of God's reconciliation to us has a distinct anti-Arminian scope. Christ's death did not just make remission possible but obtained remission. What is more, Christ did not procure this remission *sub tempore*, as Owen was willing to grant, but the sacrifice results in the immediate remission of the sins of the elect.

A third moment at which God may be said to be reconciled to us is when he first gave the promise of the Messiah: "Christ was Mediator, as soon as he was promised to be Mediator."[292] Du Moulin is thinking here of the promise of Gene-

---

288. Lewis Du Moulin, *De fidei partibus*, pp. 39-45 (in Baxter, *Confutation*, pp. 232-34).
289. Says Du Moulin: "THe words of St. *Paul* are plain: Col. *1.20. It pleased the Father to reconcile all things to himself, both things in Earth, and things in Heaven, having made Peace by the blood of his Cross.* Then are the Elect Iustified together and at once, when Reconciled: and then Reconciled when he made peace by the blood of the Cross." (In Baxter, *Confutation*, p. 237 [emphasis inverted; cf. pp. 239, 259]; "Verba Sancti Pauli diserta sunt, *Coloss.* 1.*v.*20. *Placuit patri sibi reconciliare omnia, tam quæ sunt in terra, quam quæ sunt in cælo, facta pace per sanguinem crucis:* tum demum electi justificati sunt simul & semel cum reconciliati, & tum reconciliati cum fecit pacem per sanguinem crucis ..." [*De fidei partibus*, pp. 46-47; cf. p. 59].) Du Moulin repeatedly uses the phrase *simul et semel* in these pages.
290. Says Du Moulin: "<F>or as the sin of *Adam* doth by one act involve posterity in the same guilt, so the Righteousness of Christ hath by one act Justified the sinners, for whom he dyed." (In Baxter, *Confutation*, p. 243 [emphasis inverted; cf. pp. 244-45]; "<E>tenim ut peccatum Adami uno actu posteros eodem reatu involvit; sic Justitia Christi uno actu Justificavit peccatores pro quibus mortuus est ..." [*De fidei partibus*, p. 49; cf. p. 50].)
291. Lewis Du Moulin, in Baxter, *Confutation*, p. 260 (cf. p. 236; "Omnino admittenda remissio peccatorum ante fidem: nec acutiori gladio jugulamus Arminianos asserentes, tum reconciliabilitatem non reconciliationem per Christi mortem; tum potentialem remissionem in morte Christi, non verò actualem: nec enim Christus mortuus est ut remissionem peccatorum possibilem faceret; nec tantum ut impetraret remissionem, sed ut actu remitteret electorum peccata, & conferret remissionem peccatorum: an non saltem cum mortuus Dominus noster Jesus, satisfecit ille pro omnibus electis; pretium plenarium persolvens pro omnium Electorum peccatis? an tantum impetravit in morte, ut remissionem peccatorum adipiscerentur electi cum postmodum credituri erant in Christum?" [*De fidei partibus*, pp. 59-60; cf. p. 46]).
292. Lewis Du Moulin, in *Confutation*, p. 249 (emphasis throughout in original; cf. pp. 236, 308; "Simul ac Christus promissus est in mediatorem, erat Mediator" [*De fidei partibus*, p. 55; cf. pp. 46, 105-06].).

sis 3:15. The reconciling effect of Christ's mediation precedes his sacrificial death. Here Du Moulin – as well as William Eyre – possibly took his cue from the Polish high Calvinist at the University of Franeker, Johannes Maccovius (1588-1644).[293]

Du Moulin does not indicate how these three aspects of God's reconciliation to us are related. At different points in his discussion he simply mentions the various aspects of God's reconciliation to his elect. It is not clear how he wants to overcome the tension which the juxtaposition of the three varying elements introduces into his position.

Faith Not Part of the Definition of Justification

Although Du Moulin does not indicate how the various elements of God's reconciliation to us must be connected, he leaves no doubt as to what he feels the relation is between the first and the second kind of reconciliation. The second, by which we are reconciled to God, is only the "patefaction" of the Judge's sentence to our conscience.[294] Du Moulin states that "faith is only the Manifestation and patefaction, that we are the sons of God, that we are elect, and shall obtain salvation."[295] Echoing Twisse, Du Moulin insists that "God hath set up a tribunal in our Consciences ..."[296] In this court of conscience, condemnation, remission, justification, and absolution take place after a sort (*quodammodo*).[297] This declaration or pronouncement of absolution makes known to the elect that their sins are forgiven. Du Moulin follows Twisse in his use of the verbs *innotescere* and *dignoscere*.[298] By faith the elect simply come to know or discern something which was, in fact, already a reality.

The devaluation of faith is the logical outcome of Du Moulin's thinking. When Scripture states that Abraham was justified by faith, the word "faith" must be taken for the object of faith, which is Christ.[299] Du Moulin here takes an avenue

---

293. On this very point, William Eyre appeals to Maccovius (*Vindiciæ Justificationis Gratuitæ*, pp. 24, 69). In his *Collegia theologica*, Maccovius discusses two viewpoints regarding the moment of justification: "Theologians disagree about the precise temporal circumstances. Some say that we were justified from eternity; others, only at the time at which Christ was promised to us as Mediator, Gen 3:15." ("Circa definitam circumstantiam Temporis discrepant Theologi; aliqui dicunt, nos justificatos esse ab æterno; alii hoc ipso demum tempore, quo nobis Christus promissus est in Mediatorem, Genes. 3.15" [*Collegia theologica* (Franeker, 1641), p. 129].) Maccovius excludes the former opinion because Christ, the sole author of justification, was not Mediator from eternity. Maccovius concludes: "God imputed to Christ the sins of all the elect who were, are, and shall be, as soon as he promised him to us as Mediator ... ." ("Imputavit Deus Christo omnium electorum peccata, qui erant, sunt, & futuri, simul ac eum nobis in Mediatorē promisit ..." [p. 131].) For Maccovius, see A. Kuyper, *Johannes Maccovius*, Diss. Amsterdam 1899 (Leiden: Donner, 1899); *BLGNP* 2.311-13; Bell, "Propter potestatem, scientiam, ac beneplacitum Dei."

294. Lewis Du Moulin, *De fidei partibus*, p. 10 (in Baxter, *Confutation*, p. 190).

295. Lewis Du Moulin, in Baxter, *Confutation*, p. 195 (emphasis throughout in original; "fides sit tantum manifestatio, & patefactio, nos filios Dei esse, electos esse, & salutem consecuturos ..." [*De fidei partibus*, p. 14].).

296. Lewis Du Moulin, in Baxter, *Confutation*, p. 277 (emphasis throughout in original; "constituit enim Deus in conscientiis nostris tribunal ..." [*De fidei partibus*, p. 70].).

297. Lewis Du Moulin, *De fidei partibus*, p. 70 (in Baxter, *Confutation*, p. 277).

298. Lewis Du Moulin, *De fidei partibus*, pp. 70-71 (in Baxter, *Confutation*, p. 277).

299. Lewis Du Moulin, *De fidei partibus*, pp. 8-9 (in Baxter, *Confutation*, p. 188).

which Twisse had contemplated before. Du Moulin explicitly rejects the idea that faith has a place in the definition of justification. He vehemently opposes his brother, Cyrus: "BUt it is the greatest Paralogism of the Author of the Epistle, to infer that Justification cannot be defined, but Faith must be concluded in it ..."[300] The reason why faith must not be included in the definition of justification is that it would create a confusion between justification and sanctification.[301] This is, in Du Moulin's view, the chief cause of the errors into which the moderate Calvinists have fallen:

> BUt the chief Cause of the Error is, that they make the faith which they call Justifying to be something different from Regeneration; when yet the faith of the elect is not only conjunct with Holiness in one and the same subject, but is formally our Holiness ... For seeing faith hope and charity are Inseparable, and Iustification goes before good works, it follows that Iustification must go before faith.[302]

Because Du Moulin regards faith as part of sanctification he refuses to place it before justification. It would mean a return to justification by works. Faith is not an instrument of union with Christ, but must follow this union. All graces, including faith, flow from union with Christ.[303] Where any of these graces are seen as preceding this union one falls into the trap of justification by works.

WILLIAM EYRE

Giving and Receiving of Remission

William Eyre, whose *Vindiciæ Justificationis Gratuitæ* (1654) is preceded by an epistle to the reader from John Owen, leaves behind the moderation which may perhaps be found in Owen and Kendall. Appealing to Pemble, Twisse, Rutherford, Calvin, Zanchi, Alsted, Maccovius, and Walker, Eyre insists against Baxter and Benjamin Woodbridge (1622-84) that "many Godly Learned Men have asserted the Justification of Gods Elect, *in foro Dei*, before Faith, who were never account-

---

300. Lewis Du Moulin, in Baxter, *Confutation*, p. 283 (emphasis throughout in original; "Sed maximus est paralogismus Authoris Epistolæ, ex eo quod actus Christi remittentis peccata, & fidei apprehendentis remissionem peccatorum simul fiant (si tamen fiant) inferentis Justificationem non posse definiri quin eâ fides concludatur" [*De fidei partibus*, p. 76].).
301. Lewis Du Moulin, *De fidei partibus*, pp. 76-77 (in Baxter, *Confutation*, p. 283).
302. Lewis Du Moulin, in Baxter, *Confutation*, p. 199 (emphasis inverted; cf. p. 259; "Sed præcipua causa erroris est, quod fidem quam vocant justificantem, diversum quid esse statuant a regeneratione, cum tamen fides electorum, non tantum conjuncta sit cum sanctitate in uno eodemq; subjecto, sed formaliter sit sanctitas nostra ... . <C>um enim fides spes & charitas sint inseparabiles, & Justificatio præcedat bona opera, Consequens est ut & Justificatio præcedat fidem" [*De fidei partibus*, pp. 16-17; cf. p. 59].).
303. Lewis Du Moulin, *De fidei partibus*, pp. 57-59 (in Baxter, *Confutation*, pp. 253, 259). In his response on this point, Baxter says: "I utterly deny that Union goes before Faith" (*Confutation*, p. 254). He then describes seven types of union. The most significant is the first, a "Relative Union, he being our Head, Husband, King, and we being his incorporate Members, his Spouse and Subjects: and so both make one Mystical person, that is, one Corporation, Family, Commonwealth" (p. 254).

ed *Antinomians*."[304] What is more, "all our old Protestant Divines have defined Justifying Faith to be a certain perswasion, and full assurance of the pardon of our sins; from whence it must inevitably follow, That pardon of sin precedes our Faith, for every object is before its act."[305]

For Eyre, faith does not properly justify. He makes a distinction which is similar to Du Moulin's distinction between first and second reconciliation:

> The *giving* of remission, and the *receiving* of remission, are two things; the former is Gods act, who is the onely Justifier, the latter is ours; the former is properly Justification, and not the latter; though it be called so in a passive and improper sence. We know a Prince pardons a malefactor when he gives his consent, That the Sentence of the Law should be reversed, and confirms it with his Hand and Seal: This Pardon is valid in Law, and secures the offender from punishment, though it come not to his hands for a good while after.[306]

The giving of remission, as such, secures the offender from punishment. Thus, Eyre expresses his disagreement with Kendall's statement that we are justified in God's sight when he makes it evident to our sight that we are justified. Eyre comments that "with due respect for that learned man (whom I highly honor for his worthy Labors)" he must dissent from Kendall. The terms *in foro Dei* and *in foro conscientiae* are not "equipollent and controvertible."[307] Kendall's judgement does not go quite far enough, to Eyre's mind. Justification in God's sight and in conscience must be separated. Justification *in foro Dei* may either be referred to the justice or to the understanding of God. When it refers to God's justice, we were justified "when Christ exhibited, and God accepted the full satisfaction in his Blood, for all our sins ..."[308] When it concerns the knowledge of God, we were justified in God's sight "when he willed or determined in himself, not to impute to us our sins ..."[309] The latter is from eternity. Although Eyre says he has "been sparing of calling this immanent act of God, by the name of Justification," he appeals to Twisse and says there is "very much reason" to define justification as *nolle punire*.[310] This decision of God was the outcome of the covenant between the Father and the Son.[311]

---

304. Eyre, *Vindiciæ Justificationis Gratuitæ*, p. 21.
305. Eyre, *Vindiciæ Justificationis Gratuitæ*, p. 33.
306. Eyre, *Vindiciæ Justificationis Gratuitæ*, p. 45.
307. Eyre, *Vindiciæ Justificationis Gratuitæ*, p. 61.
308. Eyre, *Vindiciæ Justificationis Gratuitæ*, p. 61.
309. Eyre, *Vindiciæ Justificationis Gratuitæ*, p. 62.
310. Eyre, *Vindiciæ Justificationis Gratuitæ*, p. 63.
311. Eyre, *Vindiciæ Justificationis Gratuitæ*, p. 64. In a separate chapter on the *pactum salutis* and the immediate effects of Christ's death, Eyre presents fourteen arguments, as well as some texts from Scripture, to prove that Christ's death immediately caused the reconciliation of the elect. The basis for this proposition lies in the covenant between God and Christ. This covenant does not allow that any conditions be interposed between Christ's death and God's reconciliation to the elect (pp. 138-46). Here, Eyre seems to give an efficacy to Christ's death which he elsewhere attributes to God's will itself.

The Manifestation of Grace and the Role of Faith

Nevertheless, God may also be said to justify men "when he reveals, and makes known to them his Grace and Kindneses within himself."[312] Eyre subdivides this "manifestation" of God's mercy and forgiveness as follows:[313] (1) First, God manifests his grace more generally, to all the elect. He does this both in his Word and in his works. In his Word, God has declared "his immutable Will, not to impute sin to his people."[314] Eyre refers here especially to the promise of Genesis 3:15. Also in his works, God has declared his sentence of pardon. He did this when he "transacted the whole debt" on Christ and also when he gave Christ his public discharge at his resurrection. This "was a solemn judicial act, whereby God the Supream Judge justified both him and us ..."[315] The elect were actually justified in Christ's justification. (2) God also manifests his grace more particularly, to individual persons. He does this externally, *in foro ecclesiae*, through baptism; as well as internally, *in foro conscientiae*, at their effectual vocation; and publicly, *in foro mundi*, on the last day.

It is the internal justification *in foro conscientiae* which Scripture means with justification by faith. Hereby "the Sentence of Forgiveness is terminated in their Consciences ..."[316] This phrase is nearly identical to Owen's statement that justification is terminated in conscience. Indeed, Eyre does not mean to distinguish a number of different justifications: "Declared Justification (whether it be *in foro Ecclesiæ*, *in foro Conscientiæ*, or *in foro mundi*) is not another, from that in the minde of God, but the same variously revealed ..."[317] Therefore, although Eyre follows Owen in speaking of justification as terminated in conscience, he does not really want to speak of a process of justification extending from the *pactum salutis* (or God's decree) to the public declaration of pardon on the day of judgement. There is but one justification, "which is perfect and compleat at once, being his fixed, and immutable will, not to deal with them according to their sins, but as Just and Righteous persons."[318] Just as Du Moulin considers justification complete in the first reconciliation, so Eyre feels that justification is complete in the giving of remission. Whereas for Owen and Kendall the termination in conscience is included in justification itself, Eyre regards it merely as the declaration of the instantaneous justification in God's mind.

The result is that Eyre, perhaps even more so than Owen, categorically rejects the notion that the covenant of grace is conditional.[319] Eyre's entire treatise fulminates against the notion of a conditional covenant. Justification is complete in

---

312. Eyre, *Vindiciæ Justificationis Gratuitæ*, p. 69.
313. Eyre, *Vindiciæ Justificationis Gratuitæ*, pp. 69-74.
314. Eyre, *Vindiciæ Justificationis Gratuitæ*, p. 69.
315. Eyre, *Vindiciæ Justificationis Gratuitæ*, p. 71.
316. Eyre, *Vindiciæ Justificationis Gratuitæ*, p. 73.
317. Eyre, *Vindiciæ Justificationis Gratuitæ*, p. 74.
318. Eyre, *Vindiciæ Justificationis Gratuitæ*, p. 74.
319. Cf. David C. Lachman, *The Marrow Controversy 1718-1723: An Historical and Theological Analysis*, Rutherford Studies in Historical Theology (Edinburgh: Rutherford House, 1988), pp. 43-44.

God's eternal counsel. No conditions need to be performed before justification is actualized. Eyre is aware that there is a diversity of opinion on this matter, also among Protestant theologians. Those Protestants, however, who regard faith as a condition or antecedent qualification for justification, "attribute as much to the *tò credere*, as *Bellarmine, Arminius*, or any other."[320] Faith may not have the role of a condition, because – as Pemble had already maintained – faith is a work. It is part of sanctification. If faith were a condition, it would mean that we are justified by works.[321]

Eyre gives an interpretation of the phrase "justification by faith" which is similar to that of Du Moulin. This expression does not mean that faith properly justifies. Romans 5:1 – "Therefore being justified by faith, we have peace with God through our Lord Jesus Christ" – must be paraphrased as follows: "Being justified *q.d.* Seeing we are justified freely, without works, by the death of Christ, by Faith we have peace with God ..."[322] Faith, in this text, must not be regarded properly, as the act or habit of faith, but relatively or metonymically, for the object of faith: the obedience and satisfaction of Christ.[323]

Faith yields justification *in foro conscientiae*. For Eyre, this means not only that faith leads to assurance, as was the case with Pemble and Twisse. Eyre insists that justifying faith includes both the assent of the understanding and the fiducial adherence of the will.[324] This means that assurance is not attained by means of a syllogistic argument. Faith gives evidence of justification in an axiomatic way, immediately.[325] Appealing to William Ames (1576-1633), Eyre states that by the act of faith "wherewith we rest and rely upon Christ, proposed to us in the Gospell, we doe immediately attaine to the assurance of this Truth [*that my sins in particular are pardoned by Jesus Christ*,] ..."[326] Eyre is not quite happy with the assertion that personal forgiveness of sins is the proper object of faith.[327] Still, the very resting on Christ implies that one is assured of remission. Says Eyre:

> <A>ccording to the degree of his affiance, or his taste of sweetnesse in Christ, is his evidence or assurance of his owne interest and propriety in him; There is no sense that doth apprehend its object with more certainty then that of Tasting; as he that tastes hony, knows both the sweetnesse thereof, and that he himselfe injoyes it; So he that tastes the sweetnesse of the Gospell Promises, and of that precious Grace which is therein revealed, knows his interest and propriety therein.[328]

---

320. Eyre, *Vindiciæ Justificationis Gratuitæ*, p. 51.
321. Says Eyre: "If we are not justified by our own works, then our believing, &c. is not that Evangelical Righteousness by which we are justified; but we are not justified by our own works, *Ergo*" (*Vindiciæ Justificationis Gratuitæ*, p. 52). Cf. p. 76.
322. Eyre, *Vindiciæ Justificationis Gratuitæ*, p. 41.
323. Eyre, *Vindiciæ Justificationis Gratuitæ*, p. 47. Cf. pp. 58, 75-76.
324. Eyre, *Vindiciæ Justificationis Gratuitæ*, pp. 80-81. Cf. pp. 33, 37.
325. Eyre, *Vindiciæ Justificationis Gratuitæ*, pp. 81-82. One of Baxter's objections to the view that justification by faith is in conscience is that it makes the duty of examination seem vain because "where God immediately by supernatural Revelation declareth to a man that he is justified, there is no use for his own reasonings and collection thereto: No more then of a Candle at noon: for Gods immediate Declaration is the fullest testimony: especially if it be so convincing and deciding as the maintainers do affirm it" (*Confession*, p. 213). Cf. pp. 191-92.
326. Eyre, *Vindiciæ Justificationis Gratuitæ*, p. 81.
327. Eyre, *Vindiciæ Justificationis Gratuitæ*, pp. 81-82.
328. Eyre, *Vindiciæ Justificationis Gratuitæ*, p. 81.

Assurance is of the very essence of faith. The degree of assurance increases and decreases along with the level or intensity of one's faith in Christ. What is more, justification is complete in God's immutable will. This means that Eyre's doctrine of justification is more high Calvinist in nature than that of Kendall and Owen or of Pemble and Twisse.

John Crandon: *Nolle Punire* and Covenant Justification

The most lengthy, and at the same time one of the most virulent responses to Baxter's *Aphorismes of Justification* is that of John Crandon, entitled *Mr. Baxters Aphorisms Exorized and Anthorized* (1654). The author is convinced of the catholicity of his doctrine of justification. No one "hath ever expressed himselfe to dissent from it: Till Doctor *Downham* excepted against Master *Pemble* for delivering it ..."[329] Like Kendall, Crandon objects to the fact that Baxter dares to call the eternity of God's immanent acts into question.[330] Like Kendall, Crandon insists that justification can both be an immanent and a transient act of God:

> For both are true, and may concurre without dashing either in the other. The Eternall Justification deposited in Christ, upon the Covenant made between the Father and the Son is immanent in God. But that Justification, which according to the tenor of the New Covenant made with man, is declared and evidenced by God unto the Conscience of man, is a transient Act of God ..."[331]

The immanent act is called God's active justification. It is a judicial act of his grace. The transient act is called passive justification "as it is terminated upon, and made out to the conscience of a man ..."[332] The former is to be justified *in Christ*, or *in God*, the latter is to be justified *by God through Christ*.[333] The former gives a right *in Christ*, the latter gives a right *to Christ*.[334] The former precedes the covenant of grace, the latter follows it.[335]

Crandon defines God's immanent justification in a similar way as Twisse did. It is

> an Act of Gods supreme Lordship or dominion, or else of his good pleasure (to use the Apostles termes) by which he freely and without necessity, in relation to his justice, willeth the salvation of one, and willeth not the salvation of another, loveth or hateth, imputeth not, or doth impute sinne, according to his own free will.[336]

In this description immanent justification is simply *nolle punire*. Crandon insists

---

329. Crandon, *Aphorisms Exorized* I.xx.245-46.
330. Crandon, *Aphorisms Exorized* I.xxi.256-58.
331. Crandon, *Aphorisms Exorized* I.xxi.259.
332. Crandon, *Aphorisms Exorized* I.xx.232.
333. Crandon, *Aphorisms Exorized* I.xx.233.
334. Crandon, *Aphorisms Exorized* I.xx.235.
335. Crandon, *Aphorisms Exorized* I.xx.233.
336. Crandon, *Aphorisms Exorized* I.xx.232.

that neither Christ's mediation, nor our faith, move God to justify us. After all, "he is God, and therefore immutable ..."[337]

Crandon describes justification by faith as "covenant justification," "federal justification," or "pactional justification."[338] This justification takes into account the covenant between the Father and the Son, Christ's satisfaction, man's faith, and the blood of the Mediator sealing the promise. Only then does God "actually pronounce and declare to the conscience of the believer" perfect absolution from sin.[339] This pronouncement adds nothing, however, to the state of the believer. Crandon could not be more explicit when he states that "although no man receiveth the sensible comfort of his justification before he actually beleeveth, yet every elect vessell hath (besides, and without his knowledge) the true benefit thereof (as to freedome from vengeance) throughout the whole time of his infidelity ..."[340] Prior to "covenant justification" only the knowledge, the comfort, the sense of remission is lacking.[341]

God's immutable will to justify even precedes – in order of nature – the covenant between the Father and the Son.[342] This means that God's will ultimately and arbitrarily determines the eternal destiny of people. As noted above, however, Crandon also speaks of immanent justification being "in Christ." Throughout his chapter on justification from eternity, Crandon speaks of the grace of justification given from eternity *in Christ*. Crandon is here thinking of the *pactum salutis*, which he also describes as a "Court" where a "transaction" between the Father and Christ (or the Son) takes place.[343] In this covenant "satisfaction was so virtually and effectually made by Christ and accepted by the Father as when it was actually accomplished."[344] The covenant of grace between the Father and the Son has great significance for the manner in which people are justified.[345] Because of this covenant, faith cannot be a condition of the covenant of grace. This covenant is absolute. It is a transaction between the Father and the Son.[346] Faith is not a condition of justification *in foro Dei* but only an instrument by which we receive Christ for consolation and salvation *in foro conscientiae*.[347]

There appears to be some inconsistency between, on the one hand, Crandon's speaking about God's will as his immanent justifying act and, on the other hand,

---

337. Crandon, *Aphorisms Exorized* I.xx.234.
338. Crandon, *Aphorisms Exorized* I.xx.234, 245, 252.
339. Crandon, *Aphorisms Exorized* I.xx.234.
340. Crandon, *Aphorisms Exorized* I.xx.237.
341. Crandon argues that justification or remission may be considered in a threefold respect: (1) as an immanent act in God; (2) as delivered into the hands of the Mediator; and (3) as in the apprehension and possession of the elect (*Aphorisms Exorized* I.x.89-91). In the third sense, justification is brought into the "apprehension and Conscience" of the elect (I.x.91).
342. Crandon, *Aphorisms Exorized* I.xx.233, 246.
343. Crandon, *Aphorisms Exorized* I.xx.244.
344. Crandon, *Aphorisms Exorized* I.xi.103. Cf. I.xi.104-07.
345. Richard A. Muller points out that John Gill, in abolishing the separation between the *pactum salutis* and the *foedus gratiae*, followed a common Antinomian pattern as set forth in Crisp, Saltmarsh, and Bunyan ("The Spirit and the Covenant: John Gill's Critique of the *pactum salutis*," *Foun*, 24 [1981], 7). By identifying the *pactum salutis* and the covenant of grace, John Crandon stands in the same tradition.
346. Crandon, *Aphorisms Exorized* I.xi.107.
347. Crandon, *Aphorisms Exorized* I.xi.106.

the connection which he makes between justification and the *pactum salutis*. Crandon separates God's will to justify and the covenant between the Father and the Son when arguing that God's will to justify precedes the *pactum salutis*. This does not prevent him, however, from attributing God's immanent justifying act to both these elements. By introducing the covenant of grace between the Father and the Son, Crandon manages to strengthen the christological element in his theory of justification. He only accomplishes this, however, with a certain loss of consistency.

WILLIAM ROBERTSON

Mental Pardon in the Breast of God

William Robertson maintains that pardon is "firstly, chiefly, and most properly" God's purpose not to punish with eternal death.[348] In his *Iggeret hammashkil* (1655), the Hebraist from London maintains that Twisse's definition of pardon can easily be vindicated against the partial, incorrect definitions of Baxter and Hotchkis. Both Hotchkis' definition of pardon – the effectual taking away of the punishment itself – and Baxter's definition – the dissolving of the obligation to punishment by the law – are deficient. Pardon can be separated from the dissolution of the obligation to punishment, as well as from the actual taking away of the punishment.[349]

To prove his point, Robertson appeals to two examples. First, suppose that a king, by his will, pardons a traitor, but that either the message of his pardon does not arrive in time or that the traitor stubbornly refuses the pardon. The traitor is killed, even though he is "really pardoned, and forgiven."[350] The conclusion must be that the essence of pardon may be separated from the effectual taking away of the punishment and that Hotchkis' definition of remission does not stand up to scrutiny.[351] Further, suppose that the king and the state are forced to capitulate and cancel all public laws against a group of traitors. The obligation to punishment has been taken away, but "the King and State doth never pardon them really, but upon the contrary they keep in their hearts a full purpose to punish them ..."[352] Robertson concludes that pardon and the dissolving of the obligation "are really different, and may be separated the one from the other ..."[353] Also the Baxterian definition of pardon appears to be fallacious.

Pardon is most properly regarded as "mental pardon" in the breast of God.[354]

---

348. Robertson, *Iggeret hammashkil*, p. 42. Cf. p. 58: "<I>t is the Kings will not to punish, that is, most perfectly, properly, and primarily pardon ... ."
349. Robertson, *Iggeret hammashkil*, pp. 44-54.
350. Robertson, *Iggeret hammashkil*, p. 48.
351. Robertson, *Iggeret hammashkil*, p. 48.
352. Robertson, *Iggeret hammashkil*, p. 53.
353. Robertson, *Iggeret hammashkil*, p. 54.
354. Robertson often uses the phrase "mental pardon" to refer to God's purpose not to punish (*Iggeret hammashkil*, pp. 37, 40, 46, 79).

This "mental pardon" is "real" pardon, even though it is secret.[355] The elect are "really pardoned in the breast of God" before faith. In this sense, pardon precedes faith.[356] Robertson acknowledges, however, that the law of grace does not absolve anyone before he believes.[357] The "condition" of faith must first be performed.[358] The elect may be pardoned in the breast of God, but prior to faith they are still not pardoned according to the law, which "threatens them, and obligeth them to punishment for their sins, even to no less then eternal punishment ..."[359]

Eternal Justification As Well As Conditionality

Whether consciously or not, Robertson follows Twisse's distinction between God's *voluntas beneplaciti* and *voluntas signi*. He places pardon in God's determined purpose not to punish but also insists that the obligation to punishment must be dissolved by the law of grace. The key question is where Robertson places the emphasis. He thinks that pardon is primarily God's determination not to punish. God's eternal will is thus placed on the foreground. Moreover, Robertson only speaks sparingly of the "condition" of faith and of the dissolving function of the covenant of grace. When he does mention it, he says that only the "sensible enjoyment" of God's favor is suspended until the condition is performed.[360]

Robertson's main concern is that the elect are "out of real danger" of punishment.[361] God has purposed not to punish the sins of the elect with eternal death. The result is that Robertson is not concerned with the perseverance of faith in the believer. Admittedly, believers do "not totally nor finally" fall away.[362] But an elect person may "fall grievously" from his first love, "not only by hainous sinning against God actually, but by continuing in an habitually sinful condition for so long a time ..."[363] Such a person is threatened "even to no less then eternal punishment."[364] Robertson even states that such an individual may live in an "impenitent and sinful condition."[365] His condition is such that "upon the *Baxterian* (Semi-Arminian) principles ... such a man in such a case should be lookt upon as quite and totally fallen away from grace ..."[366] Robertson does not base the perseverance of the saints on the certainty of their continuation in a state of grace or of their abiding conformity to the law of grace. The reason for the perseverance of the saints is that God has "immutably purposed" not to punish his elect with

355. Robertson, *Iggeret hammashkil*, p. 40.
356. Robertson, *Iggeret hammashkil*, p. 59.
357. Robertson, *Iggeret hammashkil*, pp. 59, 64.
358. Robertson, *Iggeret hammashkil*, p. 41.
359. Robertson, *Iggeret hammashkil*, p. 63. The tension between the threatening law and God's immutable purpose to save his elect is evident when Robertson denies that God ever "intended or threatned in his laws, properly to punish them as Judg out of justice ..." (p. 116).
360. Robertson, *Iggeret hammashkil*, p. 41.
361. Robertson, *Iggeret hammashkil*, p. 75.
362. Robertson, *Iggeret hammashkil*, p. 62.
363. Robertson, *Iggeret hammashkil*, p. 62.
364. Robertson, *Iggeret hammashkil*, p. 63.
365. Robertson, *Iggeret hammashkil*, p. 63.
366. Robertson, *Iggeret hammashkil*, p. 64.

eternal death. This is the reason that they can never be "unpardoned again in the breast of God."[367] The perseverance of the saints has precious little to do with the continuation of the believers' faith. All attention is shifted toward God's purpose of pardoning his elect.

Robertson places the emphasis squarely with God's immutable will not to punish. The question must be raised whether there is any real content to the condition of faith and whether the dissolution of the obligation to punishment has any real significance. Robertson speaks of the "sensible enjoyment" caused by faith.[368] He does not speak of a tribunal in conscience or of faith being nothing but assurance. Having situated pardon firmly in God's immutable will, however, it is difficult to see how Robertson can possibly attribute a more substantial role to faith in justification.

CONCLUSION

It is clear why Baxter has no hesitation in treating his high Calvinist opponents as if they represent essentially the same viewpoint. The similarities between the various authors are such that most of the arguments one might devise against the one could equally well be used against the next. This does not dissolve the present-day scholar from the obligation to gain an insight into the thought patterns of individual authors. It is understandable, however, that for Baxter – in the heat of the debate – this is a minor concern, especially because of the numerous similarities in the opinions which he rejects.

The most significant point in which Baxter's high Calvinist opponents agree is that, one way or another, justification stems from eternity. The dependance on Twisse is obvious. To be sure, there is a difference in emphasis. Owen wishes to go no further than to argue that justification begins with the *pactum salutis*. Kendall says the immanent act of God is justification "tantamount." Du Moulin, Eyre, Crandon, and Robertson, however, are all explicit in asserting justification *ab aeterno*.

Several authors (Owen, Eyre, Crandon) connect justification from eternity to the eternal covenant between the Father and the Son. By emphasizing the eternal transaction between the Father and the Son (or Christ) a christological element is introduced into the theory of justification from eternity. At the same time, however, this christological element causes a tension between the absolute will of God and the *pactum salutis*: where must pardon be situated?[369]

---

367. Robertson, *Iggeret hammashkil*, p. 62.
368. Robertson, *Iggeret hammashkil*, p. 41.
369. This tension is the result of systematizing the early Reformed emphasis on both the decree and the death of Christ as the basis of salvation. Richard A. Muller comments that "as the decree provided an eternal or metaphysical ground of salvation, so did the death of Christ offer a temporal basis; for if election was the presupposition on which human regeneration from a state of total inability was made possible, then atonement was the presupposition for the putative justification of the unworthy creature" (*Christ and the Decree: Christology and Predestination in Reformed Theology from Calvin to Perkins*, Studies in Historical Theology, 2 [1986; rpt. Grand Rapids: Baker,

There are several motives which induce Baxter's opponents to argue that justification precedes faith. Perhaps the most important one is the need to maintain the
immutability and simplicity of God. Twisse already asserted that a new act of
God's will would imply that God himself would begin *de novo*. This concern is
also the reason for Robertson's horror in reading Baxter. It further explains why
Kendall and Crandon take exception to Baxter's statements regarding the eternity
of God's immanent acts.

A second motive is the desire to ascribe as much efficacy to Christ's sacrifice
as possible. Christ's death did not just make reconciliation with God possible, but
actually obtained this reconciliation. Justification, or at least a *ius ad rem*, is said
to take place at the moment of Christ's atoning sacrifice. This anti-Arminian
element figures prominently in Owen, Eyre, and Du Moulin. It means again the
adoption of an element which was also present in Pemble and Twisse. Thus, the
efficacy of Christ's death is maintained. Reconciliation does not depend on man's
efforts or merits.

In the third place, Baxter's opponents are afraid that if faith precedes justification, man assumes God's role in justification as well as regeneration. Baxter's
opponents tend to describe faith as a good work, as part of one's sanctification.
Pemble already asserted that faith was not the root of the other graces and that it
was part of sanctification. Du Moulin and Eyre express the same opinion. Because
faith is part of one's sanctification, it may not precede justification *in foro Dei*,
lest one would run the danger of justification by works. Moreover, Pemble stated
that the first union with Christ (by the Spirit on his part) precedes faith. Similarly,
Owen tends to regard union with Christ as the basis for one's right to pardon. Also
Du Moulin maintains that all graces, including faith, flow from union with Christ.
Again, the tendency is to reduce the human role in the *ordo salutis* and to give all
honor to God's work in regeneration and in uniting the unbeliever to Christ.[370]

Finally, there is a pastoral motive. Baxter's opponents derive comfort from
the certainty that justification is in no sense dependent on faith. Kendall and
Robertson insist that there is no danger of condemnation for those who have been
pardoned from eternity. Similarly, Pemble had pleaded for the actuality of God's
eternal love for his elect.

One of the most significant results of these high Calvinist views on justification is that faith is consistently depreciated. Pemble's *Vindiciæ gratiæ* did not
speak of faith as a condition. Faith was not absolutely necessary in the elect.
Similarly, Owen, Kendall, Eyre, and Crandon insist that faith is not a condition.

1988], p. 72). Seventeenth-century high Calvinism went beyond the early Reformers because they
did more than just connect justification to the decree and to the death of Christ. These two aspects
were no longer the basis for justification but became identified with justification itself.

370. G.C. Berkouwer, in his discussion of justification from eternity, maintains that the religious motif
in the theory of justification from eternity lies in the priority of grace. The main concern is the
sovereignty of grace (*Faith and Justification*, trans. Lewis B. Smedes, Studies in Dogmatics
[Grand Rapids: Eerdmans], pp. 143-68; cf. Hae Moo Yoo, *Raad en daad: Infra- en supralapsarisme in de nederlandse gereformeerde theologie van de 19e en 20e eeuw*, Diss. Kampen 1990
[Kampen: Mondiss, 1990], pp. 175-78). Berkouwer is correct in his assessment, but mentions
only one of the high Calvinists' motives for maintaining justification from eternity.

Du Moulin refuses to give it a place in the definition of justification. Although it is true that Twisse spoke of faith as a condition, he could not do so without creating a serious tension with his view that justification is *nolle punire*. Robertson's incidental comment that faith is the condition of the covenant of grace runs into the same difficulty. Moreover, he links the perseverance of the saints not to the consistency of faith, but to eternal pardon in God's breast.

For Eyre and Du Moulin, who may have relied on a similar exegesis given by Twisse, justification by faith simply means justification by the object of faith, which is Christ. The justification which follows faith, however, is seen merely as a tribunal in conscience (Twisse, Du Moulin), as the knowledge of one's justification, as *innotescere* (Twisse, Du Moulin), as *patefactio* (Twisse, Du Moulin), or *manifestatio* (Pemble, Twisse, Du Moulin, Eyre). It is proof or evidence (Kendall), a sensible comfort (Crandon). This means that the distance between faith and assurance is diminished. Although Pemble and Twisse did not yet identify the two, Owen and Eyre do maintain that assurance is of the essence of faith. The view that assurance belongs to the essence of faith fits in with a high Calvinist doctrine in which justification precedes faith and in which faith does not have the function of a condition.

Implications of the High Calvinist Position

CHASTISEMENTS AND THE ELECT

Justification by Degrees

Baxter considers the implications of placing justification before faith as extremely dangerous. Many of his arguments against Antinomianism are based on the implications which the Antinomian position entails.[371] Although Baxter lists many dangers involved in placing justification before faith, they may be summarized under three points. The first difficulty which he sees with a high Calvinist doctrine of justification is that it can no longer be said that the elect are punished for their sins. This objection is by no means hypothetical, since several of Baxter's opponents do indeed draw this very consequence from their doctrine of justification. For this reason, and also because this aspect of the discussion sheds more light on Baxter's view of the process of justification, some detailed attention is necessary to the question if and how justification takes away the curse of the law.

The question whether the sufferings of the believers are punishments is not only an issue between Baxter and those who place justification before faith in the *ordo salutis*. The issue also plays a role in the discussion with Christopher Cartwright (1602-58), who maintains that justification in God's sight is by faith alone. Cartwright objects to Baxter's *Aphorismes* that they describe justification as, in a

---

371. For this type of argument, see esp. Baxter, *Confession*, pp. 247-89.

sense, imperfect and as taking place in varying degrees.[372] Baxter indeed says in his first work on justification that, although all acts of constitutive justification are "in their own kind perfect at once," nevertheless they "do not fully, and in all respects, procure our freedom, so they may be said to be imperfect, and but degrees toward our full and perfect Justification at the last Judgment."[373] Cartwright insists that justification by faith is perfect at once. Sentential justification at the last judgement adds nothing: it is the same justification "more fully made manifest."[374] Baxter responds by stating that constitutive justification is not the most perfect or complete justification and that sentential justification is not perfect yet. Moreover, one must distinguish between perfection with regard to the present state of the subject and perfection with regard to his future state:

> And so I say, that we are *perfectly justified constitutivè* the first day we believe, considering it as the *present Righteousness* of us in that present state: And yet that is not *materially* so perfect a Justification, as that which we have of the same kind at our death: For we are then justified from millions of sins more than before, and all the Conditions are performed.[375]

The reason why justification is not absolutely perfect in this life lies in the fact that justification is continuous. New sins need new pardon.

Baxter insists that Christ has undertaken to remove the curse of Genesis 3 by degrees till the resurrection.[376] In several places of his polemical writings, he works this out more systematically. He mentions five ways in which justification is imperfect: (1) constitutive justification must be renewed after sin;[377] (2) continued constitutive justification remains conditional;[378] (3) perfect sentential justification will take place on the last day;[379] (4) castigatory paternal punishments continue throughout one's life;[380] (5) executive pardon remains imperfect in this life;[381] and (6) the solemnizing of all justification on the last day is still lacking.[382] Thus, justification in all three aspects – constitutive, judicial, and executive – remains imperfect in the present life.

Chastisements As Punishments

Baxter is sensitive toward possible objections to his view of justification by degrees. If constitutive justification must be renewed after new sins, and if it remains

---

372. Cartwright, in Baxter, *Account of my Consideration*, p. 160.
373. Baxter, *Aphorismes* I.194 (p. 124) (emphasis throughout in original).
374. Cartwright, in Baxter, *Account of my Consideration*, p. 160. Cf. p. 304: "Our Justification (as I have often noted before) is full here, though it be not fully manifested till hereafter." Cf. pp. 276, 286; Cartwright, *Exceptions*, p. 178; Baxter, *Substance*, p. 67.
375. Baxter, *Account of my Consideration*, pp. 167-68. Cf. p. 161.
376. Baxter, *Unsavoury Volume*, p. 26; *Confession*, p. 118.
377. Baxter, *Account of my Consideration*, pp. 160-61; *Confutation*, p. 241; *Confession*, p. 126.
378. Baxter, *Account of my Consideration*, pp. 162-65; *Confutation*, p. 241; *Confession*, p. 126.
379. Baxter, *Account of my Consideration*, p. 162.
380. Baxter, *Account of my Consideration*, p. 162; *Confutation*, p. 242.
381. Baxter, *Confutation*, p. 242; *Confession*, p. 126. Baxter does not make clear why, in his *Confutation*, he distinguishes the continuation of castigatory punishment from the lack of executive pardon.
382. Baxter, *Account of my Consideration*, pp. 165-66; *Confutation*, p. 242; *Confession*, p. 126.

conditional, it is easy to call into question the perseverance of the saints. Baxter makes a point of asserting his orthodoxy here. Although the right to perfect blessedness is "in it self. Losable," God will see to it that the justified saints will persevere.[383]

Especially Baxter's assertion that believers still undergo castigatory punishments evokes protests. Crandon maintains that the sufferings of the believers are the Father's loving chastisements, not his punishments.[384] Scripture does not speak of the afflictions of believers as punishments.[385] Sin is not the meritorious cause, but only the occasion of a believer's sufferings.[386] Similarly, Robertson insists that the Old Testament never calls the believers' afflictions punishments. The texts that Baxter adduces as evidence are all "misapplied and grossly abused."[387] If only Baxter would have done "one moneths study" of Hebrew he would have noticed that although the Authorized Version speaks of punishments of believers, the Hebrew original does not do so.[388] One and the same affliction may be a punishment out of justice for unbelievers and a mere fatherly chastisement for believers.[389]

Cartwright, who is more moderate in his approach, does not accept the distinction between chastisements of love and punishments.[390] Chastisements are punishments. But, insists Cartwright, the afflictions which are evil and a curse in their own nature, are sanctified to God's children.[391] The suffering, "though sanctified, is suffering still; but so is it not still evil and a curse, because now it works for the good of those to whom it is sanctified; even as bitter pills and potions work for the good of sick persons."[392] Unlike Crandon, Cartwright admits that sin is the "meritorious cause" of believers' afflictions.[393] God's purpose, however, is not to punish sin.

Baxter insists that chastisements cannot be separated from punishments: "My full scope ... is to prove, that *Chastisements* are a *species* of *Punishment*."[394] He admits that afflictions are often a blessing for the believer. But this is only an "*accidentally · procured Effect*."[395] The affliction is an evil or *malum poenae* as it comes from God's anger. As it arises from his love, however, the suffering comes

---

383. Baxter, *Confutation*, p. 241. It should be noted, however, that Baxter is not always equally assertive with regard to perseverance. For a more extensive exposition of his understanding of perseverance, see below, pp. 316-22.
384. Crandon appeals to Gal 3:13-14; Rom 8:1; 6:14; Col 2:14; Heb 8:12; Rom 8:15; Heb 12:5-8; 1 Cor 11:32; 1 Tim 1:9; Gal 5:18, 23; 1 Pet 1:7; Matt 5:11-12, Col 1:24; 1 Pet 4:13; John 15:1-2; Isa 43:2 (*Aphorisms Exorized* I.v.33-37).
385. Crandon, *Aphorisms Exorized* I.v.33.
386. Crandon, *Aphorisms Exorized* I.vi.41.
387. Robertson, *Iggeret hammashkil*, p. 119.
388. Robertson, *Iggeret hammashkil*, p. 155. Robertson discusses Lev 26:41, 43; Lam 3:39; 4:6, 22; Ezra 9:13; Hos 4:9; Hos 12:2; Amos 3:2; Jer 46:28; 30:11; Lev 26:18, 24 (pp. 121-71).
389. Robertson, *Iggeret hammashkil*, pp. 135, 146. Cf. Crandon, *Aphorisms Exorized* I.vi.38-40.
390. Cartwright, in Baxter, *Account of my Consideration*, p. 45; *Exceptions*, pp. 16-17.
391. Cartwright, in Baxter, *Account of my Consideration*, p. 46.
392. Cartwright, in Baxter, *Account of my Consideration*, p. 50. Cf. *Exceptions*, p. 18.
393. Cartwright, *Exceptions*, p. 18.
394. Baxter, *Account of my Consideration*, p. 46.
395. Baxter, *Account of my Consideration*, p. 47. Cf. p. 50.

from Christ's blood and is good. Although this good may be greater than the evil, yet it is only good accidentally and eventually.[396] The believers' afflictions have a mixture of God's anger and love in them, even if the latter predominates.[397]

Punishments and Satisfaction to God's Justice

Sin must be the meritorious cause of all castigatory sufferings. This, Baxter insists, is "the true state of the Question" between Crandon and himself.[398] But, one may ask, which law is it that takes the sins of the believer as the meritorious cause of his punishment? Baxter says that he "will not contend with any man" about this point, as long as it is admitted that sin is the meritorious cause.[399] He states as his own opinion, however, that the sufferings are partly the effect of the law of works as Adam knew it, partly the result of the natural law as it is in the hands of Christ, and partly by consequence of the threat of the law of grace.[400]

Baxter does not really seem to care which law gives sin its meritorious causality in the punishments of the believers. Still, his statement that also the law of works is a cause for the believers' suffering must not go unnoticed. It indicates that Baxter does not believe that the curse of Genesis 3 has been entirely removed. Indeed, he states that

> the evils there mentioned, which still lie on Believers, are fruits of that first sin, and of the threatning (or Curse, if you will so call that small part of the Threat) of that Law, which Jesus Christ hath undertaken to remove, but not at once, but by degrees, so that the last shall not be removed till the Resurrection ...[401]

Baxter's statement regarding the curse on Adam is indicative of a weak element in his argument, an aspect which John Crandon uses to the fullest. He insists that Baxter's position is "Antichristian" and "hath sundry Popish errors ..."[402] He identifies five points of doctrine in which Baxter's view coincides with – or at least comes close to – that of Trent and Bellarmine: (1) man must satisfy in part for the punishment which God's law and justice require; (2) Christ suffered for eternal punishments, leaving temporal punishments for us to bear; (3) God takes satisfaction from our sufferings; (4) purgatory is necessary to satisfy God for our venial sins; and (5) there is a life-long uncertainty with regard to salvation.[403]

Crandon's charges are exaggerated, to say the least. Certainly his comments about purgatory have no basis whatsoever in Baxter's thinking. What is more, Baxter can defend himself with rightful indignation when he argues that he has

---

396. Baxter, *Account of my Consideration*, p. 54.
397. Baxter, *Aphorismes* I.71 (p. 46); *Unsavoury Volume*, pp. 34-35; *Confession*, p. 127. Crandon disagrees with Baxter on the grounds that it is "a making of God to be in a commotion against himself" (*Aphorisms Exorized* I.vi.44-45).
398. Baxter, *Unsavoury Volume*, p. 24.
399. Baxter, *Unsavoury Volume*, p. 25. Cf. *Confession*, p. 119.
400. Baxter, *Unsavoury Volume*, p. 25; *Confession*, p. 119.
401. Baxter, *Confession*, p. 118.
402. Crandon, *Aphorisms Exorized* I.vii.49.
403. Crandon, *Aphorisms Exorized* I.vii.48-57.

never said that God requires satisfaction of us.[404] He denies that the sufferings of
the damned "satisfie Justice properly," for if they would, the damned would be
freed.[405] Further, Baxter asks rhetorically: "Will it follow that because I teach that
Justice is satisfied when the whole penalty of eternal damnation is born, therefore
it is satisfied if God leave on us but the least part, though for our own advantage?"[406]

Still, the issue is not as straightforward as Baxter makes it out to be. He is
forced to make an important concession to Crandon:

> I now disapprove ... that I used the word [Curse] though I expressed that I meant
> nothing by it, but either any part of the Threatning, or any part of the evil Threatned:
> and though the Scripture it self do frequently apply the word [Curse] even to chas-
> tisements upon Believers, as I have proved before at large: Yet because our common
> use of the word [Curse] is such as intimateth some Revenging, Destructive Punish-
> ment, that may denominate the man Accursed, I think I should have forborn it, and
> hereafter purpose so to do.[407]

Throughout his reply to Crandon, Baxter reiterates that he does not use the word
"curse" in its common meaning, denoting a destructive, vindictive punishment.[408]
He admits that God's punishments of believers are not destructive in nature. He
only wants to maintain the penal character of chastisements: sin is their meritorious cause.

Justice must be done to Baxter's use of the word "curse." He rightly says in his
own defense that he does not mean that God intends to destroy us.[409] The fact
remains, however, that by insisting on the penal character of suffering, Baxter
maintains that it is at least partly the result of the curse of the covenant of works.[410]
It is obvious that Crandon's charges are outrageous. In no way does Baxter teach
that man partly satisfies God's law and justice. The question which the sharp
interchange between Baxter and Crandon raises, however, is whether there are any
dogmatic reasons remaining for Baxter's denial that man satisfies in any way for
his sin. If the curse of Genesis 3 is still partly in force, and if the sufferings of
believers are partly the result of this curse, why do these sufferings not satisfy
God's justice? Baxter does not address this question. He simply denies that he
teaches that man must satisfy God's justice and says that he does not mean that

404. Baxter, *Unsavoury Volume*, p. 22. Cf. *Confession*, p. 127: "None of a Believers Castigatory
punishments, do in the least measure satisfie Gods Justice: Yet is there some Demonstration of
Justice in and by them so far as they are punishments; though there may be a far greater Demonstration of Love, in and by them, in regard of the good to which they are intended."
405. Baxter, *Unsavoury Volume*, p. 25.
406. Baxter, *Unsavoury Volume*, p. 25.
407. Baxter, *Unsavoury Volume*, p. 23.
408. Baxter, *Unsavoury Volume*, pp. 27-29, 33, 37, 41. Cf. *Account of my Consideration*, p. 50.
409. Cf. Crandon's hostile outcries against Baxter in charging him with "un-Christing of Christ" and
asks whether it is not "an absurdity" to think that Christ humbled himself "all to this end, that
having disabled Law and Sin from all power to Curse without him, to purchase to himself the
Monopoly of Cursing ... . But no where doth the Scripture make him a Curse-monger" (*Aphorisms Exorized* I.vii.48).
410. Baxter does not believe that the law of works is still in force with regard to its covenantal and
promissory character. Cf. below, pp. 268-73.

Christ intends to curse the believer in the sense that he wants to punish him in a destructive, vindictive way. It would certainly have strengthened Baxter's position, had he adduced substantial reasons why man may be punished according to the curse of the law of works, even though these sufferings are not able to satisfy God's justice.

THE NECESSITY OF THE SATISFACTION OF CHRIST

No Absolute Necessity: Eyre, Robertson

Baxter is of the opinion that the most dire consequence of a theory of justification from eternity lies in the disservice it does to the atoning work of Christ. Twisse was not the only high Calvinist who argued that there was no absolute need for Christ's sacrifice. William Robertson holds a similar view and so do the young Owen and William Eyre.[411] Baxter judges that it is the emphasis on justification as an immanent act of God which minimizes the need for atonement. Although Lewis Du Moulin does not discuss the question whether Christ's death was absolutely necessary, Baxter is convinced that his doctrine has the same tendency as that of Twisse. Says Baxter: "It is untrue and Antichristian, that Iustification is an immanent act of God: For then it is from eternity, and then Christs death is no cause of it, nor any other work of Christs Mediatorship whatsoever. Is not this good Christianity?"[412] Christ's death is no longer necessary to reconcile God to us. Justification is an accomplished fact prior to Christ's sacrifice.[413]

William Eyre is conscious of the possible objection that his view undermines the atonement. One of the reasons why he has been hesitant to speak of God's immanent act as justification, is the possible implication that Christ did not come to satisfy justice, "but onely to manifest the love of God."[414] But the awareness of possible pitfalls does not withhold Eyre from following Twisse in describing justification as *nolle punire*. This has consequences for the need for atonement. Having stated that the justifying act is complete by God's "eternal and unchangeable Will," Eyre continues: "Neither doth this render the death of Christ useless, which is necessary by the Ordinance of God, as a meritorious cause of all the effects of this Justification; even as the eternal Love of God, is compleat in it self, but yet is Christ the meritorious cause of all the effects of it, *Eph.* 1.3,4."[415] Eyre only speaks of Christ's sacrifice as being necessary by God's ordinance. The implication appears to be that there is no absolute need for this sacrifice.

William Robertson is still more explicit in speculating on the possibility of pardon merely because of God's will. Interspersed with appeals to the "rational

---

411. This again illustrates Owen's proximity to the view that justification is from eternity.
412. Baxter, *Confutation*, p. 269.
413. Baxter, *Confutation*, p. 270. Cf. p. 299: "Note also that you do most erroneously call Iustification *an eternal effect*: This utterly denieth Christ as Mediator to be any cause of it; and so what is it, but to deny Christ! even the Lord that bought you."
414. Eyre, *Vindiciæ Justificationis Gratuitæ*, p. 62.
415. Eyre, *Vindiciæ Justificationis Gratuitæ*, p. 67.

light of nature" Robertson makes the case that Christ's death would not have been necessary if God would not have proclaimed the law of grace after the Fall. In that case "God might, and could (if he would) have pardoned *Adam* freely without infinite satisfaction ..."[416] Christ's sacrifice would not have been necessary in such a case. Thus, "there would have been nothing here in such a pardon, but the will, aud <sic> the purpose of it, not to punish, and so freeing from deserved punishment ..."[417] Robertson's purpose is to prove that Twisse's definition of justification is correct and that pardon cannot be defined merely as the dissolving of the obligation to punishment. Robertson must weaken the necessity of Christ's sacrifice in defense of his case. If there were an absolute necessity for Christ's death, Robertson would be unable to disconnect pardon and the removal of the obligation to punishment.

Growing Awareness of Danger of Socinianism: Owen

Owen presents a similar argument. Christ's sacrifice becomes a payment, a *solutio*, by means of a separate constitution of God.[418] In other words, Christ's suffering was not absolutely necessary for salvation. With Owen, the argument has a distinct anti-Arminian scope. The Arminians maintain that Christ, by his death, obtained a right to pardon sin upon the fulfillment of a condition set by him. Against this view Owen uses the argument that there is no absolute necessity for Christ's satisfaction. He does not believe that forgiveness depends on a condition set by Christ. Says Owen: "The foundation of this whole assertion seems to me to be false and erroneous, – namely, that God could not have mercy on mankind unless satisfaction were made by his Son."[419] It is a mistake of the Arminians that they insist on the absolute necessity of the atonement. Owen instead argues that the only reason why Christ's satisfaction was necessary was the decree, purpose, and constitution of God. There was no antecedent or absolute necessity for this satisfaction.[420]

Owen changes his stand in the midst of his debate with Baxter. In *A Dissertation of Divine Justice* (1653) he berates William Twisse as well as Samuel Rutherford for holding the same position which he himself has held previously.[421] Owen now repudiates his former view as filling him "with confusion and astonishment"[422] because he is no longer able to withstand the criticism to which his

---

416. Robertson, *Iggeret hammashkil*, p. 68.
417. Robertson, *Iggeret hammashkil*, p. 69.
418. Owen, *Of the Death of Christ*, in *Works* 10.443.
419. Owen, *Death of Death*, in *Works* 10.205.
420. Owen, *Death of Death*, in *Works* 10.205.
421. Owen, *A Dissertation of Divine Justice* (1653), in *Works* 10.505-08. Cf. pp. 498-99; 512, 514, 516-17, 550-53, 583-618. I have been alerted to this change in Owen's thinking by Wallace, "Life and Thought of John Owen." pp. 169-70, 271-72. Cf. Wallace, *Puritans and Predestination*, pp. 152-53; Wright, "John Owen's Great High Priest," pp. 142-44.
    For Rutherford, see Andrew A. Bonar, "Sketch of Samuel Rutherford," in *Samuel Rutherford, Letters of Samuel Rutherford*, ed. Andrew A. Bonar (1891; rpt. Edinburgh: Banner of Truth, 1984), pp. 1-30; Rcid, *Memoirs*, II, 345-62.
422. Owen, *Dissertation of Divine Justice*, in *Works* 10.508.

previous position gave rise. He admits that such views give room for Socinian error. Against the Socinian view Owen now maintains:

> Between their sentiments and ours on this point there is the widest difference; for we affirm the justice by which God punishes sin to be the very essential rectitude of Deity itself, exercised in the punishment of sins, according to the rule of his wisdom, and which is in itself no more free than the divine essence.[423]

From 1653 onwards, therefore, Owen maintains that God's vindicatory justice is one of his essential attributes and is not dependent on his will.

Baxter does not hesitate to point out that the position of Du Moulin and the early position of Owen is akin to Socinianism. In discussing 2 Peter 2:1, for instance, he opposes Owen's exegesis. Baxter states that the text speaks of a purchase by Christ's blood when it refers to those "denying the Lord that bought them." He does not accept Owen's interpretation that the text merely refers to a purchase "in respect of the enjoyment of the knowledge of the truth," rather than to the washing in the blood of the Lamb.[424] Retorts Baxter:

> He that will well prove that God can and doth so far relax his Law, as to give all these mercies without Christ's satisfying for them to whom they are given, *viz.* washing, escaping the Worlds pollutions by the knowledge of the Lord and Saviour; yea, clean escaping from them who live in errour, *ver.* 18. &c.) will do the *Socinians* a greater pleasure, and say more against the necessity of Christ's satisfaction, than ever I saw yet done by any.[425]

Baxter points out to Owen that by basing the character of Christ's sacrifice as *solutio* on a separate decree or will, rather than in God's vindicatory justice, he opens up the possibility that God does not demand satisfaction to the law at all. This would bring Owen dangerously close to the Socinian position which he abhors: perhaps God did not require satisfaction for sins at all.

CONFUSION BETWEEN KINGDOM OF GRACE AND KINGDOM OF GLORY

Baxter: Forgiveness Not Perfect Yet

Baxter's opposition to the view that the present afflictions in the lives of believers are in no sense punitive and his fear that the doctrine of the atonement might lose its central significance play a prominent role in his opposition to the theory of justification from eternity. But, in Baxter's view, there are further dangerous corollaries to the position which he rejects. These can, for the sake of conven-

---

423. Owen, *Dissertation of Divine Justice*, in *Works* 10.506.
424. Owen, *Death of Death*, in *Works* 10.363.
425. Baxter, *Universal Redemption*, p. 321. For essentially the same charge, see pp. 334-35 (confused pagination; sigs. Y8ᵛ-Z1ʳ), 420-21, 477-78. Cf. Baxter's charge that Du Moulin's position is "down-right Socinianism" (*Confutation*, p. 269).

ience, best be subsumed under a general tendency to confuse the kingdom of grace with the kingdom of glory.

Crandon is of the opinion that Baxter confuses God's eternal, immanent act of justification with justification in time. He insists that "to conjoyn what the Lord hath divided in point of time, his constitutive justifying us in his own brest thorow Christ before time, with his declarative justifying us in our own consciences in time, were to confound heaven and earth, eternity and time, together in one."[426] Crandon's accusation is based on his view that Baxter situates constitutive justification in time, whereas it really is an immanent act of God's will. Baxter, however, is convinced that Crandon is the one who makes a mistake, by reducing justification to eternity. When Crandon thinks that justification is perfect in our present state he

> doth hereby confound the Kingdom of Grace and Glory (a small mistake!) and while he takes himself to be perfected (in those particulars, though not in holiness) he destroyeth Christs Kingdom, and dreameth that he is in another, that the good man never yet did see. Perfection is reserved to the Kingdom of Perfection.[427]

By introducing perfection into the present state, Crandon acts as if he is no longer in the kingdom of grace, but has already progressed to the kingdom of glory. Lewis Du Moulin also maintains that forgiveness yields "perfect Blessedness" in this life.[428] Baxter then comes with a similar accusation in his direction: "SUre this man lives in some Paradise, where ever it is, that thinks he hath perfect blessedness already."[429]

Prayer for Pardon?

The confusion between the kingdom of grace and the kingdom of glory leads, in Baxter's view, to several problems. First, the need to pray for forgiveness disappears. Cyrus Du Moulin accuses his brother, Lewis, that his position means that someone who has once been assured of remission "should no more have need for the time to come to implore Gods mercy even for his most grievous sins."[430] In his reply, Lewis Du Moulin admits that the prayer for forgiveness is not just a prayer for "the confidence of Remission." Instead, it is a petition in which we ask that we may not be punished. Du Moulin agrees that "it may well be said that God doth through a mans whole life forgive him his sins, in as much as he doth not punish

---

426. Crandon, *Aphorisms Exorized* I.xxi.261-62.
427. Baxter, *Unsavoury Volume*, p. 27.
428. Says Du Moulin: "ANd when *David* saith, that *He is blessed whose sins are forgiven;* it is certain that he speaks of a perfect Blessedness; that is, when all sins are Remitted." (in Baxter, *Confutation*, p. 241; emphasis inverted; "Tum cum *David* dicit beatum esse cui remittuntur peccata; certum est eum loqui de beatitudine perfecta; hoc est, cum omnia peccata remittuntur" [*De fidei partibus*, p. 48].)
429. Baxter, *Confutation*, p. 241.
430. Cyrus Du Moulin, in Baxter, *Confutation*, sig. Mm2ᵛ ("non amplius in posterum opus haberet implorare Dei misericordiam pro peccatis vel gravissimis ..." [in *De fidei partibus*, p. 129].).

him ..."[431] Baxter is happy with Du Moulin's acknowledgement that prayer for pardon is more than just a request for assurance of faith. Especially the admission that there is executive pardon in this life and that God may renew pardon time and again are significant. Baxter concludes that he has found "more solidity, Iudgement and sobriety in this Section" than in Du Moulin's entire book.[432]

Meanwhile, Du Moulin's admission that God really pardons sin upon the believer's prayer is out of line with the remainder of his treatise. He consistently argues that justification takes place in God's will, because of Christ's sacrificial death, or at the time of the first promise of the Mediator to Adam. If justification by faith is but the patefaction or manifestation of God's justifying act, it is no longer consistent to argue that God remits sin when the believers pray for it. Moreover, as Baxter notes, "You confess, that our chastisements in this life, such as *David* suffered, are indeed punishments."[433] The issue of the nature of the chastisements in the lives of believers does not play a role in the debate between Baxter and Du Moulin. But the latter's position that justification is *simul et semel* cannot logically go together with the position that the believers are still punished for their sins. Justification cannot be both *simul et semel* and by degrees.

It is understandable, therefore, that when Baxter discusses the opinion that justification precedes faith he attacks the consequence that prayer for pardon is thus bereft of contents: "If we are pardoned, absolved or have Right to heaven from eternity (by the Decree) or from the time of Christs death, then may no man wicked or Godly pray for any such pardon of sin, absolution, or Right to heaven. But the Consequent is Antinomian: therefore so is the Antecedent."[434]

The Means of Grace and the Intercession of Christ

Baxter detects the same danger of Antinomianism in the fact that the means of grace become useless if justification *in foro Dei* precedes faith. If it is true that because of our union with Christ we satisfied and merited in or by him, "then we are as righteous while Infidels, as Christ himself ..."[435] Indeed, since the elect unbelievers are justified already, "we may not with any infidels or wicked men ... convince or perswade them of their misery, as being under guilt ..."[436] Preaching and baptism, as means of grace used for remission, become not only useless but even illicit.

Also Christ's intercession in heaven has lost all meaning, insists Baxter. Du Moulin defends himself by stating that Christ in heaven

---

431. Lewis Du Moulin, in Baxter, *Confutation*, p. 306 (emphasis throughout in original; "probè dici, Deum per totam vitam hominis, ei remittere peccata, quatenus eum non punit ..." [in *De fidei partibus*, p. 103].).
432. Baxter, *Confutation*, p. 307. Baxter is not completely satisfied by Du Moulin's position. In his *Confession* Baxter rejects the view that in praying for pardon we only mean it of temporal punishment: "<M>e thinks the Antinomians should think the perfect satisfaction of Christ hath as well remitted the temporal punishment as the eternal" (p. 182).
433. Baxter, *Confutation*, p. 307.
434. Baxter, *Confession*, p. 281.
435. Baxter, *Confession*, p. 279.
436. Baxter, *Confession*, p. 279.

seeketh that believers be admitted to a right of the Kingdom <*jus regni*>, (but not that they may be made heirs of the Kingdom, or believers) and in the mean time that the force and merit of Christs death be aplyed to us: For continually are the satisfaction of Christ and his obedience, the price of Redemption so before Gods eyes, that God gives us nothing but for the sake thereof ...[437]

Du Moulin states that Christ's intercession is for the *ius regni* of the believers. Furthermore, Christ makes our prayers acceptable to God and intercedes that the righteous may be preserved in grace.[438]

Baxter responds by pointing out an ambiguity in Du Moulin's statement. What sort of genitival construction is intended with the expression *ius regni*? If Du Moulin means *ius ad regnum*, this means an admission that Christ intercedes that the believers may gain a right to the kingdom – which is nothing but constitutive justification. It is more likely, therefore, that Du Moulin means *ius in regno*: "But if you have made this word <*i.e., ius regni*> but a cover for your deceitful erroneous sense, and will say, that you mean not *Ius ad Regnum*, but *Ius in Regno*, you will but plead against Christs intercession, by which I hope he is pleading for you ..."[439] In other words, either Christ's intercession has real meaning, and he prays for our justification, or Du Moulin derogates from the real content of this intercession. Furthermore, when Du Moulin admits that Christ intercedes "that the force and merit of Christs death be aplyed to us," does this not mean that justification as the fruit of Christ's death is applied to us as a result of his intercession?[440] Baxter's response to Du Moulin shows that whatever contents one may be able to attribute to Christ's intercession, justification is not part of it if justification precedes faith or is not continuous throughout one's life.

Conclusion

The influence of Pemble and Twisse is not restricted to the early years of Baxter's development. Although Baxter distances himself at an early stage from their view that justification precedes faith, he continues to make use of several aspects of especially Twisse's theology. Twisse's distinction between God's *voluntas beneplaciti* and his *voluntas signi*, his decree and his law, lies behind Baxter's opposition to the idea that justification precedes faith and is even *ab aeterno*. Baxter is able to use Twisse's distinction in his opposition to high Calvinist theories of justification

---

437. Lewis Du Moulin, in Baxter, *Confutation*, p. 316 (emphasis throughout in original; "Respondeo, Christum ... petere, ut admittantur fideles ad jus regni (non verò ut hæredes regni aut fideles fiant) & interim ut applicetur nobis vis & meritum mortis Christi: nempe jugiter satisfactio Christi ejusq; obedientia, pretium redemptionis, sic ob oculos Dei versantur, ut nihil Deus nobis indulgeat nisi in earum gratiam ..." [*De fidei partibus*, p. 113].).
438. Lewis Du Moulin, *De fidei partibus*, pp. 113-14 (in Baxter, *Confutation*, p. 316).
439. Baxter, *Confutation*, p. 317.
440. Baxter, *Confutation*, p. 318.

despite the fact that Twisse himself defined justification as an eternal, immanent act of God. The reason for this awkward situation, in which Twisse's weapon of a bifurcation of God's will is turned against himself, lies in the fact that Twisse was inconsistent in his use of the distinction of God's will. Corresponding to God's decree, Twisse maintained that Christ's death absolutely procured faith and regencration. Corresponding to God's law, Twisse argued that Christ's death conditionally procured pardon, life, and salvation. Accordingly, one would have expected Twisse to say that justification follows the condition of faith. He did not do so. By classifying justification under God's *voluntas beneplaciti* Twisse introduced an inconsistency into his thinking. When Baxter adopts Twisse's distinction in God's will he does not place justification under God's will *de rerum eventu* but under his will *de debito*. Thus, he avoids the tension in Twisse's thinking and is able to use the distinction between God's decree and his law to oppose high Calvinist theories of justification in which justification is seen as eternal.

Baxter distinguishes a threefold justification: constitutive, which consists in conformity to the law of grace; sentential, in which God as Judge declares the believer just; and executive, which is the actual taking away of the punishment. Baxter uses this view of justification to measure the validity of the theories of others, such as Thomas Hotchkis, Cyrus Du Moulin, George Kendall, and Lewis Du Moulin. Constitutive justification demands a corresponding change in the way that God looks at a person. When someone fulfills the condition of the law of grace God becomes willing to justify such a person. This means that his *propositum iustificationis* arises in him *de novo*. But Baxter is not willing to admit that God's decree changes. He also does not want to say that God himself changes. He is therefore reluctant to say that some of God's immanent acts are not eternal. Thus, Baxter's thinking displays a tension between his inclination toward the view that all God's immanent acts are eternal and his insistence that God's will to justify a believer arises in him *de novo*.

Chapter IV

Faith and Justification

Thus all on Earth have some degrees of Grace,
Which Reason tells us, they should not abuse,
Which bringeth some so far to *Adam's* case,
They stand or fall as they these Mercies use.

But God will not his Grace at randome give,
And leave the event to uncertainty,
But hath his Chosen, who shall surely live,
In whom his saving Grace shall never die.[1]

(Richard Baxter)

Common and Special Grace

INTRODUCTION

Baxter developed his theory of justification in direct opposition to the notion that justification precedes faith. The previous chapter has given some indication of the prominence of this view in the seventeenth century. Having traced Baxter's reaction to this tendency in high Calvinism, the main questions regarding the relation between faith and justification have not yet been answered. The previous chapter has discussed their relative positions within the order of salvation. According to Baxter, faith precedes justification. Little has been said, however, about the role of faith as such. Numerous questions arise. Not all are relevent to the present chapter. Those issues which were the topic of discussion in Baxter's polemical writings will be discussed. Baxter's practical writings and systematic theological treatises give valuable insights into his views on sufficient grace, free will, and irresistible grace. These non-polemical writings will only be used to clarify some matters which come to the fore in Baxter's controversial writings on these topics.[2] Second, the present chapter does not give a description of Baxter's entire doctrine of the application of redemption. His theories are only discussed insofar as they have a bearing on his doctrine of justification.

---

1. In Banks, "Poems of Richard Baxter," p. 164.
2. For Baxter's position with regard to irresistible grace, see appendix C.

With these restrictions in mind, three soteriological questions must be dealt with: (1) Baxter's doctrine of common grace; (2) his insistence that justifying faith entails faith in Christ as Lord as well as Savior; and (3) his denial of the instrumentality of faith. The first issue, that of common grace, is of importance because some of Baxter's opponents felt that he underestimated the difference between common and special grace. Related questions, such as the origin of saving grace, the assurance of faith, and preparation for special grace – all of which are intimately connected to the doctrine of justification – came to play key roles in this debate. The discussion on the difference between common and saving grace will indicate that Baxter saw sincerity as the only real distinguishing mark of true, justifying faith.

Further disagreement existed about the object of this justifying faith. While most of his antagonists would agree that it entails the accepting of Christ as Prophet, Priest, and King, most would argue that faith *as it justifies* (*fides qua*) is restricted to Christ's Priesthood, his blood, or his righteousness. This chapter will demonstrate that Baxter's objections to the distinction between *fides quae* and *fides qua* centered around a different conception of the formal reason of faith's interest in justification. This leads to the third issue: the role of faith as an instrument. Baxter denied that faith is an instrument in justification. It will be seen that he charged his opponents with self-justification and was convinced that he himself limited the role of faith by describing it as *conditio sine qua non*.

INITIAL OUTLINE OF BAXTER'S POSITION

Natural and Supernatural Condition

Certain passages in the second edition of Baxter's *Saints Everlasting Rest* (1651), in which he asserts that the difference between a hypocrite and a true Christian lies materially only in the degree, led to the controversy over common grace.[3] Baxter comes to this statement by first distinguishing between the natural truth of an act or habit, the moral or virtuous truth of an act or habit, and the truth of the justifying or saving nature of an act or habit.[4] He states that, in order to attain assurance of faith, one must first know whether or not he believes and loves Christ. This is an inquiry after the truth of the act or habit. Baxter warns against two forms of hypocrisy:

> 1. To take on us to repent, believe, love Christ, &c. when we do not at all: this is the grossest kind of hypocrisy, as wanting the very natural truth of the act.
> 2. To seem to believe, repent, love God, &c. virtuously ... and yet to do it but in subserviency to our lusts and wicked ends, this is another sort of gross hypocrisy.[5]

---

3. Baxter, *Saints Rest*, in *Works* III.198 (23.27). Baxter speaks of common grace in its soteriological sense of *gratia praeveniens*. The discussions do not center around the much-debated (and related) question of how much "goodness" may (still) be found in unbelievers.
4. Baxter, *Saints Rest*, in *Works* III.190-92 (23.5-10).
5. Baxter, *Saints Rest*, in *Works* III.192 (23.10).

In other words, if one only pretends to believe in Christ, then even the natural truth of the act is lacking. Or, if one does believe in Christ, but one does it for the wrong motives, the natural act of faith may be present, but the act is not virtuous because it is not in accordance with Christ's precepts. Only conformity to the precepts of Christ assures us of the virtuous character of a particular act or habit.[6]

There is still a more common form of hypocrisy, however. This third form occurs when both the truth and the virtue of the act or habit are present, but when the sincerity of faith is still lacking: "When men have some repentance, faith, hope, love, &c. which is undissembled and hath good ends, but yet is not saving; this is the unsoundness which most among us in the church perish by, that do perish, and which every christian should look most to his heart in."[7] Here it is not obedience to the Gospel precepts as such which is decisive, but the fulfillment of the tenor of the covenant of grace. The precepts are here considered not by themselves but in conjunction with the sanction of the covenant.[8]

Baxter then explains that there are two parts to the condition: a natural and a supernatural part.[9] The natural part concerns the "pure Godhead." It is taking the Lord only for our God as opposed to all idols.[10] This part of the condition may also be described as one's end or purpose. The second part is taking Christ as one's Savior and Lord. This is the only way and means to God.[11] Whereas the natural part of the condition is written in the nature of every reasonable creature, the supernatural part is supernaturally revealed by the Gospel.[12]

Baxter's exposition of the two parts of the covenant illustrates how he views the relation between nature and grace. As Sidney H. Rooy captures Baxter's thoughts: "Love of Christ is but the means to right love of our Creator. The image of the Creator is upon his world. Nature and providence are God's books to teach, but they are insufficient. Grace is medicinal to nature. Where natural light ends, supernatural begins."[13] For Baxter, the natural is a preparatory step to the supernatural.

Grace follows nature. It is not possible, however, to equate the distinction between nature and grace with the distinction between common and special grace. In both conditions, the natural as well as the supernatural, "there is contained somewhat common, which an unregenerate man may perform, and somewhat

6. Baxter, *Saints Rest*, in *Works* III.192 (23.10).
7. Baxter, *Saints Rest*, in *Works* III.192 (23.10).
8. Baxter, *Saints Rest*, in *Works* III.192 (23.11). Baxter summarizes his exposition as follows: "To love, is common to every man; to love God and Christ, is common to a christian with a hypocrite or wicked man; but to love Christ savingly, that is, as I shall show you presently, sovereignly, or chiefly, this is the form or constitutive difference of love which is saving. To take or accept, is common to every man; to take or accept of God and Christ, is common to a true christian and a false; but to take or accept of God and his Christ sincerely and savingly, is proper to a sound believer ..." (III.194 [23.15]).
9. Baxter, *Saints Rest*, in *Works* III.192 (23.12). Cf. III.187-88 (22.537-38).
10. Baxter, *Saints Rest*, in *Works* III.192 (23.12).
11. Baxter, *Saints Rest*, in *Works* III.192-93 (23.12-13).
12. Baxter, *Saints Rest*, in *Works* III.193 (23.14).
13. Rooy, *Theology of Missions*, p. 86.

special and proper to the saints."[14] Common grace may extend to the virtuous act
of faith and love in Christ. The only difference between such acts of faith in
unregenerate people and faith in true Christians is the degree. There is no natural
difference between the faith of a saint and the faith of a wicked person.

Baxter: Love of Christ in Unregenerate People

Any theory of common grace raises the question how seriously sin is taken. A
frequent objection to the notion of common grace is that it does not do justice to
the Calvinist theory of total depravity.[15] The early Reformers, perhaps most notably Luther, rejected the possibility of preparation for the reception of grace. As
Steinmetz referred to Luther's position: "The sole precondition for authentic conversion is real sin: the sole preparation which matters is the preparation which
God has made in the gospel."[16] The absence of the possibility of preparation
implies that faith and love to Christ are not found in the unregenerate. Baxter's
position seems to make a radical break with such a view. By distinguishing between the natural truth and the moral truth of an act he reckons with the possibility
that the unregenerate has faith in Christ. Baxter refuses to make a physical, specific distinction between the faith of a hypocrite or unregenerate person and the faith
of someone who has saving faith. Says Baxter:

> Now, for these acts of grace, who can produce any natural, specific difference
> between them, when they are special and saving, and when they are common and not
> saving? Is not common knowledge and special knowledge, common belief and spe-
> cial belief, all knowledge and belief; and is not belief the same thing in one and in
> another, supposing both to be real, though but one saving? Our understandings and
> wills are all, physically, of the like substance; and an act and an act, are accidents of
> the same kind; and we suppose the object to be the same: common love to God, and
> special saving love to God, be both acts of the will upon an object physically the
> same.[17]

---

14. Baxter, *Saints Rest*, in *Works* III.193 (23.15). Thomas W. Jenkyn wrongly states that Baxter does
not distinguish common grace from natural ability (introd., in Baxter, *Making Light of Christ and
Salvation*, p. liii). As will be noted below, it is Thomas Barlow, Baxter's opponent, who identifies
the two.
15. One of the objections of the Protestant Reformed Church to the theory of common grace as
espoused in the Christian Reformed Church is that it does not take the result of the Fall seriously.
In a recent booklet on the issue, Barret L. Gritters comments: "I believe that common grace
undermines the Reformed Confession of total depravity" (*Grace Uncommon: A Protestant Reformed Look at the Doctrine of Common Grace* [Byron Center, MI: Evangelism Society of the
Byron Center Protestant Reformed Church, n.d.], p. 11; cf. Herman Hoeksema, *Reformed Dogmatics* [Grand Rapids: Reformed Free Publishing Association, 1966], p. 207). The warning not to
ignore the doctrine of total depravity is also sounded within the Christian Reformed Church.
Gordon J. Spykman, for instance, comments in his recent systematic theology: "No doctrine of the
so-called 'remnants' or 'vestiges' of goodness which presumably survived the devastations of the
fall may be allowed to blunt the reality of total depravity or take the edge off the antithesis. Only
God's grace can restrain total depravity and soften the antithesis" (*Reformational Theology: A
New Paradigm for Doing Dogmatics* [Grand Rapids: Eerdmans, 1992], p. 320).
16. David C. Steinmetz, "Reformation and Conversion," *ThTo*, 35 (1978), 28.
17. Baxter, *Saints Rest*, in *Works* III.199 (23.30).

According to Baxter, there is no natural, specific difference between common knowledge and saving knowledge, between common faith and special faith. He insists that there is not "any one truth" which a wicked man may not believe as well as a true Christian.[18] A wicked man may believe that his sins are pardoned;[19] he may "undissemblingly rest on Christ";[20] indeed, he may love God and the Mediator.[21] Baxter refuses to believe that the unregenerate only love the benefits. They do love God and Jesus Christ, even though it is indeed for the sake of the benefits.[22]

FUNDAMENTAL DIFFERENCE OF OPINION

Kendall and Barlow: Specific Difference between Common and Special Grace

George Kendall adamantly opposes this section of Baxter's *Saints Everlasting Rest*. It is simply not true that a wicked man may believe that Scripture is the Word of God. The devils may *know* that Scripture is God's Word, but they do not *believe* it.[23] The unregenerate can by no means believe this because faith is an assent founded on the sole authority of God. This assent is implanted in us by the immediate inspiration of the Holy Spirit.[24] Kendall also does not accept that a wicked man may believe that he is pardoned. The plain reason is that such a man has no authority of God on which to base his belief. This means that he cannot believe it with the same kind of faith as a saint does.[25] The saint's faith and the wicked man's presumption are of a different kind.[26] Also, the wicked have little reason to look on the things which God gives them as mercies. Temporal blessings do not draw a wicked man to God, but they estrange him from God.[27]

When Baxter says that common and special faith are both faith, Kendall retorts that he should distinguish between the *genus* and the *species*. First of all, love of virtue and of vice are both love. They are of one and the same *genus*. The objects make a difference in *species*. But even if the object is materially the same – for instance, God and Christ – then this object is still apprehended under differing formal considerations.[28] The difference in nature is caused by the fact that not the least love to God is possible, without dissembling, if we love other things more than him.[29]

---

18. Baxter, *Saints Rest*, in *Works* III.201 (23.37).
19. Baxter, *Saints Rest*, in *Works* III.201 (23.37).
20. Baxter, *Saints Rest*, in *Works* III.202 (23.39).
21. Baxter, *Saints Rest*, in *Works* III.200, 202 (23.34, 40).
22. Baxter, *Saints Rest*, in *Works* III.203 (23.41).
23. Kendall, *Sancti sanciti* IV.117.
24. Kendall, *Sancti sanciti* IV.118.
25. Kendall, *Sancti sanciti* IV.120.
26. Kendall, *Sancti sanciti* IV.121.
27. Kendall, *Sancti sanciti* IV.125.
28. Kendall, *Sancti sanciti* IV.135.
29. Kendall, *Sancti sanciti* IV.137.

The position of Thomas Barlow is similar. In the greater part of his refutation of Baxter, he wants to prove that common and special graces differ in nature. He gives a methodical analysis of the various graces that the unregenerate and the regenerate have in common, in order to conclude that they are all specifically different from special graces. Barlow mentions five kinds: (1) Corporeal graces, such as bodily strength and beauty, obviously differ in kind from the habit of saving faith.[30] (2) Knowledge of natural things, as it was in Solomon, Plato, Aristotle, and others is immediately infused in some, whereas in others it is acquired with the help of outward means. The difference with saving faith is obvious.[31] (3) Barlow gives a more lengthy discussion of the faith of miracles.[32] Many who have this faith are not regenerated by the Spirit.[33] The faith of miracles may be in wicked people, whereas "<j>ustifying faith may be where faith of miracles never was, nor will be ..."[34] Justifying faith assents to the whole Gospel; but the belief that God will assist me in working miracles is not part of the Gospel. This latter kind of faith must depend on a particular revelation.[35] (4) The gift of tongues and prophecies differs specifically from saving grace. This gift may be found in wicked men, not just in justified saints.[36] (5) Barlow then comes to temporary or historical faith, which gives the "greatest difficulty."[37] This faith includes real knowledge and assent to Gospel truths.[38] Against those who assert a "final Apostasy of the Saints" Barlow argues that this common faith does not justify.[39]

Natural and Supernatural Origin of Common and Special Grace

The remainder of Barlow's tract discusses eight reasons why common graces and special grace are specifically different. A number of these arguments are similar to the ones that Kendall uses. First, Barlow insists that common faith is an acquired disposition or habit, whereas saving faith is immediately infused by the Holy Spirit.[40] Barlow describes these two different types of habit as *habitus ordinis naturalis* and *habitus ordinis supernaturalis*. The distinction runs parallel to that between *fides humana* and *fides divina*. The conclusion follows logically: "Now if an *Infused*, and *acquired*, a *supernaturall and naturall*, an *humane* and *divine* habit differ onely gradually; I, (and very many more) am much mistaken in my Metaphysiques."[41]

---

30. Barlow, in Sheppard, *Sincerity and Hypocricy*, pp. 337-38.
31. Barlow, in Sheppard, *Sincerity and Hypocricy*, pp. 338-39.
32. Barlow, in Sheppard, *Sincerity and Hypocricy*, pp. 339-48.
33. Barlow, in Sheppard, *Sincerity and Hypocricy*, p. 339.
34. Barlow, in Sheppard, *Sincerity and Hypocricy*, p. 341.
35. Barlow, in Sheppard, *Sincerity and Hypocricy*, pp. 343-46.
36. Barlow, in Sheppard, *Sincerity and Hypocricy*, p. 349.
37. Barlow, in Sheppard, *Sincerity and Hypocricy*, p. 349. Barlow does not distinguish between temporary and historical faith. This faith is called temporal in the sense that it may be lost and will, in fact, be lost, if persecution arises. But a person may continue in his temporal faith until death (p. 351).
38. Barlow, in Sheppard, *Sincerity and Hypocricy*, p. 350.
39. Barlow, in Sheppard, *Sincerity and Hypocricy*, pp. 352-59.
40. Barlow, in Sheppard, *Sincerity and Hypocricy*, p. 359.
41. Barlow, in Sheppard, *Sincerity and Hypocricy*, pp. 360-61.

Barlow's second argument against Baxter's position is closely related to the first. Common belief is not part of our spiritual life. It belongs to our natural life. This is evident from the fact that it does not justify or sanctify the person who has it.[42] This spiritual life is not present in those who have common faith.

In his third argument, Barlow states that even if this common faith grows into a rooted habit, it is never able to attain to "the very lowest degree of saveing faith."[43] Again, he refers to the supernatural origin of saving grace. Regeneration is solely an act of God's Spirit, "aud <sic> so a *supernaturall* Act, and how any a *naturall*, or artificiall product of our understandings ... can be a Disposition to supernaturall Grace, and such a disposition (as we now speake of) which differs from that supernaturall Grace onely in degree, I am yet to learne."[44] Kendall uses a similar argument. He maintains that the least faith, even as small as a grain of mustard seed, is a most precious pearl. He then continues:

> Nay, which is more, it is evident that there is somewhat in the *belief* and *love of the Saints*, though never so *small*, which is *more accepted* then *greater belief in others*, and *love*, such as it is; which shewes that the *Saints smaller faith* and *love* are of a *different kind* from that of *others*, which may seem *greater* ...[45]

According to Kendall, God accepts even the smallest possible amount of saving faith.

Jacobus Koelman (1632-95), a Dutch divine who attacked Baxter's view on common grace in a lengthy preface to his Dutch translation of Thomas Hooker's *The soules humiliation*, also employed this same argument.[46] Koelman's preface was written twenty years after Baxter's discussion with Kendall and Barlow. But Koelman touches on the very same issues. Against Baxter, he maintains: "The least saving grace, which is special for the regenerate, is spirit and has a spiritual being and can by no means be taken from the principles of nature (John 3:6). In its nature it is a new creature, regardless of how small it is."[47] In Koelman's view, it is possible that the grace in God's children is sincere, even if it does not prevail over their depravity.[48] Kendall, Barlow, and Koelman agree against Baxter that the smallest degree of faith is justifying.

Faced with this argument, Baxter retorts that "when the business is well

---

42. Barlow, in Sheppard, *Sincerity and Hypocricy*, p. 363.
43. Barlow, in Sheppard, *Sincerity and Hypocricy*, p. 365.
44. Barlow, in Sheppard, *Sincerity and Hypocricy*, p. 368.
45. Kendall, *Sancti sanciti* IV.110.
46. Jacobus Koelman, Pref., in Thomas Hooker, *De ware zielsvernedering en heilzame wanhoop*, trans. Jacobus Koelman (1678; rpt. Houten: Den Hertog, 1988), pp. 13-30. Cf. W. Van Gent, "Koelman's kommentaar op enkele Engelse schrijvers," *DNR*, 2 (1978), 29-32. For Koelman, see *BLGNP* 3.212-19; W. Van 't Spijker, "Jacobus Koelman (1632-95)," in *De Nadere Reformatie: Beschrijving van haar voornaamste vertegenwoordigers*, ed. T. Brienen, et al. (The Hague: Boekencentrum, 1986), pp. 127-63.
47. "De minste zaligmakende genade, die bijzonder is voor de wedergeborene, is geest en heeft een geestelijk wezen en is geenszins te trekken uit de beginselen der natuur (Joh. 3:6). Zij is in haar natuur een nieuw schepsel, hoe klein zij ook is" (Koelman, Pref., in Hooker, *De ware zielsvernedering en heilzame wanhoop*, p. 22).
48. Koelman, Pref., in Hooker, *De ware zielsvernedering en heilzame wanhoop*, pp. 24-25.

opened ... then men will see that it is *their* bringing Grace *materially lower* then I do, and not their *advancing it formally higher* that is our Difference."[49] The reason for this accusation is that for Kendall, Barlow – and, later, also for Koelman – even the least quantity of faith is saving. Baxter thinks that this means a debasing of saving grace. He rejects it because as long as faith is very small the worldly desires are still much stronger. As will be noted below, it is questionable whether this difference between Baxter and his opponents is more than verbal. It is nevertheless intriguing that Baxter, under attack for lowering grace, maintains that not he, but his opponents are guilty of degrading it.

In his fourth argument, Barlow returns to the immutable character of the habit of saving grace. Common grace may be lost because it is produced by "our natural understandings." Saving faith, however, being "immediately produced" by the Holy Spirit, is incorruptible and eternal.[50] Barlow adduces precisely the same reason to prove – in his fifth argument – that the habit of saving grace has a different object. Like Kendall, he is willing to admit that common faith may have the same *objectum materiale*, "to witt sacred truthes revealed by God in the Ghospel."[51] But habits are distinguished by their formal objects. And formally, the objects are different because they have a different *tendentia* and *habitudo*. This difference is clear from the different means and motives. Common faith comes from the "natural understandings of irregenerate persons," while saving faith comes from the Spirit of Christ and is built on his "immediate illumination and testimony."[52] The former means of attaining knowledge is more uncertain. It is only human, "opinative" assent. The latter is divine, "infallibly certaine" assent.[53]

In his next argument, Barlow refers back to Baxter's distinction between the natural and the moral truth of an act or habit. Barlow denies that wicked men can be "truely vertuous."[54] Says Barlow:

> If saveing and common grace be essentially the same, then irregenerate, and impious persons (who may, and many times have common graces) might be call'd (and indeed were) as truely gracions <sic>, and as truely beleivers as the best Saints, and Sonns of God, although not in so high a degree.[55]

Barlow is of the opinion that both philosophically and theologically it is wrong to call unregenerate people believers. Aristotle says that a vicious person cannot be prudent. Therefore, wicked people cannot be truly virtuous.[56]

Theologically, it is even more clear that those who lack faith are fools.[57] Barlow elaborates on this in a separate argument. Although hypocrites may indeed believe the history of Scripture to be true, they can only conclude from it that

49. Baxter, *Of Saving Faith*, pp. 18-19.
50. Barlow, in Sheppard, *Sincerity and Hypocricy*, p. 377.
51. Barlow, in Sheppard, *Sincerity and Hypocricy*, p. 380.
52. Barlow, in Sheppard, *Sincerity and Hypocricy*, p. 381.
53. Barlow, in Sheppard, *Sincerity and Hypocricy*, p. 382. Cf. p. 393.
54. Barlow, in Sheppard, *Sincerity and Hypocricy*, p. 395.
55. Barlow, in Sheppard, *Sincerity and Hypocricy*, p. 394.
56. Barlow, in Sheppard, *Sincerity and Hypocricy*, p. 395.
57. Barlow, in Sheppard, *Sincerity and Hypocricy*, pp. 395-96.

God's wrath lies on them. They cannot accept Christ as their Lord and Savior because they do not fulfill the condition of faith and repentance.[58] In Scripture, only regenerate people are said to love God.[59] Only they obey the Gospel.[60] Barlow provocatively concludes: "I hardly ever heard of any (save a Pelagian, or Socinian) who believed that Hypocrites, and irregenerate persons either did, or could really love Jesus Christ as their Lord and Saviour ..."[61]

In his last argument, Barlow again charges that Baxter's position means that we owe the essence of saving faith "to our selves and naturall abilities."[62] The distinction between the natural and the supernatural is the cornerstone of Barlow's opposition to Baxter. All eight arguments can, in one way or another, be reduced to this distinction. It was noted earlier that Baxter does not equate the distinction between common and special grace with the difference between natural and supernatural origin. This also implies that Barlow's objection is only valid if he is able to substantiate his claim that common grace has a natural origin, whereas special grace has a supernatural origin. Unfortunately, he does not attempt to prove this presupposition.

Baxter: Common Grace Not Merely Natural

Baxter is aware of the significance of Barlow's use of the distinction between natural and supernatural gifts, between acquired and infused habits, and between human and divine faith. In response to Barlow's first argument, he immediately touches on the heart of the issue:

> You seem here and all along this Paragraph, flatly to maintain that Temporary faith is only thus of our selves, or only Acquired, and not wrought by any other help of God, and his Spirit, then what is Generally necessary to all Acts. But that common or temporary Faith is the work of Gods Spirit as well as saving faith, is most express in Scripture: And that it may as truly be called *Infused*, and that it is from a *special assistance* of the Spirit, I shall prove: (*speciall* I say, as opposed to *meer general help or concurse*, though not *special*, as that signifieth what is proper to the saved.)[63]

Baxter rejects Barlow's use of the distinction between the natural and the supernatural spheres of influence. If temporal faith is purely natural, rather than a special work of the Holy Spirit, this would – at least on Baxter's principles – mean that man is able to come to conversion on his own strength, without God's gracious assistance. Therefore, Baxter scorns Barlow's appeal to man's depravity. He makes the highest grace of the unregenerate but a natural product of our understanding: "Mans corrupted heart seems too much exalted by you, while you call

58. Barlow, in Sheppard, *Sincerity and Hypocrisy*, pp. 398-400.
59. Barlow, in Sheppard, *Sincerity and Hypocrisy*, p. 401.
60. Barlow, in Sheppard, *Sincerity and Hypocrisy*, p. 401.
61. Barlow, in Sheppard, *Sincerity and Hypocrisy*, p. 402.
62. Barlow, in Sheppard, *Sincerity and Hypocrisy*, p. 403.
63. Baxter, *Of Saving Faith*, p. 26. Baxter's position on the infusion of saving grace is briefly dealt with in appendix C. Cf. also his *Catholick Theologie* I.iii.53-54; II.162-69.

him *Dead*, and yet think he can Acquire the highest Graces of Temporary Believers without supernatural Grace."[64] Baxter warns his opponent against Pelagianism.[65] He explicitly states that Barlow's view on the acquisition of temporary faith enables people to merit *de congruo* the first grace.[66]

It is necessary to pause and analyze what Baxter is doing. Faced with the charge that he obliterates the distinction between natural and supernatural gifts, between common and special grace, and that he thus lowers God's grace, Baxter reverts the charge. He does not lower God's grace. Instead, Baxter insists that his opponent exalts man's natural abilities to such a height that he espouses the Roman Catholic doctrine of congruous merit and even approximates a Pelagian anthropology.

PARTIAL AGREEMENT

Historical Faith Equivocally Called "Faith"

Perhaps one of most intriguing features of Baxter's response to Barlow is that he repeatedly insists that he agrees with him.[67] Much of Barlow's opposition, says Baxter, arises from misunderstanding. For instance, Baxter agrees with Barlow that common and special graces differ in kind, not only in degree.[68] Further, it is true that even "the lowest degree" of saving faith justifies us.[69] An unregenerate person does not "believe or love God heartily *at all*."[70] Baxter is at a loss why Barlow does not grasp the exact meaning of his words: "Taking faith for that which is truly Christian and saving, you might easily have known if you had desired it, that I consent to your conclusion, that the unregenerate do not believe."[71]

The question is whether Baxter is perhaps terribly confused or whether he is indeed misunderstood. Several times, he refers his opponent to the fifth disputation in his *Certain Disputations Of Right to Sacraments*, which had been published a year earlier, in 1657.[72] When Barlow says that the habit of special grace is not gradually, but specifically distinct from the habits and acts of common grace, Baxter replies: "I am wholly on your side; and where you have wrote a leaf for it, I think I have written many: so that if bulk might go for worth and weight, I had over-merited you in this Controversie."[73]

Indeed, Baxter's controversy with Thomas Blake over the admission to the

---

64. Baxter, *Of Saving Faith*, p. 40.
65. Baxter, *Of Saving Faith*, p. 45.
66. Baxter, *Of Saving Faith*, p. 29.
67. Baxter, *Of Saving Faith*, pp. 11, 13-16, 20, 22, 36, 48, 50, 72, 87.
68. Baxter, *Of Saving Faith*, p. 16.
69. Baxter, *Of Saving Faith*, p. 36.
70. Baxter, *Of Saving Faith*, p. 34.
71. Baxter, *Of Saving Faith*, p. 63.
72. Baxter, *Of Saving Faith*, pp. 8, 22, 50, 64.
73. Baxter, *Of Saving Faith*, p. 22.

sacraments touches on the very same issue. In this discussion, Baxter asks Blake what exactly historical faith is.[74] Baxter calls the faith of the devils "false Faith." It is only "pretended to be Faith in Christ."[75] He goes even further and almost seems to deny the possibility of historical faith:

> If you think ... that a man may Assent to the Truth of the Gospel with all his heart, and yet be void of Justifying Faith, you do not lightly err. Though an unregenerate man may believe as many truths, as the Regenerate, yet not with all his heart; Christ saith *Math.* 13. *The word hath not rooting in him.* Doubtless, whether or no the Practical understanding do unavoidably determine the Will, yet God doth not sanctifie the understanding truly, and leave the Will unsanctified: which must be said, if the Dogmatical Faith, that is the Intellectual Assent of a wicked man, be as strong as that of a true Believer.[76]

Baxter considers it impossible that an unregenerate person would assent "with all his heart" to the truth of the Gospel. The understanding and the will are too interrelated to admit of such a separation between assent and consent.

In the fifth disputation of his *Certain Disputations Of Right to Sacraments* Baxter refuses to call hypocrites true believers. If hypocrites are called believers

> it's plain that this *faith* it self is not the same with that of sound Believers; no not of the same *species*, Mr *Blake* himself beeing Judg, who so keenly gird's mee, for making saving & common faith to differ but in degree, when in the very writings that hee must fetch the slander from, I again and again profess that they differ morally in *specie*."[77]

Throughout this disputation, Baxter maintains that if "bare Professors" are denominated believers, Christians, or saints, they are called so only analogically or equivocally.[78] Those church members who are *merely* visible members are only equivocally called church members "becaus they participate only of the accidental form, and not at all of the essential."[79]

Baxter's near denial of historical faith, combined with his insistence that historical faith is only equivocally called faith, may seem to indicate that he is indeed contradicting himself. This position may hardly seem in line with his view that unregenerate people may believe and love Christ. Still, Baxter appears to choose his words with some care. When he says that an unregenerate person cannot assent to the truth of the Gospel he twice adds the phrase "with all his heart." When he seems to deny the possibility of historical faith he is, in fact, only severely restricting it. Common grace does not include a wholehearted assent to the truth of the Gospel.

Someone with a mere historical faith may assent to the truth of the Gospel. He may be called a believer. But he cannot be called a believer in the strict sense of

74. Baxter, *Account*, pp. 105-06; *Certain Disputations*, pp. 8, 163-75, 505-08.
75. Baxter, *Account*, p. 93.
76. Baxter, *Account*, p. 94.
77. Baxter, *Certain Disputations*, pp. 448-49.
78. Baxter, *Certain Disputations*, pp. 442-51, 473-77, 479-80.
79. Baxter, *Certain Disputations*, p. 479.

the word. This is not really different from what Baxter maintains in his debates against Kendall and Barlow. He admits, also to them, that temporary faith is only called "faith" in an equivocal sense.[80] Indeed, nowhere in his polemics against Kendall and Barlow does Baxter go as far as to suggest that common faith and love are *properly* called faith and love, even though they may be virtuous and in accordance with God's commands. Common faith may not be called spiritual life because it is not "the Christian faith, nor the person a Christian, but Analogically."[81] Only in an analogical, improper sense, may common faith be called faith. This faith is "another sort of faith."[82]

It is now clear why, at a certain point of the debate, Barlow appeals to some of Baxter's own statements in his *Aphorismes of Justification*. Did Baxter himself not say that the will's acceptance of Christ is the essential form of saving faith?[83] Did he himself not maintain that love to Christ as Savior and Lord is essential to this acceptance?[84] How, then, can he now say that unregenerate people may believe and love Christ? What Barlow fails to acknowledge, however, is that Baxter only calls the faith of unbelievers "faith" in an improper sense and that he does hold to a specific difference between common and special grace.

That there is a difference between Baxter's opposition to Kendall and Barlow and his disagreement with Blake is obvious. In his dispute with Blake, Baxter is concerned to minimize historical faith because he does not want to admit that it may entitle a person to the sacraments. In his discussions with Kendall and Barlow, Baxter approaches the same issue from the opposite angle. Now he is concerned to emphasize the positive role of the common graces found in unregenerate people. This leads him to some remarkably positive statements regarding the faith of wicked people.

More Than a Gradual Difference

It has become clear that despite a fundamental difference of opinion regarding the origin of common and saving grace, Baxter admits that the faith of unregenerate people is only equivocally called faith. This reduces the real difference of opinion substantially. Furthermore, in evaluating the debate, fair consideration must be given to Baxter's insistence that the controversy arises from misunderstanding or misrepresentation of his position. According to Barlow, Baxter only holds a gradual, rather than a specific difference between common and special grace.[85]

It is true that Baxter consistently emphasizes that common and special grace differ in degree rather than *in specie*. Wicked men, says Baxter, may have "some degree of love to godliness."[86] He adds rhetorically, "<W>hat did it want but a

---

80. Baxter, *Of Saving Faith*, pp. 3, 8, 35; *Of Saving Faith*, p. 91 (*Saints Rest*, in *Works* III.352 [23.474]).
81. Baxter, *Of Saving Faith*, p. 35.
82. Baxter, *Of Saving Faith*, p. 63.
83. Barlow, in Sheppard, *Sincerity and Hypocricy*, p. 396. Cf. Baxter, *Aphorismes* I.277 (p. 177).
84. Barlow, in Sheppard, *Sincerity and Hypocricy*, p. 396. Cf. Baxter, *Aphorismes* I.266 (pp. 169-70).
85. Barlow, in Sheppard, *Sincerity and Hypocricy*, pp. 325, 329, 332-33.
86. Baxter, *Saints Rest*, in *Works* III.203 (23.42).

more intense degree, which might have prevailed over their love to carnal things?"[87] The real distinguishing mark of special grace lies "in the prevalency of Christ's interest in the soul, above the interest of inferior good; and so in the degree, not in the bare nature of any act."[88] Throughout, Baxter emphasizes that it is only the "supremacy," "precedency," or "prevalency" of the interest in God and the Mediator over the interest in the flesh, which makes the difference.[89] Saving grace means that Christ has the "main bent" of one's heart and endeavors.[90] What is more, this prevalency is not always discernible. Where saving grace is at its smallest – in other words, where the love of God barely prevails over the love of inferior goods – there saving faith is indiscernible.[91]

Baxter nevertheless maintains that his opponents misinterpret him. They fail to appreciate the qualifications of his assertion that the difference between common and special grace is only gradual. Baxter mentions three clarifying restrictions to prevent misunderstandings.[92] The first is his distinction between a physical or natural specification and a moral specification. When he denies that common and special grace differ specifically, he means that in a *natural* sense they differ only in degree. He does, however, maintain a specific *moral* difference. Thus, insists Baxter, "a little anger, and a great deal, and little love to creatures, and a great deal, though they differ but gradually in their natures, yet they differ specifically in morality; so that one may be an excellent virtue, and the other an odious vice ..."[93] Baxter finds this distinction between a natural and a moral specification important to avoid controversies and confusion. These are often caused by "confounding of our physics and ethics in divinity."[94]

The specific moral difference between common and special grace is also the reason why Baxter calls the faith of unregenerate people faith in an analogical sense only.[95] An act is suited to its object when it has a prevalent degree. This prevalency of faith determines its formal nature. This prevalency determines whether it is suitable to its object.[96] The second clarification which Baxter makes, therefore, is "that sincerity of grace, as saving, lieth in the degree, not formally, but, as it were, materially only; for I told you before, the form of it consisteth in their being the condition on which salvation is promised."[97] Materially, there are only varying degrees of faith. Formally, however, there is a specific difference between

87. Baxter, *Saints Rest*, in *Works* III.203 (23.43).
88. Baxter, *Saints Rest*, in *Works* III.204 (23.45).
89. Baxter, *Saints Rest*, in *Works* III.194-96, 198-200 (23.16-17, 21, 23, 27, 31, 34-35); *Confession*, sig. Aaaa2ᵛ (*Saints Rest*, in *Works* III.350 [23.469]); *Of Saving Faith*, pp. 92-93 (*Saints Rest*, in *Works* III.353 [23.476]).
90. Baxter, *Confession*, sig. Aaaa3ᵛ (*Saints Rest*, in *Works* III.351 [23.471]); *Of Saving Faith*, p. 93 (*Saints Rest*, in *Works* III.353 [23.476-77]); *Right Method* (1653), in *Works* II.911 (9.93); *Of Saving Faith*, p. 12.
91. Baxter, *Saints Rest*, in *Works* III.205 (23.49); *Right Method*, in *Works* II.907 (9.81, 83). Cf. Rooy, *Theology of Missions*, p. 87.
92. Baxter, *Saints Rest*, in *Works* III.199 (23.30-31).
93. Baxter, *Saints Rest*, in *Works* III.199 (23.30).
94. Baxter, *Saints Rest*, in *Works* III.205 (23.48).
95. Baxter, *Confession*, sig. Aaaa4ʳ (*Saints Rest*, in *Works* III.351 [23.471]).
96. Baxter, *Saints Rest*, in *Works* III.194 (23.16-17).
97. Baxter, *Saints Rest*, in *Works* III.199 (23.31).

common and special grace. As the degree of grace increases, there is a specific point at which a person may be said to be a sincere believer. At that point, he has fulfilled the condition. This fulfillment of the condition is the formal difference between common and saving grace. The distinction between form and matter may be explained in terms of the threefold truth mentioned earlier: natural truth, moral truth, and the truth of the justifying nature of the act. The formal difference between common and special grace is identical to the difference between the moral or virtuous truth of the act and the justifying nature of the act. It will be remembered that the latter is the condition of the covenant. Thus, the condition is the formal, specific difference between common and saving grace.

There is little reason for misinterpreting Baxter. The proposition which caused the controversy is the following: "Therefore the sincerity of saving grace, as saving, lieth *materially*, not in the bare nature of it, but in the degree; not in the degree, considered absolutely in itself, but comparatively, as it is prevalent against its contrary."[98] The very controverted passage states that, although the difference between common and special grace lies in the degree, this is true only in a material sense. In his exposition, Baxter makes clear what he means with the word "materially." It is a physical, gradual difference.[99]

To be sure, this physical, gradual difference receives far more attention than the specific, moral difference between common and special grace. In his reply to Barlow, Baxter gives the reason for this. In his pastorate, he has come across many people who continue in sin – especially drunkenness – and yet profess that they are confident of pardon by Christ's blood. To say to such people that they dissemble and do not really have faith or love, would be useless: they would never believe their pastor. Baxter concludes that such people rightly say they have faith and love, but they do not "have them in such a predominant degree, as is suited in its Essentials to the Object, and will overcome their contraries in the main bent of heart and life, and prove predominant habits in the soul ..."[100] Baxter's concern in his *Saints Everlasting Rest*, therefore, is to point out the gradual, material difference, rather than the specific, formal difference. By telling people who continue in sin that their lives do not exhibit a sufficient degree of grace, he wants to encourage them to strive for higher degrees of grace. Baxter insists that Barlow's failure to observe the distinction between a formal and a material difference has led to his opposition: "<T>his Learned, Reverend man doth build all his opposition on a meer mistake, supposing me to speak of the *Form*, who spoke only of the *Nature* of the Act, or the *Physical Matter*, (as before expressed.)"[101]

The third clarification concerns Baxter's use of the term "prevalency." Says Baxter:

> Lastly, consider, especially, that I say not that sincerity lieth in the degree of any act in itself considered, as if God had promised salvation to us, if we love him so much,

98. Baxter, *Saints Rest*, in *Works* III.198 (23.27; emphasis added).
99. Baxter, *Saints Rest*, in *Works* III.198-99 (23.27, 31).
100. Baxter, *Of Saving Faith*, p. 12.
101. Baxter, *Of Saving Faith*, p. 13. Cf. pp. 17, 19.

or up to such a height, considered absolutely; but it is, in the degree, considered comparatively, as to God compared with other things, and as other objects or commanders stand in competition with him; and so it is in the prevalency of the act or habit against all contraries.[102]

This last point is of great significance. If the difference between common and special grace is indiscernible, the question arises which degree of love is saving. The "chief part" of Baxter's answer is that there is not a set degree which must be attained. Rather, the interest in Christ and heaven must predominate over the interest in all things below.[103]

Kendall refuses to denominate saving grace by means of a comparative analysis. Every bit of saving grace prevails over all degrees of the contrary.[104] But, grants Kendall, possibly Baxter's meaning is "that sinceritie of *saving grace* lies in such a degree as is prevalent, or greater, viz. *appretiative*, though not *intensive*. As for instance, a mans love to *God* and holy duties may be *appretiative* greater, and yet his love to his *children intensive* greater ..."[105] If Baxter means this, he is correct, though it remains "unhappily exprest."[106] To value the things of God above all things of the world in this sense does not mean that saving grace lies in a different degree of grace, but in an apprehension of the dignity of Christ, "in comparison whereof, *all things* are but as *dross* and *dung*."[107] Saving grace, therefore, must not be measured by the intensity of love, but by the appreciation of its object. When Baxter reads this, he concludes that there is no real difference between him and Kendall: "So oft he yeeldeth that all sincere Love to God doth prefer him before all other. Where then is our difference?"[108]

Perfection and Sincerity

According to Baxter, saving faith consists of the prevalency of the love of Christ over the love of inferior goods. Does this mean that God no longer demands perfection? Is it enough simply to have an interest in Christ and heaven which prevails over one's love of inferior goods? Such a conclusion would be incorrect. As noted, Baxter distinguishes between the moral truth of an act or habit and the justifying nature of an act or habit. The latter is the condition of the covenant. According to Baxter, God does not demand perfect conformity to his precepts – the moral truth of an act or habit – by way of condition.

Thomas Blake disagrees with this position. In his *Vindiciæ foederis* (1653), he opposes the opinion

> that the Covenant of grace requires perfection in the exactest way, without help of these mens distinctions in an equall degree with the Covenant of works, but with this

---

102. Baxter, *Saints Rest*, in *Works* III.199 (23.31).
103. Baxter, *Saints Rest*, in *Works* III.205-06 (23.50).
104. Kendall, *Sancti sanciti* IV.98-99.
105. Kendall, *Sancti sanciti* IV.99. Cf. IV.133, 140.
106. Kendall, *Sancti sanciti* IV.99.
107. Kendall, *Sancti sanciti* IV.99.
108. Baxter, *Confession*, sig. Aaaa4ʳ (*Saints Rest*, in *Works* III.351 [23.472]).

difference; In the Covenant of works there is no indulgence or dispensation in case of failing, but the penalty takes hold, the curse follows upon it; But the Covenant of Grace, though it call for perfection, such is the exactnesse of it, yet it accepts of sincerity, such is the qualification of it through grace, or the mercy in it.[109]

Blake refuses to accept a dualism between perfection and sincerity, in which perfection would be called for but sincerity accepted in its place. This would lead to unacceptable consequences. It would mean that God accepts covenant breakers. What is more, all would then be equally guilty of breaking the covenant. No one could ever say that he had lived according to the commandments. Our baptismal vow would then imply the promise never to sin against God. Sincerity would become something negative, a blemish, rather than something positive, a duty.[110] All these consequences indicate for Blake that Baxter's dualism between required perfection and acceptable sincerity must be rejected.

To be sure, Blake agrees with Baxter that sincerity is the condition of the covenant of grace.[111] This is an important point of unanimity. Blake states that "God in Covenant calls for obedience, requires integrity of heart in it, will not accept where sincerity of heart is wanting, and where it is he crowns it with happinesse and glory."[112] In short, according to Blake, God asks for sincerity. Baxter is also of the opinion that sincerity is the only condition of the covenant.[113] It is sincerity that counts and makes the difference between common and saving grace. It may be concluded that when Baxter makes a prevalent degree of love of Christ the condition or the distinguishing mark between common and saving grace he is speaking of the sincerity of faith.[114] What then is the difference between

---

109. Blake, *Vindiciæ foederis* (London, 1653), p. 107. Blake continues to say that the "reverence deservedly due to him that (I suppose) first manifested himself in it, hath caused it <*i.e.*, the opinion which has just been related> to finde great entertainment ..." (p. 108). The author to whom Blake here refers is mentioned on several other occasions in the debate (see Baxter, *Account*, pp. 144, 146, 152; Blake, *Covenant Sealed*, pp. 638, 642). At no point does it become completely clear who is meant. Baxter says that he first thought John Ball (1585-1640) was meant, but since he could not be the "author" of the opinion, it "is therefore sure some one much elder" (*Account*, p. 144). It might seem that the person is John Cameron (1580-1625). He could justifiably be described as the "author" of an (Amyraldian) school of thought which by the 1650s had great attraction. The opinion would certainly fit Cameron's theological views (cf. Armstrong, *Calvinism and the Amyraut Heresy*, p. 52). Blake does not seem to have him in mind, however, considering Baxter's reference to "some one much elder" than John Ball. Another possibility is that Blake refers to Jacob Arminius (1560-1609) and thus indirectly accuses Baxter of Arminianism.

110. Blake, *Vindiciæ foederis*, p. 109.

111. John Von Rohr illustrates that sincerity was a key concept in seventeenth-century English Calvinist theology, and that more than one Calvinist theologian applied the term "perfection" to this attitude of sincerity (*Covenant of Grace*, pp. 182-85).

112. Blake, *Vindiciæ foederis*, p. 114.

113. Baxter, *Account*, pp. 144-52.

114. Baxter gives a number of *dicta probantia* in defense of his position that sincerity of faith lies in the degree: Matt 10:37; Luke 14:26, 33; Matt 25; Luke 19:20ff.; Luke 13:24; 1 Cor 9:24, 26-27; Heb 12:1; Matt 6:33; John 6:27; Heb 11:6, 14, 16, 25-26, 35; 13:14; Col 3:1; Rom 2:7; Luke 17:33; 12:30-31; Amos 5:4, 8, 14; Isa 58:2-3; 1:17; Prov 8:17; Ps 119:2; Rom 8:1-14; Gal 5:17, 24; Rom 13:14; 1 John 2:16; Eph 2:3; Gal 5:16-19; John 1:13; 3:6; Matt 13:5, 23ff.; Rev 2:7, 11, 17, 26; 3:5, 12-13; 21:7; 1 John 5:4-5; 2:13; 4:4; Luke 11:22; 2 Pet 2:19-20; Ps 73:26-27; Ps 63:3; 2 Tim 3:4; John 12:43; Job 3:21; 23:12; Ps 47; 19:10; 52:3; 119:72 (*Saints Rest*, in *Works* III.204-05 [23.45-47]).

Baxter and Blake? Baxter believes that God demands more than he accepts by way of condition. Unlike Blake, Baxter does not believe that sincerity is the only requirement of the law: "A Covenant which is also a Law as well as a Covenant, may by the preceptive part Constitute much more Duty then shall be made the Condition of the Promises."[115] Thus, the duty or requirement of the covenant extends beyond its condition. The duty is perfect obedience; the condition is only sincerity. Every moral or virtuous act is not a justifying act.

Baxter and Blake agree that sincerity is the condition of the covenant. Only Baxter adds to this that the actual requirements extend beyond sincerity. Still, there is more mutual agreement. For Baxter, the condition for justification is perfect evangelical personal righteousness. This is the same as sincerity. He does not speak here of perfection of integral parts or of accidents, but of essential parts only.[116] Also here, Blake is willing to go the extra mile: he admits to a perfection of the subject (as opposed to hypocrisy) and of the object (respecting all rather than some of the commandments).[117] One might be tempted to ask: is this admission not simply a (somewhat scholastic) description of sincerity? Are Baxter and Blake, therefore, not basically on one line when it comes to the relation between perfection as the demand, and sincerity as the required condition for justification?

This would be too hasty a conclusion. More is at stake. When Blake and Baxter say the same thing they do not always mean the same thing. This can be demonstrated by an analysis of the use of the terms "perfection" and "righteousness" by the respective authors. With an appeal to Isaiah 64:6, Blake maintains that evangelical personal righteousness remains imperfect. It is all just filthy rags. Personal righteousness remains imperfect because of an imperfect conformity to the requirements of the law. Despite this imperfection, a person may retain his sincerity and can, therefore, still be called righteous: "As an image carrying an imperfect resemblance of its samplar, is an image, so conformity imperfectly answering the rule is conformity likewise."[118] When Baxter thereupon distinguishes between righteousness and holiness, the former being perfect and the latter imperfect, Blake perceives that they appear to be bickering about words. They apply the words "righteousness" and "perfection" to different entities. Baxter uses both words for the same thing: for the evangelical righteousness required as the condition of the covenant. This relation, this evangelical righteousness, is perfect because the condition has been met. Blake does not use the terms "righteousness" and "perfection" as synonyms. He speaks of "righteousness" to express (partial) conformity to the rule of the covenant, which is only the demand of sincerity. Perfection is not attained in this scheme of thought, except of course by Christ.

John Crandon and Christopher Cartwright have positions similar to that of Blake.[119] Crandon agrees "that the righteousnes by which we are perfectly justi-

115. Baxter, *Account*, p. 148.
116. Baxter, *Account*, p. 43. In other words, Baxter does not mean a perfection in the sense of the highest possible perfection, but in the sense of an essential perfection, "a Metaphisical Transcendental Perfection ... which hath no contrary in Being" (p. 43).
117. Blake, *Vindiciæ foederis*, p. 110.
118. Blake, *Vindiciæ foederis*, p. 111.
119. Cartwright buttresses his position with appeals to Blake (*Exceptions*, pp. 43-44, 54, 59, 65).

fied, must needs be a perfect righteousnes."[120] He insists, however, that this is ours only by the imputation of Christ's satisfaction. Crandon "utterly" denies that we ourselves are perfect or have "any finger in the busines of Justification."[121] Also Christopher Cartwright considers personal righteousness as "one and the same with Holiness."[122] This means that there may be varying degrees of righteousness.[123] Our righteousness remains imperfect.[124]

The result is confusion. For Blake – as well as Crandon and Cartwright – partial righteousness is possible because it indicates partial conformity to the duties of the law. For Baxter, partial righteousness is impossible because righteousness is defined as conformity to the condition and must therefore be perfect in character. Baxter is therefore apprehensive of denominating someone righteous when he (partially) fulfills the duties of the law. He considers this as righteousness by the law of works. It is "dangerous doctrine."[125] At this point, Blake notes the difference in terminology: "And if we speak not of this righteousness <i.e. moral righteousness as opposed to *iustitia forensis*>, when we speak of a Rule of righteousness, I cannot but observe, that it hath been a wild discourse, and little to purpose ..."[126]

PREPARATION

Scholarly Discussion

The disagreement between Baxter and his opponents is, partially at least, verbal. He agrees that the faith of unregenerate people is only equivocally called "faith"; he willingly admits that there is a formal, moral, specific difference between common and special grace; and he agrees that sincerity is the condition of the covenant. This explains why he is able to affirm Barlow's statement that even "the

---

120. Crandon, *Aphorisms Exorized* I.xvii.184.
121. Crandon, *Aphorisms Exorized* I.xvii.184.
122. Cartwright, in Baxter, *Account of my Consideration*, p. 104. Cf. *Exceptions*, pp. 42, 54. Cartwright appeals to Luke 1:75; Eph 4:24; Ps 145:17; and Rev 22:11. Baxter finds himself cornered by these texts, because they parallel holiness and righteousness. He continues to insist that even these texts do not "tautologize" the two phrases (*Account of my Consideration*, p. 105). The one may increase, while the other may not (p. 130). Baxter is forced to add a significant admission, however: "*Righteousness* is oft taken in Scripture for that Vertue which consisteth in *tribuendo suum cuiq;*. And so especially, as it respecteth God; giving to God the things that are Gods, and to men, that which is mens; and consequently obeying him. But this is not the Righteousness now in question" (p. 131). Here, Baxter grants that Scripture often speaks of "righteousness" in the sense of "holiness" (or obedience). When Baxter says that this is "not the Righteousness now in question," he almost admits that his dogmatic use of the term "righteousness" often does not correspond with the way in which Scripture uses this word.
123. Cartwright, in Baxter, *Account of my Consideration*, p. 127; *Exceptions*, pp. 43, 55.
124. Cartwright, *Exceptions*, pp. 42, 45.
125. Baxter, *Account*, p. 54.
126. Blake, *Covenant Sealed*, p. 612. The discourse is not quite as "wild" as Blake in exasperation suggests. It is true, there is a basic consensus on the fact that sincerity is the condition of the covenant, that at least some perfection (as to object and subject) is part of this condition, and that moral righteousness remains imperfect. But, as will be demonstrated below, the two authors disagree on the abiding role of the moral law (cf. below, p. 272).

lowest degree" of special grace is justifying. But there are also important differences. As noted earlier, the fundamental difference concerns the opinion of Baxter's adversaries that special grace has a supernatural origin, whereas common grace is natural. Baxter's rejection of this distinction has some important corollaries. These concern the possibility of preparation for special grace and the assurance of salvation.

There is no agreement among students of seventeenth-century English and American Calvinism about the question whether or not the process of conversion followed a common pattern, whether or not there was a standard morphology of conversion. A related point of discussion concerns the role of preparation. Does one's preparation for special grace bind God in any way? Perry Miller and Edmund S. Morgan have been influential in pointing out that Calvinists in the late sixteenth and seventeenth centuries did indeed hold that there were a number of chronological steps leading from unbelief to regeneration.[127] In his well-known essay of 1935, "The Marrow of Puritan Divinity," Miller represents the New England Calvinist view of the relation between God and man as a bargain, a contract, in which God would do his part if man would do his. According to this view, the Calvinist doctrine of predestination was softened by a covenant theology in which God was represented as bound to his promises. Although God remained "incomprehensible and transcendent," he had now bound himself by means of a covenant and had become a "God chained."[128] The next step, insists Miller, was the notion that man had the natural capability of preparing himself for salvation: "Though God might do as He pleased, it was noted that normally those who most strove to prepare themselves turned out to be those whom He shortly took into the Covenant of Grace."[129] Morgan has emphasized that there were standard steps which led to conversion. He refers to the morphology of conversion as having the "appearance of a stereotype."[130] Both Miller and Morgan regard William Perkins as a key figure in the development toward preparationism.[131]

Subsequent scholarship has modified this picture considerably. Norman Pettit has criticized Miller in The Heart Prepared: Grace and Conversion in Puritan Spiritual Life. According to Pettit, "the idea of preparation was never discussed, in early Puritanism at least, as a term in a contract."[132] Pettit thinks that preparation

---

127. Perry Miller, "'Preparation for Salvation' in Seventeenth-Century New England," JHI 4 (1943), 253-86; Edmund S. Morgan, Visible Saints: The History of a Puritan Idea (New York: New York Univ. Press, 1963), pp. 66-73, 90-92.
128. Perry Miller, "Marrow of Puritan Divinity," p. 63.
129. Perry Miller, "'Preparation for Salvation'," 262.
130. Morgan, Visible Saints, p. 91. Cf. Charles Lloyd Cohen, God's Caress: The Psychology of Puritan Religious Experience (Oxford: Oxford Univ. Press, 1986), p. 85: "In all discussions, preparative experience follows the same pattern. Differences of detail merely strike variations on the theme of a sinner whose increasing anxiety culminates in pride's collapse." Howard M. Feinstein goes as far as to make an extended comparison between the Puritan notion of preparation and the Freudian technique of psychoanalysis. He does this on the assumption that there is a standard morphology of conversion ("The Prepared Heart: A Comparative Study of Puritan Theology and Psychoanalysis," AmQ, 22 [1970], 166-76).
131. Miller, "Marrow of Puritan Divinity," 57-58; Morgan, Visible Saints, pp. 68-72.
132. Norman Pettit, The Heart Prepared: Grace and Conversion in Puritan Spiritual Life, Yale Publications in American Studies, 11 (New Haven: Yale Univ. Press, 1966), p. 220.

is more than just a "clever way out from under predestinarian dogma."[133] Nevertheless, he agrees that adherence to a strict doctrine of predestination and preparationism do not go hand in hand.[134] He traces the development of preparationism in Perkins, Thomas Hooker (1586-1647), and others.

Further criticism – not only of Miller and Morgan, but also of Pettit – has come from Lynn Baird Tipson. His dissertation focuses on Perkins' views. The author states that "the truism that preaching conversion and preaching predestination are antithetical must finally be put to rest as far as early Puritanism was concerned."[135] Predestination was not softened by the notion of preparation for saving grace.[136] R.T. Kendall goes even further in his criticism of Pettit – and, implicitly, of Miller. Kendall not only rejects Pettit's notion that predestination and preparation are mutually exclusive, but insists that the doctrine of reprobation lay behind the quest for preparation. Preparation gave one the assurance of being elected: "The very idea of preparation emerged as a rationale by which anxious souls could determine as soon as possible that they were not eternally damned."[137]

Influence of Preparationists

It is not the task of the present study to evaluate this scholarly debate in detail. It should be pointed out, however, that the origin of this discussion does not lie with Perry Miller. Undoubtedly, the preparationists themselves had their thoughts about how their position on conversion related to other aspects of their theology. Most interesting for the present purposes is the fact that Baxter took an unambiguous stand on the issue. On numerous occasions, he appeals to preparationist divines, such as Perkins, and more particularly, John Rogers (1572?-1636), Robert Bolton (1572-1631), and Thomas Hooker. These divines had been influential in Baxter's spiritual development. Baxter struggled long with questions surrounding the assurance of salvation. In his *Reliquiæ Baxterianæ* (1696), he comments that one of the doubts of his salvation had been related to his reading of preparationist divines:

> Because I could not distinctly trace the Workings of the Spirit upon my heart in that method which Mr. *Bolton*, Mr. *Hooker*, Mr. *Rogers*, and other Divines described nor knew the Time of my Conversion, being wrought on by the forementioned Degrees. But since then I understood that the Soul is in too dark and passionate a plight at first, to be able to keep an exact account of the order of its own Operations; and that *preparatory Grace* being sometimes longer and sometimes shorter, and the first degree of Special Grace being usually very small, it is not possible that one of very

---

133. Pettit, *Heart Prepared*, p. 221.
134. Pettit, *Heart Prepared*, p. 19.
135. Lynn Baird Tipson, "The Development of a Puritan Understanding of Conversion," Diss. Yale Univ. 1972, p. 315. Cf. p. 329: Pettit "has failed to disassociate himself from Miller's understanding of preparation as a *facere quod in se est*. Preparation is said to put a claim on God."
136. The same position is also held by Timothy K. Beougher, "Conversion," pp. 202-05.
137. Kendall, *Calvin and English Calvinism*, p. 5.

many should be able to give any true account of the *just Time* when Special Grace
began, and advanced him above the state of Preparation.[138]

This autobiographical detail gives insight into Baxter's position on conversion:
(1) for Baxter, assurance and preparation are intimately related; (2) his own conversion experience was important in determining his views on assurance and conversion; and (3) Baxter had trouble recognizing in his own experience the steps
outlined by preparationist divines.

   Perhaps more significant is the lasting influence these preparationists had on
Baxter's views. Throughout his writings, he appeals to them in support for his
view that common grace functions as preparation for special grace.[139] According
to William Eyre, it is a "Popish Tenent" to hold that faith disposes a person for
justification.[140] Baxter replies to this with an appeal to Hooker, Rogers, Bolton,
Perkins, and "the like honest old Practical Divines."[141] All these divines speak of
"a preparation necessary to Justification, yea to faith it self."[142] Also against
George Kendall, who says that an unregenerate person can do nothing toward the
reception of Christ, Baxter insists that common grace prepares for special grace:

> Cannot the Eunuch reade a Chapter and ask help of an Interpreter without faith?
> Cannot men Fast and Pray, if not as *Cornelius*, yet as *Ahab*, without faith? Is there
> not a common Grace of the Spirit, drawing men *towards Christ* that were farre from
> him, which goes before the special Grace (at least sometimes) whereby they are
> drawn to *Christ?* This that you maintain is not the doctrine of Mr. *Tho. Hooker*, Mr.
> *Joh. Rogers*, Mr. *Bolton, Perkins*, or any of our experimental practical Divines; no
> nor of any Protestants that I know; I am sure not of the Synod of *Dort*; but of the
> Libertines and Antinomists.[143]

Baxter depicts the high Calvinist views of opponents who deny the possibility of
preparation as Antinomianism. In his disputes against Eyre and Kendall, Baxter
argues that his theory of preparation for saving grace is a commonly accepted
Protestant tenet. He also appeals to Hooker and Rogers in his debate with Barlow.[144]

---

138. *RB* I.6. Cf. Packer, "Redemption and Restoration," p. 40. Packer identifies the treatises to which
      Baxter refers correctly as follows: Robert Bolton, *Instrvctions For A Right Comforting Afflicted
      Consciences* (London, 1631); Thomas Hooker, *The Sovles preparation for Christ* (London, 1632);
      John Rogers, *The doctrine of faith* (London, 1627). Baxter probably also had in mind Hooker's
      The sovles vocation or effectval calling to Christ (London, 1638). Baxter identifies all of the
      above treatises in *Admonition*, p. 35; *Catholick Theologie* I.iii.68. He also mentions Hooker's *Souls
      Justification* (*Admonition*, p. 35). With this last treatise, Baxter presumably had in mind either
      The sovles ingrafting into Christ (London, 1637) or *The soules possession of Christ* (London,
      1638).
139. *Catholick Theologie* II.267. Cf. Packer, "Redemption and Restoration," p. 40, n. 3; *Admonition*,
      p. 35; *Reduction*, p. 132; *Of Justification*, p. 388; *Of Saving Faith*, p. 42; *Catholick Theologie*
      I.iii.68.
140. Eyre, *Vindiciæ Justificationis Gratuitæ*, pp. 89-90.
141. Baxter, *Admonition*, p. 35.
142. Baxter, *Admonition*, pp. 35-36.
143. Baxter, *Reduction*, p. 132.
144. Baxter, *Of Saving Faith*, p. 42.

Elsewhere, it appears that Baxter has few objections against the statement on preparation produced by the Council of Trent (1545-63). To be sure, when John Tombes questions him on preparation, Baxter says that there are more differences between his position and that of Trent "then is worth the while to repeat."[145] But Baxter also refers to Martin Chemnitz (1522-86), who held that Trent, by speaking of "dispositions" and "preparations," introduced *meritum de congruo*.[146] Baxter then again appeals to Rogers and Hooker, who state that "not only a common preparatory contrition" precedes sanctification and justification, but "even effectual special Vocation it self."[147] Baxter does not appear to see a great deal of difference between the Council of Trent and the Calvinist preparationists.

Baxter's *Catholick Theologie* is probably most outspoken on this point. Once again, he appeals to Hooker, Rogers, and Bolton, as well as to Matthew Mead (1630?-99).[148] In a discussion between L. (a Lutheran) and R. (a reconciler) on the doctrine of merit, Baxter makes the Lutheran ask what is meant by the Roman Catholic theory of congruous merit. R. responds that, on this issue, L. holds at least as much as the Council of Trent. The reason for this is:

> 1. *De nomine* some of them deny that this is any *merit* at all, as well as you. And their Council asserteth it not (that I see.) 2. *De re:* They mean the same *thing* by *Merit* of Congruity, which Mr. *Rogers, Bolton, Hooker* and the rest call *Preparation* for *Christ* or for *Conversion*; And so the Council of *Trent* calls it: Which maketh a man a more Congruous Receiver of Grace than the unprepared, but doth not prove God obliged to give it him as a Reward. And do not you hold all this *de re?*[149]

The significance of this statement must not be underestimated. Baxter comments without any restriction that the preparationism of Rogers, Bolton, and Hooker is identical to the Roman Catholic notion of *meritum de congruo*. These preparationists hold, as does Trent, that a person is ordinarily prepared for the reception of the first saving grace.[150] In terms of the scholarly debate on Calvinist theories of

---

145. Baxter, *Of Justification*, p. 387.
146. Baxter, *Of Justification*, pp. 387-88.
147. Baxter, *Of Justification*, p. 388.
148. Baxter, *Catholick Theologie* I.iii.68: "To the same sence our English Divines commonly tell us how, ordinarily God prepareth, men for conversion before he convert them; and how far persons unconverted may go in common grace: He that readeth Mr. *Hooker* of New *England*, Mr. *John Rogers* his *doctrine* of *faith*, Mr. *Boltons instructions* for *comfort* – Mr. *Meads Almost a Christian*, and abundance such, will see that they were of the same mind <as the British delegates to the Synod of Dort>." The treatise of Matthew Mead to which Baxter refers is *The almost Christian discovered, or The false-professor tried and cast* (London, 1662). Cf. Baxter's appeal to Rogers, Hooker, and Bolton in *Catholick Theologie* II.170.
149. Baxter, *Catholick Theologie* II.267. Cf. *Universal Redemption*, p. 437: "<W>hen he <i.e., God> giveth the first Special Grace for Repenting and Believing he doth it as not pre-engaged to do it; and therefore as *Dominus Absolutus*, and not *per legem premiantem*. (And therefore the Papists in their Language say, the first Grace is not of merit, at least of Condignity.)"
150. Cf. *Catholick Theologie* II.171: "All they that hold all that Doctrine of Preparation for Conversion, which you find in the suffrages of the British Divines in the Synod of *Dort* do not (that I know of) differ from many of the Lutherans, and Jesuites, nor from many of the Arminians herein; while by the name of *merit of Congruity*, used by some, and *Preparation* by the other, no more is meant than they there assert ..." Cohen, however, states: "Puritans denied that preparation could be a 'meritorious cause' of conversion. Vocation depends only on God's will; the 'dignity, honesty, industry, or any indeavor' of those called is irrelevant" (*God's Caress*, pp. 86-87).

preparationism, it is clear that Baxter would support those who argue that by introducing preparationism, sixteenth- and seventeenth-century Calvinism returned to Roman Catholic notions of preparationism.[151]

Preparation Without a Binding Promise from God

Baxter's consistent appeal to preparationist divines makes clear that he feels strongly about the need to prepare for special grace. Barlow is afraid that this implies Arminian tendencies in Baxter's thinking: "I doe not find that saveing faith is promised us upon any precedent condition to be performed by us, and therefore I know no preparatory Dispositions to it, which can dispose, and fitt the subject ... for the Introduction of it."[152] Again, Barlow appeals to the supernatural origin of faith: there can be no natural disposition to a purely supernatural effect.[153] With this underlying presupposition Baxter disagrees. He maintains that "somewhat of the supernatural Light is given to many of the unsanctified."[154] For Baxter, the disposition of the individual is an important factor in determining the possibility of conversion: "He that is *neerer Christ* is more disposed to come to him by faith, then he that is at a further distance."[155]

Also Kendall rejects Baxter's positive way of speaking about a disposition to saving grace. Since the habits of common and special grace are of a different kind, it is impossible that common grace would be a disposition to the habit of saving grace.[156] Kendall accuses Baxter of Pelagianism, and he insists that "*Common Grace* goes no higher then either the *restraining men* from *grosser sins*, or the *enabling* them to do their *duties* in reference to *themselves* or *others* as it becomes them in their *Oeconomical* or *Politick* capacities."[157]

Baxter does not accept the charge of Pelagianism or even Arminianism. He agrees with Barlow on a significant point. Barlow rejects preparatory dispositions because he fears the next step, namely, that God will be regarded as obliged to give special grace upon the good use of common grace. Baxter supports Barlow in the rejection of this last logical deduction, and he adds: "The *Arminians* think otherwise."[158] There is no "Covenant or Promise" according to which God gives saving grace on a certain condition which man performs without grace.[159] In *Universal Redemption* (1694), Baxter foresees the following objection: "But here you vent two points of Arminianism, one, that there is sufficient Grace which is

---

151. Whether Baxter was correct or not, is another issue. It seems to me that the discussions of the development of preparationism would greatly benefit from an in depth comparative analysis with the various Roman Catholic schools of thought. Most scholarly attention, thus far, has gone to a comparison between the early continental Reformers and later Calvinists from England and New England.
152. Barlow, in Sheppard, *Sincerity and Hypocricy*, p. 369.
153. Barlow, in Sheppard, *Sincerity and Hypocricy*, p. 370.
154. Baxter, *Of Saving Faith*, p. 37.
155. Baxter, *Of Saving Faith*, p. 39.
156. Kendall, *Sancti sanciti* IV.104.
157. Kendall, *Sancti sanciti* IV.105.
158. Baxter, *Of Saving Faith*, p. 41.
159. Baxter, *Of Saving Faith*, p. 46. Cf. *Confession*, p. 30; *Catholick Theologie* II.115.

not effectual: The other, that God will give men Spiritual Blessings on the good use of natural."[160] Baxter retorts: "No Arminianism at all."[161] In clear terms, he dissents from the Arminian view of common grace. He argues that, ultimately, it does not depend on man's disposition, on his preparation, whether or not he receives saving faith. God is not tied to the *materia disposita* in giving special grace.[162] On the contrary, it is "plain *Semi-Pelagianism*, that Grace is tyed to such Dispositions of our own."[163]

Strong Encouragements To Seek Grace

From such unequivocal rejections of the Arminian position, Timothy K. Beougher has drawn the conclusion that "Baxter rejected the idea that God had promised to give men special grace, if they would use their common grace well."[164] Beougher appeals to a statement in Baxter's *Universal Redemption*, where he says that God does not give special grace as being pre-engaged but as *Dominus Absolutus*.[165] This is indeed a correct interpretation of some of Baxter's statements. But there is also evidence which shows that he has some difficulty in maintaining this position. He is not always able to make the distinction between God as *Dominus Absolutus* and as *Rector*, between his will *de rerum eventu* and his will *de debito*, as sharply as he would like to.[166] God's will *de debito* appears to be closely related to the gift of saving faith. Those who are disposed with the highest graces that the unsanctified may have are in a much better position. They "do much more ordinarily receive saving Grace, then others do."[167] The command to use the means is "a strongly incouraging intimation, that God will not deny men the end and blessing, that use the means as well as they can."[168] Although God gives no express promise, he does give much encouragement.

That Baxter remains hesitant in speaking of a conditional promise in connection with the first gift of saving grace arises from his concern for the doctrine of God. As noted in connection with his discussion with Kendall on justification from eternity, Baxter refuses to ascribe conditionality to God's decree. Still, when man's relation to the covenant of grace changes, Baxter posits a corresponding change in God's attitude. There is a new immanent act in God, a *propositum*

---

160. Baxter, *Universal Redemption*, p. 436 (emphasis inverted).
161. Baxter, *Universal Redemption*, p. 436.
162. Baxter acknowledges God as *Dominus Absolutus*, also in granting special grace, when he states: "But to unprepared Souls whom God will suddenly convert out of the ordinary way, a special extraordinary operation seemeth necessary" (*Catholick Theologie* II.189). Cf. *End of Doctrinal Controversies*, p. 287.
163. Baxter, *Universal Redemption*, p. 491.
164. Beougher, "Conversion," p. 68.
165. Baxter, *Universal Redemption*, p. 437. Cf. Beougher, "Conversion," pp. 68, 111.
166. Baxter acknowledges that the distinction between God as moral Rector and as mere Proprietor or Actor and Benefactor is important to avoid mistakes in one's view on preparation. He does not specify, however, how this distinction should function at this point (*Catholick Theologie* II.196).
167. Baxter, *Of Saving Grace*, p. 42.
168. Baxter, *Of Saving Faith*, p. 46.

iustificationis.[169] Similarly, Baxter hesitates in making God's grant of initial grace as *Dominus Absolutus* dependent upon man's fulfillment of certain conditions. God's will in himself is his essence. Strictly speaking, it is not conditional.[170] Accordingly, Baxter maintains that God does not bind himself by "a proper Promise" to give special grace upon the good use of common grace.[171]

Nevertheless, God does give strong encouragements to seek his grace. Baxter gives a prominent place to the means and secondary causes through which God works.[172] In fact, he comes close to asserting that God has bound himself to give special grace upon the right use of common grace.[173] He speaks of a "half promise, or encouragement" in which God says:

> And if thou wilt not hate and resist my motions, as enemies to thy lusts, and turn wilfully after vanity, in such a degree as thou art even Morally able to forbear; Thou shalt find that I am gracious and merciful, abundant in goodness, and truth, and forsaking none before they forsake me, and have not appointed thee these means in vain. To whom thus prepared did I ever deny the grace of faith? Name him if thou canst.[174]

Baxter maintains that "the right use of this commoner grace, in the use of the foresaid means, is a way appointed by God himself, and not in vain, by and in which men may be made fit to receive that special Grace which will call them savingly to believe."[175] Also, "no man is denied that *special grace* that deserveth it not by the *abuse* of *Common grace*".[176] It is enough to maintain that "God setteth men on no unprofitable work." Baxter adds to this: "Whether *de nomine* this encouragement shall be called a *promise* or equipollent, let them contend that list."[177] Whether it is a "proper Promise" is "a hard question."[178] Baxter even says that in a relative sense God's intrinsic will is conditional.[179]

---

169. Cf. above, p. 102.
170. Baxter, *Methodus Theologiæ* III.xxv.280: "SÆpe jam dictum est, Volitionem Dei realiter in se esse ejus ipsam Voluntatem essentialem; solùm igitur de *ejus relativâ denominatione,* & de ejus *operibus* quærendum restat." ("It has often been said already that God's will, as it is really in himself, is his essential will itself. Therefore, it only remains to enquire about its relative denomination and about its works.")
171. Baxter, *Catholick Theologie* II.118.
172. Baxter, *End of Doctrinal Controversies*, pp. 181-84; *Catholick Theologie* I.iii.16-17; II.156-69; *Methodus Theologiæ* III.xxv.292-94. Cf. Jeremias, "Richard Baxters Catholic Theology," pp. 280-81; McGrath, "Puritans and the Human Will," pp. 313-15; Beougher, "Conversion," pp. 108-25.
173. For the question whether Baxter's emphasis on the use of means leads to a rejection of irresistible grace, see appendix C.
174. Baxter, *Catholick Theologie* I.iii.23-24. For the phrase "half promise," taken from John Cotton (1584-1652), see also II.171.
175. Baxter, *Catholick Theologie* I.iii.46.
176. Baxter, *Catholick Theologie* I.iii.46.
177. Baxter, *Catholick Theologie* I.iii.57.
178. Baxter, *Catholick Theologie* II.170.
179. Baxter, *Methodus Theologiæ* III.xxv.281: "Ipsa igitur Dei intrinseca Volitio dici potest *Conditionalis relativè* ab hac *Lege* seu *Promissione Conditionali:* quâ scilicet *Donationem Conditionalem* voluit & fecit. At quamvis conditionalis dicitur quoad rem volitam, non inde opinandum est, aliquid reale in ipso Deo incertum esse, aut ex actu creaturæ dependere: Absolute vult

It is evident that Baxter comes close to asserting a promise of special grace upon the good use of common grace. His concern for the doctrine of God prevents the acceptance of a thoroughly Arminian doctrine of grace. By taking a mediating position Baxter is able to remain within his framework of the bifurcation of God's will as *voluntas de rerum eventu* and *voluntas de debito*. To be sure, it is not easy for Baxter to retain the former. His elaborate expositions on preparation for saving grace do have some tendency of minimizing God as *Dominus Absolutus*.

Still, Baxter's emphasis on preparation for saving grace does not mean that he teaches that a saving response is possible for all.[180] Such an interpretation would

---

veritatem promissionis suæ conditionalis." ("Therefore, God's intrinsic will itself may be called conditional in a relative sense from the conditional law or promise. For by this he wanted and made a conditional gift. But although it is called conditional with respect to the thing willed, it must not thence be concluded that something real in God himself is uncertain or depends on a creature's act. He wants the reality of the promise or condition absolutely."). In answering the question whether the performance of certain conditions or preparatory works are truly the cause of a certain operation of the Holy Spirit, Baxter states that God has imposed conditions in the law of grace. He is willing to speak of conditions because they are not really proper causes but only receptive moral dispositions without which the Donator does not want his donation to be efficient. ("Conditio autem ex sua natura non est causa rei, sed ut *imposita* est *Modus Donationis* ejus effectum suspendens donec præstetur, & ut *præstita* est *Dispositio receptiva moralis* sine quâ *Donator* suam donationem esse efficientem noluit" [III.xxv.294].) Man does not merit *per justitiam commutativam*. Yet, without preparation and the resulting receptive disposition he is unable to receive further grace. Baxter concludes: "Ideoque juxta justitiam Paterni regiminis distributivam, quæ spectat solum recipientis aptitudinem, mereri dicitur. Et ita Patres uno ore nos mereri à Deo dicere soliti sunt: Sine gratiâ autem divinâ etiam conditio hæc majoris gratiæ non præstatur." ("Therefore, according to the distributive justice of Paternal government, which respects only the aptitude of the recipient, he is said to merit. And, thus, the fathers always say with one accord that we merit from God. Without divine grace, however, also this condition for further grace cannot be performed" [III.xxv.294]).

Beougher, although correct both in stating that man cannot bind God by means of preparation and that God remains *Dominus Absolutus*, overstates his case when he says: "Baxter emphasized that there was no merit in the activity of preparation" ("Conversion," p. 205; cf. p. 124). As the analysis above demonstrates, Baxter had no problem admitting that a person could merit special grace *de congruo*.

180. Cf. the following comments: (1) M. Grégoire: "Avec Calvin il <*i.e.*, Baxter> admet que Dieu a prédestiné certains hommes au bonheur, sans prévision de leurs mérites. Ils ont des grâces que seuls ils possèdent, et ils seront sauvés infailliblement; mais avec Arminius, Baxter croit que les autres hommes ont éventuellement, pour parvenir au bonheur éternel, des grâces dont le bon usage peut leur procurer le salut ..." (*Histoire des sectes religieuses: Qui sont nées, se sont modifiées, se sont éteintes dans les différentes contrées du globe, depuis le commencement du siècle dernier jusqu'a l'époque actuelle*, new ed., V [Paris: Baudouin, 1829], p. 52). (2) George P. Fisher: "All men have not only the natural power to repent and believe, but they have such grace as confers *moral* ability, and if faithfully used, would lead finally to their conversion and salvation ("Theology of Richard Baxter," 152). Fisher also comments: "If men do what is in their power, their salvation is sure" ("Writings of Richard Baxter," 313). (3) A.R. Ladell: "Baxter inclined more and more to his own interpretation of Common and Special Grace, and to insist upon the possibility of Salvation including every man" (*Richard Baxter*, p. 133). (4) Hugh Martin: Baxter holds that "the salvation offered in Christ is sufficient for all, and all men, if *they* choose, can avail themselves of it" (*Puritanism and Richard Baxter*, p. 135). (5) Isolde Jeremias: "Obwohl nun alle Menschen die Freiheit und die Fähigkeit besitzen, durch die allgemeine Gnade in sich für die besondere Gnade die Voraussetzungen zu schaffen, lehnen sie diese Möglichkeit ab" ("Richard Baxters Catholic Theology," p. 82). (6) Iain Murray: "To avoid the Pelagian error that faith arises from the sinner himself, Baxter taught that God gives sufficient 'common grace' to all men to make a saving response to the gospel possible for all" ("Richard Baxter-'The Reluctant Puritan'?" p. 9).

be one-sided as well as misleading. Baxter explicitly denies that all unbelievers have sufficient grace to believe.[181] When he faces the Arminian reproach that Calvinists deny all sufficient grace to believe except that which is effectual, Baxter replies:

> You wrong them: They do not so: Have I not told you now, that they commonly grant that even the godly themselves have *sufficient Grace* to *believe*, which is not effectual as to many an act of Faith? And as to Unbelievers, 1. They say that all have not Grace sufficient or necessary to believe: And so say the *Arminians*. 2. But whether *any* one have or no, who believe not, they rather leave it to the Searcher of hearts as an unknown thing to them, than deny it.[182]

In typically Baxterian fashion, Baxter regards the question whether unbelievers have sufficient grace to believe as an issue on which Calvinists and Arminians have no real disagreement. Not only Calvinists, but also Arminians deny that all have sufficient grace to believe. The reason is obvious: all are not equally well prepared; all do not have an equally suited disposition for saving grace.[183] It is true that all men have sufficient grace to do more good and less evil than they do.[184] But this is not to say that all men are morally in a position to respond savingly to the Gospel offer.[185]

ASSURANCE OF FAITH

No Assurance With a Small Degree of Saving Grace

Baxter often expounds his views on common grace in the context of remarks on the assurance of faith. On several places in *The Right Method for a Settled Peace*

---

181. Baxter, *End of Doctrinal Controversies*, p. 170: "The common disputed question is, Whether all men have Grace *sufficient to believe*? which must be negatively answered; They have not. Those that never heard the Gospel, have not." Baxter then continues by saying that also many who have heard the Gospel may be so hardened that they are not at all in a position to believe (p. 170).
182. Baxter, *Catholick Theologie* II.131. Baxter calls the question whether unregenerate people have power to believe "the very core and true sum of all our Controversies" (II.85). Both here and elsewhere, he refuses to settle the question whether there is anyone who has sufficient grace to believe savingly, but nevertheless does not do so. He inclines, however, to an affirmative answer. Cf. II.124; *End of Doctrinal Controversies*, pp. 171-72.
183. Cf. *End of Doctrinal Controversies*, p. 165. Baxter distinguishes between natural ability and moral ability. All have the natural ability to believe, but not the moral ability or will to believe (*Catholick Theologie* I.iii.2, 35-37, 43-46; II.79-81, 86-87, 96-97; *End of Doctrinal Controversies*, pp. 176-77, 179-80). To Baxter, the solution to the controversies over grace lies in a correct apprehension of the word "can" (*Catholick Theologie* I.iii.44-45; II.86, 88, 107, 113, 146).
184. Baxter, *Catholick Theologie* I.iii.2, 43; II.107-08, 114, 131; *End of Doctrinal Controversies*, p. 164.
185. Even W. Lawrence Highfill does not quite capture Baxter's position when he summarizes: "All men, Baxter holds, have proper natural power necessary for salvation so that condemnation can never be because of a lack in basic equipment. However, this power has an indisposition to believe, though never so great that God's 'commoner sort of Grace' could not be effective to prepare for receiving God's special grace which calls man to believe" ("Faith and Works," p. 100). Baxter does not go as far as to suggest that regardless of how ill disposed one may be, common grace may ultimately lead to special grace.

of Conscience (1653), for instance, he deals with common grace amidst directions for assurance. Also the controverted chapter of *Saints Everlasting Rest* is actually an inquiry into the number and use of the marks of grace. It is no exaggeration to say that Baxter's comments on common grace serve as an aid to clarify questions concerning the assurance of faith.

There are several motives for Baxter's concern to link assurance of salvation with common grace. His interest in questions surrounding assurance is by no means academic. As noted earlier, his reading of experimental divines contributed to his lack of assurance. He lacked the preparatory steps to conversion as outlined in their practical works.[186] Baxter writes about his own experiences:

> As I lay under seven years' doubting and perplexity of spirit myself, much through my ignorance in the managing of this work, so was I very inquisitive still after signs of sincerity, and I got all the books that ever I could buy, which laid down evidences and marks of true grace, and tended to discover the difference betwixt the true christian and the hypocrite or unsound; I liked no sermon so well as that which contained most of these marks; and afterward, when I was called to the ministry myself, I preached in this way as much as most.[187]

Another factor which directly contributed to Baxter's insertion of comments on common grace into his expositions on assurance of faith was his fear of false security and complacency. If every believer would have assurance of faith people would be encouraged to sin. God has not told people just how much they may sin, because this would have promoted assurance in "those that were unfit for it."[188] God has, therefore, not linked the smallest degree of saving grace to assurance.[189] Because the natural difference between common and saving grace lies at an undiscernible point, it is understandable that, according to Baxter, only "stronger Christians" experience assurance of salvation.[190]

It is to be expected that one of Kendall's main objections to Baxter's view of common grace is that it takes away assurance. Kendall views Baxter's advise to lay Christ in one end of the balance and our carnal interests and inferior good in

---

186. Cf. above, pp. 155-56.
187. Baxter, *Saints Rest* in *Works* III.189 (23.1). As Baxter grew older, his quest for marks of grace became less pressing. In 1664, he wrote: "I was once wont to meditate most on my own *heart*, and to dwell all at home, and look little higher: I was still poring either on my Sins or Wants, or examining my Sincerity; but now, though I am greatly convinced of the need of Heart-acquaintance and imployment, yet I see more need of a higher work; and that I should look often upon Christ, and God, and Heaven, than upon my own Heart. At *home* I can find Distempers to trouble me, and some Evidences of my Peace: but it is *above* that I must find matter of *Delight* and *Joy*, and *Love* and *Peace* it self. Therefore I would have *one thought* at home upon *my self and sins*, and *many thoughts above* upon the high and amiable and beatifying Objects" (*RB* I.129).
188. Baxter, *Right Method*, in *Works* II.909 (9.88).
189. Baxter says that "those that have the smallest degree of saving grace, do not use to have any assurance of salvation" (*Saints Rest*, in *Works* III.205 [23.49]). The reason is that "it might have been a strong temptation to men to sin as far as ever they may, and to neglect their graces. I know some will say that assurance breeds not security. But that great measure of corruption which liveth with our small measure of grace, will make assurance an occasion of security and boldness in sinning. A strong christian may bear and improve assurance, but so cannot the weakest; and therefore God useth not to give assurance to weakest christians" (III.205 [23.49]).
190. Baxter, *Right Method*, in *Works* II.911-13 (9.93-101).

the other with great suspicion.[191] Says Kendall: "But this *prevailing degree* is not at *all discernable*, according to your *ground*, therefore it is *impossible* to get Assurance."[192] Kendall insists that assurance of salvation is "necessarily *included* fundamentally in every *degree of Saving Grace*."[193] He is willing to admit that assurance, as well as saving grace, may have degrees. But he rejects Baxter's argument that assurance in weak Christians might lead to presumption and sinning. Instead, the small measure of grace will further mortify corruption.[194]

Baxter does not reply to Kendall's charge that assurance will become impossible if one has to weigh the evidence to conclude where one's prevailing interest lies. It is indeed obvious that in Baxter's scheme of thought assurance becomes the privilege of stronger Christians. To Baxter, however, this is an acceptable corollary of his position on common grace. Although weak Christians do not have full assurance of salvation, Baxter is convinced that his teaching at least does not lead to the false assurance which threatens those who have heard that God accepts the least true desire for the deed. Knowing that their desires are not counterfeit, they come to assurance "on deceitful grounds."[195]

Baxter mentions four marks of sincerity, of which he rejects three as unsuitable for self-examination. First, he says that "many a soul hath been deluded" by taking the love for God's children as a mark. This is not a true mark of sincere faith because also a wicked man may have some degree of love to godliness and, therefore, some love to God's children for their godliness.[196] A second mark of sincerity which is often given is "when a man is the same in secret before God alone as he is in public before men, making conscience of secret as well as open duties."[197] Baxter thinks that this, also, is not an infallible mark because carnal interests may also affect someone's secret duties. A third common mark is that a person loves the most searching preaching. This mark may fail because a person may simply love such preaching because it discovers the hypocrisy of others or because he is strict in doctrine. Such preaching does not necessarily affect his heart.[198]

The fourth mark of sincerity which Baxter mentions is "when a man hath no known sin which he is not willing to part with."[199] This mark Baxter considers sound because it indicates that Christ's interest in the will is "prevalent" over all the interest of the flesh. In effect, this means that there are many things which may function as marks of sincerity. Baxter mentions hatred to sin, love to good, and the spirit of prayer as examples.[200] He then comments:

191. Kendall, *Sancti sanciti* IV.136.
192. Kendall, *Sancti sanciti* IV.137. Cf. IV.99.
193. Kendall, *Sancti sanciti* IV.138.
194. Kendall, *Sancti sanciti* IV.139.
195. Baxter, *Saints Rest*, in *Works* III.206 (23.50-51).
196. Baxter, *Saints Rest*, in *Works* III.203 (23.42-43).
197. Baxter, *Saints Rest*, in *Works* III.203 (23.43).
198. Baxter, *Saints Rest*, in *Works* III.203-04 (23.44).
199. Baxter, *Saints Rest*, in *Works* III.204 (23.44).
200. Baxter, *Saints Rest*, in *Works* III.204 (23.45).

I think, if I could stand to mention all the other marks of grace, so far as I remember, it would appear that the life and truth of them all lieth in this one, as being the very point wherein saving sincerity doth consist, viz. in the prevalency of Christ's interest in the soul, above the interest of inferior good; and so in the degree, not in the bare nature of any act.[201]

Taken as such, the various marks usually mentioned are not signs that a person has saving faith. If, however, Christ's interest prevails in these various duties, then one may be certain that he has a true mark of sincerity.

Common Grace and Probability of Salvation

Not only does Baxter want to avoid false security by means of his theory of common grace, but he also considers common grace itself as an important ground on which one may base the probability of his salvation. In his *Right Method*, Baxter mentions four grounds of such a probability. First, he deals with the merciful nature of God. A right estimation of God's goodness will effect love to God as well as persuasions of his love and of true grace.[202] Second, a deep apprehension of the gracious nature, disposition, and office of the Mediator is necessary.[203] The next step, Baxter points out, is to accept that Christ's sacrifice is for all.[204] The last ground of probability is the universal tenor of the new covenant of grace.[205]

Baxter then applies these four motives by distinguishing between common and special grace. He says that this distinction opens up "a rich mine of consolation."[206] One must not begin by inquiring after the sincerity of one's graces, but one must first go through the four steps in order to receive "the comforts of universal or general grace."[207] Baxter here strikes a note which is found throughout his writings. To begin by looking inward would mean to start at the wrong end. Instead, one should seek to grow in grace. By doing good works and by focusing the attention on common grace one's assurance will be increased accordingly: "Duty goeth in order of nature and time before comfort, as the precept is before the promise; comfort is part of the reward, and therefore necessarily supposeth the duty."[208] For weak Christians, the best remedy against a lack of assurance would be to do one's duty till graces increase:

> Oh! that christians would bestow most of that time in getting more grace, which they bestow in anxious doubtings whether they have any or none; and that they would lay out those serious affections in praying, and seeking to Christ for more grace, which they bestow in fruitless complaints of their supposed gracelessness![209]

201. Baxter, *Saints Rest*, in *Works* III.204 (23.45).
202. Baxter, *Right Method*, in *Works* II.889-91 (9.27-33).
203. Baxter, *Right Method*, in *Works* II.891-92 (9.33-35).
204. Baxter, *Right Method*, in *Works* II.892 (9.35).
205. Baxter, *Right Method*, in *Works* II.892 (9.35). Baxter repeats all four in II.914 (9.103).
206. Baxter, *Right Method*, in *Works* II.892 (9.36).
207. Baxter, *Right Method*, in *Works* II.893 (9.37).
208. Baxter, *Right Method*, in *Works* II.923 (9.132-33).
209. Baxter, *Saints Rest*, in *Works* III.176 (22.506). Cf. III.206 (23.52): "If they had considered, that both the saving sincerity of their graces lieth in the prevailing degree ... this would have taught

Both the performance of one's duties and the proper insight in the doctrine of common grace may further one's assurance.

Baxter extols the sufficiency of Christ's sacrifice and insists: "There is now a possibility of salvation to you. And certainly even that should be a very great comfort."[210] Baxter reiterates that people's salvation is already conditionally certain and that the condition only lies in people's willingness.[211] The four grounds of probability, related as they are to common grace, may give much spiritual comfort and peace from the mere probability of salvation, even where certainty is still lacking.[212]

The significance of these comments in *Right Method* lies especially in the overt connection between common grace and universal redemption. Common grace is based on Christ's sacrifice. Or, to put it in Rooy's words: "The redemption of Christ secured a general and sufficient grace to all, and a special and effectual grace to those who believe."[213] It is remarkable that neither Kendall, nor Barlow, have given any attention to this matter.[214] Perhaps this is due to the fact that their reactions are directed against Baxter's *Saints Everlasting Rest* rather than his *Right Method.* Had Baxter's opponents focused on the extent of the atonement, they would have come to another major source of disagreement with Baxter.

The Role of Faith in Justification

FAITH IN CHRIST AS LORD AND SAVIOR

Faith and the Threefold Office of Christ

As the discussion moves to the role of faith in justification, the central core of the disagreements between Baxter and his opponents comes into view. In his *Confession* (1655), Baxter comments that there are especially two issues that tend to offend people. The first is his teaching that "<t>he Accepting Christ as King, and Teacher, is part of that Faith which is the Condition of Justification, and so justify-

---

them to have spent those thoughts and hours in labouring after growth in grace, which they spent in inquiring after the lowest degree which may stand with sincerity, and in seeking for that in themselves which was almost undiscernible."

210. Baxter, *Right Method*, in *Works* II.894 (9.40).
211. Baxter, *Right Method*, in *Works* II.894 (9.41).
212. Baxter, *Right Method*, in *Works* II.914-15 (9.103-07).
213. Rooy, *Theology of Missions*, p. 91.
214. Several times, Koelman uses the word "special" (*bijzonder*) in referring to special graces. These graces have a "special moral relation" to Christ's mediatorial work. They are a "special part" of Christ's meritorious death. Christ's "special intercession" does not relate to the common graces of the unregenerate. By saying that Christ's "special" work leads to special grace, Koelman seems to imply that there may also be a "common" work of Christ leading to common grace. He does not work this out, however, and does not indicate how he would want to maintain limited atonement if common grace is the result of Christ's work as Mediator.

ing as well as the taking his righteousness."[215] The second offensive teaching is that obedience is a secondary part of the condition of the continuation of justification.[216] The first of these two issues will be under discussion in the present chapter. John Warner agrees that it is a significant question. The expression *fides qua iustificans* or *fides quatenus iustificans* may be taken in two different ways:

> 1. *Reduplicatively*, that is, when it doubles the subject of the proposition, as when we say, man as man is a reasonable creature: Faith as Faith, doth justifye. 2. *Specificatively*, when by the particle *quà* or *quatenùs*, there is some new or singular kind of *denomination* added to the *subject of the proposition*, as when we say, man as a reasonable creature feeleth.[217]

Warner interprets the particle *qua* or *quatenus* in the latter sense when he says that faith as justifying looks on Christ as Savior: "I dispute not what *fides qua fides* may doe, but *qua justificat*."[218] It is this distinction which has induced Warner to the writing of his discourse. In this connection he speaks of the *cardo controversiae*, the hinge of the controversy.[219] Baxter and Warner agree, therefore, that the question of justifying faith as justifying (*qua iustificans*) is of great significance.

The weight given to the issue may seem somewhat out of proportion. How great is the difference between Baxter and his opponents really? First, all participants in the debate agree that justifying faith has reference to Christ's threefold office of Prophet, Priest, and King. Warner grants "that the object of *justifying faith is* Jesus Christ, both Saviour and Lord; or that *Jesus Christ*, who is *anointed* to be *Prophet, Priest*, and *King*."[220] Similarly, Thomas Blake states that "faith accepts Christ as a Lord as well as a Saviour ..."[221] The issue is not that Baxter would regard justifying faith as the acceptance of Christ as Prophet, Priest, and King, while his opponents would view justifying faith as the embracing of Christ as Priest only. Rather, it is agreed by all that justifying faith accepts Christ in his threefold office.

Further, it is not the intention of Baxter's antagonists to make a division between the three aspects of Christ's mediatorship. The distinction between Christ as Lord and Savior is only made "for the imperfection of our understanding."[222]

---

215. Baxter, *Confession*, p. 297. Baxter considers the question whether the faith – as opposed to works – is only one physical act of the soul "the very heart of our Controversie, which most of our Disputes about the instrumentall Causality of Faith as to Justification, and the other Concomitant, are resolved into" (*Of Justification*, sig. a1ᵛ). In his account of the conference with Burgess in 1650, Baxter writes: "I told him y<a>ᵗ my Definition of faith was yᵉ very foundation of my opinion in yᵉ point of Justificat<io>ⁿ, & g̅o̅ to me of greatest moment, & if he yielded y<a>ᵗ ffaith as Justifying was a Receiving of Xᵗ as Lord & King & not to Justifye & Save only, y<e>ⁿ I desired no more" (DWL MS *BC* I, f. 263ʳ).
216. Baxter, *Confession*, p. 297. Baxter mentions the same "two great points opposed in my Doctrine" in *Of Justification*, p. 220.
217. Warner, *Diatriba fidei justificantis*, p. 29.
218. Warner, *Diatriba fidei justificantis*, p. 31.
219. Warner, *Diatriba fidei justificantis*, p. 31.
220. Warner, *Diatriba fidei justificantis*, p. 357.
221. Blake, *Vindiciæ foederis*, p. 79.
222. Warner, *Diatriba fidei justificantis*, sigs. †6ᵛ-†7ʳ (emphasis throughout in original).

Although "we should look upon all these offices joyntly in Christ," yet Warner insists that we should have "a *distinct* inspection into them according to their severall respects and uses."[223] As Prophet, Christ leads us out of a state of darkness and blindness; as Priest, he leads us out of a state of enmity and alienation to God; and as King, he leads us out of a state of impotency.[224]

Thus, the difference centers on the distinction between *fides quae* and *fides qua*. Baxter's adversaries agree that the faith which justifies (*fides quae iustificat*) is faith in Christ as Lord and Savior. They do not, however, believe that this faith, as such, justifies. When Blake has stated that faith accepts Christ both as Lord and as Savior, he continues:

> But it is the acceptation of him as a Saviour, not as a Lord that justifies; Christ rules his people as a King, teacheth them as a Prophet, but makes atonement for them only as a Priest, by giving himself in sacrifice, his bloud for remission of sins; These must be distinguished, but not divided, faith hath an eye at all, the bloud of Christ, the command of Christ, the Doctrine of Christ, but as it ties and fastens on his bloud, so it justifies.[225]

Blake lays out his position clearly. Though faith has respect to Christ in his threefold office and accepts him as such, faith does not *justify* as such. Faith in its role of instrument in justification has reference only to Christ's priesthood, or, to put it more precisely, his atoning death.

Baxter's opponents want to distinguish the object of faith without dividing it. Baxter points out, however, that they do not always succeed. Christopher Cartwright, for instance, comments that "Justification it self requires that Christ be received as King, yet not that Justification may be obtained, but because it is obtained."[226] Baxter immediately retorts: "I perceive now that you think the *receiving Christ as Priest*, and *as King*, are two distinct acts; and that the former alone justifieth us, not only without the other, as a *Condition*, but even without its *presence*, which is but to *follow* because we *are justified*."[227] Also Warner comments that the embracing of Christ as Savior is "precedaneous" to the acceptance of him as King.[228] Baxter attacks the novelty of this teaching.[229] He maintains that Warner has now shown that he not only distinguishes but divides the office of Christ.[230]

Baxter has indeed pointed out a problem in the thinking of Cartwright and Warner. On the one hand, they hold that faith looks to Christ as Savior and as Lord and that the former aspect of this faith justifies. On the other hand, they also state

223. Warner, *Diatriba fidei justificantis*, p. 407.
224. Warner, *Diatriba fidei justificantis*, pp. 404-06.
225. Blake, *Vindiciæ foederis*, p. 79.
226. Cartwright, in Baxter, *Account of my Consideration*, p. 208.
227. Baxter, *Account of my Consideration*, p. 208. In his rejoinder, Cartwright again admits that there may be "a receiving of Christ as Priest without an express and direct receiving of him as King, though implicitly and by consequence he be received as such" (*Exceptions*, p. 98).
228. Warner, *Diatriba fidei justificantis*, sig. †7ʳ.
229. Baxter, *Of Justification*, p. 300.
230. Baxter, *Of Justification*, p. 316.

that the two aspects of faith can be separated. Despite this tension, it remains clear that the main line of thinking in Cartwright and Warner is that faith in Christ as Savior and Lord may be distinguished but not divided. What is more, Baxter himself does not entirely escape the danger of putting Christ's kingship and his priesthood in opposition. For instance, he asks rhetorically: "<I>s it not much liker, if we must needs make a distinction in the matter, that God rather intended the Accepting of Christ as King, to be more the Condition of our Justification, then the accepting him as pardoner or justifier?"[231] Baxter makes a comparison to a physician, who does not say he will be someone's physician on the condition that the patient is willing to be healed. Instead, the physician will ask that the patient will take him for his physician, will trust him, will take his medicines, and will follow his directions.[232] To be sure, Baxter adds that he does not mean to "make any partition in this business."[233] It is clear, however, that he lays greater emphasis on consenting to Christ's lordship than on accepting him as Priest.

The Relation between Act and Object of Faith

Baxter's opponents have one main argument which underlies their position: acts must follow their object. Warner maintains that if there are different objects there must be different acts, "for *objects*, or *objective formalities*, doe *specifie* the acts."[234] The logical outcome is that the acts of faith differ as they have reference to Christ either as Savior or as Lord. Operating on this same principle, Cartwright comments: "The Hand may receive both Meat and Mony, yet it doth not enrich, as it receiveth Meat, nor feed as it receiveth Mony."[235]

Numerous texts are adduced to support this line of argument. Does Romans 3:25 not say that God has set forth Christ as a propitiation through faith in his *blood*?[236] Are we not said to be justified by Christ's *blood* (Rom 5:9)?[237] Did Paul not preach Christ *crucified* (1 Cor 2:2)?[238] Baxter agrees with all this. He also admits that the faith of the fathers under the Old Testament was directed to Christ as Priest.[239] He further agrees that it is true that the Levitical types pointed to Christ's sacrifice.[240] Christ as dying and as Savior did indeed satisfy God's justice.[241] Admittedly, Christ as crucified is the substance of evangelical preach-

231. Baxter, *Confession*, p. 304.
232. Baxter, *Confession*, pp. 305-06. Cf. *Account of my Consideration*, p. 208: "The Scripture calleth him *Christ, the Anointed*, more fully and frequently, in respect to the Kingly part of his Office than any."
233. Baxter, *Confession*, p. 306.
234. Warner, *Diatriba fidei justificantis*, sig. †6ᵛ (emphasis inverted). Cf. p. 366.
235. Cartwright, *Exceptions*, pp. 96-97.
236. Blake, *Vindiciæ foederis*, p. 79; *Covenant Sealed*, p. 567; Tombes, in Baxter, *Of Justification*, pp. 327, 329-30.
237. Blake, *Covenant Sealed*, p. 567; Tombes, in Baxter, *Of Justification*, pp. 329-30; Warner, *Diatriba fidei justificantis*, p. 400.
238. Warner, *Diatriba fidei justificantis*, p. 400.
239. Warner, *Diatriba fidei justificantis*, p. 412. Cf. Baxter, *Of Justification*, p. 293.
240. Blake, *Covenant Sealed*, p. 566. Cf. Baxter, *Of Justification*, p. 53.
241. Warner, *Diatriba fidei justificantis*, p. 412. Cf. Baxter, *Of Justification*, p. 293.

ing.[242] The Holy Spirit does indeed direct our faith to Christ's death, suffering, blood, and obedience.[243] It is also granted that faith must follow Christ's death to bring us to God.[244] Further, the sacraments do indeed present us with Christ as dying.[245] It is true that we have redemption and remission of sins by his blood (Col 1:14).[246] Also, we are justified by receiving Christ as priest.[247] He frees us from the curse by suffering as a sacrifice.[248] And Christ as a servant must certainly be believed in.[249] Finally, Baxter willingly grants that the promise of salvation is the proper object of justifying faith.[250]

Baxter will grant all of the above propositions. But he has one reservation. In all cases, he charges his antagonists with omitting the word "only," which is what they really need in order to defeat Baxter's position. What Baxter denies is that the faith of the Old Testament fathers was directed *only* to Christ as Priest, that the Levitical types *only* pointed to Christ's sacrifice, and so forth. This, for Baxter, is the main weakness in all the Scriptural evidence which his opponents present. Warner, however, scorns Baxter's oft repeated comment that the word "only" is lacking in his opponents' arguments. Says Warner: "The want of this *exclusive particle* being not expresly found in scripture, hath indeed made the Papists triumph before the victory; for when they grant that we are justified by faith *according to the scriptures*, yet they would have us shew where the scripture saith we are justified *only* by faith."[251] Warner maintains that the word "only" is clearly implied because of the frequency with which Scripture directs faith to Christ as Savior.[252]

Baxter insists that we must receive Christ as Christ. He declines to narrow Christ's role as Savior to his priestly task: "The word *Saviour*, comprehendeth both his Prophetical and Kingly Office, by which he saveth us from sin and Hell; as also his Resurrection, Ascension, Intercession, &c."[253] Furthermore, when Baxter does admit a differentiation in Christ's mediatorship, he consistently maintains that this only holds from the side of Christ (*ex parte Christi*), not from our side (*ex parte nostri*):

> Though, *ex parte Christi*, our several changes proceed from his several Benefits, and parts of his Office exercised for us; yet, *ex parte nostri*, i.e. *fidei*, it is one entire

242. Warner, *Diatriba fidei justificantis*, p. 413. Cf. Baxter, *Of Justification*, pp. 295-96.
243. Blake, *Covenant Sealed*, p. 567. Cf. Baxter, *Of Justification*, pp. 57-58. Also, Warner, *Diatriba fidei justificantis*, p. 414. Cf. Baxter, *Of Justification*, pp. 296-97.
244. Blake, *Covenant Sealed*, p. 568. Cf. Baxter, *Of Justification*, p. 64.
245. Blake, *Covenant Sealed*, p. 567. Cf. Baxter, *Of Justification*, pp. 55-57. Also, Warner, *Diatriba fidei justificantis*, pp. 414-15. Cf. Baxter, *Of Justification*, pp. 297-98.
246. Warner, *Diatriba fidei justificantis*, p. 415. Cf. Baxter, *Of Justification*, p. 298.
247. Cartwright, in Baxter, *Account of my Consideration*, p. 192. Cf. Baxter, *Account of my Consideration*, p. 194.
248. Blake, *Covenant Sealed*, p. 568. Cf. Baxter, *Of Justification*, pp. 64-65.
249. Warner, *Diatriba fidei justificantis*, p. 416. Cf. Baxter, *Of Justification*, p. 299.
250. Warner, *Diatriba fidei justificantis*, p. 416. Cf. Baxter, *Of Justification*, pp. 300-01.
251. Warner, *Diatriba fidei justificantis*, pp. 366-67.
252. Warner, *Diatriba fidei justificantis*, p. 368.
253. Baxter, *Of Justification*, p. 297. Cf. p. 353: "To Receive him as Redeemer is to Receive him as King; For his very Redeeming was a Purchasing them into his own hands ... though not only so."

apprehension or receiving of Christ as he is offered in the Gospel, which is the
Condition of our interest in Christ and his several Benefits; and the effect is not
parcelled or diversified or distinguished from the several distinct respects that faith
hath to its object.[254]

Ex parte Christi, Christ's tasks as Prophet, Priest, and King must be distinguished.
But *ex parte nostri* such a distinction is not possible. Baxter makes a comparison
to marriage. A rich, honorable, merciful, and powerful man enriches his wife only
with his money, honors her only because he is honorable, and saves her from
danger only because he is merciful and powerful. His wife, however, has only one,
undivided condition if she is to benefit in any way from any of these aspects: she
must accept the man to be her husband to be loved and obeyed faithfully.[255]

Baxter is willing to admit that "faith in his blood" is a more proper expression
than "faith in his obedience." When Scripture uses the former expression, it uses
faith in a relative way, as it relates to Christ as its object.[256] In other words, when
Scripture speaks of "faith in his blood" it has a more particular reference to that
which Christ does. It speaks mostly *ex parte Christi*, rather than *ex parte nostri*.

Because Baxter admits that *ex parte nostri* it is possible to distinguish various
acts of faith, the question arises how he can say that it is one act of apprehending
Christ which justifies. He does so by differentiating between physical and moral
acts. As a moral act, faith is one condition. Here, Baxter appeals to the unity of
faith as mentioned in Ephesians 4:5. Coming to Christ as Christ is the sole, undivided condition of all his benefits, including justification.[257] In his last disputation
in *Of Justification*, the main thesis is: "The faith which *Paul* opposeth to works in
the business of Justification, is not any one single Physical act in *Specie specialissima:* Nor was it ever the meaning of *Paul* to exclude all acts except some such
one, from Justification, under the name of works."[258] Baxter concentrates here on
one particular argument: the unity of faith does not deny that faith in Christ as
Christ is demanded for justification. Baxter opposes a unity of faith of a very
particular kind (*species specialissima*). He means by this that faith *qua iustificans*
does not focus on one object only.

Baxter appeals to the fact that the one sentence "I believe in Christ as Christ"
includes at least twenty acts, such as assent to the truth of the Gospel in general,
assent to the truth of Christ's sinless life, and many other acts.[259] All these are

254. Baxter, *Account*, p. 4. For the same distinction, see *Account of my Consideration*, pp. 194-95,
     205; *Of Justification*, pp. 297, 378.
255. Baxter, *Account of my Consideration*, pp. 194-95.
256. Baxter, *Of Justification*, pp. 351, 359, 379. Baxter's formulation at this point is exceedingly
     careful. He does not simply say that faith stands for Christ as its object. He explicitly rejects such
     an interpretation and prefers to speak of the act of faith as it relates most fully to Christ as the
     object (p. 351). He also states that "principally" the grace of the Giver is in view, rather than faith
     itself (p. 359). The phrase "faith in his blood" speaks "not only" of the conditionality in the act of
     faith (p. 379). Baxter must be careful to avoid substituting "Christ" for "faith" because elsewhere
     he vehemently denounces those who make use of this same substitution in interpreting the
     expression that "faith is counted for righteousness" (Rom 4:5). Cf. below, p. 287.
257. Baxter appeals to Rom 8:28, 32; 1 John 5:11-12; and John 5:40 (*Of Justification*, pp. 33-34).
258. Baxter, *Of Justification*, p. 409 (emphasis inverted).
259. Baxter lists twenty such "acts" of assent in *Of Justification*, p. 410.

essential to faith.[260] Moreover, Baxter finds it striking that none of his opponents is able to *mention* the one particular act of faith which would be opposed to all the others as works.[261] Also elsewhere, he often insists that justifying faith cannot be one single act only, because it is an act both of the understanding and of the will. It involves assent, consent, and affiance.[262] Baxter concludes, therefore, that just as marriage is one in a civil or moral sense but has many physical acts, so faith is one in a moral sense (Eph 4:5), but has many physical acts or articles.[263]

That the acceptance of Christ as Prophet, Priest, and King, is one, undivided act *ex parte nostri* is clear from the fact that Scripture teaches that the condemning sin of unbelief is the rejection of Christ in his threefold office. To Baxter, this is an important argument to which he returns on several occasions.[264] He appeals especially to Luke 19:27 and to John 3:18-19. In the parable of Luke 19, the nobleman condemns his enemies "which would not that I should reign over them." The rejection of Christ's kingship is the reason for condemnation. The opposite of this rejection of Christ as King is justifying faith. Acceptance of Christ as King is, therefore, part of justifying faith.[265] In John 3:18-19, the condemning unbelief is described as the "shunning or not coming to Christ as he is the Light to discover and heal their evil deeds."[266] The conclusion must be that justifying faith includes accepting Christ as Teacher.[267]

Union with Christ also proves the unity of faith. Union with Christ is by faith. Says Baxter: "We are united to him as to a Head, Husband and Prince, and not only as a Justifier? therefore from him received as a Head, Husband and Prince, do these Benefits of Justification and Adoption flow."[268] Furthermore, if justifying faith only had reference to Christ as crucified, this would mean that Christ's active

---

260. Baxter seems to make a minor reservation about one of these twenty articles of faith: "And of the rest, unless the fifth [*Believing that Christ was conceived by the Holy Ghost, and born of a Virgin*] may be excepted (which I dare not affirm) I know not of one thats not essential to Christianity. And I think if we had Hereticks among us that denyed Christ to be conceived by the Holy Ghost, we should scarce take them for Christians" (*Of Justification*, p. 417).
    With respect to weak and ignorant Christians Baxter comments that they truly have every particular essential article of faith, "but perhaps it may be but by a more crude imperfect Conception, that observeth not every Article distinctly, nor any of them very clearly, but his knowledge is both too dim and too confused" (p. 419). Baxter wants to distinguish this confused knowledge from the Roman Catholic doctrine of virtual or implicit faith, which is believing that Scripture is God's true Word, or which believes that the church has the true articles of faith "while they know not what the Church or Scripture doth propound: for this is not actual Christian faith ..." (p. 419).
261. Baxter, *Of Justification*, pp. 415-16. Cf. *Confession*, pp. 90-92; *Defence of Christ*, p. 21.
262. Baxter, *Confession*, pp. 90, 92-93; *Of Justification*, pp. 353-57, 360; *Catholick Theologie* II.250.
263. Baxter, *Of Justification*, pp. 402, 421. Cf. pp. 353-54; *Confession*, p. 34.
264. Baxter, *Confession*, pp. 306-10; *Of Justification*, pp. 38-41, 353.
265. Baxter, *Account*, p. 6; *Confession*, pp. 306-08; *Of Justification*, pp. 39, 175, 223-24, 353. Warner comments with regard to this text that the rejection of Christ as King is not the only condemning sin. It includes unbelief in him as Savior. The enemies would not have been condemned if afterwards they had apprehended him as Savior by justifying faith (*Diatriba fidei justificantis*, pp. 371-72).
266. Baxter, *Of Justification*, p. 38.
267. Baxter, *Confession*, pp. 309-10; *Of Justification*, p. 38. In addition, Baxter appeals to John 3:36; 1 John 5:10-12; 2 Thess 2:12; 1:8-10; John 8:24; 16:8-9; Ps 2:12; Eph 5:5-6; 1 Cor 6:9-10; Gal 5:19-21, 24; Rom 8:9, 13.
268. Baxter, *Of Justification*, p. 352.

obedience was excluded from the meritorious cause of our justification. As Baxter is quick to add, this would be "no small errour in the Judgement of most Protestants."[269]

Baxter even appeals to the Shorter Catechism of the Westminster Assembly.[270] It defines faith in Jesus Christ as "a saving grace, whereby we receive and rest upon him alone for salvation, *as he is offered to us in the gospel*."[271] Baxter's appeal is somewhat one-sided. As Warner points out, the Larger Catechism clarifies this statement somewhat.[272] It says that by justifying faith one "not only assenteth to the truth of the promise of the gospel, but receiveth and resteth upon *Christ and his righteousness*, therein held forth, for pardon of sin, and for the accepting and accounting of his person righteous in the sight of God for salvation."[273] Here, says Warner, the object of justifying faith is the promise, and the matter received is Christ's righteousness.[274]

The Formal Interest of Faith in Justification

The reason why the *fides quae/fides qua* issue engenders such heated discussion is that both sides of the debate feel that the question has consequences for more fundamental problems. Baxter's opponents are afraid that if justifying faith *qua iustificans* includes Christ's lordship for its object, works will begin to play too dominant a role. John Tombes is willing to admit that Christ is not received truly if he is not entirely accepted as King. But, he adds, "this proves not that obedience is an essential part of faith; or that subjection to Christ as King justifies as immediatety <sic>, as receiving him as Saviour."[275] The same fear of justification by works rings through in Cartwright's words that the requirement that Christ be received as King is "not that Justification may be obtained, but because it is obtained."[276] Warner says that Baxter includes "workes in the definition of *justifying faith*, making it a receiving *of Christ as Saviour, Lord and Lawgiver* for justification ..."[277] In other words, Baxter confuses justification and sanctification.[278]

Baxter is willing to run the risk of being charged with including works in the definition of faith. If, to avoid this, he would accept the distinction between *fides quae* and *fides qua*, a far more serious danger would present itself: that faith is no longer regarded as a mere *conditio sine qua non* but becomes an efficient cause in justification. This is the heart of Baxter's insistence that faith is one moral act

269. Baxter, *Of Justification*, p. 299.
270. Baxter, *Account*, pp. 6, 24; *Confession*, pp. 317-18; *Of Justification*, pp. 232, 379.
271. *Westminster Confession of Faith*, p. 310 (Answer 86; emphasis added).
272. Warner, *Diatriba fidei justificantis*, pp. 363-65.
273. *Westminster Confession of Faith*, p. 165 (Answer 72; emphasis added).
274. Warner, *Diatriba fidei justificantis*, p. 364.
275. Tombes, in Baxter, *Of Justification*, p. 329.
276. Cartwright, in Baxter, *Account of my Consideration*, p. 208.
277. Warner, *Diatriba fidei justificantis*, sig. †6' (emphasis inverted).
278. Warner, *Diatriba fidei justificantis*, p. 365. Cf. p. 416. Baxter denies that he includes works in the definition of faith (cf. below, pp. 294-99).

looking to Christ as he is offered in the Gospel. Here, Baxter also uses his most forceful language in denouncing his opponents' ideas. When Tombes says that faith as justifying is only the acceptance of Christ as our ransom, this is "either nonsense or false doctrine."[279] Baxter even goes as far as to suggest that his opponents expect justification by works in the sense disclaimed by Paul and that, therefore, they are "subverting" the Gospel.[280]

The underlying reason for the distinction between *fides quae* and *fides qua* lies, according to Baxter, in a wrong conception of the *ratio formalis*, the formal reason, of faith's interest in justification. Herein Baxter takes exception to two incorrect views. First, the formal reason of faith's interest in justification is not its goodness, as a good work.[281] But second, and for the present purpose more to the point, the formal reason is also not located in the apprehension of Christ. Says Baxter: "Faith justifieth not directly, as it apprehendeth Christ's Satisfaction ... But Faith justifieth directly or *formally*, as the *Condition of the Gift* ..."[282] His opponents err in assuming that faith directly and physically apprehends Christ or his righteousness. Baxter insists that there is no such apprehension of Christ:

> Shall I again tell you the true ground of mens mistake (as I think) in this Point? They look on Faith as if it were a natural Reception, and did make the thing received theirs immediatly aud <sic> formally, as it is such a Receiving *ex natura rei*, and not as it is *Receptio moralis*, whose effect depends wholly on, and its efficacy or Interest is derived directly from the Will, Constitution or Ordination of the Legislator and Donor, and so doth what it doth as a condition in Law-sence.[283]

Faith only apprehends Christ morally, by way of condition. Christ or his righteousness is not received directly or physically.

To say that Christ is apprehended directly by faith would mean that faith itself justifies. Baxter reiterates, therefore, that "*justifying* is not an *act or operation* of *faith*; but of *God* on the Believer."[284] To take one specific act of faith and pretend that it effects justification does an injustice to Christ: "And I would entreat you to consider. whether it were Gods Design in the Gospel, to advance any one Act of mans soul above the rest, and so to honour it? or rather to advance the *Lord Jesus* whom faith Receiveth?"[285]

In several places, Baxter gives summary statements of the various ways in which the *fides quae/fides qua* distinction may be understood.[286] The above analysis of Baxter's view of the formal reason of faith's interest in justification yields

279. Baxter, *Of Justification*, p. 310. Also in his reply to Warner, Baxter states that the distinction *fides quae/fides qua* is either "palpable false Doctrine" and a "meer begging of the Question," or there is no difference between the two (p. 294).
280. Baxter, *Catholick Theologie* II.251.
281. Baxter, *Confession*, p. 36.
282. Baxter, *Account of my Consideration*, p. 205. Cf. pp. 193-94, 229-35; *Confession*, p. 36; *Of Justification*, p. 270.
283. Baxter, *Of Justification*, p. 377.
284. Baxter, *Of Justification*, p. 311. Cf. p. 315.
285. Baxter, *Of Justification*, pp. 365-66.
286. Baxter, *Account of my Consideration*, pp. 192-94; *Account*, p. 7; *Of Justification*, pp. 294-95, 310-11.

a position from which it is easier to understand these summary statements. Baxter maintains that there are three ways in which the phrase *fides qua iustificans* may be understood. The first possible option is to take *qua* as referring to *fides*. This would mean that faith justifies as faith, by directing itself to Christ crucified. If this is the meaning, Baxter is of the opinion that the meaning is "inconveniently expressed" by the phrase *fides qua iustificans*. It would be clearer to speak of *fides qua Christum apprehendit*.[287] This clarifying expression demonstrates that this first meaning implies false doctrine. It would mean "that *hæc fides in Christum crucifixum qua talis justificat*."[288]

On the other hand, it is also possible to interpret the phrase *fides qua iustificans* in such a way that *qua* refers to *iustificans*. It may then define the material nature of the condition of justification. Here, faith does not justify *qua fides*, but as the performed condition (*qua conditio praestita*). In this sense, Baxter insists, there is no difference between *qua* and *quae*.[289] In a material sense, the condition is the acceptance of Christ as Prophet, Priest, and King. Therefore, if *qua* indicates this condition, it is identical to the *fides quae iustificat*. Finally, *qua* may also relate to the effect. In this third sense, *qua* also has reference to *iustificans*. It "would only express a distinction between *Justification* and other *Benefits*, and not between faith and faith. For then [*quâ justificans*] should be contradistinct only from [*qua sanctificans*] or the like."[290]

It will now be clear why Baxter rejects the first meaning of the phrase *qua iustificans*. It implies that faith as such (*qua talis*), in apprehending Christ's righteousness, justifies. This first sense corresponds to the erroneous position on faith's formal interest in justification which Baxter labors to confute. He is willing to accept both the second and the third interpretation of the phrase *fides qua iustificans*. In both meanings, however, the distinction between *fides quae* and *fides qua* has become superfluous. These two expressions have become identical. If the latter phrase indicates the material contents of the condition it is identical to the *fides quae iustificat*. If *fides qua iustificans* is meant to distinguish it from faith as it sanctifies, it is still the same faith which justifies and sanctifies. Baxter's conclusion is that the *fides quae/fides qua* distinction must be abandoned.

If one were to admit that faith *qua talis* has no efficient causality by directly and physically apprehending Christ, the main cause of error has been removed. The distinction no longer introduces "false doctrine." When Tombes, therefore, admits that faith is a mere condition and does not justify *qua talis*, Baxter thinks that Tombes is bound to accept the conclusion that faith in Christ as King justifies just as much as faith in Christ as Priest. Says Baxter:

> If I prove 1. that Faith justifieth as the Condition, on performance whereof the Gift is conferred. 2. And that this Faith which is the Condition, is the Accepting of Christ as Christ, or the Anointed King and Saviour: (both which are yielded me;) I must needs

287. Baxter, *Account of my Consideration*, p. 193.
288. Baxter, *Of Justification*, p. 294.
289. Baxter, *Of Justification*, pp. 294-95.
290. Baxter, *Of Justification*, p. 295.

think that I have proved that the Receiving Christ as King, doth as truly Justifie, as
the Receiving him as Priest or Justifier ...[291]

Tombes is closer to Baxter than either Cartwright or Warren. Tombes agrees with
Baxter that faith's formal interest in justification does not lie in its apprehension
of Christ but in being the condition. Because Tombes' position is close to that of
Baxter, however, he also lays himself open to criticism. What is the sense of the
fides quae/fides qua distinction once the first of the three meanings has been
abandoned? There is no difference between *fides quae* and *fides qua* either in the
second or in the third interpretation of the phrase *fides qua iustificans*.

THE INSTRUMENTALITY OF FAITH IN BAXTER'S OPPONENTS

Consistency in Baxter's Position?

Having established that justifying faith in Christ may not be distinguished *ex parte
nostri* into faith in Christ as Lord and faith in Christ as Savior, the question
remains what the role of faith is in justification. As noted already, Baxter's concern in insisting on the unity of faith is his fear that otherwise the apprehension of
Christ becomes the formal reason of faith's role in justification. Faith would then
take on an efficient causality in justification. The centrality of this concern in
Baxter's polemical writings asks for a further analysis of his position on the role
of faith.

Baxter denies Cartwright's charge that his position on the role of faith is
caused by mere partiality. He admits that it would be "a heinous crime" to reproach the views of others out of partiality. But he denies that this is the case:

> But surely, if I do know my own heart, I am partial in all my studies, for those men
> whom I am charged to be partial against, even against my self, and all others now
> living: But the light of appearing-Truth is that which forceth me to differ from them;
> and if I am mistaken, I have not yet learned a remedy. But certain I am, that partly
> *partiality for these* Reverend men, and partly the lothness to incur their censures,
> and especially lothness to occasion their offence and disquiet, have been so strong a
> temptation to me to shut my eyes, that I have been sometimes provoked to say,
> [*Depart from me; this knowledg is an ungrateful burthen, an offence to my dearest
> Friends, and makes men take me as a man of Contention:*] sed vicit veritas, (if I
> mistake not.)[292]

Baxter's refusal to shut his eyes for the evidence of the truth indicates that he is of
the opinion that important matters are at stake.

To his opponents, the denial of an inclination to partiality or singularity may
not have sounded very convincing. Cartwright, for one, seemed to think that

---

291. Baxter, *Of Justification*, p. 358.
292. Baxter, *Substance*, pp. 25-26. Cf. *Aphorismes* I.219 (p. 139): "Perhaps I shall be blamed, as
    singular from all men, in denying Faith to be the Instrument of our Justification: But affectation
    of singularity leades me not to it."

Baxter should have come to a more charitable understanding of the views of his opponents. He attempted to convince Baxter that he should not give the worst possible interpretation of a phrase like the "instrumentality of faith."[293] What is more, Baxter's charge that it was not he, but his opponents who gave too large a role to faith in justification, may well have caused his opponents to question his integrity.[294] Was it not clear that Baxter's insistence on the conditionality of faith – and even of works – made man his own Savior? Kendall was doubtless a spokesman for many when he commented:

> Man shall properly be said to *justifie himself*, (a thing which Mr. *Baxter* looks on, as well as he may, as *monstrum horrendum*,) for where there is a *promise* of a *reward* made to *all*, upon a *condition* of performing such a *service*, he that obtaines the reward, gets it by his *own service*; without which the *Promise* would have brought him never the nearer to the *reward*; and thus a man wisely *justifies himself* by *beleeving* ...[295]

Kendall clearly does not accept Baxter's assessment of the controversy: it is Baxter who teaches self-justification.

While on one occasion Baxter charges his opponents with debasing faith,[296] he elsewhere maintains that he attributes a less significant role to faith than his opponents.[297] It is understandable, therefore, that the question comes up – for Baxter's contemporaries as well as for the present-day scholar – what motivates Baxter in his discussions surrounding the instrumentality of faith. How is it possible that he reverses the charges and maintains that his adversaries teach justification by works? What, if any, is the key to a reconciliation of his apparently contradictory positions on the significance of faith and on the conditionality of the covenant? Is Baxter's position really consistent? The present section presents an attempt to clarify these matters. In the process, it will become clear that his opposition to the instrumentality of faith is of vital significance to his position on justification. With his rejection or acceptance of the instrumentality of faith Baxter's entire position on the role of faith and works in justification either stands or falls.

Faith No Instrument: Du Moulin, Eyre, and Crandon

Before coming to Baxter's own position, it is necessary to give a description of the views he opposes. It is not as if there is one particular generally accepted view to which Baxter takes exception. There is no unanimity among those whom he opposes. Lewis Du Moulin refuses to call faith an instrument: "Faith is not the Instrument of Remission of sins, unless it be made the efficient cause, though less

293. Cartwright, in Baxter, *Account of my Consideration*, pp. 169, 176; Cartwright, *Exceptions*, p. 76.
294. For Baxter's charge of self-justification, see below, pp. 186-89.
295. Kendall, *Vindication* I.iv.140.
296. Baxter, *Of Justification*, pp. 207, 224.
297. Baxter, *Of Justification*, pp. 162, 170-71, 227.

principal, why God forgiveth sins; doth an eternal cause need a temporary and transient Instrument to produce an eternal effect?"[298]

Similarly, William Eyre opposes the instrumentality of faith. Eyre, who vehemently opposes Baxter's view of the conditionality of the covenant, agrees on this point with his antagonist: "Mr. *Baxter* in my judgement disputes rationally against this notion <*i.e.*, of faith being an instrument of justification>."[299] Eyre insists that to make faith the active instrument of our justification would mean that faith is an efficient cause of justification, and that man would be made to justify himself.[300] At the most, Eyre is willing to grant that faith is a receptive, rather than an effective instrument. Thus, faith is an instrumental cause of our passive justification, whereby a person applies Christ's righteousness to himself.[301]

John Crandon also rejects the notion that faith is an instrument of active justification.[302] The reason is his idea that justification precedes faith:

> For if we should mention justification as taken meerly Actively, for that internall, eternall and immanent act in God; not transient upon an extraneous subject, but hid in God before the world was, or any justifyed or unjustifyed persons began to live or be: Mr. *Baxter* would be ready to deal with us as did the *Jewes* with *Steven, Act.* 7.57. stop his ears and cry out against us with a loud voice, Blasphemy, blasphemy: Yet in this sense we acknowledge that faith is neither Gods nor Mans instument <*sic*> of justification.[303]

In a sense, Du Moulin, Eyre, and Crandon take positions similar to that of Baxter. Eyre appeals to Baxter with regard to this issue; Baxter says that he agrees with Du Moulin's opposition to the notion of the instrumentality of faith.[304] On an essential point, there is agreement between the high Calvinism of Du Moulin, Eyre, and Crandon; and the theory of Baxter. Both viewpoints reject the notion that faith may be an efficient cause of justification. Yet there are also some important differences. Eyre and Crandon only refer to active justification when they deny faith's instrumentality. They do not object to faith as the instrument of passive justification or justification *in foro conscientiae*. There is no reason to

---

298. Lewis Du Moulin, in Baxter, *Confutation*, p. 299 (emphasis throughout original; "fides non est instrumentum remissionis peccatorum, nisi statuatur causa efficiens, quanquam minus principalis, cur Deus remittit peccata: an causa æterna indiget instrumento temporario & fluxo, ad producendum æternum effectum?" [Du Moulin, *De fidei partibus*, p. 95]). Cf. Du Moulin, in Baxter, *Confutation*, p. 193: "THis also is a cause of the error, that The cause why Christs Righteousness is made known to us and applyed, is made an efficient cause of Justification, at lest, Instrumental and less principal." ("Est & hæc causa erroris, quod causa cur nobis innotescat & applicetur Justitia Christi, constituatur Justificationis causa efficiens, saltem instrumentalis & minus principalis" [Du Moulin, *De fidei partibus*, p. 12].)
299. Eyre, *Vindiciæ Justificationis Gratuitæ*, p. 49.
300. Eyre, *Vindiciæ Justificationis Gratuitæ*, p. 49.
301. Eyre, *Vindiciæ Justificationis Gratuitæ*, pp. 31-32.
302. It must be said, however, that Crandon's argument runs opposite to that of Eyre. Eyre is intent on disproving the instrumentality of faith in active justification. Crandon, however, is bent on proving that faith is an instrument in passive justification. The result is that whereas Eyre appeals to Baxter on this issue, Crandon strongly opposes him.
303. Crandon, *Aphorisms Exorized* I.xxv.332.
304. Baxter, *Confutation*, pp. 193, 299.

suspect that Du Moulin holds a fundamentally different view, even though his opposition to the instrumentality of faith is put in more general terms. The motivations of the respective authors also clash completely. Du Moulin, Eyre, and Crandon do not want to speak of faith as an instrument of (active) justification because it is from eternity. Faith is minimized to such a degree that it can have no role in justification whatsoever: justification precedes faith. Baxter, of course, is adverse to such a position; for him, faith precedes justification.

Discussion with Burgess: Use of Natural Philosophy

Baxter's discussion with Anthony Burgess gives more insight into Baxter's opposition to the notion of the instrumentality of faith. Burgess describes his position as follows:

> Faith is passive in its instrumentality; and although to believe, be a *Grammatical action*, its *verbum activum*, yet its *physicη*, or ὑπερφυσικὴ *passive*. A man by believing, doth not *operari*, but *recipere*: As *videre, audire*, are *Grammatical actions*, but *Physical or natural passions:* now you cannot say thus of the exercises of other Graces: this is the seeming strength of your Exceptions.[305]

Baxter gives an extended critical analysis of Burgess' statement. He begins with a lengthy philosophical digression on the question whether natural acts, such as seeing and hearing, are only passive. He deals with the various philosophical views on this issue, asking whether there are, in fact, sensible and intelligible *species*, whether or not they are images caused by the object, whether they have their being already in the air, or only in the eye, or whether perhaps they are small atoms in perpetual motion.[306] With an appeal to numerous philosophers and theologians, Baxter then concludes that these have taught him "to account vision, intellection, and volition for Immanent Acts."[307] Man is not just passive in his seeing and hearing, as Burgess confidently asserts.

Baxter then takes the next step and asks whether believing is physically passive, even though it is an active verb. He thus applies the distinction between active and passive reception, as this functions in natural things, to the theological question whether faith is active or passive. He states that faith must be regarded either as a habit or as an act. But it is impossible to regard either of these as passive.[308] Moreover, if it is admitted that faith is located both in the understand-

---

305. Burgess, in Baxter, *Of Justification*, pp. 178-79. Cf. Burgess, *True Doctrine*, II (London, 1654), 225: "Though they <*i.e., credere* and *apprehendere*> be Grammatical actions, yet they are naturally passions, as *intelligere, videre*, are active verbs according to Grammar, but naturally and physically are passions: So that a man in believing is passive, that is, he receiveth Christ for his righteousnesse ..."

306. Baxter, *Of Justification*, pp. 195-97.

307. Baxter, *Of Justification*, p. 197.

308. Baxter, *Of Justification*, pp. 198-99. In his *Aphorismes*, Baxter says that it is the act of faith which justifies people, not the habit (I.225 [p. 143]). In his discussions with Cartwright and Kendall, he retracts this position. Now he says that the habit of faith may not be excepted from the condition (*Account of my Consideration*, p. 171; *Reduction*, p. 125). Cartwright and Kendall

ing and in the will, then there cannot be one particular act or passion which is a passive instrument. It is impossible, therefore, that faith would be a passive instrument. Baxter wonders which physical action could have produced the physical passion of faith in justification. There is no such act which makes faith to be the physical recipient of justification.[309]

Baxter then comes with a number of theological reasons for his opposition to Burgess' view. But it is clear that the basis of his argument has been laid already. The foundation is Baxter's conviction that faith is not passive, but active in its reception of Christ. He uses arguments derived from natural philosophy to support his thesis at this juncture.

Kendall: Faith As Passive Instrument

George Kendall has an emphasis on the passive nature of faith which is similar to that of Burgess. He states that faith is either God's or man's instrument. Although God does not believe, he is the author of my faith.[310] Kendall uses a metaphor to clarify his position:

> For example, I throw a *bowl*, the *motion* of this *bowl* is more from me then the *bowl*, aud <*sic*> I accordingly am said to have *bowled* well or ill; but the *motion* doth not denominate *me* otherwise, then in the *agent*, not the *subject* and though I be said to *bowl* well, the *Bowl* in this case is only said to *run*, not I. So the chief *author* of my *believing* is God, and he must have the glory of turning, and framing, and upholding, and workiug <*sic*> all in my heart, as being the *Author, Preserver* and *Finisher* of my *faith*, yet I alone am said to *beleeve*, not God; though my *faith* be more properly Gods *work* then it is mine *own* ...[311]

Kendall apparently has some difficulty in stating explicitly that God is the author of faith. He states that God is the "chief" author. Similarly, he comments that faith is God's instrument "as well or more" as it is my instrument.[312] Thus, God "concurres with my faith which he hath given ..."[313]

Meanwhile, faith is entirely passive. Although man is *causa secunda*, he is not a cause between God and faith. Man is "purely *passive*" when the habit of faith is

---

both insist that the habit of faith is the instrument of justification. Cartwright says that the act of faith is the reception of Christ and that the habit is the instrument of this reception, just as the act of the hand is the actual receiving of a gift, while the hand is the instrument of this reception (in Baxter, *Account of my Consideration*, p. 170; *Exceptions*, p. 74). Kendall says that because faith is not just an acquired habit, but an infused habit, it is equivalent to a new faculty. This infused habit is the instrument of giving life to the soul (*Vindication* I.iv.144). Baxter replies that the habit of faith cannot properly be the soul's instrument. He does not accept Kendall's argument that the habit is distinct from the soul. The habit of faith is nothing but the holiness or the perfection of the renewed faculty of the soul. If the habit is the soul's instrument, this would mean that it is its own instrument (*Aphorismes* I.222-23 [pp. 141-42]; *Account of my Consideration*, pp. 171-73; *Reduction*, p. 125-31).

309. Baxter, *Of Justification*, p. 204.
310. Kendall, *Vindication* I.iv.141.
311. Kendall, *Vindication* I.iv.142.
312. Kendall, *Vindication* I.iv.142.
313. Kendall, *Vindication* I.iv.142 (emphasis throughout in original).

infused. This explains why Kendall is not afraid of making man a concurring cause in justification. If man is purely passive in the reception of the habit of faith, his concurring does not have any moral value. Moreover, God remains the principal efficient cause in justification. Kendall also does not accept Baxter's reasoning that there is no such thing as a passive instrument: when a man holds up a fire shovel to receive coals the shovel is an instrument, even though it is merely passive.[314]

Faith As causa applicans: Cartwright and Blake

Christopher Cartwright and Thomas Blake are much closer to Baxter than Du Moulin, Eyre, and Crandon, and also much closer than Burgess or Kendall. Cartwright accepts the conditionality of faith. He says that it is better to call faith a condition than an instrument of our justification.[315] He does think, however, that Baxter creates needless problems. It is perfectly legitimate to call faith the instrument of justification: "The act of the hand is the actual receiving a gift; Is not the hand therefore the Instrument whereby the gift is received? and consequently whereby one is enriched?"[316] Faith is not only the believer's instrument, however. The believer himself becomes the instrument whereby God acts. We are workers together with God (2 Cor 6:1). Cartwright clarifies himself by referring to faith as the apprehensive cause (*causa apprehensiva*), by which he means that faith – unlike repentance or love – apprehends "Christ's Righteousness, by which so apprehended we are justified."[317] Cartwright's concern is to insist both on the role of faith alone in justification – as opposed to works – and on the righteousness of Christ as the only thing which justifies the believer. Only the object of faith, Christ's righteousness, justifies.

When faith justifies as *causa apprehensiva*, this does not mean that it takes the place of Christ. With an appeal to John Davenant (1576-1641), Cartwright explains: "The formal reason why Faith doth justifie, is its Apprehension, yet still that is in respect of the thing apprehended, *Causæ applicanti illud tribuitur quod immediatè pertinet ad rem applicatam. Id fidei ipsi tribuitur, quod reapse Christo debetur*, as *Davenant* ... express it, whose words you said were not against you, though none can be more in this Matter."[318] Thus, Cartwright maintains that there need not be a difference between the conditionality of faith on the one hand, and faith as *causa instrumentalis* or *causa applicans* on the other hand.

Baxter confesses that he is not sure what Cartwright means with *causa applicans*.[319] If an efficient cause is meant, Baxter disagrees. He tends to think, howev-

---

314. Kendall, *Vindication* I.iv.143.
315. Cartwright, in Baxter, *Account of my Consideration*, p. 170.
316. Cartwright, in Baxter, *Account of my Consideration*, p. 170. Cf. Cartwright, *Exceptions*, p. 178: "I so confess Faith to be the Condition of Justification, that nevertheless I hold it to justifie as apprehending Christ's Righteousness, God having in that respect required Faith of us, that we may be justified."
317. Cartwright, *Exceptions*, p. 177.
318. Cartwright, *Exceptions*, p. 183.
319. Baxter, *Substance*, pp. 20, 29.

er, that Cartwright really means nothing but a *causa dispositiva*, as William Twisse called it. Such a disposition in the recipient is not an efficient cause at all. Thus, Baxter concludes: "I verily think that you are of my mind, and do not know it ..."[320] It is questionable whether this is indeed the case. Cartwright explains clearly what he means with *causa applicans*. It is the direct apprehension of Christ's righteousness by faith. Although Cartwright does not emphasize the passive aspect of this apprehension as Burgess and Kendall do, the object remains Christ's righteousness alone. It is true that Cartwright does not speak of faith as an efficient cause. His interpretation of the instrumentality of faith is designed to carefully circumvent giving any efficiency to faith itself. Christ alone justifies. But Cartwright's disagreement with Baxter is more than a verbal quarrel. As long as the justifying aspect of faith is seen in its apprehension of Christ's righteousness, there is an immediacy in the relation between faith and justification to which Baxter cannot possibly agree.

Thomas Blake firmly agrees with Baxter that the covenant of grace is conditional. To express his concern for man's involvement in fulfilling the condition of the covenant, Blake denies that faith and repentance are God's conditions.[321] He maintains: "Whose acts they be, his conditions they are; this is evident: But they are our acts, we beleeve, we repent, it is not God that beleeves; it is not God that repents ..."[322] Blake's treatises, *Vindiciæ foederis* (1653) and *The Covenant Sealed* (1655), exude a totally different atmosphere than, for instance, Kendall's *Vindication*. Blake is much closer to Baxter on the issue of the conditionality of faith than Kendall.

Also, Blake does not want to make man an efficient cause of his own pardon and justification. He explicitly disavows this position: "Do I, or doth our *Religion* make man or faith the efficient cause of his own pardon, and justification?"[323] Blake denies that he wants to make God and man *causae principales partiales* of justification. He says that man is not an instrument of "principall efficiency."[324] God and man are not "concauses" in justification, although there is a "willing concurrence."[325] Blake carefully avoids making man the principal efficient cause in justification.

There is nevertheless a significant difference between Blake and Baxter. Blake does not regard conditional justification as incompatible with the instrumentality of faith. Rather, faith as an instrument is the condition in the covenant of grace.

---

320. Baxter, *Substance*, p. 29.
321. This section of *Vindiciæ foederis* (pp. 101-04) is actually directed against an unknown opponent of Baxter, who had argued that the bestowing of faith and repentance is part of God's condition. Faith and repentance could therefore not be our conditions. Baxter had responded to this opponent in the appendix to his *Aphorismes* (sig. Q7ʳ-II.188 [sig. M5ʳ-p. 334]). This section of Blake, therefore, is actually in defense of Baxter. Baxter's sharp opposition at this point understandably evokes Blake's indignation: "I never had it in my thoughts to oppose you; yea, I assuredly expected, that how many adversaries soever I should find, yet I should have had you here, on my party" (*Covenant Sealed*, p. 627).
322. Blake, *Vindiciæ foederis*, p. 101.
323. Blake, *Covenant Sealed*, p. 448.
324. Blake, *Covenant Sealed*, p. 449.
325. Blake, *Covenant Sealed*, p. 481.

Blake says he is "truly sorry that faith should now be denied to have the office or place of an instrument in our justification, nay scarce allowed to be called the instrument of receiving Christ, that justifies us ..."[326] When Christ is said to dwell in us by faith (Eph 3:17), and when we are said to receive the promise of the Spirit through faith (Gal 3:14), do the Scriptures not speak of faith as the soul's instrument to receive Christ?[327] Thus, Blake denies that the conditionality and the instrumentality of faith exclude each other: "I should rather judge on the contrary, that because it is a condition of the Covenant in the way as it is before exprest, that it is therefore an instrument in our justification ..."[328]

The crucial element in Blake's theory is – at least for Baxter – that he states that "neither God nor man are sole efficients."[329] There is "some kind of efficiency" in man's concurrence.[330] Blake says that faith is an instrument of *Christ* because he takes up his abode in our hearts. But faith is also *our* instrument, because it is we who believe, not Christ.[331] Blake makes a comparison with Lazarus' resurrection: "Christ was the principall efficient when he raised *Lazarus*; yet it was *Lazarus* and not Christ that did rise."[332] Blake even states that our faith is "more aptly and fitly" called an instrument than the Gospel itself, since faith, by accepting the Gospel, gives efficacy to it.[333]

Like Cartwright, Blake refers to Davenant who speaks of faith as an "applying cause."[334] In fact, Blake's entire position is remarkably similar to that of Cartwright, who also wrote a preface to Blake's *The Covenant Sealed*. Both authors think that faith can be styled a condition, an applying cause, or an instrumental cause. Both hold that man plays a role in justification, even though Cartwright does not speak of man's faith as having any efficiency in justification, as Blake (with some hesitance) does. Furthermore, both authors regard faith as God's as well as man's instrument.[335]

THE INSTRUMENTALITY OF FAITH AND BAXTER'S REACTION

Instrumentality: No Authoritative Backing and Dangerous Consequences

In his opposition to the view that faith is an instrument in justification, Baxter uses numerous arguments. First of all, Scripture does not say anywhere that faith is an

---

326. Blake, *Vindiciæ foederis*, p. 80.
327. Blake, *Vindiciæ foederis*, p. 81.
328. Blake, *Vindiciæ foederis*, p. 91.
329. Blake, *Vindiciæ foederis*, p. 81.
330. Blake, *Covenant Sealed*, p. 447.
331. Blake, *Vindiciæ foederis*, pp. 82, 101-02; *Covenant Sealed*, pp. 626-33.
332. Blake, *Covenant Sealed*, p. 633.
333. Blake, *Vindiciæ foederis*, p. 84.
334. Blake, *Covenant Sealed*, pp. 620-21.
335. This last element is also prominent in John Crandon. He argues that faith is God's instrument when God declares to a person's conscience that he is justified. Faith is man's instrument when he applies the remission to himself (*Aphorisms Exorized* I.xxv.333-35).

instrument.[336] Second, it is a novel concept. Although Baxter expected to be blamed for "affectation of singularity," already in his *Aphorismes* he denies that this is his motivation.[337] Crandon scorns what he considers to be Baxter's arrogant claim that he is "the first of men that ever saw and taught" that faith is not the instrument of justification.[338] According to Crandon, Baxter has simply taken his view from "the Priests and Jesuites."[339] Baxter's writings do not substantiate this charge. He does not refer to Roman Catholic authors in defense of his position. Nevertheless, it is true that he is of the opinion that the instrumentality of faith is a recent invention. Discussing the matter with Burgess, Baxter says that to speak of faith as an instrument is a "greater novelty" than calling it a condition.[340] According to Baxter, therefore, neither Scripture, nor tradition, supports the view that faith is instrumental in justification.

Another point of concern for Baxter is the reaction of Roman Catholics to the writings of Protestants who speak of the instrumentality of faith. Baxter is convinced that

> when Papists read this in ours <*sic*> Writings, it so hardeneth them in their Religion, that they think presently, that all the rest of our Doctrine is like this, and they cast away all in prejudice, and insult over us, and cleave the faster to all the rest of their Errours, to their souls hazard.[341]

Baxter is afraid that Roman Catholics will judge the entire Protestant church by the ill conceived notions of some extremist positions.

Baxter also presents a pastoral concern: Burgess' position is too difficult to grasp intellectually. This is dangerous, because it concerns "so fundamental a point as Justification."[342] Baxter says that he simply claims that "faith is the condition on which God hath bestowed Christ and all his benefits in the Gospel."[343] By contrast, Burgess' doctrine is almost impossible to understand: "Can every poor man or woman reach to know what a *passive Action*, or a *passive Passion*, or a *Passive Instrument* is? and how we receive Christ, as a man takes a gift in his hand? or to see through all the difficulties that I have discovered here in your Doctrine?"[344] The result of Burgess' doctrine is that people do not know

336. Baxter, *Account of my Consideration*, p. 176; *Account*, p. 16; *Of Justification*, p. 224; *Catholick Theologie* II.251.
337. Baxter, *Aphorismes* I.219 (p. 139).
338. Crandon, *Aphorisms Exorized* I.xxv.331.
339. Crandon, *Aphorisms Exorized* I.xxv.331.
340. Baxter, *Of Justification*, p. 162. Cf. Baxter's reply to Cartwright: "If I must believe as the Church believes, which Church is it? why am I not as excusable for being loth to reproach the Church of Christ for 1200, if not 1400 years after Christ (who never made Faith *the Instrument* of *justifying*, that I could yet find) as accusable for reproaching some part of the Divines of *Europe* for 150 years, by declaring the Reason of my dissent from the ill Consequence of their Opinions?" (*Substance*, p. 24)
341. Baxter, *Account of my Consideration*, p. 175.
342. Baxter, *Of Justification*, p. 221.
343. Baxter, *Of Justification*, p. 221 (emphasis throughout in original).
344. Baxter, *Of Justification*, p. 221.

what justifying faith is. This, concludes Baxter, "seemeth to me to overthrow the comfort of Believers exceedingly."[345]

Perhaps an even more serious concomitant results from the idea that faith is only a passive instrument, as Kendall and Burgess argue. When faith is merely passive in its reception of Christ's righteousness one cannot blame the unbeliever for not fulfilling his duty to believe. Baxter is afraid that "this Passive Doctrine do lay all the blame of all mens infidelity upon God, or most at least ..."[346] A person can no longer be blamed for his unbelief because his only fault is an "indisposition of the matter."[347] Thus, in essence, Baxter is afraid of accusing God to be the author of sin.

Physical Reception of Christ

The problems with a lack of authoritative backing from Scripture and tradition and the dangerous consequences of making faith into an instrument of justification are not the main issue for Baxter. More important are the doctrinal weaknesses inherent in the actual positions of his antagonists. Baxter is very apprehensive of anything which may have a tendency to changing faith into a physical reception of Christ or his righteousness. Cartwright, for instance, says that faith "immediately" makes Christ to be ours.[348] Baxter has little patience with such a view. He points out that if his opponents were consistent they should not say that justifying faith receives Christ himself, but that it receives his righteousness or justification. Only then is the reception the most direct and proper cause of justification.[349]

When Burgess says that faith is a physically passive instrument Baxter counters by saying that righteousness is but a relation and can, therefore, not be physically apprehended.[350] Christ himself can certainly not be received physically: "Who dare say so, but the *Ubiquitarians*, and Transubstantiation men? and perhaps not they. Christ is in Heaven, and we on earth. A multitude of blasphemers, Libertines, and Familists, I lately meet with that dream of this, but no sober man."[351] Besides, comments Baxter, it is impossible that the physical reception of Christ would justify a person, for then Mary would have been justified for having Christ in her womb.[352]

Instrument As Efficient Cause

Baxter does not think that people like Du Moulin, Crandon, and Eyre give faith its proper place in the *ordo salutis*. If faith follows justification *in foro Dei* it no longer plays a role as a condition of justification. But it is not just the extremists

---

345. Baxter, *Of Justification*, p. 225.
346. Baxter, *Of Justification*, p. 216. Cf. p. 224.
347. Baxter, *Of Justification*, p. 216.
348. Cartwright, *Exceptions*, pp. 97-98.
349. Baxter, *Of Justification*, p. 219.
350. Baxter, *Of Justification*, p. 209.
351. Baxter, *Of Justification*, p. 209.
352. Baxter, *Of Justification*, pp. 209, 215.

among the high Calvinists who fail to give faith its proper value. Any theory which makes faith into a passive instrument of justification fails to do justice to faith. This, says Baxter, "seemeth to me so great a debasing of faith, as to make it to be no vertue at all, nor to have any moral good in it."[353] Faith loses its moral worth if it is turned into a mere passive reception of Christ or his righteousness.

Baxter adds, however, that this "debasing" of faith takes place by means of a "self-contradiction."[354] While faith is purely passive according to the theory of his opponents, they nevertheless assert that faith is an instrument of justification. To be an instrument implies that it is an efficient cause, for an instrument is efficient in its very nature. Here lies the basis for Baxter's opposition to the instrumentality of faith:

> As an Instrument is logically and properly taken, and signifies an inferior less prin-
> cipal efficient cause, so nothing in us can have any thing to do (*i.e.* any kind of
> physical efficiency) in this work; neither is it imaginable it should, it being a work of
> Gods upon us, without us, concerning us, but not within us at all.[355]

This quotation shows Baxter's real concern: to make faith an instrumental cause means to make it an efficient cause. Baxter does not deny that the word "instrument" may have a larger meaning. But, with an appeal to Thomas Aquinas, Francis Suárez, Christoph Scheibler (1589-1653), and others, Baxter maintains that an instrument "in the proper ordinary sence" produces an effect.[356]

Crandon denies that an instrument, by its very definition, is an efficient cause. He distinguishes between effective and receptive instruments. A knife which cuts is an effective instrument. But a hand which receives something is merely a receptive instrument.[357] Crandon, therefore, insists that the definitions of Aquinas and Scheibler only hold for efficient instruments, not for receptive instruments.[358] Blake also distinguishes between "instruments *of meer reception*, and instruments *of further operation*."[359] And, as noted earlier, also Eyre and Burgess speak of faith as a receptive instrument. This disagreement as to the nature of an instrument is identical to the disagreement about the question whether an instrument can be passive. Burgess and Kendall both emphasize that faith is purely passive in justification. Thus, they deny that the instrumentality of faith implies that it is the efficient cause of justification.

---

353. Baxter, *Of Justification*, p. 207. Cf. p. 224.
354. Baxter, *Of Justification*, p. 224.
355. Baxter, *Confutation*, p. 291.
356. Baxter, *Of Justification*, p. 212. Cf. p. 207.
357. Crandon, *Aphorisms Exorized* I.xxv.335.
358. Crandon, *Aphorisms Exorized* I.xxv.336.
359. Blake, *Covenant Sealed*, p. 448. Blake continues: "A man receives a gift with his hand, as the lame man was ready to do, when he expected something from *Peter* and *John*, *Act.* 3.5. and he earnes his living with his hand, as *Paul* did, when in some exigents his hands ministred to his necessities, *Act.* 20.34. In the former mans hand concurres to his enriching, but he enriches not himself, as in the later. The denomination is from the fountaine, whence all flowes, not from the hand that accepts, or the cistern that doth receive."

Self-Justification

By contrast, Baxter denies that an instrument can be merely passive or receptive. Having defined an instrument as an active, efficient cause, he comes with his main charge: his opponents take God's place. Their doctrine implies self-justification. Again, he is deeply convinced that his opponents' accusations of justification by works are wrong, and that they are guilty of the very errors which they erroneously attribute to him. If faith is indeed a physical instrument by which Christ or his righteousness is received there can only be one conclusion: "<I>f it justifie directly as such, then it justifieth of its own Nature."[360] Accordingly, Baxter asks Blake whether he does not "seem to imply that man with God doth justifie himself, when you say [Man cannot justifie himself by beleeving without God?]"[361] When Blake says that faith gives efficacy to the Gospel in justification, Baxter exclaims: "What *Romanist* by the doctrine of merit gives more to man in the work of Justification! If our faith give efficacy and power to the Gospel to justifie us, then we justifie our selves when the Gospel justifies us! then the Gospel is our instrument of Justification!"[362]

Thus, Baxter also comes to the statement: "I give not so much as others to faith, because I dare not ascribe so much to man. And yet men make such a noise with the terrible name of *Justification by Works* (the Lords own phrase), as if I gave more then themselves to man, when I give so much less."[363] Baxter is convinced he gives a less significant role to faith because he does not make it into an efficient instrumental cause. If he errs, "it is in giving less to Faith, denying it to be the *Instrumental Cause of Justification*, but only a condition."[364] Baxter is therefore hesitant in the use of expressions such as "justifying faith" and "faith justifies us." Not only are these phrases alien to Scripture, but they also "express a Causality, if we take the word strictly."[365]

At this point, the solution emerges to the question how it is possible that, on the one hand, Baxter says that his opponents are guilty of "debasing" faith, while, on the other hand, he maintains that he gives less to faith than they do. The solution lies in the context of the various statements. When Baxter says that his disputants debase faith, his reason is that they turn faith into a merely passive instrument.

---

360. Baxter, *Of Justification*, p. 214.
361. Baxter, *Account*, p. 27. Cf. *Aphorismes* I.224 (p. 142), where Baxter says that the doctrine he opposes makes "man to be the *Causa proxima* of his own Justification." By means of a metaphor: "As if a Judge had committed Treason, and the King should give him authority to Judge, Pardon and Absolve himself" (*Account*, p. 21). Cf. *Substance*, pp. 24, 28.
362. Baxter, *Account*, p. 35. Baxter also accuses Kendall of "flat Popery" (*Reduction*, p. 141).
363. Baxter, *Of Justification*, p. 227. Similarly, when Kendall accuses Baxter of teaching that man properly justifies himself, Baxter replies that Kendall "himself is undeniably guilty of this Consequence, which here is called *Monstrum horrendum*" (*Reduction*, p. 104). Disagreeing with Kendall, Baxter says: "<I>f you make faith the proper Instrument of justifying, you make man his own pardoner, and rob God of his Soveraignty" (p. 117; cf. pp. 140-41).
364. Baxter, *Of Justification*, p. 162. Cf. *Aphorismes* I.223 (p. 142): "Here by the way take notice, that the same men that blame the advancing of Faith so high, as to be our true Gospel Rightiousnesse ... do yet, when it comes to the triall, ascribe far more to Faith, then those they blame: making it Gods Instrument in justifying." Cf. I.298-99 (p. 191); *Substance*, p. 20; *Of Justification*, pp. 170-71.
365. Baxter, *Of Justification*, p. 6.

Thereby, it is bereft of moral value. Baxter accuses his opponents of debasing faith in the sense that they take away its moral worth, its moral value as a condition. In another sense, they overvalue faith. Here Baxter does not refer to its moral worth but to its role in justification. He thinks that his opponents make faith itself – as the reception of Christ or his righteousness – into an efficient cause of justification.

It cannot be denied that Baxter's charges are at least partly to the point. When Kendall says that faith has a proper causality in passive justification he adds: "Thus then we do not *deprive* God of his glory, in *justifying us by faith*, though we *ascribe* justification to *faith*; for we ascribe our *faith* to God, and make our *believing* his *work* ..."[366] For Kendall, it is faith which justifies. His reason is that by faith Christ enters man's heart. Thus, faith is an instrument of justification. Also Blake, while denying that faith is the principal efficient cause, does assert that faith has some efficiency in justification. Only Cartwright may with some legitimacy deny Baxter's charges, because he is the most consistent of his opponents in denying any efficiency to faith. But also Cartwright does maintain that faith directly apprehends Christ as it is *causa applicans*.

If faith may not be regarded as an instrument of *justification* because it implies self-justification, is there anything against regarding faith as an instrument of apprehending *Christ*? Baxter is somewhat more lenient on this point. Repeatedly, he states that he will not fight about the word "instrument" as such.[367] At the end of his discussion with Blake on this point, Baxter proposes that he will continue to speak of faith as a condition, while allowing Blake to call faith "an instrument of receiving Christ, and consequently righteousness."[368] In that sense the word "instrument" is used "largely, vulgarly, or metaphorically."[369] Two restrictions must be noted in Baxter's willingness to accept the word "instrument." First, he says that he does not want to argue about the question whether faith is an instrument of receiving *Christ*. He does not speak of the reception of justification or of Christ's righteousness. This relation is only received *after* the reception of Christ. If faith is in any sense an instrument, it is only an instrument of accepting *Christ*, not of his righteousness. Justification is in no sense received directly, for this would always mean that faith is an efficient cause of justification. Second, if one says that Christ is accepted by faith as an instrument, then the word "instrument" must be taken in an improper, large sense. Christ is not properly or physically received. The reception of Christ by faith remains metaphorical.

Cartwright attempts to persuade Baxter that "few or none" disagree with him on this point.[370] Those who call faith the instrument of our justification simply use this terminology "because by Faith we receive Christ, by whom we are justi-

366. Kendall, *Vindication* I.iv.142.
367. Baxter, *Aphorismes* I.221-22 (p. 141); *Account*, pp. 18, 25, 40; *Reduction*, pp. 113, 122, 124, 133-34; *Unsavoury Volume*, p. 46; *Of Justification*, pp. 171, 212, 221; *Account of my Consideration*, pp. 169, 176.
368. Baxter, *Account*, p. 40.
369. Baxter, *Unsavoury Volume*, p. 46. Cf. *Reduction*, p. 124.
370. Cartwright, in Baxter, *Account of my Consideration*, p. 176.

fied."[371] Baxter, though commending Cartwright's charitable interpretation, remains unconvinced.[372] He continues to be afraid that his opponents give an efficient causality to faith in justification.

Faith As Condition for the Actual Gift

At this point, two important questions come to the fore. First, if faith is not the instrument of justification, what is its role? Second, what does Baxter think the instrument is, if it is not faith? In answering these questions it is essential to realize that Baxter distinguishes between God's conditional and his actual giving. To receive righteousness and to be pardoned in justification is an actual gift from God. But there is both an improper and a proper reception; an ethical, active, as well as a physical, passive reception. The active, improper reception – being the fulfillment of the condition – precedes the passive, proper reception. The condition, acceptance of Christ in his threefold office, must be fulfilled before there is actual justification. The receiving of Christ – as the one who redeems, satisfies, and merits – precedes the receiving of a right to him. The latter, properly called the reception of justification (*receptio iustificationis*), is entirely passive; it is to *be* justified (*iustificari*). Active reception of Christ is but a metaphoric, improper reception. Only the absolute gift of the *Donor*, commonly called passive justification, is natural and proper reception (*receptio naturalis et propria*). Says Baxter:

> It must be remembred that the thing that faith receives naturally and properly, is not Christ himself, or his righteousness; but the *species* of what is represented as its object. And that faiths reception of Christ himself and his righteousness, or of right to Christ, is but *Receptio metaphorica; vel actio ad receptionem propriam necessaria:* and that the true reception, which is *pati, non agere*, doth follow faith, and therefore Christ himself is received only *Receptione fidei ethicâ, activa, metaphoricâ: Species Christi predicati recipiatur receptione naturali, intelligendo: Jus ad Christum recipitur receptione naturali passivá, propriá:* That which is conditionally given (on condition of acceptance or the like) and offered to be accepted; this is received, *Receptione fidei ethicâ:* whereupon followeth the actual efficacious giving of that thing, (the condition being performed, which suspended it:) and this the *beleever* receiveth, *Receptione passivâ, propriâ*; but it is not his *Faith* that receiveth it.[373]

In a perhaps somewhat more accessible manner, Baxter's understanding could be laid out as follows:

371. Cartwright, in Baxter, *Account of my Consideration*, p. 169. Cf. Cartwright, *Exceptions*, pp. 75-77.
372. Cartwright, in Baxter, *Account of my Consideration*, pp. 169, 176, 180.
373. Baxter, *Account*, p. 25.

Conditional and Actual Justification

	conditionally	actually
subject	faith (and other graces)	believer
act	receptio metaphorica/ ethica/activa agere	receptio propria/ physica/passiva pati
object	Christ and his righteousness	right to Christ and his benefits

This table makes clear that faith is the necessary means for justification (*medium necessarium ad iustificari*). However, while faith is necessary as *conditio sine qua non*, this *medium* cannot properly be called an instrument. After all, when speaking of faith, Baxter only concerns himself with the conditionality, not with the actual bestowal of the right to Christ and his benefits. Moreover, faith's reception of Christ and his righteousness must be metaphorical since it is only the act which is necessary for proper reception (*actio ad receptionem propriam necessaria*). The reception of Christ itself is not the proper reception of the right to Christ. The two must be sharply distinguished. It is in no sense possible to speak of faith as an instrument in connection with the proper reception of a right to Christ. In a direct sense, Christ's righteousness is not imputed. His satisfaction and merit are only foundational.[374] When Christ is apprehended as Lord and Savior, God as absolute *Donor* grants a person the right to Christ, to the promise. Thus, he properly and absolutely receives the right to Christ and his benefits. Thus, he is constituted righteous, is justified *constitutive*.[375]

At the basis of Baxter's view of the role of faith in justification lies a bifurcation between the conditional and the actual grant of justification. This bifurcation yields the key to Baxter's opposition to the instrumentality of faith. By means of the distinction between the conditional and the actual, between faith's (ethical, improper) reception of Christ and the role of God as *Donor* in constituting the believer righteous Baxter has effectively eliminated the need for any efficient instrumental role of man, whether that be by means of faith or works.

So, when Baxter charges his opponents with self-justification he is most serious. They shortchange the role of God as absolute *Donor*. The gift of the *Donor*, the covenant of grace, has an absolute element which must be acknowledged. The

---

374. For an elaboration on Baxter's view of imputation, see below, pp. 231-45.
375. Cf. Baxter, *Reduction*, p. 103: "*Conditionally* God Justifieth *All* by his Covenant, at least All to whom it is Revealed. *Actually* he Justifieth only them that have the Condition. I oppose *Actually* to *Conditionally*, because that while it is but *Conditional*, it is not *Actual* in Law sense, that is, Effectual ..."

conditional element may not infringe upon the absolutely gratuitous character of passive, forensic justification. Ultimately, the covenant does not depend on man for its efficacy.

The Covenant As Instrument

Baxter's main objection to the instrumentality of faith is that it would give to man what properly belongs to the *voluntas Dei*. As Baxter puts it in one of his many analogies:

> What if your father bequeath by his Testament 1 10^l a piece to each of his sons? to one on condition he will ask it of his elder brother, and thank him for it: to another, if he be married by such a time: to a third, if he will promise not to wast it in prodigality: Do any of these conditions give efficacy and power to the Testament? No: Yet the Testament doth not *efficaciter agere* till they are performed. Why is that? Because all such instruments work morally, only by expressing *ut signa* the Will of the Agent ...[376]

The covenant is the proper instrument of justification. Strictly speaking, only God may be said to justify.

For Baxter, there are two efficient causes of justification. He describes them as "the Will of the Donor; and the Law or Covenant which is his Instrument."[377] The law signifies God's will, and is therefore God's instrument in justification.[378] The absolute Donor has given his law. He justifies the believer by this law as his instrument.

When the proper instrumentality of the covenant comes into focus Baxter's language tends to become rather emotional. When Kendall states that God improperly gives Christ's righteousness by means of the covenant, Baxter fulminates against him: "Could any words (not certainly destructive to Christianity it self) have fallen from this Learned man more unworthy a Divine?"[379] The matter ought to be plain, according to Baxter. A law condemning traitors is most properly disabled by an act of pardon.[380] It is a common principle in politics and morality that a law or testament is a proper instrument in conveying a certain right.[381]

Blake objects that the covenant cannot be said to justify because it may just as well function as a means of condemnation as of justification:

> A sword is not an instrument of slaughter, where it slayes not; nor an axe an instrument to hew, where it cuts not: Neither is the Gospel an instrument of justification, where it justifies not; where the Minister is a Minister of condemnation, the savour of death to death, there the Gospel becomes an instrument of condemnation and of death. The efficacy that is in the Gospel for justification, it receives by their faith to whom it is tendred.[382]

376. Baxter, *Account*, p. 36.
377. Baxter, *Reduction*, p. 126.
378. Baxter, *Reduction*, p. 134.
379. Baxter, *Reduction*, p. 98.
380. Baxter, *Reduction*, p. 99.
381. Baxter, *Reduction*, p. 122; *Of Justification*, pp. 333-34.
382. Blake, *Vindiciæ foederis*, p. 83.

Baxter has no problem admitting to Blake that God's threat is the proper instrument of condemnation. But this implies, says Baxter, that the promise or the gift is the proper instrument in justification.[383]

Furthermore, the fact that God's covenant, law, or Gospel grant justifies does not mean that justification takes place as soon as God makes this instrument known. Cartwright objects that the Gospel covenant cannot justify as an instrument because it is offered to many who nevertheless do not accept Christ.[384] Similarly, Tombes suggests that justification must be in the past if the covenant is a past act.[385] Baxter gives two identical replies to these objections. He distinguishes between a natural or physical act of the covenant and a moral act of the covenant. The former is God's making the conditional covenant or gift. This natural act took place long ago. The moral act of the covenant remains imperfect until the fulfillment of the condition. After the condition has been performed, the covenant justifies: "But when the *Condition is performed*, then the Law or Covenant doth *truly agere* or *significare*, and *give Christ* and *Righteousness*. For though the Instrument were in *being before*, yet it did not *agere vel efficere*, till the Condition was performed."[386] The covenant actually effects something only after the condition of the covenant has been fulfilled.

Baxter's sharp distinction between the natural and the moral acts of the covenant results in a temporal distinction. He maintains that the physical act of "Legislation or Covenant granting" was in the past, while the moral action of this covenant is continuous.[387] A moral cause does not need to have an immediate effect. It now also becomes clear why Baxter has an eye for more than just the conditionality of the covenant of grace. Throughout his writings, Baxter emphasizes this aspect. But when it comes to the point, it is God alone who justifies the believer by means of his covenant grant. When man has performed the condition, God's will – or God himself – justifies the believer by a proper moral act of the covenant grant.

Baxter feels that he is wrongly accused of teaching self-justification. According to Kendall, Baxter "saith, *The Condition being performed, the conditional grant becomes absolute*; *Ergo*, say I, He that *performes the Condition, makes* the grant to be *absolute*, and so doth *more* to his Justification then God, who made only a *conditional* grant ..."[388] According to Baxter, this conclusion does not follow. It is not true that the performer "makes" the grant to be absolute "if by *making*, you mean *causing*."[389] Instead, says Baxter, it is the Donor "that makes the Conditional grant become Actual or Absolute when the Condition is performed."[390] Baxter rebuts the charge of self-justification by insisting that the condition is no more than *conditio sine qua non*, which itself does not cause the effect.

383. Baxter, *Account*, p. 30.
384. Cartwright, in Baxter, *Account of my Consideration*, p. 205.
385. Tombes, in Baxter, *Of Justification*, p. 332.
386. Baxter, *Account of my Consideration*, p. 206.
387. Baxter, *Justification*, p. 386.
388. Kendall, *Vindication* I.iv.141. Cf. Crandon, *Aphorisms Exorized* I.xxv.336.
389. Baxter, *Reduction*, p. 110.
390. Baxter, *Reduction*, p. 110.

Conclusion

Baxter's insistence that the material difference between common and special grace is only gradual has significant implications for the way in which he views the difference between the acts of faith of unregenerate and of regenerate people. His distinction between the natural truth, the moral truth, and the justifying truth of an act allows him to grant that also unregenerate people may have faith and love for God and Christ. The positive way in which he evaluates the moral acts of unbelievers is opposed by high Calvinists. There are two fundamental differences regarding the distinction between common and special grace when comparing Baxter and his high Calvinist opponents. The first is that his adversaries consider common grace as something natural, whereas special grace is regarded as having a supernatural origin. Baxter rejects the idea that a supernatural habit is infused prior to the act of faith. This corresponds to his view that the material difference between common and special grace is not specific, but gradual. The second important difference of opinion concerns the relation between Christ's work as Mediator and common grace. Baxter sees a direct connection between the two. His opponents, while neglecting to debate this issue with Baxter, do not make such a connection. Nevertheless, part of the debate on common grace is only verbal. Baxter acknowledges that the faith of unregenerate people is only equivocally called "faith." He does accept a specific moral, formal difference between common and special grace. Also, he agrees that sincerity is the condition of the covenant.

Because of his different view on the nature of common grace, Baxter emphasizes its positive role in preparing for saving grace. His consistent emphasis on the means and on God's universal offer of grace increases the difference with his high Calvinist opponents. Baxter's view on assurance of salvation also has its distinct characteristics. Where high Calvinist divines tend to include assurance in the essence of faith, Baxter states that only few Christians attain such assurance. Those whose interest in Christ barely prevails over their carnal interests will not attain this certainty. On the other hand, Baxter contends that the very gift of common grace provides a basis for comfort because it yields a probability of salvation.

Despite the agreement between Baxter and his opponents that saving faith includes faith in Christ as Savior and Lord, there is disagreement on the question whether faith justifies by looking to Christ as Lord. Baxter's antagonists give a negative answer to this question. Their main argument is that since there is a threefold object of faith, there must also be a threefold act of faith. Faith as it justifies (*qua iustificans*) only has reference to Christ as Savior. While Baxter admits that there are many physical acts of faith, he insists that the performance of the condition of faith is one, undivided moral act. The distinction *ex parte Christi* between his work as Prophet, Priest, and King does not give a license to make a corresponding distinction *ex parte nostri*. Baxter's refusal to make such a distinction leads to his opponents' fear that he includes works in the definition of faith.

In the analysis of this chapter, two features of Baxter's approach figure prominently. First, Baxter is a skillful disputant. Realizing that his high Calvinist opponents will seek to accuse him of lowering special grace by erasing the distinction between common and special grace, Baxter argues that not he, but his opponents degrade saving faith. They are the ones who exalt man's natural abilities by maintaining that common grace has no supernatural origin at all. Again, faced with the accusation that he exalts the role of faith, Baxter not only refutes the charge, but even argues that his opponents make faith into an efficient cause of justification through their concept of the instrumentality of faith. This is also the reason why, in the discussion on the object of faith *qua iustificans*, he focuses his arguments on the question of the formal reason of faith's interest in justification. In doing so, he effectively turns the tables: while denying that he includes works in the definition of faith, he charges his opponents with subverting the Gospel by teaching justification by works in an unscriptural sense.

A second characteristic is the manner in which Baxter relates the two aspects of God's will: his *voluntas de rerum eventu* and his *voluntas de debito*. Secondary scholarship on Baxter's soteriology has tended to emphasize the conditional aspect of his doctrine of justification. The result is that his "political method" is seen as the key to unlock his system.[391] Accordingly, he is charged with being legalistic in his outlook.[392] It must indeed be admitted that Baxter consistently emphasizes God's role as *Rector per leges*. Baxter pays more attention to the gradual, physical difference between common and special grace than to the specific, moral difference. Special grace is usually given when a person is properly disposed through preparation by means of common grace. Baxter even speaks of "half promises" of special grace to be given once the "condition" of a good use of common grace has been performed. He does not even object to the Roman Catholic notion of congruous merit. Further, Baxter insists that, for justification, Christ must be accepted in his threefold office as Prophet, Priest, and King. Throughout, he stresses the role of faith as a condition of the new law of grace. He even describes man's fulfillment of this condition as perfection. All of this points to a prominent place for God's will *de debito*.

Yet, although it must be acknowledged that God's role as *Rector per leges* receives a dominant place in Baxter's theology, he does leave room for God's will *de rerum eventu*. By limiting the attention to only one aspect, an incomplete picture of Baxter's theology unfolds. Baxter's argument that he gives a less significant role to faith than his high Calvinist opponents must be taken seriously. Whether or not he is correct in this evaluation, his argument is that man does not effect his own justification. Faith is only the condition without which God does not justify. Moreover, it must not be ignored that, according to Baxter, God gives special grace as *Dominus Absolutus*. God generally uses means, but he is not bound to them. Thus, Baxter hesitates to speak of a "proper promise" of special grace upon the good use of common grace. His bifurcation of God's will, as adopted from William Twisse, determines his view of grace, even though the emphasis remains with God's will *de debito*.

---

391. Packer, "Redemption and Restoration," p. ii.
392. Mair, "Sanctification," pp. 232, 269, 280-81; C. Harinck, *De Schotse verbondsleer: Van Robert Rollock tot Thomas Boston* (Utrecht: De Banier, 1986), pp. 67, 69.

Chapter V

Atonement and Justification

From guilt and reigning power of sin,
And Satan's slavery:
From fire of Hell us to redeem,
God gave his Son to die.
Christ suffer'd in our stead, he was
More harmless than the Dove:
That God should lay our sins on him:
This, this indeed is Love.[1]

(Richard Baxter)

Influences on Baxter's Thinking

WILLIAM TWISSE

The prominent role of Baxter's distinction between God's will *de debito* and *de rerum eventu* not only plays a role in his view of the role of faith in justification. The same bifurcation determines Baxter's position on the extent and the nature of the atonement. Also here, the immediate background appears to lie in the impact of William Twisse on Baxter's thinking. Repeatedly, he appeals to Twisse in support of his theory of universal redemption.[2] Baxter even says that he was brought to his view on universal redemption "by reading *Dr Twisse*, and meditating of it ..."[3]

Baxter's appeal to a high Calvinist, such as Twisse, may seem out of place. Are not Twisse's view of justification from eternity and Baxter's emphasis on the conditionality of the covenant miles apart? Is there any basis for Baxter's insistence that Twisse "is down right for universal Redemption in this middle way"?[4] After all, in several other places, Baxter admits that Twisse opposes universal redemption.[5] An analysis of Twisse's views on the extent of redemption may shed some light on the background to Baxter's thinking. Twisse makes his views on the extent of the atonement and the offer of grace subservient to his conception of

---

1. In Banks, "Poems of Richard Baxter," pp. 719-20.
2. Baxter, *Aphorismes* II.168, 172-73 (pp. 321, 324-25); *Plain Scripture Proof*, p. 276; *Confession*, sig. e3ᵛ; *Universal Redemption*, pp. 287-88.
3. Baxter, *Certain Disputations*, sig. b3ᵛ (emphasis inverted).
4. Baxter, *Plain Scripture Proof*, p. 276.
5. Baxter, *Universal Redemption*, pp. 116, 170, 377.

God's twofold will. Since Christ did not merit the remission of sins for all, he did not die for all.[6] It is not true that God wants all men to be saved. When Scripture does say that God wants all to be saved (1 Tim 2:4), this must not be interpreted as referring to *singula generum* but to *genera singulorum*.[7] God does not want every one of all sorts of men to be saved, but only some of all sorts. Scripture references that seem to express God's desire that all the people of Israel would listen to him must be understood as "a figure of speech called ἀνθρωποπάθεια."[8] It is, therefore, an "abominable opinion" to think that God does as much for the salvation of the reprobates as he does for the salvation of his elect.[9] God does not proffer salvation to all that perish, and, where he does proffer it to any that perish, this does not mean that "he doth all that he could doe" for their salvation.[10]

All of the above comments belong to God's *voluntas beneplaciti*. Apart from his *voluntas beneplaciti*, however, God's *voluntas signi* must be taken into account. Twisse says that he has no problem admitting that according to his *voluntas conditionata* God "will have all to be saved, to witt, in case they beleeve."[11] What is more, Twisse repeatedly argues that he has a broader view of the extent of redemption than the Arminians do. To make this point clear he distinguishes between two kinds of benefits procured by Christ, some "only conditionally, and some absolutely."[12] Pardon and salvation are conditionally procured benefits, while faith and regeneration have been merited absolutely.[13] The conclusion should be obvious, insists Twisse:

> <L>et the indifferent consider who they be that streiten the extension of Christs merits most, we, or the Arminians. For when the question is for whom he merited pardon of sinne, and salvation of soule, therin we all agree, as before hath bene shewed, none of us extending the merits of Christ farther then other; none of us streitning them more then other. But when the question is, whether Christ merited faith, and regeneration for us; we readily maynteyne, that even these allso Christ merited for his Elect; but Arminians spare not to professe, that these benefits Christ merited for none at all.[14]

---

6. Twisse, *Vindiciæ gratiæ, lib.* II, *crim.* 4, *sect.* 4, p. 79: "But Christ did not merit remission of sins and reconciliation with God for each and every one. Therefore, Christ did not die for each and every one." ("At non pro omnibus & singulis meruit Christus remissionem peccatorum, & cum Deo reconciliationem; Ergo pro omnibus & singulis Christus non est mortuus.")

7. Twisse, *Doctrine of the Synod of Dort*, pp. 60-62; *Discovery*, pp. 512-14. This distinction goes back via John Calvin and Gregory of Rimini (d. 1358) to Thomas Aquinas (Jonathan H. Rainbow, *The Will of God and the Cross: An Historical and Theological Study of John Calvin's Doctrine of Limited Redemption*, Princeton Theological Monograph Series, 22 [Allison Park, PA: Pickwick, 1990], p. 35, n. 2; pp. 40, 139).

8. Twisse, *Treatise of Mr. Cottons* (London, 1646), p. 107.

9. Twisse, *Discovery*, p. 626.

10. Twisse, *Discovery*, p. 625.

11. Twisse, *Doctrine of the Synod of Dort*, p. 61. It should be noted, however, that this does not mean that Twisse is of the opinion that God wants anyone besides his elect to be saved. It will be recalled that, according to Twisse, God's *voluntas signi* is only improperly called his will. It merely indicates the command or condition to be fulfilled.

12. Twisse, *Doctrine of the Synod of Dort*, p. 143.

13. Twisse, *Doctrine of the Synod of Dort*, pp. 144-45; *Discovery*, pp. 527, 550-51.

14. Twisse, *Doctrine of the Synod of Dort*, p. 145. Cf. pp. 170, 194.

The conditional procurement of pardon and salvation is for all. Twisse argues that there is no difference on this issue between himself and the Arminians.[15] The difference comes in with the question whether this condition – faith – is also procured by Christ's death. The Arminian denial proves that they limit the merit of Christ's death, says Twisse.

Twisse is willing to extend the conditional procurement of salvation beyond the elect. The saying in 1 John 2:2 – that Christ is the reconciliation for the sins of the whole world – Twisse prefers to explain as referring to the elect. Even if this exegesis does not hold, however, "we willingly confesse, that Christ dyed to obtaine salvation for all and every one that beleeve in him."[16] Accordingly, Twisse reproaches John Cotton for proving "that which no man denyes: namely, that God purposed life to the world, upon condition of obedience and repentance: provided, that you understand it aright: namely, that obedience and repentance is ordained of God, as a condition of life; not of Gods purpose."[17] Twisse does not want to fall into the Arminian extreme of a conditional decree. God's purpose itself is not conditional. Pardon, salvation, and life, however, are conditional.

Now it becomes clear why Baxter is able to appeal to Twisse in defense of universal redemption. Twisse and Baxter see eye to eye in that they both assert the conditionality of salvation. Pardon and salvation is for all on the condition that they repent and believe. Baxter also admits – against the Arminian view – that Christ died with a special intent to save the elect. Thus, Baxter accepts both the conditional and the absolute aspects of redemption. But Baxter does not mention that he has an important disagreement with Twisse: Baxter is unwilling to admit that faith and repentance are the immediate fruit of Christ's death. As Baxter's debate with Owen makes clear, Baxter does not believe that Christ procured faith and repentance either conditionally or absolutely, in a direct way.[18]

AMYRALDIANISM

The view of Baxter as an Amyraldian theologian needs some modification, especially in light of the view that he did not derive his position on the extent of the atonement from Moyse Amyraut. When, in his *Parænesis ad ædificatores Imperii in Imperio* (1656), Lewis Du Moulin denounces Amyraut's theology, he com-

---

15. William Eyre argues that Twisse speaks of conditions only in an improper sense: "<A>ll certaine and constant Antecedents ... may in a vulgar sense, be called conditions of those things that follow them; and in this sense our Divines doe commonly call one benefit of the Covenant a condition of the another <sic>; as that which is given first, of that which is given after. Thus Dr. *Twisse* makes inherent holinesse to be *causa dispositiva*, or the *sine qua non*, (not of Justification) but of Salvation, or Glorification, because the one alwaies precedes the other ..." (*Vindiciæ Justificationis Gratuitæ*, p. 185). Eyre erroneously thinks that, for Twisse, justification is not conditional. This is incorrect inasmuch as Twisse speaks of a condition not only of salvation and glorification, but also of pardon itself.
16. Twisse, *Doctrine of the Synod of Dort*, p. 15.
17. Twisse, *Treatise of Mr. Cottons*, p. 74. Cf. pp. 95, 117.
18. Cf. below, pp. 263-64.

ments that "in England only one Baxter is exceedingly pleased with his meth-od."[19] Baxter denies being a proselyte of Amyraut, saying that "this *unus Baxterus* did write a Book for Universal Redemption in this middle sens, before ever hee saw either *Amyraldus, Davenant,* or any Writer (except *Dr Twisse*) for that way ..."[20]

Yet, Baxter is not adverse to the views of John Cameron and Amyraut on redemption. On the contrary, when John Tombes reproaches Baxter for his view on universal redemption, Baxter replies: "And to tel you freely my thoughts, that is the point of universal Redemption wherein I think *Amyrald* doth best, and in that ... I approve of most he saith."[21] What is more, when Baxter distinguishes the absolute promise of the first grace for the elect and the legal moral donation for all, he specifically appeals to Cameron, Amyraut, Davenant, Samuel Ward, and the Canons of Dort for support.[22] Thus, while it does not appear that Amyraut had an immediate impact on Baxter's view on the extent of the atonement, there is an obvious congeniality between the two authors. Some comments on Cameron's and Amyraut's view of the atonement – and, related to it, on their doctrine of the covenant – are in place.

Essential to Cameron's thinking is his distinction between the *foedus absolutum* and the *foedus hypotheticum.*[23] In the former, God acts as Father, according to his *voluntas absoluta.* In the latter, he acts as Lawgiver, according to his *voluntas conditionata.* The Ramist method of dichotomizing may have been conducive to such a view.[24] The background to Amyraut's thinking goes deeper, however, and goes back to the *via moderna* of Duns Scotus, with its distinction between the two aspects of God's will.[25]

Cameron distinguishes the *foedus hypotheticum* into three covenants: "We say, therefore, that one covenant is of nature, that another is of grace, and that yet another is subservient to the covenant of grace (which in Scripture is called the old covenant)."[26] These three covenants trace the various periods of the history of redemption. The covenant of nature was the covenant with all mankind through Adam, in which the mediation of Christ remained less obvious than in the second covenant, the *foedus subserviens* or *vetus foedus.* This legal covenant was made with Israel through Moses and carried the promise of the land of Canaan. The last

---

19. "in Anglia uni Baxtero apprimè placet ejus Methodus" (Du Moulin, *Parænesis,* sig. g1ᵛ). Cf. sig. g4ᵛ.
20. Baxter, *Certain Disputations,* sig. b3ᵛ (emphasis inverted). Cf. *RB* I.110.
21. Baxter, *Plain Scripture Proof,* p. 275.
22. Baxter, *Plain Scripture Proof,* p. 316. Cf. p. 332.
23. Moltmann, "Prädestination und Heilsgeschichte," 276-77; Armstrong, *Calvinism and the Amyraut Heresy,* pp. 51-52; Strehle, *Calvinism, Federalism, and Scholasticism,* pp. 198-99.
24. Sabean and Armstrong argue that Amyraut was influenced by Ramist philosophy (Sabean, "Theological Rationalism of Moïse Amyraut," 213-15; Armstrong, *Calvinism and the Amyraut Heresy,* pp. 51-52).
25. Strehle, *Calvinism, Federalism, and Scholasticism,* p. 200; Strehle, "Universal Grace and Amyraldianism," 355-56.
26. "Dicimus ergo Fœdus aliud esse *Naturæ,* aliud *Gratiæ,* aliud Fœderi gratiæ *subseruiens* (quod in Scriptura *a Fœdus vetus* appellatur ..." (Cameron, *Opera* [Geneva, 1642], p. 544). Cf. Moltmann, "Prädestination und Heilsgeschichte," p. 280, n. 41.

covenant, the *foedus gratiae*, promised life to all men on the condition of faith.[27]

It is understandable that Moltmann has asked attention for the three covenants in order to emphasize the redemptive historical aspect of Amyraldian theology. In line with this, Armstrong interprets Amyraldianism as a reaction against the scholasticism of Theodore Beza (1519-1605) which had replaced the biblically and experientially based theology of Calvin. The emphasis on the hypothetical covenant led to Amyraut's understanding of a *mutatio consiliorum Dei*. As Moltmann puts it: "Der in ewiger Unwandelbarkeit über der Geschichte thronende Wille Gottes wird in seinem Verhältnis 'erga nos' und 'sec. nostrum modum considerandi' zu einem vielgestaltigen, veränderlichen Willen, der sich den heilsgeschichtlichen Stufen der Menschheit akkommodiert."[28] In other words, Amyraut's emphasis on the *foedus hypotheticum* calls into question the doctrine of the immutability of God. It will be recalled that William Robertson and George Kendall levelled the same accusation against Baxter because of his view that an immanent act could arise anew in God. Both Amyraut and Baxter are accused of endangering the immutability of God because of their emphasis on the conditionality of the covenant between God and man.[29]

Although it may be proper to highlight Amyraut's emphasis on the redemptive historical nature of God's covenantal dealings with man, it is too much to argue that his theology represented a return to Calvin's more biblically based theology. First of all, as has recently been demonstrated by C. Graafland, Calvin's own theology was marked by a significant tension between covenant and election. This tension is closely interwoven with his use of the scholastic distinction between the revealed and the hidden will of God.[30] It is debatable, therefore, in how far a return to Calvinian theology would mean an abandonment of scholasticism. More to the point, perhaps, is the fact that regardless of its emphasis on the *foedus hypotheticum*, Amyraut's theology continues to be based on the distinction between God's revealed and his hidden will. In that sense, some form of continuity with Calvin does, indeed, remain.

This bifurcation may be illustrated in several ways. First, Cameron's order of the decree has four phases: the first decree is to restore the image of God in the creature. Then follows the decree to send the Son, who will save everyone who believes in him. The third decree is to cause men to believe. The last decree is to save those who believe. Cameron then adds: "The former two degrees are general, the latter two special."[31] The general decrees belong to God's revealed will. They set forth Christ and the demand to believe. The special decrees concern God's

27. Moltmann, "Prädestination und Heilsgeschichte," 280-82; Armstrong, *Calvinism and the Amyraut Heresy*, pp. 143-47; Strehle, *Calvinism, Federalism, and Scholasticism*, pp. 201-05; Graafland, *Van Calvijn tot Barth*, p. 190.
28. Moltmann, "Prädestination und Heilsgeschichte," 287-88.
29. It should be borne in mind, however, that Baxter rejects Amyraut's view of a conditional decree (*Plain Scripture Proof*, p. 275).
30. C. Graafland, *Van Calvijn tot Comrie: Oorsprong en ontwikkeling van de leer van het verbond in het Gereformeerd Protestantisme*, I (Zoetermeer: Boekencentrum, 1992), 147-70, 177-84.
31. "Priora duo Decreta generalia sunt, posteriora duo specialia" (Cameron, *Opera*, p. 529). Cf. Strehle, *Calvinism, Federalism, and Scholasticism*, p. 205, n. 58.

secret will. The first two decrees correspond to God's antecedent love, his general will to save all men. The last two decrees correspond to his consequent love, his special will to save the elect.[32] This bifurcation of God's will also determines Amyraut's theology. Stephen Strehle sharply criticizes this view:

> Here the significance of Christ's work is extrapolated from the "secret will" of God, God's ultimate teleological rationale for designing the cross. Here the intrinsic sufficiency and essential propitiatory value of that work is delimited by divine *acceptatio* – a device of Duns Scotus and Nominalism which negates the intrinsic meaning of the Son's work by the extrinsic consideration of the Father's will. Here the *Deus absconditus* is the real God, hidden behind the mask of the revelation and work of the Son.[33]

Strehle is not convinced that Amyraldianism means a return to a more biblically oriented theology. Instead, it remains firmly anchored within the framework of Scotist thinking on the doctrines of God and the atonement.

This bifurcation is also evident in Amyraut's approach to the extent of the atonement. He insists that Christ died equally for all because the covenant of grace is universal in its extent. It is clear that Amyraut is here thinking of God's revealed will and of his general decrees. After the Synod of Alençon (1637) decides that Amyraut should forbear such language, he complies.[34] Because Amyraut thinks that the atonement is, in a very real sense, also limited, he is able to accommodate. For the redemption acquired by Christ remains hypothetical. It is only a hypothetical universalism. God wills the salvation of all men hypothetically. If someone does not fulfill the condition God also does not decree to save such a person. Thus, "Christ's acquisition of salvation remains *in suspenso* until the condition is fulfilled."[35] Amyraut is, thus, able to view the extent of the atonement from the vantage point of God's revealed will as well as from the viewpoint of his secret will. The similarity with Baxter's position is striking.[36] It is understandable that Baxter feels attracted to the theology of Cameron and Amyraut. It presents him with the same bifurcation which he has already found in Twisse and has subsequently made the cornerstone of his theology.

HUGO GROTIUS

J.I. Packer's dissertation on Baxter recognizes Baxter's indebtedness to the Arminian theologian, Hugo Grotius. Packer goes as far as to suggest that Grotius' political

---

32. Cf. Armstrong, *Calvinism and the Amyraut Heresy*, pp. 57-58.
33. Strehle, "Universal Grace and Amyraldianism," 356.
34. Armstrong, *Calvinism and the Amyraut Heresy*, p. 93. Cf. pp. 152, n. 98; 169, n. 28; 183, n. 64; 211, n. 148.
35. Armstrong, *Calvinism and the Amyraut Heresy*, p. 210.
36. Strehle states that Amyraut first makes use of God's universal will and regards Christ's work as unlimited, and that he then considers his work as limited to the elect because God then determines its efficacious effect ("Universal Grace and Amyraldianism," 355). As will be noted below, Baxter does exactly the same thing.

method is the key to Baxter's theology.[37] Without denying the profound influence of Grotius on Baxter, I would suggest that this picture needs some modification. As suggested above, Baxter also underwent the impact of others, of whom Twisse was first and foremost. With regard to the shaping of Baxter's theology, Twisse's bifurcation of God's will takes precedence over Grotius' theory of the atonement.[38] As Packer recognizes, Baxter insists that he had almost finished his *Aphorismes* before reading "a leaf of *Grotius*."[39]

It is true, however, that without an understanding of Grotius' theory of the atonement Baxter's own theology cannot be properly understood.[40] Baxter freely admits that Grotius changed his thinking about redemption.[41] In what follows, it will become clear that especially Baxter's controversy with John Owen must be interpreted with the person of Grotius figuring prominently in the background. The reason is that Baxter engaged with Owen in an intense discussion about the question whether Christ suffered the exact same punishment as was threatened by the law (the *idem*) or whether he only suffered so much (the *tantundem*). It is precisely this distinction which lies at the heart of the Grotian governmental theory of the atonement.

Grotius employs the distinction between the *idem* and the *tantundem* in his *Defensio fidei catholicæ de satisfactione Christi Adversus Faustum Socinum Senensem* (1617).[42] In this book, he opposes the Socinian view of the atonement. He maintains that in the doctrine of the atonement God must be considered as Governor.[43] Against Socinus Grotius insists that God exacts payment: "But any Governour, and God himself also is called therefore Just, and Praised, upon the account of Justice, because he forgives not punishment, but exacts it severely."[44]

---

37. Packer, "Redemption and Restoration," pp. ii-iii, 458.
38. Cf. the comment of William M. Lamont that Baxter "would never sound more totally at one with Grotius than when he was expounding God's rectorial function" and that he would also never "sound more like Twisse than when he was developing the theme of God's power as *dominus*" (*Richard Baxter and the Millennium*, p. 137). Lamont does not appear to realize that it is because of the bifurcation of God's will that Baxter is able to expound God's rectorial function as well as his role as *Dominus*. Both aspects are rooted in Twisse's theology. Baxter is able to fit Grotius' emphasis on God's rectorial characteristics into Twisse's dual structure. Lamont rightly states, however, that both Grotius and Twisse influenced Baxter.
39. Baxter, *Unsavoury Volume*, p. 6. Cf. Packer, "Redemption and Restoration," p. 233.
40. Already in his *Aphorismes*, Baxter often refers to Grotius (cf. above, p. 26, n. 9). Also elsewhere, Baxter expresses his agreement with Grotius' view on the nature of the atonement (*Confutation*, p. 262; *Of Imputation*, pp. 76, 172, 174; *Scripture Gospel defended*, p. 109; *Universal Redemption*, pp. 76, 84-85).
41. Baxter, *Grotian Religion Discovered* (London, 1658), p. 4. Cf. *RB* I.108; *CCRB* 234, n. 1.
42. Cf. the discussions of this book in G.C. Joyce, "Grotius," *ERE* 6.441-42; A.H. Haentjens, *Hugo de Groot als godsdienstig denker* (Amsterdam: Ploegsma, 1946), pp. 91-97; H.D. McDonald, *The Atonement of the Death of Christ: In Faith, Revelation, and History* (Grand Rapids: Baker, 1985), pp. 203-07; Hugo Grotius, *Opera theologica*, I, ed. Edwin Rabbie, trans. Hotze Mulder (Assen: Van Gorcum, 1990), pp. 63-77. This last book is a critical edition of Grotius' *Defensio*. I am indebted to Prof. J. Van den Berg for alerting me to it.
43. Grotius, *Defensio* (Leiden, 1617), pp. 33-46 (*Defence*, trans. W.H. [London, 1692], pp. 55-78). For English translations I am using this 1692 edition.
44. Grotius, *Defence*, p. 71 ("At quivis rector, atque ipse Deus, justus ob id dicitur, & justitiæ nomine laudatur, quod pœnas non remittat, sed severè exigat" [*Defensio*, p. 42].).

Grotius' theory of the atonement is strongly juridical in character.[45] It was not unjust for God to punish Christ for our sins, as Socinus had maintained.[46] This punishment is "a true exchange" between Christ and the believer;[47] it is "a certain true substitution."[48]

Nevertheless, the satisfaction of Christ involved a relaxation of the law.[49] As Grotius argues: "But if furthermore, we look back to the Sanction, or the Penal Act, the Act it self will be a way to Indulgence, or a Moderation of the same Law, which Indulgence at this day we call Dispensation ..."[50] This relaxation of the law implies that the exact penalty of the law has not been executed on Christ. Grotius, therefore, maintains:

> But though we hitherto shewed that satisfaction was made to God by the punishment of Christ, yet we desire not to deny that the force of satisfaction is in the very action of Christ. For oftimes an acceptable action useth to be admitted instead of a punishment. *A benefit coming after*, saith *Seneca, suffereth not an injury to appear*, Lib. 6. cap. 5. In which place he sheweth, that to render is to give a thing for a thing, and that by payment the same thing <*idem*> is not paid, but so much <*tantundem*>.[51]

Grotius is of the opinion that Christ's death did not constitute the exact execution of the penalty of the law. There has been no *solutio eiusdem*, but only a *solutio tantidem*.

45. Cf. the comment of G.H.M. Posthumus Meyjes: "The Christian humanist program was given its characteristic stamp by the strong and fertile influence of Grotius' legal notions. Even in his theology he remains first and foremost a jurist, one who sees religion and everything associated with it through legal eyes" ("Hugo Grotius As an Irenicist," in *The World of Hugo Grotius (1583-45)*, Proc. of the International Colloquium organized by the Grotius Committee of the Royal Netherlands Academy of Arts and Sciences, 6-9 April 1983 [Amsterdam: APA-Holland Univ. Press, 1984], p. 45).
46. Grotius, *Defensio*, pp. 52-65 (*Defence*, pp. 89-112). Rhetorically, Grotius asks: "Who judgeth it unjust, if, the highest Power relaxing the Law, some man useful to the Common-wealth, but deserving Banishment for a Fault, is retained in the Common wealth, yet another of his own accord obliging himself to Banishment to satisfie the Example?" (*Defence*, p. 111; "quis injustum putet, si summa potestate legem relaxante vir aliquis reipublicæ utilis, sed ob culpam exsilium meritus, retineatur in Republicâ, alio tamen sponte suâ se ad exsilium obligante, ut exemplo satisfat?" [*Defensio*, p. 64])
47. Grotius, *Defence*, p. 201 ("Commutationem ergo illa locutio δοῦναι ἀντὶ πολλῶν veram indicat ..." [*Defensio*, p. 117].).
48. Grotius, *Defence*, p. 205 ("sed & ex ipsius sententia vera quædam substitutio indicibatur" [*Defensio*, p. 119].).
49. Grotius, *Defensio*, pp. 46-51 (*Defence*, pp. 79-88).
50. Grotius, *Defence*, p. 80 ("Si verò præterea rescipiamus sanctionem sive legem pœnalem, erit actus ipse via ad indulgentiam seu temperamentum ejusdem legis, quam indulgentiam hodie dispensationem vocamus ..." [*Defensio*, p. 47].).
51. Grotius, *Defence*, p. 153 ("Quamquam verò hactenus ostendimus Christi pœnâ Deo satisfactum, negare tamen nolumus vim satisfactionis esse etiam in ipsa Christi actione. Solet enim sæpe etiam actio grata admitti velut in pœnæ compensationem. *Beneficium superveniens*, inquit Seneca *injuriam apparere non patitur*: De benef. lib. vi, cap. v. quo loco ostendit reddere esse rem pro re dare, & solutione non idem solvi, sed tantundem" [*Defensio*, p. 89].).

WILLIAM BRADSHAW

In defense of his theory of imputation, Baxter repeatedly appeals to the moderate nonconformist minister, William Bradshaw.[52] Baxter places him on a par with Grotius[53] and acknowledges his indebtedness to both.[54] According to Baxter, Grotius and Bradshaw held essentially the same view of imputation. The work of Bradshaw to which Baxter appeals is his *Dissertatio De iustificationis doctrina* (1618), which is a translation and expansion of his *Treatise of Ivstification* (1615).[55]

For Bradshaw, the need for satisfaction is obvious. God is not able to absolutely remit sin without satisfaction. He hates all sin. His justice must be satisfied.[56] But neither man, nor any other creature, is able to do this.[57] Rather, it suffices for a just imputation that satisfaction is made by someone else.[58] To deny the possibility that a person may be just through the righteousness of someone else would be to overthrow the main foundation of all Christianity.[59]

Bradshaw devotes little attention to the question for whom Christ undertook his work of mediation. On the one hand, the reason for this mediation lies in the sin of the whole world.[60] God's justice required punishment for all the sins of all men. The covenant between the Father and the Son does not take away the fact that Christ's sacrifice is "a most true and full price."[61] This sufficiency of Christ's sacrifice does not mean, however, that he satisfied also for the reprobates: "But those for whom satisfaction has been made by Christ are not all the world as a whole – although Christ is called Savior of the world (John 4:42; 1 John 4:14; 2:2) – but the elect only (1 Tim 2:10; Eph 5:23)."[62] Christ fullfilled the moral law "most fully" for the elect.[63]

---

52. Baxter, *Aphorismes* I.52, 55, 59 (pp. 35, 37, 40); *Account of my Consideration*, pp. 27-28; *Confutation*, p. 184; *Appeal* (London, 1674), p. 2; *Of Imputation*, pp. 20, 47, 76, 172-174; *Breviate*, p. 24; *Scripture Gospel defended*, p. 109; *End of Doctrinal Controversies*, p. 266; *Naked Popery* (London, 1677), pp. 51, 54.
   For Bradshaw, see *GBD* 6.419-20; Brook, *Lives*, II, 264-70; R.C. Simmons, introd., *English Puritanisme and Other Works*, by William Bradshaw (rpt. Westmead, Farnborough, Hants.: Gregg International, 1972), pp. i-viii; R.C. Simmons, introd., *Puritanism and Separatism: A Collection of Works by William Bradshaw*, by William Bradshaw (rpt. [Westmead, Farnborough, Hants.]: Gregg International, 1972); Peter Lake, *Moderate Puritans and the Elizabethan Church* (Cambridge: Cambridge Univ. Press, 1982), pp. 262-78, 337-41; Peter Lake, "William Bradshaw, Antichrist and the Community of the Godly," *JEH*, 36 (1985), 570-89.
53. Baxter, *Aphorismes* I.55 (p. 37); *Of Imputation*, pp. 76, 172, 174; *Scripture Gospel defended*, p. 109.
54. Baxter, *Unsavoury Volume*, p. 6.
55. Baxter uses the Latin edition in his quotations. Some of the crucial ideas of Bradshaw to which Baxter appeals are only mentioned in the Latin edition.
56. Bradshaw, *Dissertatio* (Leiden, 1618), pp. 64-68.
57. Bradshaw, *Dissertatio*, pp. 68-74.
58. Bradshaw, *Dissertatio*, p. 46.
59. Bradshaw, *Dissertatio*, p. 48.
60. Bradshaw, *Dissertatio*, p. 56.
61. "verissimum plenissimumque pretium" (Bradshaw, *Dissertatio*, p. 102).
62. "Illi verò pro quibus satisfactum est a Christo, non sunt totus in universum mundus (licet mundi servator dicitur Christus *Ioh.* 4.42. 1. *Ioh.* 4.14. & 2.2.) sed Electi duntaxat. 1. *Tim.* 4.10 <2:10>. *Ephe.* 5.23" (Bradshaw, *Dissertatio*, p. 75). Cf. p. 79.
63. "plenissime" (Bradshaw, *Dissertatio*, p. 81).

It might be expected that Bradshaw, because he holds to limited atonement, would insist that Christ's passive righteousness – and, perhaps, also his active righteousness – becomes strictly and properly ours. This is not the case, however. When Bradshaw discusses the issue of double imputation – of Christ's active as well as passive obedience – he does so after denouncing the papal heresy which puts the greatest, if not all hope in one's own merits and satisfaction.[64] But even "amongst ourselves" there are several disagreements on this issue.[65] There are two views, says Bradshaw: "One of them is that we are justified because of both aspects of that obedience, and because of both aspects imputed; the other, however, is that we are indeed justified because of both aspects of the obedience, but only because of the passive obedience imputed."[66] Bradshaw points out that there is a serious difficulty with twofold imputation: if active obedience is imputed, why did Christ still have to suffer?[67] Bradshaw then presents his alternative:

> For what prevents it being determined that someone's liability to the penalty will be taken away by both aspects of Christ's obedience and that the forgiveness for all our sins will necessarily follow? What hinders our saying that it suffices for the imputation of both aspects that God has admitted both aspects of this obedience for our good and that he regards us as accepted because of both aspects of it, as if we ourselves – in a way which was equal – had fulfilled the divine law, or had sustained the eternal punishments by which we were doomed to be among the dead?[68]

Bradshaw wants to solve the double imputation question by moving the discussion to a higher plane. The error of both parties in the debate is that they suppose our sins to be imputed to Christ and his righteousness to become ours. When Scripture says that Christ became sin for us, this is "not because the sins committed by us have truly been transferred to him, or as if God in the conception of his mind (as we speak about God from a human standpoint) judged Christ to have committed those very sins which we ourselves had committed ..."[69] Our sins do not become Christ's.

Likewise, his righteousness does not really become ours. Speaking of Christ's obedience to the law, Bradshaw says that it is "in a certain way" (*modo quodam*) said to be imputed, but not "as if each of the elect is regarded by God in entirely

---

64. Bradshaw, *Dissertatio*, pp. 3-4.
65. "inter nostros ipsos" (Bradshaw, *Dissertatio*, pp. 4-5; emphasis throughout in original).
66. "Harum altera est, Nos propter utramque illam Obedientiam, & imputatam utramque justificari: altera verò, Nos propter utranque quidem Obedientiam justificari, sed passivam tantummodo imputatã" (Bradshaw, *Dissertatio*, pp. 5-6; emphasis throughout in original).
67. Bradshaw, *Dissertatio*, p. 9.
68. "Quid enim prohibet, quominus utraque Christi Obediẽtia ad peccati cujusque reatum tollendum, & ad peccatorum nostrorum omnium veniam consequendam necessaria statuatur? Quid obstat, quo minus etiam ad Imputationem utriusque hoc sufficere dixerimus, quòd Deus utramque eam bono nostro Obedientiam admiserit, & propter eam utramque perinde nos acceptos habeat, ac si nos ipsi eo quo par erat modo legem divinam implevissemus, aut pœnas æternas ex eadem nobis debitas apud inferos sustinuissemus?" (Bradshaw, *Dissertatio*, pp. 10-11; emphasis throughout in original)
69. "non quia Peccata a nobis commissa in illum revera translata sint, aut quasi Deus mentis suæ conceptu, (ut de Deo ανθρωποπαθως loquamur) Christum existimaverit ea ipsa Peccata commisisse quæ nos ipsi commisseramus ..." (Bradshaw, *Dissertatio*, p. 77).

the same position by virtue of his obedience, and as if he himself, in manner as well as degree, had entirely performed the same obedience to the law."[70] By way of proof, Bradshaw appeals to the fact that Christ did not just observe the universal law of creation, but also the judicial and ceremonial Mosaic laws, as well as evangelical laws.[71] Furthermore, Christ suffered many infirmities for us and was humiliated for our sake.[72] All of this implies that we did not simply fulfill the law of creation in Christ.

It also must not be thought that in Christ's sufferings we ourselves suffered, "each in his own person."[73] Christ did not suffer exactly that which we owed. Where Grotius distinguishes between the *idem* and the *tantundem*, Bradshaw comments: "It suffices that the surety of the debtor, in his name or place, pays either a very large amount of money owed, or something else which is of the same value and price, in a way in which the creditor wishes to allow."[74] Bradshaw then comes to a significant statement which clearly denies a strict theory of imputation even of Christ's passive righteousness:

> And it is therefore neither said that they are imputed in this sense also strictly speaking, as if Christ had either endured those things in the place of us all and in our position; or as if we ourselves had borne those same things in Christ. But they are said to be imputed to us for righteousness also with the remaining things performed by Christ because they are admitted by God instead of those eternal torments themselves, which otherwise we ourselves would have borne among the dead. Neither are we said to be crucified and to die with Christ as if God would judge that we had then suffered those same things in him; but because his death or crucifixion destroyed the power of death, and, applied to us through faith, is an efficacious instrument through which we die to sin, that is, by virtue of which we are truly sanctified. We are said to be crucified and to die with Christ, not, in fact, inasmuch as we are justified, but inasmuch as we are sanctified or born again and practise true repentance.[75]

According to Bradshaw, then, there is no strict or direct imputation of Christ's righteousness at all. Christ has only undergone the equivalent of what the law demands. Baxter's appeal to Bradshaw is justified, therefore, although it must be

---

70. "ac si Electorum quisque Obedientiæ istius virtute eodem Planè loco a Deo haberetur, atque si eandem ipse planè, tum modo, tum gradu, Legi Obedientiam præstitisset" (Bradshaw, *Dissertatio*, pp. 84-85).

71. Bradshaw, *Dissertatio*, pp. 87-91.

72. Bradshaw, *Dissertatio*, pp. 91-94.

73. "in persona quisque propria" (Bradshaw, *Dissertatio*, p. 100).

74. "Sufficit ut Fidejussor Debitoris Nomine locovè vel summam Pecuniæ debitam persolvat, vel quid aliud quod ejusdem Valoris & Pretij sit, modo Creditor illud admittere velit" (Bradshaw, *Dissertatio*, p. 45). Bradshaw says that Christ has borne that which is judged to be "equal in worth and merit to that which is owed ("debitis dignitate & merito æquale" [p. 47]).

75. "Ac proindè neque ista etiam strictè loquĕdo eo sensu imputata dicatur, ac si aut Christus nostro omnium loco nostraque vice ea pertulisset. Aut nos ipsi in Christo eadem illa sustinuissemus; Sed ideo cum reliquis etiam a Christi præstitis ad justitiam nobis imputari dicantur, quia pro cruciatibus eis ipsis æternis a Deo admittuntur, quæ apud inferos alioqui nos ipsi sustinuissemus. Neque ideo cum Christo Crucifixi mortuique dicimur quasi Deus judicarit nos tunc in ipso eadem ipsa perpessos esse. Sed quia mors ejus seu Crucifixo, peccati potestatem abolebat, & nobis per fidem applicata, instrumentum sit efficax per quod peccato moriamur, hoc est, cujus virtute verè Sanctificemur, Non enim ut justificemur, sed ut Sanctificemur sive renascamur & Pœnitentiam veram agamus cum Christo Crucifixi mortuique esse perhibemur" (Bradshaw, *Dissertatio*, pp. 100-01).

kept in mind that Bradshaw does not base his theory of imputation on universal redemption.

JOHN BALL

Another theologian frequently appealed to in Baxter's *Aphorismes of Justification* is John Ball.[76] Ball used to be a nonconformist minister at Whitmore, near New-castle, Staffordshire. In 1637, he had published *A Treatise of Faith*, and after his death Simeon Ashe (d. 1662) published Ball's *A Treatise of the Covenant of Grace* (1645).[77] Baxter's esteem of Ball's writings is obvious. This becomes clear when John Crandon attacks Ball, who being "raised to a prosperous state in the world, and who seeing the Court infected with Popery *Socinianism* and *Arminianism* ... might possibly as far as Conscience would permit him, make use of the language there held most authentick."[78] Baxter is incensed with this insinuation of Crandon:

> Unworthy man! to publish such base surmises and slanders of the dead! to talk of his eying a Court infected with Popery, Socinianisme and Arminianisme, for prefer-ment, and making a bridge to that in his writings, that never saw the light till he was dead? He that was known to live (and dye) a Nonconformist, in a poor house, a poor habit, a poor maintenance of about 20[lb] *per an.* in an obscure Village, and teaching school all the week for a further supply, deserving as high esteem and honour as the best Bishop in *England*, yet looking after no higher things, but living comfortably and prosperously with these.[79]

Crandon's attack on Ball can by no means be taken at face value. Crandon's *Aphorisms Exorized and Anthorized* (1654) proves that he did not shrink from using the most vituperative language in order to disqualify his opponents. Further, the question must be asked whether Baxter had a right to appeal to Ball in defense of his own position. Even if Baxter's admiration of Ball would suffice to make the latter suspicious in the eyes of some, the question remains whether Ball was really as "Baxterian" as Baxter makes him out to be.

That Baxter feels attracted to Ball is doubtless due to the latter's doctrine of the conditionality of the covenant. Baxter insists that, according to Ball, works – or a purpose to walk with God – justify as the passive qualification for justification.[80] Ball, says Baxter, maintains that a covenant has both a promise and a stipulation. Indeed, Ball delivers "the most of *Amiraldus* doctrine."[81] It is indeed true that Ball emphasizes the conditionality of the covenant. In his *Treatise of the Covenant of Grace*, he distinguishes between the covenant of works and the covenant of prom-

---

76. For Ball, see *GBD* 3.385-87; Brook, *Lives*, II, 440-44; *DNB* 3.74-75. For Baxter's references to Ball in his *Aphorismes*, see above, p. 26, n. 9.
77. For Ball's *Treatise of the Covenant*, see Karlberg, "Mosaic Covenant," pp. 174-81; Karlberg, "Reformed Interpretation," 35-38.
78. Crandon, *Aphorisms Exorized* II.xiv.207. Cf. I.xxiv.298-99.
79. Baxter, *Unsavoury Volume*, p. 6. Baxter also expresses his high regard of Ball in *Aphorismes* I.54 (p. 36); *Confession*, p. 385.
80. Baxter, *Aphorismes* I.332 (p. 213).
81. Baxter, *Aphorismes* II.185 (p. 332).

ise. The latter is made with Adam "immediately upon the fall" and manifests itself more and more clearly, in various degrees: first from Adam to Abraham, secondly from Abraham till the Sinaitic covenant, and thirdly from Moses to Christ.[82] The covenant of promise is actually part of the covenant of grace, which was in force even under Moses. After the coming of Christ, the covenant of grace is called the new covenant or testament.[83] Already in the covenant of works, Adam would have continued in his blessed state if he had obeyed. Of course, this does not mean that he would have deserved or merited this reward.[84] But the conditional aspect of the covenant is clearly in the picture. The conditional promise of remission becomes absolute when the condition is fulfilled.[85]

Ball qualifies the conditionality of the covenant, however, in at least three different ways. In the first place, he strenuously argues against the doctrine of universal redemption as taught by Jacob Arminius (1559-1609) and Conrad Vorstius (1569-1622). Ball retains the distinction between Christ's death being effective for some and sufficient for all.[86] It is not true that Christ died for every particular man in the world. If the impenitent and the obstinate depart from the covenant, how can they possibly believe that Christ died for them?[87]

Ball is especially intent on disproving that Christ died "equally" for all, with an intent and purpose to save all.[88] He does not deny that Christ died "in some sense" for the reprobate.[89] The false prophets mentioned in 2 Peter 2:1 were "in a sort" bought by the blood of Christ.[90] Some benefits of Christ's death are "common to all men."[91] Accordingly, the sufficiency of Christ's death is a basis for the universal offer of grace. The way to comfort the distressed is "to informe him that his sins are pardonable, because in Christ forgivenesse is offered unto him ..."[92] Ball retains the invitation of the Gospel, an invitation which is both general and serious.[93] Indeed, he even says that believers know "that Christ died in generall for sinners, and that they shall be saved who beleeve in him."[94] This means that the rejection of the Gospel is not due to inability but due to unwillingness:

> And though I cannot say, God hath given to every man to believe if he will: Yet sure, God is not wanting to any man in that which either in justice or promise he is bound to give: and did men deny themselves, nourish the motions of Gods Spirit, and earnestly desire to believe, without question they should find the Lord gracious.[95]

---

82. Ball, *Treatise of the Covenant* (London, 1645), p. 36.
83. Ball, *Treatise of the Covenant*, pp. 194-203.
84. Ball, *Treatise of the Covenant*, pp. 9-10. Cf. Karlberg, "Mosaic Covenant," p. 175.
85. Ball, *Treatise of Faith*, 3rd. ed. (London, 1637), p. 86; *Treatise of the Covenant*, p. 225.
86. Ball, *Treatise of the Covenant*, p. 222.
87. Ball, *Treatise of the Covenant*, p. 223.
88. Ball, *Treatise of the Covenant*, pp. 224, 233, 238-39.
89. Ball, *Treatise of the Covenant*, p. 238.
90. Ball, *Treatise of the Covenant*, p. 240.
91. Ball, *Treatise of the Covenant*, p. 233.
92. Ball, *Treatise of the Covenant*, p. 226.
93. Ball, *Treatise of Faith*, p. 82; *Treatise of the Covenant*, pp. 226, 243.
94. Ball, *Treatise of Faith*, p. 81.
95. Ball, *Treatise of the Covenant*, p. 226. Ball insists that man's inability is not from any impossibility outside of man himself, but from his "voluntary perversnesse" (p. 244). Cf. *Treatise of Faith*, p. 45.

Thus, while denying that Christ died equally for all, Ball makes the invitation of
the Gospel as broad as possible. As will be noted below, there are similarities
between Baxter's and Ball's views regarding the extent of redemption. It should
be remembered, however, that Ball denied that Christ died equally for all, and that
most of his comments implying a more extended redemption are incidental and are
couched in lengthy digressions against the Arminian view of universal atonement.
Baxter is far more concerned to defend universal redemption against high Calvinist restrictions. The choice of an opponent colors the position one cherishes.

A second manner in which Ball restricts the conditionality of the covenant is
that he does not accept the possibility of believers apostatizing. Baxter appeals to
Ball in arguing that it is possible to be unpardoned and unjustified for the non-
performance of the conditions.[96] The passage to which he refers, however, presents
a somewhat different picture. Ball states that those who fall away did not believe
"sincerely and unfainedly" in Christ.[97] Their sins were only remitted "in a sort."
They did not receive "perfect remission" and were not "perfectly redeemed."[98] It
appears, then, that Baxter interprets Ball too much in line with his own views.

Finally, Ball keeps faith and works separate with regard to justification.[99] Also
here, Baxter is at least one-sided in his interpretation. Baxter states that according
to Ball obedience or the purpose to walk with Christ is part of the condition; works
are necessary to the continuation of justification.[100] Christopher Cartwright takes
exception to this interpretation. He points out that Baxter is incomplete in his
quotation. He has left out Ball's explanatory statement that works qualify justifying faith, and that faith alone justifies.[101] The reason why works are necessary to
continued justification is that faith is only able to claim the promises inasmuch as
it leads us forward in the way to heaven.[102] Thus, it is still faith alone which
justifies.

Ball's writings confirm Cartwright's understanding of Ball. With reference to
Bellarmine, Ball comments:

> It is further objected, if faith cannot be without charitie, then faith alone doth not
> justifie. This followeth not, for it is one thing to say, faith alone doth not justifie,
> another that faith which justifieth is not alone. This latter we yeeld unto, the first wee
> deny. Faith alone doth justifie, that is, privatively considered without hope or chari-
> tie, as causes concurring therewith in justification: but this faith cannot really be
> separated from, or negatively considered without hope and charity.[103]

Works do not justify. Ball maintains that faith is the only instrument of justifica-

96. Baxter, *Aphorismes* I.197 (p. 126).
97. Ball, *Treatise of the Covenant*, p. 240.
98. Ball, *Treatise of the Covenant*, p. 240.
99. Baxter's views on the relation between faith and works are discussed in the next chapter. Ball's
    views are discussed at this point in order to present a more unified picture of his position.
100. Baxter, *Confession*, pp. 385-86.
101. Cartwright, in Baxter, *Account of my Consideration*, p. 298.
102. Cartwright, *Exceptions*, p. 174.
103. Ball, *Treatise of Faith*, p. 56.

tion.[104] Nevertheless, it is true that works are important in Ball's view. Faith itself contains obedience. Faith is an "obedientiall confidence."[105] As it unites the heart to the promises, "so it glueth fast to the Commandements ..."[106] Christ is received both as Lord and as Savior.[107]

Because of their significance, works also play a role in the quest for assurance. Here, Baxter's interpretation of Ball is more true to fact.[108] Justifying faith is not an assured persuasion of pardon.[109] Instead, it is "to rest on Christ obeying to the cursed death of the crosse."[110] Justifying faith is to receive Christ as he is offered in the Gospel. It is "not to bee assured that our sinnes are already pardoned."[111] Thus, Ball rejects justification from eternity.[112] The fruits of faith are necessary to gain assurance. According to Ball, "no man can bee assured of remission of his sinnes, who doth not walk before God in uprightnesse and integritie ..."[113] The notion of "uprightnesse" or "sincerity" is the key element of the condition and, thus, also in determining the state of one's soul.[114]

The Extent of the Atonement

BIFURCATION *VERSUS* ONE-END TELEOLOGY

Baxter's Bifurcation and the Extent of Redemption

In his introduction to Owen's *Death of Death* (1647), J.I. Packer has commented that the doctrine of limited atonement may not be dismissed by anyone "until he has refuted Owen's proof that it is part of the uniform biblical presentation of redemption, clearly taught in plain text after plain text. And nobody has done that yet."[115] It is not the purpose of the following discussion to determine whether Owen's proof for the position of limited atonement has been successfully refuted or not. Nevertheless, Baxter has attempted to do exactly that.

---

104. Ball, *Treatise of the Covenant*, p. 20. Baxter admits to Cartwright that he differs from Ball. While Ball makes both faith and works the condition *sine qua non* of justification, he also affirms that faith is the instrumental cause of justification. In accordance with his opposition to the instrumentality of faith, Baxter states that Ball gives more to faith than he does (*Account of my Consideration*, p. 299; *Confession*, p. 386).
105. Ball, *Treatise of Faith*, p. 24.
106. Ball, *Treatise of Faith*, p. 31.
107. Ball, *Treatise of Faith*, p. 33.
108. Baxter, *Aphorismes* I.317 (p. 203).
109. Ball, *Treatise of Faith*, pp. 82-90.
110. Ball, *Treatise of Faith*, p. 85.
111. Ball, *Treatise of Faith*, p. 87.
112. Ball, *Treatise of Faith*, p. 89.
113. Ball, *Treatise of Faith*, p. 113.
114. Ball, *Treatise of the Covenant*, pp. 166-94. Cf. Baxter, *Aphorismes* I.317 (p. 203).
115. Packer, "'Saved by His Precious Blood'," p. 136.

It has thus far gone unnoticed that Baxter, in his *Universal Redemption*, published posthumously in 1694, engages in an extensive debate with Owen's position.[116] Part of the reason why Baxter's refutation of Owen's *Death of Death* has gone unnoticed may be the repetitive character of Baxter's work, which may tempt his readers simply to distill the main arguments from his book and leave the remainder unread. Another reason lies probably in the fact that Baxter does not mention Owen by name very often.[117] Most of the time Baxter simply gives quotations from *Death of Death* without referring either to the author or to the title of the book which he is quoting. Baxter repeatedly challenges Owen, for instance, on the latter's view that Christ's suffering constituted the identical payment required in the law, rather than a mere equivalent payment. He also questions Owen's exegesis of several New Testament texts: John 3:16;[118] John 3:17-19;[119] John 6:32, 33, 35, 36, 40, 51, 64, 66;[120] 2 Peter 2:1;[121] and Hebrews 10:26-29.[122]

Because Baxter interacts continually with Owen in *Universal Redemption*, an analysis and comparison of the two different positions is required. The difference in starting points must be noted first. A fundamentally different pattern of theological thinking is the cause of the divergence in views on the extent of the atonement. Influenced as he is by Twisse, Baxter's thinking is bifocal. A brief glance at the structure of *Universal Redemption* illustrates this: the first 480 pages deal with a defense of universal redemption, while the last 22 pages defend special redemption. At the back of this distinction lies his understanding of the will of God. Baxter is aware that his view on the will of God is fundamental to the determination of the controversy: he argues that

> we must most carefully distinguish between *Gods Will de Rerum Eventu*, and his *Will de Debito*, as such. The clear distinguishing of these two is a singular Key to the opening of the sence of Scripture, and in particular of this Controversie. For indeed, it is to distinguish between our Physicks and our Ethicks. Gods will about Natural Beings as such stands at the top of Physicks, as the first Cause. Gods *will de Debito* as such, stands at the top of our Ethicks, as the first Cause.[123]

Baxter makes clear that a two-tier approach to God's will lies at the basis of any interpretation of Scripture. This bifurcation is a "singular Key to the opening of the sence of Scripture."[124] It is therefore also the key to determining the question

---

116. Baxter debated the extent of the atonement only with John Owen. For Baxter's more systematic expositions on the issue, see *Directions and Persuasions to a Sound Conversion* (1658), in *Works* II.617-20 (8.117-28); *Catholick Theologie* I.ii.51-53; II.50-72; *Methodus Theologiæ* III.i.55-61; *End of Doctrinal Controversies*, pp. 154-62.
117. Baxter does so in *Universal Redemption*, pp. 70, 78, 81, 84, 115, 139.
118. Baxter, *Universal Redemption*, pp. 286-302.
119. Baxter, *Universal Redemption*, pp. 302-09.
120. Baxter, *Universal Redemption*, pp. 312-14.
121. Baxter, *Universal Redemption*, pp. 314-31.
122. Baxter, *Universal Redemption*, pp. 333-43.
123. Baxter, *Universal Redemption*, p. 28.
124. Cf. Baxter, *Universal Redemption*, p. 307: "And by this may very many Scriptures be interpreted, which ascribe such Velleities and Unaccomplished willings to God: Yea were these few lines given in answer to this question well weighed, (if through partiality I over-value them not) I think they might give much light to shew the true mean in the greatest of the Arminian Controversies."

of the extent of redemption. The quotation also makes clear that Baxter does not base the distinction on the teaching of Scripture, but on the basis of a philosophical distinction: "Who knows not that Naturality and Morality, Physicks and Ethicks, *Event and Right* are different things, and consequently we may and must distinguish of Gods willing them accordingly."[125] Baxter is careful to note that it is not "as if we feigned two wills in God, and one of them contrary to the other."[126] They are but distinct in man's apprehension.

The result of this bifurcation is that Baxter also distinguishes "between the antecedent and consequent Acts and Will of Christ as Ruler of Mankind."[127] According to the former, Christ grants justification by his deed of gift "equal to all." This will is conditional, and since it precedes man's obedience it is called antecedent. Christ's consequent will is that by which he judges men as he finds them obedient or disobedient.[128] Although Baxter does not appeal to Cameron or Amyraut here, the similarity in thinking is obvious. Cameron's distinction between God's antecedent and his consequent love, between his general and his special decrees, is similar to Baxter's distinction between Christ's antecedent and his consequent will.

Owen's One-End Teleology

Owen's approach is entirely different from the one described above. There is nothing in Owen which vaguely resembles a bifocal approach. Alan C. Clifford correctly points out that a "one-end teleology" determines Owen's approach.[129]

125. Baxter, *Universal Redemption*, p. 31.
126. Baxter, *Universal Redemption*, p. 31.
127. Baxter, *Universal Redemption*, p. 32.
128. Baxter, *Universal Redemption*, p. 32. Meanwhile, a subtle shift has occurred. While Baxter first spoke of a two-fold will in *God*, he now speaks of a corresponding two-fold act and will of "Christ as Ruler of Mankind." One would have expected a distinction between God as absolute Donor of faith – corresponding to his will *de rerum eventu* – and God as the Ruler – corresponding to his will *de debito*. Or, if one wants to shift from God to Christ as subject, one would expect a distinction between Christ the Owner of mankind who grants faith absolutely, and Christ as Ruler who dispenses his benefits by way of conditions. Baxter does not do so. When he turns from God to Christ as the subject he abandons the distinction between the absolute and conditional. He leaves the track of "the absolute" to focus only on Christ who rules by establishing certain conditions. Baxter explicitly states at this point that "we speak not now of Eternal Decrees, but of the will of Christ in this Relation as he is the Ruler of the World and Church, and as he is the conveyer of his mercies according to and by his Covenant, and as he judgeth the World according thereunto" (p. 32). Christ's antecedent will precedes the fulfillment of the condition, his consequent will follows the fulfillment or non-fulfillment of the condition.
129. Clifford, *Atonement and Justification*, pp. 95-110. I have borrowed the phrase "one-end teleology" from Clifford. He speaks of a "'one-end' Aristotelian teleology" (p. 104). Clifford traces this one-end teleology to the influence of Aristotelian metaphysics. This is, indirectly, indeed the case. I will not elaborate on the obvious affinity with Aristotelian thought patterns at this point, since the use of Aristotelian concepts in the defence of one's theology was common place. Baxter also makes use of it when it suits him. (For an interesting, though somewhat exaggerated, account of Thomist/scholastic influence on Baxter, see Phillips, "Between Conscience and the Law," pp. 5-6, 21, 120-31, 170-71, 183, 223, 292-93). It has rightly been pointed out that the Amyraldian scheme of theology was scholastic in outlook (Strehle, *Calvinism, Federalism, and Scholasticism*, pp. 212-14; Strehle, "Universal Grace and Amyraldianism," 354-57; Rainbow, *Will of God and the Cross*, pp. 48, 185).

Owen begins his *Death of Death* (1647) as follows: "By the end of the death of Christ, we mean in general, both, – first, that which his Father and himself intended *in* it; and, secondly, that which was effectually fulfilled and accomplished *by* it."[130] Owen begins by defining his terms, such as "end," "means," and "agent." This is the point where the direction of the argument is established. Owen insists that

> the end of every free agent is either that which he effecteth, or that for whose sake he doth effect it. When a man builds a house to let to hire, that which he effecteth is the building of a house; that which moveth him to do it is love of gain. The physician cures the patient, and is moved to it by his reward... The end which God effected by the death of Christ was the satisfaction of his justice: the end for whose sake he did it was either supreme, or his own glory; or subordinate, ours with him.[131]

The glory of God is the only supreme end, according to Owen. Any other end, such as man's salvation, is only intermediate and subservient to the glory of God.[132].

Just as Baxter is aware that a bifurcation in the will of God is essential to his view on the extent of the atonement, so Owen realizes what lies at the foundation of his argument: "THE main thing upon which the whole controversy about the death of Christ turneth" is the question "about the proper end of the death of Christ."[133] While both Baxter and Owen have their exegetical ammunition, it is clear that their differences in exegesis stem from their respective systematic theological starting points.[134]

The Role of the pactum salutis

This difference in starting point is intimately related to several other points of doctrine. The first is the eternal covenant between the Father and the Son regarding man's redemption. For Owen this *pactum salutis* is of the utmost importance. In the face of trials, it gave confidence and assurance to the Savior.[135] When Owen wants to prove that Christ's oblation and intercession are co-extensive and have the same purpose, he bases this view partly on the compact between the Father and the Son.[136] Further, the Old Testament saints were saved because Christ's death was in God's mind already accounted as accomplished, "the compact and cove-

---

130. Owen, *Death of Death*, in *Works* 10.157.
131. Owen, *Death of Death*, in *Works* 10.162.
132. Owen, *Death of Death*, in *Works* 10.202.
133. Owen, *Death of Death*, in *Works* 10.200.
134. I can therefore not agree with John Macleod, who maintains that "Owen's work belongs to the department of Exegetical Theology rather than to Dogmatics or Systematic Theology" ("John Owen and the Death of Death," p. 71).
135. Owen, *Death of Death*, in *Works* 10.169-70.
136. Owen, *Death of Death*, in *Works* 10.185. B. Loonstra points out that, in a sense, Owen's view of the *pactum salutis* is exceptional. He does not discuss it in connection with the doctrine of the covenant. Rather, he uses the covenant of redemption as the first cause of union with Christ and, thus, of the imputation of Christ's righteousness. In other words, the *pactum salutis* gives certainty of justification (*Verkiezing – verzoening – verbond*, pp. 105-06).

nant with Christ about it being surely ratified upon mutual, unchangeable promises ..."[137]

Crandon also emphasizes the covenant between the Father and the Son. He denies that the law of nature or the covenant of works is the rule of Christ's mediation.[138] The reason Christ's sufferings are meritorious lies in the *pactum salutis*. Christ was made God's righteousness to us "not by the rule of the Law or Covenant of works, but of the secret and sacred Covenant made between the Father and him."[139] That the Father sent Christ and does not impute to us the breach of the law is not the fruit of the covenant of works, but it is "the fruit of his grace and in conformity to the Gospel and Covenant of grace."[140] Crandon identifies the covenant of redemption between the Father and the Son and the covenant of grace.[141]

Baxter does not need an eternal *pactum salutis* to secure the efficacy of Christ's work of redemption. He argues that God has the right to cut off the elect before they have come to faith. The only reason why God does not do this lies in his decree. Baxter then foresees the objection: does not a possible condemnation of the elect, prior to faith, do injury to Christ? Is their salvation not secured in the covenant of redemption between God and Christ? Baxter's response is revealing:

> I am indifferent how this is answered, seeing we are agreed in the sense, that God never will condemn his Elect: But by [the Covenant between the Father and Son] either they mean, somewhat from eternity, or before the Fall; and this is but Gods Decree; and is no more a Covenant indeed, than any other Decree of God is: Doth God make Covenants with himself?
> 2. Or else they mean the Prophecies and Promises in the Old Testament (or Scriptures before Christs Incarnation) made to or of Christ as God-man to be Incarnate: and these are more properly Predictions *de futuro*, as other Prophecies are, (which God cannot but fulfil because he is immutable and infallible) than the Divine Obligations, (which God must fulfil because he is Just:) ...[142]

For Baxter, that which is commonly regarded as the covenant between the Father and the Son is either nothing but his decree, or it refers to the Old Testament prophecies concerning Christ. God does not make covenants with himself. It is one of the errors of the Antinomians that they "feign God to have made an eternal Covenant with his Son; that is, God imposing on God, the Law of Mediation."[143] To be sure, there is a covenant between the Father and the incarnate Christ.[144] But there should be no speculation about an eternal covenant of God with himself.

The implications of this elimination of a separate, eternal covenant of redemption must not be underestimated. Firstly, it means that an important support sys-

---

137. Owen, *Death of Death*, in *Works* 10.248. Owen further mentions the *pactum salutis* in pp. 164-65, 253. For Owen's views on its role in the process of justification, see above, pp. 106-08.
138. Crandon, *Aphorisms Exorized* I.xiii.129-30.
139. Crandon, *Aphorisms Exorized* I.xiii.130.
140. Crandon, *Aphorisms Exorized* I.xiii.130.
141. Cf. Crandon, *Aphorisms Exorized* I.xi.107; I.xx.244; I.xxi.259; above, pp. 118-20.
142. Baxter, *Universal Redemption*, pp. 410-11. Cf. pp. 418-19.
143. Baxter, *Defence of Christ*, p. 10.
144. Baxter, *Breviate*, p. 4; *End of Doctrinal Controversies*, p. 121.

tem for the doctrine of limited atonement has been removed. The divine covenant, in which the sacrifice of Christ was exchanged for the salvation of the elect, has disappeared. Thus, room has been created for other ends of Christ's sacrifice. God's glory by means of the salvation of the elect no longer needs to be the only end of Christ's death. Secondly, although Baxter retains a temporal covenant of mediation between the Father and the Son, he distinguishes it sharply from the covenant of grace which is made with believers and their seed. The identification of the *pactum salutis* with the covenant of grace was common in high Calvinist theology.[145] The result was a tendency to take up the temporal economy into eternity.[146] Baxter's greatest fear with regard to a supra-temporal covenant between the Father and the Son is that it will be confounded with the covenant of grace. Repeatedly, Baxter insists that the covenant made with Christ is "not the same that is made between Christ and us."[147] By separating the temporal covenant of mediation between the Father and the Son from the covenant of grace Baxter facilitates the broadening of the extent of redemption and the introduction of the conditionality of the covenant as well as a view on imputation which denies a strict imputation of Christ's righteousness.

The Failed Intent of the Atonement

A second issue which arises from the two mutually exclusive starting points is the question whether the intent of Christ's death is fully reached.[148] It can be stated without exaggeration that Owen's main argument against universal redemption is that God would fail in his purpose. Owen's one-end teleology cannot be accommodated by universal redemption. That which Christ intended with his death is not accomplished if he died for all. With an appeal to Romans 4:25 Owen claims:

> For whose offences he died, for their justification he rose; – and therefore, if he died for all, all must also be justified, or the Lord faileth in his aim and design, both in the death and resurrection of his Son; which though some have boldly affirmed, yet for my part I cannot but abhor the owning of so blasphemous a fancy.[149]

Since universal redemption implies that "the Lord faileth in his aim and design" Owen cannot but reject this position. He uses this argument more than any other.[150]

---

145. The identification of the covenant of redemption and the covenant of grace was taught by Johannes Cloppenburg (1592-1652), Herman Witsius (1636-1708), Francis Turretin (1623-87), Petrus Van Mastricht, Tobias Crisp, John Saltmarsh, Edward Fisher, John Bunyan, and John Crandon (cf. Greaves, *John Bunyan*, pp. 103-11; Loonstra, *Verkiezing – verzoening – verbond*, pp. 109-11).
146. Cf. Richard A. Muller, "Spirit and the Covenant," 12.
147. Baxter, *Breviate*, p. 10. Cf. p. 19; *Defence of Christ*, pp. 8, 10. Baxter criticizes the Larger Catechism of the Westminster Standards for holding that the covenant of grace was only made with Christ (*Breviate*, p. 10; cf. Larger Catechism, Question and Answer 31).
148. Another related point is the question whether or how Christ's death procured faith. This issue will be dealt with below, pp. 263-64.
149. Owen, *Death of Death*, in *Works* 10.182.
150. It is found throughout the treatise (Owen, *Death of Death*, in *Works* 10.149, 159, 176, 182, 193, 209, 224, 238, 241, 258, 288, 296, 312, 322, 329, 335, 345, 359, 381, 417).

Baxter, however, denies the charge. His main argument is again based on a rejection of Owen's teleological approach. Christ's death was not in vain, because by his death he did not intend to lead all to salvation. Christ's satisfaction "is the ground of his New Title of Lord-redeemer, as to Dominion and Rectorship ..."[151] His death is not in vain just because something is not accomplished which Christ never intended to accomplish in the first place, namely, the salvation of all those for whom he died. Baxter also argues by way of analogy to creation: God did not make Adam capable of life in vain, just because he did not obtain the life for which he was created.[152] Furthermore, the justice of Christ and God "will be everlastingly glorified on the rejectors of Grace." Since Christ thus attained his own and his Father's glory he did not die in vain, maintains Baxter.[153]

Moving one step ahead, Baxter even reverses the charge. It is the proponents of limited atonement who, by implication, argue that Christ suffered in vain. To those who think that it is the universalist position which entails that Christ suffered in vain, Baxter replies: "This is a strange Objection for those Men to make, who say that Christ suffered enough for all, or paid a Ransom sufficient for all, without any intent that it should be *loco omnium* in their stead, or should satisfie God's Justice for all."[154] The idea behind this statement is that advocates of limited atonement acknowledge that more suffering was necessary for all the world than for one particular sin or for one man's sin.[155] If Christ's death was sufficient for all but was not actually intended for all, this would imply that Christ suffered more than was strictly necessary to redeem those for whom he died. This would mean that some blood was shed in vain, argues Baxter.[156]

THE SUFFICIENCY/EFFICIENCY DISTINCTION

Owen: Internal Sufficiency

The previous issue, regarding the "failed intent" of God's purpose and Christ's suffering, may serve as a stepping stone to a discussion of a more exact analysis of the two diverging opinions. As noted, Baxter objects to the idea that Christ suffered more than was actually necessary for redemption. In Baxter's mind this

---

151. Baxter, *Universal Redemption*, p. 61.
152. Baxter, *Universal Redemption*, p. 447.
153. Baxter, *Universal Redemption*, p. 450.
154. Baxter, *Universal Redemption*, p. 444.
155. Baxter, *Universal Redemption*, p. 143. Baxter strongly opposes the idea that the same degree of suffering is sufficient for a thousand men as for one. This may lead to dangerous consequences: one might as well say next "that one sigh or groan, or one drop of Christs Blood had been sufficient for all: And next they may as well say, it had been sufficient though he had only been willing to suffer; and next, that his suffering was needless. *Socinianism*, if not Infidelity, may easily creep in at this Gap" (p. 144). This comment is of interest because Owen does hold the view that satisfaction was not absolutely necessary (cf. above, p. 130).
156. Says Baxter: "As if he would rather when three Men owe 100 *l.* a piece, pay 300 *l.* for one of the three, than the other 200 *l.* should be tendred for the rest ..." (*Universal Redemption*, p. 232). Cf. p. 266.

would imply that Christ partly suffered in vain. At this point, he crosses swords with Owen, quoting him at length.[157] Owen's use of the distinction between the sufficiency and efficiency of Christ's death is deprived of any meaning at all, according to Baxter.

Owen has an ambivalent attitude to the issue. He mentions the opinion of some that it is wrong to say that the blood of Christ was a sufficient price for all and everyone, "not because it was not sufficient, but because it was not a ransom."[158] These people, says Owen, argue that Christ did not die for all, simply because his sacrifice was not a sufficient ransom for all. Owen is willing to accept this opinion because the sufficiency/efficiency distinction is easily misunderstood. If it is understood to mean that Christ died, in a sense, also for the non-elect, Owen rejects the distinction.[159]

Owen insists, therefore, on interpreting the distinction in a different manner. The dignity of the person that suffered and the greatness of the pain endured mean that Christ's sacrifice was sufficient for all and everyone. The meaning of this sufficiency of Christ's death is the following:

> It was, then, the purpose and intention of God that his Son should offer a sacrifice of infinite worth, value, and dignity, sufficient in itself for the redeeming of all and every man, if it had pleased the Lord to employ it to that purpose; yea, and of other worlds also, if the Lord should freely make them, and would redeem them. Sufficient we say, then, was the sacrifice of Christ for the redemption of the whole world, and for the expiation of all the sins of all and every man in the world.[160]

Three things must be noted in this statement. First, the sufficiency of Christ's death is asserted in bold terms. His death was of infinite worth, sufficient to save even other worlds. In fact, Owen makes this sufficiency the basis for the universal proclamation of the Gospel.[161] Second, the sufficiency is located strictly in the value of the sacrifice, not in the breadth of its scope. The sufficiency is strictly internal. Finally, the twice repeated "if" is striking. The sacrifice of Christ is sufficient for all *if* indeed it were meant for all.[162]

These last two factors form a severe restriction on Owen's view on the sufficiency of Christ's death. Although he acknowledges Christ's sufficiency for all, at the same time he limits it to the elect only. The sufficiency refers only to the internal value of Christ's death, not to any extension to the world. It has therefore

157. Baxter mentions and quotes Owen in *Universal Redemption*, pp. 139-40.
158. Owen, *Death of Death*, in *Works* 10.296.
159. Owen, *Death of Death*, in *Works* 10.296.
160. Owen, *Death of Death*, in *Works* 10.295-96.
161. Owen, *Death of Death*, in *Works* 10.297: "If there were a thousand worlds, the gospel of Christ might, upon this ground, be preached to them all, there being enough in Christ for the salvation of them all, if so be they will derive virtue from him by touching him in faith; the only way to draw refreshment from this fountain of salvation."
162. Beza and Perkins have the same interpretation of the sufficiency of Christ's death. Cf. E. Dekker, *Rijker dan Midas: Vrijheid, genade en predestinatie in de theologie van Jacobus Arminius (1559-1609)*, Diss. Utrecht 1993 (Zoetermeer: Boekencentrum, 1993), pp. 206-07.

no real reference to the non-elect.[163] As Clifford comments: "For Owen, the atonement is only sufficient for those for whom it is efficient."[164]

Baxter: Christ's Death As a Price for All

Baxter is well aware of the weakness in Owen's argument and therefore makes it the occasion of a special argument for universal redemption.[165] He chides "our new Divines," who "have utterly forsaken the old common opinion, and in stead of saying that [Christ died for all Men *sufficienter*] They will not so much as say that [His Death was *sufficiens pretium pro omnibus*] But only that [It is sufficient to have been a price for all.]"[166] Although he realizes that Owen explicitly adopts this position Baxter does not mention him at this point. When he does mention Owen's idea of an internal sufficiency of Christ's death, he comments: "I have disproved this in what is said before; and shewed that Christs death cannot be affirmed sufficient for any Mans Salvation, for whom it never satisfied, though he should believe."[167]

In his own explanation of the sufficiency/efficiency distinction, Baxter maintains that if Christ's death is a sufficient price for all, it must necessarily be a price for all.[168] This is something which had already been acknowledged by John Ball. He had also admitted that Christ died "in some sense" for the reprobate. Baxter distinguishes three sorts of effects of Christ's death. The first effect, satisfaction to God, "is both sufficient and effectual for all ..."[169] The second, more remote effects, are also sufficient and efficient for all. They concern general common benefits, such as the freeing of all people from an absolute necessity of perishing. With regard to the third type of effects Baxter comments: "And as for the great particular special benefits of Pardon and Sanctification and Glory, I say Christs Death is sufficient for all; but effectual only for the Elect."[170]

---

163. This weakness in Owen's position is not always recognized. William Orme, for instance, insists that had Owen strictly adhered to his views concerning the sufficiency of Christ's sacrifice, "the controversy concerning its extent would be reduced within very narrow limits" (*Memoirs*, p. 83). Andrew Thomson also by-passes the problem in Owen's position when he states that Owen "argues for the true internal perfection and sufficiency of the sacrifice of Christ, as affording a ground for the indiscriminate invitations of the Gospel, in terms as strong and explicit as the most liberal Calvinist would care to use" ("Life of Dr Owen," in *Works* 1.xxxviii). Cf. Gavin John McGrath's comment on this issue: "His <i.e., Owen's> defense of this position <on the extent of Christ's death> had not so much to do with the sufficiency of Christ's death (for he did suggest that Christ's death was sufficient for the sins of the whole world) as it did with the end of his death" ("Puritans and the Human Will," p. 205). It is true that the end of Christ's death was the major factor in Owen's view on the extent of the atonement. But the result was that he structured his understanding of the sufficiency of Christ's death accordingly.

164. Clifford, *Atonement and Justification*, p. 74.

165. Baxter, *Universal Redemption*, pp. 133-42.

166. Baxter, *Universal Redemption*, p. 134. Cf. pp. 59-60, 115-16, 336, 345, where Baxter also opposes this restricted view.

167. Baxter, *Universal Redemption*, p. 140.

168. Baxter, *Universal Redemption*, p. 134.

169. Baxter, *Universal Redemption*, p. 135.

170. Baxter, *Universal Redemption*, p. 136. Similarly, Baxter distinguishes between a "double sufficiency": (1) a material sufficiency, antecedent to satisfaction, which suffices for all men to satisfy God; and (2) a sufficiency of this satisfaction to pardon and save all that will believe (p. 289).

218 A HOT PEPPER CORN

Baxter: Christ's Death Equal for All

Baxter's careful definition of the sufficiency of Christ's sacrifice for all men also gives insight into the question whether he died equally for all men. Here, again, Baxter makes a distinction. It will be remembered that Baxter differentiates between Christ's antecedent and his subsequent will.[171] The former precedes the condition; the latter follows it. In similar fashion, Baxter holds that prior to the consideration of the fulfillment of any condition, "Christ giveth Pardon, Justification and Right to Glory, equally to all ..."[172] Taking the fulfillment of the condition into consideration, however, he died only for true Christians.[173] Baxter makes basically the same point when he distinguishes between Christ as Legislator and as absolute Owner:

> Though Christ *dyed equally for all Men*, in the foresaid *Law-Sence*, as he satisfied the offended *Legislator*, and as giving himself *to all alike* in the *conditional Covenant*; Yet he never properly intended or purposed the actual justifying and saving of all; nor of any but those that come to be justified and saved. He did not therefore dye for all, nor for any, that perish, with a Decree or Resolution to save them much less did he dye for all alike, as to this intent.[174]

Baxter refuses to give a straightforward answer to the question whether Christ died equally for all. Does one refer to the general covenant grant, established on the basis of Christ's satisfaction, then the answer is positive. If, however, the absolute decree is in view, the answer is negative.[175] On this crucial point of the equality of Christ's death for all, Baxter differs from Ball, who attempted to disprove that Christ died "equally" for all.

When Baxter, therefore, continually insists that Christ died for all sins except final impenitence and unbelief he does so in view of Christ's role as Legislator.[176] Christ has died equally for all; the Legislator has universally promised salvation.

---

171. Cf. above, p. 211.
172. Baxter, *Universal Redemption*, p. 32.
173. Baxter, *Universal Redemption*, pp. 32-33.
174. Baxter, *Universal Redemption*, p. 63. Baxter holds that the wrong understanding of "*Christ dying loco nostro*" is "the vety <sic> turning point to Antinomianism" and "the Heart of the whole System of their Doctrine" (*Of Justification*, p. 382). Baxter then explains that Christ as Mediator made satisfaction to God's justice so that people could have remission or salvation on a condition. In this way, "Christ died *loco omnium*: this is sound Doctrine. That at the same time it was the secret Will or Eternal Decree of the Father; and the Will of the Mediator *de eventu*, to give effectually Grace to believe to his Chosen only; and consequently that they only should be actually saved, and thus he died only *loco Electorum*, is also sound Doctrine" (p. 383).
175. George P. Fisher is not entirely accurate in rendering Baxter's position as follows: "Christ died for all, but not for all equally" ("Theology of Richard Baxter," 160). Baxter does use this very same phrase (*Catholick Theologie* I.ii.53; II.55; *End of Doctrinal Controversies*, p. 160). He even states: "It cannot, in a congruous manner, be said that Christ died *equally* for all." ("Non tamen congruè dicitur Christum pro omnibus *æqualiter* mortuum esse" [*Methodus Theologiæ*, III.i.57].) The context of these statements, however, is always God's decree, design, or intent. In that sense, Christ did not die equally for all. But according to his antecedent will, prior to the fulfillment or non-fulfillment of the condition, Christ did die equally for all, insists Baxter (cf. *Catholick Theologie* II.55).
176. Baxter refers to this in *Universal Redemption*, pp. 24, 33, 90, 344, 358, 383-88, 393.

If, however, the condition is not performed this non-performance is not atoned for. For Baxter it "is plain that Christ dyed not for all the Sins of all Men for whom he dyed, excepting by his new Law, the final *Non-performance* of the Conditions of the Promise, in whomsoever without exception."[177] Christ did not die for final impenitence and unbelief because that constitutes the non-performance of the condition of the new covenant.

It must be concluded that most, if not all, of the differences between Baxter and Owen regarding the extent of the atonement, can be reduced to a difference in theological starting points. Owen's one-end teleology makes him argue entirely from God's decree and the covenant of redemption between the Father and the Son. Baxter's bifurcated view creates room to accommodate both God's absolute decree and his dealing with men by way of a conditional covenant.[178] Owen's teleological thinking cannot allow for any extension of the atonement beyond the elect, while Baxter's two-tier approach accepts that redemption has been purchased for all mankind.

The Nature of the Atonement

RELATION BETWEEN EXTENT AND NATURE OF ATONEMENT

Important as the discussion regarding the extent of the atonement may be, the main scope of the debate between Baxter and Owen lies in a closely connected area: the nature of the atonement and its immediate benefits. This does not mean that either Baxter or Owen fails to recognize the significance of the question of the extent of redemption. Rather, they realize that the real issues lie deeper. Already in his *Death of Death* (1647) Owen indicates that this is the case. When speaking of the "spreading persuasion there is of a *general ransom* to be paid by Christ for all" he indicates that this universalist opinion leads to an intolerable dilemma: either God and Christ failed in their intent of Christ's death, or all men must be saved.[179] Since this dilemma is unacceptable to the universalists they simply end up denying the absolute purpose of Christ's death:

---

177. Baxter, *Universal Redemption*, p. 387.
178. Perhaps it should be noted that the difference between Owen and Baxter is not one of predestinarian theology as opposed to covenant theology. Both authors hold to absolute predestination, and the theology of both can be characterized as covenant theology. Owen, however, argues from the eternal covenant of redemption – thereby excluding a conditional covenant between God and man – while Baxter places all emphasis on the conditionality of the new covenant. The result is clearly two completely different types of federal theology.
    John Von Rohr therefore underestimates the differences between the various types of federal theology. He speaks of a "fruitful" interrelationship between the absolute and the conditional in Puritan theology (*Covenant of Grace*, p. 1; cf. pp. 81, 85, 123, 190-91). In reality, the tension was not resolved as easily as Von Rohr suggests. This is illustrated by the difference in approach between Baxter and Owen. For similar criticism on Von Rohr's position, see McGrath, "Puritans and the Human Will," p. 207.
179. Owen, *Death of Death*, in *Works* 10.159.

> Wherefore, to cast a tolerable colour upon their persuasion, they must and do deny that God or his Son had any such absolute aim or end in the death or blood-shedding of Jesus Christ, or that any such thing was immediately procured and purchased by it, as we before recounted; but that God intended nothing, neither was any thing effected by Christ, – that no benefit ariseth to any immediately by his death but what is common to all and every soul, though never so cursedly unbelieving here and eternally damned hereafter, until an act of some, not procured for them by Christ, (for if it were, why have they it not all alike?) to wit, faith, do distinguish them from others.[180]

Owen is keenly aware that if adherents to universal redemption are to maintain particular salvation they have to deny the absolute procurement of salvation through Christ's death. This procurement must then become conditional, mediated by the believer's faith. Owen insists, therefore, that Christ paid the exact payment demanded in the law. He uses this mercantile language as a direct result of his view of limited atonement.

While Baxter, following Grotius, also uses the commercial analogy for the guilt incurred by sin, he insists that to speak of "debts" does not truly convey the reality of the damaged relationship with God. Baxter states that "though we may well use the word [debt] in this Case, because the Scripture doth, yet we must acknowledg it but a Metaphor ..."[181] For Owen the use of mercantile language is more fundamental. As a direct result of his theory of limited atonement he insists on the payment of the exact debt owed by man. Alan C. Clifford rightly comments, therefore, that "it is to Owen's credit that he saw the commercial theory as the *raison d'être* of the doctrine of limited atonement."[182] One's understanding of the nature of the atonement must change if one modifies his position on its extent. This is confirmed by Baxter's controversies regarding the nature of the atonement.

ACTIVE AND PASSIVE OBEDIENCE

Historical Background

Within Christ's obedience, often an active and a passive part are distinguished: his fulfillment of the law which man has transgressed and his suffering of the penalty as a result of this transgression. Theodore Beza was the first to differentiate sharply between the various aspects of Christ's righteousness.[183] Beza maintained that there was a threefold imputation. Christ's suffering and death served to oppose the accusation that we were covered with sins; his perfect obedience to the law cancelled the accusation that we were not perfectly righteous; and his perfectly holy

---

180. Owen, *Death of Death*, in *Works* 10.159-60.
181. Baxter, *Universal Redemption*, p. 79. Cf. pp. 25, 83, 89; *Of Imputation*, p. 75; *Scripture Gospel defended*, p. 114.
182. Clifford, *Atonement and Justification*, p. 127.
183. Cf. John Crandon's comment: "Mr. *Beza* in his Exposition of the Epistle to the *Romans*, by appropriating the severall parts of Christs righteousness to make up the severall parts of Justification, gave the occasion of the dispute, as I conceive" (*Aphorisms Exorized* I.iii.22).

nature from the moment of conception made up for our original sin. Thus, Christ's passive, active, and habitual righteousness were all imputed.[184] To be sure, Calvin had already argued that Christ's innocence is imputed to us and that he merited God's grace by his obedience to the law.[185] Calvin thought that Christ obeyed the law for our sake. But he stopped short of stating that Christ's obedience to the law was imputed to us. Calvin made no explicit mention of a substitutionary fulfill-ment of the law. Far less did he distinguish between the imputation of the various aspects of Christ's righteousness. This theological refinement is typical of the way in which Calvin's colleague and successor, Beza, continued his teaching.

Johann Piscator (1546-1625), professor at the University of Herborn, rejected Beza's distinction, instead asserting that Christ's active obedience was only a cause without which his passive obedience could not be imputed to us. Christ had to be perfect according to the law in order to be a "lamb without blemish and without spot" (1 Pet 1:19), a high priest who is "holy, harmless, undefiled, sepa-rate from sinners" and who could only thus be "made higher than the heavens" (Heb 7:26).[186] Piscator was not the only one who denied that Christ's active obedience was imputed. Baxter mentions numerous theologians who held this position, both on the continent and in England.[187] It was rejected, however, by the Formula of Concord (1576) as well as by several synods of the French Reformed

---

184. Beza, *Confessio christianæ fidei* (Geneva, 1595), pp. 23-30; *Tractationes Theologicæ*, 2nd ed. (Geneva, 1682), I, 670-71. Cf. F.L. Bos, *Johann Piscator: Ein Beitrag zur Geschichte der Reformierten Theologie* (Kampen: Kok, 1932), pp. 73, 78-84; A.D.R. Polman, *Onze Nederland-sche Geloofsbelijdenis: Verklaard uit het verleden geconfronteerd met het heden* (Franeker: Wever, n.d.), III, 53; Toon, *Emergence of Hyper-Calvinism*, pp. 15-16.

185. Calvin's overriding concern is the remission of sins by means of Christ's suffering and death, *i.e.*, his passive obedience. Arts. XVI-XVIII of the Gallican Confession (1559) clearly have this in mind. Calvin also identifies forgiveness with righteousness (*OS* 4.206 [*Inst.* III.xi.22]: "idem prorsus"). We possess this righteousness through Christ's atoning death. Thus we are partakers in Christ due to his obedience (*OS* 4.206-07 [*Inst.* III.xi.23]). This does not mean, however, that Christ's obedience was restricted to his suffering and death. The reason why the Apostle's Creed by-passes Christ's life is that Scripture ascribes the way of salvation as "peculiar and proper" (*peculiare ac proprium*) to his death. But the "remainder of the obedience that he manifested in his life is not excluded" (*OS* 3.486 [*Inst.* II.xvi.5]). With reference to Gal 4:4-5 Calvin says that the basis of pardon is the whole life of Christ (*Inst.* II.xvi.5). Cf. *Comm.* Gal 4:4: Christ became subject to the law "<n>ostro nomine." His submission to the yoke of the law "was certainly not on His own account" ("Nam sua certe causa non fecit" [*CO* 50.227]. Cf. *Comm.* Matt 26:17). Again, these statements must not be overemphasized. Calvin never systematized Christ's obedi-ence into two equal parts: an active and a passive part. But the basic idea of active obedience is – in a subordinate way – present in Calvin's theology. Cf. Polman, *Nederlandsche Geloofsbel-ijdenis*, III, 52-53.

186. Albrecht Ritschl, *A Critical History of the Christian Doctrine of Justification and Reconcilia-tion*, I, trans. John S. Black (Edinburgh: Edmonston and Douglas), 248-56; Bos, *Johann Pisca-tor*, pp. 71-146; Polman, *Nederlandsche Geloofsbelijdenis*, III, 53-54.

187. On the continent, this position was held by Zacharias Ursinus (1534-83), Caspar Olevianus (1536-87), David Pareus (1548-1622), Abraham Scultetus (1566-1624), Christian Becmann (1580-1648), Marcus Friedrich Wendelin (1584-1652), and Jacob Alting (1618-76). With respect to England, Baxter mentions William Twisse, George Lawson, John Ball, Thomas Gataker, John Goodwin, and Anthony Wotton. He also refers to the Amyraldian divines, John Cameron, Moyse Amyraut, Lewis Cappel (1585-1658), Joshua Placaeus, Jean Daillé (1594-1670), and David Blondel (1590-1655) as having the same view (Baxter, *Aphorismes* I.53-54 [p. 36]; *Account of my Consideration*, p. 30; *Of Imputation*, pp. 75, 172, 174; *Breviate*, pp. 24, 109; cf. Heppe, *Reformed Dogmatics*, p. 460).

Churches.[188] Interestingly, at the Synod of Dort, Sibrandus Lubbertus (1555-1625) and Johannes Bogerman (1576-1637) appeared to incline to the same position. But the synod decided against it and reaffirmed double imputation by means of an addition to the Belgic Confession (1561).[189]

Those who opposed double imputation did so because of various theological considerations. The main arguments against it were the following: (1) Christ's active obedience was required both because of creation and in order that his sacrifice might be pleasing to God; (2) by assigning the several benefits to differing aspects of Christ's obedience the unity of this obedience would be endangered; (3) if Christ's active obedience gives eternal life, then he suffered in vain; and (4) if Christ obeyed in our place, then we no longer have to obey. Those accepting twofold imputation, however, would point out (1) that to deny the imputation of Christ's active obedience would imply an unwarranted isolation of his passive obedience;[190] (2) that Christ lived his life in his human nature not as a private person but as the second Adam under the law of works; and (3) that it is an unwarranted conclusion to say that now we no longer have to obey simply because Christ obeyed in our stead: our redemption is not applied all at once in its entirety; just as we still suffer despite Christ's suffering, so we also still have to obey the law despite his obedience.[191]

Baxter's "new Scheme of Divinity"

Already in his *Aphorismes of Justification*, Baxter appears to be have found his

---

188. Cf. Formula of Concord III.I-III (in Philip Schaff, *The Creeds of Christendom: With a History and Critical Notes*, 6th ed., rev. David S. Schaff [1931; rpt. Grand Rapids: Baker, 1983], III, 115-16). Cf. Otto Weber, *Foundations of Dogmatics*, II, trans. Darrell L. Guder (Grand Rapids: Eerdmans, 1983), p. 192. For the condemnation by French synods, see Bos, *Johann Piscator*, pp. 110-28.

189. Article XXII now came to read as follows: "But Jesus Christ, imputing to us all his merits, and so many holy works, which he hath done for us and in our stead, is our Righteousness" (in Schaff, *Creeds of Christendom*, III, 408). The phrase "in our stead" was added by the Synod of Dort (cf. *Acta of Handelingen der Nationale Synode in de naam van onze Heere Jezus Christus Gehouden door autoriteit der Hoogmogende Heren Staten-Generaal der Verenigde Nederlanden te Dordrecht in de jaren 1618 en 1619*, ed. J.H. Donner and S.A. Van den Hoorn, pref. W. Van 't Spijker [1885; rpt. Houten: Den Hertog, 1987], p. 943; H.H. Kuyper, *De Post-acta of nahande-lingen van de Nationale Synode van Dordrecht in 1618 en 1619 gehouden, naar den authen-tieken tekst in het latijn en nederlandsch uitgegeven en met toelichtingen voorzien, voorafgegaan door de geschiedenis van de acta, de autographa en de post-acta dier synode en gevolgd door de geschiedenis van de revisie der belijdenisschriften en der liturgie, benevens de volledige lijst der gravamina op de Dordtsche Synode ingediend: Een historische studie* [Amsterdam: Höveker & Wormser, (1899)], pp. 338-44, 515-16; Polman, *Nederlandsche Geloofsbelijdenis*, III, 55).

190. Both sides of the debate accused the other party of endangering the unity of Christ's mediatorial work. G.C. Berkouwer rightly concludes: "Both groups were therefore concerned with the unity of Christ's work and obedience" (*The Work of Christ*, trans. Cornelius Lambregtse, Studies in Dogmatics [Grand Rapids: Eerdmans, 1965], p. 323).

191. For discussions on the issue, and for arguments used on both sides of the debate, see Ritschl, *Critical History*, I, 248-67; H. Bavinck, *Gereformeerde dogmatiek*, III, 4th ed. (Kampen: Kok, 1929), 363-66; Heppe, *Reformed Dogmatics*, pp. 460-65; Polman, *Nederlandsche Geloofsbe-lijdenis*, III, 51-55; Berkouwer, *Work of Christ*, pp. 319-26; Alister E. McGrath, *Iustitia Dei: A History of the Christian Doctrine of Justification* (Cambridge: Cambridge Univ. Press, 1986), II, 45-47.

Denies imputation

way into the intricacies of this discussion. He mentions three different views on this issue. He acknowledges that most divines say that "Christ did as properly obey in our roome and stead, as he did suffer in our stead; and that in Gods esteem and in point of Law wee were in Christ obeying and suffering ..."[192] He adds that some even insist that also Christ's habitual righteousness and the righteousness of his divine nature are imputed. Although Baxter does not mention any names, he probably had Beza and Andreas Osiander (1498-1552) in mind.[193] The former insisted that Christ's habitual righteousness was imputed to us, and the latter maintained that we are accounted righteous by virtue of the infusion of Christ's divine righteousness.

Baxter gives eleven objections to the teaching that Christ's active and passive obedience are both imputed. Some of these objections are identical or similar to those mentioned above. Baxter says, for instance, that this opinion "maketh Christs sufferings (by consequence) to be in vain ..."[194] Baxter also avers that this view unduly separates Christ's righteousness in a number of ways: it posits a *medium* between someone who is guilty and someone who is just, between someone who has his guilt taken away and someone who is positively righteous. Further, it makes our righteousness to consist of two parts: the putting away of our guilt and the imputation of righteousness. It ascribes these two parts to Christ's passive and his active obedience, respectively. Also, this opinion makes a vain distinction between deliverance from death and right to life.[195]

In addition to these familiar objections, Baxter mentions a number of others, that focus on the strict sense of imputation implied by this theory. Baxter does not accept that we were legally in Christ before we believed, that Christ's righteousness is imputed "in so strict a sense," or that Christ paid the exact penalty demanded by the law.[196] These objections are remarkable. They do not just impugn the theory of twofold imputation, but also the position which only accepts the imputation of passive righteousness. With these objections, Baxter not only argues against the imputation of active obedience but also opposes *any* theory which holds a strict imputation of Christ's righteousness, whether that be active or passive.

---

192. Baxter, *Aphorismes* I.45 (pp. 30-31).
193. At least twice, Baxter explicitly mentions Osiander. In his *Breviate of the Doctrine of Justification*, Baxter distinguishes four different views on imputation. The first is that only Christ's sufferings are imputed; the second that both his active and passive righteousness are imputed; the third that also his habitual righteousness is imputed; and the last that even Christ's divine nature is imputed: "*Andrew Osiander* is for our Justification by the Divine Essence, but I think rather by Communication than Imputation. Thus hath our weakness distracted and disgraced us" (*Breviate*, p. 24; cf. *Defence of Christ*, sig. A4ʳ). For Osiander's views, see Wilhelm Niesel, "Calvin wider Osianders Rechtfertigungslehre," *ZKG*, 46 (1927), 410-30; Edward Boehl, *The Reformed Doctrine of Justification*, trans. C.H. Riedesel (Grand Rapids: Eerdmans, 1946), pp. 13-20, 34-46; M.J. Arntzen, *Mystieke rechtvaardigingsleer: Een bijdrage ter beoordeling van de theologie van Andreas Osiander*, Diss. Amsterdam 1956 (Kampen: Kok, 1956); Berkouwer, *Faith and Justification*, pp. 93-100; Gunter Zimmermann, "Die Thesen Osianders zur Disputation 'de iustificatione'," *KuD*, 33 (1987), 224-44; Gunter Zimmermann, "Calvins Auseinandersetzung mit Osianders Rechtfertigungslehre," *KuD*, 35 (1989), 236-56.
194. Baxter, *Aphorismes* I.48-49 (p. 33).
195. Baxter, *Aphorismes* I.49-52 (pp. 33-35).
196. Baxter, *Aphorismes* I.47-48 (pp. 31-32).

The second view which Baxter discusses is that

> God the Father doth accept the sufferings and merits of his Son as a full satisfaction
> to his violated Law, and as a valuable consideration upon which he will wholly
> forgive and acquit the offendors themselves, and receive them again into his favor,
> and give them the addition of a more excellent happiness also, so they will but
> receive his Son upon the terms expressed in the Gospel.[197]

Baxter here describes satisfaction as a "valuable consideration" which is sufficient for justification. He then subdivides this view into two opinions. The first, to
which most of these divines adhere, is that only Christ's passive righteousness
satisfies. It is the *iustitia meriti*. His active righteousness, the *iustitia personæ*,
only serves for "qualifying him to be a fit Mediator." Baxter then mentions a
number of divines who, according to him, hold this particular view.[198]

Others, who also think that Christ's satisfaction is a "valuable consideration"
for justification, hold basically the same view, "yet the Active Righteousness
considered as such is part of this Satisfaction also, as well as his Passive, and
Justitia Meriti, as well as *Justitia Personæ* ..."[199] Baxter then mentions Hugo
Grotius and William Bradshaw as proponents of this position. And indeed, Baxter's dependence on Bradshaw is obvious. As noted above, Baxter appeals to him
repeatedly. What is more, the structure of Baxter's overview of the various views
on imputation is identical to Bradshaw's outline in the preface to his *Dissertatio
De ivstificationis doctrina*. Following Bradshaw, Baxter moves the discussion
about imputation to a different level. He does not want to solve the theological
problems associated with the imputation of Christ's active obedience by denying
it but by interpreting it differently.

Baxter has carefully thought out his position before making it public. He reveals the historical sources behind his position and also indicates that it has changed
through the reading of Bradshaw and Grotius. Prior to this, he had been "ten years
of another mind for the sole Passive Righteousness."[200] It would not be correct,
therefore, to argue that Baxter, like the theologians of Saumur, denied that Christ's
active obedience was imputed to believers.[201] On this point, Baxter's later critic,
John England (fl. 1701-15), rightly said that Baxter went beyond the Salmurian

---

197. Baxter, *Aphorismes* I.52 (p. 35).
198. Baxter, *Aphorismes* I.53 (p. 36). Baxter describes this second view in such a way that it seems as
     if all these divines reject a strict imputation of Christ's righteousness. Thus, Baxter depicts this
     position as closely allied to his own. This analysis is not correct, however. The simple fact that
     high Calvinists like Twisse, Crandon, and Warner thought that only Christ's passive obedience
     was imputed invalidates Baxter's thesis. A worthwhile topic of further research would be to
     analyze the "strictness" of the imputation of Christ's passive obedience according to the various
     divines in this second group mentioned by Baxter.
199. Baxter, *Aphorismes* I.54 (p. 37).
200. Baxter, *Aphorismes* I.55 (p. 37). For Baxter's change of mind on this issue, see Packer, "Re-
     demption and Restoration," pp. 277-83. Baxter does not indicate whether his earlier position
     coincided with a strict view of imputation, in other words, that he used to hold that Christ's
     passive righteousness was strictly imputed to us. This would be in accordance with his great
     indebtedness to Twisse during this early stage.
201. As is maintained by Peter Toon, *Puritans and Calvinism* (Swengel, PA: Reiner, 1973), p. 86.

professors.[202] The latter held that Christ's passive righteousness was properly imputed to us. According to Baxter, neither Christ's active nor his passive righteousness is imputed in the strict sense of the word. England, therefore, did not overstate his case all that much when he said that Baxter "goes beyond them, and so hath laid a compleat foundation, for the erecting a new Scheme of Divinity."[203]

When John Crandon analyzes Baxter's description of the three views on imputation he says that the third opinion mentioned by Baxter, that of Bradshaw and Grotius, is "wholly one with the first in substance."[204] Comments Crandon:

> And what is the difference betwixt the opinion which he spewes out as filth and garbage, and that which he sucks and swallowes as the bread of life, and food from heaven? Forsooth, this only, that the one opinion makes the active righteousnes of Christ, together with his passive, to be imputed to us for righteousnes; the other makes the active, together with the passive righteousnes of Christ, satisfactory to God's justice, to put us into the participation of Righteousnes or Justification.[205]

Crandon, who himself holds that only passive righteousness is imputed, refuses to recognize any difference between the view of those who teach a strict double imputation and the position of Baxter. Obviously, Crandon is mistaken. The difference between the two positions is real, and it is important. By setting aside the notion that only Christ's passive obedience is imputed Baxter at the same time, and more significantly, changes the meaning of imputation itself.

Crandon's understanding of the reason why Baxter changed his view is equally misguided. Crandon argues as follows:

> But since he <i.e., Baxter> hath cast himself into the Channels of Popish Writers, and thence derived Justification by works, it concern'd him to cast off his former Opinion, for the sole passive righteousnes, as being much repugnant to Justification by works, and to take up this as authentick, and somewhat conducing and helpfull to his Cause. For if Christs active obedience should not be held meritorious and satisfactory to God, with what face could Mr. *Baxter* attribute a prevalency and power herein to our best works and actions?[206]

This argument is somewhat remarkable. One of the objections often made against the double imputation view is the implication that it takes away man's duty to obey the law. Crandon, by contrast, argues that Baxter takes the double imputation view because it allows for justification by works. Crandon is right in his suspicion that Baxter wants a theory of imputation which allows for works in justification. But Baxter does not manage that simply by substituting a double imputation theory for a view which only accepts the imputation of passive obedience.

---

202. England, *Man's Sinfulness* (London, 1700), pp. 415-63.
203. England, *Man's Sinfulness*, p. 415.
204. Crandon, *Aphorisms Exorized* I.iii.23.
205. Crandon, *Aphorisms Exorized* I.iii.23.
206. Crandon, *Aphorisms Exorized* I.iii.24.

No Imputation of Passive Righteousness Only

To follow Baxter's line of argument, it is necessary to take a look at his discussions on the issue with John Warner, Christopher Cartwright, and John Wallis. Warner and Cartwright both argue for the sole imputation of Christ's passive obedience. Warner, with an appeal to Piscator, maintains that Christ is made unto us righteousness (1 Cor 1:30) by a metonymy of the effect. Christ is here "he by whose satisfaction imputed to us, we are reputed just."[207] It is his passive obedience which Scripture calls the obedience by which we are justified.[208] Jesus' entire life was "nothing but a continued passion."[209] Cartwright, appealing to some of the same texts as Warner, maintains that because Christ took on the form of a servant and was, as a creature, under the law, he was now bound to observe the will of God, the Creator.[210] Says Cartwright: "The Apostle saying, That *Christ was made under the Law* <Gal 4:4>, it seems to be without doubt, That it was the Will of God that he should observe the Law. For is it not the Will of God that his Law should be observed by such as are under it?"[211] Christ as a man was obliged to perform even the ceremonial observances.[212] For Cartwright, then, Christ's active obedience was not directly for others, but primarily for himself.

Perhaps most important in Baxter's attempt to counter Cartwright is his assertion that some of Christ's acts of obedience were not for himself. Baxter does not believe that Christ had to observe the ceremonial law simply because he was under the law. Ceremonies are for the recovery from sin. Christ did not need this recovery. Thus, he did not use the ceremonies for the same purpose as others did. Baxter concludes that Christ performed ceremonial laws as "separated from their Legal ends, to other ends of his own, that his primary obligation to them was *ex vi sponsionis propriæ* (as was all his obligation to suffer) and not *ex Lege* ..."[213]

What is more, Baxter reminds Cartwright of the fact that Christ did not become subject to the law in the same way as others:

> If I being a Free-man, do bind my self to be your Servant, or your slave (I mean to be absolutely at your command *quoad actiones serviles*) on Condition that you give me for my service 20 *l. per annum*: Doth my service deserve none of this wages after, because I being once bound, my service is necessary? And remember, that thus Christ became bound by *quasi-Contract*, and so *Conditionally*; and the Condition was, That his service should be accepted as Meritorious and Satisfactory, towards the Recovery of sinners.[214]

---

207. Warner, *Diatriba fidei justificantis*, p. 166. Warner also appeals to 2 Cor 5:21 and Jer 23:6.
208. Warner appeals to Rom 5:19; Phil 2:8; Ps 40: 6-7; and Heb 10:10 (*Diatriba fidei justificantis*, pp. 166-67).
209. Warner, *Diatriba fidei justificantis*, p. 165.
210. Cartwright, in Baxter, *Account of my Consideration*, pp. 29-30, 32. Cartwright disagrees with Baxter's interpretation of Rom 5:19 and also appeals to Phil 2:8.
211. Cartwright, *Exceptions*, p. 12.
212. Cartwright, *Exceptions*, p. 13.
213. Baxter, *Account of my Consideration*, p. 31.
214. Baxter, *Account of my Consideration*, p. 33.

Christ's obedience to the law was, as it were, by contract. His service was voluntary. There is no reason, then, why his active obedience should not be imputed to others. Also, Baxter insists that Christ's divine nature was never subjected to the law. His divinity gave his actions their "chief Dignity."[215] Both because of this dignity of the divine nature and because of its inherent freedom from the law Christ's actions are "highly *Meritorious*."[216]

Finally, Baxter does not believe that the penalty of the law as such can be meritorious. Although he is willing to speak of "passive obedience," he considers it a "very dark" phrase.[217] Suffering as such is not obedience; rather, it is the punishment for disobedience. Christ's voluntary submission is properly and directly obedience. The sufferings which result from this are not obedience in the same proper and direct sense. Therefore, Christ's sufferings may only remotely be called "passive obedience."[218] This implies, according to Baxter, that the penalty of the guilt as such (*poena culpae propriae*) is not meritorious. Christ's voluntary submission to the penalty *made* it meritorious.[219] As Baxter puts it:

> Take all plainly in this one word as the sum. Christ's *sufferings*, as *sufferings*, were not the *immediate matter* of his *merit*; but his *Willingness* the *immediate*, and the *suffering-willed* was the *remote*. His *sufferings* were *first in order Satisfactory*, and after that *remotely Meritorious*; and therefore *Meritorious*, because first Satisfactory: But his *Active Obedience* (or to speak more properly, his *obedience*, as *obedience*, or good-works) was first *Meritorious* (in order of Nature) and then *Satisfactory*; and therefore *Satisfactory*, because *first Meritorious*.[220]

Baxter's involved statement may seem more cryptic than plain. What Baxter means, however, is that Christ's obedience as such merits. This obedience may be his active obedience to the law as well as his voluntary submission or willingness to undergo the penalty. Both of these are directly meritorious, because they are obedient acts. This obedience is also satisfaction, but only in an indirect sense. On the other hand, Christ's suffering satisfies directly. It contains no intrinsic merit. His suffering is only meritorious in a secondary, remote sense.[221] What is the conclusion of this sophisticated line of reasoning? If Christ's sufferings do not

---

215. Baxter, *Account of my Consideration*, p. 34 (emphasis throughout in original).
216. Baxter, *Account of my Consideration*, p. 34.
217. Baxter, *Account of my Consideration*, pp. 28-29. Baxter thinks that the phrase "passive obedience" is "tolerable" (DWL MS *BT* ii.21[1], f. 5ᵛ).
218. Baxter, *Account of my Consideration*, pp. 28-29. Cf. his statement: "And g̅o̅ Punishm<en>ᵗ or Suffering cañot im̅ediatly & in yᵉ neerest sence be called Obedience" (DWL MS *BT* ii.21[1], f. 5ᵛ).
219. Cf. DWL MS *BT* ii.21(1), f. 5ᵛ: "Im̅ediatly it was but his willing Submission to this Suffering y<a>ᵗ was Commanded ..."
220. Baxter, *Account of my Consideration*, p. 38. Cf. *Breviate*, p. 63.
221. Cf. Baxter, *Of Imputation*, pp. 24, 97. To Wallis, Baxter describes his position as follows: Christ's whole obedience – active and passive – makes up his satisfaction, "but in severall respects: The Sufferings having no thing in y<e>ᵐ pleasing to God before their Satisfactory use & their aptitude to Demonstrate Gods Justice: but yᵉ Obedience being in & for its.<elf> pleasing to God, & therby first Meritorious & so Satisfactory: And y<a>ᵗ in this Satisfaction Consisteth all o<u>ʳ Righteousnes (Legall) strictly & p<ro>p<er>ly so called ..." (DWL MS *BT* ii.21[1], f. 5ᵛ).

carry any intrinsic merit, his passive obedience is not the only righteousness imputed.[222]

Denial of "Negative Righteousness"

Whereas Warner and Cartwright plead for the imputation of Christ's passive obedience only, John Wallis, in his private animadversions on the *Aphorismes*, speaks in defense of strict, double imputation. He focuses on Baxter's charge that this view creates a *medium* between *iustum* and *iniustum*. Wallis uses the example of a prince who employs a soldier to hold a fort against an enemy, with the promise of a reward if he holds it faithfully, but with the threat of severe punishment if he betrays it. Says Wallis: "The souldier ows fidelity, & therefore you can, no more admit a *medium* between *fides* & *perfidia* in that case, than in ye case in hand."[223] If the soldier hands over the fort to the enemy he becomes guilty of treachery (*reus perfidiae*). If, for some reason or another, the prince grants him pardon, this does not yet imply that he also gets the reward that was promised if he would hold the fort faithfully. If he wants to actually lay claim to the reward "it must bee upon consideration of somewhat which shall bee accounted in ye nature of *Merit*, & not onely in the nature of Satisfaction for a *Demerit*." There is a "middle condition" between merit and demerit.[224] Wallis grants that when the penalty is taken away the party is restored to his former happiness. But he denies "that thereby hee doth acquire a right to a mere happynesse which before he had not: and to wh<i>ch he'd had no other claim, but a conditionall right upon supposition of service ..."[225] Wallis then distinguishes between satisfaction and merit. Adam was restored to his initial happiness by Christ's satisfaction. But he needed Christ's merit to obtain the reward which had initially been promised.[226] Passive satisfaction, which is "the full *Debt*," only yields a negative righteousness, "as if we had not sinned." Active obedience, however, is the price for purchasing heaven.[227]

Baxter does not accept this concept of "negative righteousness." It would be like a servant who both obeys and disobeys. It would seem to imply that there is "a non-bonum between Bonũ & Malum, & so a non-justum, between Justum & injustum."[228] Baxter insists that Adam was not in a "neutrall state" between happiness and unhappiness, "though perhaps he was but in via ad sũmam felicitatem."[229] Baxter here touches upon an anthropological issue with an important bearing on the doctrine of justification: was Adam created *in patria* or *in via*? Was the glory which was promised to him simply the continuance of his paradisaic state or would he be transformed to a greater degree of blessedness? In his *Aphorismes*,

---

222. Cf. Baxter's comment: "What if I should prove to you, that *no suffering*, either *as suffering*, or as *punishment* can *merit?*" (*Account of my Consideration*, p. 37)
223. DWL MS *BT* ii.21(2), f. 27^r.
224. DWL MS *BT* ii.21(2), f. 27^r.
225. DWL MS *BT* ii.21(2), f. 27^v.
226. DWL MS *BT* ii.21(2), f. 27^v.
227. DWL MS *BT* ii.21(2), f. 24^r.
228. DWL MS *BT* ii.21(1), f. 6^v.
229. DWL MS *BT* ii.21(1), f. 6^v.

Baxter defends the former position. He expresses his disagreement with Johannes Maccovius (1588-1644), who thought that in addition to the continuance of his original happiness Adam would have merited some further reward if he had stood the test. Accordingly, Maccovius maintained that after the Fall, Christ's satisfaction procured a return to the original state of happiness, while his active obedience resulted in the reward.[230] Baxter considers this "meer fiction. For where doth the scripture talk of *Adams* meriting any more? or where doth it promise him any more then the continuance of that happinesse which he then had?"[231]

Sometime between 1649 and 1652, Baxter changes his mind. This alteration in his theological position was mainly the result of his reading of John Duns Scotus and John de Rada (c. 1550-1606).[232] As a result of his investigations, Baxter admits to Cartwright, who attacks his *Aphorismes* on this point: "I dare not now be so bold, as to affirm, That *Adam* was created *in Patriâ*, and not *in Viâ*; that is, in the full fruition of his Happiness; rather in the way to it, with an imperfect taste of it."[233] Baxter's change in view puts him in a distinctly less favorable position in his discussion with Wallis. Wallis' argument for double imputation is very similar to that of Maccovius: Christ's passive obedience yields a "negative righteousness" and results only in the restoration of the original happiness. His active obedience merits the superadded glory. Now that Baxter has changed his view, he is no longer able to simply retort that Scripture does not know of such a superadded glory. Accordingly, he admits that Adam did not have the full right to confirmation, and that therefore remission

> doth not restore y<e>^m to a plenary Right; but only to such a Right as they lost by Sin; y<a>^l is, being Possessed of so much felicity as Adam enjoyed ... And ḡo there is need of something more y<a>^n bare Remission to give us y<a>^l Right to Consumate Happynes w<hi>^ch Adam never had.[234]

Baxter's newly acquired position with respect to the *status originalis* puts him in a quandary. He is forced to admit that pardon alone is not sufficient to place someone in a position of superadded glory. One might well ask: is it not true then, as Wallis argues, that pardon places someone in a "middle" condition between merit and demerit? And should one not divide Christ's righteousness accordingly?

Baxter is unwilling to grant this conclusion. Although his change in view with regard to Adam's state of happiness has weakened his position, he continues to deny that it is the imputation of Christ's passive obedience which gives pardon, while the imputation of his active obedience merits further glory. Baxter appeals

---

230. Baxter, *Aphorismes* II.136-37 (pp. 300-01).
231. Baxter, *Aphorismes* II.136-37 (p. 301). Cf. I.15 (p. 10): "That this life promised was onely the continuance of that state that *Adam* was then in in Paradice, is the judgement of most Divines ..."
232. Baxter, *Account of my Consideration*, p. 19; DWL MS *BT* ii.21(2), f. 9ᵛ. Rada had become a follower of Duns Scotus after examining the differences between Aquinas and Scotus. Baxter had Rada's *Controversiarum theologicarum inter S. Thomam et Scotum* (1620) in his personal library (cf. Nuttall, "Transcript," 212, items 146-47).
233. Baxter, *Account of my Consideration*, p. 19. Also when Thomas Blake challenges him on this issue, Baxter acknowledges that his position has changed (*Account*, pp. 111-12).
234. DWL MS *BT* ii.21(1), f. 7ᵛ.

to the fact that Adam was created in a state of happiness. Remission of sin does not just yield a "negative righteousness." It "will do much more y<a>ⁿ [save us from going to Hell] ffor yo<u>rs.<elf> say it will put us in yᵉ same Condition as if we had never siñed."[235] Baxter wants to maintain the unity of the meritorious cause of justification. He refuses to divide Christ's righteous in such a way that each part gives a different benefit. Thus, his disagreement with Wallis remains despite the fact that his argument has lost much of its force.

Although Baxter refuses to divide Christ's righteousness into different parcels which are directly given to the elect, he does admit that there is a difference between the imputation of Christ's passive and active righteousness. Says Baxter: "He suffered, to save us from suffering; but he *obeyed not to save us from obeying*, *but to bring us to Obedience*."[236] Christ did not represent us in the same way in his obedience as he did in his sufferings.[237] There is a difference between the imputation of Christ's passive and his active and habitual righteousness. The former is more properly imputed than the latter. This difference serves to avoid the conclusion that works are no longer needed for justification. Having said that Christ's passive, active, and habitual imputation are all imputed, Baxter goes a step further. He is willing to admit that even Osiander's view of imputation contains an element of truth. Also Christ's divine righteousness must be taken into account, albeit that Baxter does not say that it is imputed to us:

> But in the just sense of Imputation all is imputed to us, that is, Christs Habitual, Active and Passive Righteousness, fulfilling his own part of the Covenant, advanced in dignity by the Union of the Divine nature and perfection was the true meritorious cause of our Justification, and not any one of these alone.[238]

In a sense, Baxter's concept of imputation is even more comprehensive than that of many divines defending double imputation. Christ's divinity further enhances the meritorious character of his obedience and sufferings. All of this, however, is only possible because Baxter, following Bradshaw and Grotius, has adopted a different meaning of imputation than is customary in Calvinist theology. Thus, the question must be asked: what exactly does Baxter mean when he says that Christ's righteousness is imputed? Granted that his active, passive, and habitual righteousness are all imputed, what kind of imputation is Baxter speaking of? It is this question which must now become the focus of investigation.

---

235. DWL MS *BT* ii.21(1), f. 6ᵛ.
236. Baxter, *Of Imputation*, p. 58.
237. Cf. Baxter, *Of Imputation*, p. 68: "As Christ is less improperly said to have Represented our Persons in his satisfactory Sufferings, than in his personal perfect *Holiness* and *Obedience*; so he is less improperly said to have *Represented all mankind as newly fallen in Adam, in a General sense, for the purchasing of the universal Gift of Pardon and Life, called The new Covenant; than to have Represented in his perfect Holiness and his Sufferings, every Believer considered as from his first being to his Death*."
238. Baxter, *Breviate*, pp. 24-25. Cf. p. 96; *Of Imputation*, p. 87; *Methodus Theologiæ* III.xxvii.309.

IMPUTATION OF CHRIST'S RIGHTEOUSNESS

The Imputation of Christ's Righteousness Not Denied

Secondary scholarship has repeatedly charged Baxter with denying the imputation of Christ's righteousness. As one scholar states it: "Baxter is consciously rejecting the teaching of the Westminster Confession, that is to say, that God justifies sinners by imputing to them the righteousness of Christ."[239] This accusation is by no means new. Thomas Tully, one of Baxter's opponents, was also convinced that Baxter denied the imputation of Christ's righteousness.[240] As already indicated in the previous section, Baxter's handling of the double imputation question indicates that the issue for him is not whether, but how Christ's righteousness is imputed.

Further corroboration for the thesis that Baxter does not deny that Christ's righteousness is imputed is found in his explicit statements to this effect. Baxter calls it an "oft repeated Forgery" that he would deny all imputation of Christ's righteousness.[241] He is furious about Tully's accusation on this point, because in his *Aphorismes* he had "profest the Contrary."[242] After discussing how Christ represents the believers, he concludes with the comment: "Thus Christs Righteousness is ours."[243] When asking the question whether Christ's righteousness is imputed to us, he answers: "Yes; If by imputing you mean reckoning or reputing it ours, so far as is aforesaid, that is such a Cause of ours."[244] Accordingly, Baxter says that Christ's righteousness is indeed imputed to us: "I have shewed you that it is true, in a sound sense." Again, he comments: "There is no question but all the Righteousness that we have is given us by God: But the very heart of the Controversie is, *How the Righteousness of Christ is given us and made ours* ..."[245] Baxter does not question the fact that Christ's righteousness is imputed to us; he only disagrees with the way in which this imputation is often interpreted in high Calvinist circles.

In a sense, Christ's righteousness may even be considered as our only righteousness. Says Baxter: "But as to the *satisfying* of the Justice of the offended Majesty, and the meriting of life with pardon, *&c.* So the Righteousness of Christ

---

239. Iain Murray, "Richard Baxter-'The Reluctant Puritan'?" p. 8. Cf. Alan P.F. Sell: "In urging that what is imputed to man with a view to justification is not Christ's righteousness but, rather, man's faith in Christ's righteousness, Baxter was setting his face against that antinomianism which, he thought, removed man ultimately from the sphere of moral agency altogether" (*Great Debate*, p. 32); C. Harinck: "To take a firm position against the Antinomians, Baxter fell prey to the strange idea that we are not justified by the vicarious righteousness of Christ, but by our faith in Christ's vicarious atonement." ("Teneinde zich krachtig teweer te stellen tegen de antinomianen verviel Baxter tot de wonderlijke gedachte, dat wij niet gerechtvaardigd worden door de borgtochtelijke gerechtigheid van Christus, maar door ons geloof in Christus' borgtocht" [*Schotse verbondsleer*, p. 68].)

240. Tully, *Justificatio Paulina*, p. 117. Cf. Baxter, *Of Imputation*, p. 180.

241. Baxter, *Of Imputation*, p. 180.

242. Baxter, *Answer*, p. 75.

243. Baxter, *Of Imputation*, p. 59.

244. Baxter, *Of Imputation*, p. 87.

245. Baxter, *Scripture Gospel defended*, p. 99.

is our only *Righteousness*."[246] In a sense, it must be said that "it is onely Christs righteousness that is our Iustification or our righteousness; and that faith or repentance is not the least part of it."[247] To be sure, Baxter carefully qualifies and restricts such statements. Nevertheless, it is safe to conclude that Baxter does accept the imputation of Christ's righteousness and that, in a sense, this is our only righteousness.

Analogy Between Adam and Christ

This conclusion raises the question how it is possible that Baxter has been misinterpreted so often and on such a crucial aspect of his doctrine of justification. The reason for this lies, at least partly, in the way in which he describes the imputation of Christ's righteousness. First of all, it must be acknowledged that he is not fond of speaking of the imputation of Christ's righteousness. Already in his *Aphorismes*, and throughout his writings, he agitates against teaching imputation in a strict sense because it does not agree "with the phrase of Scripture which mentioneth no imputation of Christ or his Righteousnesse to us at all ..."[248] When Baxter has mentioned his understanding of imputation, he asks the question what, according to his opponents, is lacking in his description:

> What is wanting? Why, we must say that *Christs Righteousness is Imputed to us as ours, and that Christ satisfied for our sins!* Well; The thing signified seemeth to us true and good and needful, (though the Scripture hath as good words for it as any of us can invent.) We consent therefore to use these Phrases, so be it you put no false and wicked sence on them by *other words* of your own: Though we will not allow them to be *necessary*, because not in Scripture ...[249]

Thus, although admitting that it may be proper to speak of the imputation of Christ's righteousness, Baxter thinks that the expression as such is unnecessary and that it is liable to misinterpretation.

This wrong understanding of imputation is seen, according to Baxter, in the careless use of the analogy between Adam and Christ. John Crandon, for instance, distinguishes between two covenants, the covenant of works and the covenant of grace. The first was made with the first Adam, the second with the second Adam, Jesus Christ. According to Crandon, the issue is whether or not the first and the second Adam relate as type and antitype. After asking how Adam was a figure of Christ, he comments:

---

246. Baxter, *Of Justification*, p. 268.
247. Baxter, *Admonition*, p. 26. Speaking of universal justification, Baxter comments that "the Righteousness of Christ is the sole Meritorious Cause" (*Unsavoury Volume*, p. 44). In regard to justification from the condemnation of the first law, "*Christ's Satisfaction* is our *only Title*" as to merit (*Account of my Consideration*, p. 82).
248. Baxter, *Aphorismes* I.47 (p. 32).
249. Baxter, *Of Imputation*, sig. A2ᵛ. For similar statements in which Baxter insists that "imputation of Christ's righteousness" is not a Scripture phrase, see *Of Imputation*, pp. 53, 175; *Methodus Theologiæ* III.xxvii.309; *Breviate*, pp. 22, 33.

Doubtles not onely in this that as by him the one and first man, sin and death by sin immediately came upon all men: so by Christ, righteousnes, and by it life came upon all the elect: But also in the manner of the agreements of the Type and Antitype together. That as *Adam* representing all mankinde, by his unfaithfullnes in breaking the Covenant brought sin and death upon all that he represented: so Christ representing all the elect, by his faithfullnes in performing the Covenant &c. brought righteousnes and justification of life upon all the elect represented in him.[250]

For Crandon, it is not sufficient to say that as Adam brought death to all, so Christ came with righteousness for the elect. Of central importance is the representation of Adam and Christ as the respective heads of the covenant of works and the covenant of grace.

Baxter demurs at such a parallelism between Adam and Christ. To be sure, there is a parallel:

As *Adam* was a Head by *Nature,* and therefore conveyed Guilt by natural Generation; so Christ is a Head (not by nature but) by Sacred Contract; and therefore conveyeth Right to Pardon, Adoption and Salvation, not by Generation, but by Contract, or Donation.[251]

This statement contains most of the important elements of Baxter's critique of what he considers a superficial parallel between Adam and Christ. The parallel which does exist lies in the fact that Adam and Christ are both heads of the covenant. The most important difference, however, lies in the formal reason for this headship. Adam is head by natural generation, Christ by contract. One belongs to Christ by means of *re*generation. The saints "have no real sanctity but what shall be derived from him by Regeneration, as Nature and Sin if from *Adam* by Generation."[252]

The idea of Christ being head "by contract" rather than by nature has a number of implications. In the first place, in accordance with Baxter's universalist position, it means that Christ suffered "in the nature and room of Mankind in General, as without any condition on their part at all; to give man by an act of Oblivion or new Covenant a pardon of *Adams* sin ..."[253] Christ's headship is, therefore, conditionally for all and actually for the elect:

No<t> as being *Actually* such a Head to the Redeemed when he *Obeyed* and *Suffered*; but as a Head by *Aptitude* and *Office, Power* and *Virtue,* who was to *become a Head actually* to every one when they *Believed* and *Consented*; Being before a *Head for them,* and *over those that did exist,* but not a *Head to them,* in act.[254]

All have received the "act of oblivion." In that sense, Christ is head "for" them

---

250. Crandon, *Aphorisms Exorized* I.xi.103.
251. Baxter, *Of Imputation,* p. 66.
252. Baxter, *Of Imputation,* p. 69. Cf. *Breviate,* p. 29: "Nay our derivation from *Adam* was by *nature,* but from Christ by his *voluntary Gift and Contract.*" Cf. *Scripture Gospel defended,* p. 87.
253. Baxter, *Of Imputation,* p. 69.
254. Baxter, *Of Imputation,* p. 55.

all.[255] Christ is not "actually" a head to them, however, until they believe. Here, Baxter's distinctive notion of Christ's headship becomes clear: Christ is not just head of the elect, but is given as head for all because the act of oblivion is for all.

In the second place, Baxter maintains that Adam's natural headship did not mean that his posterity would have lived in communion with God without any condition of obedience. It would be erroneous to think that Adam represented his posterity in such a strict sense: "For if any of them under that Covenant had ever sinned afterward in their own person, they should have died for it."[256] Baxter does not believe that if Adam had conquered his temptation, all his posterity would have been "confirmed against all future sin and danger as the Angels be in Heaven."[257] In the same way, the universal gift of justification does not dissolve the obligation of fulfilling the condition of faith.[258]

Because he regards Christ, in a conditional sense, as the second Adam for all mankind, Baxter's concept of union with Christ is distinctly different from the way this theologoumenon functions among his contestants. Thus, the third implication of Baxter's notion of Christ's headship being contractual or voluntary is that Christ and the believers remain distinct persons. To begin with, Adam and his natural progeny were already distinct persons. We were only seminally or virtually in Adam.[259] If we were not one person with our natural head, Adam, we can much less be said to be one person with Christ.

Political Union

Closely related to this is a fourth consequence of Christ's voluntary headship. As noted earlier, Baxter disagrees with the way in which John Owen regards union with Christ.[260] For Baxter, union with Christ does not precede faith. What is more, this union is primarily "a Relative Union, he being our Head, Husband, King, and we being his incorporate Members, his Spouse and Subjects: and so both make one Mystical person, that is, one Corporation, Family, Common-wealth."[261] Baxter describes his understanding of the "relative union" as a corporation, a family, or a commonwealth.[262] This use of political metaphors is not coincidental. Since

---

255. Cf. Baxter, *Scripture Gospel defended*, p. 88: "It is not only the Spiritual off-spring that Christ was a second *Adam* to, but partly to all mankind: For by a resurrection (though not to glory) all men are made alive by Christ, *Joh.* 5.22, 23, 29. 1 *Cor.* 15. And all have a general conditional reconciliation and pardon, 2 *Cor.* 5.19,20. *Joh.* 3:16."
256. Baxter, *Of Imputation*, p. 69.
257. Baxter, *Breviate*, p. 29.
258. Baxter, *Of Imputation*, p. 70.
259. Baxter, *Of Imputation*, p. 69. Cf. *Scripture Gospel defended*, p. 86: "They feign us to have been *Personally in Adam*, whenas we were but seminally in him, and personally *from* him."
260. See above, pp. 106-08.
261. Baxter, *Confutation*, p. 254.
262. Cf. Baxter, *Of Imputation*, p. 55: "He did not this <*i.e.*, satisfying justice> as a *Natural* Root, or Head to man, as *Adam* was; to convey *Holiness* or *Righteousness* by *natural propagation*, as *Adam* should have done; and did by sin: For Christ had no Wife or natural Children; But as a Head, *by Contract* as a Husband to a Wife, and a King to a Kingdom, and a *Head of Spiritual Influx*."

Christ, unlike Adam, is not a natural head, the relation between Christ and his members must be conceived differently:

> Some abuse the similitude of a *Head* and *Members*; whereas Natural Head and Members make one Natural Body; but so do not Christ and Believers: And a Political Head and Members are distinct persons, and one is not guiltless, righteous, wise or good, because the other is so.[263]

Baxter describes the union between Christ and the believers in political terms.[264] J.I. Packer has appealed to Baxter's concept of union with Christ to illustrate that his "political method" regulated his dogmatic construction. Packer regards mystical union as the key to a truly catholic soteriology. Baxter did not come to grips with it:

> Antinomian abuse of this principle made Baxter shy away from it in his own dogmatic construction. He did not deny that the mystical union was a fact, but he denied strenuously that it was a theological category. He substituted for it the idea of political union between Christ and the Church, and reinterpreted the received doctrines of atonement and justification accordingly ...[265]

In the main, Packer's analysis of Baxter's position is correct.[266] Baxter indeed speaks of union with Christ in political terms and abhors "that proud and blasphemous fancy" that we are personally one with Christ.[267] Nevertheless, also in this context, he makes the important distinction between Christ as head *for* the world and as head *to* believers, between conditional and actual union with Christ. This distinction goes back to his distinction between God's will *de debito* and his will *de rerum eventu* and indicates that the bifurcation of God's will continues to play a role in the background. It is true that Baxter emphasizes that union with Christ is relative or political. This aspect comes into sharp focus because of his denial of a

---

263. Baxter, *Scripture Gospel defended*, p. 86.
264. Cf. the following comments of Baxter: "<T>he *Glory* of Gods Wisdom, Love, and Holiness, Justice and Mercy, do shine forth wonderfully in our Union with Christ, and Membership of his Political Body, in our free Pardon and Justification, Reconciliation and Adoption ..." (*How Far Holinesse*, p. 11); "A Natural Head being but a *part of a person*, what it doth the *Person doth*. But seeing a *Contracted Head*, and all the *members* of his *Body Contracted* or *Politick*, are every one a *distinct Person*, it followeth not that each person did really or reputatively what the *Head did*" (*Of Imputation*, p. 55); "But our union with Christ is political, relative, with a real participation of the same Holy Spirit ..." ("Sed unio nostra cum Christo est *Politica, Relativa*, cum ejusdem Spiritûs sancti *reali* participatione ..." [*Methodus Theologiæ* III.xxvii.308]); "In a *Political Union* Christ as the head, and the Church as the body make one Society as *parts* constituting the whole" (*Breviate*, p. 26).
265. Packer, "Redemption and Restoration," pp. 470-71.
266. Rather than say that Baxter denied that mystical union was a theological category, I would say that he was intent on interpreting union with Christ in such a way as to avoid strict imputation. The following quotation may illustrate Baxter's attempt to avoid strict imputation, while at the same time acknowledging that union with Christ is more than a relative or political union: "For though it be agreed on, that the same Spirit that is in Christ is (operatively) also in all his Members, and that therefore our *Communion* with him is more than *Relative*, and that from this *Real-Communion*, the name of a *Real-Union* may be used; yet here the *Real-Union* is not *Personal*" (*Of Imputation*, p. 112).
267. Baxter, *Confutation*, p. 255.

strict parallelism between Adam and Christ. But this political union comes about by faith: the gift of God as Absolute Donor. Thus, the idea of "political union" lies ultimately embedded within Baxter's concept of the twofold will of God.

Reatus culpae *and* reatus poenae

The impact of Baxter's notion of a "political union" must not be underestimated. It is closely connected to his understanding of Christ's substitutionary atonement. Baxter consistently opposes the idea that not only the guilt of the penalty (*reatus poenae*), but that also the guilt of the fault (*reatus culpae*) is imputed to Christ.[268] When Baxter distinguishes between the *reatus culpae* and the *reatus poenae*, he means to include the guilt of the deed (*reatus facti*) with the *reatus culpae*.[269] Baxter makes this threefold distinction of guilt in order to indicate that Christ did not take our place in the sense that he himself became the sinner as bearing the guilt of the deed (*reatus facti*) or as being guilty of the fault (*reatus culpae*). Christ only took the penalty which we deserved. His vicarious suffering was only the suffering of our penalty.[270] Man truly remains a sinner (*revera peccator*).[271]

To be sure, there is a sense in which also the *reatus culpae* is imputed to Christ. Baxter adds this "lest the Wrangler make a verbal quarrel of it."[272] In common language, we say we forgive someone his fault, when we actually only forgive him the penalty.[273] Thus, as it is the basis of the guilt of the penalty (*fundamentum reatus poenae*), it may be said that also the *reatus culpae* is forgiven. But it is actually the obligation to punishment which is remitted. Therefore, the *reatus culpae* can never be remitted in itself (*in se*).[274]

Baxter is afraid that a wrong understanding of substitution denies the essence of justification. As noted earlier, he is of the opinion that constitutive justification means the dissolution of the obligation to punishment. Consequently, he argues that if the *reatus culpae* is done away as well as the *reatus poenae*, "then the *Reatus Pœnæ*, the obligation to punishment, or the *dueness* of punishment, cannot be said to be dissolved or remitted, because it was never contracted."[275] In other words, if Christ takes our *reatus culpae*, the *reatus poenae* is automatically removed as well. Forgiveness then becomes redundant, according to Baxter. In fact, we may then well be said to merit justification ourselves.

Precisely on this point, Baxter opposes John Owen's theory of imputation. Owen insists that remission and satisfaction are not mutually exclusive. Pardon

---

268. Baxter, *How Far Holinesse*, p. 16; *Of Imputation*, pp. 50, 62-63, 77; *Breviate*, p. 31; *Scripture Gospel defended*, pp. 89, 104; *Defence of Christ*, pp. 3, 10, 59. Cf. Fisher, "Theology of Richard Baxter," 160; Richards, "Richard Baxter's Theory of the Atonement," p. 30.
269. Baxter, *Two Disputations*, pp. 113-14, 231-32; *Of Imputation*, pp. 78, 92.
270. Baxter, *Defence of Christ*, pp. 3, 10.
271. Baxter, *Of Imputation*, p. 122.
272. Baxter, *Of Imputation*, p. 126.
273. Baxter, *Of Imputation*, p. 77.
274. Baxter, *Of Imputation*, pp. 122, 126.
275. Baxter, *Of Imputation*, p. 77. Cf. pp. 58, 94, 99-102, 195; *Confutation*, pp. 224-25; *Appeal*, p. 2; *Methodus Theologiæ* III.xxvii.322-23.

only excludes payment or satisfaction of very same person whose sin is forgiven. Says Owen: "If all this <*i.e.*, the payment> were done by the persons themselves, or any one in their stead procured and appointed by themselves, then were there some difficulty in these questions; but this being otherwise, there is none at all, as hath been declared."[276] Baxter perceives a problem in this position. He states that here lies part of the reason why Owen "giveth up the cause." [277] Indeed, it cannot be denied that Owen is in some difficulty. On the one hand, he maintains that the party which receives pardon does not make the payment. On the other hand, however, he strongly emphasizes union with Christ as the basis for imputation. The elect are "under merit." They have a right to justification because of their union with Christ.[278]

This is where Baxter challenges Owen. Here, he states, is "the heart of the whole Controversie, and (if I may have leave to speak as confidently as your self,) the Root of many dangerous errors, I think very plainly subverting the Christian Religion."[279] In coming to an explanation of his objections he says:

> I confess, he that merited, hath a Right unto the thing merited as of Debt. But we that go on lower Principles then you, dare not say to God, *Lord, I have merited salvation in Christ, therefore it is mine of debt.* I do not think you are Christ: nor that you were in Christ when he Merited: nor that you merited in him. What then though Christ hath of Debt a Right to Pardon and save you? Will it follow that you have of debt, (and that before you believe, and before you are born) a Right to Pardon and Salvation? I shall think not, till I see better proof.[280]

Several things must be noted here. First, when Owen states that those who are united to Christ are "under merit," Baxter interprets this to mean that they themselves have merited salvation in Christ.[281] Whether this would be a logical inference from Owen's position or not, it is clear that the latter does not go as far as to explicitly put it this way. From one's union with Christ Owen does, however, infer that one is "under merit." In other words, what Christ merited is put on man's account due to union with Christ. Christ's right becomes the right of those who are united to him. Owen has not cleared himself of the charge that his concept of mystical union is ill suited to his position that Christ, rather than the debtor, pays the penalty.

Much of the discussion on this issue comes to a head in the exegesis of Isaiah 53:6 ("and the LORD hath laid on him the iniquity of us all") and 2 Corinthians 5:21 ("For he hath made him to be sin for us, who knew no sin; that we might be made the righteousness of God in him"). These texts play a prominent role in the

---

276. Owen, *Of the Death of Christ*, in *Works* 10.446. Cf. pp. 474-75.
277. Baxter, *Aphorismes* II.143 (p. 305).
278. Cf. above, pp. 106-07.
279. Baxter, *Confession*, p. 266.
280. Baxter, *Confession*, p. 262.
281. In a similar manner Baxter objects to justification from eternity: "It seems to me therefore that they do by their Doctrine of eternal Justification or pardon not only destroy Justification by Faith, but also all the Merits of Christ and leave nothing for them to do, for the causing of our pardon or Justification before God" (*Confession*, p. 219).

way in which Tobias Crisp understands imputation.[282] According to Crisp, "the fault of the transgression it selfe" is laid upon Christ.[283] With respect to the distinction between *reatus culpae* and *reatus poenae*, Crisp comments:

> For that objection about guilt, that the Lord layes the guilt and punishment, but not simply the sin it selfe, for ought that I see, it is a simple objection: For first, you shall never find this distinction in all the Scripture, that God laid the guilt of sin upon Christ, and not the sin it self; as for the guilt of sin, it is not mentioned all the Scripture through, that God layes the guilt of sin, or that Christ doth beare the guilt of sin; nay further, to affirme that the Lord did lay upon Christ the guilt of sin, and not the sin it selfe, is directly contrary to Scripture: for you have many testimonies of Scripture affirming that sin and iniquity the Lord doth lay upon Christ: what presumption then is it for a man to say the Lord layes on Christ the guilt, and not the sinne it selfe?[284]

Crisp's insistence that the very sin of the elect is laid upon Christ runs directly counter to Baxter's use of the distinction between *reatus culpae* and *reatus poenae*.

One of the reasons why Crisp's theology is particularly upsetting to Baxter was the uncompromising way in which Crisp alleges that our sins lay on Christ. Whether one has been an idolater, a blasphemer, a murderer, a thief, a liar, or a drunkard, there is no need to worry, for "if thou hast part in the Lord Christ, all these transgressions of thine become actually the transgressions of Christ, and so cease to be thine ..."[285] Crisp posits vicarious atonement in its most uncompromising form. He insists to his audience that if they have part in Christ, "you are all that Christ was, Christ is all that you were, 2 *Cor.* 5.21."[286] According to Crisp, there is a "direct change" between Christ's person and condition and our persons and condition.[287]

It is passages like these to which Baxter strongly objects.[288] Christ was not the greatest blasphemer or the greatest murderer in the world, insists Baxter.[289] To say that Christ is the greatest sinner would mean that he was really hated by God. Baxter mentions this objection a number of times, but he does not really dwell on it.[290] Still, it is a significant corollary of his view of imputation. Because Christ did not bear the *reatus culpae*, he was not hated by God.[291] God only hates those

---

282. Fifteen of the seventeen sermons in the second volume of Crisp's *Christ Alone Exalted* are devoted to Isa 53:6 (Tobias Crisp, *Christ Alone Exalted* [n.p., 1643], II, 69-514).

283. Crisp, *Christ Alone Exalted*, II, 88.

284. Crisp, *Christ Alone Exalted*, II, 91-92.

285. Crisp, *Christ Alone Exalted*, II, 88-89.

286. Crisp, *Christ Alone Exalted*, II, 89.

287. Crisp, *Christ Alone Exalted*, II, 89.

288. See Baxter, *Defence of Christ*, sig. A8ʳ.

289. Baxter, *Appeal*, p. 1; *Breviate*, p. 31; *Defence of Christ*, pp. 3, 10.

290. Although Baxter did not discuss the issue at length – and so perhaps avoided a controversy on it – Daniel Williams (1643?-1716) adopted the idea as well. Thus, it became the focus of controversy between Williams and Isaac Chauncy (cf. Toon, *Puritans and Calvinism*, p. 94).

291. Baxter, *Of Imputation*, pp. 53, 92; *Breviate*, p. 64; *Scripture Gospel defended*, p. 89. Cf. McGrath, "Puritans and the Human Will," p. 195. Baxter's comments on Jesus' complaint ("My God, my God, why hast thou forsaken me?") illustrate his view. In his *Paraphrase on the New*

whom he reputes to be truly ungodly.[292] When 2 Corinthians 5:21 speaks of Christ as sin it means a sacrifice for sin.[293] Baxter says that if Christ's accidents become ours it would imply that we were gods.[294] In this connection, he warns against blasphemy:

> The false notion of God's strict imputing all our sins to Christ, and esteeming him the greatest sinner in the World, being so great a Blasphemy both against the Father and the Son, it is safest in such Controversies to hold to the plain and ordinary words of Scripture.[295]

To say that Christ righteousness become ours in a strict sense and that our sins become properly Christ's sins is, according to Baxter, a serious form of blasphemy. Moreover, it implies making God the author of sin: he is then regarded as making Christ the greatest sinner in the world by making all the sins of the elect to be really Christ's own.[296]

No Strict Legal "Personating" of the Believers

Because he denies a strict imputation of Christ's righteousness, Baxter also opposes the notion that Christ becomes one natural person with the elect. Baxter lists union with Christ among the relative graces, rather than among those that make a physical change on us. Already in his *Aphorismes*, after acknowledging a real union and communion with Christ, he comments:

> But <I> am very fearful of coming so near, as to make Christ and sinners one real Person, (as the late elevated Sect among us do,) lest blasphemously I should deifie man, and debase Christ to be actually a sinner. And if we are not one real Person with Christ, then one what? It sufficeth me to know as abovesaid, and that we are one with Christ in as strict a bond of relation as the wife with the husband, and far stricter; and that we are his body mystical, but not natural.[297]

Baxter denies that union with Christ implies that the believer becomes one natural person with him.[298] Thomas Tully, however, is not impressed with this exposition. He charges Baxter with confounding a natural and a political person. Although Christ and the believers are not the same natural person, they are the same political

---

Testament (1685) (*ad* Matt 27:46 and Mark 15:34), Baxter explains Jesus' being forsaken as (1) God leaving him to the power of wicked men who are servants of Satan; (2) Jesus' being deprived of life; (3) God's withdrawing from Christ's human nature the sense of complacence; and (4) Christ's having a sense of God's justice against sin, which was his penalty as our surety. Baxter insists, however, that God's love and esteem of Christ was in no sense abated.

292. Baxter, *Of Imputation*, p. 92.
293. Baxter, *Of Imputation*, pp. 56, 126; *Methodus Theologiæ* III.xxvii.324; *Paraphrase on the New Testament, ad loc.*
294. Baxter, *Appeal*, p. 2.
295. Baxter, *Of Imputation*, p. 57. Cf. p. 126; *Defence of Christ*, pp. 4, 59.
296. Baxter, *Defence of Christ*, pp. 10, 39.
297. Baxter, *Aphorismes* I.211 (p. 134).
298. Cf. Baxter, *Of Imputation*, p. 56.

person. Imputation is not a natural, but a legal matter.[299] According to Tully, Baxter first sets up a straw man which he then proceeds to knock over. Tully questions: "I would fain know how He should be a *Representer* at all, if He were not *another* Person."[300]

By arguing against the notion of Christ becoming one natural person with the elect, Baxter indeed does not oppose a notion actually held by any of his opponents. This weakens his position. He basically gives his high Calvinist opponents the opportunity to discard his objections as irrelevant. Still, such a dismissal would be too hasty. Baxter's comments do impinge on his contestants' position. He not only states that Christ and the believer remain separate natural persons, but he also rejects that Christ becomes our person in a legal or civil sense (*in sensu legali vel civili*). Baxter regards this idea as "the very root and master vein of all Antinomianism."[301] The wrong understanding of Christ's dying *nostro loco* is "the very turning point to Antinomianism."[302] Christ did not represent us in such a way as if we had been and done what he was and did. This is "the very heart of all the Controversie."[303] The idea that Christ absolutely represents the elect "subverteth" the sum of the Gospel.[304]

Baxter's emphatic language indicates the importance which he attaches to this issue. Even if one only argues that Christ is one person with the believers in a civil or legal sense, Baxter still does not agree. In *Scripture Gospel defended*, he says that he regards it entirely erroneous to think

> that though Christ and *Adam* were two *Natural Persons*, yet they were *One Person* in a *Civil*, *Legal* or *Reputative* sense, in Christs obeying and suffering; and so that what Christ did and suffered in his *own Natural Person*, he did and suffered in *Adams*, and every Elect mans *Civil*, *Legal*, or *Reputative Person*.[305]

Although Baxter does not mention Tully by name at this particular point, he refutes precisely the position which Tully holds.

Baxter warns that Scripture does not speak of a legal or reputative personal union.[306] He insists that it is important to define one's terms. The words "person," "personating," and "representing" are ambiguous terms.[307] Baxter admits that the word "person" does not have to mean an individual intelligent substance. It may have other meanings. But if the word is used in a different sense, people are obliged to give their definition.[308] It may be possible, therefore, to say that Christ suffered in the person of a sinner. Baxter appeals to George Lawson, whose *Theopolitica* (1659) could by no means be accused of high Calvinists sympathies. Still,

---

299. Tully, *Justificatio Paulina*, pp. 80-81; *Animadversions*, sig. G2ᵛ.
300. Tully, *Animadversions*, sig. G2ᵛ.
301. Baxter, *Confutation*, p. 224.
302. Baxter, *Of Justification*, p. 382.
303. Baxter, *Breviate*, p. 22.
304. Baxter, *Breviate*, p. 23. Cf. *Scripture Gospel defended*, pp. 81, 83.
305. Baxter, *Scripture Gospel defended*, p. 83.
306. Baxter, *Breviate*, pp. 27-28.
307. Baxter, *Of Imputation*, pp. 67, 104.
308. Baxter, *Of Imputation*, pp. 105-06.

the latter states: "If we enquire of the manner, how Righteousness and Life is derived from Christ being One, unto so many, we shall find that this cannot be, except Christ be a general Head of Mankind, and one person with them, as *Adam* was."[309] When Lawson explains how Christ is one person with us, he says that Christ became liable to the punishment for us, and that we are thereby freed from that obligation. Lawson adds, however, that "yet Christ is not the sinner, nor the sinner Christ."[310] Baxter uses Lawson's exposition in order to illustrate that it is possible to say that Christ is one person with the elect.[311] Baxter does not want to dispute about mere words.[312] But he insists that if Christ is described as being one person with the believers it is important not to understand this in the strict sense of the word.

Christ As Mediator and causa sine qua non

Despite the admission that Christ and the believers may be said to be one person, Baxter remains unimpressed with this terminology. He does not even like to speak of Christ as our representative.[313] If such language is used, it should be clear that this is not proper terminology. Says Baxter:

> It belongeth to him as Mediator to undertake the sinners punishment in his own person. And if any will improperly call that, the *Personating and Representing* of the *sinner*, let them limit it, and confess that it is not *simply*, but *in tantum*, so far, and to such uses and no other, and that yet *sinners did it not in* and *by Christ*, but only Christ for them to convey the benefits as he pleased; And then we delight not to quarrel about mere words; though we like the phrase of Scripture better than theirs.[314]

In opposition to the notion that Christ is one legal person with the elect, Baxter insists that Christ is Mediator in his own person.[315] Baxter takes exception to Tully's understanding of the word ἔγγυος in Hebrews 7:22 ("By so much was Jesus made a surety <ἔγγυος> of a better testament"). The word "surety" or "sponsor," maintains Baxter, may have a number of different meanings.[316] It is not sufficient to argue that Christ is our legal representative or person simply because of the word "surety" in Hebrews 7:22. Again appealing to Lawson, Baxter main-

---

309. Lawson, *Theo-politica*, p. 100. Cf. Baxter, *Of Imputation*, p. 71.
310. Lawson, *Theo-politica*, p. 101. Cf. Baxter, *Of Imputation*, p. 72. Lawson adds that we are accounted "as one person in Law with him by a *Trope*."
311. Says Baxter: "How far those Divines who do use the phrase of *Christs suffering in our person*, do yet limit the sense in their exposition, and deny that we are reputed to have fulfilled the Law in Christ: because it is tedious to cite many, I shall take up now with one, even Mr. *Lawson* in his *Theopolitica*, which ... I must needs call an excellent Treatise, as I take the Author to be one of the most Knowing men yet living that I know" (*Of Imputation*, p. 71). Cf. p. 68.
312. Baxter, *Account of my Consideration*, p. 73; *Of Imputation*, pp. 56, 75, 96, 106.
313. Baxter, *Breviate*, p. 23; *Of Imputation*, pp. 56, 96.
314. Baxter, *Of Imputation*, p. 96.
315. Cf. Baxter, *Appeal*, p. 1: "But Christ did all this in the person of a Mediator; and not as our Delegate, Servant or Agent; nor full Representer of our persons; that is, his person, and the person of each sinner were not the same indeed, or in Law-sense, nor did God so judge them ..."
316. Baxter, *Of Imputation*, pp. 110-11; *Scripture Gospel defended*, p. 80.

tains that the word "surety" is used here in the sense of "mediator."[317] A mediator "is *not of one*, but doth somewhat on the behalf of *both parties*."[318] According to Baxter, Hebrews 7:22 speaks of Christ's mediatorial office in the covenant of grace.[319]

When Baxter posits a sharp distinction between Christ as our representative and as Mediator this has implications also for the way in which he regards the role of Christ's atoning work. Baxter regards Christ's righteousness as the meritorious cause of justification.[320] He refuses to place Christ's righteousness as meritorious cause on a par with man's righteousness. Only the former is the meritorious cause of justification.[321] Nevertheless, Baxter does speak of Christ's merit as *causa sine qua non* of justification:

> Christs Satisfaction hath several ways of causing our Justification. 1. That it is the Meritorious Cause, I know few but Socinians that will deny. 2. That it is besides properly a *Causa sine qua non*, cannot be denied by any that consider, that it removeth those great Impediments that hindered our Justification.[322]

Baxter's assertion that Christ's satisfaction is *causa sine qua non* for justification angers high Calvinists like William Eyre and John Crandon. Both authors maintain that Baxter has thus placed Christ's satisfaction "in the same kind of causality" with faith and works,[323] making Christ and faith to differ "onely *secundum magis & minus*."[324]

Christ's Righteousness As Material Cause

Eyre and Crandon are certainly correct in their observation that Baxter insists that Christ's satisfaction as well as man's faith and works are *causae sine quibus non*. Whether this indeed means that Baxter does not differentiate between these two "causes" remains to be seen.[325] What is important for the present purpose, however, is that Baxter's understanding of Christ's sacrifice as *causa sine qua non* precludes the idea of his satisfaction being the direct *causa materialis* of justifica-

---

317. Baxter, *Of Imputation*, p. 109.
318. Baxter, *Of Imputation*, p. 109.
319. Baxter, *Scripture Gospel defended*, p. 78. Cf. *Paraphrase on the New Testament, ad loc.*: "The word translated [*Surety*] signifieth an interceding Administrator and Mediator, giving Man *Assurance* of the Will of God (as *Moses* did in delivering the Law) and *consenting* to receive God's Terms and Promises in the nature of Man, and to perform his own part and undertaking, for the gathering and glorifying his Church thereby: But not that he undertook that all that he mediated for, should do all that is their duty."
320. Cf. Baxter, *Aphorismes* I.213-17 (pp. 135-38); *Confutation*, p. 221.
321. Baxter, *Admonition*, p. 10.
322. Baxter, *Aphorismes* I.215 (p. 136).
323. Crandon, *Aphorisms Exorized* I.xxiv.322. Cf. Baxter, *Unsavoury Volume*, pp. 69-70.
324. Eyre, *Vindiciæ Justificationis Gratuitæ*, p. 29. Cf. Baxter, *Admonition*, pp. 10-11, 21. Cf. also John Eedes: "I could not well brooke that he <*i.e.*, Baxter> made Christ but *causa sine qua non*, when the Scripture declares him to be not only the meritorious cause of our justification, but the author of our salvation, and that God doth blesse us with all spirituall blessings in Christ Jesus" (*Orthodox Doctrine* [London, 1654], p. 57).
325. Cf. below, pp. 289-99.

tion.[326] To be sure, Eyre exaggerates when he accuses Baxter of denying that Christ's obedience is the material cause of justification.[327] Baxter is willing to say that Christ's satisfaction is, in a sense, the material cause; but this appellation is "much more properly" given to his own righteousness than to ours.[328] Christ's material righteousness was perfect conformity to the law of innocence.[329] Only in a remote sense, therefore, can Christ's righteousness be called the matter of our justification. In that sense, it is merely the matter of the merit. Says Baxter: "Yea though some deny it, his Righteousness may *be called the material cause* of our *Righteousness*, as ours is our *Jus ad impunitatem & vitam*, because it is the *matter* of it's *meritorious cause*."[330] Baxter is only willing to grant that Christ's righteousness is the matter of the meritorious cause of justification. Thus, it is only indirectly the matter of our righteousness. Strictly speaking, only the effect of Christ's righteousness is imputed to us.[331] Although Baxter is willing to speak of Christ's satisfaction as the "material cause" of justification, he has actually little use for such a description because it remains a remote, improper appellation, nothing but an "unnecessary Logical name."[332]

Christ's Righteousness No Formal Cause

Whereas Baxter is willing to characterize Christ's righteousness, in a carefully circumscribed sense, as the material cause of our justification, he consistently denies that this righteousness of Christ is the *causa formalis* of justification.[333] In his *Aphorismes*, Baxter describes the formal cause as "the acquitting of the sinner from Accusation and Condemnation of the Law, or the disabling the Law to accuse or condemn him."[334] Because the form is that which gives something its name, Baxter denies that imputation is the form of justification: "Imputation and Justification denote distinct Acts: And how then can Imputing be the Forme of

---

326. The material cause is "the substantial basis of the motion or mutation, the *materia* on which the *causa efficiens* operates" (Muller, *Dictionary*, p. 61).
327. Eyre, *Vindiciæ Justificationis Gratuitæ*, p. 29. Responds Baxter: "I did not deny Christs obedience to be the material cause in the sense as Divines commonly so called it ..." (*Admonition*, p. 20).
328. Baxter, *Of Imputation*, p. 63. Since righteousness indicates a relation, Baxter thinks that it can never really have a material cause, whether it refers to Christ's individual righteousness or to imputed righteousness. Therefore, he often does not speak of the matter (*materia*) of Christ's (or of our own) righteousness but of its *quasi materia* (*Account of my Consideration*, pp. 80, 83, 181; *Of Imputation*, pp. 85-86, 108).
329. Baxter, *Of Imputation*, p. 63.
330. Baxter, *Scripture Gospel defended*, p. 101. Cf. pp. 108-09 (incorrect pagination; sigs. H8ᵛ-I1ʳ); *Admonition*, p. 20; *Confutation*, p. 221; *Of Imputation*, pp. 85-86, 119, 154; *Breviate*, pp. 25-26; *End of Doctrinal Controversies*, pp. 262-63.
331. Baxter often speaks of Christ's righteousness being given to us in its "effects" or "benefits" rather than in itself (*Appeal*, p. 2; *Of Imputation*, pp. 59, 67, 115-16; *Methodus Theologiæ* III.xxvii.308; *Scripture Gospel defended*, pp. 99, 104).
332. Baxter, *Scripture Gospel defended*, p. 109 (incorrect pagination; sig. H8ᵛ).
333. The *causa formalis* is "the *essentia* ... or *quidditas* ... of the thing, and which is determinative of *what* the thing caused is to be" (Muller, *Dictionary*, p. 61).
334. Baxter, *Aphorismes* I.213 (p. 135) (emphasis throughout in original).

Justifying."[335] Eyre takes exception to this distinction between imputation and justification. He insists that Christ's righteousness is the form of our justification.[336] This forces Baxter to deal with the issue once more. Somewhat remarkably, he then comments that he has "much altered" the pages of his *Aphorismes* in which he discusses the various causes of justification, "as finding the expressions unfit, and therefore do revoke them."[337] He now says that all he had meant in his *Aphorismes* is that the donation of the covenant (which he had styled "imputation") logically precedes sentential justification.[338] He now admits that, indeed, there are ways in which imputation is the form of justification. All depends on one's meaning of the words "imputation" and "justification."[339] Thus, imputation as the donation of Christ's righteousness is the form of constitutive justification; the sentential adjudication of Christ's righteousness to us is the form of sentential justification; and when God begins to approve of us and imputes righteousness to us by mental acceptation, this is the form of mental justification. Baxter concludes that in all these different ways imputation is the form of justification. What he objects to, however, is that "one sort of Imputation" is made the form of "another sort of Justification."[340]

When Baxter says that the imputation of Christ's righteousness may be called the form of justification, he does not admit to a strict theory of imputation. Speaking of justification – whether constitutive or sentential – he is referring to a relation which results from Christ's righteousness. Christ's righteousness is not identical to the imputation of this righteousness. Christ's personal righteousness precedes the imputation of it. Whereas Baxter grants that the latter, rightly understood, is the form of justification, he consistently denies that Christ's righteousness itself is the *causa formalis* of our justification. The form of a person's righteousness is simply his being not guilty; it is *non debitum poenae*.[341] Despite his high esteem of John Davenant, Baxter is forced to dissent from him on this issue when Cartwright appeals to him. Says Baxter: "I do highly reverence *Davenant* ... But far am I from owning this Doctrine which he makes to be *communis nostrorum sententia*; *viz*. That Christ's Righteousness is *formalis causa Justificationis*. I hold it to be *causa efficiens meritoria, quæ est quasi materialis*; but not *formalis*."[342] To Baxter, it is logically impossible that Christ's individual formal righteousness would become our formal personal righteousness. Christ's righteousness

335. Baxter, *Aphorismes* I.218 (p. 138).
336. Eyre, *Vindiciæ Justificationis Gratuitæ*, p. 29.
337. Baxter, *Admonition*, p. 21.
338. Baxter, *Admonition*, p. 20.
339. Cf. Baxter, *End of Doctrinal Controversies*, p. 263: "They that will dispute what is the *form* of *Justification*, must first confess the Ambiguity of the Word, and tell us in which Sence they take it: There are so many things that are truly the *form* of *Justification* taken in many Sences, that without such distinguishing to dispute of the *form* of *Justification*, is worse than to say nothing ..."
340. Baxter, *Admonition*, p. 21.
341. Baxter, *Account of my Consideration*, p. 76. From Baxter's description it is clear that he is here speaking of constitutive justification.
342. Baxter, *Account of my Consideration*, p. 181. Cf. *Of Imputation*, p. 85; *Methodus Theologiæ* III.xxvii.323.

is a relation and an accident specifically belonging to his person. Therefore, it cannot be translated from the one subject to the other.[343] Baxter compares this to the logical impossibility of the Roman Catholic notion of transubstantiation.[344]

By denying that Christ's righteousness is the formal cause of justification Baxter has taken a highly significant step. It has been argued that the "only theological unanimity" in the seventeenth-century debate on justification is "a universal assumption that the formal cause of justification is the key to the problem of soteriology."[345] Indeed, the question of the formal cause of justification is highly significant. Perhaps Baxter devotes relatively little space and attention to the question of the formal cause of justification. But this does not mean that the issue itself does not play a role in the various controversies. Baxter's consistent denial of strict imputation, his opposition to a high Calvinist understanding of mystical union with Christ and his denial that our *reatus culpae* is imputed to Christ all come down to the same thing: Christ's righteousness is the formal cause of his own righteousness as Mediator, not of the righteousness of those who belong to him by faith. This explains why Baxter consistently denies that Christ's righteousness is the formal cause whenever he does deal with this question. In the debate, Baxter takes sides with those who deny Christ's righteousness to be ours in a strict or formal sense. In this way he creates room for a place of man's own righteousness in justification.[346]

SOLUTIO EIUSDEM OR *SOLUTIO TANTIDEM*

Idem/Tantundem *and the Conditionality of the Covenant*

Baxter denies a strict imputation of Christ's righteousness. The theological necessity for this has not yet sufficiently come to the fore, however. It is intimately connected to the Baxter's understanding of Christ's personal righteousness. This righteousness is of such a nature that it cannot be directly reputed to be the righteousness of the elect. Direct imputation would only be possible if Christ's righteousness were the exact fulfillment of the obligation of the law. The controversy with Owen makes clear that Baxter is unable to accept this. At this point, Baxter's reliance on Grotius comes into focus.

Owen makes use of the distinction between *solutio eiusdem* and *solutio tantidem* which Grotius coined. Unlike Grotius, however, he insists that Christ's sacrifice was a payment of the same thing as threatened in the law. Owen rejects the view that Christ only paid the *solutio tantidem*.[347] In *Death of Death* Owen carefully distinguishes the two:

---

343. Baxter, *Of Imputation*, pp. 58, 94; *Methodus Theologiæ* III.xxvii.308, 322; *Breviate*, p. 25; *Defence of Christ*, pp. 41-42.
344. Baxter, *Methodus Theologiæ* III.xxvii.322; *Defence of Christ*, p. 42.
345. Allison, *Rise of Moralism*, p. 178.
346. That Christ did not perform the obedience of faith, repentance, and works which we owe is something which Baxter points out throughout his *Of Imputation* (pp. 54, 56, 95, 116).
347. Owen, *Death of Death*, in *Works* 10.267-73.

Now, there may be a twofold satisfaction: – First, By a solution, or paying the *very thing* <*solutio eiusdem*> that is in the obligation, either by the party himself that is bound, or by some other in his stead: as, if I owe a man twenty pounds, and my friend goeth and payeth it, my creditor is fully satisfied. Secondly, By a solution, or paying of so much <*solutio tantidem*>, although in another kind, not the same that is in the obligation, which, by the creditor's acceptation, stands in the lieu of it; upon which, also, freedom from the obligation followeth, not necessarily, but by virtue of an act of favour.[348]

From this statement of Owen several important points should be noted. First, he does not say what the value of Christ's death is according to those who hold to a *solutio tantidem*. A little later, however, again describing the same distinction, he refers to the "*solutio tantidem*, of that which is not the same, nor equivalent unto it, but only in the gracious acceptation of the creditor ..."[349] Owen understands the *solutio tantidem* to mean that Christ did not make an equivalent payment.

Baxter takes issue with Owen's description of the *solutio tantidem* as not being equivalent. Christ's payment certainly is of equal value, maintains Baxter.[350] But, he admits, if Owen means to say "that it is not equivalent in procuring its ends, *ipso facto*, delivering the debtour, without the intervention of a new concession or contract of the creditour, (as *solutio ejusdem* doth,) then I confesse *Grotius* is against him; and so am I."[351]

Baxter here refers back to what Grotius said about the immediate procurement of the benefits of Christ's death. Grotius argued that "one Payment frees *ipso facto*, and another not *ipso facto*, at the very time of Payment. The Payment of a thing that is wholly the same with what was in the Obligation, frees *ipso facto*: and it is the same sense, whether a guilty Person himself pay, or another for him, to this intent that he may be freed."[352] What Baxter, in line with Grotius, opposes, is the idea that Christ's payment frees *ipso facto*, as if no condition were interposed. In other words, Baxter does not want to quibble about the word "equivalent" as such. If it is taken to mean that it immediately, *ipso facto*, procures the blessings, then indeed he denies that it is an equivalent payment.

---

348. Owen, *Death of Death*, in *Works* 10.265.
349. Owen, *Death of Death*, in *Works* 10.267.
350. Baxter, *Aphorismes* II.138 (p. 301).
351. Baxter, *Aphorismes* II.138 (p. 302). Grotius' influence on Baxter's theory of the atonement is obvious. Baxter maintains that "*Grotius de satisfact.* alone, well studyed, without prejudice, might profit some Divines more then many years study of many large volumes hath hitherto done. (It was written before his defection.)" (*Confutation*, p. 262) This does not mean that Baxter simply adopted his theory of the atonement from Grotius. Baxter writes about Grotius' *Defensio fidei* – "a book written while he remained with the orthodox" – that he had "almost finished those Aphorismes before ever I read a leaf of *Grotius*, having only heard of him by no encouraging fame; and being at that time in speech with Mr. *Tombes*, upon his high commendations of it, I borrowed it of him to peruse, and found it fully to answer his commendations: and I confess, I learned more out of it, then I did out of any book except the Scriptures, of many a year before" (*Unsavoury Volume*, p. 6; cf. *Of Imputation*, p. 189; Packer, "Redemption and Restoration," pp. 233-34).
352. Grotius, *Defence*, p. 135-36 ("Sed alia solutio ipso facto liberat, alia non ipso facto. Ipso facto liberat solutio rei planè ejusdem quæ erat in obligatione. Perinde autem est ipse reus solvat, an alius pro eo hoc animo ut ipse liberetur ..." [*Defensio*, p.78].).

God's gracious acceptance is not for that reason the acceptance of something which is of less value. On the contrary, it is the acceptance of something "equal in value," even though it is as such a "refuseabe <sic> payment."[353] That Baxter maintains this equality in value is also clear when he opposes the *aequivalens* to the *idem* in other places.[354] Christ's payment is equivalent in value, though not equivalent in what it *ipso facto* procures. The benefits of Christ's death are applied by means of a condition. The procurement of salvation is not immediate.

The importance of this somewhat technical issue lies in its relation to the conditionality of the covenant. What Baxter opposes, is an *ipso facto* procurement of benefits. That is the reason for his opposition to a *solutio eiusdem*. If the law has been fulfilled there is no place left for the imposition of a condition in the new covenant. The debate is not as esoteric as it may seem, therefore. It concerns the question whether the benefits are applied directly or indirectly by Christ's death.

Owen's position that the benefits of Christ's sacrificial death are procured *ipso facto* is somewhat weakened, at least in the early years of his career, by his denial of the absolute necessity of Christ's death. The young Owen holds that a separate decree of God is needed to make Christ's sacrifice a *solutio*.[355] This view has implications for the *idem/tantundem* debate. Some of the poignancy of his insistence on the *idem* is lost when it appears that he does not accept the absolute need for satisfaction itself. Christ's sacrifice may by its very nature be identical to the punishment threatened. But this identical suffering only becomes a *solutio*, a payment, because of God's antecedent decree. To have the *idem* as such does not automatically imply the *solutio eiusdem*. To be sure, Christ's death is by its very nature identical to the punishment threatened in the law. But this does not yet make his suffering into a punishment. It acquires this penal character only because of God's separate decree. God's will becomes the determining factor in giving Christ's satisfaction a penal character.

When Owen changes his mind about this in *A Dissertation of Divine Justice* (1653), he implicitly strengthens his position that Christ's sacrifice is *solutio eiusdem*. In his reply to Baxter, appended to *Vindiciæ Evangelicæ* (1655), Owen touches only briefly on the distinction between *solutio eiusdem* and *solutio tantidem*.[356] He does not mention here that he has altered his position. On the surface, therefore, Owen's change of mind does not affect the debate. It remains a fact, however, that his modified position strengthens the commercialist basis of his view on the atonement. Any distinction between *satisfactio* and *solutio* has become impossible because the need for payment is now grounded in the essence of God. Any thought of a refusable payment has now become irrelevant: not only is Christ's satisfaction identical (*idem*) to the punishment threatened in the law; his satisfaction has now, by its very nature, become a payment (*solutio*).

---

353. Baxter, *Aphorismes* II.138 (p. 302). Grotius also referred to Christ's sacrifice as *recusabilis* (*Defensio*, p. 78 [*Defence*, p. 136]).
354. Baxter, *Confession*, p. 273; *Universal Redemption*, pp. 34, 49, 60, 75, 78, 378, 390.
355. Cf. above, p. 130.
356. Owen, *Vindiciæ Evangelicæ*, in *Works* 12.613-14.

Solutio eiusdem *and Substitution*

As indicated above, Owen describes the *solutio eiusdem* as "paying the *very thing* that is in the obligation, either by the party himself that is bound, or by some other in his stead."[357] Baxter is of the opinion that this implies a serious defect in his adversary's position:

> The *Idem* is the perfect Obedience, or the full Punishment of man himself; and in case of personal Disobedience, it is personal punishment that the Law requires. It is *Supplicium ipsius Delinquentis*. The Law never threatned a Surety: Nor granteth any liberty of substitution: that was an Act of God as Above the Law.[358]

The question emerging at this point is: is *solutio eiusdem* compatible with substitution? Or does the nature of a *solutio eiusdem* require the *supplicium ipsius delinquentis*, the punishment of the transgressor himself? Baxter is convinced that *solutio eiusdem* and substitution cannot go hand in hand. He argues that Owen's opinion

> denyeth X¹ to have Satisfyed p<ro>p<er>ly, or to have offered an expiatory Sacrifice for Sin, or made attonement, & become a propitiation or Ransome for us. ffor Solutio ejusdem is inconsistent with Satisfaction strictly so called, & a Sacrifice is not Solutio ipsius Debiti, id est, supplicium Delinquentis. And o<u>ʳ Divines hitherto have judged it necessary to maintaine Xᵗˢ Satisfactory Sacrifice: & so do I.[359]

There are two mutually exclusive answers to the question whether *solutio eiusdem* and substitution are compatible. Baxter denies it on the grounds that substitution is not provided for in the law: the law requires that the transgressor himself make the payment.[360] To Baxter, this is an important argument. Also apart from his debate with Owen he repeatedly uses it. He consistently maintains that the law of innocence did not say to Adam that either he or his vicar could obey, or that either he or a surety could pay the penalty. The law did not provide for substitution.[361] Accordingly, Christ never satisfied the law of innocence:

> I do not think, that Christ's Righteousness of Satisfaction, is that which the Law required (for it required *supplicium delinquentis, & non Mediatoris;*) nor yet that the Law was satisfied strictly by it (except *quoad finem remotum:* For it is an Act of the *Rector as above Laws*, to admit *Satisfaction*, which is *redditio æquivalentis*; and it supposeth a *Relaxation* of the Law, and the Law cannot relax it self:) ...[362]

Christ only satisfied the law in an improper sense: its remote ends are obtained.[363] God is pleased by Christ's perfect holiness and obedience, and the holiness of the

---

357. Owen, *Death of Death*, in *Works* 10.265.
358. Baxter, *Confession*, pp. 289-90.
359. DWL MS *BT* ii.21(1), f. 14ʳ.
360. Cf. Baxter, *Universal Redemption*, pp. 75-76, 84, 88.
361. Baxter, *Of Imputation*, pp. 83, 93, 145, 151; *Scripture Gospel defended*, pp. 81-82, 114; *Defence of Christ*, pp. 8, 57.
362. Baxter, *Account of my Consideration*, p. 100.
363. Cf. Baxter, *Of Imputation*, p. 151; *Scripture Gospel defended*, pp. 82-83.
364. Baxter, *Of Imputation*, p. 76.

law is honored "in this grand Exemplar."[364] Strictly speaking, however, only the Lawgiver himself – who is above the law – is satisfied.[365] It is better to speak of Christ's righteousness as "pro-legal" righteousness than as "legal" righteousness.[366] This implies – and in this Baxter again follows Grotius – that Christ's satisfaction was *solutio recusabilis*: God had the right to refuse it.[367]

For Owen, substitution and *solutio eiusdem* are compatible because substitution does not impinge on the nature of the punishment as such. The punishment remains the same, regardless of the person on whom it is executed. He admits, and even insists, that the law was relaxed with respect to the person who suffers.[368] Says Owen: "That the law was relaxed as to the person suffering, I positively assert; but as to the penalty itself, that is not mentioned."[369] Owen maintains that the penalty of the law, the *debitum ipsius*, is fully executed; only, it is executed on a different person than initially threatened by the law.

To Baxter, this means that Owen gives up the cause: "Here he confesseth that the sureties name was not in the Obligation; and that God relaxed the Law to put it in."[370] Baxter is of the opinion that Owen's admission to a relaxation of the law is the fatal blow to his theory. Whether this is indeed the case depends on how strictly the commination of the law is bound to the person threatened. Owen thinks that it is possible simply to argue that the penalty of the law as such is still exacted, regardless of the change in person. Baxter argues that this is not so, since the law says that the sinner – not his surety – must die for his sin.

Idem formale *and Substitution*

The debate has reached an impasse. Neither Baxter, nor Owen, indicates why the identity of the person threatened does or does not affect the issue at hand. Baxter attempts to come to a solution in an unpublished manuscript, "The Learned, Moderate, Animadversions of Mr John Wallis, Considered," as well as in his *Universal Redemption*. Here he goes beyond the earlier debate. In the former treatise he elaborates on some points that he feels have been insufficiently dealt with in his *Aphorismes*:

> I can yet find no considerable false doctrine in it <*i.e.*, the *Aphorismes*>: but two or three mistakes in ye mañer of explicating some Truthes, (w<hi>^ch I shall p<ar>ticularly acknowledge w<he>^n I come to y^ou.) But many things are Delivered too nakedly & briefly, wanting y<a>^t explication & Confirmation w<hi>^ch I now see was necessary, but did not y<e>^n ...[371]

365. Baxter, *Account of my Consideration*, p. 89; *Of Imputation*, pp. 54, 76, 151; *Scripture Gospel defended*, pp. 82, 114-15.
366. To be sure, Baxter usually speaks of Christ's righteousness as legal righteousness. When he wants to indicate, however, that there has never been a proper fulfillment of the law of innocence, he speaks of "pro-legal righteousness" (*Of Justification*, p. 264; *Of Imputation*, p. 83).
367. Baxter, *Aphorismes* I.169; II.138, 142, 149 (pp. 109, 302, 304, 309); *Confutation*, p. 262.
368. Owen, *Death of Death*, in *Works* 10.270; *Of the Death of Christ*, in *Works* 10.440-44, 447.
369. Owen, *Of the Death of Christ*, in *Works* 10.440.
370. Baxter, *Aphorismes* II.145 (p. 306).
371. DWL MS *BT* ii.21(1), f. 2^r.

It is well possible that one of the things that Baxter considers as having been delivered "too nakedly & briefly" in his *Aphorismes* (1649) – and in his *Confession* (1655) – is his exposition on the *idem/tantundem* issue.

In his unpublished response to John Wallis, Baxter makes a distinction, for the first time, between the *idem formaliter* and the *idem materialiter*. Says Baxter: "The question is not whether it be ye Idem materialiter or ejusdem speciei quoad naturam passionis; but whether it be ye Idem formaliter, i.e. ye same Punishm<en>^{t} w<hi>^{ch} ye Law threatened."[372] Baxter is now willing to admit some kind of material identity between Christ's suffering and the punishment threatened by the law.[373] Baxter considers the requirement of the law that the sinner himself be punished as the *idem formaliter*. This requirement has been set aside by God. Christ's suffering as Surety is therefore not the suffering of the *debitum eiusdem formaliter*.

Baxter goes into much more detail on this point than he has previously. Interestingly, he involves the relation between law and gospel in the debate. He argues that the law never threatened Christ. If he, as a Surety, were threatened in the law, he would have been a Surety before the Fall. This would have been a confusion of law and gospel. Says Baxter:

> 2° Hereby you make X^t to have bin mans Surety, (& y<a>^{t} in ye sence of ye Law) Before he fell, w<hi>^{ch} you have no Scripture for y<a>^{t} I know of, but much ag<ains>^{t}.// 3° Hereby you confound ye Law & Gospell, or at least, give y<a>^{t} to ye Law (as anteceding ye fall) w<hi>^{ch} is p<ro>p<er> to ye Gospell ...[374]

Thus, Baxter formulates a new argument against Owen's position. The punishment cannot be identical, formally at least, because Christ cannot have been threatened in the law. Baxter elicits support from the Aristotelian form/matter distinction to argue against a *solutio eiusdem*. There can be no identical payment where formal identity is lacking.[375]

---

372. DWL MS *BT* ii.21(1), f. 13^r. Baxter also makes this distinction in *Universal Redemption*, in sections probably written between 1655 and 1657: pp. 23, 49, 79, 91, 389 (cf. appendix A). Although p. 91 might at first sight seem to belong to the section dating from the late 1640s (pp. 90-376), it should be noted that the form/matter distinction occurs here as part of some introductory comments to the chapter. These may well have been added at a later point in time.
Baxter's use of the distinction in his *Universal Redemption* is probably of a somewhat later date than in his unpublished reply to Wallis. In the former treatise, the comments on this point are scattered and more condensed than in the latter. In his reply to Wallis, Baxter sets out exactly what he means by the distinction. This might indicate that Baxter uses the distinction for the first time when he replies to Wallis, and that he is able to use this earlier acquired opinion in scattered statements later in his *Universal Redemption*.

373. Cf. DWL MS *BT* ii.21(1), f. 14^r: "And though I have told you y<a>^{t} it is ye Idem formale (i.e. Ipsum Debitum p<er> hanc Legis obligationem Constitutum) & not ye Idem materiale, or a suffering of ye same kind. Yet I think we should be cautelous even about this how far we affirme it to be ye same." And a little further: "But seing so much of ye very Matter of o<u>^{r} Suffering is such as X^t was not capable of, we may see with w<ha>^{t} further limitation we must affirme y<a>^{t} he suffered ye Idem materiale, quoad speciem pœnæ." For the same distinction, see also Baxter, *Universal Redemption*, pp. 22-23.

374. DWL MS *BT* ii.21(1), f. 13^r.

375. Baxter has more arguments, but they do not present anything new when compared to his earlier writings against Owen.

It is intriguing that Baxter cautiously acknowledges a material identity. But here, also, he builds in reservations. He distinguishes temporal, spiritual, and eternal death.[376] Of temporal death he says that it is by far the least of the three. "And for Death spirituall, I know no sober man y<a>^{t} doth Believe y<a>^{t} X^t was Dead in Sin, devoid of Gods Image, or of ye least measure of it." With respect to eternal death he comments that Christ did not suffer death eternally as to the duration.[377]

Baxter then distinguishes between suffering in body and in soul. With regard to the former, Christ "suffered not ye flames of Hell fire on his Body ..."[378] The suffering of the soul consists especially in

> ye worme of Conscience, or selfe Accusation, & self tormenting, by continuall app^r<e>hensions of ye exceeding folly & wickednes y<a>^{t} they were Guilty of, in refusing X^t & Grace & p^r<e>ferring ye Creature & excluding y<e>^{m}s.<elves> from ye hopes of Glory. Now X^t was not capable of ye least measure of this ...[379]

To this he adds, as if by way of concession, "Yet I doubt not but X^t felt y<a>^{t} Sorrow in his Soule w<hi>^{ch} was ye effect of Gods displeasure at o<u>^{r} Sin ..."[380] To some extent, Baxter acknowledges an *idem materiale*.[381]

Baxter's reservations on this point parallel his earlier noted view that Christ, when he was hanging on the cross, was not hated by God. Christ did not bear the very *reatus culpae*, and consequently God did not hate him. Baxter's insistence that Christ did not take the very *reatus culpae* upon himself is closely connected to his view that Christ did not suffer the *solutio eiusdem*: Christ did not become a transgressor and therefore did not have to bear the formally identical punishment which the law threatened to the transgressor himself.

Baxter's recourse to Aristotelian logic, with its distinction between form and matter, may clarify matters. If Owen would want to maintain a formal identity he would be forced to limit this formal identity to the punishment, rather than to the law as such, which mentions both person and punishment. He does almost exactly this when he discusses the duration of Christ's suffering. While Baxter classifies the duration of the punishment as belonging to the matter of the punishment, Owen states that the duration of Christ's suffering need not be the same as the penalty threatened in the law: "When I say *the same*, I mean essentially the same

---

376. Also this distinction reoccurs in the same context in *Universal Redemption*, again in a condensed form when compared to the animadversions on Wallis (p. 79).
377. DWL MS *BT* ii.21(1), f. 14^r.
378. DWL MS *BT* ii.21(1), f. 14^r. Baxter added "(I think)," but later crossed it out.
379. DWL MS *BT* ii.21(1), f. 14^r. Cf. *Defence of Christ*, pp. 15-16: "They <*i.e.*, the "anti-gospellers"> say, That Christs satisfaction by Sacrifice, was the the <*sic*> *solutio ejusdem*, the payment of the same debts of suffering that was due to us; and not properly satisfaction, which is, *Redditio æquivalentis*, or *tantidem alias in debiti*: as if he had suffered death Spiritual by loss of Holiness, and the torments of Hell by an accusing Conscience, and the hatred of God."
380. DWL MS *BT* ii.21(1), f. 14^r.
381. Cf. Baxter, *Of Justification*, p. 264.

in weight and pressure, though not in all accidents of duration and the like ..."[382]
When Baxter retorts that one cannot speak of an *idem* if the accidents are not the
same,[383] Owen says that accidents like duration "follow and attend the person
suffering, and not the penalty itself."[384] Thus, Owen effectively separates penalty
and person. There is (formal) identity with regard to the former, not the latter. The
demand with respect to the person can be relaxed without any effect on the penalty
as such. The law is relaxed because of a substitution in person, but the penalty is
not changed.[385]

Baxter's use of the form/matter distinction does not really open a way out of
the impasse. The question still remains unanswered why a relaxation of the law
with respect to the person does or why it does not imply that one can no longer
speak of a *solutio eiusdem*. All in all, the debate is not decided in any conclusive
manner. Nevertheless, Baxter has accomplished something by his use of the form/
matter distinction and by forcing Owen to admit that the duration of the suffering
is only accidental to the person threatened. The debate has made it very clear that
there are a number of elements in the punishment threatened by the law that do not
pertain to Christ's suffering.

It may seem as if the differences between Baxter and Owen on the *idem/
tantundem* issue are not overly significant. After all, does Owen not admit that the
law is relaxed? And does Baxter not acknowledge that, materially at least, Christ
suffered much of the punishment threatened by the law? The discussion should
indeed not blind one to the fact that there is important agreement on several points.
Nevertheless, the answer to the question whether Christ formally fulfilled the law
or not is more than a metaphysical nicety. J.I. Packer rightly suggests that, according to Baxter, "there is no reason why He <*i.e.*, God> should not modify or repeal
the penal sanctions of His law, if the principles of good government would not be
thereby violated."[386] Indeed, by allowing for a relaxation of the law rather than
insisting that Christ underwent the penalty of the law Baxter makes a fundamental
decision. By opting for Grotius' and Bradshaw's notions of the atonement Baxter
creates room for a continuation of the commination and penal effects of the law of
innocence, for the conditionality of the new law of grace and, consequently, for
man's righteousness as a necessary condition for continued and consummate justification.

---

382. Owen, *Death of Death*, in *Works* 10.269-70. Owen has been criticized for his use of Aristotelian
metaphysics in distinguishing between essence and attributes (Alan Clifford, "Geneva Revisited
or Calvinism Revised: The Case for Theological Reassessment," *ChM*, 100 [1986], 327-28;
Clifford, *Atonement and Justification*, pp. 129-30). Clifford's observation is correct. It should be
borne in mind, however, that Owen is not the only one to buttress his argument by using
Aristotelian logic. On precisely the same issue, the *idem/tantundem* question, Baxter also takes
recourse to Aristotelian metaphysics.
383. Baxter, *Aphorismes* II.144 (p. 305).
384. Owen, *Of the Death of Christ*, in *Works* 10.447.
385. At this point, one cannot but question Owen's motives for regarding the duration as an accident
belonging to the person rather than the penalty. It seems to be a rather arbitrary move, solely
intended to safeguard the *idem* with regard to the penalty.
386. Packer, "Redemption and Restoration," p. 458.

Packer's analysis is one-sided, however, and this makes him overstate his case. He describes Baxter's position as follows:

> Baxter's "political method" led him to a very different idea of God's law. To him, God's justice is merely a rectoral attribute, a characteristic quality of His government, and His laws are no more than means to ends. Like all laws, they may under certain circumstances be changed, if the desired end is attainable by other means. When man had fallen, and God purposed to glorify Himself by restoring him, He carried out His plan, not by *satisfying* the law, but by *changing* it. God's law is thus external to Himself. The penal law of works, with its sanction of death for sin, was enacted, not because it was a natural and necessary expression of the Divine character, but simply because efficient government required it. The demand for retribution was grounded in the nature of government rather than in the nature of God, and could be dispensed with if it seemed wise. Where orthodox Calvinism taught that Christ satisfied the law in the sinner's place, Baxter held that Christ satisfied the Lawgiver and so procured a change in the law. Here Baxter aligns himself with Arminian thought rather than with orthodox Calvinism.[387]

Baxter indeed thought that God modified the law, that Christ satisfied the Lawgiver rather than the law, and that this was due to rectorial considerations. Nevertheless, a number of qualifying comments are in order. In the first place, although God did, in a sense, "repeal" the penal sanctions of his law, Baxter qualifies this by insisting on a certain measure of material identity between Christ's suffering and the penalty threatened in the law. Second, as Alan C. Clifford has pointed out, despite Grotius' pervasive influence on Baxter, he kept some distance from the Dutch lawyer.[388] In his *Catholick Theologie* (1675), Baxter reflects:

> Though I owe much thanks to God for what, near thirty years ago, I learned from *Grotius de satisfact.* yet I must say that in this great question, whether Christ *satisfied* God for Sin as *Domino absoluto, vel ut parti læsæ, vel ut Rectori*, which he asserteth *alone*, I take him to come short of *accurateness* and *soundness* ...[389]

Baxter does not accept Grotius' thesis that Christ satisfied God as Rector only. After expressing his disagreement with Grotius, Baxter continues by saying that God relates to man as *Dominus Absolutus* or Owner, as *Rector Supremus*, and as *Amicus* or *Benefactor*. Sin injures God in all three of these relations. Thus, God must also be satisfied in all three relations, even though his punishing justice belongs formally only to God as Rector and satisfaction is made first and foremost to God as Rector.[390] It must be admitted, however, that Baxter does not present this slight modification of his view in his controversial writings and that his emphasis on God as Rector is pervasive whenever he speaks of Christ's satisfaction.

The third and most important objection to Packer's interpretation is that it dissociates God's rectorial function from his essence. According to this under-

387. Packer, "Redemption and Restoration," p. 305. Cf. Kevan, *Grace of Law*, pp. 66-68.
388. Clifford, *Atonement and Justification*, p. 130.
389. Baxter, *Catholick Theologie* I.ii.69.
390. Baxter, *Catholick Theologie* I.ii.69.

standing, Baxter held that God's justice is "merely" a rectorial attribute, grounded
in the nature of government "rather" than in the nature of God.[391] Thus, a false
dilemma is created. Nowhere does Baxter suggest that God's rectorial function is
not an essential characteristic. According to Packer, Baxter's Grotian view of the
atonement means that he asserts "explicitly that the necessity of punishing sin was
external to God, and not, therefore, unconditional."[392] As it is, however, Baxter
nowhere contemplates such an idea. It would fit better in the theological framework of the young Owen. It is not Baxter, but the young Owen, along with several
other high Calvinists, who deny the absolute necessity of satisfaction. Whereas
Baxter's "middle way" retains the notion that God's justice demands punishment
in a way consistent with his role as *Rector*, the extremes of the young Owen's high
Calvinism and Socinianism meet in their denial of the absolute necessity of satisfaction.

Conclusion

The differences between Baxter and his high Calvinist opponents come out clearly
in his understanding of the doctrine of the atonement. This makes it all the more
striking that Baxter buttresses his defense of the universality of redemption with
appeals to William Twisse. Twisse was able to assert that he had at least as broad
a view on this as the Arminians he opposed, because of his bifurcation of the will
of God. This same bifurcation lies at the basis of Baxter's view of the extent of the
atonement. To be sure, the influence of Hugo Grotius and William Bradshaw on
Baxter has been pervasive. Also, the similarities between Baxter and the Amyraldian school of thought are too obvious to be ignored. Baxter assigns a place to the
elements taken from these various theologians, however, within the bifocal system of thought which he has adopted from William Twisse.

The bifurcation of Baxter's theology becomes manifest in his explanation of
the extent of redemption. John Owen's one-end teleology argues entirely from
God's eternal plan of redemption and regards Christ's satisfaction of God's justice
as a means to God's glory. Owen further maintains that universal redemption
implies that God fails in his purpose. Baxter denies this charge, for he thinks that
Christ never intended to give faith to all those for whom he died.

The result is two different ways of handling the distinction between the sufficiency and efficiency of Christ's death. Owen only acknowledges an internal
sufficiency: a sufficiency located in the infinite value of Christ's sacrifice itself. It
would only be sufficient for the whole world *if* indeed it were meant for all.
Baxter, however, asserts the sufficiency of Christ's death for all in bold terms.
There are even a number of benefits which are not only sufficient, but also effi-

---

391. Packer, "Redemption and Restoration," p. 305. Cf. p. 458.
392. Packer, "Redemption and Restoration," p. 458.

cient for all. Pardon, sanctification, and glory belong to the fruits that are sufficient for all and efficient for the elect. Baxter goes as far as to suggest that
according to Christ's antecedent will his death is equal for all. According to his
subsequent will it is only for the elect. Thus, Baxter also explains the questions
surrounding this issue against the background of his understanding of the twofold
will of God.

Baxter's understanding of the extent of redemption also results in an outlook
on the nature of the atonement which differs from that of his high Calvinist
detractors. He does not take sides in the debate whether only Christ's passive or
also his active obedience is imputed. Instead, following Bradshaw and Grotius, he
moves the discussion to an altogether different level: neither Christ's active, nor
his passive obedience is imputed in a direct or proper sense. Both, however, and
also his habitual righteousness, are the "valuable consideration" on the basis of
which forgiveness is granted. Baxter therefore disagrees with John Crandon, John
Warner, and Christopher Cartwright, who all plead for the imputation of passive
righteousness only. Baxter maintains that Christ obeyed the ceremonial law not
for the recovery from his own sins but for the sake of others. He was not subject to
the law in the same way as others. His obedience was voluntary and by contract.
Moreover, his sufferings are only meritorious because of his obedient willingness
to undergo the penalty. Baxter concludes that passive obedience is only part of
Christ's imputed righteousness. But this does not mean that there is a strict or
direct double imputation, of passive obedience for pardon and of active obedience
for superadded righteousness. Against John Wallis, Baxter denies the existence of
a "negative righteousness," a *medium* between *iustum* and *iniustum*, which would
be the result of a strict double imputation view.

Baxter does accept that Christ's righteousness is imputed. Only, he disagrees
with the way in which some interpret this. John Crandon, for instance, argues that
just as Adam represented all mankind in breaking the old covenant, so Christ
represents the elect in the new covenant. Against this, Baxter objects that Christ is
head by contract. This means that he died not just for the elect but for all mankind.
Just as Adam's posterity would have had to withstand temptation in order to be
confirmed in a state of innocence, so also Christ's headship does not dissolve one
of the obligation to fulfill the condition. Christ and the believers remain distinct
persons. Union with Christ is primarily a political or relative union, not a personal
union. He is head *for* all mankind and is the actual head *to* all those who believe in
him. The former relates to God's will *de debito*, the latter to his will *de rerum
eventu*.

Baxter's opposition to personal union with Christ makes him also oppose
Tobias Crisp's notion that Christ took upon himself the very guilt of the fault
(*reatus culpae*) of the elect. Baxter denies that Christ took upon himself the person
of a sinner and thereby became the greatest sinner in the world. Christ only took
the guilt of the penalty (*reatus poenae*). If Christ had taken the *reatus culpae* as
well, this would have meant that man himself merits salvation and is no longer in
need of pardon. Baxter sees this consequence in the thinking of John Owen, who
maintains that Christ's representation of the elect means that they are "under

merit." According to Owen, union with Christ gives the elect a right to justification.

Baxter goes beyond a denial that Christ and the elect are one natural person. When Thomas Tully insists that Christ and the elect are not one natural, but one political person, because imputation is a legal matter, Baxter still objects. Christ is also not one person with the elect in a civil or legal sense. The only way in which Christ may be said to have suffered in the person of the sinner is if the word "person" is not meant in the ordinary sense of the word, if Christ is seen as the general head of all mankind. According to Baxter, Christ is Mediator in his own person. His merit is the mere *causa sine qua non* of justification. This means that his personal righteousness is not the material cause of our righteousness, except in a remote, indirect sense. Also, while Baxter admits that imputation may be called the formal cause of justification, he strenuously denies against William Eyre and Christopher Cartwright that Christ's personal righteousness is the formal cause of our justification. This is a most significant step in Baxter's thinking, for it is the way in which he creates room for man's personal righteousness in justification.

The denial of direct imputation leads to a corresponding view of the way in Christ is regarded as having fulfilled the law. Owen insists that Christ paid the very penalty threatened in the law (*solutio eiusdem*). Thus, he procured the benefits *ipso facto*, immediately delivering the debtors. Baxter opposes such an *ipso facto* delivery. Christ did not satisfy the law, but only the Lawgiver. His payment was only an equivalent payment (*solutio tantidem*). The law threatened the transgressor himself. It did not provide for substitution. Substitution is not compatible with a strict payment of the penalty demanded in the law. Owen attempts to salvage his position by maintaining that the penalty of the law is fully executed, but that the law is relaxed with regard to the person on whom the penalty is executed (as well as with regard to some other accidents, such as the duration of the suffering). Baxter, however, counters that a change in person means that there is no formal identity (*idem formale*) between the penalty as it was threatened and as Christ suffered it. To be sure, Baxter still considers God's justice as an essential attribute. In fact, God's rectorial function is more firmly entrenched in God's nature for Baxter than for those high Calvinists who deny the absolute necessity of satisfaction. God is not just *Dominus Absolutus*, but also *Rector*, demanding that his justice be satisfied.

Chapter VI

Works and Justification

Look not on Grace in one divided notion:
But the concordant perfect frame and motion:
Take not one single part, but view the whole,
As it's the Health and Beauty of the Soul;
The Life, the Strength, the Glory, the Delight,
And that which makes it lovely in God's sight;
The honour, safety, gain, and true content;
And that which must the pains of Hell prevent:[1]

(Richard Baxter)

Introduction

The discussions surrounding the atonement make clear that Baxter's scheme of thought creates room for man's fulfillment of the condition. Christ's righteousness is not imputed in a direct or immediate sense, insists Baxter. Strictly speaking, Christ's righteousness is neither the material, nor the formal cause of our justification. What is more, Christ never took upon himself our *reatus culpae*. He was not hated by God. Accordingly, Christ did not suffer the *solutio eiusdem*, as it was threatened in the law. All of these ideas are consistent with other elements of Baxter's theology. A doctrine which creates some distance between Christ's righteousness and the righteousness of the believer logically makes room for man's personal righteousness in connection with justification. Baxter's emphasis on constitutive justification, especially in his discussions with Thomas Hotchkis and Cyrus Du Moulin make sense because of the rejection of immediate imputation. Also Baxter's insistence that justification is, in a sense, by degrees and that chastisements of the believers are God's punishments may well be regarded as the natural outcome of Baxter's view on the atonement. What is more, when he denies that faith is the instrument of justification and regards faith instead as a mere condition, his motivation lies in his fear of attributing efficiency to faith itself. According to Baxter, faith itself does not receive Christ's righteousness in a direct way. Thus, the various elements of Baxter's position find their point of confluence in his understanding of the atonement as laying the meritorious foundation rather than being the righteousness by which man is directly or immediately justified.

---

1. In Banks, "Poems of Richard Baxter," p. 136 (emphasis throughout in original).

At several points in the preceding chapters, reference has been made to the impact of the various elements of Baxter's thinking on man's role in justification. Baxter's opponents are afraid that he introduces justification by works and returns to a Roman Catholic doctrine of justification. It has been noted that Lewis Du Moulin and William Eyre place justification prior to faith in the *ordo salutis* partly because they are afraid of justification by works: since faith is a good work and belongs to sanctification, it must necessarily follow justification *in foro Dei*. Also, Crandon insists that when Baxter regards the chastisements of the elect as punishments he comes close to the doctrine of Rome, which holds that by suffering man may satisfy God's justice. Finally, the large role which Baxter assigns to common grace as preparative for special grace also points to works being significant for justification, even in the unregenerate.

Baxter's general tendency to emphasize the necessity of works for justification is beyond doubt. Other questions, however, still remain unaddressed. What, for instance, is the relation between his theory of the atonement and his emphasis on man's role in justification? Also, given the fact that man's role in justification is important, what is the relation between Christ's righteousness and man's righteousness? What is the relation between faith and works in justification? Is it true that when Baxter highlights the need for works he abandons the Protestant line of thinking about justification?

The first question which must be investigated is the relationship between the atonement and the role of works in justification. That Baxter's theory of the atonement plays a pivotal role in his doctrine of justification is not only evident from the way in which he connects the nature of the atonement as *solutio tantidem* with his understanding of indirect imputation, but also from the fact that his view on the atonement determines his understanding of the covenant and of twofold righteousness. It is necessary, therefore, to analyze Baxter's view of the covenant as well as his theory of twofold righteousness as the link between his interpretation of the atonement and the role of works in justification.

Atonement and the Covenant

THE POSITION OF CHRIST

Christ under a Threefold Law

Baxter's doctrine of the covenant provides the basis from which he legitimizes the role of works in justification. As noted already, unlike some of his high Calvinist opponents, Baxter does not believe that there is an eternal covenant of redemption between the Father and the Son in addition to God's decree and the Old Testament promises. To my knowledge, Baxter nowhere indicates the historical source of his denial of an eternal *pactum salutis*. Nevertheless, his position is eminently conducive to the introduction of a conditional element in justification.

Some might want to question whether Baxter really and unequivocally abandons the notion of an eternal *pactum salutis*. Does Baxter not repeatedly charge his opponents with the confusion of two covenants: the pact between the Father and the Son, and the covenant of grace?[2] Does the possibility of such a confusion not assume the existence of an eternal covenant of redemption? This would be a misunderstanding. When Baxter admits that there is a covenant between the Father and the Son, he does not refer to an eternal covenant but to the temporal law which the Father imposed on Christ. It is this temporal covenant between the Father and the Mediator which, according to Baxter, high Calvinists have a tendency to confuse with the covenant of grace: "They confound Gods Covenant with Christ as Mediator, imposing on him his Mediatorial part, and the Covenant of the Father and Son, with faln Man, imposing on them the terms of Recovery and Life."[3] That Baxter is merely referring to a temporal covenant of the Mediator is also clear from the position which this covenant receives within the *locus* of the covenant. Baxter sometimes deals with the covenant of the Mediator in between the covenant of innocence and the covenant of grace;[4] at other times, he locates it in between the period of the covenant of grace before the incarnation and the subsequent period.[5] Both positions of the mediatorial covenant underline its historical character.

Baxter maintains that Christ as Mediator was under a different law or covenant than the believers are. In his *Aphorismes of Justification*, Baxter argues that Christ performed several works that he was not obliged to perform. By way of example, Baxter mentions

> all the works that are proper to his office of Mediator, his assuming the Humane Nature, his making Laws to his Church, his establishing and sealing the Covenant, his working Miracles, his sending his Disciples to convert and save the world, enduing them with the Spirit, his overcoming Death and rising again, &c.[6]

All these tasks are specific to Christ's mediatorial office. Accordingly, Baxter insists that "all the works proper to the office of Mediatourship" were only required of Christ, not of the believers.[7]

In his later writings, Baxter systematizes these thoughts. The law to which Christ was subject, was "peculiar to himself."[8] Baxter then continues by saying that

> this Law given to our Mediator had three parts. 1. That he should perfectly obey the Law of Innocency so far as it was fitted to his case, and overcome the Tempter. 2. That he should perfectly keep the Law of *Moses*, so far as it agreed to him. 3. That

---

2. Baxter, *Of Justification*, p. 263; *Breviate*, p. 10. Cf. p. 19; *Defence of Christ*, pp. 8, 10.
3. Baxter, *Defence of Christ*, p. 8.
4. Baxter, *Of Imputation*, pp. 80-84; *Defence of Christ*, p. 57; *End of Doctrinal Controversies*, pp. 121-26.
5. Baxter, *Catholick Theologie* I.ii.37-42; *Breviate*, p. 4.
6. Baxter, *Aphorismes* I.57 (p. 39).
7. Baxter, *Aphorismes* II.128 (p. 295).
8. Baxter, *Breviate*, p. 4.

he should perfectly do all that was proper to the Redeemer, in being a Sacrifice for sin, clearing and publishing the New Covenant; sealing it by Miracles, rising again, instituting his Word, Sacraments and Ministry, ascending, giving the Spirit, interceding in Heaven, &c. his promised reward being the success of his undertaking, the saving of his Church and his Glory, in the glorifying of God the Father: This is the peculiar Law to the Mediator.[9]

Baxter's opposition to the notion that Christ's righteousness is directly and properly ours may now be understood from a different angle. Baxter insists that Christ had a law or a covenant of mediation which was proper to himself and which must be distinguished from the law of grace. As Isolde Jeremias puts it: "Christi Gerechtigkeit kann nicht auf irgendeinen Gläubigen Übertragen werden, weil sie einem anderen Bund, dem Bund der Vermittlung, angehört."[10]

All Things in the Hands of Christ

By making a sharp distinction between the law of mediation and the law of grace, Baxter makes room for new conditions within the law grace, conditions which were neither part of the law of nature or innocence, nor of Christ's law of mediation. The question must be asked, however, in which way Baxter comes to posit a new law of grace after he has disconnected the covenant of the Mediator and the covenant of grace. In other words: what is the relationship between the covenant of the Mediator and the covenant of grace?

The basis for this new law of grace comes to the fore when Baxter gives a description of the immediate benefit of Christ's work of redemption. In the eighth thesis of his *Aphorismes*, Baxter describes it as follows: "WHerefore the Father hath delivered all things into the hands of the Son; and given him all power in heaven and earth, and made him Lord both of the dead and living. Joh. *13.3*. Mat. *28.18*. Joh. *5.21,22,23,27*. Rom. *14.9*."[11] Baxter acknowledges that by his divine nature Christ was one with God the Father and had an "absolute soveraignty" over everything. He then adds, however, that "there is further a power given him as Mediator to dispose of all at his pleasure, to make new laws to the world, and to deal with them according to the tenor of those laws ..."[12] Christ has thus purchased "all things under his power or dominion."[13] Although the Father has properly not lost any power, nevertheless, Christ is more than just the Father's vicegerent, insists Baxter.[14] Indeed, by giving Christ the power to suspend or dispose of the strict covenant of works, "God having parted with that advantage which his Jus-

---

9. Baxter, *Breviate*, p. 4. Baxter makes exactly the same division of the law that Christ was under in *Catholick Theologie* I.ii.41; *Of Imputation*, pp. 82, 126; *Methodus Theologiæ* III.i.15; *Breviate*, p. 61; *End of Doctrinal Controversies*, pp. 121-22. Cf. Packer, "Redemption and Restoration," p. 245.
10. Jeremias, "Richard Baxters Catholic Theology," p. 76. Baxter indeed speaks of a "covenant of redemption," although it is clear that he does not mean an eternal covenant of redemption.
11. Baxter, *Aphorismes* I.61 (p. 41) (emphasis inverted).
12. Baxter, *Aphorismes* I.63 (p. 42).
13. Baxter, *Aphorismes* I.64 (p. 43).
14. Baxter, *Aphorismes* I.64 (p. 43).

tice had against the sinning world, and having relaxed that Law, whereby he might have judged us, is therefore said to judg no man, but to give all judgment to the Son. *Joh.* 5.22,27."[15] Thus, the upshot of Baxter's argument is that Christ has received the right to relax the law of works. Consequently, when discussing the immediate benefits of his death, Baxter comments: "The suspending of the rigorous execution of the sentence of the Law, is the most observable immediate effect of Christs death; which suspension is some kinde of deliverance from it."[16]

Christopher Cartwright takes exception to Baxter's idea that God has relaxed the law. He comments that God himself will still judge, although not in an immediate sense, but through Christ.[17] Baxter retorts that it is clearly Christ's office as rightful King to judge all people *ex officio*. Christ is King not only of the believers, but – at least *de iure* – of the whole world.[18] Referring to John 5:22 – "For the Father judgeth no man, but hath committed all judgment unto the Son" – Baxter insists:

> I think the Text means plainly, that God as mere Legislator of the Law of Works, judgeth no man, but hath given all judgment to the Son, as Redeemer and Legislator of, or Judg according to a Law of Grace, or on terms of Grace. It is not now *Deus-Creator secundum fœdus operum solum, sine Remedio: Sed Deus-Redemptor.*[19]

Cartwright says that Baxter's arguments are beside the point because he had never meant to deny that Christ would judge the world according to his office as King.[20] There is indeed some kind of formal agreement between the two opponents on this point. Yet, there is an underlying difference which perhaps does not surface sufficiently in the discussion. Although Cartwright admits that the Father judges through the Son, the Son's right to judge does not have a central theological function in Cartwright's thinking. For Baxter, however, it is important that the Father has given all judgement to the Son. The Son's power to rule underlies Baxter's doctrine of the covenant of grace. Thus, Baxter distinguishes between God as *Deus Creator* and *Deus Redemptor*. *Deus Creator* made the first law, which required perfect obedience. But, says Baxter, God receives satisfaction, "he giveth up all to the *Redeemer*, and *himself judgeth no man, but giveth all judgment to the Son* ..."[21] Baxter, unlike Cartwright, needs the notion that the Son has received all judgement because it enables Baxter to posit the origin of a new law of grace.

---

15. Baxter, *Aphorismes* I.65 (p. 43).
16. Baxter, *Aphorismes* I.67-68 (p. 44).
17. Cartwright, in Baxter, *Account of my Consideration*, p. 39; Cartwright, *Exceptions*, pp. 15-16, 23.
18. Baxter, *Account of my Consideration*, p. 41. Cf. *Of Imputation*, p. 81.
19. Baxter, *Account of my Consideration*, p. 40. In defense of his position, Baxter appeals to John Calvin, Hugo Grotius, Christoph Pelargus (1565-1633), and David Pareus. Scripture texts to which Baxter refers are John 5:22, 27; Luke 19:27; Matt 25; 28:18; Rom 14:9; Rev 1:18; Acts 17:31; 1 Cor 15:28; Dan 7:13; Acts 17:31; 1 Pet 4:5; and Ps 72:1.
20. Cartwright, *Exceptions*, pp. 15-16.
21. Baxter, *Account of my Consideration*, p. 80. Cf. *Substance*, p. 40: "God's first Law of Nature was made by him as *Creator*, or as *Rector ex jure Creationis*: But his Law of Grace is made by him as *Redeemer*, or as *Rector ex jure Redemptionis.*"

In later writings, Baxter refines his argument by taking recourse to a distinction which runs parallel to the distinction between God's *voluntas de rerum eventu* and his *voluntas de debito*. As noted earlier, Baxter distinguishes between the antecedent and the consequent acts of Christ as Ruler.[22] Baxter similarly maintains that Christ, having satisfied God as Lawgiver, now receives a double right: a *novum ius dominii* and a *novum ius imperii*.[23] The former corresponds to God's will *de rerum eventu*, the latter to his will *de debito*.

In his *Universal Redemption*, Baxter gives a careful description of what Christ does as Owner of all mankind and what he does as Ruler of all mankind. As Owner, or *Dominus Absolutus*, having a new right of property over mankind, Christ grants many outward and inward means. The degree to which these means succeed, varies according to his absolute disposal. Thus, Christ gives special grace to some. To these people

> he giveth his Spitit <*sic*> to work in such seasons, manner and measure, (accompanied with congruous providential occurrences and removal of temptations and hindrances) as shall infallibly prevail, 1. For to bring them to Faith; and 2 To further Sanctification and Perseverance. In a word he useth such means with all his Elect as shall infallibly succeed, to bring them to Faith and Perseverance; and so much with all the World, as shall leave them all without excuse.[24]

As *Dominus Absolutus* Christ dispenses means and establishes the success of their use. As *Rector*, however, he deals with people by means of laws. He takes down the old law, establishes new ones, and gives relative benefits – such as union with Christ, justification, adoption, and membership of the universal church – as well as real benefits – such as sanctification, eternal life, and sentential justification.[25]

Baxter's intention is clear. He wants to distinguish between two aspects of God's dealing with man: the sovereign, absolute relation between the Owner and his creatures as well as the relation between the Ruler and his rational, responsible subjects. Baxter therefore adopts the distinction between God's absolute will and his conditional will, between Christ's *novum ius dominii* and his *novum ius imperii*. The distinction between these two aspects of God's dealing with man coincides with the distinction between absolute predestination and the conditional covenant. According to God's eternal decree he "may do with his own as he list."[26] In the covenant of grace he intends that "Faith shall be the prescribed means to Glory, and Glory the end promised to all that perform that condition; and so conditionally giveth it."[27]

---

22. Cf. above, p. 211.
23. Baxter, *Universal Redemption*, pp. 11-12, 430. As far as I am aware, Baxter first makes this distinction in *Admonition*, p. 25.
24. Baxter, *Universal Redemption*, p. 20.
25. Baxter, *Universal Redemption*, p. 15. Throughout his treatise, Baxter uses the distinction between Christ as Owner or *Dominus Absolutus* and as *Rector* or Legislator (*Universal Redemption*, pp. 12-20, 28, 186-88, 305, 346-47, 364-65, 381-82, 414-15, 424-26).
26. Baxter, *Universal Redemption*, p. 305.
27. Baxter, *Universal Redemption*, p. 306.

Faith As Procured by Christ

When Baxter considers Christ's new right to the world as the immediate effect of his death, one might ask what the relation is between his death and faith. Did Christ not procure faith by means of his death? Did he only obtain the new right over all things? This question is the subject of a profound disagreement between Baxter and Owen. Owen regards sanctification and faith as a "proper immediate fruit and procurement of the death of Christ in all them for whom he died ..."[28] He demands an answer to the question whether Christ merited faith for us. If he did, he must have done so either absolutely or conditionally. If he did it absolutely, all must absolutely believe. If, however, he did it on condition, then Owen wants to know what the condition is. Surely, it must be faith. Concludes Owen rhetorically: "So the condition of faith is faith itself. *Christ procured that they should believe, upon condition that they do believe!* Are these things so?"[29]

Baxter resorts to his distinction between Christ as *Rector per leges* and as *Dominus Absolutus*.[30] Christ gives some fruits of his death as Ruler, while he gives others as Absolute Lord. Baxter rejects the idea that God gave faith in exchange for Christ's bloodshed.[31] Rather, says Baxter,

> Jesus Christ as a Ransom dyed for all, and as *Rector per Leges*, or Legislator he hath conveyed the Fruits of his death to all; that is, those Fruits which it appertained to him as Legislator to convey, which is right to what his New Law or Covenant doth promise. But those Mercies which he gives as *Dominus Absolutus*, arbitrarily besides or above his engagement, he neither gives nor ever intended to give to all that he dyed for ...[32]

Faith is one of the mercies that Christ gives "arbitrarily." He does not do so as Legislator, but as Absolute Lord, having acquired a new right of ownership, a *novum ius dominii*.

This also means that Owen's rhetorical questions do not really affect Baxter. Baxter does not argue that Christ has procured faith conditionally. Therefore, he can not be held to argue that Christ has procured faith on the condition of faith. For Baxter, faith is given absolutely. It is Christ's gift as Absolute Owner. Since God has given to him all men on the basis of his redemption, Christ now has the right both to make new laws as Legislator, and to "give further mercies, over and above

---

28. Owen, *Death of Death*, in *Works* 10.253.
29. Owen, *Death of Death*, in *Works* 10.254. In addition to interrogating his imaginary opponent Owen also gives five positive reasons why faith is procured by Christ's death: (1) Christ purchased sanctification, of which faith is formally a part; (2) all fruits of election are purchased by Jesus Christ, and faith is a principal fruit (Eph 1:4; Rom 8:30; Eph 1:9; 1 Cor 4:7; Acts 13:48; Rom 11:7); (3) all blessings of the new covenant are procured by Christ, and faith is one of these (Jer 31:33-34; Heb 8:10-12; Ezek 36:25-27); (4) that without which one cannot be saved must be procured by him who fully saves, and faith is of such necessity for salvation (Heb 11:6; Mark 16:16; Matt 1:21; Heb 9:12; 7:25); and (5) Scripture expressly states that faith is procured by Christ's death (Phil 1:19; Eph 1:3; Heb 12:2).
30. Baxter, *Universal Redemption*, pp. 42, 414, 424-26.
31. Baxter, *Universal Redemption*, p. 425.
32. Baxter, *Universal Redemption*, pp. 425-26.

what he giveth right to by that Law, being absolute Lord, he may do with his own as he list ..."[33]

Owen maintains that if it is true that Christ's death procures faith absolutely, universal redemption would logically imply universal salvation as well. His argument does not really impinge on Baxter's position. His view is not that faith is procured absolutely; rather, it is procured indirectly. Faith, maintains Baxter, is only a remote fruit, flowing not directly from Christ's death, but from the new right to ownership which he has received by means of his death.[34] In a direct sense, Christ's death did not purchase faith at all. The expression that Christ purchased faith is an "improper and unfit phrase," even though "rightly explained" it has some truth in it.[35] Baxter's position may be charted as follows:

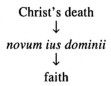

Christ's death
↓
novum ius dominii
↓
faith

Faith is not procured conditionally. Neither is it the absolute direct effect of Christ's death. Rather, it is something which his death has made possible. It is given directly by Christ as *Dominus Absolutus*, on the basis of his new ownership which he has acquired by his death.[36]

THE COVENANT AND JUSTIFICATION

The Federal Structure of Baxter's Theology

Baxter's doctrine of the covenant is based on his understanding of the twofold new right acquired by Christ. This becomes clear especially in the disagreement between Baxter and Cartwright concerning the role of the law of nature after the Fall. To properly evaluate this difference, some understanding of the basic outline

---

33. Baxter, *Universal Redemption*, pp. 423-24.
34. Baxter, *Universal Redemption*, pp. 417, 419, 430-31.
35. Baxter, *Universal Redemption*, p. 430.
36. Although Baxter's argument is mainly based on the distinction between Christ as *Rector per leges* and as *Dominus Absolutus*, he also uses the following arguments: (1) personal faith in Jesus as Christ is not needed for infants or for those who died before the incarnation. Therefore, it cannot be a direct fruit of Christ's death (*Universal Redemption*, p. 413). (2) Christ's death is not pleasing to God as such, but only as it is satisfaction. Therefore, any following effects of Christ's death presuppose satisfaction. God esteems this satisfaction meritorious of further benefits, such as faith (pp. 418-19). (3) Christ does not give all the fruits of his death to all that he died for (*e.g.*, prophecy, tongues, teaching, health, etc.). Hence, Christ's death did not procure these gifts directly (pp. 426-28). (4) God created all mankind in Adam for further happiness. Yet, in creating them he did not have the decree to save all people. There is no reason why it would be different in the case of Christ's satisfaction (pp. 433-34).

of Baxter's doctrine of the covenant is required.[37] Several people have commented on the central place of the covenant in Baxter's theology. Richard A. Muller goes as far as to suggest that "Baxter's entire system, doctrinal and practical, coalesces around the concept of the divine covenanting."[38] In a sense, this is perhaps somewhat of an exaggeration. Baxter's doctrine of justification was frequently the subject of controversy, but no one really focused his attack on Baxter's view of the covenant. Also, Baxter never devoted a single treatise to the doctrine of the covenant.

Nevertheless, Muller's comment is perceptive. Baxter's *Aphorismes of Justification* begin which a large section in which he explains the nature of the covenants. In this section, he discusses numerous aspects of his understanding of atonement and justification. Also, when he deals with the doctrine of the covenant in later treatises, he often touches upon various soteriological issues. It would by no means be impossible to give a systematic description of Baxter's soteriology centered around the doctrine of the covenant.[39] On several occasions, scattered throughout his writings, Baxter presents his understanding of the doctrine of the covenant, usually in an organized fashion.[40] Although his understanding of the covenant as such has never been the subject an extended controversy, Baxter disagrees with Cartwright on an important aspect of the doctrine of the covenant, an aspect which has an immediate bearing on the doctrine of justification as well. It is useful, therefore, to give a brief description of Baxter's understanding of the doctrine of the covenant.

By way of terminological clarification, it should be mentioned that Baxter often uses the terms "law" and "covenant" indiscriminately. Technically speaking, there is a difference between the two. The word "law" signifies one's duty with its retribution, while the word "covenant" implies a mutual contract.[41] But whenever Baxter is not concerned to draw attention to these specific elements, he is satisfied to use both words interchangeably. He thinks that there are essentially two covenants: the covenant of nature and the covenant of grace. The law of nature comes to expression in the prelapsarian covenant with Adam. Although he was unable to merit anything from God by way of commutative merit, God did

37. For Baxter's doctrine of the covenant, see Fisher, "Theology of Richard Baxter," 166; Highfill, "Faith and Works," pp. 64-68; Packer, "Redemption and Restoration," pp. 236-51; Jeremias, "Richard Baxters Catholic Theology," pp. 52-77; W.C. De Pauley, "Richard Baxter Surveyed," *CQR*, 164 (1963), 34-35; Kevan, *Grace of Law*, pp. 150, 152-55, 204-07; Richard A. Muller, "Covenant and Conscience in English Reformed Theology: Three Variations on a 17th Century Theme," *WThJ*, 42 (1980), 327-34.
38. Muller, "Covenant and Conscience," 328. Cf. Fisher: "Baxter's view of Justification is best learned by observing his doctrine of the Covenants" ("Theology of Richard Baxter," 166); also De Pauley: "Baxter's basic biblical idea throughout is that of 'covenant' ... ("Richard Baxter Surveyed," 34).
39. I do not agree with Isolde Jeremias, who asserts that Baxter was an unsystematic thinker and says: "Baxter definiert in keinem seiner Werke die Termini der Bünde Gottes zusammenhängend, setzt aber auf der anderen Seite ihr Verständnis voraus" ("Richard Baxters Catholic Theology," p. 53).
40. Baxter, *Catholick Theologie* I.ii.27-51; *Of Imputation*, pp. 80-84; *Account of my Consideration*, pp. 144-56; *Breviate*, pp. 1-5; *End of Doctrinal Controversies*, pp. 99-154, 188-202. Baxter's *Methodus Theologiæ* is centered around the various stages of the kingdom of God, for which one might well substitute the various stages of the covenant of works and of grace.
41. Baxter, *End of Doctrinal Controversies*, pp. 99-100.

promise life to Adam on the condition of perfect love and obedience. Because the "covenant of innocency" contained a promise it may rightly be called a covenant.[42] Sin made such a covenant with the condition of perfect obedience impossible. Baxter concludes that "every Sin maketh Punishment so far due to the Faithful, as that they have need of the *Grace of Christ*, and the *new Covenant* to *pardon* it."[43]

This leads Baxter to the second covenant: the covenant of grace. Within this covenant, he distinguishes two editions.[44] The first was introduced in Genesis 3:15 and was made with Adam as the head of mankind. The law of grace is therefore universal in scope.[45] This first edition was renewed with Noah as "a second Head and Father to the generality of all Mankind."[46] At that time, God also made some small additions to the covenant.[47] It is important to understand what this first edition of the law of grace entails: all people receive continuation of life out of grace. This implies that, to some degree, there is forgiveness for all.[48] There is now a demand to repent and return to God. There is hope of mercy, and all people are obliged to use the means that God gives.[49] As time progresses, the supernatural revelation of redemption in Christ becomes clearer.[50]

Baxter considers the covenant with Abraham as part of the first edition of the covenant of grace. The reason why God renewed the covenant with Abraham was that he wanted to reward him for his eminent faith and obedience.[51] This Abrahamic covenant is also called a "covenant of peculiarity." Not only is it a renewal of the covenant made with Adam and Noah, but Abraham also received the peculiar promise "that his *Seed* should be a *holy Nation* chosen out of all the world to God, and that of him the *Messiah* should come, of *both* which *Promises* (the *common* and the *special*) *Circumcision* was a Seal."[52]

With Moses came the "full Establishment" of this covenant of peculiarity.[53] Baxter considers it an "appendix" to the common law of grace.[54] His doctrine of

42. Baxter, *End of Doctrinal Controversies*, pp. 114-15.
43. Baxter, *End of Doctrinal Controversies*, p. 120.
44. Baxter speaks of two editions of the covenant of grace, thereby suggesting that the two editions together constitute one covenant of grace. When he explicitly discusses the question whether these two editions form one or two covenants, whether they are the same or diverse, he comments that these "are but needless questions about the bare *Name* of *Oneness*, as long as we agree wherein they differ, and wherein they differ not" (*End of Doctrinal Controversies*, p. 140). Baxter then proceeds to list a number of differences between the two editions.
45. Says Baxter: "This Law or Covenant in this *first Edition* was made with *Adam* as the Father of all Mankind, and so with *all Mankind in him*, as truly and as much as the Covenant of Innocency was ..." (*End of Doctrinal Controversies*, p. 131). Cf. *Breviate*, p. 2.
46. Baxter, *End of Doctrinal Controversies*, p. 131.
47. Comments Baxter: "It's very probable, that not only the Decalogue in sence; but also all, or most of the particular Mosaical Precepts, which are but the Instances, Explications, and Applications of those Generals, were given before the Flood ..." (*End of Doctrinal Controversies*, p. 194).
48. Baxter, *End of Doctrinal Controversies*, p. 128.
49. Baxter, *End of Doctrinal Controversies*, p. 129.
50. Baxter, *End of Doctrinal Controversies*, p. 130; *Breviate*, p. 4.
51. Baxter, *Catholick Theologie* I.ii.32; *Breviate*, p. 3; *End of Doctrinal Controversies*, p. 132.
52. Baxter, *Catholick Theologie* I.ii.32.
53. Baxter, *End of Doctrinal Controversies*, p. 134.
54. Baxter, *End of Doctrinal Controversies*, pp. 134, 137.

the covenant is slowly turning into an intricate system of interrelated laws. The Israelites were not just bound by the Sinaitic law. Baxter mentions four parts of God's law, that all obliged the nation of Israel.[55] First, the preceptive part of the law of nature was still in force. Second – and for the present purpose of great importance – the Jewish nation still had the "Universal Covenant of Grace made with all mankind in *Adam* and *Noah*." Third, the special promise to Abraham and his seed was for the whole nation. Finally, the Israelites were bound to the law of Moses with its political elements. According to Baxter, it is this last covenant of peculiarity, as made with the nation of Israel under Moses, which Paul usually calls the law of works. He does this

> because of the great and burdensome and costly Externals before mentioned, and because as a *political* Law it so much insisteth comparatively on those Externals, and the Doctrine of Grace is comparatively more obscure in it than in the Gospel; and because the Jews had by their abusive Interpretation overvalued the Externals and operous Ceremonies and Sacrifices of it.[56]

Baxter warns against a mistaken interpretation of Paul's quotation from Moses, that "the man which doeth those things shall live by them" (Rom 10:3; Gal 3:12). Paul does not mean to say that the condition of the Jewish covenant of peculiarity was identical to that of the law of innocence.[57] Perfection was only the condition of the latter.

The second or last edition of the covenant of grace was inaugurated by the coming of Christ. Baxter describes it as a covenant of grace as well as a covenant of peculiarity. In the latter sense it far excels the Jewish covenant of peculiarity.[58] As in the case of the covenant with the nation of Israel, so also here the universal covenant of grace is still in force. Says Baxter:

> For as the Jews had both the common *Covenant of Grace*, and also the *Covenant of Peculiarity*, setting them above all others; so the *Christian Church* hath both the common *Covenant of Grace*, and by the *second edition* of it a Covenant of *Peculiarity* ...[59]

As was the case in the first edition, so also here the precepts are more encompassing than the condition. It is noteworthy to examine what Baxter all regards as precepts of the law of Christ. Broadly speaking, Baxter identifies both the law of (lapsed) nature and the new remedying laws of grace (both faith and special institutions of church order, ministry, worship, etc.) as part of Christ's commands.[60] By mentioning these two elements Baxter indicates again that the universal covenant of grace remains in force.

---

55. Baxter, *Catholick Theologie* I.ii.35.
56. Baxter, *End of Doctrinal Controversies*, p. 137. Cf. *Scripture Gospel defended*, pp. 90-91.
57. Baxter, *End of Doctrinal Controversies*, p. 137.
58. Baxter, *End of Doctrinal Controversies*, p. 141.
59. Baxter, *End of Doctrinal Controversies*, p. 200.
60. Baxter, *Catholick Theologie* I.ii.43; *End of Doctrinal Controversies*, pp. 142, 149; *Breviate*, p. 71; *Universal Redemption*, p. 38.

The Law of Nature after the Fall

It is somewhat difficult to grasp the difference of opinion between Baxter and Cartwright on the role of the covenant of nature after the Fall. At times, Baxter minimizes the role of the law of nature, whereas Cartwright emphasizes its continuing function. On other occasions, Baxter agrees with his opponent that the precepts and threats of the law of nature are still in force. This does not mean that Baxter's view on the law of nature is inconsistent. Rather, his shifting attitude is caused by the difference in understanding which the respective authors have regarding the immediate benefits of Christ's work of redemption. Within the framework of Baxter's interpretation of the atonement, his attitude toward the law of nature is both understandable and consistent.

Baxter minimizes the role of nature when he discusses the possibility of salvation for those who are unfamiliar with the Gospel. According to Cartwright, those who have never heard the terms of the Gospel will be judged according to the covenant of works. Those to whom the covenant of grace has not been revealed will not be condemned as if they had despised it. Says Cartwright: "That the Covenant of Grace wherein Mercy is promised, being not revealed unto some, nor any way dispensed unto them, they cannot be said to be under it, nor shall be judged as transgressors of it."[61]

Baxter, however, does not believe that people are still under the law of works without any remedy. Against Cartwright, he insists that the numerous mercies which God shows to "the poorest Indians" means that he does not deal with them "merely on the terms of the Covenant of Works."[62] Also, unlike the mercies given according to the covenant of works, the mercies for pagans are intended to lead them to repentance.[63] Moreover, Christ as Mediator and King will judge all wicked men as his subjects *de iure*. They are rebellious subjects, judged according to the laws by which he rules.[64] Finally, Matthew 25 and other passages from Scripture indicate that all people will be judged according to their use of the talents of mercy: "No Scripture that I know of, doth once intimate, that God will say at last to any men, [*Go ye Cursed, because ye once sinned;*] or merely, [*because ye sinned,*] but because ye *sinned against Mercy that tended to Recovery.*"[65]

The conclusion may seem to be justified that Cartwright insists on the abiding role of the covenant of nature, whereas Baxter thinks that people will be judged according to the edition of the law of grace which applies to them. Cartwright seems to uphold the law of nature, and Baxter seems to minimize it. Although this is largely correct, some further scrutiny of the discussion between the two disputants yields a somewhat more refined picture. As noted already, Baxter maintains that since the Fall the prescriptions of the covenant are broader in scope than the condition. But the incision made by the Fall does not mean that the law of nature is

---

61. Cartwright, *Exceptions*, p. 9.
62. Baxter, *Account of my Consideration*, p. 23.
63. Baxter, *Account of my Consideration*, p. 23.
64. Baxter, *Account of my Consideration*, pp. 23-24.
65. Baxter, *Account of my Consideration*, p. 24.

simply abrogated. Baxter continues to speak of a "law of lapsed nature," which is a law of nature all the same. He calls it the "law of lapsed nature" in comparison to the old law as the law of innocent nature.[66]

In his *Aphorismes*, Baxter even argues that the law of works continues to command, prohibit, promise, and threaten. A few years later, after having received some private animadversions from George Lawson, Baxter changes this position. In 1655 he writes in his *Confession*: "In this point I retract what I delivered in my Aphorisms."[67] He now thinks that the covenant of works is – at least as a covenant – "null and void."[68] Lawson has convinced him that the promise of the covenant of works has ceased and that it is therefore no longer a covenant.[69] Baxter prefers to forbear the name "covenant of works" for the postlapsarian situation, because it was called a covenant "from Gods promise of life in that Law."[70] After the Fall, the promise has ceased:

> The promisory part of the Covenant or Law of Innocency became null or ceased with man's first sin, *cessante subditorum capacitate*; and so the *Condition* which is its *modus*. So that no man ever since was under the Obligation of that Law as a Covenant of life, saying [*Be Perfect or Innocent and Live*], nor obliged to *perfect personal perpetuall* obedience as the condition of Life; for it was become naturally impossible. And God maketh not Promises and Covenants upon *Natural* impossibilities, whatever we say of *Moral* ones.[71]

Since the Fall, God no longer posits the condition of perfect obedience. Man no longer has the natural capacity for such obedience.[72] Baxter means with this that God cannot command anyone to be sinless or perfectly obedient, because every person is already a sinner.[73] Cartwright rejects this argument. Why should one not

---

66. Baxter, *Catholick Theologie* I.ii.33; *End of Doctrinal Controversies*, p. 128.
67. Baxter, *Confession*, p. 101. On several occasions, Baxter acknowledges his indebtedness to Lawson on this point (DWL MS *BT* ii.21[1], f. 8ʳ; *Account of my Consideration*, pp. 56-57; *End of Doctrinal Controversies*, p. 192. Cf. Packer, "Redemption and Restoration," pp. 241, n. 1; 485-86; Kevan, *Grace of Law*, p. 150).
68. Baxter, *Confession*, p. 101. Cf. p. 106; *Substance*, p. 14.
69. Also in his *Theo-Politica*, Lawson states that when Christ was promised (Gen 3:15), God set up a new constitution. Lawson then continues: "By this promise the Covenant of *Works* was made *voyd*, and the *Law*, as promising life onely upon condition of *Perfect, Personall*, and *Perpetuall* obedience, without any Promise of *Pardon* of any the *least* sin was repealed ..." He adds that the sentence passed on man for his disobedience remains in force. Also, although "the Law of Works as a Condition, and only condition, of life be repealed, yet the pure Morals continue in force to bind man to obedience or punishment in generall, but not to obedience perfect, as the condition of life; or to punishment, as no wayes removeable" (*Theo-Politica* I.xiii.70).
70. Baxter, *Confession*, p. 106.
71. Baxter, *Catholick Theologie* I.ii.29. Cf. *Methodus Theologiæ* I.ii.391; *Breviate*, p. 70; *Scripture Gospel defended*, p. 91; *End of Doctrinal Controversies*, pp. 120, 193.
72. Cf. Packer, "Redemption and Restoration," pp. 240-41. Ernest F. Kevan says that Baxter's "reason for the abolition of the Covenant of Works arises from the humanistic philosophy which defines responsibility in terms of ability, and therefore regards man as no longer 'a capable subject' of such a covenant" (*Grace of Law*, p. 150). Kevan appeals to other Puritans, who distinguished between natural and moral ability and thought that man only had a moral inability to keep the law of works. This meant that man remained responsible (pp. 151-52). Kevan seems to be unaware that Baxter also makes the distinction between natural and moral inability. He insists that man has become not only morally, but also naturally incapable of fulfilling the law of innocence.
73. Baxter, *End of Doctrinal Controversies*, p. 192.

argue instead that because the precept does not cease – despite man's inability to perform it – therefore also the promise remains?[74]

Faith As a Requirement of the Law of Nature

Baxter's rejection of the continuing promissory character of the law of nature has several important implications for his theory of justification. Because the law of nature no longer has a promise it is properly no longer a covenant. It is no longer possible to be justified on the terms of the covenant of innocence. Baxter calls this "one of the chief points of all our difference."[75] According to Baxter, Christ did not fulfill the law of innocence but the law of the Mediator. Baxter is of the opinion that Christ, by fulfilling this law (which included the law of nature), received a new right over all things.

Baxter maintains that it is only the covenantal character of the law of nature which has ceased. This makes it impossible to speak of a law of innocence after the Fall. The promise is no longer valid. But the precepts of the law of nature remain. The law of (lapsed) nature itself continues: "You must distinguish between the Law of Natures obliging Man in Innocency, and the same Law as continued, obliging man faln ..."[76] In his *Aphorismes*, Baxter comments that Christ did not die for sins that were merely against the new covenant. The Gospel only threatens death for the sin of final unbelief and rebellion. Christ never died for this sin.[77] Cartwright disagrees: "I see not how final Unbelief, or any sin whatsoever, can be against the Gospel only, and not also against the Law; sin, as sin, being a transgression of the Law, 1 *John* 3.4. And there being no sin prohibited in the Gospel, which is not a breach of some Precept in the Decalogue ..."[78] Cartwright is of the opinion that all sin is sin against the law of works, and that Christ has satisfied by fulfilling this law.

Baxter goes a long way in expressing his agreement with Cartwright. He uses Cartwright's animadversion to enter on a lengthy digression about the relation between the law of works and the law of grace. Baxter explains that it is indeed true that faith is, in a sense, a requirement of the law of nature: "For now I think that all duties, with all their ends, are required by the Law of Nature, or that Law obligeth to them; and so to Faith, as it is a means of Remission, though this seemed strange to me heretofore."[79] Why and how does Baxter include faith in the law of nature? Is faith not obviously a demand of the law of grace? Baxter does not deny this. But he regards the law of nature as something which is more comprehensive than the law of grace:

---

74. Cartwright, *Exceptions*, p. 64.
75. Baxter, *Breviate*, p. 44. Cf. *End of Doctrinal Controversies*, p. 154: "It is of great importance in the Controversies of Justification, to know whether, or how far we shall be judged by the Law of Innocency, or whether only by the *Law of Grace*." Cf. p. 121.
76. Baxter, *Account of my Consideration*, pp. 145-46.
77. Baxter, *Aphorismes* I.159-60 (p. 103).
78. Cartwright, in Baxter, *Account of my Consideration*, p. 144.
79. Baxter, *Account of my Consideration*, p. 145.

As to the Decalogue and preceptive part of the Law of Works, as it is merely in *nature*, and was delivered at the first, I conceive it doth command *obedience* in *general*, and specifie all *natural duties*, and so forbid the *contrary* sin: But it doth not *specifie each particular duties* that *after* were added. I conceive that the Law of Nature, or Works, doth leave room after the first Institution, for the adding of new-*positives*, without making a new-*form* of the Law as to the *Sanction*.[80]

When man fell, new positive duties were added to the law of nature: faith and repentance. Baxter does not believe that faith and repentance only belong to the law of grace. The reason is that the law of nature binds us to all that God commands "when it is *made known*."[81] If this were not so, Baxter insists, there would have been a new law with every new command given by Moses.[82]

Baxter explains his meaning with an illustration:

Even as the earth that man's body was made of, ceased not to be truly earth when it was made man, nor ceaseth to be a proper or essential part of man, because it is earth. Or as a cup of water taken out of the River, and made Beer, ceaseth not to be water, nor yet can be denied to be Beer. Only it ceaseth to be mere or common water, as our bodies do to be mere common earth. So here the preceptive part of the Law of Nature, is comprehensive of the Law of Grace, and all Laws that ever will be ...[83]

According to Baxter, the law of nature remains in force. It even includes the law of grace because it is more comprehensive than the latter. In a manner strikingly reminiscent of John Cameron, Baxter describes the new law as "a *subservient Law* to the *Law of Nature*, being but *Lex remedians*."[84]

The question remains, of course, *how* the law of nature remains in force. As noted, Baxter does not believe that the law of nature retains its promise and its covenantal character. He thinks that the moral law remains part of the law of nature but also becomes part of Christ's law. There is a sense in which the deca-

---

80. Baxter, *Account of my Consideration*, p. 144.
81. Baxter, *Account of my Consideration*, p. 146.
82. Says Baxter: "So of *sacrificing before* Moses, *&c.* the sence of the Law was, [Obey God in all that he now doth, or hereafter shall command;] and Nature speaks so plainly. And when-ever the *Positive-Command* is added in any age, it is a fresh discovery of God's will, which *nature* obligeth us to obey: The Obligation is as much from the *general Precept* in *Nature*, as from the *particular* superadded ..." (*Account of my Consideration*, pp. 144-45).
83. Baxter, *Account of my Consideration*, p. 148. Cf. pp. 150, 256-57. Cf. Cartwright's reply: "This (I confess) to me is strange Philosophy, That the Earth, of which Man's Body was made, ceased not to be Earth still, when it was made Man. As well may you say, That *Adam*'s rib, of which *Eve* was formed, ceased not to be a Rib still; and so that all the Elements retain their several Natures in all mixt Bodies" (*Exceptions*, p. 63). Baxter himself also nuanced his position somewhat later on. In a marginal note added to the debate with Cartwright, Baxter comments: "If any had rather say, that the general Obligation to Obedience is more properly said to be our very *subjection*, and a result of God's Relation to us, than the effect of any Law, and so that it is neither the Old-Covenant nor the New that causeth this general Obligation, and so that Faith in Christ is a duty of the New-Covenant only, because it is there only commanded *in specie*, I think he will speak more properly than either Mr. *C.* or I have here done" (*Account of my Consideration*, p. 256).
84. Baxter, *Account of my Consideration*, p. 149. Baxter more often describes the law of grace as *lex remedians*, thereby indicating its subserviency to the law of nature (pp. 83, 257; *Admonition*, p. 25; *Confession*, p. 107). Baxter is aware of Cameron's teaching of the Mosaic covenant as subservient (*Aphorismes* I.145 [p. 94]).

logue remains in force. The decalogue is "done away" as it was part of the covenant of peculiarity with the people of Israel.[85] Baxter repeatedly argues that we are
no longer under the law of Moses as such.[86] Blake, however, maintains that the
moral law "as delivered by *Moses*, is binding on Christians."[87] He sees two ugly
extremes join hands in Baxter's demand of perfect righteousness in terms of conformity to the new law of grace: on the one hand those who add prescriptions to
the moral law: Papists, Socinians (and Arminians), and even Mohammedans; on
the other hand those who abolish the old rule: the Antinomians.[88] Also John
Crandon states that Baxter himself is guilty of the Antinomianism of which he
accuses his opponents. Crandon insists that "while Mr. *Baxter* declaimeth against
the innocent, hee proclaimes himselfe a rank Antinomian, in teaching, and maintaining that the perfect obedience and righteousnesse of the Law are not required,
and consequentially not due under the Gospel."[89] Baxter himself is also aware of
the consequence of his teaching. When he states that we are no longer under the
law of Moses as such, he adds not without humor: "If this be Antinomianism, I am
an Antinomian that have written so much against them."[90] The decalogue as moral
law remains, however, "as the *Law of Nature* and of *Christ*."[91] The moral law has
been delivered "into the hands of Christ."[92] Indeed, the entire law of lapsed nature
belongs to Christ's law: "The Law of Nature since the fall, is part of the Mediators
Law, by which in part he governeth: For it, with all things is deliver <sic> to
him."[93]

   For Baxter, then, it is everyone's duty to accept the offer of grace, to repent and
believe, and to be thankful, according to the law of nature, albeit in conjunction
with the law of grace.[94] What is more, although the promise of the covenant of
innocence has ceased, the threat remains. This means that unbelief as a transgression of the law of nature is still threatened with death.[95] After all, as Baxter in his
Aphorismes maintains with an appeal to Hugo Grotius, the law of works is not
abrogated, but only relaxed.[96] By now, Baxter has almost succumbed to the force

---

85. Baxter, *End of Doctrinal Controversies*, p. 138.
86. Baxter, *Account*, p. 52; *Catholick Theologie* I.ii.35; *Breviate*, p. 70. Cf. Kevan, *Grace of Law*, pp. 152-55.
87. Blake, *Covenant Sealed*, p. 600.
88. Blake, *Covenant Sealed*, pp. 601, 607.
89. John Crandon, *Aphorisms Exorized* I.xxii.277. Cf. sig. A4ʳ. Crandon is mistaken in his accusation that Baxter denies the requirement of perfect obedience and righteousness of the law. Baxter does not deny it as a requirement. He only states that it is not the law of Moses as such, but that it is the law of nature in the hands of Christ which obliges to perfect righteousness. Moreover, while maintaining the demand of perfect righteousness, Baxter denies that it is the condition of the law of grace.
90. Baxter, *Breviate*, p. 70.
91. Baxter, *End of Doctrinal Controversies*, p. 138.
92. Baxter, *Aphorismes* I.156 (p. 101). Baxter more often speaks of the moral law being delivered into the "hands" of Christ (*Confession*, p. 161; *Catholick Theologie* I.ii.29; *Universal Redemption*, p. 466). This expression was common place in Calvinist theology of this period, although some were cautious about its use for fear of Antinomian interpretations (Kevan, *Grace of Law*, pp. 184-87).
93. Baxter, *Universal Redemption*, p. 38.
94. Baxter, *Account of my Consideration*, p. 150; *End of Doctrinal Controversies*, pp. 127, 142.
95. Baxter, *Account of my Consideration*, p. 147.
96. Baxter, *Aphorismes* I.80-81 (p. 52).

of Cartwright's argument. If the law of nature is still in force with regard to its precepts as well as its threat, and if the entire moral law, including the command to repent and believe, is still part and parcel of the law of nature, would the logical consequence not be that unbelief is sin both against the law and the Gospel, as Cartwright insists? When Baxter says that the new law has both the precept and the threat in common with the old law, Cartwright demands:

> Here you seem to grant, That nothing is commanded, or threatned in the New Law, which is not commanded or threatned in the Old... The Precept [*believe*] belongs to the Old Law; but as it is not only a Precept, but also a Condition, upon performance of which Salvation is promised, [*Believe; and thou shalt be saved*] so it belongs to the New Law.[97]

Baxter feels the force of this argument. He admits: "I still confess, that for *Unbelief* and *Impenitency*, men remain *obligati ad pœnam per Legem naturæ*, till they believe, and so that Obligation be dissolved."[98] But Baxter salvages his position by distinguishing between temporary non-performance of the condition of the covenant and proper violation of the covenant. It is only *final* unbelief and impenitence which properly constitutes non-performance of the condition of the covenant of grace.[99] Baxter admits to Cartwright that unbelief is sin against the law of nature as well as the law of grace. But such temporary unbelief does not yet imply that the condition of the Gospel has not been fulfilled. Thus, Baxter continues to maintain the position outlined in his *Aphorismes*: the Gospel only threatens death to final unbelief and rebellion. People are ultimately judged by the law of grace, despite the abiding validity of the law of nature.

TWOFOLD RIGHTEOUSNESS

Origin of Baxter's Position

Baxter's theory of twofold righteousness forms a second link between his doctrine of the atonement and his understanding of the role of works in justification. In his *Aphorismes*, Baxter distinguishes between legal and evangelical righteousness.[100] Both, he insists, are "absolutely necessary to Salvation."[101] Baxter describes Christ's righteousness as legal righteousness. The believers' fulfillment of the condition is their evangelical righteousness:

---

97. Cartwright, *Exceptions*, p. 64.
98. Baxter, *Account of my Consideration*, p. 153.
99. Baxter, *Account of my Consideration*, p. 153.
100. Baxter, *Aphorismes* I.98-115 (PP. 63-75).
101. Baxter, *Aphorismes* I.102 (p. 66) (emphasis throughout in original). Baxter later qualifies this position somewhat when he states that external works of holiness are not absolutely necessary because death may occur immediately after conversion. He immediately adds, however: "Though I think no man can give us one instance of such a man *de facto:* not the thief on the cross: for he confessed prayed, reproved the other, &c." (*Of Justification*, p. 263; emphasis inverted). Cf. *Protestant Religion*, ed. Daniel Williams and Matthew Sylvester (London, 1692), p. 94.

> THe Righteousness of the New Covenant, is the only Condition of our interest in, and enjoyment of the Righteousness of the old. Or thus: Those only shall have part in Christs satisfaction, and so in him be legally righteous, who do beleive, and obey the Gospel, and so are in themselves Evangelically Righteous.[102]

While legal righteousness is in Christ, personal evangelical righteousness is the condition to partake of this legal righteousness.

It is impossible to trace the exact origin of Baxter's theory of twofold righteousness. He does not explain the background himself. In his *Aphorismes*, he discusses the issue without any extensive appeal to other divines. He only briefly mentions William Pemble's understanding of a twofold righteousness.[103] Pemble, however, distinguishes between conformity to the law and satisfaction for transgressions of the law as two kinds of righteousness.[104] Both types of righteousness refer to the same law of works. This is different from Baxter's distinction between legal and evangelical righteousness. Baxter himself recognizes this difference.[105] Also in his later works, Baxter does not discuss the immediate background to his theory of twofold righteousness. He only appeals to other theologians on a few occasions, and even then he does not state whether they had a direct impact on his thinking on this particular issue.

Baxter does claim that his theory of twofold righteousness can boast of a precedent in William Bradshaw's theology.[106] Bradshaw indeed speaks of a *duplex iustitia*.[107] Justification may either be considered as universal or as particular: "Universal, when the accused party is declared to be universally and entirely righteous (Rom 8:33). But particular when only with respect to this or that particular cause (Ps 7:3; 4:5; Luke 23:14-15)."[108] He even states with regard to our new obedience:

> When <something> is required by God himself and performed by ourselves it is, according to its degree and measure, even called our righteousness, by which we are also formally, inherently, habitually, or by works – according to their measure – even truly called righteous before God; seeing that by this rule we are judged partly righteous by God himself and that in view of this we may – if that were necessary – be justified in a certain way, even at the bar of God.[109]

---

102. Baxter, *Aphorismes* I.107-08 (p. 70) (emphasis inverted).

103. Baxter, *Aphorismes* I.98-99; sigs. Q1ᵛ-Q2ʳ (pp. 63-64; sigs. M1ʳ⁻ᵛ).

104. Pemble, *Vindiciæ fidei*, pp. 2-3

105. Baxter, *Aphorismes*, sigs. Q1ᵛ-Q2ʳ (sigs. M1ʳ⁻ᵛ).

106. Baxter, *Account of my Consideration*, pp. 92, 96, 242; *Confession*, pp. 372-75, 424; *Naked Popery*, p. 51. Cf. Cartwright's rebuttal of Baxter's appeal to Bradshaw in *Exceptions*, pp. 30-31.

107. Bradshaw, *Dissertatio*, p. 118. Cf. Baxter, *Confession*, p. 373.

108. "Vniversalis cum Reus universaliter & omnimodò justus esse asseritur *Ro:* 8.33. Particularis verò cum tantum respectu hujus vel illius Causæ particularis *Psal.* 7.3, 4.5. *Luc.* 23.14.15" (Bradshaw, *Dissertatio*, p. 30). Cf. pp. 55-56, 120.

109. "Cum a Deo ipso requiratur, & a nobis ipsis præstetur, pro gradu suo & mensura etiam justitia nostra dicitur, qua & formaliter, inhærenter habitualiter sive ex Operibus justi (pro ipsius modulo, coram Deo, etiam verè dicamur; utpotè cujus ratione pro justis ex parte a Deo ipso Censeamur Cujusque intuitu, etiam Foro Divino, aliquo modo justificari (si id opus esset) possumus" (Bradshaw, *Dissertatio*, p. 116). Cf. Baxter, *Confession*, p. 372.

According to Bradshaw, it is possible to be justified before God by our new obedience. This means that Baxter rightly appeals to him. Bradshaw is more careful in the application of a *duplex iustitia*, however, than Baxter. Bradshaw qualifies the possibility of being justified on the basis of inherent righteousness with the comment "if that were necessary." Also, he only refers to this twofold righteousness on a few occasions. Remarkably, he states that there is no disagreement on it.[110] Also, although he maintains that a person needs particular justification for salvation, he adds that particular justification is common to the elect and the reprobates.[111] Even the devils partake of such justification.[112] This is understandable, considering the fact that particular justification simply means that one cannot be regarded as unrighteous "without being accused falsely and blamed unfairly, and one may consequently also thus far deservedly be justified."[113] It may be concluded that although there is no material difference between Bradshaw and Baxter with regard to twofold justification, Bradshaw is careful – perhaps even somewhat reticent – in the application of this distinction. For Baxter, it plays a key role in his theory of justification, as will be noted below.

Baxter also appeals to the distinction which Lewis De Dieu (1590-1642) – a noted Dutch Walloon pastor and linguist – makes between imputed and inherent righteousness.[114] According to De Dieu, the latter is that righteousness "whereby God partly now justifies us, being in ourselves by regeneration partly conformed to the law."[115] This law is now a servant of Christ. De Dieu speaks therefore of a "twofold Justification" (*duplex iustificatio*)[116] which corresponds to a "double accusation" (*duplex accusatio*).[117] This second justification consists of works of sincere faith. It absolves us from the charge of hypocrisy and impiety.[118] Our works, although they remain imperfect, "are nevertheless taken by God through grace because of Christ, as good, holy, and just, and therefore we are absolved from the charge of wickedness and deceitfulness, and, compared with the wicked and profane, are justified as honest. Here even works are imputed to righteousness."[119] It means that one can no longer be accused of the sins that one used to be guilty of. This second justification is what the scholastics used to call "justification of the cause" (*iustificatio causae*).[120] There are a number of elements in De

---

110. Bradshaw, *Dissertatio*, p. 121.
111. Bradshaw, *Dissertatio*, p. 121.
112. Bradshaw, *Dissertatio*, p. 31.
113. "quin falsò accusari & iniquè culpari, & consequenter etiam eatenus meritò justificari possit" (Bradshaw, *Dissertatio*, p. 31).
114. Baxter, *Account of my Consideration*, p. 96; *Confession*, pp. 342-52. For De Dieu, see *BLGNP* 2.167-69.
115. "qua nos Deus per regenerationem in nobis etiam ipsis legi ex parte conformatos, ex parte nunc justificat ..." (De Dieu, *Animadversiones* [Leiden, 1646], p. 112). Cf. Baxter, *Confession*, p. 343.
116. De Dieu, *Animadversiones*, p. 112. Cf. Baxter, *Confession*, p. 344.
117. De Dieu, *Animadversiones*, p. 336. Cf. Baxter, *Confession*, p. 351.
118. De Dieu, *Animadversiones*, p. 104. Cf. Baxter, *Confession*, pp. 345-46.
119. "habentur tamen à Deo per gratiam propter Christum, tanquam bona, sancta & justa, indeque absolvimur à criminatione nequitiæ & fradulentiæ, comparatique cum impiis ac profanis, justificamur tanquam probi. Hîc opera etiam imputantur in justitiam" (De Dieu, *Animadversiones*, p. 104). Cf. Baxter, *Confession*, p. 347.
120. De Dieu, *Animadversiones*, pp. 107-08. Cf. Baxter, *Confession*, p. 350.

Dieu's thinking that appeal to Baxter: (1) the law is placed in the hands of Christ; (2) works of sincere faith are necessary for justification; (3) there is a twofold accusation; and (4) there is a corresponding twofold justification.

Baxter also refers to Anthony Wotton.[121] Wotton distinguishes between the law and the Gospel. The former required perfect righteousness. Wotton then adds that "by the Gospel, faith is accepted insteed of righteousnes."[122] If one performs the condition of the Gospel, this means that he "is judged to have done no less according to the Gospel Covenant, then he should have been judged to have done according to the Legal Covenant, if he had performed most perfect obedience to the Law. And this is to Impute or Repute faith to Righteousness."[123] After Baxter has quoted Wotton, he comments that his affinity to this author stems from the latter's insistence on the need for "personal Gospel righteousness" as the fulfillment of the conditions of the covenant.[124]

The most significant group of theologians to which Baxter appeals are the divines from the school of Saumur, especially John Cameron and Joshua Placaeus.[125] Cameron distinguishes between a twofold judgement (*iudicium duplex*) of God: "One which is issued according to the Law: the other which is issued according to the Gospel of Christ."[126] God's twofold judgement corresponds to a double throne (*thronus duplex*), one of strict justice and one of grace.[127] Whereas all people violate the condition of the legal covenant, the condition of the Gospel covenant is only violated by those who perish.[128] Placaeus is of the opinion that the conditions of the covenant of grace have replaced those of the legal covenant. Like De Dieu, Placaeus argues that at God's bar we are presented with a twofold accusation.[129] Says Placaeus:

> First it is objected, that we are sinners: that is, guilty of violating the condition which was imposed in the Legal Covenant. Next it is objected, that we are Unbelievers, that is, that we did not perform the condition of the Covenant of Grace, *viz.* Faith. From the former Accusation, we are Justified by faith only, whereby we embrace Christs

---

121. Baxter, *Account of my Consideration*, p. 96; *Confession*, pp. 381-83.
122. Wotton, *Sermons* (London, 1609), p. 453. Cf. Baxter, *Confession*, p. 382.
123. "non minus (secundùm fœdus Evangelij) præstitisse existimari, quam secundum fœdus legale præstitisse existimandus fuerat, si obedientiam legi perfectissimam præstitisset. Atque hoc quidem est Fidem ad justitiam reputare, vel imputare ..." (Wotton, *De Reconciliatione* [Basle, 1624], p. 101; translation taken from Baxter, *Confession*, p. 382).
124. Baxter, *Confession*, p. 383.
125. Baxter appeals to Cameron (*Confession*, pp. 377-80); to Placaeus (*Account of my Consideration*, pp. 94-95; *Confession*, pp. 334-38; *Of Imputation*, p. 35); and to Paul Testard (*Confession*, pp. 339-41). He refers only briefly to Moyse Amyraut and Lewis Cappel, "because I suppose them also the approvers of the forecited words of *Placæus*, the book going under the name of all three" (*Confession*, p. 339).
126. "Judicium Dei duplex est, vnum quod peragitur secundùm Legem, alterum quod peragitur secundùm Evangelium Christi" (Cameron, *Opera*, p. 365). Cf. Baxter, *Confession*, p. 377.
127. Cameron, *Opera*, p. 365. Cf. Baxter, *Confession*, pp. 377-78. Baxter fails to mention that Cameron, in the immediate context, states that James does not speak of justification *ad tribunal Dei*, but of justification *in conscientia nostra*. This differs from Baxter's interpretation of James (cf. below, pp. 313-14).
128. Cameron, *Opera*, p. 413 (*ad* Heb 8:9). Cf. Baxter, *Confession*, pp. 379.
129. Placaeus, in Cappel, *et al.*, *Theses theologicae* (Saumur, 1641) I.33. Cf. Baxter, *Confession*, p. 335.

Grace and Righteousness. From the latter, we are justified also by works, as faith is shewed by them ...[130]

Baxter concludes from Placaeus' statement that it "is the sum of most that I am blamed for."[131] Indeed, there is a striking similarity between Placaeus and Baxter. This is not to say that all the elements of Baxter's theory of twofold justification are also found in the same way in Placaeus. Baxter does not just appeal to the divines of Saumur, but to others as well. It is possible that when he developed his own position on twofold righteousness he took various elements from different sources and created his own synthesis.

Whatever the immediate background of Baxter's thinking may be, it is clear that he feels attracted to those theologians who maintain a moderate, Reformed position on the issue of twofold righteousness. This gives him a place among Protestant divines who keep open the possibility of an agreement with Roman Catholicism. Several times, he refers to the Colloquy of Regensburg (1541).[132] At this conference, an agreement between Roman Catholic and Protestant theologians had been possible on the basis of a theory of twofold justification. Baxter is aware that a theory of twofold justification is the way along which Roman Catholic and Protestant theologians might come to a mutual appreciation.

A Terminological Problem

Baxter's proximity to some Roman Catholic schools of thought raises the question how exactly he views the role of works in justification. In his refutation of Baxter's position, John Warner denies that both legal and evangelical righteousness are absolutely necessary for justification.[133] Since God justifies the ungodly (Rom. 4:5), a person is not legally righteous when he is justified.[134] Warner then goes on to argue that only evangelical righteousness is "absolutely necessary" for justification.[135] It is vanity to add legal righteousness to complete our justification. The righteousness of faith is sufficient, maintains Warner.[136]

With Baxter's theological framework in mind, it may be difficult to make sense of these remarks. How is it possible for a high Calvinist opponent of Baxter to say that only evangelical righteousness is necessary for justification? This problem is illusory, however. Warner applies the terms "legal" and "evangelical righteousness" differently than Baxter. Warner refers to Christ's righteousness as evangeli-

---

130. "Primùm objicitur nos esse peccatores, hoc est, reos violatæ conditionis, quæ fœdere legali <sic> lata est. Deinde obijcitur <sic> nos esse infideles, hoc est, non præstitisse conditionē fœderis gratiæ, videlicet fidem. Ab accusatione *priore* sola *fide* iustificamur, qua Christi gratiam & iustitiam ampectimur <sic>; *A Posteriore* iustificamur etiam *operibus*, quatenus ijs fides ostenditur" (Placaeus, in Cappel, *et al.*, *Theses theologicæ* I.33-34). The English translation is from Baxter, *Confession*, pp. 335-36.
131. Baxter, *Confession*, p. 337.
132. Baxter, *Confession*, pp. 144-45, 148-49, 353-54.
133. Warner, *Diatriba fidei justificantis*, pp. 154-55.
134. Warner, *Diatriba fidei justificantis*, pp. 156-57.
135. Warner, *Diatriba fidei justificantis*, p. 157.
136. Warner, *Diatriba fidei justificantis*, p. 158.

cal righteousness. Says Warner: "The legall righteousnesse *not as distinct in it selfe*, but as running into, and contained *in Christ's passive obedience*, is the matter of our Euangelicall righteousnesse..."[137] Christ's evangelical righteousness is our only righteousness.His obedient suffering, his legal righteousness,is the righteousness required in the Gospel. Therefore, Warner refers to it as "evangelical."

John Crandon operates from within the same terminological framework. Distinguishing two kinds of righteousness, the Scripture calls

> the one a legall righteousnes, or righteousness of the Law, the other the Evangelicall righteousnes, or righteousnes of the Gospel. The legall Righteousness it *affirms to be a righteonsness <sic> of works which we have done*, i.e. of good qualifications within us, and good operations flowing from us; the Evangelicall righteousness to be *of meer grace and mercy*, Tit. 3.5. The latter it terms *Gods Righteousness*, i.e. that which God giveth and imputeth; the former *our own righteousness*, i.e. which is wrought within our selves, and acted by our selves, *Rom. 10.3. Phil. 3.9.*[138]

Crandon's use of the terms "legal" and "evangelical righteousness" is the exact opposite of Baxter's. Thus, Crandon charges Baxter with quarreling "against the Holy Ghost for speaking so improperly and incongruously in Scriptures."[139]

Baxter is aware of this problem of definition. Already in his *Aphorismes*, he refers to it. After commenting that he takes the appellation "legal" and "evangelical righteousness" from the respective covenants, he states: "I know also, that Christs Legal Righteousness, imputed to us, is commonly called [Evangelical Righteousness,] but that is from a more aliene extrinsecal respect; to wit, because the Gospel declareth and offereth this Righteousness ..."[140] Also in his reply to Warner, Baxter indicates that he realizes that Warner means something different with legal righteousness than he does himself.[141]

Baxter feels tempted to exploit these definition problems. When Warner states that legal righteous makes void Christ's death, Baxter comments that it is "a sad case" that Warner charges him with making void Christ's death.[142] Baxter asks rhetorically: "Is there no aptitude in Christs legal Righteousness to give us life?"[143] Baxter is fully aware, however, that this is not what Warner means, that he only means to say that any righteousness in addition to that of Christ nullifies his death. Thus, Baxter is exploiting the difference in terminology in order to score points without really contributing to the discussion.

Fear of Justification by Works

The quarrels about definition point to a significant problem, however. It is not without reason that Baxter uses the terms in a way totally different from that of his

---

137. Warner, *Diatriba fidei justificantis*, p. 169.
138. Crandon, *Aphorisms Exorized* I.xiii.127-28.
139. Crandon, *Aphorisms Exorized* I.xiii.128.
140. Baxter, *Aphorismes* I.110 (p. 71).
141. Baxter, *Of Justification*, pp. 277-78.
142. Baxter, *Of Justification*, p. 279.
143. Baxter, *Of Justification*, p. 280.

opponents. The important difference in definition does not concern the term "legal righteousness." It concerns the term "evangelical righteousness." Baxter takes this phrase from the new covenant, which is a covenant of grace. His opponents, however, speak of Christ's legal righteousness offered in the Gospel as "evangelical righteousness." Both sides of the debate are agreed that the term "legal righteousness" refers to righteousness according to the law of works. For Baxter's opponents, legal and evangelical righteousness are really the same thing, viewed either from the perspective of the law which is fulfilled or from the Gospel which offers it. But it is the one and the same righteousness: that of Christ. Thus, Warner insists that there is only one righteousness, because there is only one formal cause of justification. This formal cause is the "remission of sinnes, and imputation of righteousnesse."[144] Warner refuses to admit that we may have a personal evangelical righteousness. His understanding of the covenants differs from that of Baxter. For Warner, there is only one law by which we are judged: the law of works. Since no one can be justified by this law, justification is only possible by means of the imputation of Christ's legal righteousness.

The issue underlying the seemingly verbal quarrel about matters of definition now appears to be the following: what is the role of our personal righteousness? At a certain point, Warner admits that there is an "inherent righteousnesse" which God infuses in us. He distinguishes this from the righteousness which we have by imputation.[145] If our legal and evangelical righteousness are one and the same, and if it is Christ's only, the question must be what this inherent righteousness may be, and what role it may play. Thus, Baxter immediately objects that by acknowledging an inherent righteousness Warner is "presently contradicting" what he has been arguing for.[146]

Christopher Cartwright also maintains that it is not "properly" our righteousness, but Christ's righteousness by which we are justified.[147] He maintains that the reception of Christ may either be considered as our duty or as the condition for justification.[148] As a duty, our reception of Christ is our personal righteousness, "but that is not it by which we are justified."[149] As the condition of pardon, our reception of Christ is no righteousness at all. The condition of faith is "only that whereby we receive Righteousness, *viz.* the Righteousness of Christ, that Righteousness indeed by which we are justified."[150] Thus, Cartwright even speaks of a twofold righteousness. He only denies that the fulfillment of the condition is a righteousness by which we are justified.[151]

---

144. Warner, *Diatriba fidei justificantis*, p. 161.
145. Warner, *Diatriba fidei justificantis*, p. 178.
146. Baxter, *Of Justification*, p. 284.
147. Cartwright, *Exceptions*, p. 27.
148. Cartwright, *Exceptions*, p. 27.
149. Cartwright, *Exceptions*, p. 28.
150. Cartwright, *Exceptions*, p. 29.
151. Cf. Cartwright's statement: "The necessity of a Two-fold Righteousness is not denied, but only the necessity of a Two-fold Righteousness unto Justification" (*Exceptions*, p. 29). Cf. Cartwright, in Baxter, *Account of my Consideration*, pp. 104, 283; *Exceptions*, p. 41. John Crandon holds essentially the same position. He states that the difference between Baxter and the "Orthodox Teachers" is "<t>his onely, that they will not say with him, that his righteousnesse ... is the personall righteousnesse by which men are justified before God" (*Aphorisms Exorized* I.xv.158-59).

The motivation of the opposition to Baxter's theory of twofold righteousness lies in the fact that he gives man's personal righteousness a role in justification. Warner, Crandon, and Eyre, all agree that there is an inherent righteousness. Cartwright even admits that there is a twofold righteousness. But they deny that man's personal righteousness plays a role in justification. This is the real reason why Crandon and Eyre adamantly refuse to call man's inherent righteousness his "evangelical righteousness." Man's inherent righteousness always remains imperfect. He is never able to live up to the law of works. This means that inherent righteousness can never play a role in justification. The real motivation of the opposition to Baxter's understanding of twofold righteousness is the fear of justification by works.

This motivation is brought to the fore on several occasions. Thus, Warner maintains that the apostle Paul is "utterly against a twofold righteousnesse" in justification. To prove this, he comments: "For to what purpose did *Paul* dispute against justification by the workes of the law, if the righteousnesse of faith were not sufficient."[152] If evangelical righteousness were in ourselves, we would be perfectly righteous.[153] Baxter's concept of twofold righteousness "derogates from the excellency of faith ..."[154] God has honored faith above other graces. Warner appeals to Philippians 3:9 ("not having mine own righteousness, which is of the law, but that which is through the faith of Christ, the righteousness which is of God by faith") and concludes that Paul "*shewes that it is not to be had by workes, but by faith*, and therefore is not a righteousnesse of workes but of faith ..."[155] Warner is also very concerned to give Christ his rightful place. Baxter's opinion "derogates" from the excellency of Christ. Says Warner: "Thus when God out of his riches of grace shall please to make Christ our righteousnesse, from whom we receive all, shall we say, that is in our selves which is in him; or can we thinke or say so, without detracting from the praise of his glory."[156]

William Eyre speaks in a similar vein when he lists his arguments against the notion that we are justified by faith or faithful actions as evangelical righteousness. As the very first argument against this position, Eyre states: "If we are not justified by our own works, then our believing, &c. is not that Evangelical Righteousness by which we are justified; but we are not justified by our own works, *Ergo*."[157] Furthermore, Eyre insists that we are justified by a perfect righteousness and, consequently, not by our obedience to Gospel precepts.[158] Scripture always maintains that we are justified by the righteousness of God, rather than by our own obedience.[159]

Cartwright also voices his concern about confusing justification and sanctification. When he denies that one's personal righteousness justifies, he states that

152. Warner, *Diatriba fidei justificantis*, p. 156.
153. Warner, *Diatriba fidei justificantis*, p. 172.
154. Warner, *Diatriba fidei justificantis*, p. 176.
155. Warner, *Diatriba fidei justificantis*, p. 177.
156. Warner, *Diatriba fidei justificantis*, p. 174.
157. Eyre, *Vindiciæ Justificationis Gratuitæ*, p. 52.
158. Eyre, *Vindiciæ Justificationis Gratuitæ*, p. 53.
159. Eyre, *Vindiciæ Justificationis Gratuitæ*, p. 55.

this righteousness "is not that whereby we are justified, but that whereby we are sanctified ..."[160] Cartwright is afraid that sanctification (or "evangelical right-eousness") becomes the basis for justification. Baxter fails to see the coherence in this position:

> But is it not a strange *Righteousness* that will *not justifie?* either you mean, that [we are not *universally* justified by it,] and that I know no man that will affirm. Or you mean, that we are not justified by it against the *Accusation* of being *breakers of the first Law:* But so we are justified by it only as *the Condition* of our interest in Christ. Or else you mean, that we are not *at all justified by it*, that is, not against the Accusation of *non-performing the Conditions of the New-Covenant*; (and this you must mean, or you speak not to me:) And this is very untrue.[161]

Baxter does not accept a separation between righteousness and justification. If one is personally righteous this must imply justification of some kind. That this leads to some form of justification by works is obvious. According to Baxter, one must be able to plead innocent in order to be personally righteous.

Twofold Accusation

What is the accusation against which people plead their personal righteousness? The answer to this question gives insight into the heart of Baxter's understanding of twofold righteousness. Against Lewis Du Moulin, Baxter insists that there is not just one, but that there are two accusations:

> When we are accused before God, or Conscience, of meer sin, as sin simply, or that the Law of works doth oblige us to punishment; we must plead the Gospel pardon in and for the blood of Christ: and this is our *Justitia Causæ* here. But when we are accused of final non-performance of the Conditions of the New Covenant, and so of final Impenitency, Infidelity and Rebellion against the Redeemer, here we must be justified by producing our performance of the Conditions, and denying the truth of the accusation: and not by pleading that Christ dyed for our final non-performance of these Conditions. So that here Faith and sincere Obedience is it self the very matter of our righteousness, to be pleaded.[162]

Baxter distinguishes between sin as sin on the one hand and final impenitence and unbelief on the other hand. The latter is the non-fulfillment of the condition of the new covenant. This means that Baxter regards the performance of the condition as the evangelical righteousness which is necessary for justification. The accusation of final impenitence and unbelief must be false, for Christ's blood will not avail against this accusation.

As noted earlier, Baxter appeals to William Bradshaw in support for this posi-tion.[163] But Bradshaw's incidental and careful way of handling the notion of a

---

160. Cartwright, in Baxter, *Account of my Consideration*, p. 104.
161. Baxter, *Account of my Consideration*, pp. 104-05.
162. Baxter, *Confutation*, p. 185.
163. Cf. above, pp. 274-75.

twofold righteousness creates a different impression than Baxter's consistent emphasis on it. Throughout his controversial writings, the latter insists that there is a twofold accusation.[164] In his *Aphorismes*, he still maintains that there is no danger of a false accusation before God.[165] In his discussion with Cartwright, however, he says that he must "explain or reverse" this comment. Although there is indeed no danger for those who are in Christ, yet Matthew 25 and other descriptions of the last judgement indicate

> that the main point that will be in question and tryal will be, *Whether we were true Believers or Performers of the Condition of the Covenant of Grace, or not?* and so, *Whether we have that personal Inherent Righteousness, which is the Condition of our interest in Christ and his benefits.* And therefore the *Accuser* hath no hope in any other Plea against any man, but that he is an *Unbeliever*, or Rejecter of recovering mercy.[166]

The question concerning one's personal evangelical righteousness will be "the main point" at the last judgement. It will be "the great enquiry of that day."[167] The reason is that Satan knows that it is impossible for him to accuse Christ's work of redemption of being insufficient.[168] He must accuse the people themselves of not fulfilling the condition. Baxter even describes this accusation as the only question which will then be dealt with, because "it is not Christ that is to be judged, *but we by Christ*."[169] As W. Lawrence Highfill captures the gist of Baxter's position: "In order for one to be ultimately judged just by God, he must be first made righteous."[170]

Twofold Justification

Baxter's understanding of a twofold accusation – and, therefore, also of a twofold righteousness – corresponds to his distinction between the law of works and the law of grace. This means that his view of a twofold righteousness is rooted in the

---

164. Baxter, *Aphorismes* I.201-05 (pp. 128-31); *Account of my Consideration*, pp. 80-84, 92, 94; *Confutation*, pp. 184-85, 224, 281; *Admonition*, pp. 25-26; *Confession*, pp. 49-52; *Of Imputation*, pp. 9, 31-32; *Breviate*, pp. 8-9, 53-54; *Defence of Christ*, pp. 31-34.
165. Baxter, *Aphorisms* I.203 (p. 129).
166. Baxter, *Account of my Consideration*, p. 92.
167. Baxter, *Confutation*, p. 224.
168. Cf. Baxter's comment: "If any say, It is not proved that there is any Accusation of the Saints at Judgement, or any such particular proceedings in their Justification; I Answ... Yet that Satan is the Accuser of the Brethren I know, and that we shall be Iudged according to what we have done in the body, whether it be Good or Evil ..." (*Confession*, p. 54; emphasis throughout in original).
169. Baxter, *Of Imputation*, p. 9. For almost identical expressions, see *Confession*, pp. 52, 300, 405. Cf. *Of Justification*, pp. 135-36: "In Judgement, if you be accused to have been finally impenitent, or an Infidel, wil you not plead your personal faith and repentance, to justifie you against that accusation? or shall any be saved that saith, [*I did not repent or believe, but Christ did for me?*] ... Nay is it like to be the great business of that day to enquire whether Christ have done his part or no? or yet to enquire, whether the world were sinners? or rather to judge them according to the terms of grace which were revealed to them, and to try whether they have part in Christ or not; and to that end, whether they believed, repented, loved him in his members, improved his Talents of Grace, or not? Or can any thing but the want of this personal righteousness then hazard a mans soul?"
170. Highfill, "Faith and Works," p. 71.

doctrine of the covenant. Baxter's disagreement with Eyre illustrates this. By way of objection to the theory of a twofold righteousness, Eyre insists that "we are made perfectly just" by Christ's righteousness. There is no other righteousness which "concurs" with his.[171] Baxter regards this as a simplification:

> All is granted, if you speak of the matter or form of our principal Righteousness; The Addition of a Condition is through no defect or imperfection in it: but God hath made it necessary to our participation of that which was not done by our selves, but by another. It is not true that we are made righteous by Christs Righteousness, till the condition be performed: but when it is performed, we are justified perfectly by Christs Righteousness alone, as to the principal general Justification; the condition performed being but a subservient particular righteousness.[172]

This statement of Baxter reveals some important elements of his thinking. In the first place, he distinguishes between general or universal and particular righteousness. This is a distinction which plays an important role throughout his controversies.[173] The universal righteousness is performed by Christ and imputed to us. It may be called our legal righteousness since it saves from the condemnation of the law of works. More properly, however, it is called a pro-legal righteousness because we do not really have our righteousness from the law of innocence. The pro-legal righteousness is *"instead of it <i.e.,* righteousness according to the law>, *in* and *by* our perfect Saviour."[174]

Our particular righteousness is our personal fulfillment of the condition. That this personal righteousness is necessary means that Christ's merit cannot be ours in the immediate sense of the word. His universal righteousness becomes ours by way of a condition: "So that now Christ's Satisfaction is not *simpliciter* our *universal Righteousness*; for then there were no need of any other of any sort, to any end, no not the Inherent Righteousness, as commonly acknowledged."[175] One's personal particular righteousness is the performance of the condition. When Baxter discusses twofold righteousness he almost invariably speaks of the conditionality of the covenant of grace. His distinction between universal and particular righteousness is doubtless a tool in creating room for the conditionality of the covenant. This means that from a historical theological point of view Baxter must be placed squarely in what J. Wayne Baker has termed "the other Reformed tradition," with its strong emphasis on the conditionality of the covenant of grace.[176]

171. Eyre, *Vindiciæ Justificationis Gratuitæ*, p. 57.
172. Baxter, *Admonition*, p. 30.
173. Baxter also makes this distinction in *Account of my Consideration*, pp. 91-92; *Substance*, pp. 10-12; *Confutation*, pp. 263-64; *Admonition*, p. 12; *Unsavoury Volume*, pp. 43-44; *Of Imputation*, pp. 31-32.
174. Baxter, *Of Imputation*, p. 144. Cf. pp. 156, 166; *Confession*, p. 50; *Of Justification*, p. 274.
175. Baxter, *Account of my Consideration*, p. 91.
176. Greaves, "Origins and Early Development of English Covenant Thought," 21-35; J. Wayne Baker, *Heinrich Bullinger and the Covenant: The Other Reformed Tradition* (Athens: Ohio Univ. Press, 1980), esp. p. 166, *et passim*; Charles S. McCoy and J. Wayne Baker, *Fountainhead of Federalism: Heinrich Bullinger and the Covenantal Tradition*, with trans. of *De testamento seu foedere Dei unico et aeterno* (1534), by Heinrich Bullinger (Louisville: Westminster/Knox, 1991), pp. 11-44; Graafland, *Van Calvijn tot Comrie*, I, 51-67, 81-82.

A second element in Baxter's understanding of twofold righteousness is that he refers to both kinds of righteousness as justification. This means that there is not just a twofold righteousness, but also a twofold justification, one which is universal and another which is particular. In his *Aphorismes*, Baxter only refers to a twofold righteousness. He even states here that justification is the acquittal from the charge of breaking the law, and "not from the charge of violating the new Covenant."[177] He states that he is afraid of "a dangerous error" which will "overthrow the Righteousness of Christ imputed."[178] He even goes as far as to suggest: "There is no room for Scripture-justification where our own Works are not first acknowledged unjustifiable: because there is no place for Satisfaction and Justification thereby from another, where we plead the Justification of our own Works in respect of the same Law."[179] Three years later, however, in his discussion with Cartwright, Baxter feels that he has to "recant these words."[180] He now maintains against Cartwright:

> I should next hence shew you the necessity of a twofold *Justification*. But it is so evident from what is said, that I will add but this much: If there be a twofold *Covenant*, with distinct *Conditions*, and a twofold *Accusation, viz.* for not-performing the one or the other, then there must needs be a twofold *Justification* ...[181]

Cartwright is unpleasantly surprised that Baxter now also speaks of a twofold justification. He speaks of a "new conceit" and observes that Baxter did not yet mention it in his *Aphorismes*.[182] According to Cartwright, Baxter has now taken a crucial step: he regards personal righteousness no longer as a mere requirement but also as the condition by which we are justified. Comments Cartwright: "But the Scripture speaks of Justification by Christ, and Justification by Faith, as of one and the same Justification, *Acts* 13.39. *Rom.* 5.1."[183]

That there is a difference between Baxter's positions of 1649 and 1652 is obvious. Yet, the difference is not as great as might at first sight be suspected. The only reason why Baxter initially refuses to refer to personal righteousness as justification is that he limits justification to the acquittal from the charge of breaking the law of works. When he later applies the term "justification" to one's personal righteousness, he does not mean to put this in opposition to the imputation of Christ's righteousness.[184] Precisely because this personal righteousness is

177. Baxter, *Aphorismes* I.135 (p. 88).
178. Baxter, *Aphorismes* I.135 (p. 89).
179. Baxter, *Aphorismes* I.136 (p. 89).
180. Baxter, *Account of my Consideration*, p. 137.
181. Baxter, *Account of my Consideration*, pp. 93-94. Cf. *Confession*, pp. 298-99: "As therefore we are constituted, pardoned sinners, purely by Christs Merits, and not any thing of our own; so we are constituted evangelically, Inherently righteous, as being performers of the new Covenants Conditions of our Interest in Christ and Pardon, &c."
182. Cartwright, *Exceptions*, p. 29. Cf. pp. 25, 56, 58.
183. Cartwright, *Exceptions*, p. 25.
184. Thus, Baxter comments to Cartwright: "Yet I maintain still the dangerousness of this speech, that our *Actions* are justified (through Christ's merits) by the Law of Works ..." (*Account of my Consideration*, p. 138). Baxter is still afraid of placing our works on a par with those of Christ as if our works can be justified by the law of works just as his were. Baxter's change in position does not affect this underlying concern.

evangelical righteousness, because it is the fulfillment of the *Gospel* condition, Baxter is able to use the term "justification" without derogating from the universal (pro-) legal righteousness of Christ. Thus, in his discussion with Cartwright, Baxter simply draws the consequence of his earlier position: when a distinction is made between legal and evangelical righteousness there is no reason to shy away from a corresponding concept of twofold justification.

Evangelical Righteousness a "Pepper Corn"

The third aspect to be considered is the relation between Christ's universal righteousness and man's particular righteousness. Man is not a "Co-ordinate Concause" with Christ in justification.[185] It is important to take note of this. Baxter is very careful not to place Christ's righteousness and man's righteousness on the same level. This secondary role of personal righteousness is the direct result of Baxter's position that this righteousness is not legal and does therefore not detract from Christ's righteousness. In his *Aphorismes*, Baxter clarifies the fulfillment of the condition by means of a metaphor:

> A Tenant forfeiteth his Lease to his Landlord, by not paying his rent; he runs deep in debt to him, and is disabled to pay him any more rent for the future, whereupon he is put out of his house, and cast into prison, till he pay the debt; his Landlords son payeth it for him, taketh him out of prison, and putteth him in his house again, as his Tenant, having purchased house and all to himself; he maketh him a new Lease in this Tenor, that paying but a pepper corn yearly to him, he shall be acquit both from his debt, and from all other rent for the future, which by his old Lease was to be paid; yet doth he not cancel the old Lease, but keepeth it in his hands to put in suite against the Tenant, if he should be so foolish as to deny the payment of the pepper corn. In this case the payment of the grain of pepper is imputed to the Tenant, as if he had payed the rent of the old Lease: Yet this imputation doth not extol the pepper corn, nor vilifie the benefit of his Benefactor, who redeemed him: Nor can it be said, that the purchase did only serve to advance the value and efficacy of that grain of pepper.[186]

Baxter speaks of the payment of a "pepper corn" in order to indicate the subordinate character of the condition.

This does not satisfy his opponents. John Crandon is horrified that Baxter dares to open his mouth "to vomit out all the *poyson* in his belly in one floud."[187] He is convinced that Baxter even goes beyond the Arminians and is blatantly popish in his doctrine. Whereas the Arminians only say that God graciously accepts faith as righteousness at his tribunal, Baxter, along with Rome, "makes the righteousness of Faith a collateral with the righteousness of Christ to our justification."[188] Regardless of Baxter's metaphor, Crandon charges him with teaching a

---

185. Baxter, *Of Justification*, p. 263.
186. Baxter, *Aphorismes* I.127-28 (pp. 83-84). Cf. I.153-54 (pp. 99-100).
187. Crandon, *Aphorisms Exorized* I.xvi.169.
188. Crandon, *Aphorisms Exorized* I.xvi.169. Crandon charges Baxter with making man a "collaterall and concause in the same order and degree of efficacy to justification, with the vertue of Christ glorifyed" (I.xxiv.319). Baxter makes Christ's sufferings and man's qualifications "collaterall causes of Justification" (I.xxiv.322).

"collateral" righteousness, a righteousness "parallell" with that of Christ,[189] a righteousness of "equall power" with his, "if not a power above, and superiour to it."[190] Crandon has no use for Baxter's "pepper corn." How can free grace possibly be acquired and maintained with a payment?[191] The payment of a "pepper corn" implies conditional, imperfect, and mutable justification.[192] Crandon scorns Baxter's insistence that the "pepper corn" is not extolled. This is the "very language of the Papists and Arminians" who also claim that they are the "sole advancers" of grace.[193]

Cartwright – although much less vehement in his disagreement – does not accept Baxter's metaphor either. He does not think that it is possible to say that we "truly and properly" purchase the benefits of the new covenant.[194] Like Crandon, he is afraid that man will usurp Christ's place. Cartwright admits that faith is the condition of partaking of Christ's righteousness. But, he continues,

> that Faith is a distinct Righteousness, by which, together with Christ's Satisfaction, we must be justified, seems to be as if we should make the Medicine and the applying of it two things co-ordinate each with other, when as the one is but subordinate and subservient, as it were, to the other, to work the cure; the Medicine being to no purpose, except it be applied.[195]

Cartwright is afraid that if one's evangelical righteousness becomes justifying, it will lose its "subordinate and subservient" character.

Baxter professes his amazement at Cartwright's misunderstanding of his position. Baxter precisely used the metaphor of a "pepper corn" to indicate the subservient character of the condition. He entirely agrees with Cartwright that faith is not part of our legal righteousness. Baxter then adds:

> I fully profess that they are *not co_ordinate*; but that the very *New-Law* or *Covenant* is but *subordinate* to the *Old*; and consequently the *Righteousness* required by it, is but *subordinate* and *subservient* to the Righteousness of Christ's Satisfaction for our sins against the Law; and that it is the *Condition* of enjoying it: And therefore *our Righteousness so far, because a Condition instituted by a New-Law*.[196]

Baxter here refers to the subservient role of the law of grace. Since the Gospel is subordinate to the law, evangelical particular righteousness is also subservient to legal universal righteousness. In his *Aphorismes*, Baxter does not yet systematize these thoughts. Nevertheless, all the constitutive elements are present, as is clear from his metaphor of the "pepper corn." Alerted by Cartwright that a misunder-

189. Crandon, *Aphorisms Exorized* I.xiii.120. Cf. Baxter's indignant reaction: "Never did it once enter into my thoughts, or fall from my mouth or pen, that our Inherent Righteousness is collaterall with Christs sacrifice and Righteousness, to salvation: or that we are saved by and for works, as by and for Christ!" (*Unsavoury Volume*, p. 54; cf. p. 68)
190. Crandon, *Aphorisms Exorized* I.xiv.139.
191. Crandon, *Aphorisms Exorized* I.xvi.173.
192. Crandon, *Aphorisms Exorized* I.xvi.173-74.
193. Crandon, *Aphorisms Exorized* I.xvi.175.
194. Cartwright, *Exceptions*, p. 50. Cf. Cartwright, in Baxter, *Account of my Consideration*, p. 117.
195. Cartwright, in Baxter, *Account of my Consideration*, pp. 69-70.
196. Baxter, *Account of my Consideration*, p. 99.

standing might possibly be derived from his *Aphorismes*, however, Baxter now
states that the condition is a "subservient particular righteousness."[197] In later
discussions, he hardly ever speaks of twofold righteousness without immediately
qualifying this by stating that man's evangelical righteousness is "subordinate" or
"subservient" to that of Christ.[198] One's evangelical righteousness is only the
condition to partake of Christ's legal righteousness.[199]

Imputation of Faith and the Formal Cause of Justification

Baxter's understanding of personal evangelical righteousness causes him to maintain that faith itself is imputed for righteousness. He does not agree with the
standard high Calvinist interpretation of Romans 4:5. When it says that "faith is
counted for righteousness" faith must not be regarded as a reference to Christ as
the object of faith. Baxter is convinced that this violates the clear meaning of the
text: "Read over the Texts and put but [*Christs Righteousness*] every where instead of the word [*Faith*;] and see what a scandalous Paraphrase you will make.
The Scripture is not so audaciously to be Corrected: It's wiser to believe Gods
Word than to contradict it on pretence of expounding it."[200] Baxter strongly objects to the way in which the Savoy Declaration (1658) – mainly drawn up by John
Owen – speaks of imputation. According to the Savoy Declaration, God justifies
not "by imputing Faith it self, the act of believing, or any other Evangelical
obedience to them, as their righteousness" (art. XI.I).[201] Baxter dislikes the statement that "it is not Faith, but Christ's Righteousness that we are justified by,
whenas it is both; and the Scripture often saith the contrary."[202] Accordingly,
Baxter opines that "it is better to justifie and expound the Scripture, than flatly to
deny it ..."[203] He insists that our own personal righteousness is the matter of our
subordinate justification.[204] This makes him disagree both with the Westminster
Confession and with the Savoy Declaration.[205]

---

197. Baxter, *Admonition*, p. 30.
198. Baxter, *Account of my Consideration*, pp. 93, 98-90, 126; *Substance*, p. 54; *Confutation*, pp. 185, 203, 287; *Admonition*, pp. 12, 23, 26-28; *Unsavoury Volume*, p. 68; *Of Justification*, pp. 261, 266, 268, 270, 278-79, 282, 284; *Appeal*, p. 3; *Of Imputation*, pp. 145, 148; *Breviate*, pp. 7, 35; *Defence of Christ*, sig. A5ʳ; p. 42.
199. Baxter maintains that "the second Righteousness (personal) is required *propter aliud*, in subordi- nation to the first, as a means to its end ..." (*Account of my Consideration*, p. 93). Cf. *Of Imputa- tion*, p. 145.
200. Baxter, *Breviate*, p. 32. Cf. p. 72; *Defence of Christ*, sigs. A5ᵛ-A6ʳ; pp. 18-19.
201. Williston Walker, *The Creeds and Platforms of Congregationalism*, introd. Elizabeth C. Nord- beck (1893; rpt. New York: Pilgrim, 1991), p. 379.
202. Baxter, *Account of the Reasons* (London, 1684), p. 8. Baxter also claims that "some worthy persons of that Assembly, upon conference, assure me, That how ill soever it be worded, they themselves did mean it as I and other Protestants do, and did disclaim the obvious ill sence" (*End of Doctrinal Controversies*, p. 266).
203. Baxter, *Of Imputation*, p. 28.
204. Baxter, *Account of my Consideration*, p. 179; *Of Justification*, p. 285; *Scripture Gospel defended*, p. 97.
205. It is interesting that with his objection to Savoy, Baxter implicitly attacks the WCF as well, since the Savoy Declaration simply adopts the wording of the WCF in rejecting the imputation of faith. Thus, Baxter acknowledges that "the same words are in the Assemblies Confession, though they might better have been left out" (*Of Imputation*, p. 26; emphasis throughout in original).

This brings up the thorny question of the formal cause of justification. It has already been noted that Baxter thinks that the formal role of faith in justification is its conditionality.[206] Nevertheless, C.F. Allison has argued that Baxter regards faith as the formal cause of justification: "It is by this <personal> righteousness that we are justified, and it is this righteousness which obtains our justification under the conditions of the new covenant. Thus, according to Baxter, the imputation of our *own* faith is the formal cause of justification."[207] Allison's interpretation of Baxter is incorrect.[208] When Baxter discusses the question whether or not faith is the formal cause of justification, he maintains that first the meaning of justification must be cleared. Every distinct sense of justification has "its proper Being and Form."[209] He insists that the question should either be left alone or be handled exactly.[210]

In practice, Baxter himself usually takes the former approach. He hardly ever discusses what the formal cause of justification is. When he does deal with this issue, however, he explicitly denies that faith is the formal cause of justification. Instead, the formal cause is "the acquitting of the sinner from Accusation and Condemnation of the Law, or the disabling the Law to accuse or condemn him."[211] To be sure, Baxter revokes this section of the *Aphorismes* in his discussion with Eyre.[212] But he never says that he has come to regard faith as the formal cause of justification. When Calvin calls faith the formal cause of our righteousness, Baxter comments that this "is more then I will say."[213] Faith only has a certain "aptitude" to its interest in justification. There is only a certain "fitness" in the nature of faith, so that God has made it the condition of justification.[214] Faith is "not the formal cause" of justification itself.[215] When Crandon attacks Baxter's under-

206. Cf. above, pp. 173-76.
207. Allison, *Rise of Moralism*, p. 157. Cf. pp. 161, 176.
208. Cf. Gavin John McGrath's disagreement: "This interpretation is unwarranted: it comes from reading Baxter's implications rather than his precise declarations" ("Puritans and the Human Will," p. 259). Timothy K. Beougher also criticizes Allison's charge ("Conversion," pp. 102-03).
209. Baxter, *End of Doctrinal Controversies*, p. 264.
210. Baxter, *End of Doctrinal Controversies*, p. 265.
211. Baxter, *Aphorismes* I.213 (p. 135) (emphasis throughout in original).
212. Baxter, *Admonition*, pp. 20-21.
213. Baxter, *Confession*, p. 333. Cf. Highfill, "Faith and Works," p. 93.
214. Baxter, *Aphorismes* I.231-32 (pp. 147-48); *Account of my Consideration*, p. 98; *Account*, p. 27; *Confutation*, p. 206; *Unsavoury Volume*, p. 58; *Confession*, pp. 37-40, 89, 335; *Of Justification*, pp. 75-77, 242-43; *Of Imputation*, p. 178; *Breviate*, pp. 12-13. It will be recalled that Baxter denies that faith justifies efficiently of itself, and that he thinks that the formal interest of faith in justification is its conditionality (cf. above, pp. 173-76). Baxter often combines such statements with the additional comment that God has chosen faith to be the condition because of its aptitude. The following statement may serve as an example: "Yet though no Ethical worth or Aptitude in faith be the formal Reason of its interest in Justification, it is nevertheless its immediatly-prerequisite Aptitude for this office and honor: And so far as we may give a reason of Gods appointments and will, from any thing without him, in the object, we may say, that therefore God made it the Condition of the Covenant, or of his gift of Christ and Justification, because it was the fittest morall Grace for this work. So that it was some Ethical or Moral excellency or worth in that grace, that caused God (as we may speak) to make it the condition, and so which is its Aptitude to the office, and the remote reason of its interest in Justification; though not the formal and neerest reason" (*Confession*, p. 96).
215. Baxter, *Of Justification*, p. 75. Baxter also denies that faith is the formal cause of justification in *Of Justification*, p. 100; *Breviate*, p. 13.

standing of the role of faith, he retorts that "if Mr. *Cr.* would intimate that I make the τò *credere* to justifie formally as such, *sub hac ratione,* I do as constantly deny it, as he is constant in false accusing."[216] Faith justifies "not as such, but as a condition."[217] When Baxter insists that faith itself is imputed for righteousness, he does not mean to say that faith itself is the formal cause of justification. He only means that God reckons faith as righteousness because he has made it the condition of the covenant of grace. When this condition of righteousness is fulfilled, God himself justifies the believer. In terms of Baxter's theory of twofold justification, this means that personal evangelical righteousness is the condition to partake of Christ's universal legal righteousness.

Allison's analysis fails because he does not realize that Baxter distinguishes between evangelical and (pro-) legal righteousness. When a person has a right to Christ and his benefits, he partakes of his universal righteousness. In Baxter's view, it is impossible that faith would be the formal cause of this righteousness, because strictly speaking it remains Christ's own righteousness only. Man's share in it is indirect by way of a foreign grant of God as *Donor,* as *Dominus Absolutus.* As illustrated earlier by means of a table, Baxter distinguishes between conditional and actual justification.[218] Now it becomes clear that man's evangelical righteousness is the condition of being actually justified, of partaking of Christ's universal righteousness. Man's own evangelical righteousness – the condition of faith – can never be the formal cause of Christ's universal righteousness.

There is nevertheless a very real sense in which Baxter's theory would allow him to speak of faith as the formal cause of justification. After all, God's grant as absolute *Donor* is not the only justification. Man's own faith constitutes him evangelically righteous. Evangelical justification is the condition to partake of legal justification. Thus, although faith cannot be styled the formal cause of legal justification, Baxter's theory demands that it is the formal cause of one's personal righteousness, of one's evangelical justification. Baxter only gives some hints that this is indeed the implication of his theory of twofold justification.[219] As far as I am aware, he does not explicitly state that faith is the formal cause of evangelical justification. Such an admission would probably have created a furor. By simply denying that faith is the formal cause of justification, Baxter avoids this. Meanwhile, his insistence that, on the one hand, faith itself is imputed for righteousness and that, on the other hand, faith is not the formal cause of justification, are two propositions about two different aspects of justification. Both statements can only be held together by means of his theory of twofold justification.

---

216. Baxter, *Unsavoury Volume,* p. 46. It should be noted that Crandon carefully avoids accusing Baxter of making faith the formal cause of justification.

217. Baxter, *Unsavoury Volume,* p. 46.

218. Cf. above, p. 190.

219. As a mature theologian, Baxter distinguishes only three distinct causes: efficient, constitutive, and final causes. He subdivides the constitutive cause into three parts: matter, receptive disposition, and form (*Methodus Theologiæ* I.i.4-9; *End of Doctrinal Controversies,* pp. xii, 91). Therefore, when Baxter first denies that faith justifies efficiently, and then says that it justifies "*constitutively,* so far as it is it self our *personal inherent Righteousness*" (p. 270), he clearly implies that faith is the formal cause (as part of the constitutive cause) of particular justification (cf. p. 244). Cf. Packer, "Redemption and Restoration," p. 74.

To conclude, Baxter's denial that faith is the formal cause of justification is intimately related to his understanding of how God relates to mankind. Man's evangelical particular righteousness or justification is the condition demanded by God as *Rector per leges*. His share in Christ's (pro-) legal universal righteousness is the absolute gift of God as *Dominus Absolutus* once the condition has been fulfilled. This means that Baxter's distinction of the twofold will of God is the framework in which he develops his theory of twofold righteousness.

Justification by Works?

WORKS MINIMIZED

Works No Cause of Justification

Baxter's understanding of the role of works in justification is a natural result of his doctrines of the covenant and of twofold righteousness. When Baxter regards man's fulfillment of the condition of the covenant of grace as his particular justification at God's bar of judgement, the charges with regard to the role of works become predictable: (1) his opponents are convinced that Baxter gives too large a role to works, whereas all works should be excluded from justification; (2) this emphasis on works as the condition of the new covenant calls into question the perseverance of the saints; and (3) by assigning a role to works in justification Baxter has put forward an essentially Roman Catholic theory of justification.

Since the charges of a loss of the doctrine of the perseverance of the saints and of a surrender to Rome are mere corollaries of the accusation that works are too prominent in Baxter's doctrine of justification, the analysis must focus mainly on the latter issue. When Anthony Burgess deals with it, he describes the heart of the matter as follows:

> *Neither is the Question about* the necessity of holinesse and sanctification in those that are justified; Justified persons will abound in the fruits of holinesse, that sweet fountain within will also bring forth sweet streams; This good tree will bear good fruit; *onely the Question is,* Upon what account these are required in justified persons? Whether in some causality or concurrence as faith is, onely not with such a degree of excellency? Whether good works be required as well as faith, so that we may say, Justifying Repentance, Justifying Law <love>, as well as Justifying Faith?[220]

Burgess agrees with Baxter that good works are necessary in those who are justified. Burgess denies, however, that works are a cause of justification – even if they are regarded a less important cause than faith – and that it would be legitimate to speak of justifying repentance or justifying love. Similarly, John Crandon accuses

---

220. Burgess, *True Doctrine*, II, 220 (emphasis inverted).

Baxter of making works into "concauses" with faith.[221] When William Eyre wants to prove that Baxter "gives as much unto Works and lesse unto Christ" as the papists, he adds that Baxter "makes Works, by vertue of Gods Promise and Covenant, to be the meritorious causes of Justification and Salvation, and in no other sence doe the Papists affirm it."[222]

Baxter professes his amazement at these descriptions of his position. They illustrate, according to him, the fact that his opponents have not understood his position at all. The above cited passage from Burgess irritates Baxter particularly because he thinks that he has been perfectly clear that the condition of works is not a cause at all.[223] Against Crandon, Baxter comments that he does not even give faith any proper causality as to justification, "and how can I then give works a concausality?"[224] It is indeed a striking feature throughout Baxter's controversial writings that he disclaims any causality for works in justification.[225]

Burgess is nevertheless able to point to Baxter's *Aphorismes*. There he had stated that faith justifies as "the great principal master duty of the Gospel" and that works justify as "the secondary, less principal parts of the condition."[226] Baxter had maintained that faith and works

> both justifie in the same kinde of causality, *viz.* as *Causæ sine quibus non*, or mediate and improper Causes; or as Dr *Twisse) Causæ dispositivæ:* but with this difference: Faith as the principal part; Obedience as the less principal. The like may be said of Love, which at least is a secondary part of the condition: and of others in the same station.[227]

When Baxter complains that Burgess is unfair in charging him with making faith into a cause of justification, it is clear that the latter is able to appeal to an explicit statement from Baxter himself.

Burgess nevertheless misrepresents his opponent. When Baxter speaks of a *causa sine qua non*, he means "only a causality improperly so called, which indeed is no causality."[228] He is using a technical term which expresses a condition. But he does not mean that works have any efficiency in justification at all. Rather than works being an efficient cause, "<t>he highest Interest that they can

---

221. Crandon, *Aphorisms Exorized* II.xv.214. Cf. II.xiv.205; II.xxiii.275.
222. Eyre, *Vindiciæ Justificationis Gratuitæ*, sig. A3ᵛ (emphasis throughout in original).
223. Baxter, *Confession*, sigs. e1ᵛ-e2ʳ; *Of Justification*, p. 96.
224. Baxter, *Unsavoury Volume*, p. 53.
225. Baxter, *Substance*, p. 15; *Admonition*, pp. 9-10; *Unsavoury Volume*, pp. 53, 71, 78; *Confession*, sigs. e1ᵛ-e3ʳ, pp. 31, 50, 88, 314-15, 321; *Of Justification*, pp. 75-76, 96-100, 127-28, 169, 182, 188.
226. Baxter, *Aphorismes* I.289-90 (p. 185) (emphasis throughout in original).
227. Baxter, *Aphorismes* I.290 (pp. 185-86) (emphasis inverted). Cf. Burgess, *Expository Sermons*, sig. A4ᵛ.
228. Baxter, *Of Justification*, p. 99.
229. Baxter, *Of Justification*, pp. 75-76. Baxter's frequent insistence that we are justified "because of" our works might create some confusion. Baxter appeals to various texts from Scripture which seem to grant a causality to man's actions (Gen 7:1; 22:16-18; 2 Chron 34:26-27; Ps 91:9, 14; Matt 25:21, 23, 34-35, 40, 46; Mark 7:29; Luke 19:17, 27; John 3:22-23; 16:27; 1 John 3:22-23; Rev 3:4, 10; 7:14-15 [*Account of my Consideration*, pp. 280-82; *Confession*, pp. 57-58; *Of Justification*, pp. 82-83]). Cf. *Confession*, p. 315. It is clear from the above, however, that when

have, is but to be a condition of our Justification ..."[229] Baxter's reason is: "Justification is not a means of our using, but an act of God."[230]

Baxter objects when works are regarded as a cause. This is in accordance with his rejection of faith as the instrumental cause of justification.[231] Neither faith nor works are a proper cause of justification. When Baxter's opponents charge him with making works into a cause of justification, this is because they are thinking in a different framework. Because they hold that faith is a proper cause of justification, they read Baxter accordingly. When they hear him say that works have the same kind of causality as faith, they wrongly interpret this to mean that works are a proper cause of justification.

This implies that for Baxter the key issue does not lie in the role of works but in the role of faith. He is convinced that he does not exalt works any more than his opponents. But by making faith into an efficient, instrumental cause, his opponents give a more important role to faith. Says Baxter:

> Lay the blame then where it should lye, and speak the truth: say that I deny that Faith justifieth us as the Instrumental cause, and say that I give less to Faith, and so to man in Justification then others do; and do not say I give more to other acts, as Repentance, Love, &c. When you know that others make them *sine qua non*, and necessary Conditions as well as I.[232]

Baxter is convinced that he does not advance the role of works at all. Therefore, when Burgess accuses him of advocating "justifying repentance" and "justifying love" Baxter retorts that he "never owned" such phrases.[233] He also does not think that "justification by works" is an appropriate phrase. It is not "fit to be used, unless rarely, or to explain such texts of Scripture as do use it, or terms equipollent."[234] He is afraid that this phrase might be an occasion for people to ascribe too much to their works. Works are only part of the covenant condition.[235] But we must be thus "Evangelically qualified" if we are to be justified at the last judgement.[236] Baxter concludes: "If this be Justification by Works, I am for it."[237]

Baxter insists that God justifies us *because* we are just, he does not mean to suggest a proper causality. He only wants to say that Scripture uses words that seem to imply a causality when it speaks of the *conditio sine qua non* (*Account of my Consideration*, p. 277; *Unsavoury Volume*, pp. 72-73).

230. Baxter, *Of Justification*, p. 100.
231. Cf. above, pp. 176-92.
232. Baxter, *Confession*, p. 301. Baxter often states that he does not "give more" to works, but less to faith than his opponents (*Substance*, p. 15; *Plain Scripture Proof*, p. 191; *Confession*, p. 89; *Of Justification*, pp. 184, 188).
233. Baxter, *Of Justification*, p. 97.
234. Baxter, *Of Justification*, p. 287. Baxter also disavows the phrase "justification by works" in *Account of my Consideration*, p. 284; *Confession*, p. 83. Cf. *Of Justification*, pp. 189, 347.
235. To be sure, there is a reason why God has chosen works as part of the condition of justification. Just as faith has a certain "aptitude" to its role in justification, so there is also a reason why God has made works part of the condition: "Not because they have any such Receptive nature as faith, but because Faith being an Acceptance of Christ as Lord also, and delivering and resigning up the soul to him accordingly in Covenant, this Duty is therefore necessarily implyed ..." (*Of Justification*, p. 243).
236. Baxter, *Of Imputation*, p. 163.
237. Baxter, *Of Imputation*, p. 163.

Works Excluded From Initial Justification

When Baxter states that one's evangelical righteousness justifies at the last judgement, he places another important restriction on the role of works. The first act of saving grace by which a person is justified is not accompanied by works. Baxter retains the *sola fide* of the Reformation, albeit in a restricted sense:

> I have ever understood most of our Divines, when they speak of Justification by faith alone, to mean by Justification, Gods first putting us into a justified and pardoned estate, upon our first believing. And if so, either I give no more to works to our Justification then they, or else I know not my own thoughts. I say therefore as they use to do, *Bona opera sequuntur Justificatum non precedunt Justificandum*, and therefore they cannot Justifie. Which Reason can hold of Iustification in no other sence then this.[238]

Baxter denies that works play a role in initial justification. At this stage, faith is alone.[239] Justification is not *simul et semel*, however, but a continued process which culminates in the great judgement on the last day. This means that renewed repentance is part of the condition of continued justification.[240] Forgiving others is also a condition.[241] To be sure, even at the last judgement, "faith hath still the principall interest."[242] But obedience does play a secondary role in continued and consummate justification.[243] At this point, Burgess dissents: "If in the continuance and progresse of our Justification, we are justified after the same manner we were at first, then its not by faith and works, but by faith only as distinct to works."[244] Burgess grants that justification is not a once for all event. But he denies that this would imply that works become a condition for continued justification. Also Cartwright insists that "as our Justification is begun, so it is continued."[245] This means that justification is only continued by faith. Baxter replies to Burgess that our first faith is "our Contract with Christ."[246] If we do not perform what we promised, we do not receive the benefits. To clarify his position, Baxter takes recourse to the following comparisons:

> And in humane contracts it is so. Barely to take a Prince for her husband may entitle a woman to his honours and lands: But conjugal fidelity is also necessary for the continuance of them: for Adultery would cause a divorce. Consent and listing

---

238. Baxter, *Confession*, p. 88. Cf. *Answer*, p. 22: "But did I ever deny that it is [*by Faith alone and without Works*]? Where, and when? But may it not be, *by Faith alone* in one sense, and not *by Faith alone* in another sense?"
239. Baxter, *Aphorismes* I.302 (pp. 193-94); *Account of my Consideration*, pp. 251-53; *Unsavoury Volume*, pp. 52, 71; *Confession*, pp. 52, 84, 97, 311-12; *Of Justification*, pp. 109, 123, 129, 149, 182, 184; *Of Imputation*, pp. 161, 183.
240. Baxter, *Aphorismes* I.235 (p. 150); *Account of my Consideration*, p. 252; *Confession*, p. 302; *Of Justification*, p. 123.
241. Baxter, *Aphorismes* I.236 (p. 150); *Account of my Consideration*, p. 252; *Confession*, p. 47.
242. Baxter, *Confession*, p. 97.
243. Baxter, *Aphorismes* I.290 (p. 185).
244. Burgess, *True Doctrine*, II, 226 (emphasis throughout in original).
245. Cartwright, in Baxter, *Account of my Consideration*, p. 251.
246. Baxter, *Of Justification*, p. 123.

may make a man your Souldier: but obedience and service is as necessary to the Continuance, and the Reward. Consent may make a man your servant, without any service, and so give him entertainment in your family. But if he do not actually serve you, these shall not be continued, nor the wages obtained. Consent may enter a Scholar into your School: but if he will not Learn of you, he shall not be continued there. For all these after-violations cross the ends of the Relations.[247]

Baxter's reply to Cartwright is similar. Cartwright errs in maintaining that justification is continued in the same way as it begun: "It is *continued* by the same *God, Christ, Merit, Covenant:* But not by the same *condition* only."[248] He again uses the same kind of metaphors to make his point.[249] According to Baxter, Cartwright's failure to distinguish between the conditions of initial and continued justification is "the root of most of <his> mistakes in this point."[250]

WORKS IN THE DEFINITION OF FAITH?

Faith and Repentance

Baxter wants to exclude works from initial justification. His opponents, however, are convinced that he does not succeed. As noted earlier, they oppose his conviction that faith *qua iustificans* includes faith in Christ as Lord as well as Savior. John Tombes, Christopher Cartwright, and John Warner are convinced that this means that sanctification and justification will be confused.[251] Baxter reacts particularly hostile to Warner's charge that he includes works in the definition of justifying faith: "Gross untruths! contrary to large and plaine expressions of my mind in several Volumes ... I ever took Works to be a fruit of faith, and no part of it ..."[252] Baxter says that he only includes *consent* to Christ's lordship in the definition of faith. He does not include obedience itself.[253] Warner, in turn, refuses to regard consent as a part of faith. Consent to Christ's lordship is but an intention, a purpose. Peter had such a purpose to die with Christ, "yet ah, alas!"[254] The intention is not the actual believing or obeying. Intentions or purposes may

247. Baxter, *Of Justification*, pp. 123-24.
248. Baxter, *Account of my Consideration*, p. 252.
249. Baxter, *Account of my Consideration*, pp. 252-53. Cf. also *Confession*, p. 47.
250. Baxter, *Account of my Consideration*, p. 253.
251. Cf. above, p. 173.
252. Baxter, *Of Justification*, p. 319 (wrong pagination; sig. Ss3ᵛ; emphasis throughout in original). Cf. p. 349, where Baxter says that Tombes also misunderstands him, "as if I thought that justifying faith contained essentially such obedience or works." William Eyre also charges Baxter with including all works of obedience to evangelical precepts in the definition of faith (*Vindiciæ Justificationis Gratuitæ*, pp. 90-91). Baxter denies the charge in *Admonition*, pp. 31-32. Cf. also *Unsavoury Volume*, pp. 46-47; *Confession*, pp. 89-90.
253. When, in *A Breviate of the Doctrine of Justification*, Baxter discusses the question whether obedience is a part of faith, he answers: "To believe in Christ at first is an act of obedience to God, who commandeth us so to do: But it is but *Subjection* to Christ which that act includeth, that is, taking him for our Lord and Saviour to be obeyed, which is virtually all future obedience as its root, but not actually" (*Breviate*, p. 46).
254. Warner, *Diatriba fidei justificantis*, p. 419.

also be found in hypocrites and reprobates.[255] Baxter retorts that he never spoke of purposes or intentions. What is at stake is the accepting or believing in Christ as Lord and Teacher.[256] Justifying faith consists of assent, consent, and affiance. The consent, or accepting, is the heart of faith. It is mere volition.[257] Of course, there are superficial purposes, "yet if no Purposes and Intentions will prove men Saints, then nothing in this world will prove them Saints ..."[258]

Baxter's angry denial that he includes works in the definition of justifying faith is understandable. For Baxter, good works follow both faith and one's initial justification. Nevertheless, some qualifications are in order. In the first place, Baxter often says that faith and repentance together make up the condition of initial justification. In his *Aphorismes*, he comments that the "bare Act of beleeving" is not the only condition of the new covenant.[259] Baxter then mentions repentance as the condition of pardon and salvation.[260] He does not just mean that repentance is a condition of continued justification. It is also a condition of "our first admission into a state of Justification."[261] Crandon maintains that Baxter here manifests himself to be even "worse" than Bellarmine.[262] According to Crandon, repentance and faith are indeed often related in Scripture. In those cases, repentance and faith are really "two acts of the same gift of grace."[263] Repentance, therefore, does not justify in addition to faith, as Baxter wrongly maintains. Comments Crandon:

> For (as our Divines well say against the Papists) though these two acts must needs cooperate together, *viz.* the casting out of self and the receiving of Christ; yet it is the latter alone that doth properly and instrumentally justifie by receiving the justifyer and his righteousnesse; the former act doth but *disponere materiam* ... doth but put a man as it were in a justifiable posture and capacity, doth but *obicem tollere*, pluck out and cast away the barre that might fasten the door against Christs entrance; and this it doth not as a distinct vertue from faith, but as a subservient act of faith to its receiving of Christ.[264]

At this point, Baxter focuses on what he perceives to be the basic error of Crandon's charge. Baxter says that Crandon gives just as much to repentance "as ever I gave to it."[265] When Crandon states that repentance only disposes the matter and takes away the bar he is simply describing the position which Baxter holds as well. The difference, insists Baxter, lies in the fact that Crandon makes faith the instru-

---

255. Warner, *Diatriba fidei justificantis*, p. 417.
256. Baxter, *Of Justification*, p. 303.
257. Baxter, *Of Justification*, p. 302.
258. Baxter, *Of Justification*, p. 304.
259. Baxter, *Aphorismes* I.235 (p. 149) (emphasis throughout in original).
260. Baxter, *Aphorismes* I.235 (p. 150). Baxter appeals to Prov 1:23; 28:13; Mark 1:15; 6:12; Luke 13:3, 5; Acts 2:38; 3:19; 8:22; 17:30: 26:20; 5:31; 11:18; Luke 24:47; Heb 6:1; 2 Pet 3:9; Ezek 18:27-28; 33:12; Hos 14:2; Joel 2:14-15; Deut 4:30; 30:10.
261. Baxter, *Of Justification*, p. 81. Cf. *Confession*, p. 97; *Breviate*, p. 68.
262. Crandon, *Aphorisms Exorized* II.iii.26.
263. Crandon, *Aphorisms Exorized* II.iii.30.
264. Crandon, *Aphorisms Exorized* II.iii.30.
265. Baxter, *Unsavoury Volume*, p. 61.

mental cause.[266] Again, Baxter is convinced that he does not "give more" to repentance, but that he "gives less" to faith than his opponents.

It may be asked whether Baxter really succeeds in excluding works from the condition of initial justification. His reply to Crandon indicates that he regards repentance as a mere *conditio sine qua non*. But does this not introduce the requirement of good works before justification? Baxter is aware of the difficulty of this issue.[267] By making repentance a condition for initial justification he obliges himself to separate this repentance carefully from other external works. Therefore, he distinguishes between "outward works" which follow initial justification and "inward works" which precede one's first justification.[268] Repentance does not belong to one's external obedience.[269] Repentance, says Baxter, signifies "our change from *Unbelief* to *Faith*, and so is *Faith* it self."[270] The relation between repentance and faith is like "the breaking off from other Suitors and Lovers, and turning the mind to this one."[271]

Baxter's attempt to separate repentance from external works may seem to result in a levelling of faith and repentance. Nevertheless, he does maintain a difference between the two. God has made faith the condition because it has a certain aptitude to receive pardon. He has made repentance the condition because it is the only way in which Christ is able to bring us back to God. But repentance does not have the same receptive nature which faith has.[272] Repentance has a natural necessity. It implies a return to God. Faith and trust in Christ has, in addition, an instituted necessity.[273] This means that repentance, as a turning to God, is the end which supposes faith in Christ as the means: "Holiness is the Souls health, and Christ believed in is the remedy: Repentance and Holiness are necessary as the end for themselves, and Faith in the Mediator is necessary as the use of the Remedy."[274] Baxter obviously links repentance to holiness, despite his insistence that repentance is not part of one's external obedience. Highfill rightly comments that Baxter emphasizes repentance "as a corrective to the antinomian idea that pardon was given automatically and eternally through the merit of Christ, eliminating the necessity for repentance."[275]

Baxter's opposition to Antinomianism means that he is forced to defend himself against those who fear that he takes works as a condition of initial justification. In this defensive position, he is walking a tight rope. On the one hand, he

266. Baxter, *Unsavoury Volume*, pp. 61-62.
267. Baxter admits that it is "easier" to avoid the charge of equalling faith and obedience than the charge of levelling faith and repentance (*Confession*, p. 97).
268. Baxter, *Confutation*, p. 201.
269. Baxter, *Of Justification*, p. 109.
270. Baxter, *Of Imputation*, p. 161. Cf. *Breviate*, p. 38.
271. Baxter, *Confession*, p. 90.
272. Baxter, *Confession*, p. 39; *Of Justification*, p. 76.
273. Baxter, *End of Doctrinal Controversies*, p. 142.
274. Baxter, *Breviate*, p. 38. Cf. *Confession*, p. 39: Without repentance "God and the Redeemer cannot have their end in pardoning us, nor can the Redeemer do all his work, for which we do accept him. For his work is, upon the pardoning of us, to bring us back in heart and life to God, from whom we were fallen and strayed" (emphasis throughout in original).
275. Highfill, "Faith and Works," p. 79.

must closely identify faith and repentance in order to avoid the charge that he repudiates initial justification by faith alone. On the other hand, he needs to keep some distance between faith and repentance in order to retain the receptive character of faith in distinction repentance.

Love As an Essential Part of Faith

In his *Aphorismes*, Baxter states: "I take love to Christ as our Saviour and Lord, to be essentiall to this Acceptance: and so some degree of Love to be part of Justifying Faith, and not properly a fruit of it, as it is commonly taken."[276] Baxter feels that the Reformed tradition allows for his position.[277] Love, argues Baxter against Tombes, is an essential part of faith, because consent is an essential part of it.[278] Love, unlike desire and hope, may consider its object as present. Therefore, unlike love, desire and hope are not essential to faith.[279] Baxter does not accept the corollary that love justifies as well as faith. That is to say, he does not think that this is a "meet phrase."[280] In a sense, love does justify, since it is an essential part of faith. But love, being an act of the will, only accepts an object as it is good.[281] When love is considered as an essential part of faith's acceptance, it "loseth its name, as a lesser River that falleth into a greater; therefore it is not said that Love Justifieth; but Faith that worketh (even in its essentiall work of Accepting) by Love <Gal 5:6>."[282]

Baxter's view on the relation between faith and love is the cause of a rather lengthy discussion with Cartwright.[283] The latter maintains that love is properly a fruit of justifying faith. For this assertion he appeals to 1 John 4:19: "We love him,

---

276. Baxter, *Aphorismes* I.266 (pp. 169-70).
277. Baxter buttresses his position with appeals to Daniel Chamier and Johannes Maccovius. Chamier maintains that faith is love because of the volitional character of faith. Maccovius states explicitly that *amor complacentiae* is required in faith. In answering the objection that he confounds faith with charity, Maccovius appeals to Martin Chemnitz, who distinguishes between love to Christ as the meritorious cause, and charity to God and our neighbor. Only the former is included in faith (Baxter, *Confession*, pp. 390, 399-400; *Of Saving Faith*, pp. 83-84).
278. Baxter, *Of Justification*, p. 348. Cf. *Confession*, p. 34.
279. Baxter, *Aphorismes* I.267 (p. 170). Cf. *Account of my Consideration*, pp. 199-200.
280. Baxter, *Of Justification*, p. 347.
281. Baxter, *Aphorismes* I.267 (p. 170); *Of Justification*, p. 346. Cf. *Catholick Theologie* I.ii.84: "Faith as it signifieth meer *Assent*, differeth from *Love*, as the act of the *Intellect*, from *Volition:* And Love formally taken presupposeth the *Assent*, and doth not contain it. But *Faith* taken largely in the sence of the Baptismal Covenant, containeth in it *Consent*, which is the *Wills Volition*, and therefore must needs have some *initial Love* in it as it acteth in *Desire*."
282. Baxter, *Aphorismes* I.268 (p. 171). Baxter also compares the relation between faith and love to the case of a condemned beggar who is offered pardon, and who will be made a queen if she will take the prince for her husband. Baxter then asks: "*Is it then a meet phrase to say, that she is pardoned and dignified by loving such a Prince?* Answ. It hath some Truth in it, but it is not a fit speech; but rather that it is *by marrying him*, because Love is but a part, or as it were an Affection of that *Marriage Covenant* or *consent*, which indeed doth dignifie her. Love may be without marriage, but not Marriage (cordially) without Love. So in our present case, justifying faith is the very Marriage Consent or Covenant with Christ; It is therefore fitter to say, we are justified by it, then by love; because the former expresseth the full condition: the latter not" (*Of Justification*, p. 348).
283. Baxter, *Account of my Consideration*, pp. 196-204; Cartwright, *Exceptions*, pp. 92-96.

because he first loved us."[284] Especially since Baxter's *Aphorismes* speak of love
which has its object present (*amor complacentiae*), the conclusion must be that
this love follows faith: "Christ must be received by Faith, that so he may be
present and *enjoyed*, and consequently, that he may be loved as such. And therefore Love in this sense is rather a fruit of Faith, than a part of it, as you endeavour
to prove."[285] Consent goes before the enjoyment of the object of faith. The embracing of Christ presupposes a love of desire (*amor desiderii*). It is followed,
however, by *amor complacentiae*.[286] The former is to love something which is
absent (*amare quod abest*), the latter is to love something which is present (*amare
quod adest*).[287] Cartwright distances himself from Baxter's appeal to Galatians
5:6, and he appeals to Calvin, who states in his exposition on Galatians:

> In the present passage Paul does not dispute whether love cooperates with faith in
> justifying; but, lest he should seem to make Christians idle and like blocks of wood,
> he indicates the true exercises of believers. When you discuss justification, beware
> of allowing any mention of love or of works, but resolutely hold on to the exclusive
> adverb.[288]

With regard to this appeal to Calvin, Baxter only comments: "*James* took not
Calvin's counsel in his phrase of Speech."[289] Baxter further insists that our love to
God does not arise from the belief that he loves me in particular more than others,
but from the apprehension of God's common love to mankind in giving Christ.[290]
This offer of Christ makes the object of faith present. This present offer must be
accepted.[291]

The distance between Baxter and Cartwright should not be exaggerated. Cartwright admits that *amor desiderii* precedes faith, or is included with it, and Baxter
shies away from the explicit assertion that *amor complacentiae* is the antecedent
condition for God's love to a person.[292] Nevertheless, the fear of Baxter's oppo-

---

284. Cartwright, in Baxter, *Account of my Consideration*, p. 196; Cartwright, *Exceptions*, pp. 92-93, 95.
285. Cartwright, in Baxter, *Account of my Consideration*, p. 198.
286. Cartwright, *Exceptions*, p. 93.
287. Cartwright, *Exceptions*, p. 94.
288. John Calvin, *The Epistles of Paul the Apostle to the Galatians, Ephesians, Philippians and Colossians*, trans. T.H.L. Parker, ed. David W. Torrance and Thomas F. Torrance, Calvin's Commentaries (Edinburgh, 1965; rpt. Grand Rapids: Eerdmans, n.d.), p. 96. ("Quantum ad prae-sentem locum attinet, Paulus nequaquam disputat an caritas ad iustificandum cooperetur fidei, sed tantum indicat quae nunc sint vera fidelium exercitia: ne Christianos videatur otiosus facere et quasi truncis similes. Ergo quum versaris in causa iustificationis, cave ullam caritatis vel operum mentionem admittas, sed mordicus retine particulam exclusivam" [*CO* 50.247].)
289. Baxter, *Account of my Consideration*, p. 202. Baxter later clarifies that he had no "taunting intent" with his remark on Calvin: "The words signifie but this, [James *his practice was contrary to the counsel that* Calvin *there gives, not to use the terms, of being justified by Works*:] I thought the Emperor or the Pope would have endured as hard language as this" (*Substance*, p. 29).
290. Baxter, *Account of my Consideration*, p. 197.
291. Baxter, *Account of my Consideration*, p. 199.
292. Baxter comments in a clarifying remark: "I never thought that *all Love* considereth its Object as *present*, (much less *as enjoyed*; but only *amor complacentiæ*" (*Account of my Consideration*, p. 199). Nevertheless, Cartwright has good reason to assume that in his *Aphorismes* Baxter was, in fact, speaking of complacential love as a condition for God's love. In his *Aphorismes* Baxter had

nents that he includes works in the definition of justification is understandable. When Baxter makes love an essential aspect of faith, Cartwright concludes that works become part of faith. But Cartwright does not want to deny that faith presupposes love to God. Consequently, he argues that only *amor desiderii* is an antecedent condition for God's love to man.

WORKS AND CONTINUED JUSTIFICATION

Works, Justification, and Salvation

Baxter's opponents are not convinced that he really excludes works from initial justification. They are equally worried by Baxter's frank admission that works are a condition for continuing justification. It is to be expected that Baxter's most hostile accusers disagree with him on this score. It can hardly be expected from someone who denies conditionality of the covenant that he attributes a significant role to works. The opposition of Eyre, Crandon, and Warner is understandable.[293] But also Calvinists of a more moderate character are convinced that Baxter makes a fundamental mistake in making works a condition for continued and consummate justification. Anthony Burgess insists that "faith is only the condition justifying,"[294] and that "good works are not Conditions."[295] Works "of all sort" are excluded by the apostle Paul.[296] It is not only meritorious works that are excluded, "for the Apostles Argument <in Romans 4:4> is *à genere*, if it be by works, its of

---

stated that "desire and hope, as such, do properly consider their object as absent, which this Justifying Faith doth not" (*Aphorismes* I.267 [p. 170]). Because he differentiates between desire and hope on the one hand, and love on the other, it is clear that Baxter had *amor complacentiae* in mind. That Cartwright is correct in this assumption is clear also from the fact that Baxter's clarifying statement does not really deny that *amor complacentiae* is part of justifying faith. He merely states that love may either consider its object as absent (like desire and hope) or as present. Love is, therefore, just a broader term than desire or hope. Also, Baxter states unequivocally that God's offer makes the object of faith present, and that, therefore, "<f>aith and Love here do consider their object as alike present" (*Account of my Consideration*, p. 199). Baxter later seems to be somewhat more careful in describing the love which is part of faith. In contradiction to his *Aphorismes*, Baxter then describes faith as "desire." He maintains that faith "hath in it essentially somewhat of Initial Love to God, to Christ, to Recovery, to Glory; that is, of Volition; and so of Desire" (*Of Imputation*, p. 162; cf. *End of Doctrinal Controversies*, p. 277).

293. Cf. Eyre's vehement charge: "Though Mr. *B.* seems to mince the matter, calling his conditions but a *sine qua non*, and a *Pepper corn, &c.* he attributes as much, if not more to works, then the Papists, Arminians, and Socinians, have done ..." (*Vindiciæ Justificationis Gratuitæ*, p. 190). Also Crandon has nothing but disdain for Baxter's understanding of the conditionality of the covenant: "But this *mouth-almighty Condition, when like Bel and the Dragon*, she hath eaten up and swallowed into her bowels, Christ, faith, and works; doth of, and by her self alone justifie, such a Justifyer, and such a Justification" (*Aphorisms Exorized* II.v.83). Warner states that justification does not depend on good works, "because when good works, the fruits of faith, are *interrupted* yet our justification abides by the *single influence* of Faith, only as a totall cause of its being, and conservation" (*Diatriba fidei justificantis*, p. 245).
294. Burgess, in Baxter, *Of Justification*, p. 177.
295. Burgess, *True Doctrine*, II, 220.
296. Burgess, *True Doctrine*, II, 222.

debt."[297] Also Cartwright maintains that all good works are works of the law and that, consequently, "<t>he Apostle doth simply and absolutely exclude Works from Justification."[298] Finally, John Eedes insists that "*Paul* excludes all Works."[299]

Burgess does not want to downplay the necessity of works. If a person does not continue in good works, justification also "cannot be continued."[300] But, adds Burgess:

> for all that they are not *Conditions* of his *Justification*, they are *qualifications* and *determinations* of the *Subject* who is *justified*, but no *Conditions* of his *Justification*... Its a thousand times affirmed by our Divines, Many things are required to the constitution of some Subject, which yet are not either causes or conditions of such and such an effect: Light is necessarily required, and drinesse, as qualities in fire, ye<t> it burneth as its hot, not as light or dry. To the integral being of a man, are required his head and shoulders, so that the eye could not see, if not seated there, yet a mans shoulders are not the *Causa sine quâ non* of his seeing.[301]

Burgess acknowledges that a godly life is "a necessary qualification of a man for pardon."[302] Good works are *media ordinata* for pardon.[303] The real issue is, according to Burgess, that by works a person cannot apply Christ's righteousness.[304] This is the reason for his refusal to call works a condition of justification. Burgess is afraid that by speaking of works as a condition Baxter will attribute a causal role to man's obedience.

Because Burgess maintains that good works necessarily characterize a justified person, he maintains that more is necessary for salvation than for justification: "Seeing therefore that *Justification* is *antecedent* to an holy life, good works cannot be any *Condition* of it; and by this we may see, That more things are required to our *Salvation*, then to our *Justification*; To the possession of heaven, and the entituling us thereunto ..."[305] By sharply distinguishing justification from salvation Burgess can maintain, on the one hand, that justification is only by faith as an instrument and a condition, and, on the other hand, that works are qualifications of those justified people who will ultimately be saved.

This position raises several questions. Baxter immediately brings these forward. He questions what Burgess means when he says that justification can only be continued in the way of a godly life. If good works are an ordained means for pardon, does this not at least imply that they are a condition? "If *medii*, then what

297. Burgess, *True Doctrine*, II, 223.
298. Cartwright, in Baxter, *Account of my Consideration*, p. 217. Cf. pp. 259-60.
299. Eedes, *Orthodox Doctrine*, p. 59. Cf. pp. 60-61.
300. Burgess, *True Doctrine*, II, 230.
301. Burgess, *True Doctrine*, II, 230. Burgess employs the well known adage that faith justifies *quae viva*, not *qua viva* (in Baxter, *Of Justification*, p. 178; for Baxter's reply, see p. 192). Also John Crandon states that *fides solum iustificat, non autem fides sola* (*Aphorisms Exorized* II.vi.100). Cf. Warner, *Diatriba fidei justificantis*, pp. 31-36. Baxter denies the validity of these distinctions (*Aphorismes* I.298 [p. 191]; *Account*, p. 14).
302. Burgess, in Baxter, *Of Justification*, p. 179.
303. Burgess, in Baxter, *Of Justification*, p. 177.
304. Burgess, in Baxter, *Of Justification*, p. 180.
305. Burgess, *True Doctrine*, II, 230.

medium is it? not a cause. If not a condition, then tell us what, if you can."[306] With
regard to Burgess' distinction between justification and salvation, Baxter comments that the doing of Christ's commandments is the condition of our right to
salvation. And what is justification but a right or title to salvation?[307]

Baxter regards the separation of justification and salvation as an illegitimate
attempt to explain the texts in Scripture that connect salvation to good works,
while at the same time opposing justification by works. Cartwright's disconnec-
tion between justification and salvation has the same background. He maintains
that we are "not fully possessed of Salvation, not glorified without good Works, as
we are fully justified without them."[308] According to Baxter, Cartwright fails to
distinguish properly between the various stages of justification. To retain one's
justification, a further condition is necessary. Moreover, Baxter continues, "*sentential Justification* is the most proper Justification and full; and that is not full (if
at all) till Judgment."[309] This means, in Baxter's view, that when Burgess and
Cartwright separate justification and salvation, they in fact deny sentential justification at the last judgement, even though this is justification in the most proper
and full sense of the word.[310]

Work For or From Life?

Because Baxter maintains that works are a condition of continued and consummate justification, sanctification receives a central place in his soteriology. This
may be illustrated by means of two issues. The first is the question whether one
may work only *from*, or also *for* life and justification. Baxter takes issue on this
point with the teaching of the *Marrow of Modern Divinity*, which had been published anonymously in 1645 by Edward Fisher, described by Baxter as "an honest
Barber."[311] The *Marrow* contains a number of features which later created the
Marrow Controversy (1718-23) in Scotland.[312]

---

306. Baxter, *Of Justification*, p. 131.
307. Baxter, *Of Justification*, p. 130. Baxter also discusses the relation between justification and
     salvation in *Aphorismes* I.310-13 (pp. 199-200); *Account of my Consideration*, pp. 264-74, 276-
     77, 285-88, sigs. X5ʳ-X8ᵛ; *Substance*, pp. 62-65, 67-69; *Confession*, pp. 48, 55, 310-12; *Of
     Justification*, pp. 171, 415; *Breviate*, pp. 52-53.
308. Cartwright, in Baxter, *Account of my Consideration*, p. 267.
309. Baxter, *Account of my Consideration*, p. 265.
310. Baxter, *Account of my Consideration*, p. 271. As noted earlier, Cartwright regards the last judge-
     ment only as the "full manifestation" of what we now already have by faith (in Baxter, *Account of
     my Consideration*, p. 276; cf. above, p. 125).
     Baxter supports his identification between consummate justification and a right to salvation by
     means of several arguments: (1) Paul excludes the same works from justification and salvation
     (Rom 3:23-24; 4:4, 13, 16; 5:17-18; 6:23; 8:1-2, 6, 13-14, 17; Eph 2:4-9; 5:8-9; Tit 3:5-7; Heb 11)
     (*Confession*, pp. 310-11; *Of Justification*, p. 415; *Breviate*, p. 52); (2) justification at the last
     judgement is a proper judgement (1 Pet 4:5; 2 Tim 4:1; Acts 17:31; John 5:22, 24, 26-27; Rev
     20:12-13; 1 Cor 4:4; 1 Pet 1:17; Luke 10:14; Heb 6:2; 9:27; Eccl 12:14; 11:9; Rom 14:10; 2 Cor
     5:10; Matt 25) (*Substance*, p. 68); (3) justification at the last judgement has the same condition as
     glorification (Matt 12:37; Matt 25) (*Confession*, p. 311; *Breviate*, p. 53).
311. Baxter, *Catholick Theologie* II.255.
312. For the *Marrow* and the controversy in Scotland, see D.M. McIntire, "First Strictures on 'The
     Marrow of Modern Divinity'," *EvQ*, 10 (1938), 61-70; John Macleod, *Scottish Theology in*

The *Marrow* is divided into two sections. The first part discusses the relation between the law of works, the law of grace, and the law of Christ. The second section discusses the ten commandments. The *Marrow* strongly emphasizes the free offer of the Gospel. It does so on the basis of what may seem to be universal redemption. It states that God "hath made a deed of gift and grant unto them all"[313] and that everyone "without exception" should be told that "Christ is dead for him."[314] One's personal application of this truth is saving faith. When Paul and Silas told the jailor to believe, they told him to "be verily persuaded in your heart that Jesus Christ is yours, and that you shall have life and salvation by him; that whatsoever Christ did for the redemption of mankind, he did it for you."[315] The *Marrow* combines this emphasis on the free offer and assurance of faith with a strict doctrine of substitution, by which Christ "entered into the same covenant that the first Adam did ..."[316] As all people sinned in Adam as a public person, so the believers died and rose in Christ.[317] This means that his obedience is imputed to believers, so that they are "dead" to the covenant of works.[318] The *Marrow* carries the spiritual marriage with Christ so far, that it comments that the law can no longer demand good works for salvation,

> for in Christ I have all things at once; neither need I any thing more that is necessary to salvation. He is my righteousness, my treasure, and work; I confess, O law! that I am neither godly nor righteous, but yet this I am sure of, that he is godly and righteous for me. And to tell the truth, O law! I am now with him in the bridechamber, where it maketh no matter what I am, or what I have done; but what Christ, my sweet husband is, has done, and does for me: and therefore leave off, law, to dispute with me, for by faith "I apprehend him who hath apprehended me," and put me into his bosom.[319]

The believer has no righteousness of his own, but can only rest on Christ, who has fulfilled the law for him. Holiness becomes underrated as a result. The law of Christ is the moral law. It is the same in substance and matter as the law of works. The form, however, differs: "<T>he one saith, 'Do this and live'; and the other saith, 'Live, and do this'; the one saith, Do this *for* life; the other saith, Do this *from* life ..."[320] Thus, it is wrong to avoid evil for fear of hell or to do good works

Relation to Church History since the Reformation, 2nd ed. (Edinburgh: Publications Committee of the Free Church of Scotland, 1946), pp. 139-66; Sell, *Great Debate*, pp. 56-57; Karlberg, "Mosaic Covenant," pp. 166-74; Karlberg, "Reformed Interpretation," 33-35; M. Charles Bell, *Calvin and Scottish Theology: The Doctrine of Assurance* (Edinburgh: Handsel, 1985), pp. 151-80; John J. Murray, "The Marrow Controversy: Thomas Boston and the Free Offer," in *Preaching and Revival*, Proc. of the Westminster Conference, 1984 (Thornton Heath, Surrey: Westminster Conference, [1985]), pp. 34-56; Harinck, *Schotse verbondsleer*, pp. 142-45; Lachman, *Marrow Controversy.*

313. Edward Fisher, *The Marrow of Modern Divinity: In Two Parts*, annotated Thomas Boston (Rpt; Edmonton, AB: Still Waters Revival, 1991), p. 126.
314. Fisher, *Marrow*, p. 127.
315. Fisher, *Marrow*, p. 118.
316. Fisher, *Marrow*, p. 106.
317. Fisher, *Marrow*, p. 108.
318. Fisher, *Marrow*, p. 109.
319. Fisher, *Marrow*, pp. 167-69.
320. Fisher, *Marrow*, p. 174.

in anticipation of heaven. This would be a "slavish" obedience.[321] At this point, the *Marrow* appeals to Luke 1:74-75 ("that we being delivered out of the hand of our enemies might serve him without fear, In holiness and righteousness before him, all the days of our life").[322]

Tobias Crisp's teaching is similar to that of the *Marrow*. He is afraid that people humble themselves, fast, pray, and weep in order to avoid evils or to attain assurance. Comments Crisp: "Beloved, I tell you plainly, there is none of all these things that you doe conduce a jot towards the obtaining of any of these ends, you propose to your selves: All you doe gets not a jot; nay, doth not concurre in it."[323] Crisp warns his hearers that it is impossible for a person to establish his "own righteousnesse to expect the dealings of God to him ..."[324] Christ is the end of both the curse and the life of the law.[325] Therefore, one cannot expect life by obedience to the law.[326] There are no conditions in the covenant:

> We say, the Lord hath firmly established upon his own people every thing, that concernes the peace, comfort and good of his people, simply and meerly for his own sake, without respect or regard to any thing his people doe performe: That they are to doe, they are not to doe it with any eye to their own advantage, that being already perfectly compleated to their hands before they doe any thing; but simply with an eye to glorifie God, and to serve their generation, and therein to serve the Lord, and therein to set forth the praise of the glory of his grace, that hath done so abundantly for them.[327]

According to Crisp, one must not do good works "with any eye" to one's own advantage. This would make one "lyable to the covenant of works" with its principle of "Do this and live."[328]

In his *Aphorismes*, Baxter briefly objects to the teaching of the *Marrow* that "we must not Act for justification or salvation; but onely in thankfulness for it."[329] When Baxter is questioned on his denunciation of this doctrine, he gives a lengthy rebuttal of the *Marrow* in the appendix to his *Aphorismes*.[330] He acknowledges Edward Fisher's "godlinesse and Moderation" and values "the greatest part" of the book.[331] Nevertheless, Baxter opposes some central aspects of the *Marrow*'s doctrine. Also elsewhere, he continues to warn against the Antinomian implications of the *Marrow*.[332] He warns that the inclusion of assurance in the definition

---

321. Fisher, *Marrow*, p. 200.
322. Fisher, *Marrow*, p. 203.
323. Crisp, *Christ Alone Exalted*, I (London, 1643), 301-02.
324. Crisp, *Christ Alone Exalted*, I, 306.
325. Crisp, *Christ Alone Exalted*, I, 308.
326. Crisp, *Christ Alone Exalted*, I, 308-09.
327. Crisp, *Christ Alone Exalted*, I, 305.
328. Crisp, *Christ Alone Exalted*, I, 307. Baxter opposes these notions of Crisp without presenting any extended argumentation (*Defence of Christ*, sigs. A8ʳ⁻ᵛ, B1ᵛ-B2ᵛ, pp. 29, 37). Baxter's arguments are more elaborate in his refutation of the *Marrow*.
329. Baxter, *Aphorismes* I.330 (p. 212).
330. Baxter, *Aphorismes* II.8, 76-106 (pp. 228, 262-81). Cf. on this the discussion of McIntyre, "First Strictures," 67-69.
331. Baxter, *Aphorismes* II.99 (p. 276).
332. Baxter, *Admonition*, p. 19; *Unsavoury Volume*, p. 26; *Confession*, pp. 123-24, 127, 177-78.

of faith implies that "we must believe a lye to make it a truth."[333] He does not agree that it is only "slavish" obedience if one works for the reward of heaven.[334] He particularly opposes the assertion that we must not work *for* life, but only *from* life.[335] The Gospel also says, "Do this and live."[336] Luke 1:74-75 does not speak about the fear of hell but only about the fear of our enemies.[337]

Baxter mentions five ways in which God commands us to act for life: (1) an unbeliever must use the means of grace "that so he may obtain the first life of grace and faith";[338] (2) a believer is permitted to "act for the increase of this spirituall life";[339] (3) we "may and must act for" reconciliation, justification, and adoption;[340] (4) we "may act for" the obtaining of assurance;[341] and (5) we "may act for eternall life and salvation."[342] Baxter uses several arguments to support his thesis that one must work for salvation. If one is allowed to act for the preservation of one's natural life, it is certainly permitted to do so for one's soul, seeing it is more important.[343] Also, if one may not work for life, how can one pray for it?[344] One would erroneously infer that he is already in heaven and that "all the work is done."[345] Considering the fact that heaven simply means the eternal enjoyment of God, "is it such a legall slavish mercenary thing for a Christian to seek after the fruition of God?"[346] God has created the "love of our selvs" as a natural power of the soul with the purpose to "labour for God in Heaven, or for nothing."[347] Baxter points out that "especially, I would have you throughly consider" the purpose of God's conditional promises and threats.[348] This can only be the fruition of God in heaven. There is "almost nothing else" to work for.[349] At this point, Baxter once again appeals to the Scriptures, that make it obvious that one must strive to enter,[350] and that we must fear going to hell.[351]

---

333. Baxter, *Aphorismes* II.104 (p. 279).
334. Baxter, *Aphorismes* II.100 (p. 277). Cf. *Confession*, pp. 177-78.
335. Baxter, *Aphorismes* II.101 (p. 278).
336. Baxter, *Aphorismes* II.77 (p. 263).
337. Baxter, *Aphorismes* II.100 (p. 277).
338. Baxter, appeals to Isa 55:3, 6, 7; Jonah 3:8-10; Prov 1:23-25; Amos 5:4; Acts 2:37; Isa 1:16; Matt 11:15; 13:43; Luke 16:29, 31; John 5:25; Acts 10:1-2, 22-23; Rom 10:13-14; 1 Tim 4:16; Heb 3:7; Rev 3:20; Joel 2:12-14; Zeph 2:3; Exod 32:30 (*Aphorismes* II.78-79 [p. 264]).
339. Baxter appeals to 1 Pet 2:1-2; 1:22; 2 Pet 1:5-8; 3:18; Matt 25:26-28, 30 (*Aphorismes* II.79 [p. 264]).
340. Baxter appeals to Isa 1:16-18; 55:6-7; Acts 8:22; Jas 5:15 (*Aphorismes* II.80 [p. 264]).
341. Baxter appeals to 2 Pet 1:10; 2 Cor 13:5 (*Aphorismes* II.80 [p. 264]).
342. Baxter appeals to Rev 22:14; John 5:39-40; Matt 11:12; 7:13; Luke 13:24; Phil 2:17; Rom 2:7, 10; 1 Cor 9:24; 2 Tim 2:5, 12; 1 Tim 6:12, 18-19; Phil 3:14; Matt 25; 1 Cor 15:58; 2 Cor 4:17; 5:10-11; 2 Pet 1:10-11; Luke 11:28; Heb 4:1; Luke 12:5; 1 Cor 9:17 (*Aphorismes* II.80-81 [pp. 264-65]).
343. Baxter, *Aphorismes* II.83-84 (pp. 266-67).
344. Baxter, *Aphorismes* II.84-85 (pp. 267-68).
345. Baxter, *Aphorismes* II.86 (p. 268).
346. Baxter, *Aphorismes* II.87 (p. 269). Cf. *Confession*, p. 178.
347. Baxter, *Aphorismes* II.88 (p. 270).
348. Baxter, *Aphorismes* II.90-91 (p. 271).
349. Baxter, *Aphorismes* II.92 (p. 272).
350. Baxter appeals to John 5:39-40; Matt 6:33; Phil 3:14; 1 Tim 6:12, 18-19; Phil 2:12; Rev 22:14; 2:7, 10-11, 13-14, 16-17, 19, 23, 26-29; 3:2-5; 8:10-13, 15-16, 20-22; Matt 18:8-9; John 5:29;

John Crandon hastens to the *Marrow*'s defense.[352] He first remarks that he never knew who the author of the *Marrow* was and that he has only read "here and there a fragment" of it.[353] He adds, however, that this is sufficient to judge that the book is "not onely orthodox but singularly usefull."[354] He defends the *Marrow*'s use of Luke 1:74-75. He maintains that this text speaks of deliverance not just from wicked men but from sin, death, and hell. There is no longer any need to be afraid of condemnation: "Is not deliverance heere the same thing with the salvation mentioned ver. 77, which Iohn was to preach? but that was salvation, and so is this deliverance, *by the remission of sins*; and consequently we must serve (who are in Christ,) *without feare of vengeance and Hell*."[355] According to Crandon it is impossible that fear of hell could arise "from the apprehension of the pardon of his sin."[356] Thus, he maintains with the *Marrow* that the difference between the two covenants is that "<t>he one bids us to seeke it <*i.e.*, life> by Works, the other by Fayth."[357]

Also William Eyre states that he disagrees with Baxter, who characterizes the following position as Antinomian: "That we must not perform duty for Life and Salvation, but from Life and Salvation; or that we must not make the attaining of Justification or Salvation, the end of our endeavors, but obey in thankfulness, and because we are justified and saved, &c."[358] According to Eyre, this is common Protestant teaching. Baxter's horrified response is: "Now God forbid!"[359] Baxter maintains that numerous Protestants teach that we must work for life and salvation. He moderates his opinion somewhat, however, by acknowledging that thankfulness and love must be "the chiefest spring" of duty, that there is much in "Christs common love in his satisfaction" to be thankful for ("which I suppose you deny") and that Christians must act from the "principle of our new spiritual life" and from God's love which precedes ours.[360] This is a somewhat more balanced presentation than Baxter gives in his *Aphorismes*, although he does not detract from anything he has said there.

Acts 2:28; 1 Tim 4:8; Jas 1:12; 1 Pet 3:10; Rom 2:7; Tit 1:2; 2 Tim 4:18; Matt 5:12; 6:1; 19:21; Luke 10:20; Phil 1:19; 1 Pet 1:9; Heb 2:3; 2 Tim 2:10; 1 Thess 5:8-9; Acts 16:17 (*Aphorismes* II.94-95 [pp. 273-74]).

351. Baxter appeals to Luke 12:5; Heb 4:1; Prov 15:24; Mark 3:29; 16:16; Matt 5:25; Rom 11:21, 44; 1 Cor 10:12; Heb 12:15-16; Jas 5:9, 12 (*Aphorismes* II.96 [p. 274]).

352. Crandon, *Aphorisms Exorized* II.x.153-65.

353. Crandon, *Aphorisms Exorized* II.x.154.

354. Crandon, *Aphorisms Exorized* II.x.154.

355. Crandon, *Aphorisms Exorized* II.x.156.

356. Crandon, *Aphorisms Exorized* II.x.157.

357. Crandon, *Aphorisms Exorized* II.x.158.

358. Eyre, *Vindiciæ Justificationis Gratuitæ*, p. 26. Cf. Christopher Cartwright: "It is one thing to work for *Life* and *Salvation*, that is, the bliss and happiness of the Life to come; another thing to work for *Justification*, or that we may be justified: The Scriptures teach us as well to deny this, as to assert the other" (in Baxter, *Account of my Consideration*, p. 285).

359. Baxter, *Admonition*, p. 19.

360. Baxter, *Admonition*, p. 19. Leo F. Solt wrongly states: "In Baxter's view the true believer performed his duties *for* life and salvation and not *from* life and salvation" (*Saints in Arms*, p. 37). For Baxter, the issue is not either/or, but both/and, even though he emphasizes the former in reaction to the denial that one may work for life. Cf. Beougher's criticism on Solt in "Conversion," p. 104.

Holiness the Design of Christianity

Baxter's emphasis on the need for sanctification also comes to the fore in his reaction to a treatise of the Latitudinarian divine, Edward Fowler, entitled *The Design of Christianity* (1671). In his reply, *How Far Holinesse is the Design of Christianity* (1671), Baxter refuses to identify his position with that of Fowler: "I am responsible for no mans Writings but my own ..."[361] Nevertheless, he maintains that Fowler's book is "of very much worth and use."[362] It is helpful to give a brief overview of Fowler's argument, both because Baxter's reluctance to criticize Fowler is indicative of his sympathy for Fowler's Latitudinarianism and because there are some notable similarities between the views of both authors.

Fowler gives an extended description of holiness at the beginning of his treatise:

> It is so sound and healthful a Complexion of Soul, as maintains in life and vigour whatsoever is Essential to it, and suffers not any thing unnatural to mix with that which is so; by the force and power whereof a man is enabled to behave himself as becometh a Creature indued with a principle of Reason; keeps his Supreme Faculty in its Throne, brings into due Subjection all his Inferiour ones, his sensual Imagination, his Brutish Passions and Affections.
>
> It is the Purity of the Humane Nature, engaging those in whom it resides, to demean themselves sutably to that state in which God hath placed them, and not to act disbecomingly in any Condition, Circumstance, or Relation.
>
> It is a Divine or God-like Nature, causing an hearty approbation of, and an affectionate compliance with the Eternal Laws of Righteousness; and a behaviour agreeable to the Essential and Immutable differences of Good and Evil.[363]

Fowler's definition may function as a brief summary of his understanding of the doctrine of sanctification. Several elements are unacceptable from a high Calvinist perspective, such as that of John Bunyan, whose *Defence of the Doctrine of Iustification* (1672) vehemently opposes Fowler's doctrine. First, Fowler's description of holiness as a "sound an healthful" complexion of the soul raises the question how seriously he takes the depravity of man. Bunyan maintains that "there is no such thing as the purity of our Nature, *abstract* and *distinct* from the *sinful* pollution that dwelleth in us."[364] Bunyan's suspicion is enhanced by Fowler's enthronement of human reason as the supreme faculty. Fowler thus contents himself "to rest within the confines of the human Nature," charges Bunyan.[365] It is not true that the Christian acts from the principle of human reason. He acts from a "better Principle": the Holy Spirit.[366] Bunyan accuses Fowler of a humanizing tendency: he fails to mention the Holy Spirit, faith in Christ, and a new heart, all three of which are essential to true sanctification:

---

361. Baxter, *How Far Holinesse*, p. 2.
362. Baxter, *How Far Holinesse*, p. 2.
363. Fowler, *Design* (London, 1671), p. 6 (emphasis inverted).
364. Bunyan, *Defence* (1672), in *Works* 4.12.
365. Bunyan, *Defence*, in *Works* 4.17.
366. Bunyan, *Defence*, in *Works* 4.18.

> Without these three, there is no such thing as Gospel holiness in Man, as before I have also hinted at. But now as there is none of these three found in your description of inward Holiness; so neither can you, or other, by all your inclinations, either to those you call first principles of natural reason, or the dictates of humane nature, obtain or fetch in the Soul, the least dram of that which is essential, to that which is indeed according to the Gospel description of inward Gospel holiness ...[367]

Thus, according to Bunyan, Fowler has replaced faith in Christ with the "dictates of human nature." This leads to a moralism without Christianity, a holiness which is "no other then what is common to all the men on Earth."[368]

Bunyan's critique is not based on a careful analysis and evaluation of Fowler's position. His accusation, for instance, that Fowler undermines the doctrine of man's depravity by exalting human reason is not altogether correct. Fowler explicitly states that people, "by their Apostacy from God, and sinking into Brutish sensuality, did they sadly dispossess themselves of it <i.e., man's true holiness>, and so became like the Beasts which perish."[369] Fowler then goes on to speak of God's sending his Son "for the Recovery of Fallen Mankind."[370] It is nevertheless true that Fowler's christology and his doctrine of the atonement have a moralizing and humanizing tendency. His overriding concern is to prove that holiness is the "Ultimate Design" of the Savior's coming.[371] Fowler even maintains that holiness is the "only Design" of the Christian precepts.[372] The promises and threats of the Gospel "have most apparently the promoting of *Holiness* for their onely Design."[373] Everything else in the discussion becomes subservient to this ultimate design of holiness. As a result, Christ is pictured as someone who promotes holiness. Fowler discusses at length the purpose of Christ's discourses and actions, of his miracles, of his death, his resurrection, and his coming again to judge.[374] After discussing Christ's disposition, Fowler characteristically concludes:

> And thus we have sufficiently and fully enough proved, that it was the whole business of our Saviour's life to make men in all respects *Vertuous* and *Holy*; and that thereunto were subservient, as his *Discourses* with them, so his *Actions* likewise and whole Behaviour. *Plus docent exempla quàm præcepta:* Examples are the most natural and easie way of teaching, and they are so by reason of Mankinds being so greatly addicted to imitation; and, I say, it doth from our past discourse sufficiently appear, That our Saviour's whole Conversation was a rare exemplification of all kinds of Vertue and true Goodness.[375]

---

367. Bunyan, *Defence*, in *Works* 4.27.
368. Bunyan, *Defence*, in *Works* 4.21.
369. Fowler, *Design*, p. 11. Fowler does emphasize the role of reason. Yet, he also warns against having "too high" an opinion of our own rationality. Reason must be submitted to divine revelation, not the other way around (pp. 274-75).
370. Fowler, *Design*, p. 12.
371. Fowler, *Design*, sig. A3ᵛ.
372. Fowler, *Design*, p. 18.
373. Fowler, *Design*, p. 28.
374. Fowler, *Design*, pp. 36-98.
375. Fowler, *Design*, pp. 67-68.

Fowler's entire christology centers around its connections with the ultimate design: holiness. The nature of the atonement is only briefly referred to.[376] Fowler
makes no mention of God's justice being propitiated. Without expressing his own
view on the matter, he comments that many "do not question but that God could
have pardoned sin without any other Satisfaction than the Repentance of the
Sinner ..."[377] Within this system of thought there is no place for any imputation of
Christ's righteousness to unrighteous people.[378] The condition is that man must be
"sincerely willing" to repent and obey Christ.[379] Justifying faith includes a sincere
resolution to obedience and the reception of Christ "for a *Lord*, as well as for a
Saviour."[380] Rejecting the "dangerous errour" of Antinomianism, Fowler explains
the imputation of Christ's righteousness as follows:

> <I>t consists in dealing with *sincerely* righteous persons, as if they were *perfectly*
> so, for the sake and upon the account of Christ's Righteousness. The *grand* intent of
> the Gospel being to make us partakers of an *Inward* and *Real* Righteousness, and it
> being but a *secondary* one that we should be *accepted* and rewarded as if we were
> *completely* righteous... .[381]

Fowler insists on holiness as the condition of the covenant.[382] More precisely,
sincerity, rather than perfection, is the key element in the fulfillment of the condition.[383] Fowler adds that the imputation of Christ's righteousness is only a secondary concern. It is a means leading to holiness. Justification is only a means toward
sanctification. The latter is the grand intent of the Gospel.

There is only one point in this understanding of the Gospel to which Baxter
takes exception. Unlike Fowler, he maintains that "*Personal Holiness* is not the
only end (or design) of God in mans Redemption, nor in instituting the Christian
Religion."[384] Baxter had earlier already denied that one's own sanctity is "the
Ultimate End" of Christ's satisfaction.[385] Still, he adds some extenuating circumstances. He believes that Fowler uses the word "only" as a "hyperbolical expression."[386] He does not think that Fowler intended to exclude all other ends. Moreover, holiness is indeed one of Christianity's "great and noble ends."[387] And even if
Fowler errs somewhat on the one extreme, "it ill beseemeth those to be their
censurers, who haue tempted them to it, by erring more on the contrary extream."[388]

376. Fowler, *Design*, pp. 80-81, 83-87.
377. Fowler, *Design*, p. 84.
378. Fowler, *Design*, p. 120.
379. Fowler, *Design*, p. 223.
380. Fowler, *Design*, p. 222.
381. Fowler, *Design*, pp. 225-26.
382. Fowler, *Design*, pp. 33, 81, 91-92.
383. Fowler, *Design*, p. 27. Fowler also mentions the condition of sincerity in pp. 81, 92, 108, 221,
    223, 296.
384. Baxter, *How Far Holinesse*, p. 12.
385. Baxter, *Confession*, p. 43 (emphasis throughout in original).
386. Baxter, *How Far Holinesse*, p. 13.
387. Baxter, *How Far Holinesse*, p. 13.
388. Baxter, *How Far Holinesse*, p. 14. Cf. p. 20: "And he that with one eye looks on that disease <*i.e.*,
    of erroneously "crying up the Gospel"> and its effects, and with the other looks on the Book you
    tell me of, and such like, will quickly see what Sore this Plaster was provided for, and how much
    excellent matter there is in it, which the foresaid persons and diseases need."

Baxter finds it remarkable that these same "censurers" are usually the ones who are quick to lament the loss of church discipline and the confounding of the holy and the profane. They should not be so hasty in condemning "such Writings, as drive harder for the promoting of Holiness than themselves."[389]

Because Baxter detects in Fowler an ally against Antinomianism he refuses to treat him as an adversary. Several elements in Fowler's position are appealing to Baxter. They share a dislike of a theory of strict imputation and of justification of unrighteous people, a strong emphasis on sincerity as the condition of the covenant, and on the place of reason.[390] Also, both authors have an inclusive concept of justifying faith: it is the acceptance of Christ as Lord as well as Savior. Most significant for the present purpose is that Fowler is not really alone in regarding holiness as the purpose of imputation and justification. Baxter makes a similar statement:

> As elsewhere I have often said, we must carefully distinguish between the Primitive or Primary and Natural part of Holiness; which is GODLINESSE or our LOVE to God as such; and the *mediate* remedying, subservient Part, which is *Faith in Christ*, or *Christianity* as such. The first is as *our Health*, the second as our *Medicine*.[391]

By distinguishing between love to God as the natural part of holiness and faith in Christ as the "remedying, subservient Part," Baxter makes the latter a means to the former. This is reinforced by his statement that faith is related to holiness in the same way as medicine is to health. At the same time, Baxter's language is reminiscent of his understanding of the covenants. The law of grace relates to the law of nature as a "remedying" law.[392] This means that Baxter's agreement with Fowler is not just superficial. Their respective frameworks have important similarities.

Significant differences between Baxter and Fowler remain, however. Baxter's description of holiness differs from that of Fowler. Baxter maintains that

> it is the Active Habitual and consequently relative, Separation, Dedication, & Devotion, of Intellectual free agents, by Life, Light and Love, to God our Father as his Children; or to God our Absolute *Owner, Ruler* and Benefactor, our Creator, Redeemer and Sanctifier, as his own peculiars, his Subjects and his Lovers.[393]

Baxter's description has a vertical dimension which is far less evident in Fowler's view on holiness. Thus, Isabel Rivers rightly observes that Baxter's understanding of holiness is different from Fowler's Latitudinarianism: "Despite his sympathy for Fowler – and in this dispute he is certainly closer to Fowler than to Bunyan – Baxter is critical of the self-interested, prudential, and human-oriented emphasis

---

389. Baxter, *How Far Holiness*, p. 19.
390. The place of reason in Baxter's theology has frequently been noted, but never systematically analyzed. A detailed study of his understanding of the role of human reason, of the relation between nature and grace, and of his relationship to Latitudinarianism and the Cambridge Platonists on this point would be worthwhile.
391. Baxter *How Far Holinesse*, p. 10.
392. Cf. above, p. 271.
393. Baxter, *How Far Holinesse*, p. 6.

of latitudinarian religion."[394] For Baxter, the primary object of holiness is God himself. Holiness is conformity to God's will.[395] The secondary object is the impressions or image of God in his works. This "secondary holiness" refers to the second table of the law.[396] Consequently, Baxter regards "morality" as an ambiguous term. Properly, it refers to all virtue and vice. This means that also faith in Christ is "a great part of our true Morality."[397] If unbelievers only have "secondary holiness," without any reference to God, this "is but Analogically called either *Holiness* or *Morality* ..."[398] Baxter's emphasis on holiness as one of the ends of Christianity retains a christological foundation and a vertical dimension that have all but disappeared in Fowler.[399]

Paul and James

Baxter's emphasis on inherent righteousness as a necessary condition for continued and consummate justification results in a harmonization between Paul and James which differs from that of his opponents. To be sure, Baxter's understanding of the role of works in justification does not depend solely on James. In his discussion with Christopher Cartwright, Baxter comments: "It is not only *James*, but multitudes of other plain Texts that must be forced, if your Opinion must stand."[400] On various occasions, Baxter mentions other texts that prove that not all works are excluded from justification.[401] Matthew 12:37 ("For by thy words thou shalt be justified, and by thy words thou shalt be condemned") and James 2:24 ("Ye see then how that by works a man is justified, and not by faith only") are his favorite texts.[402] The conclusion from these two texts is unmistakable: we are justified by our "words and works."[403]

---

394. Rivers, *Reason, Grace, and Sentiment*, p. 144.
395. Baxter, *How Far Holinesse*, p. 10.
396. Baxter, *How Far Holinesse*, pp. 6-7.
397. Baxter, *How Far Holinesse*, p. 9.
398. Baxter, *How Far Holinesse*, p. 9.
399. In his *Confession*, Baxter comments that holiness is one of the ends of Christ's satisfaction. He adds that he does not mean to say that sanctity is better than Christ's satisfaction, for (1) holiness is "but one part" of the end; and (2) the end is only better than the means in the formal notion of a means, but not simply and materially (p. 43).
400. Baxter, *Account of my Consideration*, p. 269.
401. Baxter appeals to Gen 7:1; 22:6, 16-18; Ps 2:12; 58:11; 91:9, 14; Prov 8:17, 21; 28:13, 18; 1 Kgs 8:30, 39; 2 Chr 34:26-27; Isa 1:16-19; 55:6-7; Ezek 14:16; 18:28-32; 33:11, 16; Matt 5:1-13, 16, 20, 44, 46; 6:1-2, 4, 6, 12, 14-15, 18; 7:13, 21, 23-24; 10:22, 37-38, 41-42; 11:12, 28-30; 13:49; 16:27; 18:35; 19:29; 25:21, 23, 34-36, 40-42, 46; Mark 1:4; 7:29; 11:11, 25-26; 13:34; Luke 6:27, 35, 37; 11:4, 28; 13:3, 5, 24; 16:9-10; 18:13-14; 19:17, 27; 24:47; John 3:19, 22-23; 5:22, 27-29; 10:11-12, 17; 12:26; 14:13-14, 21; 15:2-3, 10, 14; 16:27; Acts 2:21, 38; 3:19; 8:22, 24; 10:35; 17:30-31; 22:16; Rom 2:5-10, 13-14; 6:16; 8:4, 13, 28; 10:8-10, 13; 1 Cor 2:9; 3:8, 14; 9:17, 24-27; 16:22; 2 Cor 5:9-10; 9:6, 9; Gal 6:4-10; Eph 6:24; Phil 2:12; 4:17; Col 1:23; 2:18; 3:23-24; 2 Thess 1:5-6; 1 Tim 4:8, 16; 6:18-19; 2 Tim 2:5, 12; 4:7-8; Heb 5:9; 6:10; 10:35; 11:26; 12:14; Jas 1:12, 22-24; 2:5, 14; 5:15; 1 Pet 1:2, 16-17, 22; 3:21; 4:18; 1 John 1:9; 3:7, 10, 22-23; 5:15; Rev 2:5, 7, 16-17, 22, 26; 3:4, 10, 19; 7:14-15; 14:13; 20:12-13; 22:12, 14 (*Aphorismes* I.235-36, 310-13 [pp. 150-51, 199-200]; *Account of my Consideration*, pp. 262-64, 277-78; *Confession*, pp. 51, 57-64; *Of Justification*, pp. 81-83, 121, 130, 149, 245-46).
402. For Matt 12:37, see *Aphorismes* I.310 (p. 199); *Account of my Consideration*, pp. 262, 282; *Unsavoury Volume*, p. 44; *Confession*, pp. 58, 83, 311-12; *Of Justification*, pp. 70, 79-80, 94, 112,

The harmonization of James and Paul involves several exegetical problems. In the first place, the question is what James means with "faith" and "works" when he states that the former is not enough for justification. Cartwright maintains that the "dead" faith of which James speaks (2:17, 20) is a "barren and idle" faith.[404] According to Cartwright, James states that Abraham was not justified by such a dead faith, but by a "fruitful and working" faith.[405] Thus, "dead" and "working" are both adjectives referring to the nature of faith.[406] Baxter does not believe that James contrasts two different types of faith. The "dead" faith of which James speaks is mere assent.[407] The reason why this faith is called "dead" is not because there is something inherently wrong with it. The word "dead" does not refer to the nature of faith at all. Baxter even calls it "a good Belief."[408] But this good faith, this good assent, does not have a justifying and saving effect.[409] It is unprofitable.[410] Says Baxter: "I am the more confirmed, when I consider, that the death of Faith without Works here, *v.* 20, 14, 26, 24. is not merely the hypocrisie or seemingness of it: (He likeneth it to the real Faith of the Devils,) but the *inutility* of it as to justifie and save ..."[411] According to Baxter, therefore, the word "dead" refers to the result of this faith.[412] The assent of faith is unprofitable because works are needed in addition.[413]

This means that Baxter interprets James' question as follows: "What is the Condition of our Justification by this Righteousness of Christ? Whether Faith onely? or Works also?"[414] Baxter maintains that James places the assent of faith over against works. The former is not a sufficient condition. In his *Aphorismes,*

122; *Answer,* p. 22; *Of Imputation,* p. 197. For Jas 2:24, see *Account of my Consideration,* pp. 219, 282; *Confession,* pp. 58-59, 83; *Of Justification,* pp. 79-80, 94, 112, 122; *Answer,* p. 22; *Of Imputation,* p. 197.

403. Baxter, *Of Justification,* pp. 79, 183.

404. The King James Version speaks of a "dead" faith in 2:17, 20, 26. The word used in vv. 17 and 26 is indeed νεκρός (dead). In v. 20, however, either the word αργός (idle; unproductive) or κενός(empty) is used, depending on which textual variant is correct.

405. Cartwright, in Baxter, *Account of my Consideration,* p. 211.

406. Crandon, Burgess, and Warner hold essentially the same view as Cartwright (Crandon, *Aphorisms Exorized* II.vi.97-103; Burgess, *True Doctrine,* II, 237; Warner, *Diatriba fidei justificantis,* pp. 258-59, 274, 283-84).

407. Baxter, *Account of my Consideration,* p. 222.

408. Baxter, *Account of my Consideration,* p. 238 (emphasis throughout in original). The devils have a real faith, according to Baxter. They may even "really consent" that Christ will justify and save them (p. 240).

409. Baxter, *Account of my Consideration,* p. 223.

410. Baxter, *Account of my Consideration,* p. 225.

411. Baxter, *Account of my Consideration,* p. 238. Cf. Crandon's comment: "We grant that the hypocriticall profession of Faith which *James* reproveth, is as all other sinne, alive to condemne the unbelievers and unjustified, but dead to the use of justifying us in our consciences before God, or outwardly before men. But that the addition of workes to such a dead Faith can make it alive to justifie a man before God, we deny ..." (*Aphorisms Exorized* II.vi.101).

412. Cf. Baxter, *Account of my Consideration,* pp. 224-25.

413. Baxter does acknowledge that Paul and James do not use the word "faith" in the same way. Paul speaks of assent combined with acceptance of Christ. James only means "a bare ineffectual Assent to the Truth of the Christian Religion, snch <sic> as the Devils themselves had" (*Of Justification,* p. 155).

414. Baxter, *Aphorismes* I.308 (p. 198).

Baxter takes exception to the interpretation of William Pemble and Johann Piscator, who maintain that by "works" James means "a working faith." Says Baxter: "I dare not teach the holy Ghost to speak; nor force the Scripture; nor raise an exposition so far from the plain importance of the words, without apparent necessity ..."[415] Cartwright follows the interpretation of Pemble and Piscator.[416] When James speaks of "works" he simply means "a working faith."[417] Cartwright believes that James does not really compare works to faith at all. When Abraham was willing to sacrifice his son, this simply demonstrated that Abraham really believed. Explains Cartwright:

> His <*i.e.*, Abraham's> willingness to obey God in so great a work, shewed that he believed indeed, and that his Faith was such, as whereby he was justified. So when St. *James* saith, That by Works *Abraham*'s Faith was made perfect; the meaning is, that his Works shewed his Faith to be perfect, that is, a true justifying Faith ...[418]

According to Cartwright, Abraham's later works proved that his faith was a working faith. Only the initial act of faith, however, justified him. Baxter does not believe that James speaks of initial justification. This is impossible, for "how can *James* prove by Works many years after, that the Faith was fruitful, when he was first justified by it."[419] According to Baxter, James speaks of continued, rather than of initial justification. He maintains that this is one of the differences between Paul and James.

Baxter rejects the interpretation of "works" as "a working faith." James speaks of "works" twelve times in thirteen verses, "and never by the name of [*working Faith,*] or, [*that Faith which worketh:*]."[420] To substitute "a working faith" for "works" would make the entire passage unintelligible.[421] Even if Cartwright's interpretation were correct, however, it would still mean that he "granteth as much as I plead for."[422] If the adjective "working" is a "true, necessary, secondary" part of the condition, then works are still necessary for continued justification.[423] Bax-

---

415. Baxter, *Aphorismes* I.297 (p. 190).
416. Cartwright, in Baxter, *Account of my Consideration*, pp. 221-22. Cf. Thomas Blake, who appeals to Piscator, Pareus, and Pemble in maintaining "that *Paul* and *Iames* handle two distinct questions; The one, whether faith alone justifies without works, which he concludes in the affirmative. The other, what faith justifies, whether a working faith only, and not a faith that is dead and idle" (*Vindiciæ foederis*, p. 80). Baxter replies to Blake in *Account*, pp. 12-14. Cf. also Warner, *Diatriba fidei justificantis*, pp. 275-84.
417. Cartwright, in Baxter, *Account of my Consideration*, p. 236.
418. Cartwright, in Baxter, *Account of my Consideration*, p. 211.
419. Baxter, *Account of my Consideration*, p. 212.
420. Baxter, *Account of my Consideration*, p. 237. Cf. *Confession*, p. 313.
421. Baxter, *Account of my Consideration*, pp. 238-39. Baxter gives several examples. One may suffice: "And in *Vers.* 20. *Works* must needs mean *Works*; else it must run thus, [*Faith without a working Faith is dead.*]" (p. 238)
422. Baxter, *Account of my Consideration*, p. 215. Cf. *Confession*, pp. 313-14: "For example; A man is promised his freedom if he pay 100 l. currant money. That it be money, is the substance of the Condition: but that it be currant, is a modification of it, and part of the Condition; and without it he shall no more be freed then if he paid none at all. So if God say, [He that believeth with a working Faith, shall be Justified] that it be working, is as necessary a part of the Condition as that it be Faith. And it is but the Conditionality that I assert."
423. Baxter, *Account of my Consideration*, p. 215.

ter is afraid, however, that Cartwright will say that works do not justify the person, but that they justify only faith itself.[424] Baxter rejects this use of the distinction between *iustificatio causae* and *iustificatio personae*. The former necessarily implies the latter as well.[425] Moreover, James does not say that faith, but that a man is justified by works (2:24).

Another question concerns the type of justification about which James speaks. Is it merely a justification before men (*coram hominibus*) or is it justification before God (*coram Deo*)? Cartwright admits that James speaks of the latter, and Baxter recognizes this.[426] For precisely this reason, however, it is imperative for Cartwright to maintain that James does not really speak of works, but only of a working faith. If he were to admit that James speaks of works, this would entail that people are justified by works *coram Deo*, which is an unacceptable conclusion for Cartwright. Not all Baxter's opponents are agreed with Cartwright on this point. According to Crandon, James explicitly mentions justification before men:

> *James* himselfe even in expresse words affirming it ver. 18 Shew me thy Faith without thy workes, and I will shew thee my Faith by my works, where he tels us that by Iustifying, he means the shewing or declaring our Faith, and Justification (not to God) but one to another. And thus he denieth Faith which is not *Shewed by Works*, to Iustifie *i.e.* to *Shew* or declare us to men Iustified.[427]

Not only does James assert positively that he means justification before men, but this is also obvious from the fact that Abraham was justified by sacrificing his son on the altar (2:21). It is impossible that James speaks of justification *coram Deo*, because Abraham was justified by faith "many yeares before."[428] Furthermore, how could James possibly adduce Rahab as an example of justification before God and pardon from sin even though she probably had never even heard of "a Christ to come"?[429]

John Warner has a similar evidentialist interpretation. He also insists that James is speaking of justification before men. This is clear from the fact that this justification is evidenced by clothing the naked and feeding the hungry (2:15-16).[430] Like Crandon, Warner appeals to James' challenge to his readers to show him their faith without works (2:18).[431] Moreover, James speaks of a justification

---

424. Cf. Baxter, *Account of my Consideration*, pp. 225-26: "Now if (as I have said) *Piscator, Pemble, &c.* by [*working Faith,*] mean not only [*Faith it self as Faith,*] but [*Faith as working,*] i.e. *first as Faith, and secondarily as Working,* they say as much as I (but yet I will not accuse or refuse this oft repeated Scripture-phrase: But if they mean by [*working Faith,*] only [*that Faith which hath Works as only* quoad præsentiam *necessary,* and not at all *ad effectum Justificationis,*] I think they utterly forsake plain Scripture-words and sense."
425. Baxter, *Account of my Consideration*, pp. 215-17.
426. Baxter, *Account of my Consideration*, p. 241.
427. Crandon, *Aphorisms Exorized* II.vi.91. In opposition to Burgess, Baxter replies to this same argument that although James "mention *shewing faith by works to men,* as an argument for his main conclusion, yet he nowhere expoundeth the word Justification by it" (*Of Justification*, p. 151).
428. Crandon, *Aphorisms Exorized* II.vi.91.
429. Crandon, *Aphorisms Exorized* II.vi.92.
430. Warner, *Diatriba fidei justificantis*, p. 248.
431. Warner, *Diatriba fidei justificantis*, pp. 248-49.

which is known to men as life and death are known to men (2:20).[432] Finally, the example of Abraham makes it clear that James can speak "only of the *manifestation*, *declaration*, and *approbation* of that faith before men, whereby justification was *passed* on *Abraham long before*, by faith alone."[433] This justification was at that time only known to Abraham himself, but is "now made knowne to others."[434]

Baxter, however, thinks that James speaks of a justification which is "of greater moment."[435] He speaks of salvation (2:14).[436] The world neither has the authority nor the ability to judge someone's relation to the law of God.[437] This is certainly clear in Abraham's case, who could hardly be justified before men "for a secret Action."[438] Moreover, God rather than man is said to impute righteousness (2:23).[439] The conclusion must be that James speaks of justification *coram Deo*.[440]

Baxter is not afraid to assert the role of works in justification in bold terms. An important question should now be addressed: how does Baxter attempt to reconcile his explanation of James with Paul's rejection of justification by works? Part of the answer lies in what has already been noted: Baxter is of the opinion that James only speaks of continued justification, whereas Paul speaks of initial justification.[441] The latter remains by faith alone. Baxter also maintains that Paul speaks of a different type of works than James. The works which Paul rejects are "justifying by their value."[442] They make the reward not of grace but of debt (Rom 4:4).[443] Moreover, the works of which James speaks are subordinated to Christ. They are not in competition with or even in coordination with his merit. James

---

432. Warner, *Diatriba fidei justificantis*, pp. 249-50.
433. Warner, *Diatriba fidei justificantis*, p. 250. Burgess also argues that "hitherto the reformed Churches have generally agreed" that "the scope of the Apostle *Paul* is to treat upon our Justification before God, and what is the instrument and means of obtaining it; and this he doth against those Jewish teachers, *That we were justified by the works of the Law*. But the Apostle *James* takes Justification for the declaration and manifestation of it before men ..." (*True Doctrine*, II, 237).
434. Warner, *Diatriba fidei justificantis*, p. 251.
435. Baxter, *Aphorismes* I.294 (p. 188).
436. Baxter, *Aphorismes* I.295 (p. 188); *Account of my Consideration*, p. 241; *Methodus Theologiæ* III.xxvii.343. Cf. Crandon, *Aphorisms Exorized* II.vi.95; Warner, *Diatriba fidei justificantis*, pp. 273-75.
437. Baxter, *Aphorismes* I.295 (pp. 188-89); *Account of my Consideration*, p. 241. Cf. Crandon, *Aphorisms Exorized* II.vi.95-96.
438. Baxter, *Aphorismes* I.296 (p. 189). Cf. *Account of my Consideration*, p. 248; Crandon, *Aphorisms Exorized* II.vi.96.
439. Baxter, *Aphorismes* I.296 (p. 189); *Account of my Consideration*, p. 241; *Of Imputation*, p. 151; *Methodus Theologiæ* III.xxvii.343. Cf. Crandon, *Aphorisms Exorized* II.vi.96-97.
440. Isolde Jeremias erroneously attributes to Baxter an evidentialist position: "Die Werke stehen also auf einer ganz anderen Stufe als das Verdienst Christi und die Gnade Gottes. Sie sind das Zeichen <!>, daß der Mensch nicht nur durch Assent, sondern auch in Consent und Affiance Christus als Herrn angenommen hat und seinen Willen als maßgeblich anerkennt. In ihm wird deutlich sichtbar <!>, daß der Mensch wirklich den rechtfertigenden Glauben besitzt... Die guten Werke sind das sichtbare Zeichen <!> dafür, daß der Mensch im Gehorsam lebt und Christus als Herrn angenommen hat" ("Richard Baxters Catholic Theology," pp. 113-14).
441. Cf. Baxter, *Account*, p. 13; *Of Justification*, pp. 103-04, 155.
442. Baxter, *Of Justification*, p. 102.
443. Baxter, *Plain Scripture Proof*, p. 191; *Account of my Consideration*, pp. 219-20; *Account*, p. 13; *Admonition*, p. 27; *Confession*, pp. 67, 94, 301; *Of Justification*, pp. 70, 75, 102; *Protestant Religion*, p. 95. Cf. Jeremias, "Richard Baxters Catholic Theology," pp. 112-13.

presupposes Christ's satisfaction and merit.[444] This also means that when Paul opposes works he rejects only a legal justification by means of legal works.[445] Unlike James, he does not speak of evangelical works.[446] For Paul, being justified by works is identical to being justified by the law.[447] Yet, Baxter grants that also if people were to perform evangelical works – such as believing in Christ – for legal ends, this would be against Paul's intentions. Baxter summarizes his view as follows:

> I will therefore suppose some men to be so unreasonable, as to expect a Legal Justification, by their believing or confessing that Christ only can Legally justifie them, and not themselves; and so I will grant you, that *Paul* doth (consequentially) exclude *all works*, even Evangelical works from Justification: But though he exclude *all works*, yet not in every notion, nor doth he exclude *All interest* of All works in our Justification. All works as *valuable offerings*, he excludes, and so as meritorious, not only in point of Commutative Justice, but also in point of Legal worth and Legal Justice, as the Pharisees supposed them meritorious. All works he excludes from all proper Causality. But he doth not exclude all works from having any Interest at all in subordination to Christ.[448]

In addition, Paul and James do not have the same people as adversaries. Paul argues against Jews who thought that they would be justified by obeying the Mosaic law and by sacrificing for any sins that they had committed, and who "lookt for the *Messias* but to free them from captivity, and repair their Temple, Law, &c."[449] James, on the other hand, disputes against Christians who thought that it was enough "barely to believe in Christ."[450] The conclusion is justified that Baxter is sharply at odds with his opponents with regard to the exegesis of James 2 and the manner in which Paul and James should be harmonized.[451] Baxter rejects

---

444. In accordance with his position that one's personal, evangelical righteousness is subordinated to Christ, Baxter also insists that the justification of which James speaks is in subordination to and is subservient to Christ's righteousness (*Account of my Consideration*, pp. 218-19; *Account*, p. 13; *Confutation*, pp. 204-05; *Admonition*, p. 27; *Unsavoury Volume*, p. 16; *Confession*, p. 30; *Of Justification*, pp. 70, 76, 102-03, 106, 109, 140, 153-55, 166, 190, 288; *Of Imputation*, p. 164). Cf. Jeremias, "Richard Baxters Catholic Theology," p. 113.
445. Baxter recognizes that when Paul rejects justification by the law of works he does not mean the law of innocence but the law of Moses. Baxter maintains, however, that "consequently *à fortiore*, it's certain that we have no works by which that <law of innocence> will justify us (either personal or imputed)" (*Breviate*, p. 50).
446. Baxter, *Confession*, p. 301; *Of Justification*, pp. 104-05, 155; *End of Doctrinal Controversies*, p. 253.
447. Baxter, *Of Justification*, pp. 104, 154.
448. Baxter, *Of Justification*, pp. 105-06.
449. Baxter, *Of Justification*, p. 154. Cf. *Confutation*, p. 204; *Admonition*, p. 28; *Confession*, p. 94.
450. Baxter, *Of Justification*, p. 154.
451. This conclusion differs from that of Packer, who maintains that "the difference between Baxter and the others is for practical purposes non-existent; since all agree that James is warning 'gospel hypocrites' against expecting final salvation without works, and reminding them that a barren profession saves nobody; a point on which Manton and Owen insisted no less than Baxter" (Packer, "Redemption and Restoration," p. 308). Packer does not trace Baxter's debates with his opponents on the harmonization between Paul and James. Such an analysis, as given above, makes clear that the disagreements on this point are illustrative for the different ways in which the various disputants regard the role of works in justification.

the notion that James contrasts dead faith and working faith; he maintains that James speaks of the justification of people, not just of the justification of one's faith; and he also rejects an evidentialist exegesis of the passage in question: the justification of which James speaks is *coram Deo*, not *coram hominibus*.

God's Decree and the Conditionality of the Covenant

Baxter's insistence that continued faith and obedience are necessary for continued and consummate justification has implications for his understanding of the perseverance of the saints. Because he insists that justification is a continuous process he is required to maintain that the promise also remains conditional. Since people are only conditionally pardoned, they "may be unpardoned and unjustified again for their non-performance of the conditions, and all the debt so forgiven be required at their hands; and all this without any change in God, or in his Laws."[452] Baxter guards this comment with an appeal to God's twofold will:

> And for that which intimates in the following Position, the falling away of the justified, understand, that I speak only upon supposition, and of a possibility in the thing, and of the Tenor of the Gospel: But in regard of Gods Will of Purpose, which determineth eventually, whether they shall fall quite away or not, I do beleeve, that the justified by Faith never do, or shall fall away.[453]

Baxter's position seems straightforward enough: according to God's will *de debito* it is possible to be "unpardoned and unjustified." From his will *de rerum eventu*, however, we know that this shall never happen. Baxter often mentions in one breath the conditionality of the covenant of grace and the impossibility of the apostacy of the saints according to God's decree.[454]

Nevertheless, Baxter's understanding of God's will introduces a tension in his thinking on perseverance. Since perseverance may be linked both to God's will *de debito* and to his will *de rerum eventu* Baxter is able to speak of being "unpardoned and unjustified," and he is also able to say that people will never fall away. The question can hardly be suppressed: which of the two is God's real will? Crandon is afraid that Baxter opts for God's will *de debito*, thereby making room for apostacy of the saints. According to Crandon, Baxter's position implies that

---

452. Baxter, *Aphorismes* I.196-97 (p. 126) (emphasis inverted). Baxter appeals to John Ball, who refers to people who "were called into the Covenant, accepted the condition, beleeved in Christ, for a time rejoyced in him, and brought forth some fruit." Yet these people did not believe in Christ "sincerely and unfainedly." Ball adds that such men did not receive "perfect remission" and were not "perfectly redeemed" (*Treatise of the Covenant*, p. 240). Ball does not use Baxter's terminology of being "unpardoned and unjustified." Baxter also comments that "should" people "cease to believe and repent, the Promise would cease to justifie them, and give them right to Christ and Life" (*Confession*, p. 118).
453. Baxter, *Aphorisms* I.197-98 (p. 126).
454. Baxter, *Account of my Consideration*, pp. 57-78, 63; *Unsavoury Volume*, pp. 48-49; *Confession*, pp. 102, 116.

"by beleeving and unbeleeving, obeying and rebelling we may be justifyed and unjustifyed again a thousand times before we die ..."[455] It is one of Baxter's "Popish errors"[456] to hold that "they that are in Christ may fall away and be damned if they continue in their Apostasy, or may after their many apostacies, oft renew again their union with Christ, and so at last be justified."[457]

Baxter denies Crandon's accusation. When God threatens his people, this is a means to keep them from apostasy: "Cannot God make a conditional grant, as certainly to be accomplished as an absolute?"[458] Baxter calls it a "forgery" to assert that by "believing and unbelieving" we may repeatedly be "justified and unjustified."[459] With indignation, he retorts: "When I still affirm that God will preserve us from turning unbelievers, notwithstanding the conditionality of this promise, yea by the means of this conditionality to excite us to vigilancy and care for perseverance."[460] Crandon makes a caricature of Baxter. Baxter's *Aphorismes* keep the conditionality of the covenant and the certain perseverance of the saints side by side.

No Certainty of Perseverance

Despite Crandon's misrepresentation, he is correct in detecting a tension in Baxter's theology. It would not be correct to state, without careful qualification, that Baxter accepts the doctrine of the perseverance of the saints.[461] He has some difficulty in maintaining both that continued justification is conditional upon continued faith and works, and that all justified saints persevere. Baxter himself is aware of this tension, but he does not really know how to deal with it. In *The Right Method For a settled Peace Of Conscience, and Spiritual Comfort* (1653), he plays down the perseverance of the saints. To be sure, he still says: "It is my strong opinion that no man who hath attained to a Rootedness in the Faith, and so is throughly sanctified, doth ever totally and finally fall away ..."[462] He is "much perswaded that the Rooted in Grace do never fall quite away."[463] He is "perswaded that all the Rooted, through-Christians, are elect."[464] But he fails to say how deeply "rooted" one must be in order to persevere.[465] Consequently, he states:

455. Crandon, *Aphorisms Exorized* I.xxvi.350. Cf. I.xxiv.300.
456. Crandon, *Aphorisms Exorized* I.ix.78.
457. Crandon, *Aphorisms Exorized* I.ix.79.
458. Baxter, *Unsavoury Volume*, p. 65.
459. Baxter, *Unsavoury Volume*, p. 50.
460. Baxter, *Unsavoury Volume*, pp. 50-51. Cf. p. 75; *Confession*, p. 118.
461. It is sometimes thought that Baxter maintains the perseverance of the saints. See Bass, "Platonic Influences," p. 197; Packer, "Redemption and Restoration," p. 99; Beougher, "Conversion," p. 76 (but cf. pp. 93-95).
462. Baxter, *Right Method*, p. 165.
463. Baxter, *Right Method*, p. 167.
464. Baxter, *Right Method*, p. 166. Cf. *Account*, sig. a4^r. In *End of Doctrinal Controversies*, Baxter says that there is a degree of holiness that is never lost (p. 305; cf. pp. 307-08).
465. In a *The Protestant Religion Truely Stated and Justified*, Baxter does identify rooted and saving grace (p. 98). In *Right Method*, however, he is so vague on what he means with "rooted" Christians that one cannot help but wonder whether he deliberately keeps open the possibility that people may lose saving grace when they are not "throughly" "rooted" in it. This interpretation agrees with the fact that he later openly expresses his doubt whether all the justified persevere.

> But yet I dare not say, that *I am Certain of this*, that all are elect to salvation, and shall never fall away totally and finally, who sincerely Believe and are Justified. It is my opinion, but I dare not put It Into my Creed among either the Points of absolute Necessity or undoubted Verity. I know how many Texts of Scripture seem to speak otherwise: and I know how generally the Primitive Fathers thought otherwise, if a man can know their mindes by their Writings: I know that *Austin* himself, the Mall of the Pelagians, seems to be either unresolv'd, or more against this Perseverance then for it. I know how many Learned, Godly men do differ from me, and deny the certainty of Perseverance: I know how sad and shaking Examples this age hath afforded: And therefore I am not Certain, properly, strictly Certain of my Perseverance, and so not fully, strictly Certain of my Salvation.[466]

Baxter is strongly persuaded that "rooted" Christians do persevere, and he is even inclined to think that all the justified will persevere. But with respect to this latter proposition he expresses his uncertainty. The clarification in his "Apologie" (1653) and the substitution of *Richard Baxter's Account of His present Thoughts concerning the Controversies about the Perseverance of the Saints* (1657) for the controverted section in *Right Method* present by and large the same view. In his "Apologie," Baxter defends himself with the evasion that he "never questioned the Certainty of the Object."[467] He says that he only confesses his own "Darkness" because he has "not yet attained to an Absolute subjective Certainty of this Certainty objective."[468] Baxter is nevertheless forced to admit that he is still not sure that all the justified will persevere.[469] Isolde Jeremias rightly states: "Baxter wagt es nicht, den Lehrsatz aufzustellen, daß der 'habitual faith', der echte Glaube, unverlierbar sei oder daß er so eindeutig die Erwählung beweise, daß der Mensch zwar teilweise, aber nie gänzlich von Gott abfallen könne."[470]

Baxter feels attracted to the position of the British delegates to the Synod of

---

466. Baxter, *Right Method*, p. 166.
467. Baxter, *Right Method*, 2nd ed., sig. Cc2^r.
468. Baxter, *Right Method*, sig. Cc2^r.
469. Baxter, *Right Method*, 2nd ed., sigs. Cc2^v, Cc9^v-Cc10^r. Also in *Certain Disputations*, Baxter comments: "But wee are not certain <!> whether *Solomon* were justified and in a state of salvation at that time <*i.e.*, when he lived in sin>: It is a Controversie among wise godly learned men; and many of the Antient Fathers thought that hee was not" ([London, 1657], p. 328). Baxter adduces the example of Solomon probably because he considered this a case where sin was not obviously "contrary to the main bent and scope" of his life, as was the case with Lot, Noah, David, and Peter (*Catholick Theologie* II.204). Cf. *Account*, p. 88: "Vocation throughly effectual, is of the same extent as justification, and (I think) Election."
470. Jeremias, "Richard Baxters Catholic Theology," p. 120. Cf. also Highfill, "Faith and Works," pp. 79-80. Jürgen Moltmann erroneously links Baxter to William Perkins, William Ames, and others in attributing to him the high Calvinist idea that perseverance is certain because of the *habitus fidei* which precedes and transcends the act of faith. Moltmann comments with regard to Baxter's distinction between habitual and active holiness that it must be understood "als Wiedergabe der reformierten Perseveranzlehre, nach deren orthodoxer Gestalt das habituelle Sein im Glauben allen aktuellen Betätigungen des Glaubenslebens vorhergeht und über den Wechselfällen der aktiven Heiligung die Kontinuität bewahrt" (*Prädestination und Perseveranz: Geschichte und Bedeutung der reformierten Lehre "de perseverantia sanctorum"*, Beiträge zur Geschichte und Lehre der Reformierten Kirche, 12 [Neukirchen: Neukirchener Verlag, 1961], p. 164). Moltmann fails to take note of the fact that Baxter takes some distance from the idea that the habit precedes the act of faith (cf. above, pp. 76-77). Also, his stand on perseverance is much less adamant than Moltmann thinks.

Dort. He quotes their Suffrage at some length.[471] This is understandable, since the British delegates had tried to maintain a similar delicate balance.[472] On the one hand, when some apostatize from the faith, one must not draw the wrong conclusion. These people were never justified, "and therefore by the Apostasie of these men, the Apostasie of the Saints is very erroneously concluded."[473] On the other hand, justified people do sometimes fall into "hainous sinnes."[474] While they are in this condition, "they lose the fitnes, which they had of entring into the Kingdome of Heaven ..."[475] Such people "cannot but fall into everlasting death" if they should die in such a state.[476] The only reason why such people will be saved is that according to God's decree they will be brought to repentance.[477] Only then are they "actually absolved."[478] The British delegates grant, however, that the period between the grievous sin and the renewed act of faith and repentance is not the same for the faithful and the wicked: "<T>o the unfaithfull, this inward active cause is wanting, to wit, faith, without which the remedy ... is as if it were layed afarre off, out of reach, neither can it be made their owne, or actually applyed to them."[479] Baxter summarizes the position of the Suffrage as follows:

> In all this it appeareth that they take holyness and sincere obedience as an absolutely necessary Condition of continuing or not losing our state of Justification and Salvation And that as great sins do actually bring guilt of death, and make uncapable of salvation till we return by Repentance, so if God should permit us totally to fall from Sanctification, we should thereby fall also from our state of Iustification and salvation; and that as God hath decreed that we shall not fall from justification, so hath he Deereed <sic> our not falling from sanctification as the means thereof, and the keeping our state of Justification.[480]

Baxter still seems to maintain that, because of God's decree, the state of justification is not intermitted. A few years earlier, however, in 1651, he already admits in a letter to John Tombes that the issue of perseverance has "long troubled" him.[481] Baxter speaks of a "knot" that he is unable to untie: how is it possible that a man is guilty of death and is yet "perfectly justified"?[482] In a postscript added more than six years later, Baxter himself offers a solution to this difficulty. He distinguishes between a "Plenary Guilt or Remission" and a guilt and remission that are "imper-

471. Baxter, *Confession*, pp. 437-40; *Catholick Theologie* I.ii.94-95. Cf. *Certain Disputations*, p. 347; *Of Justification*, p. 396.
472. For the position of the British divines at Dort, see Peter White, *Predestination, Policy and Polemic: Conflict and Consensus in the English Church from the Reformation to the Civil War* (Cambridge: Cambridge Univ. Press, 1992), pp. 195-96.
473. *Collegiat Suffrage* (London, 1629), p. 112 (emphasis throughout in original).
474. *Collegiat Suffrage*, p. 121 (emphasis throughout in original).
475. *Collegiat Suffrage*, p. 123.
476. *Collegiat Suffrage*, p. 124.
477. *Collegiat Suffrage*, pp. 123-26.
478. *Collegiat Suffrage*, p. 128.
479. *Collegiat Suffrage*, p. 127.
480. Baxter, *Confession*, pp. 439-40.
481. Baxter, *Of Justification*, p. 395.
482. Baxter, *Of Justification*, p. 396. Cf. Baxter's acknowledgement of the "difficulty" of the issue in *End of Doctrinal Controversies*, p. 314.

fect and of a middle sort."[483] When Peter denied the Lord, he retained his plenary remission. Because his sin went against the "Habitual bent" of his heart he remained in a state of justification.[484] Yet, his sin made him guilty of death. This guilt was instantly forgiven by means of an "imperfect Remission" of a "middle sort" because Peter still had the habit of faith.[485] He was in a "middle condition."[486] After his repentance he received a full pardon.[487] The former is a "vertual Pardon," the latter an "actual Pardon."[488] If someone were to die in a "middle condition" – which Baxter does not think will ever happen – he would probably be pardoned at the instant of death, "because the Lord knoweth that he repented Habitually and vertually, and would have done it actually, if he had had time for consideration."[489] Baxter is forced to posit an "imperfect remission," a "middle condition," to untie the knot. This illustrates that he has great difficulty in maintaining the perseverance of the saints along with the conditionality of continued justification. When he feels forced to opt between the two aspects of God's will, Baxter veers toward the *voluntas de debito*.

Fear of Singularity and Pastoral Motives

Apart from Baxter's theological question how the doctrine of the perseverance of the saints can be made to match with his understanding of justification, he has at least two other motives not to insist too strongly on perseverance. The first is that he is afraid of singularity on this point. He notes that for at least "a thousand years" after Christ it had not been denied by anyone that truly justified people might perish.[490] Moreover, the Greek Church, the Roman Church, the Lutherans, the Arminians, and most Anabaptists are all against the doctrine of the perseverance of the saints.[491] As noted already, Baxter is aware that Augustine only insisted that the elect will persevere. He did not exclude the possibility that some justified people may fall away. Baxter refers to him often and at length.[492] Only at one point, does he state that he disagrees with a particular exegesis of Augustine with regard to perseverance.[493] In his *Catholick Theologie*, he leaves the question open whether or not Augustine's position is correct.[494] And in *End of Doctrinal*

---

483. Baxter, *Of Justification*, p. 397 (emphasis throughout in original).
484. Baxter's solution is very close to – and perhaps even borrowed from – that of the *Suffrage* of the British delegates to Dort, which also makes use of an "inward active cause" to describe the difference between the faithful and the wicked after they have fallen into a grievous sin.
485. Baxter, *Of Justification*, p. 397 (emphasis throughout in original).
486. Baxter, *Of Justification*, p. 398 (emphasis throughout in original).
487. Baxter, *Of Justification*, p. 397 (emphasis throughout in original).
488. Baxter, *Of Justification*, p. 397.
489. Baxter, *Of Justification*, p. 398 (emphasis throughout in original).
490. Baxter, *Catholick Theologie* I.ii.93; II.216; *End of Doctrinal Controversies*, p. 314. Cf. *Present Thoughts*, p. 18; *Catholick Theologie* I.ii.100.
491. Baxter, *Right Method*, 2nd ed., sigs. Cc8^{r-v}; *Present Thoughts*, pp. 18-20; *Catholick Theologie* I.ii.93; II.210, 216.
492. Baxter, *Right Method*, p. 166; *Present Thoughts*, pp. 4-8, 14-17; *Catholick Theologie* I.ii.93, 97-100; II.57-58, 214-17; *End of Doctrinal Controversies*, pp. 308-09, 313; *Protestant Religion*, p. 98.
493. Baxter, *Present Thoughts*, p. 15.
494. Baxter, *Catholick Theologie* II.215-18.

Controversies, Baxter frankly admits: "<W>hether many also are truly *sanctified* and *justified* that are *not elect*, and so *do not persevere*, as *Austin* held, I said before, I do not know."[495] Baxter's hesitation with regard to Augustine's position is in agreement with the uncertainty expressed in *Right Method*, in 1653.

The disagreement among Christians implies, according to Baxter, that the perseverance of the saints is not a fundamental article which must be in the church's creeds or confessions.[496] The creeds must "express the Fundamentals only, or only those Points which we expect all should subscribe to, with whom we will hold communion."[497] The perseverance of the saints is not such a point. Baxter even comments: "I never found the Doctrine of certain Perseverance in any Creed of the Church."[498] Accordingly, when he draws up a catechism of faith for the Worcestershire Association, he purposely omits this doctrine.[499]

Baxter also has some pastoral motives for being lenient on the doctrine of the perseverance of the saints. He is not convinced by the Calvinist argument that this doctrine provides the necessary comfort for believers. Many of those who insist on this argument admit that they themselves do not yet have assurance of their own sincerity.[500] Baxter concludes that there is no sense in insisting on the necessary consolation of perseverance if one is not even certain of his present state before God:

> Now if Assurance of sincerity and Justification be so rare (and imperfect in the best) then it must needs follow that certainty of their own Perseverance must be as rare. And all these Persons that are uncertain of their Perseverance, can fetch no comfort from that certainty which they have not.[501]

Not only does the lack of assurance of present justification imply a corresponding uncertainty of one's perseverance, but the theory of the perseverance of the saints may even be the cause of uncertainty. When an apparently godly Christian falls away, others may well start wondering whether they themselves are any stronger in faith than the person who fell away. Baxter admits that he has "found it no easie

---

495. Baxter, *End of Doctrinal Controversies*, p. 309.

496. Baxter, *Right Method*, 2nd ed., sigs. Cc3^{r-v}; *Present Thoughts*, pp. 18, 23-25; *Catholick Theologie* I.ii.94; II.198, 206-08, 218, 258; *End of Doctrinal Controversies*, p. 313. Cf. Packer, "Redemption and Restoration," p. 99; Beougher, "Conversion," p. 76.

497. Baxter, *Present Thoughts*, p. 23.

498. Baxter, *Right Method*, 2nd ed., sigs. Cc3^{r-v}. Cf. McGrath, "Puritans and the Human Will," p. 362: "Baxter's argument was that the issue of perseverance was relatively new, and should not divide the church of his day."

499. Cf. Baxter's defense of this omission in *Present Thoughts*, pp. 23-25.

500. Baxter, *Right Method*, 2nd ed., sig. Cc6^{v}.

501. Baxter, *Present Thoughts*, p. 21. Cf. *End of Doctrinal Controversies*, p. 310. Kendall admits that "none are more troubled with such anguish fits in their spirits, then those who are most zealous for this our Doctrine <i.e., of the perseverance of the saints>" (*Sancti sanciti*, sig. ****3^{r}). He objects to Baxter (1) that the certainty of perseverance is grounded in God's decree, not the knowledge of the saints; (2) that even if the saints have sufficient ground for subjective certainty, they do not always see on what ground they stand; (3) that God may bring them close to the gates of hell so that they may with the more humility cast themselves on him; and (4) that Baxter's very objection is proof that the doctrine of perseverance does not make people presumptuous (sigs. ****3^{r-v}).

matter to quiet the minds of some that were troubled with this doubt."[502] Furthermore, he is afraid that people will use the recollection of their past sincerity as a
license for present immorality. Such sinners may "quiet their Consciences with
this, that they were once sincere, and they are certain true Grace cannot totally be
lost ..."[503] Finally, if someone has no absolute certainty of his perseverance, Baxter insists that this problem must be reduced to its proper proportions. No one can
be sure that he will not sin like Lot, Noah, David, and Peter.[504] But this does not
have to disturb his peace: "For we have strong Probabilities, though we have not
Certainties."[505]

Baxter never actually denies the certain perseverance of all the justified. In his
early writings – his *Aphorismes* (1649), his *Apology* (1654), and his *Confession*
(1655) – he positively asserts this doctrine. Already at this early stage, however,
he speaks of the (merely hypothetical) possibility of being "unpardoned and unjustified." Also, already in *Right Method* (1653) he admits that he is not certain of
the perseverance of all who are justified. This hesitation is also apparent in his
Confession (1655). Here, Baxter expresses his doubts about perseverance and
appears attracted by the Augustinian view. God's will *de rerum eventu* comes
under pressure from his will *de debito*. Baxter finds it difficult to maintain both
aspects of God's will. In three ways, he is tempted to abandon the doctrine of the
perseverance of the saints. Most important is his theological motive: the conditionality of continued and consummate justification. But Baxter is also afraid to
take a stand which is at variance with the early church – especially Augustine –
and with traditions outside the Calvinist fold. Finally, Baxter does not think that
pastoral motives require him to accept a Calvinist position. That, despite these
motives, he never actually denies the perseverance of all justified saints means
that he wants to do justice to both aspects of God's will, however difficult this
may be.

BAXTER AND ROMAN CATHOLICISM

Baxter's Attitude toward Roman Catholicism

Baxter's theory of justification has emerged as a highly eclectic whole, with
elements from numerous moderately Calvinist divines. The framework of a bifurcation of God's twofold will appears to be derived directly from the high Calvin-

---

502. Baxter, *Present Thoughts*, p. 26. Baxter states that his answer to this objection is usually that God
      has not made the hearts or lives of others the standard to go by, because he does not reveal the
      secrets of the heart to other people (pp. 27-28). Cf. *Catholick Theologie* I.ii.97.
503. Baxter, *Right Method*, 2nd ed., sig. Cc4^r. Baxter's response to this objection is (1) that if they had
      true assurance, this would have kept them from living in sin; and (2) that the doctrine of persever-
      ance is "controverted and of some obscurity" and is denied by "very Godly and Learned Divines"
      (sigs. Cc4^r-Cc5^r).
504. Baxter, *Right Method*, 2nd ed., sig. Cc5^v; *Present Thoughts*, pp. 22-23.
505. Baxter, *Right Method*, 2nd ed., sig. Cc6^r. Cf. *Present Thoughts*, p. 32; *Catholick Theologie* I.ii.93;
      II.211, 217. For Kendall's opposition to this argument, see his *Sancti sanciti*, sigs. ****3^r-****6^v).

ist, William Twisse. The emphasis within this pattern lies with God's rectorial attributes, which shows the influence of Hugo Grotius and William Bradshaw. An important question has not yet been addressed, however: what is Baxter's relation to Roman Catholic theories of the role of works in justification? Does the fact that Baxter's theory lies embedded within Protestant thinking preclude any similarity to or agreement with Roman Catholicism? Baxter was keenly aware that a possible affinity of his teaching with Roman Catholic schools of thought was, for some, the outstanding question. The establishment of such a link would effectively disqualify his theory of justification. Several of his opponents, therefore, focused on this element as the easiest way of invalidating Baxter's position. Especially his tolerance toward the use of the word "merit" elicited furious responses from William Eyre and John Crandon.[506] Eyre, for instance, insisted: "Mr. *Baxter* will tell you, That the performers of a condition, may be said to merit the reward. The Papists never pleaded for merit upon any other account ..."[507]

Baxter does not seem to have been greatly disturbed by this criticism: "If the *Papists* be nearer to us then I take them to be, it is cause of joy and not sorrow."[508] The question remains, however: is Baxter's understanding of the role of works akin to Roman Catholicism? This accusation is not restricted to those who first responded to his *Aphorismes of Justification*. A Pinner's Hall lecture held by Baxter in 1673 resulted in an outcry in London.[509] He was forced to defend himself against the charge that he had said that there were only verbal differences between Protestants and Roman Catholics.[510] Moreover, the accusations were not only voiced by Baxter's most severe critics. Also one of his more careful disputants, Anthony Burgess, was afraid that Baxter had fallen victim to a Roman Catholic understanding of justification.[511] Modern scholarship has generally tended to regard the charges as unfounded rhetoric. James I. Packer, for instance, comments:

> Baxter's alleged heterodoxy amounted merely to this: he had assimilated the four characteristic Protestant positions concerning justification (that it is a forensic act, done in this life; that it is grounded on Christ's satisfaction; that it is secured through faith; and that a dead faith justifies nobody) to his 'political' doctrine of the new covenant as a legal instrument for its conveyance; and he had distinguished two decisive moments in justification, one present and one future, where other Protestants recognised only the first. The charges brought against him were ludicrous.[512]

---

506. Crandon, *Aphorisms Exorized* I.xvii.190-92; II.xv.214. For Baxter's response, see *Unsavoury Volume*, pp. 78-80. For similar charges by Thomas Tully, see his *Justificatio Paulina*, p. 127; *Letter*, pp. 16-17. For Baxter's response, see *Of Imputation*, pp. 195-96.

507. Eyre, *Vindiciæ Justificationis Gratuitæ*, p. 190. Cf. p. 30; and Baxter's response in *Admonition*, pp. 22-23, 38-40. Baxter added a separate chapter to his *Confession* in which he answered the question: "Whether it be true that the Papists do maintain no other merit than I do, as Mr. *Eyre*, and Mr. *Crandon* fearlessly affirm" (*Confession*, pp. 131-50; emphasis inverted).

508. Baxter, *Of Justification*, p. 246. Cf. *Answer*, p. 24; *Of Imputation*, p. 196.

509. Cf. above, p. 60.

510. For Baxter's reactions, see his *Appeal to the Light* and *Catholick Theologie* II.263-99.

511. Burgess, *True Doctrine*, II, 223. For Baxter's response, see *Of Justification*, pp. 109-10. Burgess lards his arguments with subtle references to Bellarmine, without explicitly accusing Baxter (*True Doctrine*, II, 221; in Baxter, *Of Justification*, p. 180).

512. Packer, "Redemption and Restoration," pp. 302-03.

Packer does not accept the stigmatization of Baxter's theory of justification as Roman Catholic. Other modern scholars have also not detected any connection with Roman Catholic views on justification. The only exception is C.F. Allison, who finds it difficult to distinguish between Baxter's position and that of the Council of Trent.[513]

It is not the purpose of this study to make a comparison between Baxter's theory of justification and that of the various Roman Catholic schools of thought. In this section, I will analyze Baxter's attitude toward Roman Catholicism and consider the question whether Baxter's attitude toward merit is similar to that of certain Roman Catholic thought patterns. Few authors have been as voluminous as Baxter in opposing Roman Catholicism. He has written at least twenty books against it.[514] He opposes especially the Roman Catholic doctrine of the church, revelation, Scripture, tradition, church offices (especially papacy), idolatry of worship in the mass and transubstantiation, worship of saints and images, and purgatory. There should be no question, therefore, that Baxter was vehemently opposed to Rome as a hierarchical institution and to numerous Roman Catholic doctrines.

Nevertheless, there is a remarkable lacuna in these polemical writings: Baxter rarely deals with soteriological issues. When he does bring them up, he consistently minimizes the differences between Roman Catholic and Protestant positions. In several places, Baxter lists a number of issues where the differences are not nearly as great as is commonly thought:

> We must not untruly fasten on them any Errour which they hold not, nor put a false sence on their words, though we may find many Protestants that so charge them; nor may we charge that on the Party which is held but by some whom others contradict. How far many Protestants herein mistake and rashly wrong them (In the Doctrine of Predestination, Free-will, Grace, Merits, Justification, Redemption, Perseverance, &c.) I have freely shewed in my Catholick Theology and End of Doctrinal Controversies; and Ludovicus le Blank after others hath excellently opened.[515]

Baxter distinguishes the soteriological questions sharply from other divisive issues. When William Hutchinson accuses the Protestants of teaching only an imputative righteousness, Baxter does not attempt to refute his opponent's position, but merely sets forth his own view and concludes that it is "impudent Slander" to say that Protestants deny the need for inherent righteousness.[516] In The Protestant Religion Truely Stated (1692), one of the few polemical writings against Roman Catholicism in which Baxter discusses soteriological questions, he reproaches Matthew Kellison (1560?-1642), president of Douay College and author of The

---

513. Allison, Rise of Moralism, p. 163.
514. An analysis of Baxter's controversial writings against Roman Catholicism would be an interesting topic for further research.
515. Baxter, Against the Revolt, p. 533. Baxter gives similar lists of soteriological issues with the purpose to minimize the differences in Full and easie Satisfaction (London, 1674), sig. A4ʳ; Appeal, p. 5; RB I.131 (probably written in 1664).
516. Baxter, Naked Popery, p. 55. Baxter's treatise was a reaction to W<illiam> H<utchinson>, The Catholick Naked Truth. Or, the Puritan Convert, to Apostolical Christianity (1676). For the authorship of this work, see RB III.180; William Orme, "Life and Writings," in Works 1.654; CCRB 1002.

Touch-Stone of the Reformed Gospel for falsely accusing the Protestant position.[517] Roman Catholics disagree on free will just as much "among themselves"
as with the Protestants.[518] Baxter concludes his discussion on merit with the comment that the Protestants do not differ from many of "<y>our own Doctors."[519]

Baxter frequently applauds Lewis Le Blanc – the learned and moderate professor of theology at the University of Sedan – as someone who adopts a moderate
position between Protestantism and Roman Catholicism.[520] Le Blanc originally
requested Baxter to publish his *Theses theologicæ* (1675) in England.[521] Baxter's
willingness to comply is based on his congeniality to Le Blanc's position. In his
preface, Le Blanc states that he wants to elucidate the state of the controversies
between the Roman church and those who have separated from it.[522] He is convinced that many of the controversies are merely verbal:

> For it is often the case that when contending parties use the same words, they
> nevertheless take them in a different sense. If this is not noticed, it makes for many
> useless controversies, or rather logomachies and disputes about words, even though
> there is agreement on the issue itself. Many such disputes have been entertained in
> the schools, and that – which is unworthy of good and serious men – with great
> bitterness.[523]

Le Blanc sets out to prove his conviction that many of the controversies between
Rome and the Reformation are only verbal quarrels.[524] Baxter's affinity with such

---

517. Matthew Kellison's *The Touch-Stone of the Reformed Gospel* was first published in 1623 as *The
    Gagge of the Reformed Gospell*. It was republished several times under its new title. Baxter
    presumably reacted to the revised edition of 1687. For Kellison, see *DNB* 30.344-45.
518. Baxter, *Protestant Religion*, p. 83.
519. Baxter, *Protestant Religion*, p. 97. Cf. *Confession*, p. 132; *Of Justification*, p. 94; *Answer*, p. 24.
520. Baxter, *Full and Easie Satisfaction*, sig. A4ʳ; *End of Doctrinal Controversies*, pp. 16, 21; *Against
    the Revolt*, pp. 101, 533. Cf. *CCRB* 1160. For Lewis Le Blanc, see Peter Bayle, *The Dictionary
    Historical and Critical of Mr Peter Bayle*, I, 2nd ed., pref. Des Maizeaux (London, 1784), pp.
    705-08; *La France protestante ou vies des protestants Français qui se sont fait un nom dans
    l'histoire depuis les premiers temps de la Réformation jusqu'a la reconnaissance du principe de
    la liberté des cultes par l'assemblée nationale*, Eug. and Em. Haag, VI (Paris: Cherbuliez, 1856),
    pp. 453-54; *CCRB* 1025.
521. *RB* III.177: "AT this time Mr. *Le Blank* of *Sedan* sent to me his desire that I would publish here his
    Scatter'd *Theses* in one Volume, which I purposed, and Wrote an *Epistle* to it: But some Conform-
    ists, hearing of it, would not have the Publication to be a Nonconformists work, and so my
    Bookseller took 50 Books for his Title to the Copy which I gave him, and quit his Interest in it to
    a Conformist: But *Le Blank* sent an *Epistle* of his own, to prevent the Conformists; and died as
    soon as it was Printed and Published." Cf. *End of Doctrinal Controversies*, p. 21; *Against the
    Revolt*, p. 101.
522. Le Blanc, *Theses theologicæ* (London, 1675), sig. A2ʳ.
523. "Nam sæpe sit, ut cum partes contendentes iisdem Vocibus utantur, illas tamen sensu diverso
    accipiant: quod non animadversum multas inanes facit Controversias, seu potius λογομαχιας &
    de Vocibus dissidia, cum in re ipsa consensus: qualia multa in Scholis agitantur, & quidem quod
    Viris bonis & gravibus indignum est, magna cum acerbitate" (Le Blanc, *Theses theologicæ*, sig.
    A2ᵛ).
524. Le Blanc's chapters end with assessments in which he concludes that the differences are at least
    much smaller than they are often thought to be. Some of the most significant ideas are the notion
    that works are only excluded as properly meritorious, as works of the law, which make the reward
    to be of debt rather than of grace (*Theses theologicæ*, pp. 249, 251, 256, 261). With appeals to
    John Davenant, Le Blanc insists that our inherent righteousness is the formal cause of our justifi-
    cation. But this justification is not that which answers to the strict examination of the Judge. In the
    latter sense, we are only justified because of Christ's merits (pp. 269, 276).

a treatise is a further indication that he is of the opinion that with regard to soteriological issues the distance from Rome is but small.

The Meritorious Character of Works

The way in which Baxter speaks of merit supports this thesis. It is sometimes thought that he completely rejects the meritorious character of works.[525] It is indeed possible to point to a number of statements which seem to exclude merit as such. When Eyre accuses Baxter of making works the meritorious cause of justification "in no other sence" as the Papists, Baxter retorts: "I have ever professed that our best works are not in the least degree meritorious, no not of a bit of bread, much less of Justification and Salvation."[526] Baxter even states that "there is something within me that disliketh and abhorreth" the word "merit."[527] It is clear, however, that when he denounces human merit as such, he is thinking of works that deserve the reward as a debt, by way of commutative justice. Commutative merit is only found in Christ.[528] No human creature is able to merit in commutative justice, as if he could profit God and make the reward to be of debt.[529] Thus, Baxter often states that we cannot *properly* merit anything from God.[530] Eyre maintains that by speaking of merit Baxter ascribes at least "as much unto works, as Papists do."[531] Baxter's denial is characteristic:

> Did ever I say *The word Merit may be admitted.* Shew where if you can. I said indeed that in that large improper sense, *Works may be called Merits,* thereby intending no *Moral admission* of it: but only a *capacity in the term,* to signifie such a thing by improper use. But I never said that it is no sin in them that do use the words so improperly, or that *it may be admitted.* For my part, I think the danger is so great,

525. N.H. Mair, "Christian Sanctification," p. 132; McGrath, "Puritans and the Human Will," p. 190; Beougher, "Conversion," pp. 92, 96, 99, 104.
526. Baxter, *Admonition,* p. 9. Cf. Eyre, *Vindiciæ Justificationis Gratuitæ,* sig. A3ᵛ. Baxter makes similar general statements disclaiming merit in *Plain Scripture Proof,* p. 192; *Account of my Consideration,* p. 266; *Unsavoury Volume,* p. 53; *Confession,* pp. 52, 71-72, 88, 137; *Of Justification,* p. 78.
527. Baxter, *Confession,* p. 71.
528. Cf. Baxter, *Unsavoury Volume,* p. 16: "But I that am, with this man <i.e., Crandon> the great enemy of free Grace, do profess to believe, that it was the Value of Christs performance that made it Meritorious, as it was a most excellent Means to the attainment of Gods Ends: and that it made the Reward to be of Debt to Christ, and not of meer Grace; and that it was Merit in the strictest sense, even on the termes of Commutative Justice, considering it as undertaken and dignified by the second Person in Trinity, who was never obliged by subjection but by voluntary sponsion; and that afterward as performed by God-man, under the Law, it was strictly and properly meritorious from Distributive Justice."
529. Baxter, *Confession,* p. 80; *Of Imputation,* pp. 160, 183; *Breviate,* pp. 40, 45; *End of Doctrinal Controversies,* p. 290; *Protestant Religion,* p. 95. Baxter gives more weight to Adam's works than to ours. Adam's obedience would have been perfect obedience of a perfect creature. Unlike Adam's works, ours are purely receptive (*Unsavoury Volume,* p.73; *Confession,* pp. 67-68, 80-81).
530. Baxter, *Aphorismes* I.137-41 (pp. 89-91); *Admonition,* pp. 10, 22; *Unsavoury Volume,* p. 53; *Confession,* pp. 69, 132; *Of Justification,* p. 75. Baxter takes the Scriptural term ἄξιος (worthy) in the same improper sense as the word "merit" (*Confession,* pp. 76-78).
531. Eyre, *Vindiciæ Justificationis Gratuitæ,* p. 30.

that the very use of the word is to be avoided by us, except in interpretations of others, or with them that will use it whether we will or not; and so we must speak to men in their own language sometime, or say nothing.[532]

The church fathers used the word "merit" in an improper way, without intending to speak of merit in a commutative sense. This should make one careful before rashly condemning a mere word.[533] Improperly, therefore, we may be said to merit justification and salvation. But this is only merit for evangelical works, according to distributive justice.[534]

It now becomes clear why Baxter does not think that the distance from Roman Catholic ideas on justification is very great. He rejects the understanding of Robert Bellarmine, who argues that good works are properly meritorious *ex condigno* and that they are accepted by God not only *ratione pacti*, but also *ratione operis*.[535] The Scotists, however, affirm that "*Merit* ariseth but *ex pacto*, from God's *Promise*; and to be *meritorious*, is no more than to be a *Work which God hath promised a Reward* to: And do any of us deny this?"[536] When God rewards us, he does it from his "ordinate Justice."[537]

Baxter explicitly states that his understanding of the worthiness of one's personal righteousness does not differ from the Scotist view. This does not mean, however, that he severs himself from the Reformed tradition. Baxter's firm entrenchment within this tradition has already been noted. It would be remarkable if his view on the role of works would be an exception. In his *Confession*, Baxter presents a lengthy section with citations from Reformed divines "ascribing as much to works as I."[538] Of the numerous theologians to whom he appeals, Baxter states that he especially agrees with Davenant, "and next him *Bradshaw, Bergius,*

---

532. Baxter, *Admonition*, p. 22. Although Baxter's understanding of the role of works in justification does not really change, in later years he is more willing to accept the word "merit." In *End of Doctrinal Controversies* (probably written in 1674; cf. appendix B), Baxter says that "formerly" he thought it would be best to omit the word because of its abuse by the Papists. Now, however, he thinks it may be best to keep the word because (1) "all the ancient Churches" used it; (2) to abandon it might "harden Papists, Greeks and others"; and (3) there is no substitute: "The word [*Rewardable*] is long and oft harsh: And what other have we? And it is nothing else that we mean" (pp. 295-96). Cf. Packer, "Redemption and Restoration," p. 299.

533. Baxter, *Admonition*, p. 9; *Unsavoury Volume*, p. 53; *Confession*, p. 74; *Of Justification*, p. 100; *Of Imputation*, p. 185. In his *Confession*, Baxter distinguishes fourteen different meanings of the word "merit" (pp. 68-69). He concludes: "Now among all these senses, it is not fair to condemn any man of Error for the bare use of the word, till you know what sence he takes it in" (p. 69).

534. Cf. Highfill, "Faith and Works," pp. 85-86: "Even the term merit need not be condemned so long as the sense is clear and guarded."

535. Baxter, *Admonition*, p. 39; *Confession*, pp. 135-36. Cf. *Of Justification*, p. 190.

536. Baxter, *End of Doctrinal Controversies*, pp. 296-97. Baxter more frequently appeals to Scotus' understanding of merit (*Admonition*, p. 10; cf. *Confession*, pp. 144-45; *Protestant Religion*, p. 97). He expresses his disagreement with Scotus when he makes merit the instrumental cause with respect to the reward (*Confession*, p. 143).

537. Baxter, *Aphorismes* I.141 (p. 91).

538. Baxter, *Confession*, p. 316 (emphasis throughout in original). This section covers pp. 316-455 (incorrect pagination; sig. Nnn1ʳ).

Lud. Crocius, and Dr. *Twiss*."[539] Baxter's quotations of these divines show a great similarity to the theory which he himself espouses. Baxter is able to show that Davenant, Twisse, and Conrad Berg reject faith and works as efficient causes of justification.[540] God has simply "ordinated" works as conditions, according to his promise.[541] Works, in the opinion of these divines, are simply conditions *sine quibus non* of continued justification.[542] Berg and Crocius state that only those works are excluded that expect justification and eternal life as wages of debt.[543] They maintain that there is no commutative merit, but only merit *ex pacto*, which is merit "improperly" so called.[544] Baxter insists – with some legitimacy – that his position with regard to works and merit is no different from that of other moderate Calvinists.

Conclusion

Works play an important role in Baxter's doctrine of justification. The basis for this significance lies in his understanding of the covenant and in his theory of twofold righteousness. He denies the existence of an eternal *pactum salutis* and instead maintains that Christ was under a mediatorial covenant. After he had fulfilled its conditions, all things were placed into his hands. Christ now has a *novum ius dominii* and a *novum ius imperii*, which corresponds to the distinction between God's will *de rerum eventu* and his will *de debito*. God has given all judgement to the Son, who now judges according to the tenor of the law of grace which he has established as *Rector*. As *Dominus Absolutus*, he gives faith arbitrarily, according to his *novum ius dominii*. According to Baxter, therefore, faith is procured indirectly, and it is bestowed absolutely.

Apart from the law of nature, Baxter distinguishes between two editions of the covenant of grace: one from Adam to Christ and one following the coming of Christ. The universal covenant of grace is not superseded when covenants of peculiarity are added (with Moses, Abraham, or the Christian church). Unlike Cartwright, Baxter does not believe that those who are unfamiliar with the Gospel

---

539. Baxter, *Confession*, p. 455 (incorrect pagination; sig. Nnn1ʳ). Baxter's esteem of Davenant is worth noting: "D*Avenant* (that light of *Dort*, *Cambridge*, *England*) expresseth himself concerning the interest of works in justification in the same phrase and sense (as far as I can understand him) as I do: I therefore recite his words, not as a bare Testimony, but as an Explication of my own meaning, as fully as I can tell how to explain it. And if any will make a difference, let them on the same grounds set me at odds with my self. For I do hereby subscribe to these words of his as heartily as to any of my own" (p. 318). Cf. p. 150; *Account*, pp. 56-57; *Admonition*, p. 13; *Substance*, pp. 16-19.
540. Baxter, *Confession*, pp. 321, 323, 326, 329, 367.
541. This expression is used by Davenant, Twisse, and Berg (*Confession*, pp. 323, 325-27, 364).
542. Baxter cites Davenant, Berg, and Crocius (*Confession*, pp. 321-22, 324, 364, 367, 371).
543. Baxter, *Confession*, pp. 366, 369-70.
544. Baxter, *Confession*, pp. 368-69, 371. Davenant allows the word "merit" as used by the church fathers, but not the "proud and false opinion of Merit of Condignity" (p. 324).

are judged only by the law of nature. They will be judged according to the edition of the covenant of grace which applies to them. The covenant of innocence has ceased after the fall. Its precepts and threats, however, remain, for the law of nature is broader in scope than the law of grace and encompasses also the duties of the law of grace. The law of grace is subservient to the law of nature. The abiding validity of the law of nature implies that it still threatens unbelief with death. When people continue in unbelief, however, they will be condemned according to the law of grace because of the non-performance of its condition.

The immediate background to Baxter's theory of twofold righteousness remains obscure. However, he considers himself in line with William Bradshaw, Lewis de Dieu, John Cameron, and Joshua Placaeus. Baxter does not agree with his opponents that our evangelical righteousness is Christ's legal righteousness imputed. He carefully distinguishes the two. Baxter gives man's personal evangelical righteousness a subordinate role in justification. This causes his opponents to fear that he derogates from the role of Christ and of faith and that he introduces justification by works. Baxter indeed distinguishes between the accusation of sin as sin, against which Christ's righteousness must be pleaded, and the accusation of final unbelief, against which one must be personally justified. The former is our universal righteousness, the latter our particular righteousness. The result is a strong emphasis on the conditionality of the covenant and a twofold justification. Nevertheless, the fulfillment of this condition remains subordinate to Christ's righteousness. Although faith is imputed for righteousness, it is not the formal cause of our universal justification. Yet, although Baxter does not explicitly put it this way, his theory demands that one's personal righteousness be regarded as the formal cause of one's evangelical justification. One's personal righteousness is the condition demanded by God as Ruler, according to his *voluntas de debito*; one's universal righteousness is God's gift according to his *voluntas de rerum eventu* as Absolute Lord.

In reply to the charge that he gives too prominent a role to works in justification, Baxter denies that they are a cause of justification at all. Furthermore, in initial justification, they are not even a condition. Nevertheless, both repentance and love are important ingredients of the condition of this first justification. This enhances the fear of Crandon and Cartwright that he is unable to exclude works from initial justification. Baxter positively asserts that works are part of the condition of continued and consummate justification. Therefore, he rejects the attempt of Burgess and Cartwright to distinguish between conditions for justification and conditions for salvation. The central role which sanctification receives in Baxter's theology is evident from (1) his insistence – especially against the *Marrow of Modern Divinity* and Tobias Crisp – that one must not only work *from* but also *for* life; and (2) his sympathy for Fowler's Latitudinarian emphasis on holiness as the ultimate end of Christianity. Baxter also harmonizes James and Paul in accordance with the position that works are a condition of continued justification before God.

Baxter's understanding of the twofold will of God allows him to retain both the perseverance of the saints and the conditionality of the covenant. He is strongly inclined, however, to lessen the tension which his understanding of God's will introduces. Beginning with his *Right Method* (1653), Baxter persistently expresses his sympathy for the Augustinian denial of the certain perseverance of all justified saints. He is afraid of singularity on this point and does not believe that the doctrine of the perseverance of the saints affords greater comfort than the denial of this theory.

Baxter's doctrine of justification has emerged as an eclectic whole which has elements from numerous moderately Calvinist divinses. Baxter is convinced that this theological position implies some affinity to Roman Catholic soteriological thought patterns. This is clear from his highly selective opposition to Roman Catholicism and from his agreement with Le Blanc's *Theses theologicæ*. Also Baxter's willingness to speak of merit in an evidently Scotist fashion supports this thesis. Despite this eclectic agreement with some Roman Catholics, Baxter remains firmly entrenched within the Reformed tradition.

Epilogue

Baxter's adoption of Twisse's distinction between God's *voluntas beneplaciti* and his *voluntas signi* permeates much of his theology. The bifurcation of God's will constitutes the framework within which Baxter seeks to come to a solution of many of the issues surrounding the doctrine of justification. Baxter associates justification with God's will *de debito*. Justification follows the condition of faith. This means that Baxter is able to employ Twisse's distinction in opposition to high Calvinist notions of justification. Baxter detects many dangers in the theory that justification is from eternity. His opposition to this doctrine is an important motive for his emphasis on God's will *de debito*.

This emphasis may also be noted in his understanding of the role of common grace and preparation for justification. Both imply a conditional covenant, even though God does not bind himself to give special grace upon the good use of common grace. Baxter approves of the Roman Catholic notion of congruous merit and thinks that assurance is restricted to stronger Christians only. Christ must not only be believed in as one's Savior. Part of the condition is the acceptance of him as Lord. For continued justification, works belong to the condition as well. Baxter minimizes the differences with Roman Catholicism on the question of merit. It is nevertheless clear that he wants to stand in the Reformed tradition.

Baxter's predilection for God's will *de debito* does not nullify his concern for God's will *de rerum eventu*. The main reason why Baxter does not want to speak of faith as an instrument in justification is that it would make man's faith an efficient cause of justification. Moreover, he argues that God ultimately does not give faith conditionally. It is a gift from God as *Dominus Absolutus*. Also, despite his obvious interest in universal redemption, Baxter maintains that, according to his subsequent will, Christ died only for the elect. Furthermore, despite his sympathy for the Augustinian view on perseverance, Baxter does not dare to openly abandon the idea that all justified people will persevere according to God's decree.

Baxter is indebted to Hugo Grotius and William Bradshaw for his theory of the atonement. According to Baxter, Christ's righteousness is imputed only in an indirect sense. Still, God's demand for justice remains grounded in his nature. The satisfaction of God's justice is more essential from Baxter's perspective than from a high Calvinist point of view. By his death, Christ has acquired a *novum ius dominii* and a *novum ius imperii*. These correspond to God's will *de rerum eventu* and his will *de debito*. Baxter's distinction between universal and personal righteousness – which plays a key role in his understanding of justification – reveals the same bifurcation. The latter is the condition to partake of the former. Once the condition is fulfilled, it is God who grants universal justification. Baxter attempts to do justice to both elements. Nevertheless, when he softens the tension, it is at the cost of God's will *de rerum eventu*. Baxter is intent on maintaining that God is in earnest when he comes down to deal with people.

Appendix A

The Date of Composition of Baxter's *Universal Redemption* (1694)

Apart from its intrinsic value, insight into the origin of Baxter's *Universal Redemption* (1694) is a prerequisite for a careful analysis of the debate between Baxter and Owen. It will be clear that if it predates the controversy, which extended from 1649-55, this would mean that the treatise has no direct bearing on the dispute itself, however interesting an analysis of the publication might be. If, on the other hand, it is written during the period of the debate this changes the picture. Especially if it can be established that major sections of Baxter's treatise are, in fact, reflections on the debate, this would necessitate the use of *Universal Redemption* in a discussion of the controversy. In this appendix I try to establish which part of *Universal Redemption* was written at what time period. It may be concluded with a fairly high degree of probability (1) that the entire book post-dates Owen's *Death of Death* (1647); and (2) that the largest part of the tract must be dated at a time when the controversy had already come to an end.

Transcribing *Universal Redemption* was among the first tasks which Baxter gave Joseph Read ... to when he became Baxter's assistant in 1657. Read maintained that Baxter used the disputations for the monthly lectures of the Worcestershire Association, which began its meetings in 1653.[1] According to Read, Baxter wrote the book around 1655:

---

1. Baxter, *Universal Redemption*, sig. A3ᵛ. The Worcestershire Association was an association of ministers set up by Baxter in 1653. He reports that "every first *Thursday* of the month was the Ministers meeting for Discipline and Disputation: And in those Disputations it fell to my lot to be almost constant Moderator; and for every such day (usually) I prepared a written Determination" (*RB* I.84; cf. II.149-50). The association was intended to further Christian unity: "In our Association in this County, though we made our Terms large enough for all, Episcopal, Presbyterians and Independants, there was not one Presbyterian joyned with us that I know of, (for I knew but of one in all the County, Mr. *Tho. Hall*) nor one Independant, (though two or three honest ones said nothing against us) nor one of the New Prelatical way (Dr. *Hammonds*) but three or four moderate Conformists that were for the old Episcopacy; and all the rest were meer Catholicks; Men of no Faction, nor siding with any Party, but owning that which was good in all, as far as they could discern it ..." (*RB* I.97).

   For secondary literature on the Worcestershire Association, see Powicke, *Life*, pp. 163-76; Morgan, *Nonconformity*, pp. 45-48; Geoffrey F. Nuttall, "The Worcestershire Association: Its Membership," *JEH*, 1 (1950), 197-206; Nuttall, *Richard Baxter*, pp. 66-74; Brown, "Richard Baxter's Contribution," pp. 18-27; Wood, *Church Unity without Uniformity*, pp. 32-34, 101-05; H.A. Lloyd Jukes, "Gunning and the Worcestershire Agreement," *MCM*, NS 7 (1964), 184-86; Paul, "Ecclesiology,", pp. 373-75.

> Let it suffice to assure the Reader that this Disputation of Universal Redemption was composed by him in the strength of *his day*, about the *40th* year of his Age, when the opposition of the Learned of differing Opinions had sharpen'd his Pen, and made him critically exact in considering what he intended for the Press.[2]

If Read's account is correct, Baxter must have written *Universal Redemption* between 1653 and 1657, between the date of the first monthly meetings of the Worcestershire Association and of Baxter's request that his assistant transcribe the material.

James I. Packer, in a meticulous bibliographical note on the origin of *Universal Redemption*, argues that Read was mistaken.[3] Packer does so by showing that Baxter already referred to his papers on universal redemption in his *Aphorismes* (1649) and in a postscript to *Plain Scripture Proof* (dated November 12, 1650).[4] Packer proves beyond doubt that Baxter had already been writing on the topic of the universality of redemption by 1649. Also Baxter's numerous references in his *Universal Redemption* to Owen's *Death of Death* (1647) also suggest that Baxter began writing on universal redemption not long after 1647.

It is doubtful, however, whether the entire work, as published in 1694, was identical to the material Baxter had written in the late 1640s. It seems unlikely that Joseph Read would be mistaken in a such a matter. He was, after all, a native of Kidderminster, and Baxter himself had financially secured Read's education at Trinity College, Cambridge.[5] It is difficult to imagine that Read would not know the immediate background of the material on which he must have worked for quite a number of weeks.

There are also indications in the structure of *Universal Redemption* which make it highly improbable that all the material of *Universal Redemption* stems from the late 1640s. First, Baxter refers to his material written in the forties as being "a few pages" only,[6] "a small Tract."[7] This does not correspond well to the final laborious treatise of 502 pages.

In the second place, the book has a peculiar structure. It commences with three introductory chapters which present numerous distinctions and give a basic outline of Baxter's views on the atonement.[8] The book then comes to a defense of four propositions. The first three concern the nature of the atonement. They argue (1) that Christ in his suffering did not properly represent the persons of the elect; (2) that Christ's sufferings were not the *idem*, but the equivalent or *tantundem* of the punishment threatened in the law; and (3) that Christ, by his suffering, did not satisfy the law, but the lawgiver. Baxter neglects entirely to point out the relation between his stand on these matters and the extent of the atonement. This is a peculiar omission in a book designed to defend the universality of redemption. It

---

2. Baxter, *Universal Redemption*, sig. A4ʳ (emphasis inverted).
3. Packer, "Redemption and Restoration," pp. 473-76.
4. Baxter, *Aphorismes*, sig. Q6ᵛ; II.164 (sig. M4ᵛ, p. 319); *Plain Scripture Proof*, p. 345.
5. Cf. Nuttall, *Richard Baxter*, p. 62; *CCRB* 133, n. 7.
6. Baxter, *Aphorismes*, sig. Q6ᵛ (M4ᵛ).
7. Baxter, *Aphorismes* II.164 (p. 319).
8. Baxter, *Universal Redemption*, pp. 1-21, 22-33, 33-67.

suggests that the defense of these three propositions is somewhat extraneous to the actual argument of the book.

In the third place, while the defense of these first three propositions is rather brief, Baxter elaborates extensively on the fourth proposition.[9] It deals very pointedly with the extent of the atonement, giving thirty different arguments for universal redemption, along with lengthy exegetical support for it. This chapter ends with the peculiar comment: "*Here* Amyraldus *and* Dallæus *coming forth stopt me*."[10] However, the treatise does not conclude at this point. In the subsequent chapter Baxter refutes five arguments against universal satisfaction.[11] Here Baxter ends by commenting: "When I had gone thus far, *Dalleus*'s Defence of Universal Redemption, and Grace came out with *Blondels* Preface, where are so great a number of Witnesses cited of all Ages, that I not only stopt my work but cast away a multitude of Testimonies which I had collected; even of English *Anti-Arminians* ..."[12] The book then closes with a disputation of twenty pages on special redemption.[13]

Finally, most striking about this set-up is the fact that it divides naturally into a number of relatively short sections. These sections would lend themselves well for disputations held at the monthly meetings of the Worcestershire Association. The only section which is not suitable for such a purpose is the one containing thirty arguments defending universal redemption followed by extensive exegetical commentary.

The above arguments lead to the suspicion that the lengthy defense of the fourth proposition may have constituted the original papers which Baxter wrote between 1647 and 1649. The remaining material would then have formed the disputations that Baxter held for his fellow ministers between 1655 and 1657. The scattered nature of the material created in such an *ad hoc* manner would explain the need for Joseph Reid to transcribe it all.

Apart from arguments taken from the structure of the book, the actual contents of some parts of the book also gives some important clues. The book clearly bears the mark of Baxter's polemic with Owen. In particular those discussions in *Universal Redemption* that deal with the nature of the atonement are clearly subsequent to the debate with Owen.[14] The material covered in these three sections lay at the heart of the discussion between Baxter and Owen. As noted already, Baxter makes no mention of a relation between these issues and the extent of the atonement. It would be difficult to identify the essence of the debate between Baxter and Owen in a more sharp and concise manner. It is therefore almost impossible that these three sections were part of the original papers on universal redemption.

Interestingly, the matters debated with Owen regarding the nature of the atone-

---

9. The first three propositions are defended in pp. 67-78, 78-85, 86-90; the last proposition in pp. 90-376.
10. Baxter, *Universal Redemption*, p. 376.
11. Baxter, *Universal Redemption*, pp. 376-412, 412-38, 438-43, 443-51, 451-79.
12. Baxter, *Universal Redemption*, p. 480.
13. Baxter, *Universal Redemption*, pp. 481-502.
14. Baxter, *Universal Redemption*, pp. 67-78, 78-85, 86-90.

ment are not confined to the three sections referred to above. They also occur in the three introductory chapters of the book. It therefore seems that these are the result of the debate between Baxter and Owen as well. Owen is mentioned four times in these chapters.[15] This relatively small number of explicit references to Owen is understandable, considering Baxter's resolve that Owen would have the last word in the debate.[16]

In his original objections to Owen, in the *Aphorismes*, Baxter is not as refined in his criticism as he is in *Universal Redemption*: in the latter book Baxter constantly uses the word "equivalent" alongside *tantundem* in describing his view on the satisfaction of Christ.[17] This is probably due to Owen's charge that Baxter's use of the word *tantundem* meant a denial of the equivalence between the punishment threatened in the law and Christ's suffering.[18] Furthermore, in *Universal Redemption* Baxter employs arguments that he also uses in his unpublished reply to the correspondence he had received from John Wallis. These arguments do not yet surface in the debate with Owen. They must therefore be dated later than the controversy with Owen. In these arguments Baxter makes use of the difference between a formal and a material *idem* and gives an analysis of Christ's temporal, eternal, and spiritual death in order to minimize the similarity with the death which was threatened in the law.[19] Baxter's manner of presentation presents a clarity of thought not yet present in the *Aphorismes* (1649).

Also the type of arguments used, yields support for the hypothesis that Baxter had written some of the material in the late 1640s, and that he added material between 1655 – when Owen closed the debate with Baxter by means of his *Vindiciæ Evangelicæ* – and 1657 – when Joseph Read was asked to transcribe the material. This hypothesis also explains the odd reference to Amyraut and Daillé at the end of the most lengthy section of the book: the end of this chapter was the point at which Baxter originally terminated his work in 1648 or 1649 because of the publication of Amyraut's book against Frederic Spanheim, *Specimen animadversionvm in exercitationes de gratia universalis* (1648).[20] Baxter was confirmed

---

15. Baxter, *Universal Redemption*, pp. 60, 78, 81, 84.
16. Cf. above, p. 43, n. 141.
17. Baxter, *Universal Redemption*, pp. 34, 49, 60, 75, 78, 378, 390.
18. Owen, *Death of Death*, in *Works* 10.267. Cf. above, p. 246.
19. Cf. above, pp. 250-51.
20. Baxter identifies this book of Amyraut as being the cause of his doubt whether he should proceed with his work on universal redemption: "But the last week I have received *Amiraldus* against *Spanhemius* exercitations, who hath opened my very heart, almost in my owne words; and hath so fully said the very same things which I intended, for the greater part, that I am now unresolved whether to hold my hand, or to proceed" (Baxter, *Aphorismes* II.164 [p. 319]).
    This reference seems to indicate that Amyraut's book was the main initial reason for Baxter's suspending the publication of his papers. As noted, Baxter also refers twice to Daillé in his *Universal Redemption*. Daillé's arguments were also part of the reason Baxter halted his publication on the extent of the atonement (Baxter, *Universal Redemption*, pp. 376, 480). The identification of the second reference to Daillé is not open to doubt. Baxter does not identify this treatise of Daillé, but Packer rightly considers that it must concern a treatise of 1655, *Apologia pro duabus ecclesiarum* (Packer, "Redemption and Restoration," p. 475). Keeble and Nuttall think Baxter refers to *Apologie for the reformed churches* (1653; *CCRB* 314, n. 2). This is a translation of a different work, *Apologia pro ecclesiis reformatis* (1652). Packer's suggestion is probably correct

in his resolution to lay aside his manuscript by the publication of two other books on the subject, a posthumous treatise by John Davenant in 1650 and a tract by Jean Daillé (1594-1670), the Amyraldian pastor of Charenton in France, in 1655.[21]

There were additional reasons for Baxter not to publish his *Universal Redemption*. Lack of time, partly due to a continuous poor state of health, as well as fear that the material would unnecessarily offend people, played a role.[22] Moreover, the numerous references – both implicit and explicit – to Owen in the book, was likely an inhibitive factor: he had resolved that Owen would have the last say in the debate. The publication of *Universal Redemption* would mean no less than a reopening of the debate with Owen. The result was that Baxter would not be swayed by the numerous requests to have his *Universal Redemption* published.[23]

It must be concluded that, in all likelihood, Baxter wrote his *Universal Redemption* in two stages. The first stage was from 1647-49, between the publication of Owen's *Death of Death* (1647) and his own *Aphorismes* (1649). In this period Baxter wrote a relatively brief treatise advocating universal redemption. It became the core of the final publication.[24] When writing disputations for the Worcestershire Association Baxter most probably wrote what turned out to be the remainder of the final publication. This was between 1655 and 1657. It concerned introductory chapters, three sections dealing with the nature of the atonement, a chapter opposing five arguments against universal satisfaction, and a disputation on special redemption.

---

since the *Apologia pro duabus ecclesiarum* (1655) deals with universal redemption. The *Apologie for the reformed churches* (1653) deals with the Rome's charging the Protestants of schism. Also, Baxter mentions that the treatise of Daillé was prefaced by David Blondel (Baxter, *Universal Redemption*, p. 480). The *Apologia pro duabus ecclesiarum* (1655) qualifies for this.

The first reference to Daillé in *Universal Redemption* is less clear. When Baxter comments, "*Here* Amyraldus *and* Dallæus *coming forth stopt me,*" he may, here just as in the second reference to Daillé, refer to his *Apologia pro duabus ecclesiarum* of 1655. If so, this would not agree with the fact that the section concluded by Baxter's comment dates from the late 1640s. It would mean that Baxter's interjection at this point is a later insertion. This is not impossible, since *Universal Redemption* also carries a reference to Baxter's *Methodus Theologiæ*, which must also be a later addition (p. 33). Another option is that this first reference to Daillé is to his *De poenis et satisfactionibvs hvmanis, libri VII* of 1649. Baxter did own this book as well (Nuttall, "Transcript," 214). This would mean that Baxter's first reference is to a 1648 publication of Amyraut and a treatise of Daillé from 1649. This accords with the hypothesis that the section preceding Baxter's comment dates from the late 1640s.

21. Baxter identifies the book of John Davenant as being *Dissertationes Duæ* (1650) (*RB* I.123). Cf. Baxter's comment in a letter of June 24, 1656 to Thomas Wadsworth: "What need more y<a>ⁿ Davenants Dissert. & Dailes Apology if there were no more" (DWL MS *BC* ii, f. 256ᵛ [*CCRB* 310]). For Daillé, see Armstrong, *Calvinism and the Amyraut Heresy*, p. 12, n. 28.
22. Baxter, *Aphorismes*, sig. Q6ᵛ (M4ᵛ); *Confession*, p. 2; *Plain Scripture Proof*, p. 345; *RB* I.123.
23. Among those who wrote to Baxter requesting the publication of *Universal Redemption* are Robert Abbott (1588?-1654?), Robert Morton, Henry Oasland (1625-1703), Peter Ince, John Horne (1616-76), and Thomas Wadsworth (1630-76). The requests for publication are noted in *CCRB* 42, 45, 47, 162, 236, 263, 310. For Robert Abbott, see *DNB* 1.25-26; *CCRB* 42. For Robert Morton, see *DNB* 39.157; *CCRB* 47. For Henry Oasland, see *DNB* 41.292-93; *CR* 370-71; *BDBRSC* 2.270-71; *CCRB* 139. For Peter Ince, see *CR* 288-89; *CCRB* 103. For John Horne, see *DNB* 27.357-58; *CR* 277; Geoffrey F. Nuttall, "John Horne of Lynn," in *Christian Spirituality: Essays in Honour of Gordon Rupp*, ed. Peter Brooks (SCM, 1975), pp. 231-47. For Thomas Wadsworth, see *DNB* 58.426-27; *CR* 505.
24. Baxter, *Universal Redemption*, pp. 90-376.

The impact of this conclusion for a discussion on the controversy between Baxter and Owen will be clear. *Universal Redemption* is intimately related to the entire polemic. Throughout the treatise Baxter is in a (partly silent) debate with Owen. Some parts are probably best described as Baxter's more mature reflections on his debate with Owen.

Appendix B

The Date of Composition of Baxter's
End of Doctrinal Controversies
(1691)

Baxter's *End of Doctrinal Controversies* – as published in 1691 – is structured as follows:

* chapter 1-5: pp. i-xxxiv (doctrine of God, trinity, hypostatic union and incarnation, diversity of God's transient operations, faith and reason)

* chapter I-VI: pp. 1-45 (two introductory chapters [pp. 1-23] and four chapters on the will of God and predestination [pp. 24-45])

* pp. 46-70 ("An Answer to Mr. Polehill's Exceptions about Futurition")

* chapter VII-XXVII: pp. 70-320 (various soteriological issues)

It is difficult to be precise about the date of composition of this treatise. In what follows, I give a hypothesis – no more than that – of its origin. Baxter himself writes in his *Reliquiæ Baxterianæ*: "Three years before this <*i.e.* before late 1677> I wrote a Treatise to end our common Controversies, in Doctrinals, about Predestination, Redemption, justification, assurance, perseverance and such like; being a Summary of *Catholick* reconciling *Theology*."[1] This statement would date the writing of *End of Doctrinal Controversies* in 1674. There are two complicating factors, however. In the first place, Baxter comments a little further on that a paper from Edward Polhill (1622-94?), "an excellent learned Gentleman occasioned the answer which perhaps may be published."[2] Baxter's response to Polhill's paper on predetermination is contained in *End of Doctrinal Controversies*.[3] Judging by the place of Baxter's comment on Polhill in his autobiography, Baxter must have written his response in 1678.[4] The question is why Baxter would insert some comments on a manuscript from 1674 in the midst of events that took place 1677

---

1. *RB* III.182.
2. *RB* III.183. For Polhill, see *DNB* 46.57-58; Geoffrey F. Nuttall, "Puritan and Quaker Mysticism," *Theol.*, 78 (1975), pp. 520-24; *CCRB* 1123.
3. Baxter, *End of Doctrinal Controversies*, pp. 46-70.
4. *CCRB* 1012 estimates c. late August 1677, presumably because it is likely that Baxter received Polhill's paper in this same month (cf. *CCRB* 1008).

and 1678. Did it simply occur to him all of a sudden that he still had to mention it? Or is there perhaps a connection with Baxter's response to Polhill, which was probably written in 1678, and which Baxter must later have added to the manuscript treatise?

In the second place, Baxter relates in *End of Doctrinal Controversies* how Lewis Le Blanc, theology professor at Sedan, had sent him his *Theses theologicæ* (1678) in order to have it published in England. The publisher, however, sold his copy to someone else.[5] This incident took place in the spring of 1676.[6] Baxter also refers to Le Blanc elsewhere in *End of Doctrinal Controversies*.[7] It is impossible that these references to Le Blanc date from 1674, when Baxter did not have the *Theses theologicæ* yet.

My hypothesis is that the solution to these two problems probably lies in the fact that Baxter wrote *End of Doctrinal Controversies* in different stages. Baxter himself relates that he wrote the first five chapters (except the last one) about twenty years after the rest of the book.[8] This means that these introductory chapters (pp. i-xxxi) were written in 1691 and were then added to the main body of the book.[9] The rest of the book was by and large finished in 1674, as Baxter relates in his *Reliquiæ Baxterianæ*. Most likely, however, the two introductory chapters of this main part of the book (pp. 1-23) and the answer to Polhill were added in 1677. This explains the curious fact that Baxter's autobiography refers to *End of Doctrinal Controversies* three years after it was actually written. At this time, Baxter had probably just added some sections to the treatise. Moreover, when Baxter wrote these additions, he had recently had the incident surrounding the publication of Le Blanc's *Theses theologicæ*. It is precisely in these additional pages that Baxter refers to Le Blanc three times, while he does not mention him elsewhere in the treatise at all. In 1678 Baxter had the memory of the affair around Le Blanc's *Theses theologicæ* fresh in his mind.

If the above hypothesis is correct, the following chronology emerges:

1674   * Baxter writes pp. 24-45, 70-320 of *End of Doctrinal Controversies*

1676   * Baxter attempts to publish Le Blanc's *Theses theologicæ*

1677   * Baxter adds pp. 1-23, 46-70 of *End of Doctrinal Controversies* (including his reply to Polhill and several references to Le Blanc)

5. Baxter, *End of Doctrinal Controversies*, p. 21.
6. *RB* III.177.
7. Baxter, *End of Doctrinal Controversies*, pp. 16, 53. The last reference is located in Baxter's response to Polhill.
8. Baxter, *End of Doctrinal Controversies*, p. xxxiv. This is presumably the reason why James I. Packer comments that Baxter wrote *End of Doctrinal Controversies* around 1670 ("Redemption and Restoration," p. 299).
9. The preface is dated January 1, 1991 (*End of Doctrinal Controversies*, sig. A4ʳ). It is not clear to me when Baxter wrote his chapter 5 (pp. xxxi-xxxiv, on faith and reason). When Baxter says that only the four preceding chapters were written about twenty years after the writing of rest of the book, this would seem to imply that he wrote chapter 5 at the same time that he wrote the rest of the book. As will become clear below, this is probably either 1674 or 1677.

* Baxter comments on *End of Doctrinal Controversies* in his *Reliquiæ Baxterianæ*

1678   * Baxter refers to his reply to Polhill in the *Reliquiæ Baxterianæ*

1691   * Baxter adds a preface and chapter 1-4 (pp. i-xxxi) for *End of Doctrinal Controversies*

Appendix C

Baxter on Irresistible Grace

There is no unanimity among scholars regarding Baxter's position on irresistible grace. Some deny that he taught that grace is irresistible.[1] Bass comments that according to Baxter all grace is resistible.[2] Others state the exact opposite. Jeremias depicts Baxter's position as follows: as God gives his clear laws, "so wählt er auch als absoluter Herrscher der Welt einen Teil der Menschen aus und läßt ihnen seine besondere Gnade zukommen und zieht sie unwiderstehlich zu sich."[3] Most scholars arguing that Baxter holds to irresistible grace clarify that he also used the term "invincible" or "insuperable."[4] Thus far, there has been no study which systematically analyzes Baxter's comments on the resistibility of grace. The disagreement among Baxter scholars on this issue illustrates the need for a more in depth analysis.

Baxter puts it beyond doubt that God's decree to save a particular person will be carried out. He has an "Everlasting secret Decree" that his chosen will "infallibly" perform the conditions of the covenant of grace.[5] This decree is "not frustrate."[6] Accordingly, Baxter is able to call this decree as such "irresistible."[7] What is more, God's "impulse" on man is sometimes so great, "as *propriâ vi*, doth change mind and will and overcome resistance, and procure our act."[8] Baxter asks rhetorically: May God not "invite multitudes that will refuse; and yet compel but his chosen only to come in? Here it is that special differencing Grace begins, in the execution ..."[9] God, "by his special effectual Grace, *contra omnem Resistentiam*, infallibly causeth" faith and repentance.[10] It is obvious that Baxter is intent on maintaining God's role as *Dominus Absolutus*. When God wants to bring someone to faith he is able to use such force as man is unable to overcome.

Still, Baxter states that "<s>ometimes" God's impulse by its own strength

---

1. Phillips, "Between Conscience and the Law," p. 250.
2. Bass, "Platonic Influences," p. 184. Cf. Alan P.F. Sell's comment that in Baxter's view, "men may render saving grace ineffectual by resisting it ..." (*Great Debate*, p. 32).
3. Jeremias, "Richard Baxters Catholic Theology," p. 95. Cf. pp. 240, 304-05.
4. Packer, "Redemption and Restoration,", pp. 256-58, 391; Richards, "Richard Baxter's Theory of the Atonement," pp. 46, 92; McGrath, "Puritans and the Human Will," p. 289; Beougher, "Conversion," pp. 75-76, 82, n. 204.
5. Baxter, *Universal Redemption*, p. 381.
6. Baxter, *Catholick Theologie* I.iii.22. Cf. II.172.
7. Baxter, *Methodus Theologiæ* III.xxv.286.
8. Baxter, *Catholick Theologie* I.iii.51. Baxter mentions Paul as an example where God suddenly changes the mind and will. Thus, "God worketh not alike on all" (I.iii.22).
9. Baxter, *Universal Redemption*, p. 347.
10. Baxter, *Account*, p. 110. Cf. *End of Doctrinal Controversies*, p. 160: "Christ doth give to some such *special Grace*, as shall and doth infallibly prevail with them to repent and believe, and also actual Pardon, Justification, Adoption and Salvation."

overcomes man's resistance.[11] The implications are that God does not always or
even usually work this way and that man does resist God's grace. Indeed, all
people, including the elect, resist it. They do this in three ways: (1) by not receiving God's grace passively, as oil resists water; (2) by not receiving God's grace
actually or morally, as one resists the light of the sun by refusing to open his eyes;
and (3) by active opposition, as someone resists an enemy. In the first sense,
man's sinful soul is indisposed to the reception of God's grace. In the second
sense, a person does not do what he can do, morally, to receive grace. In the last
sense, a person actively resists God's gracious operation by being unwilling.[12]

When, in a fictitious discussion between C. (a Calvinist) and B. (the concilia-
tor), B. asks whether C. has never repented for resisting grace, his opponent is
forced to admit that, "*in some sense*," he has, and that by "resisting" he means
"overcoming."[13] B. then retorts: "Why then did you not speak as you meant. None
dreameth that Omnipotence is overcome by a greater strength; much less by the
derived power of us worms."[14] When Baxter, therefore, speaks of irresistible
grace he means that the work of the Spirit is invincible:

> And in the word [*Infallible*] which respecteth the act of the Divine *Understanding*,
> we imply also [*Immutable*] which respecteth Gods Will: and *Invincible* as to his
> operation: and had we one word that comprehended these, it would contain our full
> sense. It is the same thing which our Divines mean by the word [*Irresistible*] or
> *Insuperable*.[15]

The grace given by God to his elect is ultimately insuperable, however much it
may be resisted. The insuperable character of this grace is given with the certainty
of the execution of his decree and with the special intention with which Christ died
to bring certain chosen persons to salvation.[16]

That all people resist God's grace implies that he does not use his omnipotence
to the fullest. God does not do all that he can do, and his works do not all equally
manifest his omnipotence.[17] To the high Calvinist objection that resistible grace
would bring dishonor to God's omnipotence, Baxter replies that this would mean
that God is the author of his own dishonor, since he has diversified instruments,
receptivities, and effects "in wonderful variety." Moreover, if it is no dishonor to
God not to will or work something at all, why should it be a dishonor to will or
operate in a limited and resistible measure?[18]

Baxter's insistence that grace is, to some extent, always resisted, is the result
of his emphasis on moral suasion as the manner in which conversion takes place.
Admittedly, he is quick to add that it is "none of my meaning" that the bare means

11. Baxter, *Catholick Theologie* I.iii.51.
12. Baxter, *Catholick Theologie* I.iii.21; II.172.
13. Baxter, *Catholick Theologie* II.172.
14. Baxter, *Catholick Theologie* II.172-73.
15. Baxter, *Universal Redemption*, pp. 482-83.
16. Baxter, *Universal Redemption*, pp. 482-83.
17. Baxter, *Catholick Theologie* I.iii.20.
18. Baxter, *Catholick Theologie* I.iii.24.

by themselves change the soul or even that they are the principal cause.[19] None-theless, moral suasion and the freedom of the will play a significant role in his theology. Baxter regards a proper understanding of the nature of the power and liberty of the will as "the very key to open all the rest of the controverted difficul-ties in these matters."[20] God has made man an intellectual free agent, so that he is a fit subject of God's moral government.[21] Man's self-determining will has the natural liberty to make choices.[22]

Baxter's emphasis on moral suasion and on man's natural freedom of the will leads him to the view that God does not "ordinarily" infuse habits of grace without means. Baxter disagrees with William Pemble, who asserted that habits are super-naturally infused and precede the act of faith.[23] Baxter has an entirely different view on the origin of habits of grace. While admitting that besides the divine operation by the Word, God has another immediate operation on the soul, he states that neither the habit, nor the act, is immediately infused. Instead, he maintains "that the thing first and properly infused is not the act of Faith it self, but the *vis impressa facultatem* <sic> ..."[24]

What Baxter means with this statement becomes clear when he distinguishes subjective grace into (1) the *vis impressa*; (2) the power; (3) the act; and (4) the disposition or habit.[25] Baxter argues that God, using means, makes an "impress" on the soul, "though extraordinarily God can do without means."[26] This "impress, or influx, or force" causes the moral power to believe. This in turn leads to the act of faith, and thus slowly a habit of faith emerges.[27]

Because God does not use his power equally on all people, the *vis impressa* differs from person to person.[28] God is not dependent on man's disposition. Man is totally passive when God makes his first impression on the soul.[29] By analogy

---

19. Baxter, *Catholick Theologie* I.iii.17. Baxter explains the term "moral suasion" in such a way that it is more than *proponere obiectum*. There is also an inward suasion by the Spirit. Although God works on the will in such a way as to preserve its liberty, yet he operates on the mind and will itself (II.161).
20. Baxter, *Catholick Theologie* I.iii.35.
21. Baxter, *Catholick Theologie* II.36.
22. For Baxter's views on free will, see Baxter, *Catholick Theologie* I.i.27-41; I.iii.35-37; II.73-129, 151-55; *Methodus Theologiæ* I.viii.209-17; *End of Doctrinal Controversies*, pp. 92-93, 164, 173-81; *Protestant Religion*, pp. 82-88. There is little disagreement among scholars with respect to Baxter's views on the freedom of the will. A comprehensive analysis of Baxter's position within the context of his ideas on predetermination and on anthropology is, unfortunately, still lacking (cf. Fisher, "Theology of Richard Baxter," 141-43, 150-51; Highfill, "Faith and Works," pp. 96-101; Packer, "Redemption and Restoration," pp. 114-15, 129, 163-65, 384-87; Jeremias, "Richard Baxters Catholic Theology," pp. 58-59; 277-78; Phillips, "Between Conscience and the Law," pp. 56, 224-26; Rooy, *Theology of Missions*, pp. 72-73; Von Rohr, *Covenant of Grace*, pp. 143-44; McGrath, "Puritans and the Human Will," pp. 237-44; Beougher, "Conversion," pp. 50-52).
23. Cf. above, pp. 75-77.
24. Baxter, *Catholick Theologie* II.164.
25. Baxter, *Catholick Theologie* II.150.
26. Baxter, *Catholick Theologie* II.150.
27. Baxter, *Catholick Theologie* II.150-51.
28. Baxter, *End of Doctrinal Controversies*, p. 186.
29. Baxter, *Catholick Théologie* I.iii.55.

of physical motion, we must call ourselves patients in this act of God.[30] While Baxter, thus, maintains that man is only passive in the first instant as he is influenced by God, he does not think that there is any real difference here between the Arminian and the Calvinist position. When the Arminians are accused of teaching that man is not merely passive in his first conversion, Baxter states that everybody is agreed that man must first be receptive of the divine influx before he can act. He then adds: "And all the world agreeth, that no man before Conversion or after doth any act of Faith, Love, &c. no nor eating, and drinking, and going, &c. but he is in the first instant *passive* as influenced by God, before he is active."[31] It is, therefore, the grace of Christ which gives us strength to fulfill the condition of the covenant.[32] Against those who deny special redemption, Baxter asks: "Do these men think that the unrenewed faculty hath need of *no Grace* but an *object* or *perswasion* from without, to cause it *to believe?*"[33] Moral suasion alone does not lead a person to conversion. God must come with his grace before it can result in man's act of faith.

This does not mean that man has no role to play in the origin of faith. Faith is the result of at least two causes: God's motion and man's faculty. But Baxter immediately adds that "*man's will* is *no Cause* (save a *recipient Cause*) of God's *Part* or *Impress*."[34] Man's disposition is a different cause of faith than God's influx. The former is only a receptive material cause, whereas the latter is the efficient cause.[35] Because dispositions vary, the same impress on different people does not have the same effect. Baxter says that if he had time, he would write a book on the common saying *Recipitur ad modum recipientis*.[36]

---

30. Baxter, *Catholick Theologie* I.iii.28. Cf. *End of Doctrinal Controversies*, p. 186: "The *first Impress* on the Soul moving it toward the Act (*e.g. Faith*) is the *first Grace internal* (*sub ratione effecti*): And this God himself worketh on man as on a *meer Patient*; tho' not antecedently to all former acts of Man, or all preparative dispositions, (usually) yet antecedent to that Act of Man to which it moveth: So that as to this, 1. Man is passive, 2. and the Divine Operation (or the *powerful Will of God*) is not only sufficient but effectual; for that *Impress* or *Motus* is effected."

31. Baxter, *Catholick Theologie* II.126.

32. Baxter, *Aphorismes* I.115-16 (p. 75). Cf. *Account*, pp. 103-04: "Renewing Grace must intercede, which is not in their <i.e., unregenerate men's> hand: how then can they promise to do the works of the truly Gracious. God may invite and command the dead to live, yea and to do the works of the living, because he gave them life, and gives them means for revival. But I know not where he calls such men to promise to do it ..."

33. Baxter, *Universal Redemption*, p. 488.

34. Baxter, *End of Doctrinal Controversies*, p. 187.

35. Baxter, *Catholick Theologie* II.174.

36. Baxter, *Catholick Theologie* II.173. Cf. *End of Doctrinal Controversies*, p. 185. The following rather lengthy quotation is illustrative of Baxter's position:
   "1. That the *Diversity of Nature*, or *Receptive Dispositions*, being presupposed, God hath an *established order of means*, and a *congruous established universal Concurse*, which *quantum in se*, as far as belongeth to it to do, worketh equally on all.
   2. That this *established measure of aid*, or *concurse, recipitur ad modum recipientis*, and operateth variously as to the effects, according to the various disposition of the Recipients: from whom the *ratio diversatis* <sic> is to be fetcht, and not from it.
   3. That this *established measure of Concurse* or *aid* may by the greatness of the *Passive* and *Active Indisposition* and *Illdisposition* of the *Recipient*, be both *resisted*, and *overcome* or frustrate.
   4. That as *Adam* did resist and overcome such Grace, so do all wicked men in some cases now. And so do all godly men, in most of the sins (if not all) which they commit.

It is true that Baxter's writings do not emphasize the primacy of the work of the Spirit and the mere passive role of man in receiving the first impression on the soul. In fact, at one place he even speaks of a concurrence between the work of the Spirit and man's will:

> There is an admirable, unsearchable concurrence of the Spirit, and his appointed means, and the will of man, in the procreation of the new creature, and in all the exercises of grace, as there is of male and female in natural generation; and of the earth, the sun, the rain, the industry of the gardener, and the seminal virtue of life and specification, in the production of plants with their flowers and fruits.[37]

Baxter objects to separating "what God hath conjoined." One may not assign the cause of conversion either to the work of the Spirit or to the will of man.[38] Several students of Baxter refer to this passage.[39] And, as one of them states, it is indeed "easy to see how Baxter could be charged with Arminianism in this, if he actually intended to say that the human will acts as a partner with the Spirit and the Word in any way that makes the human will effective in securing the benefits of grace."[40]

Baxter's comments on man's initial passive role and his disposition being only a receptive cause shed some light, however, on how the comment regarding an "unsearchable concurrence" must be interpreted. This phrase does not constitute a denial of God's first impression on the soul. Rather, because of Baxter's continuous stress on moral suasion instead of on the supernatural aspect of conversion, and because of the attention he gives to the freedom of the will and the possibility of preparation for special grace it becomes more difficult to retain the primacy of the work of the Holy Spirit in conversion. The passage about an "unsearchable concurrence" illustrates this difficulty. But Baxter's repeated comments on man's initially passive role make clear that he has not lost all sight of the primacy of the role of the Holy Spirit in conversion.

Baxter's acceptance of "invincible grace" comes under pressure from his views on moral suasion, the freedom of the will, and preparation for special grace. These same factors are the cause of yet a further limitation of irresistible grace. A number of times, Baxter raises the question whether grace which is sufficient to the act of faith may be resisted. Baxter calls this "the sticking difficulty."[41] Aware of the sensitive nature of the question, Baxter wavers. He does not dare to say with certainty that there are people who have grace sufficient to believe savingly, but

---

5. As God *rarely* worketh *Miracles*, (and we hardly know when he *violateth* his established course of nature, though we may know when he worketh beyond the power of any second cause known to us, and when he leaveth his ordinary way) but ordinarily keepeth to his *established course* and use of the second causes (even in his wonders.) So it is very probable, that in the Works of Grace, Recovery and Salvation, he ordinarily keepeth to his *established order*, his Ordinances, and fixed degree of Concurse" (*Catholick Theologie* II.176-77).

37. Baxter, *Christian Directory*, in *Works* I.70 (2.193).
38. Baxter, *Christian Directory*, in *Works* I.70 (2.193).
39. Rooy, *Theology of Missions*, p. 82; Breed, "Sanctification," pp. 273-74; McGrath, "Puritans and the Human Will," p. 304.
40. Breed, "Sanctification," p. 274.
41. Baxter, *End of Doctrinal Controversies*, p. 171.

who yet refuse to do so. After indicating his uncertainty on the point, Baxter continues: "But if we may conjecture upon Probabilities, it seemeth to me most likely, that *there is such a sufficient Grace or Power to repent and believe savingly* in some that use it not, but perish."[42] In defense of this position Baxter appeals to the examples of Adam and the fallen angels. Both had sufficient grace to have remained faithful.[43] Moreover, both the wicked and the godly often have sufficient grace to do more good than they actually do.[44]

Baxter's *non liquet* on this "sticking difficulty" could be interpreted as an ultimate *non liquet* also on irresistible grace. As noted above, Baxter does speak of irresistible or invincible grace. There is no question that God is able to employ such power that man is unable to resist his divine influx. Also, he infallibly fulfills his decree. Important is further Baxter's insistence that in the first impress which leads to the first act of saving faith God is the sole subject: man is a mere patient, a recipient cause only. In this way, Baxter tries to safeguard God's sovereignty and his role as *Dominus Absolutus*. The rejection of an infused habit of grace, the emphasis on free will, moral suasion, and preparation for saving grace, however, lead him to assert man's actual resistance to God's grace in strong terms. Thus, he even comes to the view that it is probable that some people resist grace which is sufficient to repent and believe savingly.

Does Baxter deny irresistible grace? There is no simple affirmative or negative answer to this question. First, it must be determined what someone means with "irresistible grace." It is clear that Baxter does not say that all grace, including saving grace, may be resisted.[45] All he says is that sufficient grace, grace which *could* have been saving, is probably successfully resisted by some people. This admission indicates that his emphasis remains with God as *Rector per leges*. Without denying his decree or his absolute power to effect conversion when he so desires, Baxter so emphasizes God's will *de debito* that the irresistible aspects of God's grace are usually relegated to the background.

---

42. Baxter, *End of Doctrinal Controversies*, p. 171. Cf. *Catholick Theologie* I.iii.48: "And that no *prepared soul* hath such sufficient Grace to *believe*, that yet believeth not, is a thing that is past our reach to know." Cf. *Breviate*, p. 37.
43. Baxter, *Catholick Theologie* I.iii.48; II.176; *End of Doctrinal Controversies*, p. 171.
44. Baxter, *Catholick Theologie* II.176; *Methodus Theologiæ* III.xxv.287; *End of Doctrinal Controversies*, p. 171.
45. As asserted by Bass, "Platonic Influences," p. 184; Sell, *Great Debate*, p. 32.

Appendix D

The Possibility of Salvation without Knowledge of the Gospel

The question whether those may be saved who are not familiar with the Gospel is an issue which Baxter addresses on a number of occasions. Some of these are mere incidental remarks in a different context. For instance, in the midst of a disputation against the baptism of children of ungodly parents, Baxter comments that we run the danger that people might start thinking of Christianity as being no better than other world religions if

> wee (justly <!> condemn a *Seneca, Cicero, Fabricius, Socrates*, &c. as miserable for not believing in Christ, whom they never heard of (most of them;) and priviledg the children of one wors than *Nero, Sardanapalus, Machiavel*, and that for the sake of such a Parent, and as a member of him, to bee in Covenant with Christ, and of the beloved Societie and Houshold of Faith.[1]

Baxter here maintains that the condemnation of Seneca and others "as miserable" is just.

Elsewhere, Baxter briefly mentions the issue in connection with the question of fundamental articles. He pleads for moderation and insists that Christians must not "damn, curse and kill" because of controversies that hardly anybody understands.[2] The reason for this moderation is that "it puts the wisest Divines hard to it, how far they may pronounce Damnation on all those Heathens, that live in Sincerity (though not in Perfection) according to that measure of the notification of God's Will which they are under ..."[3] In other words, if perhaps even heathens are saved, Christians ought not to condemn each other because of difficult issues. These incidental comments of Baxter illustrate the need for further investigation. This is possible because at various places of his writings he discusses the problem in more detail. The question to be addressed, then, is this: does Baxter think that all those who have not heard the Gospel will be condemned, as the first statement may seem to intimate, or does he allow for the possibility that people without an understanding and acceptance of the Gospel be saved?

Baxter repeatedly insists that it is impossible to make unequivocal statements about this issue, simply because Scripture does not reveal the answer. Baxter says that it is "safest to leave the Case of those that never heard of Christ and their Infants, as a thing unrevealed or so darkly revealed that God would not have us know any more of it, than that our condition is far better than theirs, that so we

---

1. Baxter, *Certain Disputations*, p. 300.
2. Baxter, *End of Doctrinal Controversies*, p. 17.
3. Baxter, *End of Doctrinal Controversies*, pp. 16-17.

may be thankful."[4] The "terms" on which God will judge those who have not heard of Christ are not mentioned in Scripture.[5] The lack of information in Scripture implies that the issue is not as important "as some imagine."[6]

Although Scripture may not be very clear on the issue, this does not mean that Baxter feels he is unable to appeal to Scripture for his opinion. Whenever he does this, he consistently allows for the possibility that also non-Christians will be saved. For instance, Baxter does not follow the Authorized Version in its translation of Malachi 1:11. According to Baxter, this text does not say that God's name *shall be* great, but that it *is* great among the heathen.[7] Baxter insists that there is no intimation that Jonah ever preached Christ to the Ninevites.[8] Further, Baxter appeals to God's mercy to all people in giving rain and fruitful seasons (Acts 14:17). This goodness of God is meant to lead to repentance (Rom 2:4). God is not a "respecter of persons" (Acts 10:35). He renders to every man according to his deeds (Rom 2:6). It is the duty of all pagans to seek the Lord (Acts 17:27). Wicked men are those who do not seek after God (Rom 3:11; Ps 14:2). They are without excuse (Rom 1:19-20; Acts 14:17).[9]

The way in which Baxter deals with these Scriptural data is illustrative for his approach: on the one hand, he maintains that Scripture does not really answer the question whether non-Christians may be saved. On the other hand, when Baxter does appeal to Scripture, it is always in favor of the possibility of salvation for those who do not know the Gospel. He repeatedly appeals to the limited knowledge which the Old Testament saints had of redemption by Christ. The Jews used to have only a "more general belief in the Messiah."[10] Even the apostles had only a slight inkling of Christ's work as Mediator:

> Nay, it appears by divers passages in the Gospel, that Christs own Twelve Apostles after they had long heard his Teaching, and seen his Miracles, did not believe that Christ should be put to Death, and be made a Sacrifice for Sin; much less his Resurrection, &c. And how unlikely is it then that all the true believers of the World long before should believe this?[11]

The case of the apostles proves to Baxter that a clear understanding and accept-

---

4. Baxter, *Universal Redemption*, p. 54.

5. Baxter, *Universal Redemption*, p. 475.

6. Baxter, *End of Doctrinal Controversies*, p. 199. Cf. *Methodus Theologiæ* III.i.18: "It is most certain that God has, in fact, far more obscurely revealed to us the future state of those who have never heard the Gospel (both adults and infants) than the state of others, especially Christians. Indeed, it is particularly the knowledge of our own affairs – and not so much that of others – which concerns us." ("Certissimum est de facto, Deum multò obscuriùs nobis revelâsse, statum futurum eorum qui Evangelium nunquam audivêre, (& adultorum & Infantum) quàm aliorum, præcipuè Christianorum: Notitia quippe rerum nostrarum, maximè ad nos pertinet; non ita alienarum.")

7. Baxter, *End of Doctrinal Controversies*, pp. 200-01.

8. Baxter, *Universal Redemption*, p. 120.

9. Baxter appeals to these texts in *God's Goodness Vindicated* (1671), in *Works* II.979-80 (8.527-28); *Methodus Theologiæ* III.i.23; and *Universal Redemption*, pp. 120-21.

10. Baxter, *More Reasons*, in *Works* II.222 (21.559).

11. Baxter, *Universal Redemption*, p. 477. Cf. *Of Justification*, pp. 28-30; *More Reasons*, in *Works* II.222 (21.561); *Methodus Theologiæ* III.i.21; *Dying Thoughts* (1683), in *Works* III.1060 (18.497); *End of Doctrinal Controversies*, p. 130.

ance of Christ's work as Mediator is not absolutely necessary for salvation. Baxter believes that this was also Abraham's opinion. Again and again, Baxter appeals to him by way of an example. Abraham thought that there were fifty righteous people in Sodom, "even when God had told him how much worse it was than other places. How many then proportionably did he think there was in *Canaan* and all other Countries of the World."[12]

These examples come from his theological conviction that also pagans do not receive grace in vain. He objects to the idea that the sinful world is "shut up under desperation."[13] The use of means only makes sense if there is "hope of success."[14] Says Baxter:

> The very command of God, to use his appointed means for men's recovery, doth imply that it shall not be in vain; and doth not only show a possibility, but so great a hopefulness of the success to the obedient as may encourage them cheerfully to undertake it, and carry it through.[15]

All people have a duty to use "all possible means and industry" to come to know the way of salvation.[16] Although it is true that all people do not have the sufficient means to know Christ, they are yet in the position not only to know God and to know that he is a righteous Judge, but also to know that "they cannot of themselves discover what those satisfactory grounds are, on which God so suspendeth the rigour of Justice, and dealeth with them so contrary to their deserving."[17] It is their duty, therefore, to "send to enquire of all others in the World" in order to find out how God's justice is satisfied.[18]

Consequently, it is the "abuse of sufficient Grace" which causes them to forfeit other benefits of Christ's blood.[19] The reason why people are not saved is only their wrong use of the means.[20] Indeed, "all men that perish" are condemned for this reason.[21] Sidney H. Rooy correctly summarizes Baxter's position as follows: "All nations who are without the gospel do have certain means for their salvation

---

12. Baxter, *Catholick Theologie* II.106. Cf. *Methodus Theologiæ* III.i.26; *End of Doctrinal Controversies*, pp. 17, 201.
13. Baxter, *Reasons of the Christian Religion*, in *Works* II.72 (21.126). Cf. *More Reasons*, in *Works* II.223 (21.563); *Universal Redemption*, p. 464.
14. Baxter, *Reasons of the Christian Religion*, in *Works* II.72 (21.126).
15. Baxter, *Reasons of the Christian Religion*, in *Works* II.73 (21.126).
16. Baxter, *Universal Redemption*, p. 464.
17. Baxter, *Universal Redemption*, p. 464. James McJunkin Phillips, while correctly commenting that Baxter does not hold that all non-Christians are lost, overstates the case when he says: "God's goodness is such that He can save those who have not known Him, and it is going beyond the evidence of Scripture to say that such are surely lost" ("Between Conscience and the Law," p. 258). Baxter only discusses the possibility of salvation of those who do not know the revelation of the Gospel of Christ. He thinks that everybody is able to know both the existence and a number of attributes of God without supernatural revelation. He indeed extends the possibility of salvation to those who do not know Christ, but never to those who do not know God. In Baxter's view, ignorance of God could only arise from abuse of the light of nature.
18. Baxter, *Universal Redemption*, p. 464. Cf. pp. 470-71.
19. Baxter, *Universal Redemption*, p. 473.
20. Baxter, *Account of my Consideration*, p. 24; *Universal Redemption*, p. 124.
21. Baxter, *Reasons of the Christian Religion*, in *Works* II.73 (21.128). Cf. *God's Goodness Vindicated*, in *Works* II.979 (8.525-26).

which they are obliged to use in hope, and which in neglecting add to their sin."[22]
One might even argue that Baxter is of the opinion that when God provided these
means he at the same time gave reason to believe that the proper use of the means
would lead to salvation.

What is the theological basis from which Baxter comes to such remarkably
positive statements about the possibility that non-Christians may be saved? According to his understanding of the covenant, Baxter insists that nobody is under
the mere law of works.[23] The reason why all nations have some hope is that they
will ultimately be judged by the law of grace.[24] The law of nature or of works is
now in Christ's hands; it is part of his law.[25] Christ remits transgressions against
this moral law if people accept the grace of redemption.[26]

Within this covenant of grace, Baxter distinguishes two editions. The first
edition extends from the time of the promise of Genesis 3:15 until Christ, while
the second edition came in force after this period. But there does not appear to be
a sharp line of demarcation between the two editions. Baxter distinguishes between the mere legislation or enacting of the covenant and its promulgation:

> It belongeth to the Rector after the enacting of his Law, to promulgate it: And
> though promulgation be not in the strictest sense (I think) a part of Legislation
> (though many think otherwise I confess;) yet it is a necessarily subsequent act of the
> Rector, without which his Law cannot actually oblige ... For it is the *Sense and Will*
> of the Legislator, that his enacted Law do oblige those, and only those to whom it is
> promulgate; (else it should be apparently unjust, as obliging to natural Impossibili-
> ties.) And it cannot oblige beyond his Sense and Will.[27]

According to Baxter, the mere enacting of the law does not oblige the subjects.
They must first have at least the opportunity to know the terms.[28]

The result is that those who have not heard the Gospel will not be condemned
simply for not accepting Christ. Baxter repeatedly insists that the universal covenant of grace made with Adam and renewed with Noah is still in force: "No man
can prove either a limitation of this covenant to some, (till the rest, by violating it,
became the serpent's seed, at least,) nor yet that ever God did abrogate it, as it was
made to all the world."[29] Indeed, Baxter explicitly states that if people are not able
to have the second edition of the covenant of grace, they remain under the first
edition. Baxter says that he was gradually confirmed in this opinion. At the end of

22. Rooy, *Theology of Missions*, p. 90.
23. Baxter, *God's Goodness Vindicated*, in *Works* II.980 (8.528); *Universal Redemption*, pp. 37, 456.
24. Baxter, *Universal Redemption*, pp. 37-38.
25. Baxter, *Universal Redemption*, pp. 38, 466.
26. Baxter, *Universal Redemption*, p. 466.
27. Baxter, *Universal Redemption*, p. 459.
28. Cf. Baxter, *Reasons of the Christian Religion*, in *Works* II.74 (21.129): "God will not condemn
    men for not believing a truth which mediately or immediately was never revealed to them, and
    which they had no means to know. Nor for not obeying a law which was never promulgated to
    them, or they could not come to be acquainted with: physical impossibilities are not the matter of
    crimes, or of condemnation." Cf. *Reduction*, p. 99.
29. Baxter, *More Reasons*, in *Works* II.222 (21.559).

a section of *Universal Redemption*, probably dating from around 1655-57, Baxter comments:

> Let the Reader note, that since the writing of this, I am clearer than I was then in the assurance of this Truth, that the Covenant or Law of Grace, as it is the Rule of Duty and Retribution; was made with all Mankind in the first Edition, in *Adam* and *Noah*; and is not repealed to any that have not the second Edition (in the Gospel) but the rest of the World are still under it.[30]

Baxter insists that the second edition of the covenant of grace only takes effect when people have had the opportunity to acquaint themselves with the terms of this edition. As noted, part of his reason is that otherwise God would demand not just moral, but also natural impossibilities. What is more, this would imply that the coming of Christ had made salvation more difficult. If the covenant would no longer be universal since Christ's coming, God's mercies would have diminished, and man's condition would have been made worse rather than better by Christ's coming. Baxter argues that

> if Christ since his incarnation hath diminished none of the mercies of God to the world, but rather greatly increased them, and so where the gospel is not preached, nor cannot be had, they that refuse it not are in no worse case than they were before, how can you say that they are remediless, if Christ be the Ransom and Remedy?[31]

This last statement of Baxter indicates that those who are not willfully ignorant of the Gospel will be judged according to the first edition of the law of grace.[32] At the same time, the comment makes an important clarification: Christ is the ransom and remedy also of those who will ultimately be judged according to the tenor of this first edition. Although the apostles had only a dim view of Christ's role as Mediator, he was nevertheless the one who saved them.[33] Says Baxter: "For it is most certain that without the mediation, sacrifice, and intercession of Christ, or without the sanctification of the Spirit no one, whether adult or infant, will be saved."[34] Thus, Baxter has no problem in dealing with the objection that Christ is the only way to come to the Father (John 14:6) and that there is "none other name under heaven given among men, whereby we must be saved" (Acts 4:12). The point is, insists Baxter, that even though they have never heard the Gospel, they may nevertheless obtain salvation through the Mediator without knowledge of his

---

30. Baxter, *Universal Redemption*, p. 480. Cf. *More Reasons*, in *Works* II.224 (21.566); *Methodus Theologiæ* III.i.19.
31. Baxter, *More Reasons*, in *Works* II.223 (21.563).
32. Cf. Jeremias, "Richard Baxters Catholic Theology," p. 77: "Die Menschen, die jedoch das Evangelium nie hörten, stehen unter der ersten Form des 'Law of Grace', wie es Adam und Noah gegeben wurde, und von ihnen wird nur Reue und Umkehr zu Gott verlangt. Auch über sie herrscht jedoch Christus, denn Gott hat ihm die Regierung der ganzen Welt bis zum Jüngsten Gericht übergeben, seit er durch seinen Tod die sündige Menschheit erlöste."
33. Baxter, *Of Justification*, p. 29.
34. Baxter, *Methodus Theologiæ* III.i.18 ("Certissimum enim est sine Christi Mediatione, sacrificio, intercessione aut Spiritûs sanctificatione, neminem vel adultum vel infantem salvum fore."). Cf. *Christian Directory*, in *Works* I.721 (5.551).

incarnation, death, and resurrection.[35] In this context, Baxter disagrees with William Twisse and other high Calvinist divines who deny the absolute necessity of Christ's satisfaction.[36] No one can ever be saved without his work of mediation. But our knowledge of this work of redemption does not have the same type of necessity: "And indeed the satisfaction of Christ is of greater necessity to mans Salvation, than our knowledge of Christ, or Faith in him ..."[37] It may be concluded that when Baxter allows for the possibility that non-Christians be saved, he is careful to add that this is only due to Christ's work of mediation.

Two more qualifying comments are in place. First, the possibility that those who have not heard the Gospel may be saved does not imply that mission work becomes redundant. Baxter's missionary fervor is well known and may be noticed, for instance, in his extensive correspondence with the New England missionary, John Eliot (1604-90), who is often referred to as the "apostle of the Indians," and who translated Baxter's *Call to the Unconverted* (1658) into Algonquian.[38] In his autobiography, Baxter makes the comment that he does not want to "pass a peremptory Sentence of Damnation upon all that never heard of Christ ..."[39] This comment is preceded, however, by a long paragraph in which Baxter expresses his deep desire for the conversion of "the miserable World." He is seriously bothered by the division of languages, which he regards as a plague. Baxter even comments that

> there is nothing in the World that lyeth so heavy upon my heart, as the thought of the miserable Nations of the Earth: It is the most astonishing part of all God's Providence to me, that he so far forsaketh almost all the World, and confineth his special Favour to so few: That so small a part of the World hath the Profession of Christianity, in comparison of Heathens, Mahometans and other Infidels![40]

In the second place, Baxter does not think that it is an indifferent matter whether one has heard the Gospel or not. Those who live in countries where the Gospel is preached are in a far better position to be saved than others. Again, the reason is that God usually employs means:

> But what *numbers* do perform the Condition and are saved, no mortal man can tell: But in general we know, that God usually worketh in *Congruity to his appointed means*, and consequently that *far fewer are saved* where *less means* is vouchsafed, than among *Christians* who have herein the unvaluable *pre-eminence* above others.[41]

35. Baxter, *Methodus Theologiæ* III.i.23.
36. Baxter, *More Reasons*, in *Works* II.223 (21.562); *Universal Redemption*, pp. 477-78; *Methodus Theologiæ* III.i.26-29.
37. Baxter, *Universal Redemption*, p. 120.
38. For John Eliot, see *DNB* 17.189-94; F.J. Powicke, "Some Unpublished Correspondence of the Rev. Richard Baxter and the Rev. John Eliot, 'The Apostle to the American Indians', 1656-1682," *BJRL*, 15 (1931), 138-76, 442-66; Neville B. Cryer, "Biography of John Eliot," in *Five Pioneer Missionaries*, ed. S.M. Houghton (London: Banner of Truth, 1965), pp. 171-231; Rooy, *Theology of Missions*, pp. 156-241; *CCRB* 327.
39. *RB* I.131.
40. *RB* I.131.
41. Baxter, *End of Doctrinal Controversies*, p. 199.

Repentance is both easier and more common for those who have the Gospel.[42] Thus, Baxter rejects a simple equation between the situation of those who are and those who are not in a position to hear the Gospel.

The *crux* of the issue of salvation of non-Christians has already been mentioned: it lies in Baxter's understanding of the covenant of grace with its two editions. It has not yet become clear, however, whether there are indeed people who make such use of common grace that it leads to their salvation without knowledge of Christ. N.H. Mair has stated that for Baxter the law of nature is "theoretically sufficient" to give the possibility of salvation. Having acknowledged this possibility, Mair comments: "The difficulty was, however, that such men are rare – if indeed they ever existed."[43]

The question is: does Baxter believe that such men exist? He is by no means anxious to provide an answer to this problem. Apart from the lack of Scriptural data, he points out that it is not our duty, and that it is also not possible, to know the hearts of all people: "I can read God's law, but I cannot know or read the hearts of millions whom I never saw. Must I be obliged to know the thoughts of every man in China, Tartary, Japan, or the antipodes?"[44] In other words, Baxter refuses to pry into God's will *de rerum eventu* and thinks that for guidance he can only refer to God's will *de debito*.

This does not mean that Baxter never attempts to come to a solution. As noted already, he comments in passing that Seneca and others are justly condemned "as miserable" for not believing in Christ. In this remark, Baxter stops short of denying that these people are saved. He only condemns them "as miserable." It is not very likely that he means to imply that they are eternally condemned. Such a statement would be out of line with his consistently careful attitude in passing a peremptory judgement on others with regard to their salvation. Baxter warns those who easily condemn others: "I advise those that use to assault such things with reproach, which they find reproached by their Party, to remember, that God is Love, and Christ is the Saviour of the World, and the Pharisaical Appropriators of Mercy and Salvation, do seldom know what spirit they are of."[45] Baxter calls those who are certain that all non-Christians are damned, "over-doing divines" and "undoers of the church by over-doing."[46]

Furthermore, on several occasions Baxter explicitly states that it is probable that there are also non-Christians who are saved. He says that

> it is exceedingly *probable*, at least, That God would never govern many hundred parts of the World (compared to the *Jews*) before Christ's Incarnation, and five sixth parts since his Incarnation, by a Law of Grace, which yet no person should ever have effectual Grace to keep as far as was necessary to his Salvation. Every *Law of God* is

42. Baxter, *God's Goodness Vindicated*, in *Works* II.980 (8.529); *More Reasons*, in *Works* II.226 (21.570); *Methodus Theologiæ* III.i.22.
43. Mair, "Christian Sanctification," p. 79.
44. Baxter, *More Reasons*, in *Works* II.226 (21.570). Cf. *God's Goodness Vindicated*, in *Works* II.980 (8.529).
45. Baxter, *End of Doctrinal Controversies*, p. 202.
46. Baxter, *Christian Directory*, in *Works* I.721 (5.551-52).

a *Means*, and appointeth the Subjects the use of much Means for their own Salvation: These means they are bound to use, and shall be condemned, if they use them not; and that none should ever use them savingly, is an Assertion so unlikely, that he that hath the boldness to affirm it, should bring certain Proof of it, which the Scripture, I think, doth not afford him.[47]

According to Baxter, it is extremely unlikely that all non-Christians are eternally condemned.[48] Also, if indeed it is true that all pagans are damned, then still their punishment will not be equal to that of those who have heard the Gospel: "For their Consciences will never torment them for the refusal of Christ revealed ..."[49] The more knowledge a person has, the more guilty he is for rejecting it.[50]

The conclusion must be that Baxter is somewhat hesitant to answer the question whether there are non-Christians who are saved. Scripture does not give a clear solution, and it is not really our domain to discuss the salvation of others whose hearts we do not know. Still, Baxter consistently chides those who have a narrow view on this issue, and he uses several texts and examples of Scripture to at least open up the possibility that there may be some who have never heard the Gospel but are nevertheless saved. When Baxter does allow himself to be tempted into an answer to the question he answers in the positive: it is most likely that some non-Christians are saved. The reason for this positive evaluation lies in Baxter's doctrine of the covenant. The world is no longer under the terms of the mere law of works, and those who have never heard the Gospel are to be considered under the terms of the first edition rather than the second edition of the law of grace.

---

47. Baxter, *End of Doctrinal Controversies*, p. 199.
48. Also in his *Methodus Theologiæ*, Baxter says that, according to the judgement of charity (*ex lege tamen charitatis*), we must hold that some non-Christians perform the conditions of the initial covenant and are saved (III.i.22). It is true that Baxter once comments that it is "not likely" that "any Indians or others" have used all means to come to a fuller discovery of the Gospel (*Universal Redemption*, p. 470). Although this is a somewhat uncharacteristic statement for Baxter, he does not say that this means that only Christians will be saved.
49. Baxter, *Universal Redemption*, p. 479.
50. Cf. *RB* I.131; *More Reasons*, in *Works* II.223 (21.562-63).

Select Bibliography

MANUSCRIPTS

DWL MS *BC*.
DWL MS *BT*.

PRIMARY LITERATURE[1]

Acta of Handelingen der Nationale Synode in de naam van onze Heere Jezus Christus Gehouden door autoriteit der Hoogmogende Heren Staten-Generaal der Verenigde Nederlanden te Dordrecht in de jaren 1618 en 1619. Ed. J.H. Donner and S.A. Van den Hoorn. Pref. W. Van 't Spijker. 1885; rpt. Houten: Den Hertog, 1987.

Ames, William. *The Marrow of Theology: William Ames 1576-1633*. Trans. and ed. John D. Eusden. Foreword Douglas Horton. 1968; rpt. Durham, NC: Labyrinth, 1983.

Baillie, Robert. *The Letters and Journals of Robert Baillie, A.M. Principal of the University of Glasgow. M.DC.XXXVII.-M.DC.LXII*. Ed. David Lang. 3 vols. Edinburgh: Ogle, 1841-42.

Ball, John. *A Treatise of Faith. Divided into two Parts: The first shewing the Nature, The second, the Life of Faith: Both tending to direct the weake Christian how he may possesse the whole Word of God as his owne, overcome temptations, better his obedience, and live comfortably in all estates*. 3rd ed. London, 1637.

———. *A Treatise of the Covenant of Grace: Wherein The graduall breakings out of Gospel-grace from Adam to Christ are clearly discovered, the differences betwixt the old and new Testament are laid open, divers errours of Arminians and others are confuted; the nature of Uprightnesse, and the way of Christ in bringing the soul into Communion with himself: Together with many other Points, both doctrinally and practically profitable, are solidly handled*. London, 1645.

Baxter, Richard. *An Account of my Consideration of the Friendly, Modest, Learned Animadversions of Mr. Chr. Cartwright of York, on my Aphorisms. Of God's Legislative and Decretive Will*. [London, 1675]. In *Treatise of Justifying Righteousness*.

———. *An Account of the Reasons Why the Twelve Arguments, Said to be Dr. John Owen's, Change not my Judgment about Communion with Parish-Churches*. London, 1684. In *Catholick Communion Defended*.

———. *Against the Revolt to A Foreign Jurisdiction, Which would be to England its Perjury, Church Ruine, and Slavery. In Two Parts. I. The History of Mens Endeavors to*

---

1. In transcription of titles of primary sources, I have tried to follow a consistent style. When a treatise is published as part of a larger work but with separate pagination, the larger work and the individual treatise are both listed in the bibliography. Where possible, titles have been rendered in their complete, original form. Where the length of the title was prohibitive I have indicated this by the use of "etc." or " . . . " in the title. Whenever "&c." occurs this is part of the original title. The capitalization of the primary sources has been followed, except that words that were originally completely capitalized with all letters being equal in size (e.g., "APOLOGY") have been adapted to present-day English custom (e.g., "Apology"). Any form of emphasis in the titles (e.g., enlarged letter type, italics) has been omitted.

introduce it. II. The Confutation of all Pretences for it. Fully stating the Controversie, and Proving, That there is no Soveraign Power of Legislation, Judgment and Execution over the whole Church on Earth, Aristocratical or Monarchical, but only Christs: Especially against the Aristocratists who place it in a Council or College. London, 1691.

———. *An Answer to Dr. Tullies Angry Letter.* London, 1675. In *Treatise of Justifying Righteousness.*

———. *An Answer to Mr. Dodwell and Dr. Sherlocke; Confuting an Universal Humane Church-Supremacy, Aristocratical and Monarchical; as Church-Tyranny and Popery: And defending Dr. Isaac Barrow's Treatise against it.* London, 1682.

———. *Aphorismes of Justification, With their Explication annexed. Wherein also is opened the nature of the Covenants, Satisfaction, Righteousnesse, Faith, Works, &c.* London, 1649.

———. *Aphorismes of Justification, With their Explication annexed. Wherein also is opened the nature of the Covenants, Satisfaction, Righteousnesse, Faith, Works, &c.* [Cambridge], 1655.

———. *An Appeal to the Light, Or, Richard Baxter's Account of Four accused Passages of a Sermon on Eph. 1.3. Published in hope either to procure the convincing instructions of the wise, or to humble and stop the erroneous Resisters of the Truth.* London, 1674.

———. *A Breviate of the Doctrine of Justification, Delivered in many Books, By Richard Baxter: In many Propositions, And the Solution of 50 Controversies about it. Etc.* London, 1690. In *Scripture Gospel defended.*

———. *Catholick Communion Defended against both Extreams: And Unnecessary Division Confuted, by Reasons against both the Active and Passive ways of Separation: Etc.* London, 1684.

———. *Certain Disputations Of Right to Sacraments, and the true nature of Visible Christianity; Defending them against several sorts of Opponents, especially against the second assault of that Pious, Reverend and Dear Brother Mr Thomas Blake.* London, 1657.

———. *A Defence of Christ, and Free Grace: Against the Subverters, Commonly Called, Antinomians or Libertines; Who Ignorantly Blaspheme Christ on Pretence of extolling Him. In a Dialogue Between An Orthodox Zealot, and A Reconciling Monitor. Etc.* London, 1690. In *Scripture Gospel defended.*

———. *An End of Doctrinal Controversies Which have Lately Troubled the Churches by Reconciling Explication, without Much Disputing.* London, 1691.

———. *Full and Easie Satisfaction Which is the True and Safe Religion. In a Conference Between D. a Doubter, P. A Papist, and R. A Reformed Catholick Christian. Etc.* London, 1674.

———. *The Grotian Religion Discovered, At the Invitation of Mr. Thomas Pierce in his Vindication. With a Preface, vindicating the Synod of Dort from the calumnies of the New Tilenus; and David, Peter, &c. And the Puritanes, and Sequestrations, &c. from the censures of Mr. Pierce.* London, 1658.

———. *How Far Holinesse Is the Design of Christianity. Where the Nature of Holiness and Morality is opened, and the Doctrine of Justification, Imputation of Sin and Righteousness, &c. partly cleared, and Vindicated from Abuse. In certain Propositions, returned to an unknown Person, referring to Mr. Fowlers Treatise on this Subject.* London, 1671.

———. *Making Light of Christ and Salvation, Too Oft the Issue of Gospel Invitations: A Call to the Unconverted to Turn and Live: The Last Work of a Believer; His Passing Prayer, Recommending His Departing Spirit to Christ, to Be Received by Him; Of the Shedding Abroad of God's Love on the Heart by the Holy Ghost.* Introd. Thomas W. Jenkyn. Works of the Puritan Divines. London: Nelson, 1846.

———. *Methodus Theologiæ Christianæ, 1. Naturæ rerum, 2. Sacræ Scripturæ, 3. Praxi,*

Congrua conformis adaptata Plerumque (corrigenda tamen & perficienda) etc. London, 1681.

——. *More Proofs of Infants Church-membership and Consequently their Right to Baptism: Or a Second Defence of our Infant Rights and Mercies. Etc.* London, 1675.

——. *Naked Popery; Or, The Naked Falshood Of a Book called the Catholick Naked Truth, Or The Puritan Convert to Apostolical Christianity; Written by W.H. Opening their Fundamental Errour of Unwritten Tradition, and their unjust Description of the Puritan, the Prelatical Protestant, and the Papist, and their differences; and better acquainting the ignorant of the true difference, especially what a Puritan and what a Papist is.* London, 1677.

——. *Of Justification: Four Disputations Clearing and amicably Defending the Truth, against the unnecessary Oppositions of divers Learned and Reverend Brethren.* London, 1658.

——. *Of Saving Faith: That it is not only gradually, but specifically distinct from all Common Faith. The Agreement of Richard Baxter with that very Learned consenting Adversary, that hath maintained my Assertion by a pretended Confutation in the end of Serjeant Shephards Book of Sincerity and Hypocrisie. With the Reasons of my Dissent in some passages that came in on the by.* London, 1658.

——. *Of the Imputation of Christ's Righteousness to Believers: In what sence sound Protestants hold it; And, Of the false devised sence, by which Libertines subvert the Gospel. With an Answer to some common Objections, especially of Dr. Thomas Tully, whose Justif. Paulina occasioneth the publication of this.* London, 1675. In *Treatise of Justifying Righteousness.*

——. *A Paraphrase on the New Testament, With Notes, Doctrinal and Practical. By Plainness and Brevity fitted to the Use of Religious Families, in their daily Reading of the Scriptures; and of the younger and poorer sort of Scholars and Ministers, who want fuller helps. With an Advertisement of Difficulties in the Revelations.* London, 1685.

——. *Plain Scripture Proof of Infants Church-membership and Baptism: Being The Arguments prepared for (and partly managed in) the publick Dispute with Mr. Tombes at Bewdley on the first day of Jan. 1649. With a ful Reply to what he then answered, and what is contained in his Sermon since preached, in his Printed Books, his M.S. on I Cor. 7.14. which I saw, against Mr. Marshall, against these Arguments. With a Reply to his Valedictory Oration at Bewdley; And a Corrective for his Antidote.* 4th ed. London, 1656.

——. *The Practical Works of Richard Baxter: With a Preface, Giving Some Account of the Author, and of This Edition of His Practical Works: An Essay on His Genius, Works, and Times; and a Portrait.* 4 vols. London, 1838; rpt. Introd. J.I. Packer (Vol. I). Ligonier, PA: Soli Deo Gloria, 1990-91.

——. *The Practical Works of the Rev. Richard Baxter with a Life of the Author and a Critical Examination of His Writings.* Ed. William Orme. 23 vols. London: Duncan, 1830.

——. *The Protestant Religion Truely Stated and Justified.* Ed. Daniel Williams and Matthew Sylvester. London, 1692.

——. *The Reduction of a Digressor: Or Rich. Baxter's Reply to Mr George Kendall's Digression in his Book against Mr Goodwin.* London, 1654. In *Rich. Baxters Apology.*

——. *Reliquiæ Baxterianæ: Or, Mr. Richard Baxter's Narrative of The most Memorable Passages of His Life and Times.* Ed. Matthew Sylvester. London, 1696.

——. *Rich. Baxters Account Given to his Reverend Brother Mr T. Blake of the Reasons of his Dissent from The Doctrine of his Exceptions in his late Treatise of the Covenants.* London, 1654. In *Rich. Baxters Apology.*

——. *Rich. Baxters Apology Against the Modest Exceptions of Mr T. Blake. And the Digression of Mr. G. Kendall. Whereunto is added Animadversions on a late Disser-*

tation of Ludiomæus Colvinus, aliàs, Ludovicus Molinæus, M. Dr Oxon. and an Admonition of Mr W. Eyre of Salisbury. With Mr Crandon's Anatomy for satisfaction of Mr Caryl. London, 1654.

———. *Rich. Baxter's Admonition to Mr William Eyre of Salisbury; Concerning his Miscarriages in a Book lately Written for the Justification of Infidels, against M. Benj. Woodbridge, M. James Cranford and the Author.* In *Rich. Baxters Apology.* London, 1654. In *Rich. Baxters Apology.*

———. *Rich: Baxter's Confesssion* [sic] *of his Faith, Especially concerning the Interest of Repentance and sincere Obedience to Christ, in our Justification & Salvation. Written for the satisfaction of the misinformed, the conviction of Calumniators, and the Explication and Vindication of some weighty Truths.* London, 1655.

———. *Richard Baxter's Account of His present Thoughts concerning the Controversies about the Perseverance of the Saints. Occasioned by the gross misreports of some passages in his Book, called, The Right Method for Peace of Conscience, &c; which are left out in the last Impression to avoid offence, and this here substituted, for the fuller explication of the same Points.* London, 1657.

———. *Richard Baxter's Catholick Theologie: Plain, Pure, Peaceable: For Pacification Of the Dogmatical Word-Warriours, etc.* London, 1675.

———. *Richard Baxter's Confvtation of a Dissertation For the Justification of Infidels: Written by Ludiomæus Colvinus, alias Ludovicus Molinæus, Dr. of Physick and History-Professor in Oxford, against his Brother Cyrus Molinæus.* London, 1654. In *Rich. Baxters Apology.*

———. *Richard Baxter's Penitent Confession, And His Necessary Vindication, In Answer to a Book, called, The Second Part of the Mischiefs of Separation, Written by an Unnamed Author.* London, 1691.

———. *The Right Method For a settled Peace of Conscience, and Spiritual Comfort. In 32 Directions. Written for the use of a troubled friend: and now published.* London, 1653.

———. *The Right Method For a settled Peace Of Conscience, and Spiritual Comfort. In 32 Directions.* 2nd ed. London, 1653.

———. *The Safe Religion. Or Three Disputations For the Reformed Catholike Religion, Against Popery. Proving that Popery is against the Holy Scriptures, the Unity of the Catholike Church, the consent of the Antient Doctors, the plainest Reason, and common judgment of sense it self.* London, 1657.

———. *The Saints Everlasting Rest: Or, A Treatise Of the Blessed State of the Saints in their enjoyment of God in Glory. Wherein is shewed its Excellency and Certainty; the Misery of those that lose it; the way to Attain it, and Assurance of it: and how to live in the continual delightful Foretasts of it, by the help of Meditation. Written by the Author for his own use, in the time of his languishing, when God took him off from all Publike Imployment; and afterwards Preached in his weekly Lecture.* London, 1650.

———. *The Scripture Gospel defended, and Christ, Grace and Free Justification Vindicated Against the Libertines, Who use the names of Christ, Free Grace and Justification, to subvert the Gospel, and Christianity, etc.* London, 1690.

———. *The Substance of Mr. Cartwright's Exceptions Considered.* London, 1675. In *Treatise of Justifying Righteousness.*

———. *A Treatise of Justifying Righteousness, In Two Books: I. A Treatise of Imputed Righteousness . . . II. A Friendly Debate with the Learned and Worthy Mr. Christopher Cartwright . . . All Published instead of a fuller Answer to the Assaults in Dr. Tullies Justificatio Paulina, for the quieting of Censorious and Dividing Contenders, who raise odious Reports of their Brethren as Popish, &c. who do but attempt Reconcilingly to open this Doctrine more clearly than themselves.* London, 1676.

———. *Two Disputations of Original Sin. I. Of Original sin, as from Adam. II. Of Original Sin, as from our Neerer Parents. Written long ago for a more private use, and now published (with a Preface) upon the invitation of Dr. T. Tullie*. London, 1675.

——. *Universal Redemption of Mankind, by the Lord Jesus Christ: Stated and Cleared by the late Learned Mr. Richard Baxter. Whereunto is added a short Account of Special Redemption, by the same Author*. London, 1694.

——. *An Unsavoury Volume of Mr Jo. Crandon's Anatomized: Or a Nosegay of the Choicest Flowers in that Garden, Presented to Mr Joseph Caryl by Rich. Baxter*. London, 1654. In *Rich. Baxters Apology*.

——. *Whether Parish Congregations Be True Christian Churches, And the Capable Consenting Incumbents, be truly their Pastors, or Bishops over their Flocks, And so, Whether the old Protestants, Conformists, and Nonconformists, or the Brownists, were in the right herein. And how far our present Case is the same. Written by Richard Baxter, as an Explication of some Passages in his former Writings; especially, his Treatise of Episcopacy, misunderstood and misapplied by some; and answering the strongest Objections of some of them; especially a Book called, Mr. Baxters Judgment and Reasons against Communicating with the Parish Assemblies, as by Law required. And another called, A Theological Dialogue. Or, Catholick Communion once more Defended, upon mens necessitating importunity*. London, 1684.

Benbrigge, John. *Christ above All Exalted, As in Jvstification So in Sanctification. Wherein severall Passages in Dr. Crisps Sermons are Answered*. London, 1645.

Beverley, Thomas. *A Conciliatoy* [sic] *Judgment concerning Dr. Crisp's Sermons, and Mr. Baxter's Dissatisfactions in Them*. London, 1690.

Beza, Theodore. *Confessio christianæ fidei, et eivsdem collatio cum Papisticis Hæresibus*. Geneva, 1595.

——. *Volvmen primvm Tractationum Theologicarum, in qvibvs pleraqve christianæ Religionis dogmata aduersus hæreses nostris temporibus renouatas solidè ex Verbo Dei defenduntur*. 2nd ed. Geneva, 1682.

Blake, Thomas. *The Covenant Sealed. Or, A Treatise of the Sacraments of both Covenants, Polemicall and Practicall. Especially Of the Sacraments of the Covenant of Grace . . . Together with a brief Answer to Reverend Mr. Baxter's Apology, in defence of the Treatise of the Covenant*. London, 1655.

——. *Vindiciæ Foederis; Or, A Treatise of the Covenant of God Entered with Man-kinde, In the several Kindes and Degrees of it etc*. London, 1653.

Bradshaw, William. *Dissertatio De ivstificationis doctrina, Qua via plana munitur ad eorum concordiam qui hac de re variarunt*. Leiden, 1618.

——. *English Puritanisme and Other Works*. Introd. R.C. Simmons. Rpts. Westmead, Farnborough, Hants.: Gregg International, 1972.

——. *Puritanism and Separatism: A Collection of Works by William Bradshaw*. Introd. R.C. Simmons. Rpts. [Westmead, Farnborough, Hants.]: Gregg International, 1972.

——. *A Treatise of Ivstification. Tending to proue that a Sinner is iustified before God, onely by Christs Righteousnes imputed*. London, 1615.

Bunyan, John. *The Miscellaneous Works of John Bunyan*. Vol. IV. Ed. T.L. Underwood. Oxford: Clarendon, 1989.

Burgess, Anthony. *CXLV Expository Sermons upon The whole 17th Chapter of the Gospel according to St John: Or, Christs Prayer Before his Passion Explicated, and Both Practically and Polemically Improved*. London, 1656.

——. *The True Doctrine of Ivstification Asserted, and Vindicated, From The Errors of Papists, Arminians, Socinians, and more especially Antinomians. In XXX Lectures Preached at Lawrence-Iury, London, By Anthony Burgess, Preacher of Gods Word*. London, 1648.

——. *The True Doctrine of Justification Asserted & Vindicated From the Errours of many, and more especially Papists and Socinians. Or A Treatise of the Natural Righteousness of God, and Imputed Righteousness of Christ*. London, 1654.

——. *Vindiciæ legis: Or, A Vindication of the Morall Law and the Covenants, From the*

Errours of Papists, Arminians, Socinians, and more especially, Antinomians. In XXIX. Lectures, preached at Lawrence-Jury, London. London, 1646.

Calvin, John. *Calvin: Institutes of the Christian Religion.* 2 vols. Ed. John T. McNeill. Trans. and Indexed Ford Lewis Battles. Library of Christian Classics, 20-21. Philadelphia: Westminster Press, 1960.

———. *The Epistles of Paul the Apostle to the Galatians, Ephesians, Philippians and Colossians.* Trans. T.H.L. Parker. Ed. David W. Torrance and Thomas F. Torrance. Calvin's Commentaries. Edinburgh, 1965; rpt. Grand Rapids: Eerdmans, n.d.

———. *Ioannis Calvini Opera quae supersunt omnia.* Ed. Guilielmus Baum, Eduardus Cunitz, and Eduardus Reuss. 57 vols. Corpus Reformatorum, 29-85. Brunswig: Schwetschke, 1863-97.

———. *Joannis Calvini Opera Selecta.* Ed. Petrus Barth and Guilelmus Niesel. 5 vols. Munich: Kaiser, 1926-36.

Cameron, John. *Τα σωζομενα Siue Opera partim ab avctore ipso edita, partim post eius obitum vulgata, partim nusquam hactenus publicata, vel è Gallico Idiomate nunc primùm in Latinam linguam translata.* Geneva, 1642.

Cappel, Lewis, Moyse Amyraut, and Joshua Placaeus. *Theses theologicæ in academia Salmvriensi variis temporibvs dispvtatæ.* Saumur, 1641.

Cartwright, Christopher. *Exceptions Against a Writing of Mr. R. Baxters, In Answer to some Animadversions Upon his Aphorisms.* London, 1675. In Baxter, *Treatise of Justifying Righteousness.*

The Collegiat Svffrage of the Divines of Great Britaine, concerning the Five Articles Controverted in the Low Countries. Which Suffrage was by them delivered in the Synod of Dort, March 6. Anno 1619. Being their vote or voice foregoing the joint and publique judgment of that Synod. London, 1629.

Crandon, John. *Mr. Baxters Aphorisms Exorized and Anthorized. Or An Examination of and Answer to a Book written by Mr. Ri: Baxter Teacher of the Church at Kederminster in Worcester-shire, entituled, Aphorisms of Justification. Together with A vindication of Justification by meer Grace, from all the Popish and Arminian Sophisms, by which that Author labours to ground it upon Mans Works and Righteousness.* London, 1654.

Crisp, Tobias. *Christ alone Exalted: Being the Compleat Works of Tobias Crisp, D.D. Containing XLII. Sermons, On several Select Texts of Scriptures: Which were formerly Printed in Three finall Volumes, by That late Eminent and faithful Dispenser of God's Word: Etc.* London, 1690.

———. *Christ Alone Exalted In fourteene Sermons preached in, and neare London, by the late Reverend Tobias Crispe Doctor in Divinity, and faithfull Pastor of Brinkworth in Wiltshire. As they were taken from his owne mouth in shortwriting, whereof severall Copies were diligently compared together, and with his owne Notes. And published for the satisfaction and comfort of Gods people.* London, 1643.

———. *Christ Alone Exalted; In seventeene Sermons: Preached In or neare London, by the late Reverend Tobias Crisp Doctor in Divinity, and faithfull Pastor of Brinkworth in Wiltshire, As they were taken from his owne mouth in short-writing, and compared with his Notes. Volume II.* N.p., 1643.

———. *Christ Alone Exalted, in the Perfection and Encouragement of the Saints, Notwithstanding Sins and Trials Being the Complete Works of Tobias Crisp, D.D. Sometime Minister of the Gospel, at Brinkworth, in Wiltshire: Containing Fifty-Two Sermons, on Several Select Texts of Scripture.* Ed. John Gill. 7th ed. London: Bennett, 1832. Vol. I.

———. *Christ made Sin: II Cor. V. xxi. Evinc't from Scripture, Upon Occasion of An Exception taken at Pinners-Hall, 28 January, 1689, At Re-printing the Sermons of Dr. Tobias Crisp.* London, 1691.

De Dieu, Lewis. *Animadversiones In D. Pauli Apostoli Epistolam ad Romanos, in quibus, Collatis Syri, Arabis, Vulgati, Erasmi & Bezæ versionibus, difficiliora quæque loca,*

& maximè præterita aliis illustrantur. Accessit Spicilegium in reliquas ejusdem Apostoli, ut & Catholicas Epistolas. Leiden, 1646.

A Dialogue between the Pope and the Devil, about Owen and Baxter. London, 1681.

Dirt wip't off: Or A manifest Discovery of the Gross Ignorance, Erroneousness and most Unchristian and Wicked Spirit of one John Bunyan, Lay-Preacher in Bedford, Which he hath shewed in a Vile Pamphlet Publish't by him, against The Design of Christianity. Written for the disabusing of those poor deluded people that are followers of him, and such like Teachers, and to prevent their farther deluding of others, and poisoning them with Licentious and destructive Principles. London, 1672.

Downham, George. The Covenant of Grace Or An Exposition vpon Lvke 1.73.74.75. Dublin, 1631.

Du Moulin, Lewis. De fidei partibus in justificatione Dissertatio. In qua modestè expenduntur, quæ Clar. Vir. Cyrus Molinæus profert, ut sententiam, vulgò Orthodoxam habitam, tueatur. London, 1653.

———. Parænesis ad ædificatores Imperii in Imperio; In qua Defenduntur jura Magistratus adversus Mosem Amyraldum, Et cæteros vindices potestatis Ecclesiasticæ Presbyterianæ. In Præfatione excurritur in Iohannis Dallæi Apologiam pro duabus synodis. London, 1656.

Edwards, Thomas. The Paraselene dismantled of her Cloud. Or, Baxterianism Barefac'd. Drawn from A Literal Transcript of Mr. Baxter's, And the Judgment of Others, In the most Radical Doctrines of Faith; Compar'd with those of the Orthodox, Both Conformist and Nonconformist; And transferr'd over by way of Test, unto the Papist and Quaker. London, 1699.

Eedes, John. The Orthodox Doctrine concerning Iustification by Faith Asserted and Vindicated: Wherein The Book of Mr. William Eyre, one of the Ministers of New Sarum, is examined: And Also The Doctrine of Mr. Baxter concerning Justification is Discussed. London, 1654.

England, John. Man's Sinfulness and Misery by Nature. Asserted and Opened in Several Sermons on Ephes. 2. Verses 1,2,3. Designed Chiefly For the Unconverted. Whereunto is added a Disputation concerning the Headship of Adam and Christ, and the Imputation of the Sin of the One, and the Righteousness of the Other. London, 1700.

Eyre, William. Christ's Scepter Advanc'd, Or The Righteous administrations of Christ's Kingdome, set forth for the imitation of earthly Rulers; In a Sermon Preached at the Assizes holden in the City of New Sarum, in the County of Wilts on Saturday the 31 of July, 1652. London, 1652.

———. Vindiciæ Justificationis Gratuitæ. Justification without Conditions; or The Free Justification of a Sinner, Explained, Confirmed, and Vindicated, from the Exceptions, Objections, and seeming Absurdities, which are cast upon it, by the Assertors of Conditional Justification: More especially from the Attempts of Mr. B. Woodbridge in his Sermon, Entituled [Justification by Faith] Of Mr. Cranford in his Epistle to the Reader, and of Mr. Baxter in some Passages, which relate to the same Matter. Wherein also, the Absoluteness of the New Covenant is proved, and the Arguments against it, are disproved. London, 1654.

Fisher, Edward. The Marrow of Modern Divinity: In Two Parts. Annotated Thomas Boston. Rpt. Edmonton, AB: Still Waters Revival, 1991.

Flavel, John Πλανηλογία. A Succinct and Seasonable Discourse of the Occasions, Causes, Nature, Rise, Growth, and Remedies of Mental Errors. Written some Months since; and now made publick, both for the healing and prevention of the Sins and Calamities which have broken in this way upon the Churches of Christ, to the great scandal of Religion, hardening of the Wicked; and obstruction of Reformation. Etc. London, 1691.

Fowler, Edward. The Design of Christianity; Or, A plain Demonstration and Improvement of this Proposition, Viz. That the enduing men with Inward Real Righteousness or

True Holiness, was the Ultimate End of our Saviour's Coming into the World, and is the Great Intendment of His Blessed Gospel. London, 1671.

Geree, Stephen. *The Doctrine of the Antinomians by Evidence of Gods Truth plainely Confuted. In an answer to divers dangerous Doctrines, in the seven first Sermons of Dr. Crisps fourteen, which were first published. And are here declared to be as well Anti-evangelicall as Antinomicall, absolutely overthrowing the Gospel of Jesus Christ, and perverting the Free-Grace of God.* London, 1644.

Grayle, John. *A Modest Vindication of the Doctrine of Conditions in the Covenant of Grace And the Defenders thereof, from the Aspersions of Arminianism & Popery, which Mr. W.E. cast on them.* London, 1655.

Grotius, Hugo. *A Defence of the Catholick Faith Concerning the Satisfaction of Christ.* Trans. W.H. London, 1692.

———. *Defensio fidei catholicæ de satisfactione Christi Adversus Faustum Socinum Senensem.* Leiden, 1617.

Grotius, Hugo. *Opera theologica.* Vol. I. Ed. Edwin Rabbie. Trans. Hotze Mulder. Assen: Van Gorcum, 1990.

Hooker, Thomas. *De ware zielsvernedering en heilzame wanhoop.* Trans. and pref. Jacobus Koelman. 1678; rpt. Houten: Den Hertog, 1988.

Hotchkis, Thomas. *An Exercitation Concerning the Nature of Forgivenesse of Sin. Very necessary (as the Author humbly conceiveth) to a right information, and well grounded decision of sundry Controversal Points in Divinity now depending. Directly intended as an Antidote for preventing the danger of Antinomian Doctrine. And consequently subservient for promoting the true faith of Christ and fear of God, in a godly, righteous, and sober life.* London, 1655.

Jessop, Constant. *A Preface Concerning the Nature of the Covenant of Grace, Wherein is a Discovery of the judgment of Dr. Twisse in the point of Justification, clearing him from Antinomianism therein.* In *A Modest Vindication of the Doctrine of Conditions in the Covenant of Grace And the Defenders thereof, from the Aspersions of Arminianism & Popery, which Mr. W.E. cast on them.* By John Grayle. London, 1655.

Kellison, Matthew. *The Touch-Stone of the Reformed Gospel. Wherein sundry Chief Heads and Tenets of the Protestant Doctrin (objected by them commonly against the catholics) are briefly refuted, by the express Texts of the Protestants own Bible, set forth and approved by the Church of England. With the Ancient Fathers Judgments thereon, in Confirmation of the Catholic Doctrin.* Rev. ed. London, 1687.

Kendall, George. "Dissertatiuncula de novis actibvs immanentibus sintne Deo ascribendi?" in *De Doctrina Neopelagianâ Oratio habita in Comitiis Oxonii Julii 9.1654*, pp. 141-219. In *Fur pro Tribunali.* Oxford, 1657.

———. *Fur pro Tribunali. Examen dialogismi cui inscribitur Fur Prædestinatus. Accesservnt, Oratio de doctrina neo-pelagiana habita Oxonii in comitiis julii ix. M.DC.LIV. Cl.V.G. Twissii vita, & Vindiciæ à Calumniis & Sophismatis Francisci Annati Jesuitæ. Et Dissertatiuncula de novis actibus immanentibus sintne Deo ascribendi.* Oxford, 1657.

———. *Sancti sanciti. Or, The Common Doctrine of the Perseverance of the Saints: As who are kept by the Power of God, through Faith Unto Salvation. Vindicated From the attempts lately made against it, by Mr. John Goodwin, in the Digression of his Book, which he was pleased to entitle Redemption Redeemed. Etc.* London, 1654.

———. Θεοκρατία: *Or, A Vindication of the Doctrine Commonly Received in the Reformed Churches Concerning Gods Intentions Of special Grace and Favour to his Elect In the Death of Christ: As Also His Prerogative, Power, Prescience, Providence, the Immutability of his Nature and Counsels, &c. from the attempts lately made against it, by Master John Goodwin in his book Entituled Redemption Redeemed. Together With some digressions concerning the Impossibility of new Immanent Acts in God, the Possibility of Faiths being an instrument of Justification, and the nature of the Covenants of works and Grace.* London, 1653.

———. "Twissii Vita & Victoria," in *De Doctrina Neopelagianâ Oratio habita in Comitiis Oxonii Julii 9.1654*, pp. 63-140. In *Fur pro Tribunali*. Oxford, 1657.

Lawson, George. *Theo-Politica: Or, A Body of Divinity, Containing The Rules of the special Government of God, According to which, He orders the immortal and intellectual Creatures, Angels, and Men, to their final and Eternal Estate. Etc.* London, 1659.

Le Blanc, Lewis. *Theses theologicæ, Variis temporibus in Academia Sedanensi Editæ et ad disputandum propositæ.* London, 1675.

Lobb, Stephen. *The Glory of Free-Grace Display'd: Or, The Transcendent Excellency of the Love of God in Christ, unto Believing, Repenting Sinners, in some measure describ'd. Wherein 1. The Followers of Dr. Crispe are prov'd to be Abusers of the true Gospel-Notion of Free-Grace: And 2. The Congregational clear'd from the Reproach of being Asserters of Such Errors as are found in Dr. Crispes Writings, as appears by the Prefix'd Epistle of Dr. Owen.* London, 1680.

———. *The Growth of Error: Being an Exercitation concerning The Rise and Progress of Arminianism, and more especially Socinianism, both abroad, and now of late in England.* London, 1697.

Long, Thomas. *A review of Mr. Richard Baxter's life, wherein many mistakes are rectified, some false relations detected, some omissions supplyed out of his other books. With remarks on several material passages.* London, 1697.

Maccovius, Johannes. *Collegia theologica Quæ Extant, Omnia: Tertia ab auctore recognita, emendata, & plurimis locis aucta, in partes duas distributa.* Franeker, 1641.

Owen, John. *The Works of John Owen.* Ed. William H. Goold. 16 vols. 1850-53; rpt. London: Banner of Truth, 1965-68.

Pagitt, Ephraim. *Heresiography: Or, A description of the Heretickes and Sectaries of these latter times.* London, 1645.

Pemble, William. *Vindiciæ fidei, Or A Treatise of Iustification by Faith, wherein the truth of that point is fully cleared, and vindicated from the cauills of it's [sic] Adversaries.* 2nd ed. Oxford, 1629.

———. *Vindiciæ gratiæ. A Plea for Grace. More Especially the Grace of Faith. Or, Certain Lectvres as touching the Nature and Properties of Grace and Faith: Wherein, amongst other matters of great vse, the maine sinewes of Arminivs doctrine are cut asunder.* 2nd ed. London, 1629.

A Plea For the Late Accurate and Excellent Mr. Baxter, And those that Speak of the Sufferings of Christ as he does. In Answer to Mr. Lobb's Insinuated Charge of Socinianism against 'em, in his late Appeal to the Bishop of Worcester, and Dr. Edwards. With a Preface directed to Persons of all Persuasions, to call 'em from Frivolous and Over-eager Contentions about Words, on all sides. London, 1699.

Robertson, William. אגרת המשכיל *Iggeret hammashkil. Or, An Admonitory Epistle unto Mr Rich. Baxter, and Mr Tho. Hotchkiss, About their Applications (or Mis-applications rather) of several Texts of Scripture (tending cheifly) to prove that the Afflictions of the Godly are proper Punishments. Etc.* London, 1655.

Rutherford, Samuel. *Letters of Samuel Rutherford.* Sketch of his life and biographical notices of correspondents Andrew A. Bonar. 1891; rpt. Edinburgh: Banner of Truth, 1984.

———. *A Survey of the Spirituall Antichrist. Opening The secrets of Familisme and Antinomianisme in the Antichristian Doctrine of John Saltmarsh, and Will. Del, the present Preachers of the Army now in England, and of Robert Town, Tob. Crisp, H. Denne, Eaton, and others. In which is revealed the rise and spring of Antinomians, Familists, Libertines, Swenck-feldians, Entbysiasts [sic], &c. The Minde of Luther a most professed opposer of Antinomians, is cleared, and diverse considerable points of the Law and the Gospel, of the Spirit and Letter, of the two Covenants, of the nature of free grace, exercise under temptations, mortification, justification, sanctification, are discovered.* 2 vols. London, 1648.

Saltmarsh, John. *Free-Grace: Or, The Flowings of Christs Blood freely to Sinners. Being an Experiment of Jesus Christ upon one who hath been in the bondage of a troubled Conscience at times, for the space of about twelve yeers, till now upon a clearer discovery of Jesus Christ, and the Gospel: Wherein divers secrets of the soul, of sin and temptations, are experimentally opened, and by way of Observation, concerning a natural condition, and a mixed condition of Law and Gospel: With a further revealing of the Gospel in its glory, liberty, freenesse, and simplicity for Salvation.* London, 1645.

Sheppard, William. *Sincerity and Hypocricy. Or, The Sincere Christian, and Hypocrite in their lively Colours, standing one by the other.* Oxford, 1658.

Some Considerations of a Certificate Prefixed to Doctor Crisp's Works. London, 1690.

A Theological Dialogue: Containing the Defence and Justification of Dr. John Owen from the Forty Two Errors Charged upon him by Mr. Richard Baxter, In a certain Manuscript about Communion in Lyturgical Worship. London, 1684.

Tombes, John. *Animadversiones in Librum Georgii Bulli Cui titulum fecit Harmonia Apostolica. Seu Binæ dissertationes, Quarum in priore Doctrina D. Jacobi de Justificatione ex operibus explanatur ac defenditur In Posteriore Consensus D. Pauli cum Jacobo liquido demonstratur.* Oxford, 1676.

Troughton, John. *Lutherus Redivivus: Or The Protestant Doctrine of Justification by Faith onely, Vindicated. And a Plausible Opinion of Justification by Faith and Obedience proved to be Arminian, Popish, and to lead unavoidably unto Socinianism.* Part I. London, 1677.

——. *Lutherus Redivivus: Or, The Protestant Doctrine of Justification By Christ's Righteousness Imputed to Believers, Explained and Vindicated.* Part II. London, 1678.

Tully, Thomas. *Animadversions upon a Sheet of Mr Baxters entituled An Appeal to the Light, Printed 1674.* Oxford 1675.

——. *Justificatio Paulina sine operibvs ex mente ecclesiæ anglicanæ, Omniumque Reliquarum Quæ reformatæ audiunt, Asserta & Illustrata. Contra nuperos novatores.* Oxford, 1674.

——. *A Letter to Mr Richard Baxter Occasioned by several injurious Reflexions of His upon a Treatise entituled Justificatio Paulina. For the better Information of his weake or Credulous Readers.* Oxford, 1675.

Twisse, William. *A Discovery of D. Iacksons Vanitie.* N.p., 1631.

——. *The Doctrine of the Synod of Dort and Arles, reduced to the practise. With a consideration thereof, and representation with what sobriety it proceeds.* 2nd ed. N.p., [1650].

——. *A Treatise of Mr. Cottons, Clearing certaine Doubts Concerning Predestination. Together with an Examination Thereof.* London, 1646.

——. *Vindiciæ gratiæ, potestatis, ac providentiæ Dei Hoc est, Ad Examen Libelli Perkinsiani de Prædestinationis modo et ordine, institutum a Iacobo Arminio, Responsio scholastica, tribus libris absoluta. Unà cum Digressionibus ad singulas partes accommodatis; in quibus illustriores in hoc Negotio quæstiones fusiùs pertractantur et accuratè discutiuntur, Veritasque adversus Bellarminum, Didacum Alvarez, Gabrielem Vasques aliosque tum Papistas tum Pelagianos, asseritur; Nec non opiniones nonnullæ quorun: dam modernorum Theologorum modestè examinantur.* 2nd ed. Amsterdam, 1632.

Vindiciæ Anti-Baxterianæ: Or, Some Animadversions On a Book, Intituled Reliquiæ Baxterianæ; Or, The Life of Mr. Richard Baxter. London, 1696.

Warner, John. *Diatriba fidei justificantis, qua justificantis. Or A Discovrse Of the Object and Office of Faith as Justifying. Distinct from other Objects, Acts, and Offices of the same Faith as Sanctifying. Wherein the Lutheran and Protestant Doctrine is asserted against the Pontificians, Socinians, Arminians, and others.* Oxford, 1657.

Warren, Thomas. *Vnbeleevers No subjects of Iustification, Nor of mystical Vnion to Christ, Being the sum of a Sermon preached at New-Sarum, with a Vindication of it from the objections, and calumniations cast upon it by Mr. William Eyre, in his Vindiciæ Justificationis. Etc.* London, 1654.

Woodbridge, Benjamin. *Justification by Faith: Or a Confutation of that Antinomian Error, That Justification is before Faith; Being The Sum & Substance Of a Sermon Preached at Sarum; By Benjamin Woodbridge, Minister of Newberry in Barkshire.* London, 1652.

―――. *The Method of Grace in the Justification of Sinners. Being a Reply to a Book written by Mr. William Eyre of Salisbury: Entituled, Vindiciæ Justificationis Gratuitæ, Or the Free Justification of a Sinner justified. Wherein the Doctrine contained in the said Book is proved to be Subversive both of Law and Gospel, contrary to the consent of Protestants. And inconsistent with it self. And the Ancient Apostolick Protestant Doctrine of Justification by Faith asserted.* London, 1656.

Wotton, Anthony. *De reconciliatione peccatoris, Ad Regium Collegium Cantabrigiense, libri qvattuor. In quibus Doctrina Ecclesiæ Anglicanæ de Justificatione impij explicatur & defenditur: Etc.* Basle, 1624.

―――. *Sermons vpon a Part of the First Chap. of the Gospell of S. Iohn.* London, 1609.

SECONDARY LITERATURE

Abernathy, George R. "Richard Baxter and the Cromwellian Church." *HLQ*, 24 (1961), 215-31.

Allison, C.F. *The Rise of Moralism: The Proclamation of the Gospel from Hooker to Baxter.* London: SPCK, 1966.

Arber, Edward. *The Term Catalogues.* 3 vols. London: privately printed, 1903-06.

Armstrong, Brian G. *Calvinism and the Amyraut Heresy: Protestant Scholasticism and Humanism in Seventeenth-Century France.* Madison: Univ. of Wisconsin Press, 1969.

Arntzen, M.J. *Mystieke rechtvaardigingsleer: Een bijdrage ter beoordeling van de theologie van Andreas Osiander.* Diss. Amsterdam 1956. Kampen: Kok, 1956.

Baker, J. Wayne. *Heinrich Bullinger and the Covenant: The Other Reformed Tradition.* Athens: Ohio Univ. Press, 1980.

―――. "Sola Fide, Sola Gratia: The Battle for Luther in Seventeenth-Century England." *SCJ*, 16 (1985), 115-33.

Bavinck, H. *Gereformeerde dogmatiek.* Vol. III. 4th ed. Kampen, 1929.

Bayle, Peter. *The Dictionary Historical and Critical of Mr Peter Bayle.* Vol. I. 2nd ed. Pref. Des Maizeaux. London, 1784.

Beeke, Joel R. *Assurance of Faith: Calvin, English Puritanism, and the Dutch Second Reformation.* American University Studies, Series VII: Theology and Religion, 89. New York: Lang, 1991.

Bell, M. Charles. *Calvin and Scottish Theology: The Doctrine of Assurance.* Edinburgh: Handsel, 1985.

Benton, W. Wilson. "Federal Theology: Review for Revision." In *Through Christ's Word: A Festschrift for Dr. Philip E. Hughes.* Ed. W. Robert Godfrey and Jesse L. Boyd III. Phillipsburg: Presbyterian and Reformed, 1985, pp. 180-204.

Berkouwer, G.C. *Faith and Justification.* Trans. Lewis B. Smedes. Studies in Dogmatics. Grand Rapids: Eerdmans, 1954.

―――. *The Work of Christ.* Trans. Cornelius Lambregtse. Studies in Dogmatics. Grand Rapids: Eerdmans, 1965.

Biografisch lexicon voor de geschiedenis van het Nederlandse protestantisme. Eds. D. Nauta et al. 3 vols. Kampen: Kok, 1978-88.

Biographical Dictionary of British Radicals in the Seventeenth Century. Eds. Richard L. Greaves and Robert Zaller. 3 vols. Brighton, Sussex: Harvester, 1982-84.

SELECT BIBLIOGRAPHY 367

Boehl, Edward. *The Reformed Doctrine of Justification*. Trans. C.H. Riedesel. Grand Rapids: Eerdmans, 1946.

Boersma, Hans. "Calvin and the Extent of the Atonement." *EvQ*, 64 (1992) 333-55.

Bonet Maury, Gaston. "John Cameron: A Scottish Protestant Theologian in France (1579-1625)." *ScHR*, 7 (1910), 325-45.

Bos, F.L. *Johann Piscator: Ein Beitrag zur Geschichte der Reformierten Theologie*. Kampen: Kok, 1932.

Bottrall, Margaret. "Richard Baxter." In *Every Man a Phoenix: Studies in Seventeenth-Century Autobiography*. London: Murray, 1958, pp. 111-40.

Bowle, John. *Hobbes and His Critics: A Study in Seventeenth Century Constitutionalism*. London: Cape, 1951.

Brinkley, Roberta Florence, ed. "Richard Baxter." In *Coleridge on the Seventeenth Century*. Introd. Louis I. Bredvold. 1955; rpt. New York: Greenwood, 1968, pp. 321-64.

Brook, Benjamin. *The Lives of the Puritans: Containing a Biographical Account of Those Divines Who Distinguished Themselves in the Cause of Religious Liberty, from the Reformation under Queen Elizabeth, to the Act of Uniformity, in 1662*. 3 vols. London: Black, 1813.

Brownen, George. "John Warner, M.A.: A Forgotten Nonconformist Leader in South-West Hampshire 1646-1668." *TCHS*, 7 (1916-18), 280-87.

Campbell, K.M. "Living the Christian Life: 4. The Antinomian Controversies of the 17th Century." In *Living the Christian Life*. Proc. of the Westminster Conference. 1974. n.p.: n.p., [1975], pp. 61-81.

Carter, C. Sydney. *Richard Baxter 1615-1691*. Great Churchmen, 12. London: Church Book Room Press, 1948.

Catalogue of the Pamphlets, Books, Newspapers, and Manuscripts Relating to the Civil War, the Commonwealth, and Restoration, Collected by George Thomason, 1640-1661. 2 vols. London, 1908; rpt. Ann Arbor, MI: Univ. Microfilms International, 1977.

Chadwick, Henry. "Justification by Faith: A Perspective." *OiC*, 20 (1984), 191-225.

Clifford, Alan C. *Atonement and Justification: English Evangelical Theology 1640-1790: An Evaluation*. Oxford: Clarendon, 1990.

———. "Geneva Revisited or Calvinism Revised: The Case for Theological Reassessment." *ChM*, 100 (1986), 323-34.

Cohen, Charles Lloyd. *God's Caress: The Psychology of Puritan Religious Experience*. Oxford: Oxford Univ. Press, 1986.

Coleridge, Samuel Taylor. "Richard Baxter: 1615-1691." In *Marginalia*. Vol. I. Ed. George Whalley. Vol. XII of *The Collected Works of Samuel Taylor Coleridge*. Bollingen Series, 75. London: Routledge and Kegan Paul; Princeton, NJ: Princeton Univ. Press, 1980, pp. 230-61.

Colligan, J. Hay. "The Antinomian Controversy." *TCHS*, 6 (1915), 389-96.

Collinson, Patrick. *The Elizabethan Puritan Movement*. Oxford: Clarendon, 1967.

Condren, Conal. *George Lawson's* Politica *and the English Revolution*. Cambridge: Cambridge Univ. Press, 1989.

———. "The Image of *Utopia* in the Political Writings of George Lawson (1657): A Note on the Manipulation of Authority." *Moreana*, 18 (1981), 101-05.

———. "*Sacra* before *Civilis*: Understanding the Ecclesiastical Politics of George Lawson." *JRH*, 11 (1981), 524-35.

Cornick, David. "Richard Baxter: 'Autobiography'." *ET*, 101 (1990), 259-63.

Crippen, T.G. "The Ancient Merchants' Lecture." *TCHS*, 7 (1916-18), 300-09.

Cryer, Neville B. "Biography of John Eliot." In *Five Pioneer Missionaries*. Ed. S.M. Houghton. London: Banner of Truth, 1965, pp. 171-231.

De Koeyer, R.W. "'Pneumatologia': Enkele aspecten van de leer van de Heilige Geest bij de puritein John Owen (1616-1683)." *ThRef*, 34 (1991), 226-46.

De Pauley, W.C. "Richard Baxter Surveyed." *CQR*, 164 (1963), 32-43.

Dekker, E. *Rijker dan Midas: Vrijheid, genade en predestinatie in de theologie van Jacobus Arminius (1559-1609).* Diss. Utrecht 1993. Zoetermeer: Boekencentrum, 1993.

Dorham, A. Morgan. "Richard Baxter and the Oecumenical Movement." *EvQ*, 23 (1951), 96-115.

Dictionary of National Biography. Eds. Leslie Stephen and Sidney Lee. 63 vols. London: Smith, Elder, & Co., 1855-1900.

Feinstein, Howard M. "The Prepared Heart: A Comparative Study of Puritan Theology and Psychoanalysis." *AmQ*, 22 (1970), 166-76.

Ferguson, Sinclair B. *John Owen on the Christian Life.* Edinburgh: Banner of Truth, 1987.

Fisher, George P. "The Theology of Richard Baxter." *BSTR*, 9 (1852), 135-69.

——. "The Writings of Richard Baxter." *BSTR*, 9 (1852), 300-29.

La France protestante ou vies des protestants Français qui se sont fait un nom dans l'histoire depuis les premiers temps de la Réformation jusqu'a la reconnaissance du principe de la liberté des cultes par l'assemblée nationale. Eug. and Em. Haag. 10 vols. Paris: Cherbuliez, 1846-59.

La France protestante. Eugène and Émile Haag. 2nd ed. Ed. M. Henri Bordier. 6 vols. Paris: Sandoz et Fischbacher, 1877-88.

Franklin, Julian H. *John Locke and the Theory of Sovereignty: Mixed Monarchy and the Right of Resistance in the Political Thought of the English Revolution.* Cambridge Studies in the History and Theory of Politics. Cambridge: Cambridge Univ. Press, 1978.

Fuller, Morris. *The Life Letters and Writings of John Davenant D.D. 1572-1641 Lord Bishop of Salisbury.* London: Methuen, 1897.

Fuller, Thomas. *The History of the Worthies of England.* London, 1662.

The General Biographical Dictionary: Containing an Historical and Critical Account of the Lives and Writings of the Most Eminent Persons in Every Nation: Particularly the British and Irish: From the Earliest Accounts to the Present Time. Ed. Alexander Chalmers. Rev. ed. 32 vols. London: Nichols, 1812-17.

Graafland, C. *Van Calvijn tot Barth: Oorsprong en ontwikkeling van de leer der verkiezing en het Gereformeerd Protestantisme.* The Hague: Boekencentrum, 1987.

——. *Van Calvijn tot Comrie: Oorsprong en ontwikkeling van de leer van het verbond in het Gereformeerd Protestantisme.* Vol. I. Zoetermeer: Boekencentrum, 1992.

Greaves, Richard L. *John Bunyan.* Pref. Geoffrey F. Nuttall. Courtenay Studies in Reformation Theology, 2. Appleford: Sutton Courtenay, 1969.

——. "The Origins and Early Development of English Covenant Thought." *Hist*, 31 (1968), 21-35.

Grégoire, M. *Histoire des sectes religieuses: Qui sont nées, se sont modifiées, se sont éteintes dans les différentes contrées du globe, depuis le commencement du siècle dernier jusqu'a l'époque actuelle.* New ed. Vol. V. Paris: Baudouin, 1829.

Griffin, Martin I.J. *Latitudinarianism in the Seventeenth-Century Church of England.* Annotated Richard H. Popkin. Ed. Lila Freedman. Brill's Studies in Intellectual History, 32. Leiden: Brill, 1992.

Gritters, Barrett L. *Grace Uncommon: A Protestant Reformed Look at the Doctrine of Common Grace.* Byron Center, MI: Evangelism Society of the Byron Center Protestant Reformed Church, n.d.

Haentjens, A.H. *Hugo de Groot als godsdienstig denker.* Amsterdam: Ploegsma, 1946.

Halkett, Samuel, and John Laing. *Dictionary of Anonymous and Pseudonymous English Literature.* Rev. ed. 9 vols. Ed. James Kennedy, et al. Edinburgh: Oliver and Boyd, 1926-62.

Harinck, C. *De Schotse verbondsleer: Van Robert Rollock tot Thomas Boston.* Utrecht: De Banier, 1986.

Haskin, Dayton. "Baxter's Quest for Origins: Novelty and Originality in the Autobiography." *EC*, 21 (1980), 145-61.

Heppe, Heinrich. *Die Dogmatik der evangelisch-reformierten Kirche: Dargestellt und aus den Quellen belegt.* Ed. Ernst Bizer. Neukirchen: Neukirchener Verlag, 1958.
———. *Reformed Dogmatics: Set Out and Illustrated from the Sources.* Ed. Ernst Bizer. Foreword Karl Barth. Trans. G.T. Thomson. 1950; rpt. Grand Rapids: Baker, 1978.
Hill, Christopher. *A Turbulent, Seditious, and Factious People: John Bunyan and His Church 1628-1688.* Oxford: Clarendon, 1988.
Hoeksema, Herman. *Reformed Dogmatics.* Grand Rapids: Reformed Free Publishing Association, 1966.
Holifield, E. Brooks. *The Covenant Sealed: The Development of Puritan Sacramental Theology in Old and New England, 1570-1720.* New Haven: Yale Univ. Press, 1974.
Huehns, Gertrude. *Antinomianism in English History: With Special Reference to the Period 1640-1660.* London: Cresset, 1951.
Hunt, John. *Religious Thought in England: From the Reformation to the End of Last Century.* 3 vols. London: Strahan, 1870-73.
Hutton, Sarah. "Thomas Jackson, Oxford Platonist, and William Twisse, Aristotelian." *JHI*, 39 (1978), 635-52.
Johnson, George Arthur. "From Seeker to Finder: A Study in Seventeenth-Century English Spiritualism before the Quakers." *ChH*, 17 (1948), 299-315.
Jones, Hywel R. "The Death of Presbyterianism." In *By Schisms Rent Asunder*. Proc. of the Puritan and Reformed Studies conference. 1969. n.p.: n.p., [1970], pp. 31-42.
Joyce, G.C. "Grotius." *ERE* (1913), pp. 440-43.
Jukes, H.A. Lloyd. "Gunning and the Worcestershire Agreement." *MCM*, NS 7 (1964), 184-86.
Karlberg, Mark W. "Reformed Interpretation of the Mosaic Covenant." *WThJ*, 43 (1980), 1-57.
Keeble, N.H. "The Autobiographer as Apologist: *Reliquiae Baxterianae* (1696)." *PS*, 9 (1986), 105-19.
———, ed. *The Autobiography of Richard Baxter*. Abridged J.M. Lloyd Thomas. London: Dent; Totowa, N.J.: Rowman & Littlefield,1974.
———. "C.S. Lewis, Richard Baxter, and 'Mere Christianity'." *CaL*, 30, No. 3 (1981), 27-44.
———, ed. *John Bunyan: Conventicle and Parnassus: Tercentenary Essays.* Oxford: Clarendon, 1988.
———. *Richard Baxter: Puritan Man of Letters.* Oxford English Monographs. London: Clarendon, 1982.
———. "Richard Baxter's Preaching Ministry: Its History and Texts." *JEH*, 35 (1984), 539-59.
———, and Geoffrey F. Nuttall. *Calendar of the Correspondence of Richard Baxter.* 2 vols. Oxford: Clarendon, 1991.
Kendall, R.T. *Calvin and English Calvinism to 1649.* Oxford: Oxford Univ. Press, 1979.
Kevan, Ernest F. *The Grace of Law: A Study in Puritan Theology.* London, 1964; rpt. Grand Rapids: Baker, 1976.
Knox, R. Buick. *James Ussher Archbishop of Armagh.* Cardiff: Univ. of Wales Press, 1967.
Kuyper, A. *Johannes Maccovius.* Diss. Amsterdam 1899. Leiden: Donner, 1899.
Kuyper, H.H. *De Post-acta of nahandelingen van de Nationale Synode van Dordrecht in 1618 en 1619 gehouden, naar den authentieken tekst in het latijn en nederlandsch uitgegeven en met toelichtingen voorzien, voorafgegaan door de geschiedenis van de acta, de autographa en de post-acta dier synode en gevolgd door de geschiedenis van de revisie der belijdenisschriften en der liturgie, benevens de volledige lijst der gravamina op de Dordtsche Synode ingediend: Een historische studie.* Amsterdam: Höveker & Wormser, [1899].
Labrousse, Elisabeth. "Une lettre de Moïse Amyraut à Richard Baxter." *BSHPF*, 119 (1973), 566-75.
Lachman, David C. *The Marrow Controversy 1718-1723: An Historical and Theological*

Analysis. Rutherford Studies in Historical Theology. Edinburgh: Rutherford House, 1988.

Ladell, A.R. *Richard Baxter: Puritan and Mystic*. Pref. W.H. Frere. Studies in Church History. London: Society for Promoting Christian Knowledge; New York: Macmillan, 1925.

Lake, Peter. *Moderate Puritans and the Elizabethan Church*. Cambridge: Cambridge Univ. Press, 1982.

———. "William Bradshaw, Antichrist and the Community of the Godly." *JEH*, 36 (1985), 570-89.

Lamont, William M. *Richard Baxter and the Millennium: Protestant Imperialism and the English Revolution*. Croom Helm Social History Series. London: Croom Helm; Totowa, NJ: Rowman and Littlefield, 1979.

Langley, Arthur S. "John Tombes As a Correspondent." *TBHS*, 7 (1920), 13-18.

Laplanche, François. *Orthodoxie et Prédication: L'œvre d'Amyraut et la querelle de la grâce universelle*. Études d'histoire et de philosophie religieuses, 59. Paris: Presses universitaires de France, 1965.

Letham, Robert. "The *Foedus Operum*: Some Factors Accounting for Its Development." *SCJ*, 14 (1983), 457-67.

Loonstra, B. *Verkiezing — verzoening — verbond: Beschrijving en beoordeling van de leer van het pactum salutis in de gereformeerde theologie*. Diss. Utrecht 1990. The Hague: Boekencentrum, 1990.

MacGillivray, Royce. "Richard Baxter: A Puritan in the Provinces." *DaR*, 49 (1969-70), 487-96.

Maclean, A.H. "George Lawson and John Locke." *CHJ*, 9 (1947), 69-77.

Macleod, Jack N. "John Owen and the Death of Death." In *Out of Bondage*. Proc. of the Westminster Conference. 1983. Nottingham: Westminster Conference, [1984], pp. 70-87.

Macleod, John. *Scottish Theology in Relation to Church History since the Reformation*. 2nd ed. Edinburgh: Publications Committee of the Free Church of Scotland, 1946.

Martin, Hugh. *Puritanism and Richard Baxter*. London: SCM, 1954.

Matthews, A.G. *Calamy Revised: Being a Revision of Edmund Calamy's Account of the Ministers and Others Ejected and Silenced, 1660-2*. Oxford: Clarendon, 1934.

———. "The Works of Richard Baxter." *TCHS*, 11 (1930-32), 102-12, 125-39, 189-205, 228-36.

———. *The Works of Richard Baxter: An Annotated List*. [London, 1932].

Matthews, Nancy L. *William Sheppard, Cromwell's Law Reformer*. Cambridge Studies in English Legal History. Cambridge: Cambridge Univ. Press, 1984.

McAdoo, H.R. *The Structure of Caroline Moral Theology*. London: Longmans, Green and Co, 1949.

McCoy, Charles S., and J. Wayne Baker. *Fountainhead of Federalism: Heinrich Bullinger and the Covenantal Tradition*. With trans. of *De testamento seu foedere Dei unico et aeterno* (1534), by Heinrich Bullinger. Louisville: Westminster/Knox, 1991.

McDonald, H.D. *The Atonement of the Death of Christ: In Faith, Revelation, and History*. Grand Rapids: Baker, 1985.

McGrath, Alister E. "The Emergence of the Anglican Tradition on Justification 1600-1700." *ChM*, 98 (1984), 28-43.

———. *Iustitia Dei: A History of the Christian Doctrine of Justification*. 2 vols. Cambridge: Cambridge Univ. Press, 1986.

McGrath, Gavin J. *Grace and Duty in Puritan Spirituality*. Grove Spirituality Series, 37. Bramcote: Grove, 1991.

McIntyre, D.M. "First Strictures on 'The Marrow of Modern Divinity'." *EvQ*, 10 (1938), 61-70.

McKim, Donald K. *Ramism in William Perkins' Theology*. American University Studies, Series VII: Theology and Religion, 15. New York: Lang, 1987.

McRae, Kenneth. "Ramist Tendencies in the Thought of Jean Bodin." *JHI*, 16 (1955), 306-23.

Miller, Perry. "The Marrow of Puritan Divinity." In *Errand into the Wilderness*. New York: Harper & Row, 1956, pp. 48-98.

———. "'Preparation for Salvation' in Seventeenth-Century New England." *JHI* 4 (1943), 253-86.

Moltmann, Jürgen. "Prädestination und Heilsgeschichte bei Moyse Amyraut: Ein Beitrag zur Geschichte der reformierten Theologie zwischen Orthodoxie und Aufklärung." *ZKG*, 65 (1954), 270-303.

———. *Prädestination und Perseveranz: Geschichte und Bedeutung der reformierten Lehre "de perseverantia sanctorum"*. Beiträge zur Geschichte und Lehre der Reformierten Kirche, 12. Neukirchen: Neukirchener Verlag, 1961.

Morgan, Edmund S. *Visible Saints: The History of a Puritan Idea*. New York: New York Univ. Press, 1963.

Morgan, Irvonwy. *The Nonconformity of Richard Baxter*. London: Epworth, 1946.

Muller, Richard A. *Christ and the Decree: Christology and Predestination in Reformed Theology from Calvin to Perkins*. Studies in Historical Theology, 2. 1986; rpt. Grand Rapids: Baker, 1988.

———. "Covenant and Conscience in English Reformed Theology: Three Variations on a 17th Century Theme." *WThJ*, 42 (1980), 308-34.

———. *Dictionary of Latin and Greek Theological Terms: Drawn Principally from Protestant Scholastic Theology*. Grand Rapids: Baker, 1985.

———. *God, Creation, and Providence in the Thought of Jacob Arminius: Sources and Directions of Scholastic Protestantism in the Era of Early Orthodoxy*. Grand Rapids: Baker, 1991.

———. "The Spirit and the Covenant: John Gill's Critique of the *pactum salutis*." *Foun*, 24 (1981), 4-14.

Murray, Iain. "Richard Baxter-'The Reluctant Puritan'?" In *Advancing in Adversity*. Proc. of the Westminster Conference. 1991. Thornton Heath, Surrey: Westminster Conference, [1992], pp. 1-24.

Murray, John J. "The Marrow Controversy: Thomas Boston and the Free Offer." In *Preaching and Revival*. Proc. of the Westminster Conference. 1984. Thornton Heath, Surrey: Westminster Conference, [1985], pp. 34-56.

Nelson, Robert. *The Life of Dr. George Bull, Late Lord Bishop of St. David's. With the History of Those Controversies In which he was Engaged: And an Abstract of those Fundamental Doctrines which he Maintained and Defended in the Latin Tongue*. 2nd ed. London, 1714.

New, John F.H. *Anglican and Puritan: The Basis of Their Opposition, 1558-1640*. London: Black, 1964.

Newman, A.H. "Antinomianism and Antinomian Controversies." *NSHE*. 1949 ed.

Nicole, Roger. *Moyse Amyraut: A Bibliography with Special Reference to the Controversy on Universal Grace*. New York: Garland, 1981.

Niesel, Wilhelm. "Calvin wider Osianders Rechtfertigungslehre." *ZKG*, 46 (1927), 410-30.

Nobbs, Douglas. "New Light on Louis du Moulin." *PHSL*, 15 (1936), 489-509.

———. *Theocracy and Toleration: A Study of the Disputes in Dutch Calvinism from 1600 to 1650*. Cambridge: Cambridge Univ. Press, 1938.

Nuttall, Geoffrey F. "Dr. Du Moulin and *Papa Ultrajectinus*." *NeAKG*, NS 61 (1981), 205-13.

———. "John Horne of Lynn." In *Christian Spirituality: Essays in Honour of Gordon Rupp*. Ed. Peter Brooks. London: SCM, 1975, pp. 231-47.

———. "The MS. of *Reliquiae Baxterianae* (1696)." *JEH*, 6 (1955), 73-79.

———. "The Personality of Richard Baxter." In *The Puritan Spirit: Essays and Addresses*. London: Epworth, 1967, pp. 104-17.

———. "Presbyterians and Independents: Some Movements for Unity 300 Years Ago."
    JPHSE, 10 (1952), 4-15.
———. "Puritan and Quaker Mysticism." *Theol.*, 78 (1975), 518-31.
———. *Richard Baxter*. London: Nelson, 1965.
———. *Richard Baxter and Philip Doddridge: A Study in Tradition*. London: Oxford Univ.
    Press, 1951.
———. "Richard Baxter's *Apology* (1654): Its Occasion and Composition." *JEH*, 4 (1953),
    69-76.
———. "Richard Baxter's Correspondence: A Preliminary Survey." *JEH* 1 (1950), 85-95.
———. "Thomas Lambe, William Allen and Richard Baxter: An Additional Note." *BQ*, 27
    (1977), 139-40.
———. "A Transcript of Richard Baxter's Library Catalogue: A Bibliographical Note."
    JEH, 2 (1951), 207-21.
———. "A Transcript of Richard Baxter's Library Catalogue (Concluded)." *JEH*, 3 (1952),
    74-100.
———. "Walter Cradock (1606?-1659): The Man and His Message." In *The Puritan Spirit:
    Essays and Addresses*. London: Epworth, 1967, pp. 118-29.
———. *The Welsh Saints 1640-1660: Walter Cradock, Vavasor Powell, Morgan Llwyd*.
    Cardiff: Univ. of Wales Press, 1957.
———. "The Worcestershire Association: Its Membership." *JEH*, 1 (1950), 197-206.
Oakley, Francis. *Omnipotence, Covenant, & Order: An Excursion in the History of Ideas
    from Abelard to Leibniz*. Ithaca: Cornell Univ. Press, 1984.
Oberman, Heiko Augustinus. *The Harvest of Medieval Theology: Gabriel Biel and Late
    Medieval Nominalism*. Cambridge: Harvard Univ. Press, 1963.
Ong, Walter, J. *Ramus: Method, and the Decay of Dialogue: From the Art of Discourse to
    the Art of Reason*. Cambridge, MA: Harvard Univ. Press, 1958.
Orme, William. *Memoirs of the Life, Writings, and Religious Connexions, of John Owen,
    D.D. Vice-Chancellor of Oxford, and Dean of Christ Church, during the Common-
    wealth*. London: Hamilton, 1820.
Packer, J.I. "The Doctrine of Justification in Development and Decline among the Puri-
    tans." In *By Schisms Rent Asunder*. Proc. of the Puritan and Reformed Studies
    Conference. 1969. n.p.: n.p., [1970], pp. 18-30.
———. "'Saved by His Precious Blood': An Introduction to John Owen's *The Death of
    Death in the Death of Christ*." In *A Quest for Godliness: The Puritan Vision of the
    Christian Life*. Wheaton: Crossway, 1990, pp. 125-48.
Paul, Robert S. "Ecclesiology in Richard Baxter's Autobiography." In *From Faith to Faith:
    Essays in Honor of Donald G. Miller on His Seventieth Birthday*. Ed. Dikran Y.
    Hadidian. Pittsburgh: Pickwick, 1979, pp. 357-402.
Perks, Stephen C. "Atonement and Justification: A Review Article." Rev. of *Atonement
    and Justification: English Evangelical Theology 1640-1790: An Evaluation*, by Alan
    C. Clifford. *CalTo*, 1, No. 4 (1991), 26-32.
Pettit, Norman. *The Heart Prepared: Grace and Conversion in Puritan Spiritual Life*. Yale
    Publications in American Studies, 11. New Haven: Yale Univ. Press, 1966.
Polman, A.D.R. *Onze Nederlandsche Geloofsbelijdenis: Verklaard uit het verleden gecon-
    fronteerd met het heden*. Franeker: Wever, n.d. Vol. III.
Posthumus Meyjes, G.H.M. "Hugo Grotius As an Irenicist." In *The World of Hugo Grotius
    (1583-45)*. Proc. of the International Colloquium organized by the Grotius Commit-
    tee of the Royal Netherlands Academy of Arts and Sciences. 6-9 April 1983. Am-
    sterdam: APA-Holland Univ. Press, 1984, pp. 43-63.
Powicke, F.J. "Dr. Lewis Du Moulin's Vindication of the Congregational Way." *TCHS*, 9
    (1926), 219-236.
———. *A Life of the Reverend Richard Baxter 1615-1691*. London: Cape, [1925?].
———. *The Reverend Richard Baxter under the Cross (1662-1691)*. London: Cape, 1927.

————. "Richard Baxter (1615=1691) as a Catholic Christian." *PMQR*, NS 31 (1909), 232-47.

————. "Richard Baxter and Comprehension in the English Church." *CoQ*, 7 (1919), 349-67.

————. "Some Unpublished Correspondence of the Rev. Richard Baxter and the Rev. John Eliot, 'The Apostle to the American Indians', 1656-1682." *BJRL*, 15 (1931), 138-76, 442-66.

Rainbow, Jonathan H. *The Will of God and the Cross: An Historical and Theological Study of John Calvin's Doctrine of Limited Redemption*. Princeton Theological Monograph Series, 22. Allison Park, PA: Pickwick, 1990.

Reid, James. *Memoirs of the Lives and Writings of Those Eminent Divines, Who Convened in the Famous Assembly at Westminster, in the Seventeenth Century*. 2 vols. 1811, 1815; rpt. Edinburgh: Banner of Truth, 1982.

"Richard Baxter's 'End of Controversy'." *BSABR*, 12 (1855), 348-85.

Ritschl, Albrecht. *A Critical History of the Christian Doctrine of Justification and Reconciliation*. Vol. I. Trans. John S. Black. Edinburgh: Edmonston and Douglas, 1872.

Rivers, Isabel. "Grace, Holiness, and the Pursuit of Happiness: Bunyan and Restoration Latitudinarianism." In *John Bunyan: Conventicle and Parnassus: Tercentenary Essays*. Ed. N.H. Keeble. Oxford: Clarendon, 1988, pp. 45-69.

————. *Reason, Grace, and Sentiment: A Study of the Language of Religion and Ethics in England, 1660-1780*. Vol. I: *Whichcote to Wesley*. Cambridge Studies in Eighteenth-Century English Literature and Thought, 8. Cambridge: Cambridge Univ. Press, 1991.

Rooy, Sidney H. *The Theology of Missions in the Puritan Tradition: A Study of Representative Puritans: Richard Sibbes, Richard Baxter, John Eliot, Cotton Mather, and Jonathan Edwards*. Diss. Amsterdam 1965. Delft: Meinema, 1965.

Sabean, David. "The Theological Rationalism of Moïse Amyraut." *ARG*, 55 (1964), 204-16.

Schaff, Philip, ed. *The Creeds of Christendom: With a History and Critical Notes*. 6th ed. Rev. David S. Schaff. 3 vols. 1931; rpt. Grand Rapids: Baker, 1983.

Scott, J.F. "The Reverend John Wallis, F.R.S. (1616-1703)." In *The Royal Society: Its Origins and Founders*. Ed. Harold Hartley. London: Royal Society, 1960, pp. 57-67.

Sell, Alan P.F. *The Great Debate: Calvinism, Arminianism and Salvation*. Studies in Christian Thought and History. Worthing, West Sussex: Walter, 1982.

Solt, Leo F. "John Saltmarsh: New Model Army Chaplain." *JEH*, 2 (1951), 69-80.

————. *Saints in Arms: Puritanism and Democracy in Cromwell's Army*. Stanford, CA: Stanford Univ. Press; London: Oxford Univ. Press, 1959.

Sprunger, Keith L. "Ames, Ramus, and the Method of Puritan Theology." *HThR*, 59 (1966), 133-51.

Spykman, Gordon J. *Reformational Theology: A New Paradigm for Doing Dogmatics*. Grand Rapids: Eerdmans, 1992.

Stauffer, Donald A. *English Biography before 1700*. Cambridge, MA: Harvard Univ. Press, 1930.

Steinmetz, David C. "Reformation and Conversion." *ThTo*, 35 (1978), 25-32.

Sterrett, J. Macbride. "Antinomianism." *ERE*. 1908 ed.

Stoeffler, F. Ernest. *The Rise of Evangelical Pietism*. Studies in the History of Religions, 9. Leiden: Brill, 1965.

Strehle, Stephen. *Calvinism, Federalism, and Scholasticism: A Study of the Reformed Doctrine of Covenant*. Basler und Berner Studien zur historischen und systematischen Theologie, 58. Bern: Lang, 1988.

————. "The Extent of the Atonement and the Synod of Dort." *WThJ*, 51 (1989), 1-23.

————. "Universal Grace and Amyraldianism." *WThJ*, 51 (1989), 345-57.

Strong, Augustus Hopkins. *Systematic Theology: A Compendium Designed for the Use of Theological Students*. Old Tappan, NJ: Revell, 1907.

Thomas, J.M. Lloyd, ed. *The Autobiography of Richard Baxter*. Everyman's Library, 868. London: Dent; New York: Dutton, 1931.

Thomas, Roger. *The Baxter Treatises: A Catalogue of the Richard Baxter Papers (Other Than the Letters) in Dr. Williams's Library*. Occasional Paper, 8. London: Dr. Williams's Trust, 1959.

———. "The Break-Up of Nonconformity." In *The Beginnings of Nonconformity*. By Geoffrey F. Nuttall, et al. The Hibbert Lectures. London: Clarke, 1964, pp. 33-60.

———. "Parties in Nonconformity." In *The English Presbyterians: From Elizabethan Puritanism to Modern Unitarianism*. By C.G. Bolam, et al. London: Allen & Unwin, 1968, pp. 93-112.

———. "Presbyterians in Transition." In *The English Presbyterians: From Elizabethan Puritanism to Modern Unitarianism*. By C.G. Bolam, et al. London: Allen & Unwin, 1968, pp. 113-74.

The Thomason Tracts 1640-1661: An Index to the Microfilm Edition of the Thomason Collection of the British Library. 2 vols. Ann Arbor, MI: Univ. Microfilms International, 1981.

Tolmie, Murray. "Thomas Lambe, Soapboiler, and Thomas Lambe, Merchant, General Baptists." *BQ*, 27 (1977), 4-13.

Toon, Peter, ed. *The Correspondence of John Owen (1616-1683): With an Account of His Life and Work*. Pref. Geoffrey F. Nuttall. Cambridge: Clarke, 1970.

———. *The Emergence of Hyper-Calvinism in English Nonconformity 1689-1765*. Pref. J.I. Packer. London: Olive Tree, 1967.

———. *God's Statesman: The Life and Work of John Owen: Pastor, Educator, Theologian*. Exeter: Paternoster, 1971.

———. *Puritans and Calvinism*. Swengel, PA: Reiner, 1973.

Trevor-Roper, Hugh. *Catholics, Anglicans and Puritans: Seventeenth Century Essays*. London: Secker & Warburg, 1987.

Tyacke, Nicholas. *Anti-Calvinists: The Rise of English Arminianism c. 1590-1640*. Oxford Historical Monographs. 1987; rpt. Oxford: Clarendon, 1991.

Van Gent, W. "Koelman's kommentaar op enkele Engelse schrijvers." *DNR*, 2 (1978), 29-32.

Van Leeuwen, Henry G. *The Problem of Certainty in English Thought: 1630-1690*. Pref. Richard H. Popkin. The Hague: Nijhoff, 1970.

Van Os, M., and G.J. Schutte, eds. *Bunyan in England and Abroad: Papers Delivered at the John Bunyan Tercentenary Symposium, Vrije Universiteit Amsterdam, 1988*. VU-Studies on Protestant History, 1. Amsterdam: VU Univ. Press, 1990.

Van Stam, F.P. *The Controversy over the Theology of Saumur, 1635-1650: Disrupting Debates among the Huguenots in Complicated Circumstances*. Diss. Amsterdam 1988. Studies of the Institute Pierre Bayle, Nijmegen (SIB), 19. Amsterdam: APA-Holland University Press, 1988.

Van 't Spijker, W. "Jacobus Koelman (1632-95)." In *De Nadere Reformatie: Beschrijving van haar voornaamste vertegenwoordigers*. Ed. T. Brienen, et al. The Hague: Boeken-centrum, 1986, pp. 127-63.

Von Rohr, John. *The Covenant of Grace in Puritan Thought*. Studies in Religion, 45. Atlanta: Scholars, 1986.

Walker, Williston. *The Creeds and Platforms of Congregationalism*. Introd. Elizabeth C. Nordbeck. 1893; rpt. New York: Pilgrim, 1991.

Wallace, Dewey D. *Puritans and Predestination: Grace in English Protestant Theology, 1525-1695*. Studies in Religion. Chapel Hill: Univ. of North Carolina Press, 1982.

Watkins, Owen C. "*Reliquiae Baxterianae*." In *The Puritan Experience: Studies in Spiritual Autobiography*. New York: Schocken, 1972, pp. 121-43.

Webber, Joan. "Richard Baxter: The Eye of the Hurricane." In *The Eloquent "I": Style and Self in Seventeenth-Century Prose*. Madison: Univ. of Wisconsin Press, 1968, pp. 115-48, 281-84.

Weber, Otto. *Foundations of Dogmatics*. Vol. II. Trans. Darrell L. Guder. Grand Rapids: Eerdmans, 1983.

Weintraub, Karl Joachim. "Bunyan, Baxter, and Franklin: The Puritan Unification of the Personality." In *The Value of the Individual: Self and Circumstance in Autobiography*. Chicago: Univ. of Chicago Press, 1978, pp. 228-60, 391-93.

Weir, David A. *The Origins of the Federal Theology in Sixteenth-Century Reformation Thought*. Oxford: Clarendon, 1990.

Westminster Confession of Faith. 1958; rpt. Glasgow: Free Presbyterian Publications, 1990.

White, Peter. *Predestination, Policy and Polemic: Conflict and Consensus in the English Church from the Reformation to the Civil War*. Cambridge: Cambridge Univ. Press, 1992.

Whitley, W.T. "Dissent in Worcestershire during the Seventeenth Century." *TBHS*, 7 (1920), 1-12.

Wiley, Margaret L. "Richard Baxter and the Problem of Certainty." In *The Subtle Knot: Creative Scepticism in Seventeenth-Century England*. London: Allen and Unwin, 1952, pp. 161-78, 292-93.

Wood, A. Harold. *Church Unity without Uniformity: A Study of Seventeenth-Century English Church Movements and of Richard Baxter's Proposals for a Comprehensive Church*. Pref. E. Gordon Rupp. London: Epworth, 1963.

Wood, Anthony à. *Athenæ Oxonienses: Exact History of All the Writers and Bishops Who Have Had Their Education in the University of Oxford. To Which Are Added The Fasti or Annals of the Said University*. 3rd ed. Ed. Philip Bliss. 4 vols. London: Rivington, 1813-20.

Yoo, Hae Moo. *Raad en daad: Infra- en supralapsarisme in de nederlandse gereformeerde theologie van de 19e en 20e eeuw*. Diss. Kampen 1990. Kampen: Mondiss, 1990.

Zimmermann, Gunter. "Calvins Auseinandersetzung mit Osianders Rechtfertigungslehre." *KuD*, 35 (1989), 236-56.

———. "Die Thesen Osianders zur Disputation 'de iustificatione'." *KuD*, 33 (1987), 224-44.

UNPUBLISHED THESES

Banks, Linda Jo Samuel. "The Poems of Richard Baxter: A Critical Edition with Notes and Commentary." Diss. Emory Univ. 1967.

Bass, William W. "Platonic Influences on Seventeenth-Century English Puritan Theology As Expressed in the Thinking of John Owen, Richard Baxter and John Howe." Diss. Univ. of Southern California 1958.

———. "The Theology of John Owen." M.A. Thesis. Univ. of Southern California 1955.

Beeke, Joel R. "Personal Assurance of Faith: English Puritanism and the Dutch 'Nadere Reformatie:' From Westminster to Alexander Comrie (1640-1760)." Diss. Westminster Theological Seminary 1988.

Bell, Michael Daniel. "Propter potestatem, scientiam, ac beneplacitum Dei: The Doctrine of the Object of Predestination in the Theology of Johannes Maccovius." Diss. Westminster Theological Seminary 1986.

Beougher, Timothy K. "Conversion: The Teaching and Practice of the Puritan Pastor Richard Baxter with Regard to Becoming a 'True Christian'." Diss. Trinity Evangelical Divinity School 1990.

Breed, James Lincoln. "Sanctification in the Theology of Cotton Mather." Diss. Aquinas Institute of Theology 1980.

Brown, Earl Kent. "Richard Baxter's Contribution to the Comprehension Controversy: A Study in Projected Church Union." Diss. Boston Univ. Graduate School 1956.

Daniel, Curt D. "Hyper-Calvinism and John Gill." Diss. Univ. of Edinburgh 1983.

De Koeyer, R.W. "Pneumatologia: Een onderzoek naar de leer van de Heilige Geest bij de puritein John Owen (1616-1683)." Doctoraalscriptie. Rijksuniversiteit Utrecht 1990.

Godfrey, William Robert. "Tensions within International Calvinism: The Debate on the Atonement at the Synod of Dort, 1618-1619." Diss. Stanford Univ. 1974.

Graebner, Norman Brooks. "Protestants and Dissenters: An Examination of the Seventeenth-Century Eatonist and New England Antinomian Controversies in Reformation Perspective." Diss. Duke Univ. 1984.

Haskin, Dayton William. "The Light Within: Studies in Baxter, Bunyan, and Milton." Diss. Yale Univ. 1978.

Highfill, W. Lawrence. "Faith and Works in the Ethical Theory of Richard Baxter." Diss. Duke Univ. 1954.

Jeremias, Isolde. "Richard Baxters Catholic Theology, ihre Voraussetzungen und Ausformungen." Diss. Georg August-Universität 1956.

Karlberg, Mark Walter. "The Mosaic Covenant and the Concept of Works in Reformed Hermeneutics: A Historical-Critical Analysis with Particular Attention to Early Covenant Eschatology." Diss. Westminster Theological Seminary 1980.

Keeble, N.H. "Some Literary and Religious Aspects of the Works of Richard Baxter." Diss. Univ. of Oxford 1973.

Mair, N.H. "Christian Sanctification and Individual Pastoral Care in Richard Baxter: An Analysis of the Relation between Richard Baxter's Understanding of Christian Sanctification and the Form and Content of His Individual Pastoral Direction." Diss. Union Theological Seminary 1966.

McCan, R.L. "The Conception of the Church in Richard Baxter and John Bunyan: A Comparison and Contrast." Diss. Univ. of Edinburgh 1955.

McGrath, Gavin John. "Puritans and the Human Will: Voluntarism within Mid-Seventeenth Century English Puritanism As Seen in the Works of Richard Baxter and John Owen." Diss. Univ. of Durham 1989.

Packer, James I. "The Redemption and Restoration of Man in the Thought of Richard Baxter." Diss. Univ. of Oxford 1954.

Phillips, James McJunkin. "Between Conscience and the Law: The Ethics of Richard Baxter (1615-1691)." Diss. Princeton Univ. 1958.

Richards, David J. "Richard Baxter's Theory of the Atonement." M.A. Thesis. Wheaton College 1982.

Shealy, William Ross. "The Power of the Present: The Pastoral Perspective of Richard Baxter, Puritan Divine: 1615-1691." Diss. Drew Univ. 1966.

Shields, James L. "The Doctrine of Regeneration in English Puritan Theology, 1604-1689." Diss. Southwestern Baptist Theological Seminary 1965.

Tipson, Lynn Baird. "The Development of a Puritan Understanding of Conversion." Diss. Yale Univ. 1972.

Wallace, Dewey D. "The Life and Thought of John Owen to 1660: A Study of the Significance of Calvinist Theology in English Puritanism." Diss. Princeton Univ. 1965.

Won, Jonathan Jong-Chun. "Communion with Christ: An Exposition and Comparison of the Doctrine of Union and Communion with Christ in Calvin and the English Puritans." Diss. Westminster Theological Seminary 1989.

Wright, Robert Keith McGregor. "John Owen's Great High Priest: The Highpriesthood of Christ in the Theology of John Owen, (1616-1683)." Diss. Iliff School of Theology and Univ. of Denver 1989.

Index of Names

Printed in the United States
36226LVS00004BA/19

9 781573 832823